How to Prepare for the

NCLEX-RN
Using CAT

Third Edition

By
Sadie Smalls
Arlyne M. Kellock
Luzviminda Casapao
Paula Schnabel
Leon Sutton

BARRON'S

All inquiries should be addressed to:
Barron's Educational Series, Inc.
250 Wireless Boulevard
Hauppauge, New York 11788

Library of Congress Catalog Card No. 95-13041

International Standard Book No. 0-8120-2824-4

Book/Disk Package No. 0-8120-8284-4

Library of Congress Cataloging-in-Publication Data
Smalls, Sadie.
    Barron's how to prepare for the national council licensure
examination for registered nurses, NCLEX-RN / Sadie Smalls,
Arlyne M. Kellock, Luzviminda Casapao. — 3rd ed.
        p.   cm.
    The former ed. was cataloged under title main entry.
    Includes bibliographical references and index.
    ISBN 0-8120-2824-4
    1. Nursing—Examinations, questions, etc. I. Kellock, Arlyne M.
II. Casapao, Luzviminda. III. Barron's Educational Series, Inc. IV. Title.
RT55.B37   1996
610.73'076—dc20   95-13041
                                                        CIP

PRINTED IN THE UNITED STATES OF AMERICA
6789   100   987654321

CONTRIBUTING AUTHORS

Sadie M. Smalls, R.N., Ed.D.
Clinical Administrative Liaison Nurse
The Brooklyn Hospital Center
Brooklyn, New York

Arlyne M. Kellock, R.N., Ed.M.
Instructor
Phillips Beth Israel School of Nursing
New York, New York

Luzviminda Casapao, R.N., Ed.M.
Consultant in Education and Training
New York, New York

Paula Schnabel, R.N., Ph.D.
Former Associate Professor
William Paterson College of New Jersey
Wayne, New Jersey

Leon Sutton, Ph.D.
Former Adjunct Assistant Professor
City College of the City University of New York
New York, New York
Former Director, Sutton Nursing Review

REVIEWERS/ CONSULTANTS

Julia M. Leahy, Ph.D., R.N., C.S.
Director, Certification and Advanced Practice
    Testing
National League for Nursing
New York, New York

Doretta Dick, R.N., Ed.M.
Assistant Dean and Associate Professor
School of Nursing
State University of New York at Stony Brook
Stony Brook, New York

Lenora J. McClean, R.N., Ed.D.
Dean and Professor
School of Nursing
State University of New York at Stony Brook
Stony Brook, New York

Mary D. Smith, R.N., Ed.M., Ed.D.
Assistant Professor
School of Nursing
Columbia University
New York, New York

**Patricia K. Herman, R.N., M.S., C.S.,
    C.N.A.A.**
University Hospital
State University of New York at Stony Brook
Stony Brook, New York

CONTENTS

See also the detailed Study Guide preceding each unit, and the index at the back of the book.

Part III.   MODEL EXAMINATIONS

INTRODUCTION

This book will provide you with a comprehensive, up-to-date review for the National Council Licensure Examination for Registered Nurses (NCLEX-RN), administered by Computerized Adaptive Testing (CAT), the exam that you must take to become a registered nurse in the United States, Guam, or the U.S. Virgin Islands. The book is far more, however, than just a review for the NCLEX-RN; it is also an extensive outline of expected nursing behaviors for each developmental stage of the human life cycle. It will be useful to you both as an exam preparation manual now and as a professional guide throughout your career.

In this Introduction you will learn about Computerized Adaptive Testing (CAT), the format and test plan of the exam, how to use this book effectively to prepare yourself for the exam, how this book is organized, how to prepare, and how to apply test-taking techniques to maximize your score. Also included here are a discussion of the nursing process, advice for foreign nurses, a bibliography, and the addresses and telephone numbers of the State Boards of Nursing.

FORMAT OF THE NCLEX/CAT-RN[1]

NCLEX-RN using Computerized Adaptive Testing (CAT) is a multiple-choice examination administered by computer. The computer selects test items from an item pool as the candidate progresses through the examination. The test difficulty is tailored to the candidate's knowledge and ability. The test items selected are neither too easy nor too difficult. The first test item presented is of average difficulty. An initial estimate of ability is made. As the candidate answers each question, the computer searches its question bank for the appropriate test item to measure the candidate according to the test plan and according to the person's ability level, then presents it on the computer screen. This process is repeated for each question, creating an examination tailored to the candidate's knowledge and skill while fulfilling all NCLEX-RN test plan requirements.

The *NCLEX-RN Bulletin* with a registration form is available from the Board of Nursing in the state in which the candidate wishes to obtain licen-sure (*see* listing of State Boards of Nursing). After the licensure application has been reviewed and eligibility approved, the candidate will receive an Authorization to Test (ATT) from the Education Testing Service (ETS) Data Center and a second bulletin, *Scheduling and Taking Your NCLEX-RN.* This bulletin contains the procedure for making an appointment for testing, a list of available test center locations and telephone numbers, and a toll-free number to call for information on any newly opened centers.

The only computer keys that are needed to take NCLEX/CAT-RN are the SPACE BAR and ENTER key. The SPACE BAR moves the cursor among the answer choices; the ENTER key is used by the candidate to highlight and select an answer choice, and must be struck twice in order to record the answer and proceed to the next question. Once the examination begins, all other keys are "turned off" so that they cannot be inadvertently struck. All candidates receive training prior to taking NCLEX/CAT-RN, which includes a keyboard tutorial with a practice exercise. The training provides all the information necessary to take the exam.

The NCLEX/CAT-RN uses standard multiple-choice questions. All questions are structured in one of two ways: (1) a stand-alone question and four response choices; or (2) case scenario information, a question, and four response choices. Each question will fit entirely on the computer screen at one time.

Every candidate will answer at least 60 real (scored) questions and 15 tryouts (unscored) questions. Candidates will answer a maximum of 250 real plus 15 tryouts. Each candidate is allowed five hours to complete the examination (including keyboard tutorial and rest breaks). There is one mandatory break after two hours and one optional break after an additional $1^1/2$ hours.

Pass or fail decisions are based on the following guidelines:

Candidates pass the examination by demonstrating, in any of the ways outlined below, that they have the level of competence necessary to practice entry-level nursing. Candidates must:

1. answer at least the minimum number of questions, within the time allowed and achieve a competence measure significantly above the

---

1 "NCLEX Using CAT: An Overview of It All," *Issues,* Special Edition, 1993, pp. 1, 6, 8, and 9.

passing standards. (Testing stops as soon as this level is achieved and the test plan is met.)

2. answer the maximum number of questions within the time allowed and achieve a final competence measure above the passing standard.

3. answer test questions for the maximum time allowed, answer at least the minimum number of questions, and achieve a competence measure above the passing standards *consistently for all of the last 60 questions.*

Candidates fail the examination if they:

1. answer between the minimum and maximum number of questions within the time allowed and achieve a competence measure significantly below the passing standard. (Testing stops as soon as this level is achieved and the test plan is met.)

2. answer the maximum number of questions within the time allowed and achieve a final competence measure below the passing standard.

3. answer questions for the maximum time allowed, answer at least the minimum number of questions, and do not achieve a competence measure above the passing standards *consistently for all of the last 60 questions.*

4. answer test items for the maximum time allowed and have taken less than the minimum number of items.

CONTENT OF THE NCLEX/CAT-RN

The National Council of State Boards of Nursing's test plan provides the content framework for the examination. Based on the test plan, each NCLEX-RN examination reflects the knowledge, skills, and abilities essential for application of the phases of the nursing process to meet the needs of clients with commonly occurring health problems. The test plan is based on data collected in *A Study of Nursing Practice and Role Delineation, and Job Analysis of Entry-Level Performance of Registered Nurses.*[2]

The examination includes test items at the cognitive levels of knowledge, comprehension, application, and analysis. Most items in the examination are at the application and analysis levels.

Level 1: Knowledge

The remembering of previously learned materials. This may involve the recall of a wide range of material from specific facts to complete theories.

Level 2: Comprehension

The ability to grasp the meaning of material. This may be shown by translating material from one form to another (words to numbers), by interpreting material (explaining or summarizing), and by estimating future trends (predicting consequences or effects).

Level 3: Application

The ability to use learned material in new and concrete situations. This may include the application of such things as rules, methods, concepts, principles, laws, and theories.

Level 4: Analysis

The ability to break down material into component parts so that its organizational structure can be understood. This may include the identification of the parts, analysis of the relationship between parts, and recognition of the organizational principles involved.[3]

Two areas are addressed within the framework of the test plan: the nursing process and the needs of clients.

PHASES OF THE NURSING PROCESS

The nursing process is an orderly, systematic method of determining the client's problems, making a plan to solve them, initiating the plan or assigning others to implement it, and evaluating the extent to which the plan was effective in resolving the problems identified. The phases of the nursing process to be measured in the licensure examination are grouped under the broad categories of Assessment, Analysis, Planning, Implementation, and Evaluation. *Because the five phases have equal importance, each one is represented by an equal percentage range of items in the examination.*

Assessment

(Establishing a data base): Data are collected for a data base that includes the patient's chief complaints, social data (age, sex, education, growth and development, socioeconomic and cultural/religious patterns), history of present and past illness, physical examination, base-line laboratory

[2] M. Kane, C. Kingsbury, D. Colton, and C. Estes. *A Study of Nursing Practice and Role Delineation, and Job Analysis of Entry-Level Performance of Registered Nurses.* Chicago: National Council of State Boards of Nursing, Inc., 1993.

[3] N. Gronlund. *Measurement and Evaluation in Teaching,* 2nd ed. New York: Macmillan Company, 1971, p. 528.

data, and nursing theory.[4] The nursing history is obtained through a planned interview with the client as soon as the nurse and the client meet. The data is verified and communicated to the health team.

Analysis

(Identifying actual or high-risk health care needs/ problems based on assessment):

The collected data are analyzed for possible problems and then organized into the nursing diagnosis. The nursing diagnosis is a statement that describes a health state or an actual or potential alteration in a person's life processes (physiological, psychological, sociocultural, developmental, and spiritual).[5]

The accepted diagnostic categories of the North American Nursing Diagnosis Association (NANDA) Nursing Diagnoses are arranged in a list alphabetically by the operational word in each category. Each diagnostic category has three components: the title (label), the etiological and contributing factors, and the defining characteristics.

Title: A concise description of the state (actual, risk) of the individual's health. Qualifying terms such as *altered, impaired, deficit,* and *ineffective* reflect a change in health status but do not label the degree of change (*see* NANDA Nursing Diagnoses, 1995–1996, following).

Etiological and contributing factors: The physiological, situational, and maturational factors that cause the problem or influence its development.

Defining characteristics: The cluster of signs and symptoms observed in the person with the problem.[6]

The diagnostic statement should have two parts: the diagnostic title linked with the etiological and contributing factors. The use of the words *related* to reflects a relationship between the first and the second part of the statement. Linking the diagnostic category with contributing factors also assists the nurse in validating the category. Examples include:

- Risk for injury: Trauma related to an unstable gait secondary to arthritis.
- Colonic constipation related to immobility.
- Spiritual distress related to a belief that illness is God's punishment.[7]

NANDA Nursing Diagnoses, 1995–1996[8]

Activity intolerance
Activity intolerance, risk for
Acute confusion
Adjustment, impaired
Airway clearance, ineffective
Altered family process: alcoholism
Anxiety
Aspiration, risk for

Body image disturbance
Body temperature, risk for altered
Breast-feeding, effective
Breast-feeding, ineffective
Breast-feeding, interrupted
Breathing pattern, ineffective

Caregiver role strain
Caregiver role strain, risk for
Communication, impaired verbal
Constipation
Constipation, colonic
Constipation, perceived

Decisional conflict (specify)
Decreased adaptive capacity: intracranial
Decreased cardiac output
Defense coping
Denial, ineffective
Diarrhea
Disorganized infant behavior
Diversional activity deficit
Dysfunctional ventilatory weaning response
Dysreflexia

Energy field disturbance

Family coping: compromised, ineffective
Family coping: disabling, ineffective
Family coping: potential for growth
Family processes, altered
Fatigue
Fear
Fluid volume deficit

[4] Mary Jo Aspinall and Christine Tanner. *Decision Making for Patient Care.* New York: Appleton-Century-Crofts, 1981, p. 2.

[5] Lynda Juall Carpenito. *Nursing Diagnosis: Application to Clinical Practice,* 6th ed. Philadelphia: J.B. Lippincott, 1995, p. 5.

[6] *Ibid.,* pp. 15–16.

[7] *Ibid.,* pp. 38–39

[8] Fron *NANDA Nursing Diagnoses: Definitions and Classification 1995–1996.* Philadelphia: North American Nursing Diagnoses, 1994.

Fluid volume deficit, risk for
Fluid volume excess

Gas exchange, impaired
Grieving, anticipatory
Grieving, dysfunctional
Growth and development, altered

Health maintenance, altered
Health-seeking behaviors (specify)
Home maintenance management, impaired
Hopelessness
Hyperthermia
Hypothermia

Impaired environmental interpretation syndrome
Impaired memory
Incontinence, bowel
Incontinence, functional
Incontinence, reflex
Incontinence, stress
Incontinence, total
Incontinence, urge
Individual coping, ineffective
Ineffective community coping
Ineffective management of therapeutic regimen: families
Infection, risk for
Injury, risk for

Knowledge deficit (specify)

Management of therapeutic regimen (individuals), ineffective

Noncompliance (specify)
Nutrition: less than body requirements, altered
Nutrition: more than body requirements, altered
Nutrition: potential for more than body requirements, altered

Oral mucous membrane, altered

Pain
Pain, chronic
Parental role, conflict
Parenting, altered
Parenting, risk for altered
Peripheral neurovascular dysfunction, risk for
Personal identity disturbance
Physical mobility impaired
Poisoning, risk for
Post-trauma response
Potential for enhanced community coping
Potential for enhanced organized infant behavior

Potential for enhanced spiritual well-being
Powerlessness

Rape-trauma syndrome
Rape-trauma syndrome: compound reaction
Rape-trauma syndrome: silent reaction
Relocation stress syndrome
Risk for altered parent/infant/child attachment
Risk for disorganized infant behavior
Risk for loneliness
Risk for perioperative positioning injury
Role performance, altered

Self-care deficit: bathing/hygiene
Self-care deficit: dressing/grooming
Self-care deficit: feeding
Self-care deficit: toileting
Self-esteem, chronic low
Self-esteem, disturbance of
Self-esteem, situational low
Self-mutilation, risk for
Sensory-perceptual alterations (specify): visual, auditory, kinesthetic, gustatory, factile, olfactory
Sexual dysfunction
Sexuality patterns, altered
Skin integrity, impaired
Skin integrity, imparied: risk for
Sleep pattern disturbance
Social interaction, impaired
Social isolation
Spiritual distress (distress of the human spirit)
Suffocation, risk for
Sustain spontaneous ventilation, inability to

Thermoregulation, ineffective
Thought processes, altered
Tissue integrity, impaired
Tissue perfusion, altered (renal, cerebral, cardiopulmonary, gastrointestinal, peripheral)
Trauma, risk for

Unilateral neglect
Urinary elimination, altered
Urinary retention

Violence, risk for: self-directed or directed at others

Planning

(Setting goals for meeting patients' needs and designing strategies to achieve these goals): This phase begins with the nursing diagnosis. The purposes of this phase are (a) to assign priority to

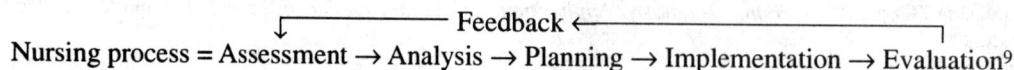

Nursing process = Assessment → Analysis → Planning → Implementation → Evaluation[9]
┌────── Feedback ←──────────────────────┐

---

[9] Helen Yura and Mary Walsh. *The Nursing Process,* 2d ed. New York: Appleton-Century-Crofts, 1973, p. 66.

the problem diagnosed; (b) to differentiate among problems that can be resolved by nursing interventions, those that can be handled by the patient and/or members of the family, and those that must be referred to other members of the health team or handled in conjunction with them; (c) to designate specific actions and overall goals of these actions, written in expected observable/measurable outcomes for the patient; (d) to write a nursing care plan; and (e) to collaborate with other health team members for delivery of the patient's care.

Implementation

(Initiating and completing actions necessary to accomplish the defined goals):   This phase consists of organizing the patient's care, performing activities of daily living, providing care to establish patient goals, and coordinating the delivery of patient care.

Evaluation

(Determining the extent to which goals have been achieved):   Evaluation aids the nurse and the patient to determine problems that have been resolved, problems that need to be reprocessed (including reassessment and replanning), and new problems that must be diagnosed.[10] This phase is always carried out in terms of how the patient is expected to respond to planned action. Elements of evaluations, like those of assessment and planning, are concurrent and recurrent with other components; evaluating the effect of actions during and after the implementation phase determines the patient's response and the extent to which goals are achieved.[11] If goals are not achieved satisfactorily, each phase is reexamined in reverse order. When the point of difficulty is discovered, the process begins again from there and the faulty step is corrected.

CLIENT NEEDS

The health needs of patients are grouped under four broad categories:

1. Safe, effective care environment
2. Physiological integrity
3. Psychosocial integrity
4. Health promotion/maintenance

The subcategories of activities listed below under the broad categories were identified in *A Study of Nursing Practice and Role Delineation, and Job Analysis of Entry-Level Performance of Registered Nurses.*[12] Activities given a weighting (percentage of test item) of less than 0.20% were excluded. All of the activities presented are of importance.

Asterisks indicate activities with heavier emphasis (above 1%).

1.   Safe, Effective Care Environment

(percentage of test items—15 to 21%)

A.   Coordinated care
1. Teach staff about confidentiality.
2. Plan assignment for staff.
3. Check on contraindicated orders.
4. Withhold medications for adverse reaction.
5. Recommend change in drug therapy.
6. Look for source of infection.
7. Document errors or accident.
8. Identify patients needing isolation.
9. Develop standards of care.
10. Intervene in inadequate care.

B.   Environmental safety
1. Arrange a room for safety.
2. Check accuracy of orders.
3. Act when patient dignity is violated.
4. Plan for patient safety needs.
5. Identify patients who need restraints.
6. Verify patient's identity.
7. Monitor the operation of a continuous mechanical ventilator.
8. Institute radiation protection measures.
9. Monitor the operation of electronic equipment.

C.   Safe and effective treatment and procedures
1. Prepare patient for diagnostic tests.
2. Verify that patient has information for consent.
3. Insert indwelling urinary catheter.
4. Explain outcome of therapy.
*5. Ask about allergies.
6. Check emotional readiness for procedure.

---

[10] Helen Yura and Mary Walsh. *The Nursing Process,* 2d ed. New York: Appleton-Century-Crofts, 1973, p. 66.
[11] *Ibid.,* p. 120.
[12] Kane et al., *op. cit.*

*7. Check readiness for procedure.
*8. Set up sterile field.
*9. Maintain asepsis for at-risk patient.
*10. Check functioning of suction equipment.
11. Stay with patient to promote safety.
12. Maintain patient's status during procedure.
13. Pass instruments during surgical procedure.

2. Physiological Integrity

(percentage of test items—46 to 54%)

A. Physiological adaptation
1. Administer blood.
2. Perform complete physical exam.
3. Report change in intracranial pressure.
4. Plan to deal with cardiac arrhythmias.
5. Perform CPR.
*6. Report changes in consciousness.
*7. Notify MD about changes in condition.
8. Interpret EKG.
9. Evaluate response to total parenteral nutrition.
10. Monitor mechanical ventilator.
11. Alter IV rate.
12. Attach monitoring equipment.
13. Provide tracheostomy care.
*14. Give emergency care to wound.
*15. Give IV meds.
16. Assess severity of chest trauma.
17. Start an infusion.
18. Counteract adverse effects of medications.
19. Manage emergency until MD arrives.
20. Order tests in emergencies.
21. Insert nasogastric tube.
22. Administer oxygen.
23. Interpret central venous pressure readings.
24. Suction respiratory tract.
25. Order routine tests.

B. Reduction of risk potential
*1. Assess respiratory status.
*2. Assess cardiovascular status.
*3. Plan to prevent circulatory complications.
4. Assess orientation.
5. Observe for side effects of chemotherapy or radiation therapy.
6. Assess tolerance for activity.
7. Check for drug interaction.

*8. Plan to maintain skin integrity.
9. Modify care based on test results.
10. Check bowel sounds.
*11. Prevent respiratory complications.
12. Record characteristics of tube drainage.
13. Plan to reduce discomfort.
14. Assess nutrition and hydration status.
15. Assess for sensory stimulation.
*16. Assess patency of tube.
*17. Check for bleeding.
18. Suggest changes in medication orders.
*19. Assess wound healing.
20. Perform complete physical examination.
21. Change medication.
22. Administer medication intravenously.
23. Start intravenous.
*24. Administer intramuscular or subcutaneous medications.
*25. Administer oral medications.
26. Position patient with spinal injury.
27. Check for complication from immobility.
28. Check traction devices.
29. Check for cast complications.
30. Plan to prevent neurological complications.
31. Assess neurosensory function.
32. Plan to minimize pain.
33. Teach pain management techniques.
34. Plan to deal with anxiety from pain.
35. Evaluate response to pain control measure.
36. Assess need for prn medications.

C. Provisions of basic care
1. Measure vital signs.
2. Modify food and fluid intake.
3. Help with activities of daily living.
4. Position or turn the patient.
5. Obtain specimen for tests.
6. Help the patient to eat.
7. Schedule the patient's rest.
*8. Label specimens for lab.
9. Give a tube feeding.
10. Test a urine specimen.
11. Give an enema.
12. Record intake and output.
13. Insert an indwelling catheter.
14. Insert a nasogastric tube.
15. Give perineal care.
16. Apply dressing to a wound.
17. Help the patient in and out of bed.

18. Record characteristics of the tube drainage.
19. Assess the patency of the drainage and compression tube.

3. Psychosocial Integrity

(percentage of test items—8 to 16%)

A. Psychosocial adaptation

1. Evaluate therapy (potential for suicide).
2. Check for alcohol/drug withdrawal.
3. Record behavior indicating delusions.
*4. Assess potential for violence.
*5. Assess environment of suicidal patient.
6. Control disruptive behavior.
7. Monitor for orientation to person, place, and time.
8. Teach early signs and symptoms of recurring depression.
9. Teach technique for managing behavior of emotionally disturbed patients by family.
10. Counsel suspected abuse victims.
11. Counsel victims with drug-alcohol problems.
12. Establish positive nurse-patient relationship.

B. Coping/adaptation

1. Assess adequacy of emotional support.
2. Help patient talk about fears.
3. Help patient deal with negative attitude related to illness.
4. Encourage persistence with therapy.
5. Report interventions.
6. Teach relaxation therapy.
7. Assess emotional adjustment in the handicapped.
8. Record mood changes.
9. Assist the patient with anxiety about dyspnea.

4. Health Promotion/Maintenance

(percentage of test items—17 to 23%)

A. Growth and development through the lifespan

1. Assess the newborn.
2. Assess the maternal progress and stress in pregnancy and labor.
3. Perform fetal assessment/monitoring.
4. Perform maternal physical assessment.
5. Take a maternal history and psychosocial profile.
6. Assess parental role and antepartal care.
7. Teach childbirth classes.
8. Care for the newborn.
9. Take care of any maternal, fetal, or newborn emergency.
10. Identify newborn complications or anomalies.
11. Report on interventions.
12. Teach newborn care classes.
13. Teach postpartum classes.

B. Self-care and integrity of support systems

1. Analyze self-care abilities.
2. Teach self-administration of medications.
3. Teach how to avoid infections.
4. Evaluate performance of breathing exercises.
5. Adapt patient's diet to special needs.
6. Teach self-care to impaired patients.
7. Suggest modification of medical therapies.
8. Evaluate compliance with therapy.
9. See to bowel and bladder retraining.
10. Teach ostomy care.
11. Teach normal nutrition and special diets.
12. Assess knowledge of the cause of illness.
13. Support terminal patients and families.
14. Teach home-care givers.
15. Help patients to adjust to role changes.
16. Assist caregiver with feelings about the stress of illness, accident, or developmental change.
17. Educate family members/significant other about the patient's therapy.

C. Prevention and early treatment of disease

1. Administer an immunizing agent.
2. Interpret skin tests.
3. Identify problems such as noncompliance, altered health maintenance, and knowledge deficit.
4. Teach health promotion and procedures such as breast and testicular self-examination.

HOW TO USE THIS BOOK

This book contains a diagnostic exam designed to assist you in identifying the subject areas where you are weakest; a comprehensive review (in outline form) of the subject matter most pertinent to the NCLEX/CAT-RN; and two complete model exams with explained answers.

You should begin your review by taking the diagnostic exam. You do not need to time yourself. When you have completed the exam, compare your answers with the answer key. The diagnostic exam is a test of factual knowledge, rather than nursing judgment, to assist you in determining the areas where your knowledge is weakest. When you have identified these areas, you may focus a greater portion of your study time on them; remember, however, that the purpose of learning more in any subject area is to enable you to make better *nursing judgments*. The NCLEX-RN tests your ability to make nursing judgments according to the nursing process. It does *not* seek to test your knowledge of subject areas, but rather is intended to test your ability to *use* that knowledge to make proper nursing judgments.

After taking the diagnostic exam, you should methodically review the subject area outline in this book, allowing yourself several weeks, at least, for this phase of your study. During this review you should refer to your own textbooks and school notes as necessary to thoroughly refresh your memory. You may also wish to study portions of the books listed in the Bibliography for the subject areas in which you are weakest.

When you have completed your review, you should take the NCLEX-RN on disk or the model exams in this book.

ORGANIZATION OF THIS BOOK

This review provides extensive coverage of common alterations of health and nursing principles and practices in outline format. The content is organized around a developmental approach across the life span. The nursing process serves as a basis for the presentation of material on health promotion/maintenance, common alterations of health, and nursing principles and practices.

The Developmental Approach

The developmental approach is based on the universal stages of development. Each stage has a qualitatively different organization from any other stage. A person who lives to old age will pass through all the stages and will do so in a fixed order. An individual cannot skip a stage, but the rate of progression through a particular stage may differ. Because of illness or death not all individuals pass through all stages.

Because the registered nurse is expected to identify the health needs/problems of clients throughout their life cycles, the developmental approach was used as an organizing framework. If your textbooks are organized in the traditional way around the five fields of nursing (medical, surgical, obstetric/gynecologic, pediatric, and psychiatric), this book will substantially increase your knowledge of (1) the specific needs of clients within the various divisions of the life cycle; (2) the alterations of health common to specific age groups; and (3) the concerns to be considered in providing nursing interventions and patient education for a wide variety of clients.

To eliminate confusion and overlap, the placement of alterations of health in developmental periods was decided upon after examining numerous nursing textbooks and periodicals. The periods covered by the various divisions of the life span are as follows:

Newborn	Birth to 1 month
Infant	1 to 12 months
Toddler	12 to 36 months
Preschooler	3 to 5 years
School-Age Child	6 to 12 years
Adolescent	13 to 18 years
Young Adult	19 to 39 years
Middle-Aged Adult	40 to 64 years
Older Adult	65 years and older

Each unit of the review section except those on the Newborn and the Terminally Ill Patient contains the following subheadings:

- Developmental Milestones/Tasks
- Health Promotion
- Alterations of Health

The units on the Young Adult, the Middle-Aged Adult, and the Older Adult contain some or all of the following subheadings under "Alterations of Health":

- Alterations in Cardiovascular Organs, Blood, and Blood-Forming Organs, and/or Alterations in Respiration and Carbon Dioxide Exchange
- Alterations That Interfere with the Meeting of Nutritional Needs

- Alterations in Metabolism
- Alterations in Fluid and Electrolyte Elimination
- Alterations in Perception and Coordination
- Alterations That Interfere with the Meeting of Sexual Needs

Behavioral alterations or maladaptive behaviors are covered under the subheading "Alterations in Behavior." A separate unit covers the care of the Terminally Ill Patient.

A standard format based on the nursing process is used to present the material under "Alterations of Health." This format is as follows: Definition; Assessment; Patient Care Management; Nursing Diagnoses/Goals/Interventions and Evaluation.

TESTS

The diagnostic test consists of 480 questions to test your factual knowledge of the subject matter.

The items in the two model examinations at the end of this book and in the NCLEX/CAT-RN simulation computer disk deal with a combination of common health problems and are drawn from the stages of the life cycle. As in the NCLEX-RN, items related to pharmacology, nutrition, accountability, mental health concepts, body structure and function, pathophysiology, principles of asepsis, growth and development, documentation, communication, and teaching are integrated throughout the model exams.

DESCRIPTION AND ANALYSIS OF A QUESTION IN EACH OF THE NURSING PROCESS CATEGORIES

The following are examples of questions in each of the categories of the new test plan that is used for the NCLEX/CAT-RN.

Assessment: collecting the data necessary to formulate a health plan for the client.

An 18-year-old male has been brought to the emergency room after a motorcycle accident with a possible fracture of the left femur. Which of the following items of information would be MOST valuable in assessing his current state?

1. The shape and length of his left leg.
2. The presence of localized swelling.

3. The presence of localized discoloration.
4. The absence of pain.

Answer—**1**
To answer this question, you need to know how to assess musculoskeletal status and the clinical manifestations of fracture of the femur. The symptoms presented in choices 2 and 3 are not seen exclusively in fractures but are present also after a sprain or contusion.

Analysis: identifying the problem and organizing a nursing diagnosis.

A 25-year-old female is hospitalized for treatment of thrombophlebitis. She rings for the nurse and says, "I am having chest pains and trouble breathing." The nurse determines that the patient's vital signs have been stable for the last 8 hours. Which of these interpretations would be accurate?

1. The client's anxiety level is high.
2. Her lungs are congested.
3. Her room is not adequately ventilated.
4. The blood supply to her lungs is obstructed.

Answer—**4**
The patient is experiencing symptoms of pulmonary emboli. As a nurse, you not only must know the complications of thrombophlebitis but also be able to recognize the symptoms of these complications.

Planning: fomulating a plan to meet the health needs of the patient.

A female patient with a transverse colostomy refuses to look at the stoma while the nurse is administering colostomy care. The BEST way for the nurse to deal with the situation is to

1. encourage the patient to look at the stoma.
2. continue to administer colostomy care.
3. notify the physician.
4. start teaching the patient how to care for her colostomy.

Answer—**2**
This question tests your knowledge of the psychological trauma experienced by a client when confronted with an alteration in body image. To choose the correct answer, you have to analyze the situation and plan the appropriate care.

Implementation: taking the necessary actions to put the plan into effect.

A 4-year-old boy is admitted to the pediatric unit with a tentative diagnosis of lymphoblastic leukemia. He is receiving a transfusion of packed cells. He complains of a sharp pain in his back and chills. His vital signs are measured by the nurse and found to be elevated. The MOST appropriate actions by the nurse at this time are to

1. slow down the transfusion and assess the child's vital signs every 15 minutes.
2. stop the transfusion, place the child in a semi-Fowler's position, and notify the head nurse.
3. slow down the transfusion and administer an antihistamine as ordered by the physician.
4. stop the transfusion, send a sample of the child's urine to the laboratory, and notify the physician.

*Answer—***4**
To arrive at the correct response, you must analyze the client's status and then transfer knowledge into action.

Evaluation: determining the extent to which the plan has been successful and the client's health needs have been met.

A 3-year-old girl has cystic fibrosis. She has been admitted to the hospital for bronchopneumonia, and placed in a mist tent with compressed air for 24 hours. Two days later she is still expectorating a small amount of secretion. Which of these actions is indicated?

1. Maintain the child in the mist tent.
2. Remove the child from the mist tent.
3. Refer the child to physiotherapy.
4. Decrease the child's fluid intake.

*Answer—***1**
This question tests your ability to measure results against expectations and to adjust the treatment accordingly. (A mist tent with compressed air provides increased humidity and therefore assists in diluting secretion in the lungs so that it can be expectorated more easily.) Since the child is expectorating a small amount of secretion, she needs to remain in the tent.

Following each model examination you will find a section entitled Rationales. The rationale for each question provides the following information:

- the correct answer
- an explanation of the correct answer
- the phase of the nursing process
- the client need
- the cognitive level of the question

Because the items on the actual NCLEX-RN are almost exclusively cognitive level 3 (application) and cognitive level 4 (analysis), the only types of questions included in the model examinations in this book are level 3 and level 4.

PREPARATION FOR THE NCLEX/CAT-RN

A few simple steps followed systematically will improve the effectiveness of your study time.

1. **Begin your review early.**
   A minimum of 4 to 8 weeks of review is recommended.

2. **Develop a readiness training plan.**
   Progressive preparation is essential.
   A. ***Set aside a fixed time period and day for study.***   Select, in advance, one or more periods for study and review. To the extent possible, allot the same time each period. This time period should be long enough to permit your full attention to be focused on your studies. Although this time will vary from individual to individual, a minimum of 2 hours per study session is recommended. Choose a quiet location if possible, and avoid studying with distracting music in the background. (Soft music without words is probably the least distracting.) Explain to friends and family members the importance of your studying, and tell them that you do not wish to be disturbed during your study periods except for real emergencies. Refrain from making or taking telephone calls during these times.

   B. ***Skim, review, summarize.***   When you begin each study period, select the material that you will cover in that period. Skim the entire batch of material quickly (this may require 10 to 15 minutes), paying attention only to the major ideas. Then go back and begin a thorough review of the material.

When you complete each logical section (say, every 10 to 20 minutes), stop your review and briefly summarize on paper the main ideas and facts of the section just reviewed, without referring to the source material. Use key words and abbreviations; do not spend more than 5 minutes summarizing each section. After you have finished your summary, briefly look over the source material to see which significant points you were unable to recall.

3. Use the examination preparation software packaged with this book to increase your comfort with a computer.

Practice using the two keys that will be used during the NCLEX-RN—SPACE BAR and ENTER.

HOW TO MAXIMIZE YOUR SCORE THROUGH PROPER TEST-TAKING TECHNIQUES

The NCLEX/CAT-RN consists entirely of multiple-choice questions, with four answer choices for each question. Your performance on this exam will be aided if you follow these guidelines:

1. Eat moderately the day of the exam and the day before.

Eating heavily can cause sleepiness and indigestion, while eating too lightly can result in fatigue and nervousness. Moderate meals the day before the exam should be followed by a moderate breakfast. Avoid drinking large quantities of coffee on the days of the exam, and do include some solid food in your breakfast. Avoid a heavy lunch on the exam days. You should have fully adequate sleep for at least two nights before exam day.

2. Bring with you the items you will need.

These include a watch and your admission ticket or other authorization to take the NCLEX-RN.

3. Leave home in plenty of time.

Allow for such contingencies as canceled trains, late-running buses, and inadequate parking spaces.

4. Remember that there are no "trick" questions.

Read each question carefully and consider all four answer choices. There is only one correct answer. You may find that none of the answers describes the action you would take in the given situation, since there are often several correct alternative actions that a nurse can take in a particular situation; however, only *one* of the listed answer choices is a correct alternative. Many questions will be difficult, but none are tricky.

5. Eliminate obviously unreasonable or incorrect answer choices immediately.

Among the four choices there is sure to be at least one (and there may well be two) that you can eliminate at once as incorrect, irrelevant, ridiculous, incomprehensible, too general, or too limited. Immediately eliminate such answers so that you will not be tempted to reconsider them. Then concentrate on the remaining choices.

6. Don't get "hung up" on any question.

You may find that you cannot decide between two or three of the answer choices for a given question, even after careful thought. In that case you must have the willpower to make a choice, even though you are torn between alternative answers. Make your choice, then put the question out of your mind so that you are free to tackle the next one.

7. Do not leave any questions unanswered.

Remember: There is no penalty for guessing. Use the process of elimination described in item 5 to narrow the choice of answers; then, after careful consideration, choose one. Even if you cannot eliminate any of the answer choices, you should still guess at the answer. The NCLEX/CAT-RN must have an answer registered to proceed to the next question.

SPECIAL TIPS FOR FOREIGN NURSES

Nurses educated in foreign countries have special hurdles to overcome in preparing for the NCLEX/CAT-RN. The role of the nurse in the health care setting differs among cultures, as does the core of common health problems and normative behaviors. The NCLEX-RN has been tailored to test the nurse's ability to handle his/her responsibilities as they are understood and accepted in the United States, in the situations that he/she is most likely to encounter. To assist the foreign nurse in becoming knowledgeable about nursing practice in the United States, the following steps are recommended.

1. Read about the nursing process in depth.

The nursing process describes the nursing behavior expected in the United States and is the basis for the test plan of the NCLEX-RN. Failure to understand it fully will greatly impair a candidate's performance on the exam. Knowledge of subject matter alone, without knowledge of how it is to be used by the nurse, will be of little help. You should study thoroughly these two reference books:

> J. B. Lederer, et. al. *Care Planning Pocket Guide.* Redwood City: Addison Wesley Nursing, 1993.
>
> Lynda Juall Carpenito. *Nursing Diagnosis: Application to Clinical Practice,* 6th ed. Philadelphia: J. B. Lippincott, 1995.

2. Allow several months for your review of nursing.

Regular study over a 2–4 month period using this book and several of the nursing textbooks listed in the Bibliography (p. xxiii) will assist you in familiarizing yourself with the role and responsibilities of the nurse in the United States. Pay particular attention to learning what the common health problems are in the American health care system, as well as what constitutes normative symptoms and behavior of wellness.

3. Make frequent use of a medical dictionary.

As a foreign nurse, you will have demonstrated a knowledge of English before being permitted to be a candidate for the NCLEX-RN. However, if your training was in a language other than English, you may continue to find, in your studies, terminology unfamiliar to you. Each time you encounter a nursing or medical term that you do not know, write it down and look it up that same day.

4. Obtain help if you need it.

If, as you study, you experience difficulty with cultural differences in the nursing role between your native country and the United States, or in understanding nursing textbooks and periodicals written in English, you will do well to seek help. Assistance in the form of tutoring by U.S.-educated nurses or teachers, or of adult education courses in English for the foreign born, may be necessary to enable you to do well on the NCLEX-RN.

5. Familiarize yourself with the computer screen and the two keys that will be used during the test (SPACE BAR and ENTER).

Use the examination preparation software packaged with this book to increase your comfort.

BIBLIOGRAPHY

Acute Pain Guideline Panel. *Acute Pain Management: Operative or Medical Procedures and Trauma. Clinical Practice Guidelines.* AHCPR Pub. No. 92-0032, *Acute Pain Management in Adults: Operative Procedures.* Rockville, MD: Agency for Health Care Policy and Research, Public Health Service, U.S. Department of Health and Human Services, February 1992.

American Psychiatric Association. *Diagnostic and Statistical Manual of Mental Disorders.* 4th ed., Washington, D.C.: American Psychiatric Association, 1994.

Ball, J. and Bindler, R. *Pediatric Nursing.* Norwalk: Appleton and Lange, 1995.

Bennett, E. G. and Woolf, D. *Substance Abuse: Pharmacologic, Developmental, and Clinical Perspectives.* 2nd ed., Albany, N.Y.: Delmar Publishers, 1991.

Betz, C. L.; Hunsberger, M.; Wright, S. *Family Centered Nursing Care of Children.* 2nd ed. Philadelphia: W. B. Saunders Co., 1994.

Bobak, I. M.; Lowdermilk, D. L.; Jensen, M. D. *Maternity Nursing.* 4th ed., St. Louis: Mosby, 1995.

Bobak, I. M. & Jensen, M. D. *Maternity and Gynecology Care,* 5th ed., St. Louis: Mosby, 1993.

Carpenito, L. *Handbook of Nursing Diagnosis.* 6th ed., Philadelphia: J. B. Lippincott, 1995.

Carpenito, L. *Nursing Diagnosis: Application to Clinical Practice.* 6th ed., Philadelphia: J. B. Lippincott, 1995.

Cataract Management Guidelines Panel. *Cataracts in Adults: Management of Functional Impairment, No. 4 Clinical Practice Guidelines,* AHCPR Pub. No. 93-0542, *Management of Cataracts in Adults Quick Reference Guide for Clinicians* No. 4. AHCPR Pub. No. 93-0543; *Cataracts in Adults: A Patient's Guidelines.* AHCPR No. 93-0544. Rockville, MD; Agency for Health Care Policy and Research, Public Health Service, U.S. Department of Health and Human Services. February 1993.

Chenitz, C.; Stone, J; and Salisbury, S. *Clinical Gerontological Nursing: A Guide to Advanced Practice.* Philadelphia: W. B. Saunders Company, 1991.

Depression Guidelines Panel. *Depression in Primary Care No. 5 Vol. 1, Detection and Diagnosis* AHCPR Pub. No. 93-0550; *Vol. 2, Treatment of Major Depression* AHCPR Pub. 93-0551; *Clinical Practice Guidelines, Depression in Primary Care: Detection, Diagnosis, and Treatment Quick Reference Guide for Clinicians* Pub. No. 93-0552; *Depression is a Treatable Illness—A Patient's Guide,* AHCPR No. 93-0553; Rockville, M.D.: Agency for Health Care Policy and Research, Public Health Service, U.S. Department of Health and Human Services, April 1993.

Doenges, M., et al. *Psychiatric Care Plans: Guidelines for Client Care.* Philadelphia: F. A. Davis. 1989.

Fischbach, F. *A Manual of Laboratory and Diagnostic Tests,* 4th ed., Philadelphia: J. B. Lippincott Co., 1992.

Gordan, Marjory. *Manual of Nursing Diagnosis, 1995–1996.* 7th ed., St. Louis: Mosby, 1995.

Gorrie, T. M.; McKinney, E. S.; and Murray, S. S. *Foundation of Maternal Newborn Nursing.* Philadelphia: W. B. Saunders Company, 1994.

Heckheimer, Estelle. *Health Promotion of the Elderly in the Community.* Philadelphia: W. B. Saunders Company, 1989.

Jackson, D. B. and Saunders, R. B. *Child Health Nursing.* Philadelphia: J. B. Lippincott Co. 1993.

Janicak, P. G.; Davis, J. M.; Preskorn, S. H.; and Ayd, F. J. *Principles and Practice of Psychopharmacotherapy.* Baltimore, MD: William & Wilkins, 1993.

Kane, M; Kingsbury, C.; Colton, D.; and Estes C., *A Study of Nursing Practice and Role Delineation, Job Analysis of Entry-Level Performance of Registered Nurses.* Chicago: National Council of State Board of Nursing, Inc. 1993.

Ladewig, P. W.; London, M. L.; Olds, S. B. *Essential of Maternal-Newborn Nursing.* 3rd ed., Redwood City: Addison Wesley Nursing, 1994.

Lederer, J. R., et al. *Care Planning Pocket Guide.* Redwood City: Addison Wesley Nursing, 1993.

Lego, S. *Fear and AIDS/HIV: Empathy and Communication.* Albany, N.Y.: Delmar Publishers, 1994.

Lehne, R. A. et al. *Pharmacology for Nursing Care.* 2nd ed., Philadelphia: W. B. Saunders Company, 1994.

Kinney, J. *Clinical Manual of Substance Abuse.* St. Louis: Mosby-Year Book, 1991.

McKenry, L. M. and Salerno, E. *Pharmacology in Nursing,* 18th ed., St. Louis: Mosby, 1992.

Mattewson, M. K. *Pharmacotherapeutic: A Nursing Process Approach.* Philadelphia: F.A. Davis Co., 1991.

Miller, B. and Keane, C. *Encyclopedia and Dictionary of Medicine, Nursing and Allied Health.* 4th ed., Philadelphia: W. B. Saunders Company, 1987.

National Pressure Ulcer Advisory Panel. *Statement On Pressure Ulcer Prevention.* Buffalo: National Pressure Ulcer Advisory Panel, 1992.

Olds, S. B.; London, M. L.; Ladewig, P. W. *Maternal-Newborn Nursing.* Redwood City: Addison Wesley Nursing, 1992.

Pagana, K. D. and Pagana, T. J. *Mosby Diagnostic and Laboratory Test Reference.* 2nd ed., St. Louis: Mosby, 1995.

Pilliteri, A. *Maternal Child Health Nursing.* 2nd ed., Philadelphia: J. B. Lippincott Co., 1995.

Poleman, C. and Peckenpaugh, N. *Nutrition Essential and Diet Therapy.* 6th ed., Philadelphia: W. B. Saunders Company, 1991.

Prediction and Prevention of Pressure Ulcers Panel. *Pressure Ulcers in Adults: Prediction and Prevention Clinical Practice Guideline No. 3* AHCPR Pub. No. 92-0047; *Preventing Pressure Ulcers Quick Reference For Clinicians No. 3* AHCPR Pub. 92-0048. Rockville, MD: Agency for Health Care Policy and Research, Public Health Service, U.S. Department of Health and Human Services. May 1992.

Rogers-Seidl, F. *Geriatric Nursing Care Plan.* St. Louis: Mosby, 1991.

Sherwin, L. N.; Scoloveno, M. A.; and Weingarten, C. J. *Nursing Care of Childbearing Family.* 2nd ed., Norwalk: Appleton and Lange, 1995.

Treatment of Pressure Ulcers Guideline Panel. *Treatment of Pressure Ulcers Clinical Practice Guideline, No. 15,* AHCPR No. 95-0652, *Pressure Ulcer Treatment Quick Reference Guide for Clinicians No. 15.* AHCPR No. 95-0652, *Treating Pressure Sores, Consumer Version No. 15,* AHCPR No. 95-0652. Rockville, MD: Agency for Health Care Policy and Research Public Health Services, U.S. Department of Health and Human Services, December 1994.

Townsend, M. *Drug Guide for Psychiatric Nursing.* St. Louis: Mosby-Year Book, 1990.

Tucker, S.; Canobbio, M. Paquette, E.; and Wells, M. *Patient Care Standards: Nursing Process, Diagnosis, and Outcome.* St. Louis: Mosby, 1992.

Urinary Incontinence Guideline Panel. *Urinary Incontinence in Adults: Clinical Practice Guideline* AHCPR Pub. No. 92-0038, *Urinary Reference Guide for Clinicians* AHCPR No. 92-0041. Rockville, MD: Agency for Health Care Policy and Research, Public Health Services, U.S. Department of Health and Human Services, March 1992.

Varcolis, E. *Foundation of Psychiatric Nursing.* Philadelphia: W. B. Saunders Company, 1990.

Wong, D. *Whaley & Wong's Essentials of Pediatric Nursing.* 4th ed., St. Louis: Mosby, 1993.

Wong, D. *Whaley & Wong's Nursing Care of Infants and Children.* 5th ed., St. Louis: Mosby, 1995.

Yura, H. and Walsh, M. *The Nursing Process,* 2nd ed., N.Y.: Appleton-Century-Crofts, 1973.

ADDRESSES AND TELEPHONE NUMBERS OF BOARDS OF NURSING FOR THE 50 STATES, THE DISTRICT OF COLUMBIA, THE U.S. VIRGIN ISLANDS, AND GUAM

Admission to the NCLEX-RN must be obtained by applying to the Board of Nursing in the state or territory where you wish to practice. Each state has its own application procedures. A complete list of addresses and telephone numbers for the Boards of Nursing in the 50 states, the District of Columbia, the U.S. Virgin Islands, and Guam is provided below.

ALABAMA

Alabama Board of Nursing
RSA Plaza, Suite 250
770 Washington Avenue
Montgomery, Alabama 36130-3900
Tel: (205) 242-4060
FAX: 205/242-4360

ALASKA

Alaska Board of Nursing Licensing
Department of Commerce & Economic
  Development
Division of Occupational Licensing
P.O. Box 110806
Juneau, Alaska 99811-0806
Tel: (907) 465-2544

ARIZONA

Arizona State Board of Nursing
2001 W. Camelback Road, Suite 35
Phoenix, Arizona 85015
Tel: (602) 255-5092

ARKANSAS

Arkansas State Board of Nursing
University Tower Building
1123 South University Avenue, Suite 800
Little Rock, Arkansas 72204
Tel: (501) 686-2700
FAX: 501/686-2714

CALIFORNIA

California Board of Registered Nursing
400 "R" Street, Suite 4030
P.O. Box 944210
Sacramento, California 95814
Tel: (916) 322-3350

COLORADO

Colorado Board of Nursing
1650 Broadway, Suite 670
Denver, Colorado 80202
Tel: (303) 894-2430

CONNECTICUT

Department of Health Services
Connecticut Board of Examiners for Nursing
150 Washington Street
Hartford, Connecticut 06106
Tel: (203) 566-1041

DELAWARE

Delaware Board of Nursing
Federal & Court Streets
Margaret O'Neill Building
P.O. Box 1401
Dover, Delaware 19901-1401
Tel: (302) 739-4522

DISTRICT OF COLUMBIA

District of Columbia Board of Nursing
Department of Consumer & Regulatory Affairs
614 "H" Street, N.W., Room 904
P.O. Box 37200
Washington, D.C. 20001
Tel: (202) 727-7461

FLORIDA

Florida State Board of Nursing
111 Coastline Drive East, Suite 516
Jacksonville, Florida 32202
Tel: (904) 359-6331

GEORGIA

Georgia Board of Nursing, Registered Nurses
Suite 400
166 Pryor Street, S.W.
Atlanta, Georgia 30303
Tel: (404) 656-3943

GUAM

Guam Board of Nurse Examiners
P.O. Box 2816
Algana, Guam 96910
Tel: 001 (671) 477-8766 or 8517
FAX: 011 671/734-2066

HAWAII

State of Hawaii Board of Nursing
P.O. Box 3469
Honolulu, Hawaii 96801
Tel: (808) 548-5086

IDAHO

Idaho Board of Nursing
280 North 8th Street, Suite 210
Boise, Idaho 83720
Tel: (208) 334-3110

ILLINOIS

Illinois Department of Professional Regulation
320 W. Washington Street
Third Floor
Springfield, Illinois 62786
Tel: (217) 782-0800

INDIANA

Indiana State Board of Nursing
Health Professions Service Bureau
402 West Washington Street, Room 041
Indianapolis, Indiana 46204
Tel: (317) 232-2960

IOWA

Iowa Board of Nursing
Executive Hills
1223 East Court
Des Moines, Iowa 50319
Tel: (515) 281-3255

KANSAS

Kansas Board of Nursing
Landon State Office Building
900 S.W. Jackson, Suite 5511
Topeka, Kansas 66612-1230
Tel: (913) 296-4929
FAX: 913/296-3929

KENTUCKY

Kentucky State Board of Nursing
312 Whittington Parkway, Suite 300
Louisville, Kentucky 40222-5172
Tel: (502) 329-7000
FAX: 502/329-7011

LOUISIANA

Louisiana State Board of Nursing
150 Baronne Street, Suite 912
New Orleans, Louisiana 70112
Tel: (504) 568-5464
FAX: 504/568-5467

MAINE

Maine State Board of Nursing
State House Station
P.O. Box 158
Augusta, Maine 04433-0158
Tel: (207) 624-5275

MARYLAND

Maryland Board of Nursing
Metro Executive Center
4201 Patterson Avenue
Baltimore, Maryland 21215-2299
Tel: (410) 764-4747

MASSACHUSETTS

Massachusetts Board of Registration in Nursing
100 Cambridge Street, Room 1519
Boston, Massachusetts 02202
Tel: (617) 727-9961

MICHIGAN

Michigan Board of Nursing
P.O. Box 30018
Lansing, Michigan 48909
Tel: (517) 373-1600

MINNESOTA

Minnesota Board of Nursing
270 University Avenue W., #108
St. Paul, Minnesota 55114
Tel: (612) 642-0567

MISSISSIPPI

Mississippi Board of Nursing
239 N. Lamar, Suite 401
Jackson, Mississippi 39201
Tel: (601) 359-6170

MISSOURI

Missouri State Board of Nursing
P.O. Box 656
Jefferson City, Missouri 65102
Tel: (314) 751-0681

MONTANA

Montana State Board of Nursing
Department of Commerce
Arcade Building, Lower Level
111 North Jackson
P.O. Box 200513
Helena, Montana 59620-0513
Tel: (406) 444-4279

NEBRASKA

Nebraska Board of Nursing
State House Station
P.O. Box 95007
Lincoln, Nebraska 68509-5007
Tel: (402) 471-2115

NEVADA

Nevada State Board of Nursing
1281 Terminal Way, Suite 116
Reno, Nevada 89502
Tel: (702) 786-2778

NEW HAMPSHIRE

New Hampshire Board of Nursing
Division of Public Health Services
Health and Welfare Building
6 Hazen Drive
Concord, New Hampshire 03301-2657
Tel: (603) 271-2323

NEW JERSEY

New Jersey Board of Nursing
124 Halsey Street, 6th Floor
P.O. Box 45010
Newark, New Jersey 07101
Tel: (201) 504-6493

NEW MEXICO

New Mexico Board of Nursing
4253 Montgomery Boulevard, N.E., Suite 130
Albuquerque, New Mexico 87109
Tel: (505) 841-8340

NEW YORK

New York State Board for Nursing
State Education Department
Cultural Education Center, Room 3013
Albany, New York 12230
Tel: (518) 474-3843

NORTH CAROLINA

North Carolina Board of Nursing
P.O. Box 2129
Raleigh, North Carolina 27602-2129
Tel: (919) 828-0740

NORTH DAKOTA

North Dakota Board of Nursing
919 South 7th Street, Suite 504
Bismarck, North Dakota 58504-5881
Tel: (701) 224-2974

OHIO

Ohio Board of Nursing
77 South High Street, 17th Floor
Columbus, Ohio 43266-0316
Tel: (614) 466-3947

OKLAHOMA

Oklahoma Board of Nurse Registration and
    Nursing Education
2915 N. Classen Boulevard, Suite 524
Oklahoma City, Oklahoma 73106
Tel: (405) 525-2076

OREGON

Oregon State Board of Nursing
800 N.E. Oregon Street #25, Suite 465
Portland, Oregon 97232
Tel: (503) 731-4745

PENNSYLVANIA

Pennsylvania Board of Nursing
Department of State
P.O. Box 2649
Harrisburg, Pennsylvania 17105-2649
Tel: (717) 783-7142

RHODE ISLAND

Rhode Island Board of Nurse Registration and
    Nurse Education
Cannon Health Building,
#3 Capitol Hill, Room 104
Providence, Rhode Island 02908
Tel: (401) 277-2827

SOUTH CAROLINA

State Board of Nursing for South Carolina
220 Executive Center Drive, Suite 220
Columbia, South Carolina 29210
Tel: (803) 731-1648

SOUTH DAKOTA

South Dakota Board of Nursing
3307 South Lincoln Avenue
Sioux Falls, South Dakota 57105-5224
Tel: (605) 335-4973

TENNESSEE

Tennessee State Board of Nursing
283 Plus Park Boulevard
Nashville, Tennessee 37427-1010
Tel: (615) 367-6232

TEXAS

Board of Nurse Examiners for the State of Texas
9101 Burnet Road, Suite 104
P.O. Box 140466
Austin, Texas 78714-0466
Tel: (512) 835-4880

UTAH

Executive Secretary
Utah State Board of Nursing
Division of Occupational and Professional
    Licensing
Heber M. Wells Building, 4th Floor
160 East 300 South
P.O. Box 45802
Salt Lake City, Utah 84145-0801
Tel: (801) 530-6628

VERMONT

Vermont State Board of Nursing
109 State Street
Montpelier, Vermont 05609-1106
Tel: (802) 828-2396

VIRGINIA

Virginia State Board of Nursing
6606 West Broad Street, Fourth Floor
Richmond, Virginia 23230-1717
Tel: (804) 662-9909

VIRGIN ISLANDS (U.S.)

Virgin Island Board of Nurse Licensor
Kongens Gade #3
P.O. Box 4247
St. Thomas, Virgin Islands 00803
Tel: (809) 776-7397
FAX: 809/779-6368

WASHINGTON

Washington State Board of Nursing
Division of Professional Licensing
P.O. Box 47864
Olympia, Washington 98504-7864
Tel: (206) 453-2686

WEST VIRGINIA

West Virginia Board of Examiners for Registered
    Nurses
101 Dee Drive
Charleston, West Virginia 25311-1620
Tel: (304) 558-3692/3728

WISCONSIN

Wisconsin Board of Nursing
Room 174
P.O. Box 8935
Madison, Wisconsin 53708-8935
Tel: (608) 266-0145

WYOMING

Executive Director
Wyoming State Board of Nursing
Barrett Building, 2nd Floor
2301 Central Avenue
Cheyenne, Wyoming 82002
Tel: (307) 777-7601

PART I

Diagnostic Test of Factual Knowledge

Purpose of the Diagnostic Test

The Diagnostic Test is a self-assessment tool to enable you to identify your strengths and weaknesses in areas of nursing practice. *It is a test of factual knowledge,* rather than of nursing judgment, and is to be utilized as a pretest before studying the units on nursing principles and practices.

Directions:

1. Read each question carefully before looking at the answer choices.

2. When you are sure that you understand the question, select the choice that provides the correct answer.

3. In marking the answer sheet, use a pencil and blacken completely the circle that corresponds to your answer:

① ● ③ ④

If it becomes necessary to change an answer, erase the original one completely.

4. Don't spend too much time on a question to which you don't know the answer. If you can eliminate one or more choices as clearly incorrect, select the best answer from the remaining ones.

5. Since there is no penalty for guessing, answer every question.

ANSWER SHEET FOR DIAGNOSTIC TEST

1 ① ② ③ ④	49 ① ② ③ ④	97 ① ② ③ ④	145 ① ② ③ ④	193 ① ② ③ ④
2 ① ② ③ ④	50 ① ② ③ ④	98 ① ② ③ ④	146 ① ② ③ ④	194 ① ② ③ ④
3 ① ② ③ ④	51 ① ② ③ ④	99 ① ② ③ ④	147 ① ② ③ ④	195 ① ② ③ ④
4 ① ② ③ ④	52 ① ② ③ ④	100 ① ② ③ ④	148 ① ② ③ ④	196 ① ② ③ ④
5 ① ② ③ ④	53 ① ② ③ ④	101 ① ② ③ ④	149 ① ② ③ ④	197 ① ② ③ ④
6 ① ② ③ ④	54 ① ② ③ ④	102 ① ② ③ ④	150 ① ② ③ ④	198 ① ② ③ ④
7 ① ② ③ ④	55 ① ② ③ ④	103 ① ② ③ ④	151 ① ② ③ ④	199 ① ② ③ ④
8 ① ② ③ ④	56 ① ② ③ ④	104 ① ② ③ ④	152 ① ② ③ ④	200 ① ② ③ ④
9 ① ② ③ ④	57 ① ② ③ ④	105 ① ② ③ ④	153 ① ② ③ ④	201 ① ② ③ ④
10 ① ② ③ ④	58 ① ② ③ ④	106 ① ② ③ ④	154 ① ② ③ ④	202 ① ② ③ ④
11 ① ② ③ ④	59 ① ② ③ ④	107 ① ② ③ ④	155 ① ② ③ ④	203 ① ② ③ ④
12 ① ② ③ ④	60 ① ② ③ ④	108 ① ② ③ ④	156 ① ② ③ ④	204 ① ② ③ ④
13 ① ② ③ ④	61 ① ② ③ ④	109 ① ② ③ ④	157 ① ② ③ ④	205 ① ② ③ ④
14 ① ② ③ ④	62 ① ② ③ ④	110 ① ② ③ ④	158 ① ② ③ ④	206 ① ② ③ ④
15 ① ② ③ ④	63 ① ② ③ ④	111 ① ② ③ ④	159 ① ② ③ ④	207 ① ② ③ ④
16 ① ② ③ ④	64 ① ② ③ ④	112 ① ② ③ ④	160 ① ② ③ ④	208 ① ② ③ ④
17 ① ② ③ ④	65 ① ② ③ ④	113 ① ② ③ ④	161 ① ② ③ ④	209 ① ② ③ ④
18 ① ② ③ ④	66 ① ② ③ ④	114 ① ② ③ ④	162 ① ② ③ ④	210 ① ② ③ ④
19 ① ② ③ ④	67 ① ② ③ ④	115 ① ② ③ ④	163 ① ② ③ ④	211 ① ② ③ ④
20 ① ② ③ ④	68 ① ② ③ ④	116 ① ② ③ ④	164 ① ② ③ ④	212 ① ② ③ ④
21 ① ② ③ ④	69 ① ② ③ ④	117 ① ② ③ ④	165 ① ② ③ ④	213 ① ② ③ ④
22 ① ② ③ ④	70 ① ② ③ ④	118 ① ② ③ ④	166 ① ② ③ ④	214 ① ② ③ ④
23 ① ② ③ ④	71 ① ② ③ ④	119 ① ② ③ ④	167 ① ② ③ ④	215 ① ② ③ ④
24 ① ② ③ ④	72 ① ② ③ ④	120 ① ② ③ ④	168 ① ② ③ ④	216 ① ② ③ ④
25 ① ② ③ ④	73 ① ② ③ ④	121 ① ② ③ ④	169 ① ② ③ ④	217 ① ② ③ ④
26 ① ② ③ ④	74 ① ② ③ ④	122 ① ② ③ ④	170 ① ② ③ ④	218 ① ② ③ ④
27 ① ② ③ ④	75 ① ② ③ ④	123 ① ② ③ ④	171 ① ② ③ ④	219 ① ② ③ ④
28 ① ② ③ ④	76 ① ② ③ ④	124 ① ② ③ ④	172 ① ② ③ ④	220 ① ② ③ ④
29 ① ② ③ ④	77 ① ② ③ ④	125 ① ② ③ ④	173 ① ② ③ ④	221 ① ② ③ ④
30 ① ② ③ ④	78 ① ② ③ ④	126 ① ② ③ ④	174 ① ② ③ ④	222 ① ② ③ ④
31 ① ② ③ ④	79 ① ② ③ ④	127 ① ② ③ ④	175 ① ② ③ ④	223 ① ② ③ ④
32 ① ② ③ ④	80 ① ② ③ ④	128 ① ② ③ ④	176 ① ② ③ ④	224 ① ② ③ ④
33 ① ② ③ ④	81 ① ② ③ ④	129 ① ② ③ ④	177 ① ② ③ ④	225 ① ② ③ ④
34 ① ② ③ ④	82 ① ② ③ ④	130 ① ② ③ ④	178 ① ② ③ ④	226 ① ② ③ ④
35 ① ② ③ ④	83 ① ② ③ ④	131 ① ② ③ ④	179 ① ② ③ ④	227 ① ② ③ ④
36 ① ② ③ ④	84 ① ② ③ ④	132 ① ② ③ ④	180 ① ② ③ ④	228 ① ② ③ ④
37 ① ② ③ ④	85 ① ② ③ ④	133 ① ② ③ ④	181 ① ② ③ ④	229 ① ② ③ ④
38 ① ② ③ ④	86 ① ② ③ ④	134 ① ② ③ ④	182 ① ② ③ ④	230 ① ② ③ ④
39 ① ② ③ ④	87 ① ② ③ ④	135 ① ② ③ ④	183 ① ② ③ ④	231 ① ② ③ ④
40 ① ② ③ ④	88 ① ② ③ ④	136 ① ② ③ ④	184 ① ② ③ ④	232 ① ② ③ ④
41 ① ② ③ ④	89 ① ② ③ ④	137 ① ② ③ ④	185 ① ② ③ ④	233 ① ② ③ ④
42 ① ② ③ ④	90 ① ② ③ ④	138 ① ② ③ ④	186 ① ② ③ ④	234 ① ② ③ ④
43 ① ② ③ ④	91 ① ② ③ ④	139 ① ② ③ ④	187 ① ② ③ ④	235 ① ② ③ ④
44 ① ② ③ ④	92 ① ② ③ ④	140 ① ② ③ ④	188 ① ② ③ ④	236 ① ② ③ ④
45 ① ② ③ ④	93 ① ② ③ ④	141 ① ② ③ ④	189 ① ② ③ ④	237 ① ② ③ ④
46 ① ② ③ ④	94 ① ② ③ ④	142 ① ② ③ ④	190 ① ② ③ ④	238 ① ② ③ ④
47 ① ② ③ ④	95 ① ② ③ ④	143 ① ② ③ ④	191 ① ② ③ ④	239 ① ② ③ ④
48 ① ② ③ ④	96 ① ② ③ ④	144 ① ② ③ ④	192 ① ② ③ ④	240 ① ② ③ ④

241 ① ② ③ ④	289 ① ② ③ ④	337 ① ② ③ ④	385 ① ② ③ ④	433 ① ② ③ ④
242 ① ② ③ ④	290 ① ② ③ ④	338 ① ② ③ ④	386 ① ② ③ ④	434 ① ② ③ ④
243 ① ② ③ ④	291 ① ② ③ ④	339 ① ② ③ ④	387 ① ② ③ ④	435 ① ② ③ ④
244 ① ② ③ ④	292 ① ② ③ ④	340 ① ② ③ ④	388 ① ② ③ ④	436 ① ② ③ ④
245 ① ② ③ ④	293 ① ② ③ ④	341 ① ② ③ ④	389 ① ② ③ ④	437 ① ② ③ ④
246 ① ② ③ ④	294 ① ② ③ ④	342 ① ② ③ ④	390 ① ② ③ ④	438 ① ② ③ ④
247 ① ② ③ ④	295 ① ② ③ ④	343 ① ② ③ ④	391 ① ② ③ ④	439 ① ② ③ ④
248 ① ② ③ ④	296 ① ② ③ ④	344 ① ② ③ ④	392 ① ② ③ ④	440 ① ② ③ ④
249 ① ② ③ ④	297 ① ② ③ ④	345 ① ② ③ ④	393 ① ② ③ ④	441 ① ② ③ ④
250 ① ② ③ ④	298 ① ② ③ ④	346 ① ② ③ ④	394 ① ② ③ ④	442 ① ② ③ ④
251 ① ② ③ ④	299 ① ② ③ ④	347 ① ② ③ ④	395 ① ② ③ ④	443 ① ② ③ ④
252 ① ② ③ ④	300 ① ② ③ ④	348 ① ② ③ ④	396 ① ② ③ ④	444 ① ② ③ ④
253 ① ② ③ ④	301 ① ② ③ ④	349 ① ② ③ ④	397 ① ② ③ ④	445 ① ② ③ ④
254 ① ② ③ ④	302 ① ② ③ ④	350 ① ② ③ ④	398 ① ② ③ ④	446 ① ② ③ ④
255 ① ② ③ ④	303 ① ② ③ ④	351 ① ② ③ ④	399 ① ② ③ ④	447 ① ② ③ ④
256 ① ② ③ ④	304 ① ② ③ ④	352 ① ② ③ ④	400 ① ② ③ ④	448 ① ② ③ ④
257 ① ② ③ ④	305 ① ② ③ ④	353 ① ② ③ ④	401 ① ② ③ ④	449 ① ② ③ ④
258 ① ② ③ ④	306 ① ② ③ ④	354 ① ② ③ ④	402 ① ② ③ ④	450 ① ② ③ ④
259 ① ② ③ ④	307 ① ② ③ ④	355 ① ② ③ ④	403 ① ② ③ ④	451 ① ② ③ ④
260 ① ② ③ ④	308 ① ② ③ ④	356 ① ② ③ ④	404 ① ② ③ ④	452 ① ② ③ ④
261 ① ② ③ ④	309 ① ② ③ ④	357 ① ② ③ ④	405 ① ② ③ ④	453 ① ② ③ ④
262 ① ② ③ ④	310 ① ② ③ ④	358 ① ② ③ ④	406 ① ② ③ ④	454 ① ② ③ ④
263 ① ② ③ ④	311 ① ② ③ ④	359 ① ② ③ ④	407 ① ② ③ ④	455 ① ② ③ ④
264 ① ② ③ ④	312 ① ② ③ ④	360 ① ② ③ ④	408 ① ② ③ ④	456 ① ② ③ ④
265 ① ② ③ ④	313 ① ② ③ ④	361 ① ② ③ ④	409 ① ② ③ ④	457 ① ② ③ ④
266 ① ② ③ ④	314 ① ② ③ ④	362 ① ② ③ ④	410 ① ② ③ ④	458 ① ② ③ ④
267 ① ② ③ ④	315 ① ② ③ ④	363 ① ② ③ ④	411 ① ② ③ ④	459 ① ② ③ ④
268 ① ② ③ ④	316 ① ② ③ ④	364 ① ② ③ ④	412 ① ② ③ ④	460 ① ② ③ ④
269 ① ② ③ ④	317 ① ② ③ ④	365 ① ② ③ ④	413 ① ② ③ ④	461 ① ② ③ ④
270 ① ② ③ ④	318 ① ② ③ ④	366 ① ② ③ ④	414 ① ② ③ ④	462 ① ② ③ ④
271 ① ② ③ ④	319 ① ② ③ ④	367 ① ② ③ ④	415 ① ② ③ ④	463 ① ② ③ ④
272 ① ② ③ ④	320 ① ② ③ ④	368 ① ② ③ ④	416 ① ② ③ ④	464 ① ② ③ ④
273 ① ② ③ ④	321 ① ② ③ ④	369 ① ② ③ ④	417 ① ② ③ ④	465 ① ② ③ ④
274 ① ② ③ ④	322 ① ② ③ ④	370 ① ② ③ ④	418 ① ② ③ ④	466 ① ② ③ ④
275 ① ② ③ ④	323 ① ② ③ ④	371 ① ② ③ ④	419 ① ② ③ ④	467 ① ② ③ ④
276 ① ② ③ ④	324 ① ② ③ ④	372 ① ② ③ ④	420 ① ② ③ ④	468 ① ② ③ ④
277 ① ② ③ ④	325 ① ② ③ ④	373 ① ② ③ ④	421 ① ② ③ ④	469 ① ② ③ ④
278 ① ② ③ ④	326 ① ② ③ ④	374 ① ② ③ ④	422 ① ② ③ ④	470 ① ② ③ ④
279 ① ② ③ ④	327 ① ② ③ ④	375 ① ② ③ ④	423 ① ② ③ ④	471 ① ② ③ ④
280 ① ② ③ ④	328 ① ② ③ ④	376 ① ② ③ ④	424 ① ② ③ ④	472 ① ② ③ ④
281 ① ② ③ ④	329 ① ② ③ ④	377 ① ② ③ ④	425 ① ② ③ ④	473 ① ② ③ ④
282 ① ② ③ ④	330 ① ② ③ ④	378 ① ② ③ ④	426 ① ② ③ ④	474 ① ② ③ ④
283 ① ② ③ ④	331 ① ② ③ ④	379 ① ② ③ ④	427 ① ② ③ ④	475 ① ② ③ ④
284 ① ② ③ ④	332 ① ② ③ ④	380 ① ② ③ ④	428 ① ② ③ ④	476 ① ② ③ ④
285 ① ② ③ ④	333 ① ② ③ ④	381 ① ② ③ ④	429 ① ② ③ ④	477 ① ② ③ ④
286 ① ② ③ ④	334 ① ② ③ ④	382 ① ② ③ ④	430 ① ② ③ ④	478 ① ② ③ ④
287 ① ② ③ ④	335 ① ② ③ ④	383 ① ② ③ ④	431 ① ② ③ ④	479 ① ② ③ ④
288 ① ② ③ ④	336 ① ② ③ ④	384 ① ② ③ ④	432 ① ② ③ ④	480 ① ② ③ ④

DIAGNOSTIC TEST

1. The average initial weight loss for the normal newborn is what percentage of his/her body weight?
   1. 0–5%.
   2. 5–10%.
   3. 10–15%.
   4. 15–20%.

2. The startle reflex present in all newborns is known as
   1. the tonic neck reflex.
   2. the Moro reflex.
   3. the Babinski reflex.
   4. the knee-jerk reflex.

3. A clinical manifestation that indicates a newborn is in distress is
   1. bluish discoloration of the hands and feet.
   2. rapid, irregular respirations.
   3. periods of loud crying.
   4. habitual extension of the arms and legs.

4. If a newborn has swollen breast tissue at birth, the mother should be instructed to
   1. rub the breasts until the swelling disappears.
   2. put ice on the breasts.
   3. leave the breasts alone.
   4. squeeze the breasts to eliminate fluid.

5. The hemoglobin of a newborn is
   1. 17–20 gm.
   2. 12–14 gm.
   3. 10–12 gm.
   4. 9–10 gm.

6. Hiccups are caused by
   1. spasms of the diaphragm.
   2. underfeeding.
   3. swallowing too much air.
   4. spasms of the cardiac sphincter.

7. Which of the following is abnormal in the newborn?
   1. Irregular respirations, 40 per minute.
   2. Slight cyanosis of the extremities.
   3. Black, tarry stools.
   4. Persistent, high-pitched, whining cry.

8. Which of the following techniques is MOST important in preventing infections in the newborn nursery?
   1. Autoclaving all clothing and linens utilized by the newborn.
   2. Wearing masks and gowns.
   3. Handwashing before each contact with an infant.
   4. Using ultraviolet lights and special ventilation systems.

9. Maternal hormones may be responsible for which of the following in the newborn?
   1. Engorgement of the breasts.
   2. Undescended testicles.
   3. Vaginal fusion.
   4. Hypertrophy of the genitalia.

10. Which of the following findings related to a newborn's umbilical cord is normal?
    1. Redness at the base of the cord.
    2. Drying of the cord.
    3. Discharge from the base of the cord.
    4. Foul odor from the cord.

11. Which of the following is NOT included on an Apgar score?
    1. Weight.
    2. Color.
    3. Respiratory effort.
    4. Muscle tone.

12. Respirations in a newborn soon after birth are usually
    1. shallow, from the chest, and rapid.
    2. effortless and slow.
    3. rapid, diaphragmatic, and irregular.
    4. slow, abdominal, and regular.

13. The tonic neck reflex in the newborn is manifested by
    1. the fencing position.
    2. a coordinated sucking and swallowing reflex.
    3. the startle reflex.
    4. rigidity of the neck when held.

14. Which of the following findings in an infant would require immediate notification of the physician?

  1. A small green stool with yellow material mixed in it.
  2. Loose yellow-orange stool in a breast-fed infant.
  3. Greenish yellow, watery stools forcefully expelled.
  4. Dark green, tarry stools.

15. Milia is a condition of the infant skin in which there is (are)

  1. presence of a yeastlike infection.
  2. small red "port wine" areas on the nose and the face.
  3. dark areas on the back.
  4. white pinhead-sized papules on the face.

16. Cephalhematoma in an infant

  1. is an engorgement of the soft tissue at the back of the head.
  2. is often due to trauma during delivery.
  3. occurs over a nonbony area.
  4. indicates a frontal presentation at delivery.

17. When a father sees his baby for the first time, he expresses concern because the baby's head appears elongated. The nurse's best reply would be that the apparent elongation is due to

  1. a collection of blood under the bones.
  2. a collection of fluid in the tissues.
  3. an overlapping of bones during birth.
  4. a genetically inherited trait.

18. Which of the following infants will be observed most closely for signs of infection?

  1. The child of a mother whose membranes ruptured prior to 24 hours before delivery.
  2. The child of a multipara pregnancy.
  3. The child delivered by cesarean.
  4. The child of a multipara who has had eight pregnancies.

19. Upon admission of a newborn, the nursery nurse notes the presence of protruding tongue and slanted eyes. These can be an indication of

  1. phenylketonuria.
  2. hypoglycemia.
  3. Down syndrome.
  4. drug addiction.

20. A nurse on the postpartum unit reports to the nursery personnel that a patient stated she had had no opportunity, before admission to the hospital with labor pains, to use the ointment given her that morning in clinic for pruritis and a thick, curdlike vaginal discharge. This information should alert the nursery staff to observe the patient's baby for signs of

  1. ophthalmia neonatorum.
  2. jaundice.
  3. conjunctivitis.
  4. thrush.

21. In giving care to a baby, the nurse observes depressed fontanels. The nurse reports this to the doctor immediately because it can be a sign of

  1. infection.
  2. dehydration.
  3. brain hemorrhage.
  4. shock.

22. In inspecting the fontanels on a newborn infant, which of the following observations would suggest an abnormality?

  1. Posterior fontanel smaller than anterior fontanel.
  2. Diamond-shaped anterior fontanel.
  3. Bulging anterior fontanel.
  4. Posterior fontanel difficult to palpate.

23. Which of the following would cause an infant to be isolated in the nursery?

  1. Physiologic jaundice.
  2. Recent circumcision.
  3. Impetigo.
  4. Subnormal temperature.

24. If a 3-day-old infant was found to have a 100°F temperature, which of the following explanations is NOT possible?

  1. The room was too warm.
  2. The infant was too warmly dressed.
  3. The infant's temperature was normal for a newborn.
  4. The infant was dehydrated.

25. For a baby who has a meningomyelocele, the FIRST priority in providing nursing care for the baby is to

  1. maintain fluid and electrolyte balance.
  2. prevent rupture of the external sac.
  3. begin passive range of motion exercises.
  4. prevent urinary tract infections.

26. The pediatrician suspects that a 1-month-old baby has hydrocephalus. The nurse assigned to the baby should

    1. monitor his blood pressure.
    2. palpate his anterior fontanel.
    3. auscultate his apical pulse.
    4. measure his chest circumference.

27. A 2-year-old child has just had a cleft-palate repair. The BEST method of feeding the child a clear liquid diet is with

    1. an Ascepto syringe
    2. a special cleft-palate nipple.
    3. a rubber-tipped syringe
    4. a plastic cup.

28. A nursery nurse feeds a baby his first water feeding. The baby becomes cyanotic. The nursery nurse should suspect

    1. pyloric stenosis
    2. congenital heart disease.
    3. respiratory distress syndrome.
    4. esophageal atresia.

29. A nursery nurse observes that a 1-day-old infant has not passed a meconium stool. Further assessment is required as the nurse should suspect that the newborn may have

    1. an imperforate anus.
    2. a congenital megacolon.
    3. biliary atresia.
    4. a rectovaginal fistula.

30. A 1-month-old baby has a patent ductus arteriosus. This anomaly occurs when

    1. the opening between the left and the right atrium fails to close after birth.
    2. the structure that shunts blood from the pulmonary artery to the aorta remains open after birth.
    3. there is a narrowing of the aortic lumen near the level of the ductus arteriosus.
    4. the aorta arises from the right ventricle and the pulmonary artery originates from the left ventricle.

31. A newborn who has an atrial septal defect is scheduled to have a cardiac catheterization for assessment of

    1. pressure and oxygen concentration within the heart and major vessels.
    2. size and position of the chambers of the heart and the status of the pulmonary vascular bed.

    3. hemoglobin and hematocrit values of arterial and venous blood.
    4. changes in the electric potential of the heart and the condition of cardiac muscles.

32. A 6-month-old child has been placed in a spica cast for treatment of congenital dislocated hip. The nurse teaches the mother how to care for the baby while she is in the spica cast. The HIGHEST priority in caring for the baby at this time is to

    1. provide appropriate toys to promote normal growth and development.
    2. keep the skin around the spica cast clean and dry.
    3. assess for signs of circulatory impairment.
    4. maintain the integrity of the cast.

33. A 2-week old baby is admitted to the pediatric unit for repair of pyloric stenosis. The BEST position to place the baby in after feeding is

    1. on her right side, with her head elevated.
    2. on her back, in an infant seat.
    3. on her abdomen, with her head turned to the side.
    4. on her left side, supported by sandbags.

34. A mother brings her 6-month-old son to the child health clinic. His birth weight was 7 pounds, 9 ounces. The nurse weighing the baby would expect him to weigh approximately

    1. 10 pounds.
    2. 12 pounds.
    3. 15 pounds.
    4. 20 pounds.

35. The nurse assesses the baby's reflexes. Which of the following responses would indicate the need for further neurological testing?

    1. A negative tonic neck reflex.
    2. A positive Moro reflex.
    3. A negative rooting reflex.
    4. A positive Babinski reflex.

36. The nurse assesses an 8-month-old child's motor development. Which of the following behaviors should she expect to observe?

    1. The child will pull herself to a sitting position.
    2. The child will pull herself to a standing position.
    3. The child will be able to walk holding on.
    4. The child will walk independently.

37. According to Erikson, the infant is in the developmental stage of trust versus mistrust. Trust is facilitated by
    1. allowing the infant to cry for increasingly longer periods of time before meeting his/her needs.
    2. exposing the infant to a variety of care-takers.
    3. receiving constant attention from the mother or mother substitute.
    4. having the mother consistently meeting the infant's needs.

38. A mother has been breast feeding her 5-month-old son. She asks the nurse when she should begin weaning him. The nurse replies:
    1. "Weaning is a gradual process that is most often begun when the baby gives cues."
    2. "Weaning must be accomplished by the time the infant's central incisors erupt."
    3. "Weaning is best accomplished after the infant is walking because he will be more interested in exploring his environment than in breast feeding."
    4. "Weaning is begun when the infant is 12 months old and is completed when he is 13 months old."

39. A 15-month-old child is brought to the child health clinic. If his immunizations are up to date, this visit he will receive
    1. his third diphtheria-tetanus-pertussis immunization.
    2. *Haemophilus influenzae* type b polysac-charide vaccine.
    3. the measles, rubella, and mumps immu-nization.
    4. a diphtheria-tetanus-pertussis booster.

40. A 6-month-old baby has been admitted to the pediatric unit with a diagnosis of pneumonia. To help the mother cope with her anxiety about her baby's hospitalization, the nurse should
    1. allow her to participate in the admission procedure.
    2. ask her to wait in the lounge.
    3. assure her that her child will get well.
    4. ask her to contact her husband.

41. The recommended site for a 3-month-old infant to receive an intramuscular injection of ampicillin is the
    1. deltoid muscle.
    2. ventrogluteal muscle.
    3. posterior gluteal muscle.
    4. vastus lateralis muscle.

42. A 3-year-old child is to receive 125 mg of ampicillin PO. The BEST approach by the nurse would be to
    1. ask the child if he would like his medica-tion now or in a half hour when he has finished watching a cartoon show.
    2. hand the child the medication cup and tell him to drink his medication now.
    3. place the medicine in a dropper, hold the child in a semireclining position, and place the medication at the side of his mouth.
    4. tell the child that if he drinks all of his medication quickly he can have a lol-lipop.

43. A 6-month-old infant is to receive 800 cc of dextrose 5% and water to run over a 12-hour period. A Volutrol that delivers 60 ml per minute will be used. The nurse adjusts the Volutrol to run
    1. 47 microdrops per minute.
    2. 57 microdrops per minute.
    3. 67 microdrops per minute.
    4. 77 microdrops per minute.

44. A couple have a 2-year-old child with phenylketonuria. They wish to have another child in the future. What is the probability of them having another child with phenylke-tonuria?
    1. There is a 50% probability that their next child will have phenylketonuria.
    2. Since the first child has phenylketonuria, all their future children will be normal.
    3. All children that the couple have in the future will also have phenylketonuria.
    4. There is a 25% probability that their next child will have phenylketonuria.

45. An 18-month-old child is admitted to the pediatric unit with a diagnosis of intussusception. Intussusception is
    1. a telescoping of one portion of the intestine into another.
    2. a herniation of the abdominal viscera at the level of the umbilicus.
    3. a faulty development of the bile ducts linking the gall bladder to the duodenum.
    4. an absence of parasympathetic ganglion nerve cells in the descending colon.

46. The nurse is teaching the parents of a child with cystic fibrosis the procedure for postural drainage. When should the nurse instruct the parents to do postural drainage?
    1. Each morning as soon as the child gets out of bed.
    2. Before each meal and at bedtime.
    3. Once or twice a day when they have time.
    4. Each night just before the child's bedtime.

47. A patient is being treated for celiac disease. Which of the following foods would be included in her diet?
    1. Crackers.
    2. Spaghetti.
    3. Oatmeal.
    4. Rice.

48. A 2-month-old baby has had green, loose, watery stools for 2 days. The nurse assesses him for signs of dehydration. The BEST way to assess for dehydration is to
    1. determine intake and output every 8 hours.
    2. obtain his weight each shift.
    3. palpate for sunken fontanels.
    4. determine a daily specific gravity.

49. A 7-month-old child is placed on Fer-In-Sol, an oral iron preparation. The nurse counseling the mother about administration of the iron supplement advises her to
    1. administer the iron preparation between meals to enhance absorption.
    2. administer the iron preparation once a day immediately after breakfast.
    3. withhold fluids for at least 1 hour after administering iron.
    4. administer the iron with a glass of milk to prevent teeth staining.

50. A 2-year-old child is admitted to the pediatric unit with a diagnosis of sickle-cell crisis. The priority nursing care goal at this time is to
    1. minimize the child's joint pain.
    2. provide genetic counseling for the family.
    3. protect the child from infection.
    4. provide an increased fluid intake.

51. A child is receiving a transfusion of whole blood for treatment of thalassemia major. The nurse assigned to the child observes that he has urticaria and is wheezing. These are manifestations of
    1. an allergic reaction.
    2. circulatory overload.
    3. electrolyte imbalance.
    4. a hemolytic reaction.

52. Which of the following toys would be appropriate for a 10-month-old child who has infantile eczema?
    1. Large wooden blocks.
    2. A rubber duck.
    3. A stuffed rabbit.
    4. A string of beads.

53. A 1-year-old child has been admitted to the pediatric unit with a diagnosis of Wilm's tumor. The MOST important nursing intervention is
    1. monitoring the child's vital signs.
    2. providing the child with diversional activities.
    3. keeping an accurate record of the child's intake and output.
    4. avoiding palpation of the child's abdomen.

54. A 3-year-old child is brought to the emergency room with multiple bruises on his body. His mother states that the child fell off his tricycle, but child abuse is suspected. Generally parents who abuse their children
    1. were abused when they were children.
    2. are alcohol and drug abusers.
    3. feel guilty and helpless.
    4. are from low socioeconomic neighborhoods.

55. Which of the following behaviors does NOT describe the autistic child?
    1. Severe withdrawal.
    2. Preoccupation with inanimate objects.
    3. Remarkable memory for poems, songs, and other rhythmic lyrics.
    4. Responsiveness to human contact.

56. The nurse at the well-child clinic is obtaining a developmental history on a 20-month-old child. The nurse expects that the child will have

 1. complete bowel and bladder control.
 2. bowel control only.
 3. daytime bladder control.
 4. both daytime and nighttime bladder control.

57. A nurse has prepared a 3-year-old child for bed. As the nurse begins to leave the room, the child cries, "My mommy always kisses me goodnight and she leaves the light on. I always sleep with my teddy bear." This is an example of

 1. autonomy.
 2. a temper tantrum.
 3. negativism.
 4. ritualistic behavior.

58. A mother tells the nurse that she is concerned about her 2½-year-old son. She has observed him frequently talking to "Ralph," a large, invisible bear. The nurse should make which of these replies?

 1. "Imaginary playmates are common at this age."
 2. "It is best to discuss this with your pediatrician."
 3. "I will observe your son and then discuss this problem further with you."
 4. "You should purchase a stuffed bear for your son."

59. A 3-year-old child is in the playroom. She tries to take a doll from another child. When she is unsuccessful, she begins to roll on the floor, thrashing her arms and legs. The MOST appropriate intervention by the nurse would be to

 1. provide her with another doll to play with.
 2. take her to her room and place her in her crib for 1 hour.
 3. protect her from injury and not comment on her behavior.
 4. explain to her that the doll belongs to another child.

60. A mother is concerned about her 18-month-old daughter's decrease in appetite. She states, "Stacy eats much less than she did when she was an infant." Which of these replies would be appropriate for the nurse to make?

 1. "You should speak to your pediatrician about providing a vitamin supplement for Stacy."
 2. "Children of this age normally have a decrease in appetite because they are more interested in exploring their environment."
 3. "You should provide Stacy with small, frequent feedings throughout the day."
 4. "I'm sure there is no need to be concerned. Her appetite will increase when she is 2 years old."

61. A mother asks the nurse when she should begin taking her 2-year-old son to the dentist. Which of these replies would be appropriate for the nurse to make?

 1. "It is not necessary to visit a dentist until your child enters kindergarten."
 2. "Most dentists like to see children for the first time when they are 4 years old."
 3. "Dental care should begin when a child is 1 year old."
 4. "Your child should first visit the dentist when all 20 temporary teeth are present."

62. A group of toddlers are in the playroom. The nurse supervising the group would expect to observe

 1. each child playing with a peer of the same sex.
 2. the group cooperating in playing house.
 3. the children playing alongside, but not with, each other.
 4. the children sharing their toys with each other.

63. A 24-month-old child was just admitted to the pediatric unit. Her mother is unable to room-in with her. Which of the following behavior patterns would be MOST likely to describe the child's response to hospitalization at this age?

 1. She lies quietly in one corner of her crib.
 2. She stands in her crib crying constantly for her mother.
 3. She readily accepts the attentions of the nurse.
 4. She asks to go to the playroom.

64. In the middle of the night the parents of a 2-year-old bring him to the emergency room where the pediatrician diagnoses the child as having acute spasmodic croup. The nurse assessing the child should expect to observe

1. retractions on inspiration.
2. slow, shallow respirations.
3. wheezing on expiration.
4. stridor on both inspiration and expiration.

65. A 3-year-old child is brought to the emergency room by her parents. She is having an asthma attack. The physician will most likely order which of the following types of medication for the child?

1. Antihistamine.
2. Antibiotic.
3. Bronchodilator.
4. Expectorant.

66. A 2-year-old child has otitis media. Drainage is present in her right ear canal. The nurse cleansing the child's ear should pull her ear lobe

1. up and back.
2. down and forward.
3. up and forward.
4. down and back.

67. A nurse is speaking to a group of mothers about safety during the toddler period. One of the mothers asks what she should do if her child ingests a poisonous substance. The BEST reply by the nurse is:

1. "Induce vomiting by stimulating the back of the child's throat."
2. "Identify what was ingested, and call the local poison control center."
3. "Have the child drink large quantities of milk."
4. "Administer syrup of ipecac immediately."

68. A 20-month-old child is brought to the emergency room by his parents after he ingested half a bottle of aspirin. The nurse assessing the child immediately takes his vital signs. The nurse would expect to observe

1. hyperventilation.
2. elevated blood pressure.
3. hypopyrexia.
4. a slow, steady pulse.

69. A 15-month-old child is being treated for lead poisoning with EDTA and BAL intravenously. These medications act to

1. promote excretion of lead via the gastrointestinal tract.
2. aid in depositing lead in the soft tissues.
3. aid in depositing lead at the ends of the long bones.
4. promote urinary excretion of lead.

70. A 2-year-old girl is brought to the emergency room with burns on both legs and her entire abdomen. She pulled a kettle of boiling water off the stove. The nurse admitting the child should FIRST observe for signs of

1. infection.
2. shock.
3. respiratory distress.
4. dehydration.

71. A 19-month-old child fell from his high chair and fractured his femur. He is admitted to the hospital and placed in Bryant's traction. The priority nursing intervention while the child is in traction is

1. frequently assessing the circulatory status in both lower extremities.
2. providing frequent skin care to the child.
3. encouraging the child to cough and deep-breathe every 2 hours.
4. providing small, frequent feedings of the child's favorite foods.

72. A 3-year-old boy is admitted to the pediatric unit with a diagnosis of nephrotic syndrome. The MOST common presenting symptom of nephrosis is

1. increased urine output.
2. hematuria.
3. hypertension.
4. periorbital edema.

73. A 3-year-old child is receiving prednisone to treat his nephrosis. The nurse assigned to the child assesses him for the side effects of this medication, which include

1. Cushing's syndrome.
2. hypotension.
3. blood dyscrasias.
4. hyperactivity.

74. A 3-year-old child has cerebral palsy. The nurse assessing the child observes that his legs are scissored, his forearms are flexed and held against his chests, and his fists are clenched. The child has which of the following types of cerebral palsy?

1. Mixed.
2. Ataxic.
3. Dyskinetic.
4. Spastic.

75. A nurse assessing the vital signs of a 4-year-old child should know that the average pulse rate for this age group is

1. 120 per minute.
2. 105 per minute.
3. 95 per minute.
4. 80 per minute.

76. A nurse assessing a 3-year-old child's ability to participate in activities of daily living should expect that the child can

1. undress herself.
2. lace and tie her shoes.
3. dress herself without assistance.
4. button her clothes.

77. The nurse is observing a 3-year-old child trying to copy geometric figures. A child of this age group can copy a

1. circle.
2. diamond.
3. square.
4. rectangle.

78. By the end of the preschool period, which of the following personal-social characteristics has emerged?

1. The child wishes to spend equal time with each of his/her parents.
2. The child identifies with the parent of the opposite sex.
3. The child prefers to spend time with his/her peers.
4. The child identifies with the parent of the same sex.

79. According to Erikson, the preschooler is in which of the following stages of development?

1. Autonomy versus shame and doubt.
2. Industry versus inferiority.
3. Initiative versus guilt.
4. Identity versus identity diffusion.

80. A group of preschoolers is observed in the playroom. Which of the following statements MOST accurately describes play in this age group?

1. The boys are playing with fire engines, and the girls are playing with dolls.
2. Both boys and girls are playing house.
3. Each child is engaged separately in an activity of his or her choice.
4. Each child is playing alongside another child of the same sex.

81. A 5-year-old child is hospitalized for viral pneumonia. Which of the following toys would be MOST appropriate for this child?

1. Modeling clay.
2. A stuffed poodle.
3. Doctor and nurse puppets.
4. A coloring book and crayons.

82. A 4-year-old boy is admitted to the hospital for inguinal hernia repair. The nurse preparing the child for surgery

1. explains in detail the surgical procedure, utilizing diagrams.
2. uses simple terms to explain preoperative and postoperative procedures.
3. explains the rationale for a hernia repair.
4. reassures the child that he will definitely go home in the afternoon following surgery.

83. A 4-year-old child has just had her tonsils removed. The nurse assessing the child would be MOST concerned if she observed which of the following symptoms?

1. Mucus containing dark blood.
2. A pulse rate of 90 per minute.
3. Frequent swallowing.
4. A temperature of 100°F.

84. A 5-year-old child is admitted to the pediatric unit with a tentative diagnosis of meningitis. To which of the following rooms should the head nurse assign this child?

1. A 2-bedded room occupied by a 4-year-old boy with pneumonia.
2. A private room across from the nurses' station.
3. A 2-bedded room occupied by a 5-year-old boy with acute glomerulonephritis.
4. A private room at the end of the hall.

85. A 3-year-old child has a history of repeated urinary tract infections. Her urinalysis will probably reveal

    1. amber, acidic urine.
    2. increased specific gravity.
    3. an absence of white blood cells.
    4. cloudy, alkaline urine.

86. A 4-year-old child is admitted to the pediatric unit with a diagnosis of acute glomerulonephritis. The MOST common presenting symptom of acute glomerulonephritis is

    1. proteinuria.
    2. pyuria.
    3. hematuria.
    4. oliguria.

87. Classical hemophilia, a defect in the clotting mechanism, is a hereditary disorder transmitted by

    1. an autosomal recessive trait.
    2. a female carrier to her male offspring.
    3. a female carrier to her children of either sex.
    4. a male carrier to his female offspring.

88. A 4-year-old child has a convulsive disorder. The nurse observes a seizure lasting 40 seconds and consisting of alternating clonic and tonic movements with loss of consciousness. This type of seizure is called a

    1. grand mal seizure.
    2. focal seizure.
    3. petit mal seizure.
    4. psychomotor seizure.

89. A 5-year-old child is admitted to the pediatric unit with a diagnosis of acute lymphoblastic leukemia. The nursing assessment should reveal that that child

    1. tires easily and has a low-grade temperature and multiple bruises on her body.
    2. has a temperature of 103°F, nuchal rigidity, and anorexia.
    3. is afebrile and has an elevated pulse rate and an elevated blood pressure.
    4. is pale and has an enlarged abdomen and a fine rash on her extremities.

90. Methotrexate is prescribed by the oncologist to treat a child. Methotrexate is a

    1. folic acid antagonist.
    2. nitrogen mustard derivative.
    3. purine derivative.
    4. steroid.

91. A mother tells the nurse that her daughter has severe anemia. She also asks the nurse for names of other physicians who might help her daughter get better sooner. In relation to the stages of death and dying, the nurse assesses the mother to be in the stage of

    1. denial.
    2. anger.
    3. bargaining.
    4. acceptance.

92. A 7-year-old child is having her annual physical examination. Since last year, she has gained 5 pounds and has grown 2 inches. This pattern of growth is

    1. above average for both height and weight for her age group.
    2. above average for weight and below average for height for her age group.
    3. below average for both height and weight for her age group.
    4. within the normal range for both height and weight for her age group.

93. Assessment of motor development during the school-age years should indicate that hand-eye coordination is fully developed at

    1. 6 years of age.
    2. 8 years of age.
    3. 9 years of age.
    4. 11 years of age.

94. Four 6-year-old children are playing a game of cards. Which of the following statements would BEST describe their behavior?

    1. A 6-year-old is able to follow the precise rules of a game.
    2. A 6-year-old is unconcerned about who will go first in a game.
    3. A 6-year-old is able to concentrate on games that last 1 or 2 hours.
    4. A 6-year-old can't bear to lose and will cheat at games.

95. Social relationships of an 8-year-old child generally center around activities shared with

    1. parents and siblings.
    2. a best friend of the same sex.
    3. peers of both sexes.
    4. a friend of the opposite sex.

96. According to Piaget, the child from ages 7 to 11 is in the

1. sensorimotor stage of development.
2. preconceptual stage of development.
3. concrete operations stage of development.
4. formal operations stage of development.

97. A 12-year-old girl who has rheumatic fever is on bedrest. Which of the following activities would be MOST appropriate, considering her illness and developmental level?

1. Making a potholder by herself.
2. Playing checkers with a 10-year-old girl with a fractured tibia.
3. Playing cards with a nurse's aide.
4. Playing Monopoly with a 9-year-old boy with pneumonia.

98. One of the major causes of accidents during the school-age period is

1. poisoning.
2. firearms.
3. aspiration of foreign bodies.
4. motor vehicles.

99. To promote a sense of industry in a hospitalized school-age child, the nurse should

1. encourage visits by his parents.
2. ask the child to bring his favorite toy from home.
3. encourage the child to telephone his friends.
4. allow the child to bathe himself.

100. A 7-year-old child is a patient on the pediatric unit. She is scheduled for surgery to correct strabismus. The nurse explaining the procedure to the child should

1. reassure her that only the specified body part will be involved.
2. explain the functions of the extraoccular muscles to her.
3. tell her that having anesthesia is just like going to sleep.
4. remind her to save her questions about the surgery for her pediatrician.

101. While playing football, an 8-year-old child fractured his humerus. Supracondylar fractures of the humerus are often treated with

1. Russell's traction.
2. Bryant's traction.
3. Buck's traction.
4. Dunlop's traction.

102. An 8-year-old child is admitted to the hospital with a diagnosis of osteomyelitis secondary to a burn of his upper thigh. A blood culture will probably reveal which of the following causative organisms?

1. *Staphlococcus aureus.*
2. Hemolytic *Streptococcus.*
3. *Escherichia coli.*
4. *Salmonella.*

103. A 7-year-old child has been complaining of a persistent pain in the right hip and has been limping. The physician believes that the child may have Legg-Calvé-Perthes disease. This is

1. an infection of the hip joint.
2. a dislocation of the femur from the acetabulum.
3. a sprain of the hip adductors.
4. an aseptic necrosis of the head of the femur.

104. A 7-year-old child fell off her bicycle, landing on the back of the head. During the admission assessment the nurse observes drainage in the external auditory canal. The MOST appropriate nursing action at this time is to

1. estimate the amount of drainage present.
2. document the color of the drainage.
3. notify the physician.
4. test the drainage for glucose.

105. A 6-year-old child is admitted to the pediatric unit with a diagnosis of medulloblastoma. The initial nursing assessment should include observing for signs of

1. motor and/or sensory dysfunction.
2. cranial nerve involvement.
3. respiratory distress.
4. increased intracranial pressure.

106. A 9-year-old child's pediatrician has ordered strict bedrest because the child has rheumatic fever. The primary reason for this intervention is to

1. reduce the swelling of the child's joints.
2. prevent respiratory complications.
3. reduce the workload on the child's heart.
4. prevent complications of the central nervous system.

107. A 6-year-old has juvenile rheumatoid arthritis. A potential complication to counsel the child's family about is

    1. iridocyclitis.
    2. aortic valve stenosis.
    3. glomerulonephritis.
    4. peripheral neuritis.

108. The preadolescent growth spurt occurs in females at approximately

    1. 8 years of age.
    2. 10 years of age.
    3. 12 years of age.
    4. 14 years of age.

109. A school nurse is teaching a group of adolescents a course in sexuality. While discussing bodily changes during puberty, she states that the first physical change that occurs in females is

    1. the development of breast buds.
    2. an alteration in vaginal secretions.
    3. the onset of menses.
    4. the growth of pubic and axillary hair.

110. In order of appearance, the last secondary sexual characteristic to appear in males is

    1. increase in size of the genitalia.
    2. growth of bodily hair.
    3. voice changes.
    4. production of spermatozoa.

111. The motor abilities of 13- and 14-year-old adolescents are

    1. equivalent to those of an adult.
    2. graceful and smooth.
    3. generalized and diffuse.
    4. clumsy and lacking in coordination.

112. The problem-solving abilities of the adolescent in Piaget's phase of formal operations are based on

    1. juxtaposition.
    2. transducive reasoning.
    3. syncretism.
    4. inductive and deductive reasoning.

113. To promote optimal growth and development during adolescence, the diet must contain a higher percentage of

    1. vitamin B.
    2. carbohydrates.
    3. vitamin C.
    4. proteins.

114. Which of the following would be considered unusual behavior for an adolescent boy?

    1. Inconsistent attitudes.
    2. Emotional equilibrium.
    3. Intense involvements.
    4. Strong peer group attachment.

115. Health maintenance of adolescents should include yearly screening for

    1. venereal disease.
    2. diabetes mellitus.
    3. tuberculosis.
    4. scoliosis.

116. When caring for a hospitalized adolescent it is important for the nurse to

    1. include the adolescent in the planning of his/her care.
    2. share the completed nursing care plan with the adolescent.
    3. discuss all plans with the parents before implementing them.
    4. provide the adolescent with complete physical care.

117. A 16-year-old male has been admitted to the hospital with multiple trauma after an automobile accident. The nurse assigned to the teenager the day after his accident should first

    1. ask him to relate the details of the accident.
    2. explain to him his treatment regimen.
    3. encourage him to verbalize his feelings about his injuries.
    4. counsel him about automobile safety.

118. A 15-year-old male has acne vulgaris. The nurse counseling the teenager recommends

    1. a decrease in his daily exercise program.
    2. a reduction of emotional tension and anxiety.
    3. application of suntan lotion prior to ultraviolet therapy.
    4. strict adherence to a high-protein, low-calorie diet.

119. A school health nurse is the leader of a group of students who are overweight. The primary advantage of the group approach to adolescent obesity is

1. to share feelings with peers who have similiar problems.
2. to hasten weight loss by encouraging competition among group members.
3. to have a health professional available to assure that a reduced caloric intake is adhered to.
4. to provide motivation to adolescents who are not interested in losing weight.

120. A teenager has infectious mononucleosis. Infectious mononucleosis is a viral infection that causes

1. inflammation and damage to connective tissues.
2. a decrease in lymphocytes.
3. enlargement of lymphoid tissue throughout the body.
4. alterations in the immunological system.

121. A female teenager reports to the adolescent health care clinic complaining of a purulent vaginal discharge and burning on urination. The nursing history reveals that she is sexually active. The clinic nurse should suspect that she may have

1. gonorrhea.
2. genital herpes.
3. syphilis.
4. genital warts.

122. A 13-year-old female has functional scoliosis. While teaching her about her condition, the nurse

1. demonstrates proper application of a Milwaukee brace.
2. emphasizes principles of cast care.
3. prepares her for the possibility of a spinal fusion.
4. helps her plan an exercise program.

123. A teenager has osteogenic sarcoma. The nurse assessing the patient should observe for signs of

1. metastasis to the liver.
2. pulmonary metastasis.
3. central nervous system metastasis.
4. metastasis to the kidney.

124. A 12-year-old female newly diagnosed juvenile diabetic was admitted via the emergency room because of hyperglycemia. Early signs of hyperglycemia include

1. nausea, vomiting, and abdominal pain.
2. pallor, tremors, and increased perspiration.
3. dilated pupils, dizziness, and sudden hunger.
4. acetone breath, little perspiration, and weakness.

125. A patient is being treated with NPH insulin. The nurse should teach the patient that hypoglycemia may be precipitated by

1. an increase in emotional stress.
2. lowering of insulin dosage.
3. an increase in exercise.
4. ingestion of excessive carbohydrates.

126. The nurse should teach a diabetic to test her own blood sugar level consistently

1. before breakfast and before bedtime.
2. before each meal and at bedtime.
3. only before breakfast.
4. before and after school.

127. For maximum benefit, which of the following positions should be assumed while douching?

1. Sitting on the toilet.
2. Lying down in the bathtub.
3. Standing over the toilet.
4. Any position that is comfortable.

128. A Class II Pap smear

1. is suggestive, but not conclusive, for malignancy.
2. is strongly suggestive for malignancy.
3. indicates atypical cells, but is not suggestive for malignancy.
4. indicates no abnormal or atypical cells.

129. A pregnant female has decided to terminate her pregnancy at 18 weeks of gestation. Which of the following is the appropriate method of abortion at this point of pregnancy?

1. Suction aspiration.
2. D and C.
3. Hysterectomy.
4. Prostaglandin instillation.

130. When a tubal ligation is performed on a woman of childbearing age, she can expect sterility

1. without menopausal symptoms.
2. with menopausal symptoms.
3. resulting in loss of libido.
4. that can be readily reversed by surgery.

131. A 50-year-old woman visits the gynecology clinic, stating that her last period was 6 months ago. Since that time, she has been experiencing palpitations and hot flashes. The nurse should suspect that her symptoms are related to

1. fibroids of the uterus.
2. menopause.
3. carcinoma of the cervix.
4. endometriosis.

132. Which of the following would be the MOST accurate description of the occurrence of ovulation in the menstrual cycle?

1. Midway in the cycle, regardless of the length of the cycle.
2. Two weeks after the onset of menses.
3. Two weeks before the onset of menses.
4. Ten days after the cessation of the menstrual flow.

133. The ovum is fertilized by the sperm

1. at the time of nidation.
2. in the fallopian tube near the uterus.
3. in the distal portion of the tube.
4. in the ovary.

134. Implantation usually occurs

1. 7 days after fertilization.
2. 21 days after the last menstruation.
3. within minutes after fertilization.
4. the 4th day after ovulation.

135. The fetal heart usually begins beating at

1. 3 to 5 weeks.
2. 10 to 12 weeks.
3. 18 to 20 weeks.
4. the 6th lunar month.

136. The sex of the fetus is determined by

1. the X chromosomes of the father.
2. the Y chromosomes of the father.
3. either of the above, depending on which the fetus receives.
4. the mother's chromosomes.

137. If a pregnant woman's last menstrual period was March 17, her estimated date of confinement would be

1. January 24.
2. January 10.
3. December 24.
4. December 10.

138. If a woman is pregnant for the third time and has had one viable delivery, she is

1. gravida 2, para 1.
2. gravida 3, para 2.
3. gravida 3, para 1.
4. gravida 3, para 0.

139. Chadwick's sign is

1. softening of the lower uterine segment.
2. quickening.
3. softening of the cervix.
4. bluish discoloration of the vaginal mucosa.

140. Frequency of micturition is experienced by the pregnant woman

1. early in pregnancy and again during the last weeks.
2. at the end of the first trimester and again in the last few weeks.
3. usually during the last few weeks only.
4. during the 4th and 8th month.

141. The approximate 50% increase in blood volume in a healthy pregnant woman causes

1. increased blood pressure.
2. increased cardiac output.
3. a tendency to pulmonary edema in the last trimester.
4. a marked increased of water retention in all body tissues.

142. A patient complains of rather painful and enlarged leg veins during pregnancy. This complaint is MOST probably the result of which of the following?

1. Infected veins.
2. Pressure of the uterus on the femoral veins.
3. Decreased fluid volume in the body.
4. Pressure on the walls of the arteries.

143. If a pregnant woman complains of a sudden pain in the calf of her leg as she lies on the examining table, which of the following would you do FIRST?

1. Massage the muscle vigorously.
2. Apply heat to the affected part.
3. Dorsiflex the foot on the affected leg while pressing the knee downward.
4. Notify the doctor immediately, and wait until he/she arrives for instructions.

144. The MOST probable cause of leg cramps during pregnancy is

1. simple calcium deficiency.
2. varicose veins.
3. thrombophlebitis.
4. excessive smoking.

145. The articular surfaces of the pelvic joints are lined with cartilage that softens during pregnancy, causing greater mobility of bones. This normally results in

1. a pelvis that enlarges during labor.
2. wobbliness of gait.
3. separation of symphysis during delivery.
4. softening of pelvic bones.

146. The precursor of human milk (colostrum) can first be expressed from the breasts of the pregnant woman at the end of the

1. first trimester.
2. second trimester.
3. third trimester.
4. postpartum period.

147. Which of the following is unnecessary in an antepartum history?

1. Date of the last menstrual period.
2. History of previous pregnancy.
3. Mother's medical history.
4. Communicable diseases other children have had.

148. How can an expectant father be MOST helpful to the mother during pregnancy?

1. By taking charge of her diet and activities.
2. By being supportive and accepting of her labile emotions and changing moods.
3. By making all decisions for the household.
4. By keeping her busy so she doesn't have time to think about the changes she is undergoing.

Questions 149–151

A 35-year-old woman, gravida 3 para 2, is first seen in the antepartal clinic at 16 weeks gestation. At 24 weeks the doctor notes that her uterus is enlarged to a size inconsistent with her estimated delivery date. He also thinks he hears two fetal heartbeats. A sonogram confirms the presence of twins. Polyhydramnios is also noted.

149. Because of the presence of twins, the nurse would expect the patient to have a greater than usual likelihood of which discomfort of pregnancy?

1. Breast tenderness.
2. Leukorrhea.
3. Varicose veins.
4. Urinary tract infections.

150. The doctor tells the patient that her delivery will probably be slightly premature because this is very common with twins. Her chances of having a premature delivery are further increased by

1. an excessive weight gain.
2. vulvar varicosities.
3. recurrent vaginal infections.
4. polyhydramnios.

151. The patient goes into premature labor at 35 weeks. Which of the following complications of labor would the nurse anticipate because of her polyhydramnios?

1. Vaginal bleeding.
2. Ineffective uterine contractions.
3. Decrease in fetal heart rate.
4. Cephalopelvic disproportion.

152. If a woman complains of nausea and vomiting during her first trimester of pregnancy but it is not severe, the nurse should advise her to

1. keep her stomach empty until nausea and vomiting disappear later in the day.
2. eat one large meal.
3. eat some dry toast or crackers before arising in the morning.
4. drink two glasses of milk before arising.

153. The principal causes of vaginal bleeding in the early months of pregnancy are

1. placenta previa and abruptio placenta.
2. cervical polyps and erosions.
3. abortion and ectopic pregnancy.
4. carcinoma of the cervix and ectopic pregnancy.

154. Which of the following is discouraged during pregnancy?
    1. Dental repairs during the third trimester.
    2. Douching with a hand-bulb syringe.
    3. Tub bathing with warm water.
    4. Intercourse during the third trimester.

155. If a patient who is 8 months pregnant suddenly becomes pale and diaphoretic while lying on an examining table, the nurse should
    1. ask if she was having contractions.
    2. check for ruptured membranes.
    3. call the doctor.
    4. turn her on her side.

156. A small amount of glycosuria is normal in a pregnant woman because of
    1. lowered renal threshold to glucose.
    2. normally high blood sugar level.
    3. dilatation of ureters.
    4. decreased reabsorption of glucose in the tubule.

157. Which of the following must be regarded as a sign of preeclampsia?
    1. Polyuria.
    2. Glucosuria.
    3. Elevated temperature.
    4. Albuminuria.

158. A patient is admitted to the labor room, stating that her "labor" has begun. The nurse knows that in true labor
    1. contractions occur at regular intervals and gradually increase in intensity.
    2. the discomfort is located chiefly in the abdomen.
    3. there will be the presence of copious watery vaginal secretion.
    4. the cervix usually remains uneffaced and closed.

159. If a woman came to the emergency room stating that her membranes had ruptured but was found not to be in labor, the action that would probably be taken would be to
    1. send the woman home and tell her to return when labor begins.
    2. admit her for observation, on the supposition that labor will soon begin.
    3. set up for a cesarean section.
    4. send the woman home, but tell her to remain in bed.

160. In a primigravida, when contractions are 10 to 15 minutes apart and regular, the nurse would BEST advise
    1. complete bedrest to conserve energy.
    2. immediate admission to the hospital.
    3. walking to enhance contractions.
    4. heavy housework to make contractions more frequent.

Questions 161–163

A 28-year-old woman is 8 months pregnant. When she awakened this morning, she found herself lying in a pool of blood. She states that she was hospitalized in her seventh month for a bleeding episode. She does not have any pain associated with the bleeding.

161. Upon the patient's admission to the labor room, the nurse should plan the nursing interventions on the assumption that the patient's diagnosis MOST probably is
    1. abruptio placenta.
    2. placenta previa.
    3. dystocia.
    4. ruptured uterus.

162. On the basis of the initial assessment of the patient the nurse withholds the routine admission soap suds enema. The primary reason for withholding an enema in this case is that it may
    1. cause infection.
    2. increase the bleeding.
    3. stimulate uterine contractions.
    4. cause the membranes to rupture.

163. Another part of the admission routine that would be omitted for the patient is
    1. rectal or vaginal exam.
    2. fetal monitoring.
    3. perineal prep.
    4. urinalysis.

164. The first stage of labor begins with
    1. true labor contractions.
    2. full dilatation of the cervix.
    3. rupture of membranes.
    4. delivery of the baby.

165. When timing contractions, the time from the beginning of one contraction to the beginning of the next is known as the
    1. duration.
    2. interval.
    3. intensity.
    4. frequency.

166. The fetal heart-rate range per minute normally is between
    1. 90 and 100.
    2. 100 and 150.
    3. 120 and 160.
    4. 130 and 180.

167. The nurse auscultates the fetal heart just above the umbilicus on a patient who is admitted in active labor. Which one of the following might the nurse suspect?
    1. Breech presentation.
    2. Anterior position.
    3. Posterior position.
    4. Face presentation.

168. Which of the following could describe the emotional reactions of a woman in the transition phase of labor?
    1. She is concentrating on working with her contractions.
    2. She may feel drowsy.
    3. She is very aware of her surroundings.
    4. She just wants to push (whether she is ready or not).

169. As the fetal head advances in the birth canal, the shape of the baby's head may also change in order to adapt to the birth canal. This is termed
    1. accommodation.
    2. molding.
    3. caput succedaneum.
    4. engagement.

170. The second stage of labor ends with the
    1. delivery of the baby.
    2. delivery of the placenta.
    3. delivery of the membranes.
    4. repair of the episiotomy.

171. Which of the following may be true of an unwed pregnant adolescent?
    1. She may not understand how she got pregnant.
    2. She will quickly establish her own independence so that she will be able to take care of the baby.
    3. She may have no difficulty forming intimate relationships in the future.
    4. She will substitute the role of mother for her previous role of daughter.

172. A patient is found to be 6 to 8 weeks pregnant upon examination. The nurse should expect her uterus to be
    1. nonpalpable abdominally.
    2. just palpable above the symphysis pubis.
    3. palpable between the symphysis and the umbilicus.
    4. palpable at the umbilicus.

173. Which of the following would NOT be included in the nursing care given during the initial postpartum period in the delivery room?
    1. Check fundus, B/P, pulse, and respirations every 15 minutes.
    2. Encourage the mother to sleep while you care for the infant.
    3. Introduce the baby to the mother and allow for inspection.
    4. Keep the mother warm.

174. Which of the following changes in vital signs is abnormal during the first 24 hours postpartum?
    1. A slight decrease in blood pressure.
    2. A temperature of 100°F.
    3. Bradycardia.
    4. Tachycardia.

175. Which of the following would predispose a woman to postpartal infection?
    1. Vaginal lacerations.
    2. Preeclampsia.
    3. Vaginal delivery.
    4. Fetal distress.

176. The postpartum mother is MOST receptive to discussion of infant care during which of the following periods?
    1. Taking-in.
    2. Taking-hold.
    3. Letting-go.
    4. Newborn.

177. A new primipara on the postpartum unit becomes agitated when her baby cries while being held, and she dissolves into tears. This MOST probably means that

1. she is too weak to stand the baby crying.
2. she feels inadequate as a mother when she can't comfort the baby.
3. she has symptoms of being an abusive mother and would spank the baby if the nurse weren't present.
4. she is rejecting her baby.

178. The BEST way for the nurse to support a patient who is anxious when her baby cries is to

1. leave the crying baby with the mother so she learns to comfort him.
2. comfort the baby, and then tell the mother that she can comfort the baby too if she tries.
3. comfort the mother and tell her she will learn gradually, as a crying baby doesn't necessarily mean poor mothering.
4. tell the mother the baby was hungry and will be fed in the nursery.

179. Which of the following is a nursing intervention for a nonnursing mother who has breast engorgement?

1. Manual expression of milk.
2. Supportive bra.
3. Restricted fluids.
4. Warm packs.

180. Which of the following nursing interventions should the nurse implement with a breast-feeding mother who complains of sore nipples?

1. Keep nipples covered after each feeding.
2. Stop breast-feeding for a day.
3. Change baby's position on nipple at each feeding.
4. Start the baby feeding on the nipple that is more painful.

181. Which of the following methods of birth control can a postpartum patient use before her 6-week checkup?

1. The pill.
2. The diaphragm.
3. Condoms.
4. The IUD.

182. A mother of a 2-year-old child asks the nurse what she can do to assist him in getting along with the new baby. The nurse should tell the mother

1. to emphasize the positive aspects of having a new little brother in order get the 2-year-old involved with the new baby.
2. to give the 2-year-old new toys and lots of love to prevent jealousy.
3. to remove the 2-year-old from his crib and put him in a youth bed so he will feel more grown up.
4. to keep the 2-year-old away from the baby and pay attention to him only when the baby is sleeping.

183. A patient, 36 weeks pregnant, is pale and apprehensive as she is wheeled into the labor room. Before admission, she experienced localized pain over the uterus along with some vaginal bleeding. Her blood pressure is 90/70, her pulse 110, and her skin cold and clammy. The admitting diagnosis is abruptio placenta. She asks the nurse whether she thinks the baby will be all right. The MOST appropriate response by the nurse would be which of the following?

1. "I understand your concern, your baby will be fine."
2. "I understand your concern, don't worry and try to relax."
3. "I understand your concern, everything possible is being done."
4. "I understand your concern, everything will work out for the best."

Questions 184–188

A 37-year-old woman is 7 days postpartum. She has been diagnosed as having endometritis, which is classified as a puerperal infection.

184. A puerperal infection is any infection

1. of the uterine cavity.
2. of the genital tract that occurs within 6 weeks of delivery.
3. of the genital tract that occurs within 1 week of delivery.
4. of the birth canal.

185. When doing assessments on postpartum patients, the nurse should be aware that a frequent manifestation of puerperal infection is
    1. diarrhea.
    2. vulval rash.
    3. excessive lochia.
    4. foul lochia.

186. The first indication that a postpartum patient has a puerperal infection might be
    1. excessive bleeding.
    2. severe abdominal pain.
    3. a chill with elevation of temperature.
    4. nausea and vomiting.

187. The postpartum patient is on complete bedrest. She asks the nurse whether she should assume any particular position in bed. The nurse should tell her to
    1. assume whatever position is most comfortable.
    2. maintain a Fowler's position.
    3. lie prone.
    4. assume a dorsal recumbent position.

188. The postpartum patient is on antibiotic therapy but has continued to breast-feed her infant. For which common newborn complication should the nursery staff carefully assess the baby?
    1. Thrush.
    2. Conjunctivitis.
    3. Diarrhea.
    4. Impetigo.

Questions 189–191

A 29-year-old patient is admitted to the obstetrical unit for a scheduled second cesarean section.

189. Preoperative preparation for a cesarean section usually includes
    1. insertion of a Foley catheter.
    2. insertion of a rectal tube.
    3. insertion of sterile vaginal packing.
    4. a betadine vaginal douche.

190. Immediate postoperative care for this patient after her cesarean section would NOT include
    1. assessing recovery from anesthesia every 15 minutes.
    2. checking her vital signs every 15 minutes until stable.
    3. checking the abdominal dressing and perineal pad for bleeding every 15 minutes.
    4. massaging the fundus every 15 minutes to keep it firm.

191. Early ambulation of the patient would NOT prevent which complication of cesarean section?
    1. Urinary retention.
    2. Hemorrhage.
    3. Abdominal distension.
    4. Thrombophlebitis.

192. The use of forceps would be contraindicated if
    1. there was a breech presentation.
    2. the cervix was only partially dilated.
    3. there was fetal distress.
    4. the mother was becoming exhausted.

193. Which of the following newborn abnormalities would NOT be caused by forcep delivery?
    1. Cephalhematoma.
    2. Brachial paralysis.
    3. Cleft lip.
    4. Facial paralysis.

194. Which of the following is NOT true in a comparison of breast milk to formula?
    1. Breast milk is more easily digested.
    2. Breast milk contains more carbohydrates.
    3. Breast milk contains sufficient iron to meet the infant's needs.
    4. Breast milk causes fewer allergic reactions.

195. The nurse should tell a patient in labor to push
    1. during the first stage.
    2. during the second stage.
    3. during the third stage.
    4. during the fourth stage.

196. Which of the following circumstances does NOT require the administration of RhoGAM to an RH negative woman?

1. A spontaneous miscarriage.
2. Delivery of an Rh-negative baby.
3. Delivery of an Rh-positive baby.
4. A voluntary abortion.

197. When assisting a patient to breast-feed her infant, what is the nurse's reason for telling the mother to get the brown-pigmented area around the nipple well into the baby's mouth?

1. The patient's nipples are most likely inverted, and this measure promotes erection of the nipple.
2. This measure minimizes breast engorgement and decreases the mother's discomfort during feeding.
3. The infant feels more secure if this position is maintained.
4. The baby can compress the lactiferous sinuses behind the areola and draw the milk into his mouth by sucking.

198. A patient who experiences "afterpains" when she nurses her baby asks the nurse whether it would be advisable to stop nursing because of this. The BEST response for the nurse is

1. "This is a rather unusual complaint, and it may be best not to nurse your baby until you see your doctor."
2. "Pain is never a serious complication, so there is no reason not to nurse your baby."
3. "Nursing tends to cause the uterine muscles to relax. This will disappear in a few days so you can postpone nursing until then."
4. "Nursing causes a reflex stimulation of the uterine muscles and helps the uterus return to its normal size. Therefore, nursing is beneficial despite some discomfort."

199. A patient, age 20, gravida 1, para 0, has a history of rheumatic fever at age 8 and a residual rheumatic heart disease, Class 1A. When the patient returns from the delivery room, the nurse should know that

1. the danger period will end after the first 24 hours postpartum.
2. the danger period will end after the first 48 hours postpartum.
3. major circulatory readjustment in the postpartum period may cause heart failure even 4 or 5 days postpartum.
4. the patient's care need be no different from that of any other postpartum patient.

200. Which of the following types of anesthesia does NOT minimize perception of uterine contractions?

1. Spinal.
2. Saddle block.
3. Continuous caudal.
4. Pudendal block.

201. The American family structure today tends to be

1. nuclear.
2. extended.
3. patriarchal.
4. matrilineal.

202. A nuclear family structure imposes certain stresses on the young primigravida. She is likely to

1. feel isolated and alone when her husband is away.
2. seek information about pregnancy and childbirth from her family.
3. seek companionship of other pregnant women.
4. not share information about pregnancy, childbirth, and infant care with her husband.

203. A side effect of epidural anesthesia that the nurse caring for an anesthetized patient must be aware of is

1. hypotension.
2. hypertension.
3. tachycardia.
4. arrhythmias.

204. Cancer cells metastasize to distant sites in the body via

1. droplets from the respiratory tract.
2. direct extension into the surrounding tissues.
3. body fluid such as circulating blood and the lymph vessels.
4. touch, the hands acting as a vector.

205. The MOST common symptom in cancer is

1. pain.
2. fever.
3. weight loss.
4. change in bowel habit.

206. Alopecia is defined as

1. chronic obesity.
2. hair loss.
3. severe back pain.
4. chronic bleeding of the gums.

207. A patient has experienced alopecia following chemotherapy. The patient would like to know if this state is permanent. The BEST answer the nurse can give is which of the following?

    1. "The condition will disappear once the treatment is discontinued."
    2. "The therapy causes permanent alopecia."
    3. "Ask your phvsician whether this condition is permanent."
    4. "We do not know the exact effect of the drug you took."

208. The nurse can BEST explain the purpose of a biopsy as

    1. removal of malignancy.
    2. establishment of tumor classification and stage.
    3. alleviation of pressure on organs and/or blood vessels.
    4. prevention of metastasis.

209. A common side effect related to chemotherapy that the nurse should be aware of is

    1. sterility.
    2. increase in body hair.
    3. stomatitis.
    4. pain.

210. Which of the following are side effects or toxic effects of cortisone therapy?

    1. Nausea, vomiting, and diarrhea.
    2. Urticaria, hypertension, and hematuria.
    3. Psychiatric disturbances, moon face, and poor wound healing.
    4. Headaches, tinnitus, and edema.

211. The main objective of administering preoperative radiotherapy is to

    1. encourage lymph drainage.
    2. prevent metastasis.
    3. alleviate pain.
    4. reduce tumor size.

212. Which of these drugs should NOT be given with anticoagulants?

    1. Aspirin.
    2. Morphine sulfate.
    3. Prednisone.
    4. Valium.

213. Which of the following activities should be avoided during radiotherapy?

    1. Sunbathing.
    2. Taking a shower.
    3. Driving a car.
    4. Traveling long distances.

214. Which of these actions would decrease the incidence of venous stasis?

    1. Alternating between sitting and standing during a 4-hour airplane ride.
    2. Wearing a girdle instead of a circular garter during a cross-country plane trip.
    3. Crossing legs at the thighs for short periods of time.
    4. Removal of support hose during a 2-hour car ride.

215. Postoperative nursing care for a patient who has had a femoropopiteal bypass and for a paitent who had a vein stripping and ligation are similiar in that after these surgeries the nurse should

    1. encourage the patient to stay in bed.
    2. compare the legs for warmth and color.
    3. keep the leg below the level of the heart.
    4. encourage the patient to sit or stand when bedrest is no longer necessary.

216. During an 8-hour period a patient has received 2000 mL of IV fluids. His ouput has been only 600 mL during this same time period. Before reporting this situation to the physician the nurse should

    1. inspect the lower extremities.
    2. discontinue IV therapy.
    3. palpate the bladder.
    4. ausculate the lungs.

217. To ensure that a patient is properly prepared for a colonoscopy, which of these measures should a nurse expect to be ordered before the procedure?

    1. Golytely the night before.
    2. A clear liquid diet the day before.
    3. A soap suds enema the night before.
    4. Valium, 10 mg, one-half hour before the procedure.

218. The primary reason for administering neomycin before intestinal surgery is to

1. reduce the bacterial content of the bowel.
2. reduce the incidence of urinary infection.
3. prevent postoperative respiratory infection.
4. reduce the incidence of postoperative infection.

219. A patient is now receiving nitroglycerin tablets, which are administered sublingually. The nurse should instruct the patient to

1. place the tablet under his tongue.
2. crush the tablet.
3. swallow the tablet.
4. chew the tablet.

220. Which of the following would be considered a clear fluid diet?

1. Tea with sugar and apple juice.
2. Black coffee and orange juice.
3. Ginger ale and milk sherbet.
4. Chicken broth and strained skim milk.

221. A patient has a moderate amount of mucus and needs suctioning. The nurse should perform which of these interventions before initiating suctioning?

1. Administer IPPB therapy.
2. Administer humidified air.
3. Spray the bronchi with normal saline via aerosol.
4. Ventilate the lungs with 100% oxygen via an ambu bag.

222. A patient has been diagnosed as having a pulmonary embolus and is being treated with an anticoagulant. A drug that fits this category is

1. dextran.
2. Inderal.
3. vitamin K.
4. heparin.

223. Teaching for a patient while he is on nitroglycerin should include the instruction to

1. place the tablets in a clear bottle.
2. carry medications only when necessary.
3. take a tablet before an emotional or exertional situation.
4. repeat the medication dosage every half hour until chest pain relief occurs.

224. Which of the following foods may be included in a sodium-restricted diet?

1. Relishes and pickles.
2. Frankfurter with sauerkraut.
3. Cheesecake.
4. Spinach and mushroom salad.

225. The doctor has prescribed a nitroglycerin transdermal patch for a patient. The nurse should instruct him to apply the patch to

1. any place in the chest area only.
2. a hairy area of the chest.
3. a nonhairy area on the chest or abdomen.
4. any hairy area of the body.

226. A nurse has reviewed a batch of serum cholesterol values obtained at a health fair. The person whom the nurse should advise to see a physician is the one whose serum cholesterol value was

1. 100 mg/dl.
2. 170 mg/dl.
3. 205 mg/dl.
4. 265 mg/dl.

227. The nursing responsibility for a patient receiving methyldopa (Aldomet) or hydralazine (Apresoline) is to

1. discontinue the drug if the blood pressure increases.
2. take the blood pressure every 4 hours in the same arm in a supine position.
3. discontinue the drug if the blood pressure decreases.
4. teach the patient to stand or sit up slowly in order to avoid dizziness or fainting.

228. Treatment for a hypertensive patient includes

1. antihypertensive drugs such as procainamide (Pronestyl).
2. diuretic drugs such as guanethidine (Ismelin).
3. a low-sodium, low-cholesterol diet.
4. restriction of fluids.

229. Nitrite intake may be reduced if a patient decreases his intake of

1. green leafy vegetables.
2. ham and bacon.
3. poultry and fish.
4. milk and eggs.

230. A patient receiving radiotherapy has experienced a weight loss of 5 pounds within 2 weeks because eating stimulates nausea and vomiting. The patient can control both the nausea and the vomiting by

1. having one large meal a day.
2. eating meals 2 to 3 hours before or after treatment.
3. taking antiemetic drugs when nausea is present.
4. restricting fluid intake on the day of treatment.

231. A post-cardiac-surgery patient has been experiencing tachycardia. The patient may be developing bacterial endocarditis. On what area should the nurse focus the assessment?

1. Measurement of temperature.
2. Inspection of skin.
3. Palpation of soft tissues of the abdomen.
4. Inspection of toes for numbness and tingling.

232. The major difference between hemodialysis and peritoneal dialysis is that in hemodialysis

1. the peritoneum is used as a semipermeable membrane.
2. a synthetic semipermeable membrane is used.
3. a dialysate solution is used.
4. selection of the dialysate solution is related to the serum electrolyte level.

233. Transmission of human immunodeficiency virus (HIV) infection may be prevented by

1. wearing a mask whenever in contact with an infected person.
2. cleansing spilled blood or body fluids with a solution of alcohol and water.
3. using gloves whenever handling items soiled with blood or equipment contaminated with blood and/or body fluids.
4. disposing of contaminated items securely wrapped in plastic.

234. Safe sexual practices advocated to reduce the risk of transmission of human immunodeficiency virus (HIV) include

1. using a condom only during vaginal intercourse.
2. instituting care during sexual activities that can tear or cut the vagina, rectum, or penis.

3. cleansing the penis, vagina, or rectum with soap and water before oral contact.
4. using a condom during sexual contact with a partner having a history of intravenous drug abuse.

235. In an upper GI series, which of the following procedures is performed?

1. Barium is swallowed under direct fluoroscopic examination.
2. A barium enema is given; then X-rays are taken.
3. X-rays are taken without the benefit of a contrast media.
4. Gastric juice is aspirated through a nasogastric tube.

236. A patient is recovering from gastrointestinal surgery. He is reluctant to perform deep breathing and coughing exercises. The nurse should encourage him to perform these exercises

1. within 15 minutes after administering an analgesic to prevent the anticipated pain.
2. in a couple of days when the pain has subsided.
3. just before administering an analgesic so the drug can relieve the expected pain.
4. as close to bedtime as possible so his tolerance will be increased.

237. Nursing care for a patient with a nasogastric tube to low suction would include

1. ausculating the abdomen for the presence of bowel sounds.
2. irrigating the tube with 3 ml every shift to maintain patency.
3. maintaining strict bedrest until the nasogastric tube is removed.
4. clamping the nasogastric tube if the patient complains of nausea.

238. The nurse notices a yellow-green drainage from a patient's nasogastric tube. The nurse should

1. notify the physician.
2. record that normal gastric secretions have returned.
3. prepare the patient for a transfusion of whole blood.
4. record the change and continue to observe the patient for further complications.

239. A patient, age 28, has had chronic ulcerative colitis for the past 5 years and has required surgery because of constant diarrhea and subsequent dehydration. The operation performed was a proctocolectomy and ileostomy. This means that the patient

1. can anticipate reanastamosis after her colon has healed.
2. will have continuous liquid drainage from the stoma.
3. might be able to irrigate the "ostomy" to attain regularity.
4. will have voluntary control over the emptying of the ileostomy.

240. A 28-year-old patient is beginning to show signs of skin breakdown around the stoma site. One preventative measure the nurse can use is

1. Maalox.
2. skin protectant.
3. pectin.
4. water-soluble jelly.

241. The primary reason for the nurse to maintain meticulous skin care around an ileostomy stoma is to prevent

1. excoriation from gastric secretions.
2. proteolytic enzyme digestion.
3. secondary infection.
4. retraction of the stoma.

242. In preparing a patient with an ileostomy for discharge, the nurse should counsel the patient to control the diet by

1. restricting fluids.
2. eliminating fruits and vegetables.
3. eating a high-calorie, high-protein, low-residue diet.
4. limiting the intake of calories.

243. To reduce the formation of uric acid crystals in a patient who has a malignancy, the nurse should expect which of the following medications to be administered?

1. Lasix.
2. Esidrix.
3. Allopurinal.
4. Diamox.

244. The nurse should know that antineoplastic drugs have a small margin of safety because these drugs

1. cannot differentiate between normal and cancer cells.
2. must be administered in large doses.
3. act very quickly.
4. are excreted slowly from the body.

245. The major problem for which the nurse should assess patients who are receiving antineoplastic drugs is

1. anemia.
2. loss of appetite.
3. loss of hair.
4. bleeding tendencies.

246. Which of the following signs and symptoms of increasing intracranial pressure should the nurse assess the patient for?

1. Drainage of clear fluids from the nose or the ear.
2. Refusal to sit up or eat, irritability, and slight drowsiness.
3. Blood pressure 180/60, pulse 64, respirations 12, and temperature 99°F.
4. Unequal dilatation of the pupils.

247. When administering dexamethasone (Decadron) to a patient who has an increased intracranial pressure, the nurse should know the therapeutic effect is to

1. decrease headache.
2. prevent infection.
3. produce rapid diuresis.
4. reduce cerebral edema.

248. The nurse should observe the patient on Decadron for side effects, which include

1. peptic ulcer.
2. hyperkalemia.
3. hypoglycemia.
4. aplastic anemia.

249. Which of the following statements applies to an epidural hematoma?

1. It is the most common of all brain injuries.
2. It is a surgical emergency.
3. The patient remains unconscious.
4. A clot develops below the dura mater.

250. Which of the following statements applies to a subdural hematoma?

1. It is a result of arterial bleeding into the space below the dura.
2. The hematoma cannot be reabsorbed.
3. Symptoms may not appear until several weeks after the head trauma.
4. It is a result of venous bleeding into the foramen magnum.

251. The primary purpose of administering Maalox with Decadron is to

1. reduce gastric irritation.
2. prevent constipation.
3. enhance the action of Decadron.
4. increase the healing rate.

252. The nurse should explain to a patient who is experiencing an acute flare-up of rheumatoid arthritis that absolute bedrest is necessary to

1. decrease the body's caloric needs.
2. prevent damage to the inflamed joints.
3. allow the body to manufacture red blood cells and antibodies.
4. reduce the metabolic activities of the muscles and nerves.

253. The nurse should observe a patient being evaluated for multiple sclerosis for signs of

1. mental deterioration with spastic paralysis.
2. spastic paralysis with speech disturbance.
3. masklike facies and tremors at rest.
4. muscle rigidity and "pill-rolling" tremors.

254. Which of the following statements BEST describes skeletal traction?

1. It consists of Buck's extension with the addition of a sling for the knee.
2. Pulley and weights are attached to the skin by Ace bandages.
3. Balanced suspension is obtained with a Thomas splint and a Pearson attachment.
4. Traction is applied to the bone by use of a metal or a wire pin inserted into the bone.

255. Which of these measures should a nurse take for a patient in continuous skeletal traction/balanced suspension?

1. Instruct the patient in the use of the trapeze bar.
2. Remove the weights when pulling the patient up in bed.
3. Adjust the level of the patient's bed to provide sensory stimulation.
4. Turn the patient from side to side every 2 hours.

256. The nurse must assess the patient with a long-leg cast for pressure on the

1. dorsalis pedis.
2. posterior tibialis.
3. popliteal artery.
4. peroneal nerve.

257. A nurse should determine that a plaster cast is dry when it

1. has a dull sound to percussion.
2. is white and shiny.
3. is warm to the touch.
4. has a musky smell.

258. Immediately after the application of a long leg plaster cast, the nursing intervention aimed at reducing edema and stimulating circulation should be

1. covering the cast with a blanket.
2. handling the wet cast only with the fingers.
3. assessing the toes for color and temperature once each 8 hours.
4. placing the cast on a pillow.

259. To prevent prosthesis dislocation after hip surgery, the leg should be kept in

1. adduction.
2. abduction.
3. internal rotation.
4. flexion.

260. X-rays show that the lower end of a patient's femur has been splintered into fragments. This type of fracture is called

1. greenstick.
2. compound.
3. oblique.
4. comminuted.

261. Which of the following are contraindicated in the care of a post-cranial-surgery patient?
    1. Nasal suctioning.
    2. Rectal temperature.
    3. Alcohol sponging.
    4. Reinforcement of the surgical dressing.

262. Which of the following responses should be monitored while a patient is on the dialysis machine?
    1. Pupillary responses.
    2. Blood pressure.
    3. Breath sounds.
    4. Deep tendon reflexes.

263. Which of the following therapeutic actions would dialysis therapy NOT accomplish?
    1. Removing accumulated waste products of protein metabolism from the bloodstream.
    2. Restoring the electrolyte balance and pH of the circulating blood.
    3. Withdrawing excess body fluid from the patient.
    4. Increasing the fluid level of the blood.

264. Which of the following should the nurse expect to observe in the patient immediately after peritoneal dialysis?
    1. Increased blood pressure.
    2. Increased pulse and respirations.
    3. Decreased blood pressure.
    4. No changes in pulse, respirations, or blood pressure.

265. A patient on hemodialysis is on a 22-gm protein and 500-mg sodium diet with potassium restriction. Which of the following lunches is allowed?
    1. Hard-boiled eggs on low-sodium bread with unsalted butter.
    2. Chicken (1 ounce) with lettuce and tomatoes.
    3. One ounce of hamburger on low-sodium bread.
    4. Shrimp salad on mustard greens.

266. A patient has returned to his room following an appendectomy. Besides measurement of pulse and blood pressure, which of these assessment skills should the nurse employ for this patient during the first 24 hours postoperatively?
    1. Inspection of the skin.
    2. Auscultation of the bowels.
    3. Percussion of the lungs.
    4. Palpation of the lymph nodes.

267. To prevent the spread of infectious hepatitis, health personnel should practice which of the following?
    1. Using mask and gown whenever entering the patient's room.
    2. Washing hands before and after contact with patient.
    3. Disposing of patient's linen and underwear.
    4. Using gloves whenever coming into contact with the patient.

268. Which of the following individuals is at risk of being infected by hepatitis B (HBV)?
    1. A person considering going on a reducing diet for 2 weeks.
    2. A person considering having her ears pierced at home using a sewing needle.
    3. A person who has diabetes switching to disposable syringes and needles.
    4. A person with a long history of alcoholism.

269. The purpose of a cholecystogram is to
    1. visualize the gallbladder.
    2. determine the bacterial agent responsible for gallbladder infections.
    3. estimate the degree of liver damage produced by obstructive jaundice.
    4. distinguish jaundice caused by hemolysis from that due to infection.

270. When irrigating a colostomy by bulb syringe, the nurse should remember that the purpose of the irrigation is to
    1. stimulate fecal return.
    2. wash the intestines.
    3. apply warmth to the intestines.
    4. prevent infection of the intestines.

271. Which of the following statements BEST describes a therapeutic approach?
    1. Use of professional knowledge and skill in such a way that they assist the patient's well being.
    2. Use of constant, probing questions to uncover the patient's hidden conflicts.
    3. Analysis of the patient's behavior in order to seek solutions for his/her problems.
    4. Ability to understand the "whys" of patient behavior.

272. Which of the following statements is LEAST descriptive of a therapeutic relationship?

1. It is goal directed.
2. The interaction between participants is guided by the patient's needs.
3. The relationship takes place in a highly permissive environment without limits.
4. The counselor recognizes his/her own needs and avoids introducing them into the relationship.

273. An environment where limits are clear and consistent is important if the patient is to learn socially acceptable interpersonal processes. In providing such an environment, which of the following approaches should the nurse avoid?

1. Constantly reminding the patient what behavior is acceptable and what is not.
2. Limiting only behaviors that are clearly destructive to the patient and others.
3. Encouraging the patient to reassess situations related to the behavior in question.
4. Assisting the patient to test alternative ways of dealing with his/her conflicts.

274. Defense mechanisms can be BEST described as

1. adaptive mechanisms that are consistently unconscious.
2. adaptive mechanisms that always foster growth when excessively used.
3. coping mechanisms that resolve one's emotional conflicts.
4. coping mechanisms used by all persons to a certain degree to relieve tension and anxiety.

275. A patient says to the nurse, "My children haven't visited me for weeks now. I don't get phone calls from them either. I don't even have any news about my new grandson. I guess nobody remembers that I am here." Which of the following responses would be MOST helpful in finding out exactly what the patient is feeling?

1. "I'm sure they did not forget you. They must be very busy with your new grandson."
2. "Why don't you give them a call and find out what's happening?"
3. "It sounds as if you are feeling sort of neglected at this time."
4. "I'll take you to bingo this afternoon to take your mind off your family for awhile."

276. Which of the following approaches would be LEAST helpful in caring for a client with posttraumatic stress disorder?

1. Allow the client to recall details of the catastrophic event without probing.
2. Assess the client's risk of suicide.
3. Provide for client participation in a support group.
4. Divert the client's attention away from any reminders of the catastrophic event experienced.

277. In establishing a nurse-client relationship, which of the following should be the initial requisite?

1. Self-awareness.
2. An understanding of the client's needs.
3. Verbalization.
4. Sympathy.

278. Which of the following BEST describes empathy?

1. It is sharing another person's feelings.
2. It is understanding the meaning of the thoughts and feelings of another person.
3. It is incorporating another person's total personality into one's own.
4. It is adapting certain attributes or characteristics of another person as part of one's own personality.

279. Which of the following statements BEST describes the state of crisis?

1. It is a form of mental disorder.
2. It is always self-limiting.
3. The problem may actually be solved during this state.
4. The person in crisis is totally dependent on the "helping" individual in resolving his/her problem.

280. Withdrawal of a psychotic nature is MOST evident in the patient who has

1. unipolar depression.
2. bipolar depression.
3. schizophrenic reaction.
4. anxiety disorder.

281. In preparing to terminate the nurse-patient relationship, which of the following topics would be MOST therapeutic?

1. The patient's plans for rejoining the work force.
2. The patient's plans for a "new life" when he/she goes home.
3. The patient's views on current social issues.
4. The patient's perspectives on the benefits he/she derived from the nurse-patient relationship.

282. During a helping interview, a female patient keeps talking about other people and consistently avoids talking about herself. Which of the following approaches by the nurse would be MOST helpful in assisting the patient to focus on herself and her concerns?

1. Make frequent use of the patient's name when responding to her.
2. Remind her that she has no business talking about other people.
3. Ask the patient why she does not seem to want to talk about herself.
4. Avoid using the personal pronoun "you" when talking to the patient.

283. A nurse may obtain valuable information concerning the background and maturing forces behind an individual's behavior by

1. employing only direct questioning.
2. asking provoking questions to elicit the expression of repressed feelings.
3. using keen observation and general conversation.
4. discussing the problem with another person.

284. To serve a patient's needs the nurse must

1. be alert and sensitive to patient cues, and ask only direct, pertinent, probing questions.
2. help the patient to express his needs verbally and be alert and sensitive to patient cues.
3. know the patient's past history and diagnosis.
4. be aware of the events that precipitated the patient s admission to the hospital.

285. Which of the following is MOST important for the nurse to be aware of when talking to a patient for the first time?

1. Hostile behavior in a patient indicates that the nurse's initial approach has been inadequate.
2. The case history must be read and discussed with the psychiatrist before talking to the patient.
3. The patient's physical appearance provides an accurate index of whether or not the patient will be receptive to the nurse's approach.
4. The patient is a stranger to the nurse, and the nurse is a stranger to the patient.

286. Which of the following concepts would be MOST likely to provide the patient with an opportunity to deal with his feelings in a healthy way?

1. The ability to express a negative emotion is not a healthy sign because strong emotions are potentially explosive and therefore dangerous.
2. The patient is accepted because his symptoms permit him to discharge his emotions without fear of retaliation.
3. An atmosphere in which all the patient's behavior is accepted meets his needs because no threat is present for him.
4. All behavior is recognized as meaningful.

287. Which of the following statements is NOT true about manipulative behaviors?

1. They are often reinforced by permissiveness and lack of consistencies in the patient's environment.
2. They represent a conflict of goals between the nurse and the patient.
3. They are always unconsciously motivated.
4. They represent the patient's lack of trust in others.

288. All emotional illnesses share a common characteristic, which is

1. complete denial of objective reality.
2. ego fragmentation.
3. faulty interpersonal relationships.
4. complete personality disintegration.

289. Anxiety differs from fear in that the stimulus for anxiety

1. is an external threat.
2. is completely unrelated to one's life.
3. lies within the patient's unconscious level of mind.
4. lies within the patient's conscious level of mind.

290. Anxiety is basically a response to

1. a change in id impulses.
2. threats to ego integrity.
3. release of repressed drives.
4. all of the above.

291. The feeling of alienation from one's feelings, body, or self is known as

1. introjection.
2. ambivalence.
3. depersonalization.
4. projection.

292. Repression can be BEST understood as

1. the barring of unacceptable id impulses from the consciousness.
2. the resumption of behavior typical of an earlier developmental level.
3. the conscious forgetting of one's acts, impulses, or desires.
4. a persistent, repetitive, unwelcome thought.

293. Concealing a motive by giving strong expression to its opposite is the defense mechanism known as

1. sublimation.
2. substitution.
3. projection.
4. reaction formation.

294. Emotional release or discharge resulting from recalling to awareness painful experiences that have been repressed is called

1. displacement.
2. abreaction.
3. rationalization.
4. projection.

295. Regression can be MOST accurately described as

1. resumption of behavior typical of an earlier level of development.
2. banishment of unacceptable wishes or ideas from conscious awareness.
3. unconscious efforts to eradicate a previous painful experience.
4. turning of interests inward to total self-preoccupation.

296. To assist a person in crisis, the "helping" individual must

1. assist the person to consider his alternatives.
2. point out the consequences of the solution.
3. be directive in resolving the problem.
4. identify to the person his strengths and weaknesses.

297. Crisis theory is reality oriented, and its basic purposes are all of the following EXCEPT to

1. avoid hospitalization.
2. maintain the patient's functioning within the family and community.
3. facilitate emotional growth through problem solving.
4. identify the solution for the person in crisis.

298. Behavior modification comes from a school of psychology known as

1. operant conditioning.
2. classical conditioning.
3. behaviorism.
4. behavior analysis.

299. Behavior modification is designed to

1. probe the unconscious motives of the patient's behavior.
2. produce a basic change in the patient's personality.
3. modify current behavioral patterns.
4. alleviate symptoms and resolve underlying conflicts.

300. Which of the following statements characterizes a therapeutic relationship?

1. The relationship is goal directed.
2. The relationship takes place within a highly permissive environment.
3. Acknowledgment and acceptance of all the patient's behaviors are important because these behaviors are meaningful to the patient.
4. There is reciprocity of need expression and gratification.

301. A 28-year-old female was admitted to a psychiatric hospital for a second time. She believes that her employer is controlling her by radar and that she is charged with electric current. During admission the nurse held out her hand to the patient and asked her for the bottle of pills she took out of her suitcase. She responded, "Don't touch me. You will be hurt. I am charged with electricity." Which of these responses would be the BEST for the nurse to make?

1. "Do you believe you're charged with electricity?"
2. "Don't worry; your electricity won't hurt me."
3. "You think my touching you is dangerous."
4. "Miss Pert, you are not charged with electricity."

302. One day a patient approaches the nurse and tells her that her employer has sent a new set of messages by radar telling her to burn all the linen in her room. What initial response by the nurse would be MOST appropriate?

1. "When did you receive the message."
2. "What time are you supposed to do this?"
3. "These messages will stop coming as your condition improves."
4. "It sounds as if you are angry about being in the hospital. Let's talk about it."

303. The nurse's primary goal in the care of a suspicious patient like the one in question 302 should be to

1. interpret her speech and behavior to her.
2. control and direct her activities.
3. anticipate and meet all her needs.
4. provide a warm human experience.

304. The primary aim of occupational therapy is to

1. force the patient to confront reality.
2. stimulate the patient's interest in his physical surroundings.
3. teach the patient social skills.
4. provide a constructive outlet for the patient's excessive energy.

305. The defense mechanism of projection consists of

1. shifting one's emotion to a less dangerous object.
2. transferring one's unacceptable impulses and thoughts to others in the environment.
3. having an awareness of disharmony between one's thoughts and feelings.
4. resuming behavior typical of an earlier developmental stage.

306. A 24-year-old male is admitted to the psychiatric unit with a diagnosis of antisocial behavior. Which of the following types of behavior would be observed in this patient?

1. Adherence to routines in the unit.
2. Demanding special privileges.
3. Marked interest in social activities.
4. Withdrawal from any form of human interaction.

307. In caring for a patient with antisocial behavior, which of the following approaches should be emphasized?

1. Encouraging him to participate in group activities.
2. Allowing him to do anything he wants.
3. Providing him with opportunities for making simple decisions.
4. Setting limits on his behavior on the unit.

308. The primary psychodynamic observed in the sociopathic personality is the absence of

1. hostility.
2. guilt.
3. self-centeredness.
4. impulsivity.

309. The nurse's primary goal in the care of a schizophrenic patient should be to

1. control and direct the patient's activities.
2. anticipate and gratify all the patient's needs.
3. provide the patient with a warm human experience.
4. interpret the meaning of the patient's behavior.

310. According to the most widely accepted theory, schizophrenia is caused by

1. metabolic imbalances produced by genetic abnormalities.
2. interaction of a variety of diverse social and biological factors.
3. establishment of poor interpersonal relationships.
4. heredity and constitutional predisposition.

311. A 32-year-old male is admitted to a psychiatric hospital because he refused to leave his room at home. For the last several weeks he had sat and stared into space at home. In the hospital he is completely mute and does not appear to recognize what is going on about him. He assumes and holds unusual body positions. At times he becomes very loud, profane, and noisy, and then returns to his motionless state. His diagnosis is schizophrenic reaction, catatonic type. A classic symptom that the patient exhibits is

1. waxy flexibility.
2. flight of ideas.
3. paranoid ideas.
4. neologism.

312. The nurse walks into the dayroom, and a patient states, "The Mie-Mie have settled on the street." The word "Mie-Mie" may be an example of

1. word salad.
2. neologism.
3. ideas of reference.
4. fabulation.

313. The withdrawal from reality that an antisocial patient exhibits is an attempt to

1. avoid stimulation of his aggressive impulses.
2. relieve tension and anxiety by seeking security in a less threatening environment.
3. provide uninterrupted periods for more concentrated thinking in an attempt to resolve his conflicts.
4. punish those who have put him in the hospital.

314. A patient comes into the dayroom and approaches the nurse. In the opposite corner a group of patients and visitors are talking and laughing together. The patient states, pointing to the group, "They're talking about me and laughing at me." This behavior on the patient's part could be interpreted as

1. a neologism.
2. a confabulation.
3. an abstraction.
4. ideas of reference.

315. The nurse should observe an antisocial patient for expressions of depersonalization, which tend to develop from

1. decreased acuity of visual, auditory, and tactile perception.
2. retardation of impulse transmission between voluntary and automatic nervous systems.
3. increasing preoccupation with self and withdrawal from reality.
4. increasing deterioration of the prefrontal lobe of the cortex.

316. Denial can BEST be understood as

1. unconscious refusal to recognize and accept unwelcome thoughts and wishes.
2. keeping one's attitude unconscious by consciously expressing the opposite.
3. an attempt to justify unacceptable behavior.
4. disharmony between feeling and affect.

317. The withdrawn, regressed patient MOST often utilizes the mechanism of

1. denial.
2. repression.
3. displacement.
4. compensation.

318. Schizophrenia is characterized by

1. disorganized behavior.
2. logical thinking.
3. gregariousness.
4. multiple personalities.

319. Projection is a defense mechanism that involves

 1. the shifting of one's emotion to a less dangerous object.
 2. the transferring of one's unacceptable impulses and thoughts to others in the environment.
 3. a disharmony between thoughts and feelings.
 4. the resumption of behavior typical of an earlier development.

320. Which of these sequences BEST illustrates the typical "vicious cycle" pattern of behavior in a drug-dependent person, most often seen in a person dependent on alcohol?

 1. Conflict; anxiety; drugs; remorse; anxiety; drugs; remorse; anxiety; drugs; etc.
 2. Conflict; anxiety; drugs; anxiety; drugs; etc.
 3. Conflict; drugs; anxiety; remorse; anxiety; drugs; etc.
 4. Conflict; anxiety; drugs; remorse; drugs; remorse; drugs; etc.

321. Which of the following statements is NOT true about the treatment of alcoholism?

 1. The most important factor is the person's motivation to rid himself of the problem.
 2. Treatments available are for the problems associated with drinking, not alcoholism per se.
 3. Alcoholism is curable.
 4. The alcoholic who wants to stop or control his drinking will find a way to do so.

322. When trihexyphenidyl hydrochloride (Artane) is given with Haldol, the primary reason is to

 1. maintain normal activity of the bone marrow.
 2. potentiate the action of Haldol.
 3. prevent liver damage.
 4. reduce the extrapyramidal effects of Haldol.

323. In patients receiving antidepressant drugs that inhibit monoamine oxidase in the body, certain foods naturally high in pressor amines should be avoided. The foods to be avoided are

 1. honey, sugar, and hard candy.
 2. butter, fats, and oils.
 3. most cheese, yeast, and chicken livers.
 4. beef, pork, and lamb.

324. Of the following, the MOST serious untoward effect resulting from administration of phenothiazine is

 1. parkinsonism.
 2. hypotension.
 3. agranulocytosis.
 4. dermatitis.

325. Which of these medications has been useful in maintaining a schizophrenic patient who is inconsistent in taking medication?

 1. Thorazine.
 2. Haldol.
 3. Parnate.
 4. Prolixin.

326. If postural hypotension occurs after administration of Thorazine, the patient should

 1. lie down with the feet higher than the head.
 2. lie down in a semi-Fowler's position.
 3. lie flat in bed.
 4. lie on the side with the head of the bed elevated.

327. The nurse should be MOST concerned about which of the following set of complaints by a patient who is taking Thorazine?

 1. Dry mouth and constipation.
 2. Malaise and scratchy throat.
 3. Weight gain and nasal congestion.
 4. Drowsiness and unpleasant taste.

328. Before giving Thorazine, the nurse should check the patient's

 1. temperature.
 2. blood pressure.
 3. pupils.
 4. apical rate.

329. All of the following statements are true about psychotropic drugs EXCEPT

 1. they may elevate a low mood or calm agitated patients.
 2. they may act against specific symptoms of mental disorder.
 3. their primary action is on the central nervous system, which includes the brain and spinal cord.
 4. they treat the underlying cause of mental illness.

330. Which of the following signs and symptoms should the nurse observe when caring for patients who are taking phenothiazine derivatives?
    1. Hypertensive crisis and urinary retention.
    2. Hypotension and parkinsonian syndrome.
    3. Dry mucous membranes and anorexia.
    4. Tachycardia and nausea and vomiting.

331. A common side effect known to occur with the administration of large doses of phenothiazine derivatives is photosensitivity. In avoiding unnecessary complications, the nurse's responsibility includes all of the following EXCEPT
    1. instructing the family and patient in the appropriate preventive measures.
    2. reporting the occurrence of dark pigmentation in the skin.
    3. keeping the patient indoors at all times.
    4. restricting the patient's outdoor activities during times of the day when sun exposure is maximal.

332. Minor tranquilizers are thought NOT to be effective for which of the following conditions?
    1. Some gastrointestinal, musculoskeletal, and cardiovascular conditions.
    2. Acute psychotic episodes marked by agitation.
    3. Psychosomatic or psychoneurotic conditions.
    4. Withdrawal reactions or delirium tremens.

333. Autistic thinking is BEST described as a kind of thinking in which
    1. such objective considerations as those of time and place, and possible and impossible (ego judgments), have little weight.
    2. an artist does his most creative work.
    3. two opposing feelings are present in equal proportions.
    4. the patient uses neologisms.

334. Delusions of grandeur serve to enable the individual to
    1. avoid the hostility of others.
    2. deny feelings of inadequacy.
    3. prove superiority over others.
    4. verbalize unfulfilled needs.

335. The physical care of the overactive patient is based on an understanding of all the following EXCEPT
    1. the patient often does not take time out to eat or drink and may sleep only 1 or 2 hours each night.
    2. the patient needs constant reminders of what is acceptable and what is unacceptable behavior.
    3. the patient may ignore constipation and bladder distention.
    4. the patient may injure himself and not be aware of it.

336. Preoperative teaching of deep breathing and coughing exercises is done to prevent postoperative
    1. pneumonia.
    2. phlebitis.
    3. incisional strain.
    4. fluid imbalance.

337. A patient is premedicated before surgery with Demerol 100 mg IM and Vistaril 50 mg IM. Understanding the effects of the narcotic, the nurse would observe the patient for which of the following untoward reactions?
    1. Bradycardia.
    2. Shortness of breath.
    3. Hypotension.
    4. Urinary retention.

338. A patient has an indwelling (Foley) catheter removed. If the patient has not voided after 8 hours, the necessary action would be to
    1. obtain an order to catheterize the patient.
    2. give the patient several glasses of water.
    3. get an order to give the patient a diuretic.
    4. palpate the patient's bladder to stimulate urination.

339. A positive diagnosis of tuberculosis is made by
    1. complete blood count.
    2. skin test.
    3. sputum examination.
    4. X-ray examination.

340. A definitive diagnosis of Hodgkin's disease is based on the result of which of these diagnostic tests?
    1. Bone marrow smear.
    2. Lymph node biopsy.
    3. Computerized axial tomography.
    4. Complete blood count.

341. Total parenteral nutrition (TPN) will accomplish which of these goals?

1. Increase fluids.
2. Provide calories.
3. Maintain negative nitrogen balance.
4. Supply fats and electrolytes.

342. Which of the following laboratory tests should be done before and after a dialysis treatment?

1. Hgt and Hct.
2. Electrolytes and serum albumin.
3. Urinalysis and CBC.
4. CBC and PTT.

343. Which of the following would NOT necessitate cancellation of surgery?

1. A temperature of 99°F.
2. An unsigned consent for the surgery.
3. CBC, urinalysis, and chest X-ray have not been done.
4. Elevated blood pressure.

344. Although all of the following tests are included in a complete eye examination, the test that would diagnose glaucoma is

1. ophthalmoscopy.
2. visual field evaluation.
3. tonometry.
4. gonioscopy.

345. Postspinal anesthesia headache may be caused by

1. overdose of anesthesia.
2. leakage of spinal fluid from the sub-arachnoid space.
3. overhydration in the preoperative period.
4. inadequate preoperative preparation.

346. Which of the following statements is true concerning Pontacaine?

1. It is used as a general anesthetic.
2. It is used for nerve block and infiltration.
3. Its effect lasts for 2 hours or more.
4. It can not be used for topical application.

347. After a spinal anesthetic the nurse should observe the patient for

1. signs of respiratory depression.
2. return of motion and sensation to the extremities.
3. increase in blood pressure.
4. signs of generalized circulatory impairment.

348. Which of the following measures aimed at easing postspinal anesthesia headaches is contraindicated?

1. Keeping the patient flat in bed in a supine position.
2. Hydrating the patient with fluids.
3. Applying a pressure dressing over the patient's puncture site.
4. Monitoring the patient's blood pressure.

349. Louise Barton is awakening from anesthesia. Which of the following statements represents what the nurse should say to her first?

1. "Louise, cough, deep-breathe, and move your extremities."
2. "Louise, the surgery is over and you are now in the recovery room."
3. "Louise, the surgery is over."
4. "Louise, please do not talk or move your body."

350. Postoperatively, in the recovery room, a female patient is just beginning to react from anesthesia. She opens her eyes when spoken to by name, moans, is very restless, and states that she is experiencing pain. Her blood pressure is stable, her pulse is 96 and regular, and her respirations are 24 and shallow. Which of the following measures would the nurse use to support the patient's continuing reaction from anesthesia?

1. Wake her up periodically and make her talk to you.
2. Administer oxygen by nasal cannula per order.
3. Have her cough and take deep breaths.
4. Give the dose of postoperative analgesic as ordered.

351. Which of the following should be assessed FIRST in the recovery room?

1. The time of admission.
2. Level of consciousness.
3. Quality of respirations.
4. Blood pressure and pulse.

352. A patient is admitted to the recovery room following bowel surgery. He has a nasogastric tube in place. The purpose of the nasogastric tube is to

1. drain the surgical wound.
2. prevent distention.
3. introduce nourishment.
4. replace lost fluids and electrolytes.

353. Which of the following is true concerning a plastic airway?

1. It is removed by the nurse as the patient enters the recovery room.
2. It is inserted by the nurse in the recovery room.
3. It is removed when the gag reflex returns.
4. The patient returns to his room with it in place.

354. Which of the following standards of interpretation should be applied in regard to a patient's blood pressure in the recovery room?

1. Keep in mind that a blood pressure below 90/60 is abnormal.
2. Use the preoperative blood pressure as a baseline for determining the quality of the blood pressure.
3. Report all changes in blood pressure.
4. Determine the quality of the patient's blood pressure based on past nursing experience.

355. A nurse bases the decision to transfer a patient from the recovery room to his/her room on which of the following indications?

1. Absence of drainage from the operative site.
2. Stable vital signs for six readings.
3. Absence of pharyngeal reflexes.
4. Presence of mild drowsiness.

356. Buck's extension can be classified as

1. skin traction.
2. skeletal traction.
3. intermittent traction.
4. suspension traction.

357. Which of the following actions should the nurse take when a patient's first-day-postoperative dressing is saturated?

1. Remove the dressing, inspect the site, and then apply a dry dressing.
2. Reinforce the dressing and notify the physician.
3. Chart this observation on the patient's record.
4. Report this observation to the head nurse.

358. Which of these interventions would demonstrate that the nurse understands the underlying principles of traction?

1. Maintaining countertraction.
2. Maintaining the patient in a prone position.
3. Maintaining the spreader in contact with the bed.
4. Maintaining the weights in a dependent position.

359. If during the administration of blood the patient experiences chills, nausea and vomiting, and a drop in blood pressure, the nurse should

1. call the doctor and then discontinue the transfusion.
2. discontinue the transfusion and then call the doctor.
3. decrease the flow rate and observe the patient.
4. realize that this is a normal reaction and observe the patient carefully.

360. When preparing to transfuse a unit of whole blood, the nurse should

1. warm the blood to room temperature.
2. check the type and cross-match slip with the unit of blood.
3. prepare a 5% dextrose solution to be used by the physician to start the transfusion.
4. obtain an intravenous administration set.

361. The nurse enters a patient's room and observes his intravenous infusing at a rate higher than originally set. He has received 200 ml in 15 minutes. He is sitting upright in bed, with a respiration rate of 32, shallow, labored, and "moist." He is also restless and anxious. The nurse should FIRST

1. place the head of the bed in a semi-Fowler's position.
2. administer oxygen at 10 liters per minute.
3. slow the intravenous rate.
4. notify the physician.

362. Tissue turgor is significant in assessing fluid and electrolyte imbalance. Which of the following is true of tissue turgor?

1. It is best palpated in the abdominal area or the sternum.
2. Dry, dehydrated, pinched skin will fall back to its normal configuration when released.
3. In its normal condition pinched skin will remain in a pinched position.
4. It is best palpated on the arms and the hands.

363. A patient on hyperalimentation (TPN) is receiving a hypertonic solution. The preferred site for the infusion in an adult is the
    1. subclavian vein.
    2. femoral vein.
    3. saphenous vein.
    4. basilic vein.

364. A major complication of hyperalimentation is
    1. infection of the infusion/port site.
    2. perforation of the pleura.
    3. protein deficiency.
    4. air embolism.

365. The physician ordered that 125 ml of 5% glucose in water be given in 1 hour. The administration set gives 10 drops = 1 ml. How many drops per minute would you give?
    1. 16
    2. 18
    3. 20
    4. 24

366. If shortness of breath, cyanosis, and distention of the vein occur during the infusion of parenteral fluids, the nurse's FIRST action should be to
    1. notify the physician.
    2. assist the patient to a sitting position.
    3. discontinue the infusion.
    4. observe the patient for further complications.

367. Signs that indicate that an intravenous has infiltrated include
    1. pain along the vein.
    2. decreased flow rate.
    3. redness around the infusion site.
    4. coolness around the infusion site.

368. Which of the following should be done after administering a preoperative medication?
    1. Place the side rails up.
    2. Have the patient void.
    3. Remove the patient's dentures.
    4. Remove the patient's jewelry.

369. The physician ordered that 1000 ml of 5% glucose in water be given in 24 hours. The microdrip to be used administers 60 drops per cubic centimeter. How many drops would you give per minute?
    1. 25
    2. 38
    3. 41
    4. 60

370. A patient's Foley catheter has been removed postoperatively. In order to determine whether the patient's output is normal, the nurse should remember that the average daily output is
    1. 500 ml.
    2. 1500 ml.
    3. 2500 ml.
    4. 3000 ml.

371. Which of these measures for reducing an elevated temperature needs a doctor's order?
    1. Ice bags to groin and axillae.
    2. Sponge with tepid water.
    3. Force fluids.
    4. Hypothermia blanket.

372. Partial to complete separation of the wound edges is called
    1. dehiscence.
    2. evisceration.
    3. singultus.
    4. cachexia.

373. A pneumothorax is treated with
    1. medications.
    2. chest tubes.
    3. postural drainage.
    4. ambulation.

374. IPPB therapy improves ventilation by doing which of the following?
    1. Humidifying the respiratory mucosa.
    2. Resisting alveolar collapsing.
    3. Increasing cardiac functioning.
    4. Calming the anxious dyspneic patient.

375. A nursing intervention to prevent the spread of infectious hepatitis is
    1. maintaining the patient on bedrest.
    2. placing the patient in a single room with toilet and bath facilities.
    3. using gloves and gown whenever entering the patient's room.
    4. utilizing universal precautions with the patient.

376. Which of these structural changes occurs in pulmonary emphysema?
    1. Accumulation of pus in the pleural space.
    2. Overdistension and rupture of the alveoli.
    3. Constriction of the capillaries.
    4. Filling of the bronchus with mucus.

377. A patient who has a fractured hip would be expected to have which of these manifestations of the affected leg?

1. Shortening.
2. Internal rotation.
3. Increased range of motion.
4. Muscle flaccidity.

378. Oxygen is given cautiously to patients with emphysema because

1. oxygen increases airway resistence.
2. the physiological stimulus for breathing can be triggered only when there is a low oxygen level in the blood.
3. it is irritating to the mucous membrane.
4. the increased oxygen tension in the alveoli may cause a rapid drop in the carbon dioxide tension.

379. Prophylactic treatment for a positive tuberculin test consists of

1. decreased physical activity.
2. bedrest for 1 year.
3. isoniazid for 1 year.
4. a low-protein, high-carbohydrate diet.

380. Chemotherapeutic agents used in the treatment of tuberculosis

1. destroy the organism.
2. attenuate the organism.
3. absorb the toxin.
4. prevent the organism from multiplying.

381. The aim of treatment in tuberculosis is to

1. cure the disease.
2. prevent the need for surgical procedures.
3. prevent remission.
4. arrest the disease.

382. An increase in which of the following, as revealed by a diagnostic test, would necessitate the administration of vitamin K?

1. Serum bilirubin.
2. Icterus index.
3. Serum transaminase.
4. Prothrombin time.

383. The purpose of the first bottle in a three-bottle water seal drainage is to

1. collect drainage.
2. provide a water seal.
3. lessen the degree of suction applied to the patient.
4. maintain negative pressure in the thoracic cavity.

384. The primary purpose of closed chest drainage (water seal drainage) is to

1. provide mild suction to the thoracic cavity.
2. help restore negative pressure within the thoracic cavity.
3. provide aseptic conditions to the thoracic area.
4. equalize the internal and the external thoracic pressures.

385. To add flavor to a sodium-restricted diet, which of the following may be used?

1. Commercial salt substitutes.
2. Fresh onion, onion salt, and garlic salt.
3. Condiments such as chili sauce and Worcestershire sauce.
4. Fresh herbs and lemon juice.

386. The two nutrients that may require close attention in the diet of a cardiac patient are

1. protein and iron.
2. fat and sodium.
3. carbohydrates and vitamin C.
4. niacin and thiamine.

387. Thrombophlebitis is BEST defined as

1. a blood clot formed in the lumen of the blood vessel.
2. inflammation of a vein accompanied by clot formation.
3. a localized clot of blood in a tissue due to a break in the wall of a blood vessel.
4. a blood clot without inflammation.

388. A factor that precipitates thrombophlebitis is

1. venous stasis.
2. increased cardiac output.
3. exercise.
4. warmth.

389. The treatment of thrombophlebitis includes
1. massaging the leg to increase the blood supply.
2. active exercise of the leg to increase circulation.
3. elevation of the leg to promote venous return.
4. restriction of fluids to decrease peupheral blood flow to the leg.

390. A positive Homan's sign is
1. pain in the calf when the foot is in plantar flexion.
2. pain in the thigh referred from the calf.
3. pain in the leg due to venous stasis.
4. pain in the calf when the foot is in dorsiflexion.

391. The pain associated with a myocardial infarction can BEST be described as
1. viselike, increasing steadily in severity.
2. severe, precipitated by exertion.
3. persistent, relieved by nitrites.
4. intense, lasting for a few minutes.

392. To prevent osteoporosis, the public health nurse should encourage young women to
1. restrict milk and milk products.
2. participate in weight-bearing exercise for 20 minutes three times a week.
3. ingest 200–400 mg of calcium daily.
4. add milk to coffee.

393. Which of the following is the major nursing problem with a patient who has pitting edema of the extremities?
1. Prevention of joint contractures.
2. Prevention of pressure ulcer.
3. Prevention of weight gain.
4. Prevention of kidney failure.

394. Which of the following groups of foods can a patient on a sodium-restricted diet consume?
1. Margarine, fresh fruit, canned vegetables, roast beef.
2. Sweet butter, chicken, puffed rice, ginger ale.
3. Tomato juice, Swiss cheese, fresh fruit, fresh vegetables.
4. Chicken, saltine crackers, ice cream.

395. Repeated prothrombin time determinations are required with the administration of
1. Coumadin.
2. heparin.
3. vitamin K.
4. protamine.

396. Which of the following statements concerning anticoagulants is INCORRECT?
1. They dissolve already existing clots.
2. They are used primarily as prophylaxes.
3. They prolong the time period for blood clotting.
4. They help to prevent the formation of new thrombi by retarding clotting.

397. Myocardial infarctions are often due to atherosclerosis of the
1. aorta.
2. coronary arteries.
3. superior and inferior vena cava.
4. valves of the heart.

398. Which of the following is NOT a true statement when digitalization has occurred?
1. There is development of early symptoms of digitalis toxicity.
2. The patient is free of symptoms of cardiac disease.
3. The failing heart is receiving maximum benefits from digitalis.
4. The heart has been slowed to normal.

399. The usual maintenance dose of digoxin is
1. 0.1 mg.
2. 0.25 mg.
3. 0.5 mg.
4. 1.0 mg.

400. A thyroidectomy patient should be observed postoperatively for evidence of
1. perforation of the lung.
2. accidental removal of the parathyroid gland.
3. removal of the laryngeal cartilage.
4. laceration of the esophagus.

401. A patient who suffers from angina pectoris asks what nitroglycerin will do for him. Which of the following would be the nurse's BEST response?

1. "Nitroglycerin will open your blood vessels so more blood carrying oxygen can reach the painful muscle that needs it."
2. "Nitroglycerin will open your blood vessels so blood can reach your heart valves, where the pain is located."
3. "This pill will relieve your heart pain."
4. "This pill will strengthen your heartbeat and relieve heart pain."

402. Anginal attacks are due to

1. vasoconstriction of coronary vessels.
2. transient hypoxia of myocardial tissue.
3. decrease in cardiac output.
4. temporary necrosis of heart muscle.

403. The nurse should be able to recognize the pain associated with angina, which may be BEST described as being

1. constant, dull aching precordially.
2. sharp, stabbing retrosternally.
3. viselike, crushing, radiating.
4. squeezing, burning substernally.

404. Cirrhosis of the liver is MOST commonly caused by

1. alcoholism.
2. previous damage from infection.
3. malnutrition.
4. parasites.

405. A patient has a nonproductive cough, although the lungs are congested. Which of these measures may be taken by the nurse to assist the patient to raise sputum?

1. Teach deep breathing exercises.
2. Administer oxygen by mask.
3. Elevate the head of the bed.
4. Increase fluid intake.

406. To prevent pressure on the suture line after parathyroidectomy, the nurse should assist the patient to sit in bed by

1. grasping both of the patient's hands and pulling forward.
2. placing the hands under the head and neck.
3. placing the bed in a low-Fowler's position.
4. rolling the patient to the side of the bed and swinging his/her feet over the side.

407. A stone in the common bile duct would cause

1. no changes in urine or stool.
2. clay-colored stool and dark urine.
3. melena and yellow urine.
4. dark stool and light urine.

408. Which of the following nursing measures is MOST important immediately after a liver biopsy?

1. Checking blood pressure.
2. Checking temperature.
3. Checking lab work such as a CBC.
4. Checking for passing of flatus.

409. While the nurse is caring for a patient who has diabetes, the patient suddenly shows symptoms of hypoglycemic reaction. Which of the following groups of symptoms would be indicative of this reaction?

1. Rapid deep respiration, acetone on breath, drowsiness.
2. Restlessness, profuse sweating, trembling.
3. Nausea, vomiting, visual disturbances.
4. Thirst, abdominal pain, headache.

410. The doctor has diagnosed a patient as having appedicitis and has written preoperative orders for surgery the following day. Which of the following orders should the nurse definitely question?

1. Nothing by mouth (NPO).
2. Normal saline enema until clear.
3. 1000 ml of 5% D/W to run for 12 hours.
4. Demerol 75 mg IM every 4 hours prn for pain.

411. The action of antithyroid drugs is specifically aimed at

1. stimulating the production of thyroid-stimulating hormone.
2. interfering with the formation, release, or action of thyroxin.
3. increasing the excretion of triiodothyronine.
4. blocking the formation of parathyroid hormone.

412. What emergency equipment should be kept at the patient's bedside after a thyroidectomy?

1. A 50-ml syringe with Solu-Cortef.
2. A tracheotomy set.
3. A rubber tourniquet.
4. A large metal clamp.

413. During the assessment of a patient with a suspected diagnosis of pericarditis, the nurse should auscultate the heart for the presence of

1. heart murmur.
2. friction rub.
3. bruit.
4. ectopic heart beat.

414. Postural drainage has been ordered. The BEST time to institute postural drainage is

1. immediately after breakfast.
2. during the evening.
3. 1 hour before lunch.
4. immediately after IPPB treatment.

415. Cushing syndrome is characterized by

1. hypertension, sodium retention, and increased gastric activity.
2. muscle weakness, "buffalo hump," and poor ability to heal.
3. hypoglycemia, bone demineralization, and headaches.
4. hypotension, hyperglycemia, and hirsutism.

416. Ketoacidosis is caused by

1. depletion of mineral stores.
2. enhanced storage of glycogen.
3. incomplete breakdown of fatty acids.
4. excessive destruction of protein.

417. Diabetes is treated by

1. insulin, rest, and exercise.
2. diet, insulin, and exercise.
3. food, stress, and weight reduction.
4. insulin, medication, and rest.

418. When the nurse brings a male patient his medication, he looks at it and says, "I think I have already had this medication. Another nurse brought me a medicine that looked the same as this." The MOST suitable and reassuring reply would be

1. "No, you have not had this medicine. I'm positive."
2. "You must be confused with yesterday's medicine. Please just go ahead and take it."
3. "I'm sure you have not received this medicine, but I will go back and check again to be certain."
4. "I have already checked, so you have nothing to worry about."

419. A patient received 10 units of regular insulin at 7 A.M. and received breakfast at 8 A.M. When would a hypoglycemic reaction be MOST likely to occur?

1. 7:30 A.M.
2. 9:30 A.M.
3. 11:30 A.M.
4. 1:30 P.M.

420. Which of the following types of insulin acts MOST rapidly?

1. Protamine zinc.
2. Regular.
3. N.P.H.
4. Globin.

421. A patient has been placed on retrovir (AZT, azidothymidine). Retrovir works biologically/therapeutically by

1. arresting the disease process.
2. blocking the replication of RNA and DNA.
3. kiling the nucleus of the AIDS virus.
4. rendering the AIDS virus harmless.

422. Oral hypoglycemics may be used when

1. the pancreas is no longer functioning.
2. the pancreas is still functioning.
3. the diabetic gets the disease in early childhood.
4. insulin is not effective.

423. Which of the following statements is true concerning long-term steroid therapy?

1. Expected body changes that occur when a patient is on steroid therapy are weight gain, increased facial hair, and moon face.
2. Hospitalized patients on steroid therapy should be placed on daily weighings, a high-sodium diet, restricted fluids, and intake and output.
3. Weakness of the proximal muscles of the arms and legs is an expected change and therefore this discomfort should not be regarded with concern.
4. Therapy should be terminated by the patient whenever he experiences complications or side effects of steroid therapy.

424. Which of the following statements about the opportunistic diseases that accompany acquired immune deficiency syndrome is true?

1. *Pneumocystis carinii* pneumonia causes disease only in immunocompromised hosts.
2. Chronic cryptococcosis is extremely contagious.
3. Kaposi's sarcoma is one of the commonest types of malignancy found in heterosexuals.
4. Esophageal candidiasis is seldom found in iummosuppressed patients.

425. A staging system is of great importance in diagnosis of carcinoma as it

1. assists in continuing investigation.
2. defines the extent of the disease at a point in time.
3. implies a regular progression of the disease.
4. predicts the outcome of the disease process.

426. To prevent a hospitalized patient from becomming confused at night, the nurse should

1. leave the light on in the patient's room.
2. reorient the patient to person, place, and time.
3. keep a calendar within the patient's view.
4. ask the physician to prescribe medication to make the patient sleep.

427. The nurse was standing outside the room talking to a patient after her radium insertion. The patient asked the nurse. "Are you afraid of me? Am I radioactive?" Which of the following responses by the nurse would be MOST appropriate?

1. "No, there is really no possibility that I could be harmed from the radium implanted in your vagina."
2. "Yes, I am afraid of radium, but I am more concerned with your welfare."
3. "No, I limit my contact with you to a safe time and distance while providing you with the care that you need."
4. "No, but are you afraid of being radioactive? Would you like to discuss this now?"

428. The nurse can BEST describe the procedure of mammography to a patient as

1. irradiation of the breasts with low-voltage X-ray that identities differences in tissue density.
2. an X-ray of the breasts after radio-opaque dye is injected into the mammary artery.

3. an infrared photo that shows areas of increased blood supply.
4. an X-ray of the breasts.

429. A patient receiving insulin for diabetes melitus is receiving a form of therapy that can be compared to which of the following?

1. Thyroid for cretinism.
2. Streptomycin for tuberculosis.
3. Cortisone for rheumatoid arthritis.
4. Morphine for severe pain.

430. Postoperative gas pain can BEST be prevented by

1. using a rectal tube to release intestinal gas.
2. initiating ambulation to promote intestinal activity.
3. administering a narcotic to ease gas pains.
4. inserting a nasogastric tube to decrease intestinal content.

431. The nurse assigned to take care of a female, a new admission, notes during the assessment that she has pitting edema (2+) of the ankles and rales in both lungs. The nurse also notes from the chart that she was given Lasix IV in the emergency room. The MOST accurate nursing measure for assessing water retention or the effectiveness of the diuretic is to

1. monitor the patient's vital signs.
2. record the patient's intake and output.
3. weigh the patient daily.
4. measure the patient's abdominal girth daily.

432. A nurse observes that a patient (1 day post-surgery for a hysterectomy) is awake and restless at 3 A.M. The nurse's assessment finds that vital signs are stable, but the patient states that she is unable to sleep. She complains of a lot of pain around her suture line and says she is afraid to turn in bed. She has not had pain or sleep medication since 9 P.M. The MOST appropriate nursing action would be to

1. administer a prn hypnotic to relax the patient and induce sleep.
2. discuss with the patient her relationship with her husband and ways to cope with his response to her surgery.
3. offer the patient some warm milk and a snack to induce drowsiness.
4. assist the patient in changing her position, and offer a prn pain medication.

433. Which one of these patients indicates the BEST acceptance of surgery ?

1. Jack Jones, who says he's been through all this before, knows what to expect, and doesn't want to talk about it.
2. Bob Smith, who is very friendly and outgoing and always directs the conversation away from himself.
3. Tom White, who is having trouble sleeping, chain smokes, and continuously asks everyone the same questions.
4. Joe Black, who listens to preoperative instructions, asks relevant questions, and has expressed his fear of pain after surgery.

434. In caring for an AIDS patient, the staff should practice which of the following universal precautions?

1. Wear a gown if the patient has a large amount of mucus.
2. Wear a mask when there is a possibility that the patient's secretions or excretions may be spattered.
3. Use gloves whenever in contact with the patient's body secretions.
4. Observe all of the above.

435. Which of the following activities would the nurse MOST probably use to prevent disuse atrophy in a patient who has recently experienced a stroke?

1. Active range of motion.
2. Passive range of motion.
3. Isometric exercises.
4. Resistant exercises.

436. The drug of choice for the control of manic behavior is

1. Tofranil.
2. Elavil.
3. lithium carbonate.
4. reserpine.

437. A severely depressed patient is to undergo ECT (electroconvulsive therapy) for the first time. Preparation for ECT therapy would include all of the following EXCEPT

1. a complete physical examination, an ECG, a CBC, a urinalysis, a chest X-ray, and an EEC.
2. maintaining NPO the night before the treatment.

3. written consent.
4. explanation to the patient and his/her family that there will be a permanent memory loss after the ECT, which is the desired outcome from the treatment.

438. Upon the patient's return to the ward from the ECT in a state of disorientation, the nurse must keep in mind that

1. nursing care should be centered on the patient's reorientation to his/her surroundings.
2. after ECT there is no intellectual impairment.
3. the memory loss is temporary and would not be a matter of concern to the patient.
4. the memory loss, though temporary, could be distressing to the patient.

439. Depression produces changes in a person's thinking, decision making ability, and reality testing. Which of the following guidelines would enhance the effectiveness of a therapeutic plan for the depressed person?

1. Assist the person to recognize that his symptoms are all in his mind and will disappear as he recognizes them as not real.
2. Convince the person of his worthiness to increase his self-esteem.
3. Assist the person to identify alternative coping methods open to him, and encourage him to make a decision.
4. Encourage the person to participate in group activities in the unit to keep his mind off his problems.

440. There is increased danger of suicide when a patient is

1. improving from severe depression.
2. becoming more extremely depressed.
3. demonstrating increased lethargy.
4. pacing frequently in the hall.

441. Which of the following nursing interventions would demonstrate a good understanding of the dynamics of the depressed person's behavior?

1. Restrain in a firm manner in the event of destructive outbursts against self and others.
2. Directly provoke the patient's repressed anger to facilitate its expression.
3. Do not reinforce feelings of dependency and helplessness by convincing the patient that he is a competent person.
4. Accept the patient because of his symptoms.

442. Which of the following are typical needs of aged persons?

1. Increased sexual activity, security, esteem, and acceptance.
2. Increased sexual activity, self-actualization, and security.
3. Sexual activity, security, esteem, and self-actualization.
4. Increased competitiveness, esteem, and sexual activity.

443. The older patient is more likely to maintain a productive level of functioning if the patient feels

1. useful and loved.
2. dependent and closely observed.
3. wanted and dependent.
4. financially secure and physically active.

444. Depression in the adolescent may be difficult to recognize because

1. the adolescent is usually active, and depression is often masked by other behaviors.
2. the adolescent is not usually aware of the meaning of depression.
3. depression is not common during adolescence.
4. depression in the adolescent is always self-limiting.

445. According to Erikson, the major developmental tasks of early adulthood include all of the following EXCEPT

1. generativity.
2. sharing feelings in heterosexual relations.
3. occupational choice.
4. firm grasp of identity.

446. Maladaptive responses during early adulthood may be manifested by

1. despair.
2. isolation.
3. somatization.
4. homosexuality.

447. Which of the following constellations of physical problems are commonly associated with drug addiction?

1. Hepatitis, skin infection, nutritional disturbances, menstrual irregularities, impotence.
2. Agranulocytosis, constipation, urinary tract infection.

3. Hypertensive crisis, acne vulgaris, hormonal imbalance, dental caries.
4. Hypotension, respiratory problems, nutritional disturbances, skin problems.

448. Finding drug use soothing and comforting BEST describes

1. physical addiction.
2. habituation.
3. psychological dependence.
4. predisposition to drug addiction.

449. Anorexia nervosa can be precipitated by

1. traumatic events.
2. bodily changes during puberty.
3. sexual experiences, particularly failures.
4. all of the above.

450. Which of the following activities is NOT considered primary prevention?

1. Providing anticipatory guidance for pregnant women.
2. Teaching the general public about acquired immune deficiency syndrome (AIDS) and the risk factors.
3. Administering immunizations.
4. Having "half-way houses" for emotionally disabled persons.

451. Community mental health services are geared toward

1. primary prevention.
2. secondary prevention.
3. tertiary prevention.
4. a combination of all three.

452. Health care services that are concerned with maintaining mental health rather than treating mental disorders are geared toward

1. primary prevention.
2. secondary prevention.
3. tertiary prevention.
4. a combination of all three.

453. Which of the following statements is LEAST descriptive of a therapeutic community?

1. A person is accepted as an individual.
2. All behavior is recognized as meaningful.
3. All behavior is accepted.
4. The environment is democratic and considerate of the individual's coping abilities.

454. An obsessive-compulsive behavior is BEST described as

1. the expression of unconscious conflict through physiological disturbances.
2. an absence of voluntary activity and a tendency to extreme negative behavior.
3. the presence of fixed, systematized, and well-conceived delusions.
4. compelling, repetitive, and ritualistic patterns of behavior.

455. Flight of ideas is an attempt to

1. increase intellectual organization.
2. test reality.
3. alleviate anxiety.
4. confuse others.

456. It is important that the nurse understand that confused behavior may be indicative of

1. functional disorders and acute stressful situations.
2. organic disorders.
3. infectious processes of the central nervous system.
4. all of the above.

457. The process by which a person is gradually emancipated from bondage to a lost person is

1. dream work.
2. grief work.
3. displacement.
4. despair.

458. Which of the following is MOST likely to make a grief reaction complicated and pathological?

1. An extremely ambivalent relationship with the lost person.
2. Identification.
3. Fantasy.
4. None of them.

459. In describing her mother to the nurse, the daughter said, "She was really a very good woman; you know what I mean?" What would be the MOST appropriate initial response by the nurse?

1. "You say that your mother was really a very good woman. Do you really mean that?"
2. "What makes you say that your mother was a very good woman?"
3. "I am not sure that I follow what you are trying to tell me."
4. "Your mother must have been a wonderful person."

460. A 42-year-old male has been a heavy drinker for the past 10 years. When the nurse walks into his room, he becomes verbally abusive and starts criticizing the hospital and its staff: "This place stinks and does nothing right." Which of the following is the BEST initial response by the nurse?

1. "We have a highly competent staff, and we try our best to help you."
2. "I am not going to permit you to talk about our institution the way you do."
3. "You seem to be very upset about something. Would you like to talk about it?"
4. "What exactly do you want from our staff?"

461. The principal pharmacological effect of alcohol is

1. depression of the cortical brain center.
2. decreased mobility of the digestive tract.
3. stimulation of the peripheral nervous system.
4. increased irritability of muscle fibers.

462. The community mental health center staff should expect an alcoholic to display all of the following EXCEPT

1. strong need for dependence on others.
2. a high threshold to frustration.
3. feeling of inferiority and unworthiness.
4. a charming but superficial personality.

463. All of the following are true about Alcoholics Anonymous EXCEPT

1. it is a form of group therapy.
2. it considers alcoholism as a physical, sociological, and spiritual problem.
3. it is a federally funded organization.
4. it appears to gratify dependency needs through identification or by caring for new members.

464. Which of the following measures would be MOST therapeutic to a patient during delirium tremens?

1. Using physical restraints.
2. Making sure the bed rails are up.
3. Reassuring the patient that the reasons for his fears are unfounded.
4. Keeping procedures to a minimum and decreasing stimulation.

465. Pilocarpine is effective in treating chronic simple glaucoma because it

1. allows aqueous fluid to drain from the anterior chamber.
2. depresses the cells of the ciliary body.
3. relaxes the extraocular eye muscles.
4. draws the smooth muscles away from the canal of Schlemm.

466. The treatment of a cataract is primarily concerned with

1. the instillation of miotics.
2. the instillation of mydriatics.
3. surgery of the lens.
4. removal of the iris.

467. A patient is on a low-cholesterol diet. Which of the following foods are allowed on this diet?

1. Shrimp salad.
2. Liver and onions.
3. Egg sandwich.
4. Skim milk in coffee.

468. A patient with rheumatoid arthritis, who is being treated with daily doses of aspirin, asks the nurse, "Why can't I have cortisone?" The MOST appropriate and helpful answer the nurse can give this patient is

1. "You doctor probably wants to take a conservative approach to your problem."
2. "Cortisone can be dangerous and produces many undesirable side effects."
3. "Aspirin is considered one of the safest and best drugs on the market for arthritis."
4. "Cortisone is a relatively expensive drug, whereas aspirin in inexpensive."

469. To involve a patient with glaucoma in the management of her condition, the nurse should teach the patient to

1. regulate dosage of medications.
2. administer eyedrops.
3. increase fluid intake.
4. visit her physician annually.

470. A patient received an intravenous push of Lasix 40 mg during an episode of congestive heart failure. The nurse should observe his output by Foley catheter, expecting to see a diuresis

1. immediately.
2. within 1/2 to 1 hour.
3. within 2 to 4 hours.
4. within 4 to 6 hours.

471. While preparing a medication, the nurse notes that the physician had doubled the usual dosage of the drug. The nurse should

1. administer the drug as ordered.
2. check the orders with several other staff nurses before administering the drug.
3. record that an overdosage was ordered.
4. check with the doctor concerning the dosage ordered.

472. Leukemia is

1. characterized by a decrease in white blood cells.
2. a result of overexposure to antibiotics.
3. characterized by weight loss.
4. characterized by bleeding from body orifices.

473. Which of the following patients who have diabetes should avoid regular exercise this morning?

1. Insulin-dependent—blood glucose level of 100 mg/dl in A.M., no ketones in urine.
2. Diet-controlled—blood glucose level 300 mg/dl in A.M., ketones in urine.
3. Insulin-dependent—blood glucose level 210 mg/dl in A.M., no ketones in urine.
4. Non-insulin-dependent—blood glucose level 150 mg/dl in A.M., ketones in urine.

474. Which of the following would be LEAST effective in preventing wound infection while a dressing is being changed?

1. Using forceps to remove the soiled dressing.
2. Washing hands before and after the dressing is changed.
3. Covering the wound with a sterile dressing.
4. Removing the soiled dressing with the hand.

475. Bulimia can BEST be described as

1. discrete, uncontrollable, rapid consumption of large quantities of food over a period of time.
2. repeated, uncontrollable ingestion of non-nutritive substances for a period of time.
3. an intense fear of becoming overweight.
4. discrete, uncontrollable, rapid consumption of large quantities of food over a period of time followed by actions to remove the ingested food from the body and thereby prevent weight gain.

476. Signs of cocaine ("crack") withdrawal would include

1. depression, irritability, anxiety.
2. psychomotor agitation.
3. insomnia.
4. all of the above.

477. Therapy for victims of sexual assault, such as rape, is MOST helpful when

1. it focuses on the restoration of the person's sense of control over her/his life.
2. it provides for expression, in an accepting environment, of feelings of helplessness, vulnerability, anger, shame, humiliation, fear, and confusion.
3. support systems that include collaboration with local law enforcement agencies are available.
4. all of the above are considered.

478. Which of the following is (are) considered predisposing factors to domestic violence such as spouse abuse?

1. Financial difficulties.
2. Substance abuse.
3. Frustration at home.
4. All of the above.

479. Which of the following characteristics may BEST describe an abusive spouse's personality?

1. Aggressive.
2. Immature, dependent, nonassertive, with feelings of inadequacy.
3. High self-esteem with feelings of superiority over the victim, who is perceived as helpless and dependent.
4. Loving but unable to express love appropriately.

480. Which of the following statements BEST describes crisis intervention?

1. It is a form of secondary prevention that seeks to prevent disorders through early intervention, allowing the person to regain equilibrium.
2. It is aimed at reducing the long-term impact of a psychiatric disorder.
3. It seeks to prevent psychiatric disorders through community education and special programs targeting high-risk groups.
4. It is primarily focused on rehabilitation.

ANSWER KEY

1.	2	49.	1	97.	2	145.	1	193.	3
2.	2	50.	4	98.	4	146.	1	194.	3
3.	4	51.	1	99.	4	147.	4	195.	2
4.	3	52.	2	100.	1	148.	2	196.	2
5.	1	53.	4	101.	4	149.	3	197.	4
6.	1	54.	1	102.	1	150.	4	198.	4
7.	4	55.	4	103.	4	151.	2	199.	3
8.	3	56.	2	104.	4	152.	3	200.	4
9.	1	57.	4	105.	4	153.	3	201.	1
10.	2	58.	1	106.	3	154.	2	202.	1
11.	1	59.	3	107.	1	155.	4	203.	1
12.	3	60.	2	108.	2	156.	1	204.	3
13.	1	61.	4	109.	1	157.	4	205.	3
14.	3	62.	3	110.	4	158.	1	206.	2
15.	4	63.	2	111.	4	159.	2	207.	1
16.	2	64.	1	112.	4	160.	3	208.	2
17.	3	65.	3	113.	4	161.	2	209.	3
18.	1	66.	4	114.	2	162.	2	210.	3
19.	3	67.	2	115.	4	163.	1	211.	4
20.	4	68.	1	116.	1	164.	1	212.	1
21.	2	69.	4	117.	3	165.	4	213.	1
22.	3	70.	2	118.	2	166.	3	214.	1
23.	3	71.	1	119.	1	167.	1	215.	2
24.	3	72.	4	120.	3	168.	4	216.	3
25.	2	73.	1	121.	1	169.	2	217.	1
26.	2	74.	4	122.	4	170.	1	218.	1
27.	4	75.	3	123.	2	171.	1	219.	1
28.	4	76.	1	124.	1	172.	1	220.	1
29.	1	77.	1	125.	3	173.	2	221.	4
30.	2	78.	4	126.	2	174.	4	222.	4
31.	1	79.	3	127.	2	175.	1	223.	3
32.	3	80.	2	128.	3	176.	2	224.	4
33.	1	81.	3	129.	4	177.	2	225.	3
34.	3	82.	2	130.	1	178.	3	226.	4
35.	2	83.	3	131.	2	179.	2	227.	4
36.	1	84.	2	132.	3	180.	3	228.	3
37.	4	85.	4	133.	3	181.	3	229.	2
38.	1	86.	3	134.	1	182.	1	230.	2
39.	3	87.	2	135.	1	183.	3	231.	1
40.	1	88.	1	136.	3	184.	2	232.	2
41.	4	89.	1	137.	3	185.	4	233.	3
42.	3	90.	1	138.	3	186.	3	234.	4
43.	1	91.	1	139.	4	187.	2	235.	1
44.	4	92.	4	140.	1	188.	1	236.	1
45.	1	93.	3	141.	2	189.	1	237.	2
46.	2	94.	4	142.	2	190.	4	238.	2
47.	4	95.	2	143.	3	191.	2	239.	2
48.	2	96.	3	144.	1	192.	2	240.	2

241. 1	289. 3	337. 3	385. 4	433. 4
242. 2	290. 4	338. 4	386. 2	434. 4
243. 3	291. 3	339. 3	387. 2	435. 2
244. 1	292. 1	340. 2	388. 1	436. 3
245. 4	293. 4	341. 2	389. 3	437. 4
246. 2	294. 2	342. 1	390. 4	438. 3
247. 4	295. 1	343. 1	391. 1	439. 3
248. 1	296. 1	344. 3	392. 2	440. 1
249. 2	297. 4	345. 2	393. 2	441. 1
250. 3	298. 1	346. 2	394. 2	442. 3
251. 1	299. 3	347. 2	395. 1	443. 1
252. 2	300. 1	348. 4	396. 1	444. 1
253. 2	301. 3	349. 2	397. 2	445. 1
254. 4	302. 4	350. 4	398. 3	446. 4
255. 1	303. 4	351. 3	399. 2	447. 1
256. 4	304. 4	352. 2	400. 2	448. 3
257. 2	305. 2	353. 3	401. 1	449. 4
258. 4	306. 2	354. 2	402. 1	450. 4
259. 2	307. 4	355. 2	403. 4	451. 4
260. 4	308. 2	356. 1	404. 1	452. 2
261. 1	309. 3	357. 2	405. 4	453. 3
262. 2	310. 2	358. 1	406. 2	454. 4
263. 4	311. 1	359. 2	407. 2	455. 3
264. 3	312. 2	360. 2	408. 1	456. 4
265. 2	313. 2	361. 3	409. 2	457. 2
266. 2	314. 4	362. 1	410. 2	458. 1
267. 2	315. 3	363. 1	411. 2	459. 3
268. 2	316. 1	364. 1	412. 2	460. 3
269. 1	317. 1	365. 3	413. 2	461. 1
270. 1	318. 1	366. 3	414. 4	462. 2
271. 1	319. 2	367. 4	415. 2	463. 3
272. 3	320. 1	368. 1	416. 3	464. 4
273. 1	321. 3	369. 3	417. 2	465. 4
274. 4	322. 4	370. 2	418. 3	466. 3
275. 3	323. 3	371. 4	419. 3	467. 4
276. 4	324. 3	372. 1	420. 2	468. 1
277. 1	325. 4	373. 3	421. 2	469. 3
278. 2	326. 1	374. 1	422. 2	470. 2
279. 3	327. 2	375. 4	423. 1	471. 4
280. 3	328. 2	376. 2	424. 1	472. 4
281. 4	329. 4	377. 1	425. 2	473. 2
282. 1	330. 2	378. 2	426. 1	474. 4
283. 3	331. 3	379. 3	427. 3	475. 4
284. 2	332. 2	380. 4	428. 4	476. 4
285. 4	333. 1	381. 4	429. 1	477. 4
286. 4	334. 2	382. 4	430. 2	478. 4
287. 3	335. 2	383. 1	431. 3	479. 3
288. 3	336. 1	384. 2	432. 4	480. 1

HOW WELL DID YOU DO?

When you have completed the Diagnostic Test and checked your answers, fill out the chart below. It will indicate the areas in which you are weakest and on which you should spend most of your study time.

UNIT	NUMBER OF QUESTIONS	NUMBER CORRECT	NUMBER INCORRECT
One	1–31 **(32)** 33		
Two	32 **(17)** 34–39		
Three	50–77 **(29)** 333		
Four	78–91 **(14)**		
Five	92–107 **(16)**		
Six	108–126 **(20)** 444		
Seven	127–203 **(234)** 204–258 260–332 334–335 445–455 460–464 467–468 471–473 475–480		
Eight	336–376 **(104)** 379–441		
Nine	259 **(11)** 377–378 442–443 456 465–466 469–470 474		
Ten	457–459 **(3)**		

PART II

Review of Nursing Principles and Practices

Meeting the Needs of the Newborn

(birth to 1 month)

STUDY GUIDE

IMMEDIATE CARE IN THE DELIVERY ROOM

A. Establishment of Respirations (First Priority of Care)
B. Maintenance of Heat
C. Apgar Scoring
D. Eye Care
E. Cord Care
F. General Observations
G. Identification
H. Bonding

MANAGEMENT OF THE NEWBORN PERIOD

A. Admission to the Nursery
B. Newborn Assessment
C. Routine Nursery Care
D. Prevention of Infection
E. Care of Circumcision

CARE OF HIGH-RISK INFANTS

A. Preterm Infants
B. Infants Small for Gestational Age (SGA)
C. Postmature Infants
D. Infants of Diabetic Mothers (IDM)
E. Infants of Substance-Abusing Mothers

ALTERATIONS OF HEALTH IN THE NORMAL NEWBORN

A. Respiratory Distress Syndrome
B. Hypoglycemia
C. Hyperbilirubinemia
D. Erythroblastosis Fetalis
E. Infection of the Newborn

CONGENITAL ABNORMALITIES

Congenital Heart Diseases

A. Acyanotic Congenital Heart Disease
   1. Coarctation of the aorta
   2. Patent ductus arteriosus
   3. Atrial septal defect
   4. Ventricular septal defect
B. Cyanotic Congenital Heart Disease
   1. Tetralogy of Fallot
   2. Transposition of the great vessels
C. Diagnostic Measures for Congenital Heart Diseases
D. Preoperative Nursing Care Plan for Congenital Heart Diseases
E. Postoperative Nursing Care Plan for Congenital Heart Diseases
F. Congestive Heart Failure

Other Congenital Abnormalities

A. Spina Bifida
B. Hydrocephalus
C. Cleft Lip and Cleft Palate
D. Esophageal Atresia
E. Intestinal Obstructions
   1. Hirschsprung's disease (congenital aganglionic megacolon)
      2. Imperforate anus
F. Pyloric Stenosis
G. Congenital Dislocated Hip

IMMEDIATE CARE IN THE DELIVERY ROOM

A. Establishment of Respirations (First Priority of Care)
   1. Observe for spontaneous respirations.
   2. Have resuscitation equipment on hand.
   3. Place the newborn in a 30° Trendelenburg position to facilitate drainage of mucus.
   4. Suction the nose and the mouth as necessary with a bulb syringe or a DeLee suction trap.
   5. Administer oxygen as necessary.
B. Maintenance of Heat
   1. Rub the infant dry so that no body heat is lost through evaporation.
   2. Wrap in warm blankets.
   3. Place in a heated crib.
   4. Expose only one part of the body at a time when doing newborn care.
C. Apgar Scoring
   1. Done at 1 and 5 minutes.
   2. Scored 0 to 2 on each of five observations.

   2. Silver nitrate is not usually used due to chemical conjunctivitis.
   3. Most hospitals use antibiotic ointments.

E. Cord Care
   1. Use a sterile clamp and scissors.
   2. Clamp cord close to the abdomen with a plastic clamp.
   3. Observe cord for the presence of two umbilical arteries and one umbilical vein.
   4. Leave cord about 8 inches long if there is a possibility that umbilical infusion or transfusion will be necessary (as in a premature infant or the infant of an Rh-negative mother).

F. General Observations
   1. Obvious congenital anomalies.
   2. Birth trauma: forceps marks, edema of the scalp, fractured clavicle.
   3. Meconium-stained skin or umbilical cord.
   4. Passage of meconium or voiding.

a.

SIGN	0	1	2
Heart rate	Absent	Below 100	Over 100
Respirations	Absent	Irregular; weak cry	Good; strong cry
Muscle tone	Flaccid	Partially flexed	Well flexed
Reflex irritability	No response	Grimace	Cry; withdrawal
Color	Blue, pale	Body pink, extremities blue	Completely pink

   b. Interpretation of scores: 0 to 4, high risk; 4 to 6, "guarded"; 7 to 10, good condition.

D. Eye Care
   1. Prophylaxis against gonorrheal conjunctivitis is mandated by state law.

G. Identification
   1. Place bands with matching numbers on the mother and on the newborn (one on the mother, two on the newborn).
   2. Footprint the newborn. The mother's index fingerprint or thumbprint will also be placed on the footprint record.

H. Bonding
1. As soon as possible, let the mother hold the newborn.
2. Allow the father to hold the infant also if he is present.
3. Allow the mother to breast-feed on the delivery table if she wishes.
4. Allow the family some time alone together before the infant is transferred to the nursery, if possible.
5. Teach parents to keep the newborn well wrapped to prevent heat loss.

MANAGEMENT OF THE NEWBORN PERIOD

A. Admission to the Nursery
1. Weigh the newborn.
2. Measure length, head circumference, and chest circumference.
3. Check temperature rectally to assess anal patency.
4. Administer vitamin K intramuscularly.
5. Place the newborn in a heated crib.
6. Check temperature every hour. The newborn may be placed in an open crib when the temperature is 98°F and bathed as soon as the temperature stablizes.
7. Check respirations and apical heart rate every hour for 4 hours and as necessary.
8. Have suction equipment ready.
9. Observe for any obvious congenital abnormalities.

B. Newborn Assessment (Complete physical assessment should be done during the first 24 hours of life.)
1. Measurements
   a. Weight: 5½ to 10 pounds.
   b. Length: usually 18 to 22 inches.
   c. Head circumference: 13½ to 14 inches.
   d. Chest circumference: 1 inch less than head circumference.
2. Vital signs
   a. Temperature: 98 to 99°F.
   b. Apical rate: 120 to 140 per minute; may be 180 during crying.
   c. Respirations: 30 to 60 per minute at rest; irregular depth, rate, and rhythm.
3. Inspection
   a. Size in relation to gestational age.
   b. Gross abnormalities.
   c. State of consciousness.
   d. Movements.
   e. Position at rest.
   f. Response to stimuli.
   g. Cry.
   h. Color.
4. Skin
   a. Color: pallor, cyanosis, jaundice.
   b. Hydration: turgor.
   c. Milia, lanugo, vernix.
   d. Pigmentation: birthmarks, variations. } *See* Newborn variations, page 60.
5. Head
   a. Shape and symmetry.
   b. Position control.
   c. Condition of the scalp.
   d. Character of the hair.
   e. Fontanelles
      (1) Anterior: diamond shaped; closes between 12 and 18 months.
      (2) Posterior: triangular; difficult to palpate; closes by the second month.
   f. Symmetry of the face.
6. Eyes
   a. Symmetry, shape, and position.
   b. Reaction to light.
   c. Red reflex.
   d. Blinking.
7. Ears
   a. Symmetry, shape, and position.
   b. Reaction to noise.
8. Nose
   a. Test nares for patency.
   b. Elicit sneeze.
9. Mouth and throat
   a. Tongue: mobility.
   b. Palate: intactness; Epstein's pearls.
   c. Mucous membranes: thrush.
   d. Teeth: any present?; check for looseness.
10. Neck
   a. Length.
   b. Mobility.
   c. Trachea in midline.
11. Chest
   a. Contour and symmetry.
   b. Rate, depth, and rhythm of respirations.
   c. Breath sounds.
   d. Location of the point of maximum impulse.
   e. Rate and rhythm of the heart.

12. Breasts
    a. Symmetry.
    b. Nipples: position, supernumerary.
    c. Axillary nodes.
13. Abdomen
    a. Contour and symmetry.
    b. Condition of the cord.
    c. Peristalsis.
    d. Liver and spleen: palpate.
14. Genitalia
    a. Size of structures.
    b. Edema.
    c. Drainage.
    d. Descent of the testes in the male.
    e. Inguinal nodes.
    f. Voiding.
    g. Femoral pulses.
15. Rectum
    a. Anus: check patency.
    b. Passage of stools
        (1) Meconium: black, tarry (within 24 hours).
        (2) Transitional: greenish yellow (2nd to 5th day).
16. Hips
    a. Symmetry.
    b. Range of motion.
    c. Abnormal clicks.
17. Back and spine
    a. Contour: should be straight.
    b. Tufts of hair: abnormal.
    c. Dermal sinus: abnormal.
    d. Symmetry of the scapulae.
18. Extremities
    a. Length and symmetry.
    b. Position of the feet.
    c. Range of motion.
    d. Webbing of the hands or feet.
    e. Polydactyly (extra fingers or toes).
    f. Simian crease on the hands.
    g. Pulses.
19. Reflexes
    a. Moro: startle reflex.
    b. Tonic neck: fencing reflex.
    c. Babinski reflex: positive in newborns; may persist until 18 months old.
    d. Rooting: the newborn turns his/her head in the direction of the cheek that is stroked.
    e. Sucking: stimulated by touching the newborn's lips.
    f. Swallowing: automatic when food is placed on the posterior portion of the tongue.
    g. Extrusion: the newborn spits out substances placed on the anterior portion of the tongue.
    h. Grasp: the newborn closes fingers on any object placed in the palm.
    i. Stepping: the newborn takes a few quick steps when held standing on a hard surface.
20. Newborn variations
    a. Harlequin sign: an infant lying on his/her side will appear red on the dependent side and pale on the upper side.
    b. Mongolian spots: slate-gray patches across the sacrum and buttocks; common in Asian and African children; disappear by school age.
    c. Vernix caseosa: cheeselike substance covering the infant's skin; is absorbed or washed away during the first 2 days.
    d. Lanugo: fine, downy hair over the shoulders, back, and arms; disappears by 2 weeks of age.
    e. Desquamation: peeling of the skin; common in postmature infants.
    f. Milia: pinpoint white papules found on the bridge of the nose and the cheeks.
    g. Erythema toxicum: "newborn rash"; pinpoint papules on an erythematous base; no treatment required; disappears in 3 days.
    h. Forceps marks: disappear in 2 to 3 days.
    i. Caput succedaneum: edema of the scalp at the area of the presenting part; not dangerous; disappears.
    j. Cephalhematoma: collection of blood between the periosteum and the bone of the skull; may be discolored; swelling stops at the bone's suture line; can cause intracranial pressure; observe for signs of irritability.
    k. Molding: head molds during delivery to fit the shape of the cervix; appears asymmetrical at birth; normal shape restored within a few days.
    l. Stork bite: light, pink patch on eyelid or nape of the neck; fades spontaneously.
    m. Nevus flammeus: dark red macular lesions on the face or thighs; called "portwine stain"; those above the nose will fade; others won't.

n. Strawberry hemangiomas: raised, red birthmarks; may grow during the first year of life; disappear by 10 years of age.

o. Cavernous hemangiomas: resemble strawberry hemangiomas but do not disappear.

C. Routine Nursery Care
1. Assessment
   a. Take temperature, pulse, and respirations each shift.
   b. Weigh daily
   c. Record voiding and stools.
   d. Observe feeding.
   e. Check for jaundice each shift.
   f. Check cord each shift.
   g. DIAGNOSTIC MEASURE: A screening test for metabolic disorders is done before discharge.
2. Physical care
   a. Bathe newborn daily.
   b. Clean cord with alcohol daily.
   c. Keep diaper area clean and dry.
3. Feeding
   a. First feeding should be given at 4 hours after birth. Sucking and swallowing reflexes should be tested with sips of sterile water, then infant should be fed.
   b. Formula feeding on demand.
   c. Breast feeding on demand.
   d. Caloric requirements: 50 calories per pound of body weight per 24 hours.
   e. Fluid requirements: $2\frac{1}{2}$ to 3 ounces per pound of body weight per 24 hours.

D. Prevention of Infection
1. Ensure that each infant has his/her own bassinet and bath equipment.
2. Use a barrier on the scale when weighing infants.
3. Wash hands before and after handling each newborn.
4. Wear gloves when giving infant his/her "first bath."
5. Wear gloves when doing heel sticks on infants.
6. Place infants at risk for AIDS on blood and secretion precautions.
7. Isolate any infant suspected of infection.
8. Ensure that personnel are carefully screened for infection.

E. Care of Circumcision
1. Observe for first voiding. Assess for presence of blood.
2. Observe for local bleeding for 12 hours after the procedure.
3. Cover area with Vaseline gauze. Leave primary dressing on until it falls off, becomes soiled with stool, or becomes constricting.
4. Teach parents to wash area gently with plain warm water at each diaper change after primary dressing falls off.
5. Teach parents to apply petroleum jelly on plain gauze to surgical area for 2–3 days after Vaseline gauze falls off.

CARE OF HIGH-RISK INFANTS

A. Preterm Infants
1. Definition: infants born before the 37th week of gestation regardless of their birth weight.
2. Contributing factors: (in the mother) low socioeconomic status, diabetes, toxemia, poor nutrition, chronic disease; (in the infant) congenital anomalies.
3. Assessment
   a. Appearance
      (1) Weight usually less than 2500 grams.
      (2) Transparency of skin.
      (3) Lack of subcutaneous fat.
      (4) Absence of vernix.
      (5) Large amount of lanugo.
      (6) Wrinkled appearance.
      (7) Head large in comparison to chest.
      (8) Small fontanelles.
      (9) Poor muscle tone.
      (10) Weak cry.
   b. Physiological characteristics
      (1) Weak or absent reflexes.
      (2) Immature enzyme system.
      (3) Poorly developed central nervous system.
      (4) Unstable heat regulation.
      (5) Immature respiratory system.

(6) Lack of passive immunity from the mother.

(7) Inability to produce own antibodies.

(8) Immature liver.

(9) Tendency toward capillary fragility.

(10) Low iron stores.

(11) Susceptibility to dehydration.

4. Nursing diagnoses/goals/interventions

a. Impaired gas exchange related to respiratory distress

Goal: Infant's arterial blood gases will be maintained within normal limits.

Interventions:

(1) Check respirations every hour.

(2) Administer oxygen as ordered.

(3) Maintain humidification of oxygen.

(4) Monitor blood gases carefully.

(5) Turn the infant every 2 hours.

b. Ineffective thermoregulation related to immaturity

Goal: Infant's body temperature will be maintained between 97.5° and 99°F.

Interventions:

(1) Keep the infant warm at all times.

(2) Cover head to prevent heat loss.

(3) Maintain temperature of warmer or isolette in response to the infant's body temperature.

c. Alteration in nutrition: less than body requirements related to inadequate intake

Goal: Infant's body weight will be maintained at or above birth weight.

Interventions:

(1) Give small, frequent feedings with head elevated after each feeding.

(2) Feed the infant slowly, allowing for rest periods.

(3) Use preemie nipple if bottle feeding.

(4) Give the infant a pacifier during gavage feedings.

(5) Observe for dehydration.

(6) Observe for hypoglycemia.

(7) Maintain strict intake and output record.

(8) Weigh the infant daily.

d. Risk for infection related to immature immune system

Goal: Infection will be prevented.

Interventions:

(1) Handle the infant gently.

(2) Maintain asepsis.

e. Altered parenting risk related to infant's physical condition

Goal: Parents will bond successfully with the infant.

Interventions:

(1) Allow the parents to touch and speak to the infant.

(2) Allow the parents to hold the infant as soon as his/her condition permits.

(3) Encourage the parents to make eye contact with the infant.

(4) Encourage the parents to discuss their feelings about the infant.

(5) Introduce the parents to a support group of other parents of preterms.

5. Evaluation

a. Respirations are unlabored.

b. Arterial blood gases remain within normal limits.

c. Body temperature is stable between 97.5°F and 99°F.

d. Infant gains weight.

e. No infection occurs.

f. Infant and his/her parents bond positively.

B. Infants Small for Gestational Age (SGA)

1. Definition: infants whose birth weights are below the 10th percentile for gestational age. SGA infants are less predisposed to complications than are preterms.

2. Contributing factors: placental insufficiency, maternal smoking, maternal substance abuse, postmaturity.

3. Nursing diagnoses/goals/interventions/evaluation. *See* preterm infants, above.

C. Postmature Infants

1. Definition: infants delivered after 42 weeks of term who shows signs of fetal hypoxia and malnutrition.

2. Assessment

a. Vernix and lanugo are absent.

b. Marked desquamation is present.

c. Newborn may be small for gestational age.

d. Newborn may develop respiratory distress.

e. Newborn may be hypoglycemic.

f. Newborn may be polycythemic in response to fetal hypoxia.

3. Nursing diagnoses/goals/interventions
   a. Alteration in nutrition: less than body requirements related to depleted glycogen stores
      Goal: Infant's blood glucose will be maintained above 40 mg per 100 ml on Dextrostix determination.
      Interventions:
      (1) Assess blood glucose levels every hour for first 6 hours of life.
      (2) Feed the infant glucose water immediately if level is below 40 mg per 100 ml.
      (3) If Dextrostix is above 40 mg per 100 ml, feed between 2 and 4 hours of life.
      (4) Do Dextrostix determinations before each feeding for first 24 hours of life.
   b. Impaired gas exchange related to meconium aspiration
      Goal: Infant's arterial blood gases will be within normal limits.
      Interventions:
      (1) Monitor respirations hourly.
      (2) Suction as necessary.
      (3) Observe skin color.
      (4) Monitor arterial blood gases if respiratory distress or cyanosis occurs.
      (5) Maintain warmth.
4. Evaluation
   a. Newborn establishes effective respiratory function.
   b. Newborn establishes stable blood glucose level.

D. Infants of Diabetic Mothers (IDM)
1. Contributing factors: usually premature, usually large for gestational age, frequently delivered by cesarean section.
2. Assessment:
   a. Infants are prone to respiratory distress.
   b. Infants are prone to hypoglycemia.
3. Nursing diagnoses/goals/interventions
   a. Impaired gas exchange related to respiratory distress
      Goal: Infant's arterial blood gases will be within normal limits.
      Interventions:
      (1) Check respirations hourly.
      (2) Administer oxygen as ordered.
      (3) Maintain humidification of oxygen.
      (4) Monitor blood gases carefully.
      (5) Maintain warmth.
   b. Alteration in nutrition: less than body requirements related to hyperinsulinemia
      Goal: Infant's blood glucose will be maintained above 40 mg per 100 ml on Dextrostix determination.
      Interventions:
      (1) Assess blood glucose levels every hour for first 6 hours of life.
      (2) Feed the infant glucose water immediately if level is below 40 mg per 100 ml.
      (3) Do Dextrostix determinations before each feeding for first 72 hours of life.
4. Evaluation
   a. Newborn establishes effective respiratory function.
   b. Newborn establishes stable blood glucose level.

E. Infants of Substance-Abusing Mothers
1. Contributing factors
   a. Alcoholism in mother may cause fetal alcohol syndrome (FAS), which is a series of malformations.
   b. Cocaine use in pregnancy leads to placental vasoconstriction and fetal tachycardia from hypoxia.
   c. Infants of substance-abusing mothers are usually small for gestational age.
   d. Onset of symptoms depends on when the mother had her last dose of drugs, usually 48–72 hours postdelivery.
   e. Severity of symptoms depends on the duration and the amount of the mother's drug usage.
   f. Methadone is stored in fatty tissue. Therefore, sometimes the infant shows symptoms after discharge from the hospital.
2. Assessment
   a. Tremors.
   b. Irritability.
   c. Sneezing.
   d. High-pitched cry.
   e. Respiratory distress.
   f. Fever.
   g. Feeding problems.
   h. Hunger.
   i. Vomiting.
   j. Diarrhea.
   k. Dehydration.
   l. Convulsions.

3. Patient care management
   a. Paregoric or phenobarbital to control symptoms.
   b. Bottle feeding to prevent transmission of drugs in the mother's breast milk.
   c. Quiet environment to prevent convulsions.
4. Nursing diagnoses/goals/interventions
   a. Ineffective breathing patterns related to effect of narcotics on respiratory reflex
      Goal: Infant will establish effective breathing patterns.
      Interventions:
      (1) Keep the infant warm.
      (2) Monitor respirations closely.
      (3) Suction as necessary.
   b. Risk for injury related to hyperactivity and seizures
      Goal: Infant will suffer no injury.
      Interventions:
      (1) Handle the infant gently and slowly.
      (2) Hold the infant firmly when feeding.
      (3) Reduce stimuli in environment.
      (4) Pad sides of bassinet.
      (5) Keep the infant swaddled when in crib.
      (6) Monitor neurological status.
   c. Alteration in nutrition: less than body requirements related to feeding problems
      Goal: Infant will gain weight
      Interventions:
      (1) Give small, frequent feedings.
      (2) Feed the infant slowly with decreased environmental stimuli.
      (3) Position the infant on side after feeding.
   d. Altered parenting risk related to hyperirritability of the infant
      Goal: Parents will handle the infant lovingly.
      Interventions:
      (1) Encourage the parents to visit frequently.
      (2) Encourage the parents to hold the infant.
      (3) Teach the parents how to hold the infant firmly to prevent injury.
      (4) Teach the parents to swaddle the baby.
      (5) Allow the parents to express their feelings about the baby's condition.
5. Evaluation
   a. Infant establishes effective breathing pattern.
   b. Infant sustains no injury.
   c. Infant tolerates feedings and gains weight.
   d. Parents learn ways to comfort their infant.

ALTERATIONS OF HEALTH IN THE NORMAL NEWBORN

A. **Respiratory Distress Syndrome**   A syndrome correlated with a lack of lung surfactant; fibrous membrane lines the alveoli and halts the exchange of gases.
   1. Incidence: common in immature infants, infants delivered by cesarean section, and infants of diabetic mothers; associated with hypothermia of the infant, fetal hypoxia, and acidosis.
   2. Assessment
      a. Respirations above 60 per minute with retractions.
      b. Expiratory grunt.
      c. Nasal flaring.
      d. Cyanosis.
      e. Increased apical pulse.
      f. Metabolic and respiratory acidosis.
      g. Atelectasis.
   3. Patient care management
      a. Oxygen administered with a hood; infant may be on a respirator with positive pressure.
      b. Administration of bicarbonate to combat acidosis.
      c. Intravenous therapy.
      d. Frequent monitoring of blood gases and electrolytes.
   4. Nursing diagnosis/goals/interventions
      a. Impaired gas exchange related to inadequate lung surfactant
         Goal: Infant's arterial blood gases will be maintained within normal limits.
         Interventions:
         (1) Check respirations every hour.
         (2) Administer oxygen as ordered.
         (3) Maintain humidification of oxygen.
         (4) Keep the infant warm.
         (5) Monitor blood gases carefully.
         (6) Turn the infant every 2 hours.
      b. Potential for alteration in bonding related to the infant's condition
         Goal: Parents will bond successfully with the infant

Interventions:
(1) Encourage the parents to touch and hold the infant as his/her condition permits.
(2) Keep the parents informed of the infant's condition.
(3) Discuss the parents' feelings with them.

5. Evaluation
   a. Respirations are unlabored.
   b. Arterial blood gases remain within normal limits.
   c. Infant and parents bond positively.

B. **Hypoglycemia**   Blood sugar level below 40 mg per 100 ml on Dextrostix determination.

1. Incidence: occurs in postmature infants, SGA infants, and infants of diabetics; following hypothermia or hypoxia and in neonatal infection.

2. Assessment
   a. Lethargy.
   b. Twitching and convulsions.
   c. Poor muscle tone.
   d. Shrill cry.
   e. Increased respirations.
   f. Cyanosis.
   g. Periods of apnea.
   h. Poor sucking.

3. Patient care management: Administration of glucose intravenously or orally, depending on the condition of the infant.

4. Nursing diagnosis/goal/interventions
   a. Alteration in nutrition: less than body requirements related to disturbance in metabolism
      Goal: Infant's blood glucose will be maintained above 40 mg per 100 ml on Dextrostix determination.
      Interventions:
      (1) Observe for signs of hypoglycemia in all newborns.
      (2) Do Dextrostix determination on any infant exhibiting signs of hypoglycemia.
      (3) Do Dextrostix determination on infants at risk every hour for first 6 hours of life.
      (4) Feed glucose water immediately to any infant with a blood glucose level below 40 mg per 100 ml.
      (5) Do Dextrostix determination before each feeding for first 24 hours of life in high-risk infants.
      (6) Do Dextrostix determination before each feeding for next 24 hours any time any infant has a hypoglycemic episode.

5. Evaluation: Infant maintains stable blood glucose level.

C. **Hyperbilirubinemia**   Elevation of indirect bilirubin above 12 mg per 100 ml of blood in full-term infants.

1. Causes
   a. Physiological jaundice: occurs 48 hours after birth.
   b. Bacterial infections.
   c. ABO and Rh incompatibilities: occur within the first 24 hours after birth.

2. Assessment
   a. Lethargy and irritability.
   b. Jaundice of the skin and the sclera.
   c. Dark urine and light stools.
   d. Rising level of bilirubin in the blood.

3. Patient care management
   a. Phototherapy: fluorescent light converts indirect bilirubin to direct bilirubin, which can be excreted in the urine.
   b. Exchange transfusion: if blood level of bilirubin approaches 20 mg per 100 ml of blood in a full-term infant; done at a lower blood level in premature infants.

4. Nursing diagnoses/goals/interventions
   a. Risk for injury related to phototherapy
      Goals:
      (1) Infant will sustain no injury while receiving therapy.
      (2) Bilirubin level will drop below 12 mg per 100 ml.
      Interventions:
      (1) Cover the infant's eyes when he/she is under the phototherapy light.
      (2) Cover the scrotal area of male infants.
      (3) Change the infant's position every 2 hours while he/she is under the phototherapy light.
   b. Risk for fluid volume deficit related to phototherapy
      Goals:
      (1) Infant will remain well hydrated while receiving therapy.
      (2) Bilirubin will be excreted in urine.
      Interventions:
      (1) Encourage frequent feedings.
      (2) Give sterile water or glucose water PO between feedings.

c. Pain related to phototherapy

Goal: Infant will experience comfort while receiving therapy.
Interventions:
(1) Do not clothe the infant while under the phototherapy lights.
(2) Take the infant out from under the lights for feedings.
(3) Cuddle the infant frequently.
5. Evaluation
a. Infant sustains no injury.
b. Infant remains well hydrated.
c. Bilirubin level returns to normal.
d. Infant experiences comfort.
D. **Erythroblastosis Fetalis** Hemolysis of red blood cells due to an antibody-antigen reaction in Rh incompatability.
1. Assessment
a. Prenatal diagnosis: by amniocentesis.
b. Postnatal diagnosis: by
(1) Direct Coombs's test to detect maternal antibodies attached to the infant's red blood cells.
(2) Anemia.
(3) Jaundice.
(4) Edema.
2. Patient care management
a. Prenatal: intrauterine transfusion with packed O-negative red blood cells.
b. Postnatal
(1) Phototherapy.
(2) Exchange transfusion if bilirubin approaches 20 mg per 100 ml (use Rh-negative blood of infant's own type).
c. Hemolysis may also occur with ABO incompatibility; is usually less severe than Rh. Treatment: phototherapy; if exchange transfusion is needed, use O blood in infant's Rh factor.
3. Nursing diagnoses/goals/interventions/ evaluation. *See* Hyperbilirubinemia, above.
E. **Infection of the Newborn**
1. Causes: prolonged rupture of the membranes (over 24 hours) or maternal infection; can also be contracted from nursery staff or other infants.
2. Assessment (Newborn does not have inflammatory response; manifestations may be vague.)

a. Jaundice.
b. Subnormal temperature.
c. Lethargy.
d. Poor sucking.
e. DIAGNOSTIC MEASURES: **cultures of blood, urine, umbilicus, mouth, and throat to determine the causative organism.**
3. Patient care management
a. **Treatment on the basis of symptoms and culture findings.**
b. **Isolation from other infants.**
4. Nursing diagnosis/goals/interventions
Risk for infection related to **immature immune system**
Goals:
a. **Infant's infection will be controlled.**
b. **Infant will not develop a superimposed infection.**
Interventions:
a. **Maintain isolation from other infants.**
b. **Use medical asepsis when handling the infant.**
c. **Monitor temperature every 2 hours.**
d. **Monitor pulse and respirations hourly.**
e. **Administer antibiotics on time to maintain blood levels.**
5. Evaluation
a. **Infection is controlled.**
b. **No secondary infection occurs.**

CONGENITAL ABNORMALITIES

Congenital Heart Diseases

A. Acyanotic Congenital Heart Disease
1. **Coarctation of the aorta** A narrowing of the aortic lumen in the region of the ductus arteriosus.
a. Assessment
(1) Auscultate for a systolic murmur at the left sternal border.
(2) Determine whether hypertension is present in the upper extremities and hypotension in the lower extremities.
(3) Palpate for a full bounding radial pulse and an absence or weakening of the femoral and pedal pulses.
(4) Assess for complaints of leg weakness and muscle spasms in the lower extremities, headaches, dizziness, and epistaxis.
(5) Assess for the clinical manifestations associated with congestive heart failure.

b. Patient care management
  (1) Surgery is deferred until 2 to 4 years of age.
  (2) The narrowed section is surgically resected with an end-to-end anastomosis of the aorta, or it is replaced with a graft.
2. **Patent ductus arteriosus**   During fetal circulation, blood bypasses the lungs and flows from the pulmonary artery to the aorta via the ductus arteriosus. This structure normally closes after birth. If it remains open, there is an abnormal passageway between the aorta and the pulmonary artery.
  a. Assessment
    (1) Auscultate for a "machinery murmur" in the left intraclavicular area.
    (2) Observe for feeding difficulties and failure to gain weight.
    (3) Observe for dyspnea on exertion and frequent upper respiratory infections.
    (4) Assess for increased pulse pressure.
    (5) Palpate for hepatosplenomegaly.
    (6) Assess for the clinical manifestations associated with congestive heart failure.
  b. Patient care management
    (1) Medical treatment, before 10 days of age, consists of administration of indomethacin to promote closure of the patent ductus.
    (2) Surgical ligation of the patent ductus is indicated for the older infant or child.
3. **Atrial septal defect**   An opening in the septum between the right and the left atrium, resulting from failure of the foramen ovale to close, inadequate development of the endocardial cushions, or failure in the formation of the superior portion of the atrial septum.
  a. Assessment
    (1) Auscultate for a soft, blowing systolic murmur over the second to third interspace near the left sternal border.
    (2) Assess for slow weight gain.
    (3) Observe for dyspnea on exertion and frequent upper respiratory infections.

b. Patient care management
  (1) Surgery is ideally performed between 2 and 4 years of age.
  (2) The defect is sutured closed or covered with a Dacron patch.
4. **Ventricular septal defect**   An abnormal opening in the septum between the right and the left ventricle.
  a. Assessment
    (1) Auscultate for a loud, blowing systolic murmur in the third or fourth left intercostal space.
    (2) Assess for feeding difficulties and slow weight gain.
    (3) Observe for dyspnea on exertion and frequent upper respiratory infections.
    (4) Observe for signs of bacterial endocarditis.
    (5) Assess for clinical manifestations associated with congestive heart failure.
  b. Patient care management
    (1) Antibiotics are administered to prevent bacterial endocarditis.
    (2) The optimal time for surgery is 2 to 4 years of age.
    (3) The defect is sutured closed or covered with a Dacron patch.
B. Cyanotic Congenital Heart Disease
  1. **Tetralogy of Fallot**   A defect consisting of four associated abnormalities: pulmonary valve stenosis, ventricular septal defect, overriding of the aorta, and right ventricular hypertrophy.
    a. Assessment
      (1) Auscultate for a harsh systolic murmur at the mid to lower left sternal border and for tachycardia.
      (2) Assess for feeding difficulties, failure to gain weight, and poor muscle development.
      (3) Inspect for cyanosis, squatting and clubbing of the fingers and toes.
      (4) Observe for dyspnea on exertion.
      (5) Assess the frequency and severity of anoxic spells.
    b. Patient care management
      (1) Palliative surgical procedures increase the pulmonary blood flow.
      (2) Complete surgical repair involves patching the ventricular septal defect and resecting the pulmonary stenosis.

(3) The optimal time for complete repair is between 2 and 4 years of age.

2. **Transposition of the great vessels** The aorta originates in the right ventricle, and the pulmonary artery originates in the left ventricle.
   a. Assessment
      (1) Auscultate for a systolic murmur and tachycardia.
      (2) Assess for growth retardation.
      (3) Inspect for deep cyanosis, and squatting and clubbing of the fingers and toes.
      (4) Observe for dyspnea.
      (5) Assess the frequency and duration of anoxic spells.
      (6) Assess for clinical manifestations associated with congestive heart failure.
   b. Patient care management
      (1) Palliative repair involves surgical creation of an atrial septal defect.
      (2) A complete repair is often done before 1 year of age.

C. Diagnostic Measures for Congenital Heart Diseases
   1. Blood tests. Polycythemia is present in cyanotic congenital heart defects: elevated red blood cells, hemoglobin, and hematocrit.
   2. Electrocardiograms
      a. Measure changes in the electric potential of the heart.
      b. Assess the condition of cardiac muscles.
   3. Echocardiography
      a. Produces an image of the structure of the heart, using high-frequency sound waves.
      b. Determines the pressure on either side of the heart valves, cardiac output, and blood flow within the heart and great vessels.
   4. Chest X-rays
      a. Reveal the size and position of the chambers of the heart.
      b. Assess the condition of the pulmonary vascular bed.
   5. Transcutaneous pulse oximetry
      a. Assesses arterial oxygen saturation.
      b. Evaluates suspected cyanosis in infants and children at rest and during rapidly changing circulatory states.

6. Cardiac catheterization with angiography
   a. Reveals anomalies of structure.
   b. Measures pressure and oxygen concentration within the heart and major vessels.

D. Preoperative Nursing Care Plan for Congenital Heart Diseases
   1. Nursing diagnoses/goals/interventions
      a. Risk for injury related to cardiac catheterization
         Goal: Child will be free from injury.
         Interventions:
         (1) Assess the blood pressure for hypotension.
         (2) Auscultate the apical pulse for evidence of arrhythmias or bradycardia.
         (3) Palpate the pulses distal to the catheterization site.
         (4) Assess the color and temperature of the involved extremity.
         (5) Inspect the site for evidence of bleeding or hematoma formation.
         (6) Maintain bedrest as ordered.
         (7) Immobilize the involved extremity.
      b. Decreased cardiac output related to structural congenital heart defects heart defects
         Goal: Child will have adequate cardiac output.
         Interventions:
         (1) Frequently assess vital signs and skin color.
         (2) Assist the child during anoxic spells by placing in a knee-chest or squatting position and administering oxygen.
         (3) Encourage frequent rest periods.
         (4) Organize nursing care to minimize interruptions of rest.
      c. Impaired gas exchange related to pulmonary congestion
         Goal: Child will have clear breath sounds and spontaneous effective respiration.
         Interventions:
         (1) Monitor respiratory rate and lung sounds.
         (2) Encourage coughing and deep breathing when age-appropriate.
         (3) Position the child in a semi-Fowler's position.
         (4) Avoid contact with infected individuals.

d. Altered nutrition: less than body requirements related to increased fatigue during feeding

Goal: Child will tolerate age-appropriate diet with adequate caloric intake to meet metabolic requirements.

Interventions:

(1) Weigh the child daily.

(2) Record intake and output.

(3) Provide small, frequent feedings to reduce fatigue.

(4) Feed the child slowly.

(5) Implement gavage feedings when necessary.

e. Knowledge deficit related to unfamiliarity with the disease process and treatment regime

Goal: Parents and child will demonstrate understanding of disease process and treatment regime.

Interventions:

(1) Clearly explain all diagnostic tests and surgical procedures.

(2) Review and clarify information provided by the physician.

(3) Encourage the child and his/her family to express their feelings and concerns.

(4) Allow the parents to participate in their child's care.

2. Evaluation

a. Child's vital signs are within normal limits for age.

b. Child experiences none of the complications associated with congenital cardiac defects.

c. Child ingests adequate nutrients to promote a normal growth pattern.

d. Child and parents understand the disease process and treatment regime.

e. Parents demonstrate increased participation in caring for their child.

E. Postoperative Nursing Care Plan for Congenital Heart Diseases

1. Nursing diagnoses/goals/interventions

a. **Impaired gas exchange related to decreased lung expansion and/or increased pulmonary secretions .**

Goal: Child will have clear breath sounds and spontaneous effective respiration.

Interventions:

(1) Assess for signs of respiratory distress.

(2) Maintain proper oxygen and humidity.

(3) Encourage coughing, deep breathing, and use of an incentive spirometer.

(4) Perform chest physiotherapy.

(5) Suction as necessary.

(6) Change the child's position every 2 hours.

(7) Ambulate the patient *ad lib*.

(8) Maintain patency of the chest tubes and underwater seal drainage.

b. Decreased cardiac output related to surgical procedure and/or cardiac disease

Goal: Child will have adequate cardiac output.

Interventions:

(1) Assess vital signs frequently.

(2) Monitor central venous pressure.

(3) Assess peripheral perfusion.

(4) Determine oxygen saturation with an oximeter.

(5) Observe for changes on the cardiac monitor.

c. Risk for infection related to surgical incision

Goal: Child will be afebrile with clean, intact surgical incision.

Interventions:

(1) Monitor for clinical manifestations of infection.

(2) Administer antibiotics as ordered.

(3) Maintain medical asepsis.

d. Pain related to surgical procedure

Goal: Child will experience minimal pain.

Interventions:

(1) Administer analgesics as ordered, especially before coughing and deep breathing and ambulation.

(2) Splint the incision during breathing exercises.

e. Altered nutrition: less than body requirements related to dietary restrictions secondary to surgery

Goals:

(1) Child will not experience dehydration or electrolyte disturbances.

(2) Child will tolerate age-appropriate diet.

Interventions:

(1) Monitor IV fluids.

(2) Measure intake and output.

(3) Monitor urine specific gravity and pH.

(4) Monitor daily weight.

(5) Evaluate nasogastric drainage.

(6) Irrigate the nasogastric tube.

(7) Measure abdominal girth.

(8) Assess for the presence of bowel sounds before beginning oral fluids.

(9) Provide progressive diet for age.

2. Postoperative evaluation

    a. Child's vital signs remain within normal limits.

    b. Child has no manifestations of surgical complications.

    c. Child's level of discomfort is minimized.

    d. Child tolerates an age-appropriate diet.

F. **Congestive Heart Failure**   Inability of the heart to pump a sufficient amount of blood to supply the metabolic needs of the body. *See also* Unit Nine, Alterations in Cardiovascular Organs, Section D: Congestive Heart Failure, page 352.

1. Assessment

    a. Auscultate for tachycardia, rales, moist respirations, and wheezing.

    b. Observe for tachypnea, dyspnea, orthopnea, and cyanosis.

    c. Assess for a dry or productive cough and hemoptysis.

    d. Inspect for distended neck veins.

    e. Assess for decreased urine output and edema.

    f. Check for decreased peripheral pulses and mottling of the extremities.

    g. Observe for diaphoresis.

    h. Palpate for liver enlargement.

    i. Assess for fatigue.

    j. Observe for feeding difficulties and failure to gain weight.

2. Patient care management

    a. Digoxin (Lanoxin) to improve myocardial efficiency.

    b. Removal of accumulated fluid and sodium.

        (1) Diuretic therapy.

        (2) Potassium supplements.

        (3) Fluid restriction.

    c. Formula containing increased calories per fluid ounce.

    d. Bedrest to decrease the cardiac workload.

    e. Humidified oxygen.

3. Nursing diagnoses/goals/interventions

    a. Decreased cardiac output related to ineffective contractions of the heart

Goal: Child will experience improved cardiac output.

Interventions:

(1) Assess vital signs frequently.

(2) Administer digoxin as ordered.

(3) Withhold digoxin for an apical pulse below 100 in infants and below 70 in older children.

(4) Observe for signs of digoxin toxicity: bradycardia, arrythmias, nausea and vomiting, and anorexia.

(5) Avoid constricting clothing or restraints across the chest and around the abdomen.

    b. Impaired gas exchange related to increased pulmonary secretions

Goal: Child will have improved gas exchange as evidenced by clear breath sounds and decreased respiratory rate.

Interventions:

(1) Assess respiratory rate and breath sounds frequently.

(2) Place the child in a semi-Fowler's position.

(3) Administer humidified oxygen.

(4) Administer chest physiotherapy and suctioning as necessary.

(5) Monitor the results of arterial blood gas studies.

    c. Fluid volume excess related to compromised cardiac function

Goal: Child will show evidence of adequate renal perfusion of at least 1 ml / kg / hr.

Interventions:

(1) Monitor edema.

(2) Weigh the child daily.

(3) Monitor intake and output.

(4) Check urine specific gravity.

(5) Monitor the results of electrolyte studies.

(6) Administer diuretic therapy and potassium supplements as ordered.

    d. Activity intolerance related to decreased cardiac output

Goal: Child will follow regimen established to preserve energy.

Interventions:

(1) Encourage frequent rest periods.

(2) Organize nursing care to minimize interruptions of rest.

(3) Anticipate needs to prevent crying.

(4) Maintain a neutral thermal environment.

e. Altered nutrition: less than body requirement related to fatigue during feedings
Goal: Child will tolerate diet reflecting adequate caloric intake to meet metabolic needs.
Interventions:
(1) Weigh the child daily.
(2) Monitor intake and output.
(3) Provide small, frequent feedings to reduce fatigue.
(4) Increase the size of the hole in the nipple when necessary.
(5) Feed the child slowly.
(6) Implement gavage feedings as ordered.

4. Evaluation
a. Child shows evidence of resolving congestive heart failure: decreased respiratory and heart rates, clear breath sounds, stabilized weight, increased urinary output, increased activity tolerance, increased ability to take oral feedings.
b. Parents understand home-care and follow-up instructions.

Other Congenital Abnormalities

A. **Spina Bifida** A congenital defect in neural tube closure in which the posterior portion of the vertebral laminae fails to close.
1. Types
a. **Spina bifida occulta** A defect in the vertebral laminae without protrusion of an external sac. No symptoms are present.
b. **Meningocele** Protrusion of an external sac containing meninges and cerebral spinal fluid through the unfused vertebral laminae without sensory or motor loss.
c. **Meningomyelocele** Protrusion of an external sac containing meninges, cerebral spinal fluid, and a portion of the spinal cord through the unfused vertebral laminae, accompanied by alterations of motor and sensory functions of the lower extremities.
2. Assessment
a. Inspect the sac by holding a light behind it. A transilluminated sac indicates a meningocele. A sac that does not transilluminate indicates a meningomyelocele.

b. Examine the lower extremities for motor and sensory deficits.
c. Assess anal sphincter control.
d. Assess for urinary retention.
e. Observe for complications: hydrocephalus, meningitis, urinary tract infections, and orthopedic abnormalities.
3. Patient care management
a. Surgical closure.
b. Long-term habilitation to promote optimal functioning.
4. Nursing diagnoses/goals/interventions
a. Risk for infection related to an open membranous sac
Goal: Infant will remain free of central nervous system infection related to contamination of the sac.
Interventions:
(1) Cover the sac with a moist, sterile dressing.
(2) Use strict sterile technique when handling the infant.
(3) Secure a sterile pad below the sac to prevent contamination by urine and stool.
(4) Observe the infant for manifestations of infection.
b. Risk for injury related to the possibility of sac rupture
Goal: The sac will remain intact.
Interventions:
(1) Handle the infant carefully.
(2) Place the infant in a prone position with hips and pelvis elevated 20 degrees.
(3) Avoid the use of diapers.
c. Reflex incontinence related to neurogenic bladder and bowel incontinence related to neurogenic bowel.
Goal: Infant will establish bowel and bladder regimen.
Interventions:
(1) Assess intake and output.
(2) Encourage fluids.
(3) Credé the bladder as necessary.
(4) Observe the infant for signs of urinary tract infection.
(5) Establishing a regular bowel program with suppositories.
d. Risk for impaired skin integrity related to immobility
Goal: Infant's skin will remain intact.
Interventions:
(1) Position the infant on a pressure-minimizing mattress.

(2) Reposition the infant every 1 to 2 hours.

(3) Perform passive range of motion exercises.

e. Risk for altered parenting related to birth of a handicapped infant
Goal: Parents will progress through grieving process, and bonding will be evident.
Interventions:

(1) Encourage the parents to verbalize their feelings and concerns.

(2) Assure the parents that their feelings are normal.

(3) Provide information about possible causes, the treatment plan, and prognosis.

(4) Provide time for the parents and infant to be alone.

(5) Encourage parental participation in the infant's care.

5. Evaluation

a. Sac shows no signs of infection or rupture.

b. Bladder and bowel elimination is established.

c. Infant's skin remains intact.

d. Parents progress through the grieving process.

e. Parental bonding occurs.

f. Parents understand the immediate and long-term treatment plans.

B. **Hydrocephalus** Excessive accumulation of cerebrospinal fluid in the ventricle system of the brain.

1. Assessment

a. Measure the head circumference.

b. Palpate the skull to determine tenseness of the fontanels and separation of sutures.

c. Observe for dilated scalp veins and a "setting sun" appearance of the eyes.

d. Listen for a high-pitched cry.

e. Observe for anorexia, vomiting, and irritability.

2. Patient care management: Performance of shunting procedures to bypass the point of obstruction and divert the cerebrospinal fluid to another body area.

a. A ventriculoatrial shunt or a ventriculoperitoneal shunt may be used.

b. Shunts are accomplished by utilizing plastic tubing and a one-way Holter or Pudenz valve that regulates the flow of cerebrospinal fluid and prevents backflow of blood.

3. Preoperative nursing diagnoses/goals/interventions

a. Alteration in tissue perfusion related to increased intracranial pressure
Goal: Infant will be assessed for increased neurologic deterioration.
Interventions:

(1) Assess level of consciousness and responsiveness.

(2) Measure head circumference daily.

(3) Palpate for tense fontanels and separation of sutures.

(4) Monitor vital signs.

b. Altered nutrition: less than body requirements related to decreased appetite and nausea and vomiting secondary to increased intracranial pressure
pressure
Goal: Infant will receive an age-appropriate diet.
Interventions:

(1) Weigh the infant daily.

(2) Record intake and output.

(3) Provide small, frequent feedings.

(4) Position the infant on the right side after feeding.

(5) Handle the infant as little as possible after feeding.

c. Risk for impaired skin integrity related to difficulty in moving enlarged head
head
Goal: Infant's skin will remain intact.
Interventions:

(1) Position the infant on a pressure-minimizing mattress.

(2) Change the infant's position every 1 to 2 hours.

d. Altered family processes related to diagnosis of a potentially life-threatening condition in the infant
Goal: Parents will experience decreasing levels of anxiety.
Interventions:

(1) Encourage the parents to verbalize their feelings and concerns.

(2) Provide information about their infant's condition and treatment plan.

(3) Encourage parental participation in the infant's care.

4. Evaluation

a. Infant's neurologic status is evaluated.

b. Skin on infant's scalp remains intact.

c. Adequate nutrients are ingested by the infant.

d. Parents are prepared for surgical intervention.
5. Postoperative nursing diagnoses/goals/interventions
    a. Altered tissue perfusion related to increased intracranial pressure
        Goals:
        (1) Infant will be assessed for neurologic baselines.
        (2) Shunt disorders will be assessed and treated promptly.
        Interventions:
        (1) Assess the infant's level of consciousness and responsiveness.
        (2) Measure head circumference daily.
        (3) Palpate for tense fontanels and separation of sutures.
        (4) Monitor vital signs.
        (5) Position the infant on the unoperative side with the head of the bed flat.
        (6) Pump the shunt if ordered.
    b. Risk for infection related to surgical placement of shunt
        Goal: Infant will remain afebrile with no signs of skin infection.
        Interventions:
        (1) Assess temperature.
        (2) Maintain a dry, sterile dressing.
        (3) Assess the surgical incision when possible for redness, drainage, swelling, and approximation.
        (4) Administer antibiotics as ordered.
    c. Knowledge deficit regarding follow-up treatment and home care
        Goal: Parents will demonstrate understanding of home-care and follow-up instructions.
        Interventions:
        (1) Review signs of shunt malfunction or infection.
        (2) Have the parents demonstrate how to pump the shunt.
        (3) Discuss the importance of ongoing assessment and medical care.
6. Evaluation
    a. Infant is alert and interactive and behaves in an age-appropriate manner.
    b. Infant's skin remains intact.
    c. Parents can state symptoms of shunt infection or malfunction.
C. Cleft Lip and Cleft Palate (These abnormalities may be present separately or simultaneously.)

1. Definitions
    a. **Cleft lip** A unilateral or bilateral defect ranging from a notch in the vermilion border of the lip to an opening extending into the nostril.
    b. **Cleft palate** This abnormality may involve only the soft palate, both the soft and the hard palate, and at times the nose.
2. Assessment
    a. Determine the extent of the cleft lip and/or palate.
    b. Assess the infant's ability to suck and to swallow.
    c. Observe for respiratory and ear infections.
3. Patient care management
    a. Surgical repair of cleft lip is usually done when the infant is 2 months old.
    b. Surgical repair of cleft palate is usually done before 2 years of age.
    c. Long-term management of cleft palate involves prevention of respiratory and ear infections, speech therapy, and orthodonture therapy.
4. Preoperative nursing diagnoses/goals/interventions
    a. Altered nutrition: less than body requirements related to ineffective sucking
        Goal: Infant will receive age-appropriate caloric intake, will gain weight, and will remain hydrated.
        Interventions:
        (1) Use a soft nipple placed in the center of the mouth.
        (2) If the infant is unable to feed with a nipple, use a rubber-tipped medicine dropper.
        (3) Feed in an upright position to facilitate swallowing and prevent aspiration.
        (4) Burp the infant frequently, since he/she swallows excessive air.
        (5) Rinse the infant's mouth with water after feedings to prevent infection.
        (6) Orient the infant to the feeding technique that will be utilized in the postoperative period: a rubber-tipped syringe for cleft lip repair, and a plastic cup or spoon for cleft palate repair.
        (7) Position the infant on the side or in infant seat after feeding.

b. Risk for infection related to inefficient drainage of the middle ear
Goal: Infant will have no signs of infection.
Interventions:
(1) Assess for signs of respiratory infection and refer for prompt treatment.
(2) Keep the infant away from persons with infections.

c. Risk for injury related to birth of an infant with a structural defect
Goal: Parent-infant relationship will be promoted, and bonding will occur.
Interventions:
(1) Encourage the parents to verbalize their feelings and concerns.
(2) Assure the parents that their feelings are normal.
(3) Provide information about possible causes, the treatment plan, and prognosis.
(4) Provide time for the parents and the infant to be alone.
(5) Encourage parental participation in the infant's care.

5. Evaluation
a. Infant has sufficient calories to meet metabolic requirements.
b. Infant is afebrile.
c. Parental bonding is evident.
d. Parents understand home care and future surgical interventions.

6. Postoperative nursing diagnoses/goals/interventions
a. Ineffective airway clearance related to increased production of secretions during the surgical procedure
Goal: Infant's airway will remain patent.
Interventions:
(1) Assess for signs of respiratory distress.
(2) Suction gently on low with a soft catheter, avoiding the suture line, only when necessary.
(3) Position the infant in infant seat or on the side after a cleft lip repair.
(4) Position the child on the abdomen after a cleft palate repair.
(5) Place the infant in a mist tent as ordered.

b. Risk for injury related to touching of incision line and/or tension to the suture line when crying
Goal: Infant's incision line will remain intact and free of injury.
Interventions:
(1) Prevent dislodgement of the Logan bow present after cleft-lip surgery.
(2) Use elbow restraints.
(3) Remove restraints, one at a time, every hour to assess the skin and circulation of the extremity and to perform range of motion exercises.
(4) Prevent crying by anticipating the child's needs.

c. Risk for infection related to the surgical incision
Goal: Infant's incision line will remain free of infection.
Interventions:
(1) Assess the incision line for manifestations of infection.
(2) Gently clean the cleft-lip suture line with sterile cotton swabs and half-strength hydrogen peroxide.
(3) Apply a bacteriostatic ointment as ordered.
(4) Rinse the mouth with water after feeding to keep the surgical site clean.
(5) Administer antibiotics as ordered.

d. Altered nutrition: less than body requirements related to inability to ingest nutrients secondary to discomfort of the healing suture line
Goal: Infant will tolerate age-appropriate number of calories.
Interventions:
(1) Provide clear liquids as tolerated.
(2) Feed the infant with a rubber-tipped syringe, away from the suture line, to prevent sucking.
(3) Feed the older child with a plastic cup or spoon.
(4) Monitor intake and output.
(5) Weigh the infant daily.

e. Knowledge deficit related to long-term care
Goal: Parents will demonstrate understanding of home-care and follow-up instructions.
Interventions:
(1) Discuss speech therapy, dental malformations, and susceptibility to ear infections.

    (2) Encourage the parents to verbalize and ask questions.

7. Evaluation
   a. Infant's airway is patent.
   b. Suture line remains free of injury and infection.
   c. Infant has sufficient calories to meet growth needs.
   d. Parents are able to care for their infant and understand the long-term treatment plan.

D. **Esophageal Atresia** During fetal development the esophagus fails to develop as a continuous passage from the pharynx to the stomach. The esophagus may consist of two blind pouches, or one segment will end in a blind pouch while the other connects to the trachea via a fistula.

1. Assessment
   a. There are excessive amounts of mucus and constant drooling.
   b. When fed, the infant chokes, coughs, and sneezes.
   c. Cyanosis occurs if fluid is aspirated into the tracheobronchial tree.

2. Patient care management
   a. Nothing by mouth, and IV therapy.
   b. Constant suctioning of the upper pouch to prevent aspiration.
   c. Antibiotics to prevent and treat respiratory complications.
   d. A gastrostomy to decompress the stomach and prevent aspiration of gastric contents through the tracheoesophageal fistula.
   e. Surgical repair
      (1) Primary repair: the tracheoesophageal fistula is ligated, and the esophageal segments are anastomosed.
      (2) Palliative repair: if the distance between the two segments is large, the fistula is ligated, a temporary gastrostomy and cervical esophagostomy are performed, and a colon transplant is done at a later date.

3. Preoperative nursing diagnoses/goals/interventions
   a. Ineffective airway clearance related to the collection of secretions in the esophageal pouch and regurgitation of stomach contents
      Goal: Infant's airway will remain patent.

Interventions:
   (1) Maintain NPO.
   (2) Suction mouth and nasopharynx whenever necessary.
   (3) Monitor continuous suctioning of esophageal pouch by sump tube.
   (4) Position the infant with the head elevated a minimum of 30 degrees.
   b. Risk for fluid volume deficit related to inability to swallow oral feedings
      Goal: Infant will remain hydrated.
      Interventions:
      (1) Assess for signs of dehydration.
      (2) Monitor IV therapy.
      (3) Monitor intake and output.
      (4) Weigh the infant daily.
   c. Altered parenting risk related to diagnosis of a life-threatening condition in the infant
      Goal: Parent will demonstrate positive bonding behavior.
      Interventions:
      (1) Encourage the parents to verbalize their feelings and concerns.
      (2) Clearly explain the infant's condition and the treatment plan.
      (3) Review and clarify information provided by the physician.
      (4) Encourage parental visiting in the intensive care nursery.
      (5) Explain to the parents the importance of talking to and touching their infant.
      (6) Allow parental participation in the infant's care when possible.

4. Evaluation
   a. Infant maintains a patent airway.
   b. Infant remains hydrated.
   c. Parents demonstrate positive bonding behaviors.
   d. Parents have a clear understanding of the infant's defect and the required surgical correction.

5. Postoperative nursing diagnoses/goals/interventions
   a. Ineffective airway clearance related to increased production of secretions during the surgical procedure
      procedure
      Goal: Infant's airway will remain patent.
      Interventions:
      (1) Assess for signs of respiratory distress.
      (2) Maintain NPO.

(3) Place the infant in a mist tent.

(4) Maintain chest tubes and underwater seal drainage.

(5) Position the infant with the head slightly elevated, avoiding hyperextension of the neck.

(6) Change the infant's position every 2 hours.

(7) Perform chest physiotherapy.

b. Risk for injury related to improper suctioning techniques
Goal: Infant will be free of trauma to the anastomosis site.
Interventions:

(1) Suction the infant's nares with a catheter marked by the surgeon as to the maximum length it can be inserted.

(2) Suction gently and as little as possible.

c. Altered nutrition: less than body requirements related to inability to ingest fluids orally
Goal: Infant will tolerate, via gastrostomy tube, diet reflecting age-appropriate caloric requirement.
Interventions:

(1) Feed a progressive liquid diet.

(2) Give gastrostomy feeding via gravity.

(3) Keep gastrostomy tube open to air.

(4) Provide a pacifier.

(5) Start oral feedings as ordered.

d. Knowledge deficit related to home care and long-term treatment plan
Goal: Parents will demonstrate understanding of home care and follow-up.
Interventions:

(1) Teach gastrostomy tube care.

(2) Teach the parents the signs of respiratory distress and esophageal stricture.

6. Evaluation

a. Infant's airway is patent.

b. Suture line will be free of trauma from suctioning.

c. Breath sounds are clear.

d. Infant is able to tolerate diet reflecting caloric requirement.

e. Parents understand the infant's home-care needs and long-term treatment plan.

E. Intestinal Obstructions

1. **Hirschsprung's disease (congenital aganglionic megacolon)**   Congenital absence of parasympathetic ganglion nerve cells of the bowel wall, resulting in an absence of peristalsis and eventual obstruction of the intestine by bowel contents.

a. Assessment

(1) Assess for a pattern of alternate episodes of constipation and diarrhea.

(2) Be aware that stools may be ribbonlike.

(3) Observe for bile-stained vomitus, abdominal distention, and anorexia.

b. Patient care management

(1) Temporary colostomy.

(2) At a later date, a pull-through anastomosis.

2. **Imperforate anus**   A congenital abnormality in which the rectum ends in a blind pouch. An accompanying fistula may be present between the rectum and the perineum, vagina, or urinary tract.

a. Assessment

(1) Determine whether the anus is patent.

(2) Observe for the passage of meconium.

(3) Observe for the presence of meconium in the urine.

b. Patient care management

(1) Surgical reconstruction of the abnormality is performed.

(2) Occasionally, a temporary colostomy is performed prior to complete repair.

3. Preoperative nursing diagnoses/goals/ interventions

a. Bowel incontinence related to presence of a congenital abnormality of the colon
Goal: Infant will show no sign of complications.
Interventions:

(1) Assess the presence or absence of stools.

(2) Assess for complications: enterocolitis, bowel perforation, peritonitis, sepsis, and shock.

(3) Administer isotonic enemas and colonic irrigations with an antibiotic solution before surgery as ordered.

(4) Maintain NPO.

(5) Monitor IV fluids.

b. Knowledge deficit related to surgical procedure to be performed

Goal: Parents will have a clear understanding of defect and required surgical correction.

Interventions:

(1) Encourage the parents to verbalize their feelings and concerns.

(2) Discuss temporary colostomy and later complete repair of the congenital abnormality.

4. Evaluation

a. Infant shows no signs of complications of intestinal obstruction.

b. Parents understand the surgical treatment plan.

5. Postoperative nursing diagnoses/goals/interventions

a. Risk for fluid volume deficit related to dietary restrictions secondary to surgery and gastric drainage

Goal: Infant will remain hydrated.

Interventions:

(1) Assess for signs of dehydration.

(2) Maintain IV therapy.

(3) Replace fluids lost through nasogastric tube as ordered.

(4) Monitor intake and output.

(5) Weigh the infant daily.

(6) Administer progressive diet for age as ordered.

b. Bowel incontinence related to colon surgery

Goal: Infant will develop normal bowel pattern.

Interventions:

(1) Measure and note color of nasogastric drainage.

(2) Irrigate as ordered.

(3) Position in semi-Fowler's position to promote drainage.

(4) Assess for the presence of bowel sounds.

(5) Monitor for passage of stools.

c. Risk for infection related to surgical incision and decreased mobility secondary to pain

Goal: Infant will be free of infection.

Interventions:

(1) Assess for manifestations of infection.

(2) Use aseptic techniques when changing dressings.

(3) Reposition the infant every 2 hours.

(4) Encourage coughing and deep breathing when appropriate.

d. Pain related to surgical procedure postoperative pain

Goal: Infant will be relatively painfree.

Interventions:

(1) Decrease environmental stimuli.

(2) Administer analgesics as ordered.

e. Risk for impaired skin integrity related to the colostomy

Goal: Infant's skin will remain intact.

Interventions:

(1) Change the collecting device as necessary.

(2) Administer care to the skin surrounding the stoma.

(3) Provide adequate fluid intake.

f. Knowledge deficit related to home care and follow-up treatment

Goal: Parents will demonstrate understanding of colostomy care and home-care needs.

Interventions:

(1) Teach care of colostomy and anal/perineal area when appropriate.

(2) Discuss appropriate diet.

6. Evaluation

a. Infant tolerates age-appropriate diet.

b. Infant is hydrated.

c. Infant develops normal bowel elimination pattern via colostomy or rectum.

d. Infant is free of wound and respiratory infection.

e. Parents understand home care and future interventions.

F. **Pyloric Stenosis**   A thickening of the pyloric muscle that impedes the emptying of the stomach contents into the duodenum.

1. Assessment

a. Observe for projectile vomiting of undigested food during or after feedings.

b. Assess for excessive hunger, decreased number of stools, and weight loss.

c. Observe for visible peristaltic waves moving from left to right in the upper right quadrant.

d. Assess for signs of dehydration, metabolic alkalosis, and electrolyte deficits.

2. Patient care management: Pyloromyotomy (Fredet-Ramstedt operation).
3. Preoperative nursing diagnoses/goals/interventions
   a. Risk for fluid volume deficit related to repeated projectile vomiting
      Goal: Infant will remain hydrated and free of electrolyte imbalance and metabolic alkalosis.
      Interventions:
      (1) Assess for manifestations of dehydration, hypochloridemia, and metabolic alkalosis.
      (2) Check results of serum electrolytes.
      (3) Weigh the infant daily.
      (4) Measure intake and output.
      (5) Maintain IV therapy.
      (6) Administer diet as ordered.
   b. Knowledge deficit related to congenital abnormality and surgical treatment plan
      Goal: Parents will have clear understanding of defect and required surgical correction.
      Interventions:
      (1) Encourage the parents to verbalize their feelings and concerns.
      (2) Explain the surgical procedure and postoperative course.
4. Evaluation
   a. Infant shows no signs of dehydration, electrolytemia, or acid-base imbalance.
   b. Parents understand the surgical treatment plan.
5. Postoperative nursing diagnoses/goals/interventions
   a. Altered nutrition: less than body requirements related to postoperative dietary alterations
      Goal: Infant will tolerate feeding sufficient to meet caloric requirement (115 Cal per kg) before discharge.
      Interventions:
      (1) Gradually progress liquid diet for age as ordered.
      (2) Weigh the infant daily.
      (3) Monitor intake and output.
      (4) Position the infant on right side after feedings.
      (5) Handle the infant as little as possible after feedings.
   b. Risk for infection related to surgical incision
      Goal: Infant will remain afebrile, and incision will remain clean and intact.

Interventions:
(1) Assess temperature.
(2) Use aseptic technique when changing the dressing.
(3) Monitor the incision line for redness, drainage, swelling, and approximation.
(4) Fasten the diaper below the incision line.
6. Evaluation
   a. Infant tolerates age-appropriate diet reflecting fluid and caloric requirements.
   b. Infant's surgical incision remains clean and intact.
G. **Congenital Dislocated Hip** The head of the femur is completely outside the acetabulum.
   1. Assessment
      a. Assess for presence of Ortolani's sign.
      b. Observe for limited hip abduction, asymmetry of gluteal and thigh folds, and shortening of leg on affected side.
   2. Patient care management
      a. In the neonate, the dislocated hip is immobilized in an abducted position by the use of double diapering, a Frejka pillow, or an abduction brace.
      b. If a contracture of the hip adductors develops, the child is placed in Bryant's traction to stretch the muscles and to bring the femoral head down to the level of the acetabulum.
      c. When hip reduction cannot be maintained, a hip spica cast is applied.
      d. Open reduction is done if all other methods are unsuccessful.
   3. Nursing diagnoses/goals/interventions
      a. Impaired physical mobility related to spica cast
         Goal: Infant will experience no complications related to hip spica cast.
         Interventions:
         (1) Maintain bedrest in prescribed position until the cast dries.
         (2) Expose the cast to air until the cast dries.
         (3) Use a bedboard or firm mattress.
         (4) Assess for circulatory impairment by checking capillary refill, color, and temperature of each lower extremity.
      b. Risk for impaired skin integrity related to immobility
         Goal: Infant's skin will remain intact.

Interventions:
(1) Inspect skin under the edges of the cast for irritation.
(2) Petal the cast edges.
(3) Keep the cast as dry as possible.
(4) Provide perineal care.
(5) Apply lotion to exposed skin areas.
(6) Change the infant's position every 2 hours.

c. Knowledge deficit regarding home care in a spica cast
Goal: Parents will demonstrate understanding of cast care.

Interventions:
(1) Teach the parents the signs of circulatory impairment.
(2) Demonstrate to the parents how to prevent skin breakdown.
(3) Instruct the parents how to provide appropriate diversional activities to promote normal growth and development.

4. Evaluation
a. Child experiences no complications related to the hip spica cast.
b. Parents understand the principles of cast care.

UNIT TWO

Meeting the Needs of the Infant

(1 to 12 months)

STUDY GUIDE

DEVELOPMENTAL MILESTONES

A. Physical Development
B. Gross Motor Development
C. Fine Motor Development
D. Language Development
E. Personal-Social Development
F. Freud's Psychosexual Theory of Development
G. Erikson's Psychosocial Theory of Development
H. Piaget's Theory of Cognitive Development
I. Play

HEALTH PROMOTION OF THE INFANT

A. Physiological Needs
B. Safety and Security Needs

THE INFANT AND THE CRISIS OF HOSPITALIZATION

A. Communicating with Parents
B. The Infant's Response to Hospitalization

ALTERATIONS OF HEALTH DURING INFANCY

Cognitive Impairment

A. Degrees
B. Nursing Care Plan for the Child with a Cognitive Impairment
C. Specific Alterations Leading to Cognitive Impairment
   1. Phenylketonuria
   2. Hypothyroidism (congenital)
   3. Down syndrome

Other Alterations of Health

A. Cystic Fibrosis
B. Celiac Disease
C. Fluid and Electrolyte Disturbances
   1. Diarrhea
   2. Vomiting
D. Anemias of Childhood
   1. Iron-deficiency anemia
   2. Sickle-cell anemia
   3. Thalessemia (Cooley's anemia)
E. Infantile Eczema (Atopic Dermatitis)
F. Intussusception
G. Wilm's Tumor (Nephroblastoma)
H. Abused Child Syndrome
I. Pervasive Developmental Disorders

DEVELOPMENTAL MILESTONES

A. Physical Development
  1. Weekly weight gain during the first 6 months is 5 to 7 ounces per week.
  2. Weekly weight gain during the second 6 months is 3 to 5 ounces per week.
  3. Height gain during the first 6 months is 1 inch per month.
  4. Height gain during the second 6 months is $\frac{1}{2}$ inch per month.
  5. Pulse rate is 110 to 140 per minute.
  6. Respirations are 20 to 40 per minute.
  7. The posterior fontanel closes at 2 months.
  8. The lacrimal ducts are opened and the infant cries tears at 2 months.
  9. The Moro, tonic neck, and rooting reflexes disappear by 4 months.
  10. The Landau reflex appears at 3 months.
  11. Tooth eruption begins with the lower incisors at 6 months.
B. Gross Motor Development
  1. Two months
    a. Turns from side to back.
    b. Lifts both head and chest a short distance when prone.
    c. Follows objects vertically and horizontally.
  2. Three to four months
    a. Turns from side to back.
    b. Balances head well in a sitting position.
    c. Follows objects 180 degrees.
  3. Five to six months
    a. Turns from abdomen to back and from back to abdomen.
    b. Shows no head lag when in a sitting position.
  4. Seven to eight months
    a. Begins crawling.
    b. Pulls self to a sitting position.
  5. Nine to ten months
    a. Pulls self to a standing position.
    b. May stand alone momentarily.
  6. Eleven to twelve months
    a. Walks holding on or alone.
    b. Can sit down from a standing position.
C. Fine Motor Development
  1. Two months
    a. Hands are frequently open.
    b. Grasp reflex is fading.
  2. Three to four months
    a. Holds a rattle placed in his/her hand.
    b. Grasps objects with both hands.
    c. Tries to reach for objects.
    d. Plays with hands.
    e. Brings objects to his/her mouth.
  3. Five to six months
    a. Uses palmar grasp.
    b. Plays with feet.
    c. Returns a dropped object.
    d. Holds own bottle.
  4. Seven to eight months
    a. Transfers objects from one hand to the other.
    b. Begins use of pincer grasp.
  5. Nine to ten months
    a. Shows preference for use of one hand.
    b. Shows beginning of crude release.
  6. Eleven to twelve months
    a. Scribbles with a crayon.
    b. Can hold a cup to drink with assistance.
    c. Eats well with fingers.
D. Language Development
  1. Two months
    a. Makes throaty noises.
    b. Utters different cries, depending on circumstances.
  2. Three to four months
    a. Laughs aloud.
    b. Coos and gurgles when talked to.
    c. Vocalizes to a familiar voice.
    d. Makes consonant sounds n, k, g, p, and b.
  3. Five to six months
    a. Babbles vowel sounds ah, eh, and uh.
    b. Vocalizes some well-defined syllables.
  4. Seven to eight months
    a. Babbles "da, ba."
    b. Imitates sounds.
    c. Combines syllables.
    d. Makes consonant sounds t, d, and w.
  5. Nine to ten months
    a. Says "mama" and "dada" with meaning.
    b. May say one other word.
    c. Understands "bye-bye."
    d. Responds to simple commands.
  6. Eleven to twelve months
    a. Has a vocabulary of two to three words besides "mama" and "dada."
    b. Uses jargon.
    c. Imitates animal sounds.

E. Personal-Social Development
1. Two months
    a. Regards face intently.
    b. Responds to a speaking voice.
    c. Has social smile.
2. Three to four months
    a. Recognizes mother.
    b. Shows anticipation for feeding.
    c. Initiates social play.
3. Five to six months
    a. Holds arms out to be picked up.
    b. Demands attention by fussing.
    c. Smiles at self in mirror.
    d. Has definite likes and dislikes.
4. Seven to eight months
    a. Displays stranger anxiety.
    b. Plays peek-a-boo.
    c. Responds to own name.
5. Nine to ten months
    a. Waves bye-bye.
    b. Plays pat-a-cake.
6. Eleven to twelve months
    a. Shows fear, anger, affection, anxiety, jealousy, and sympathy.
    b. Enjoys being the center of attention.
    c. May kiss on request.
    d. Shakes head for "no."
F. Freud's Psychosexual Theory of Development
1. The infant is in the oral stage of development.
2. The pleasure principle is operating, and id impulses dominate.
3. The infant receives pleasure through eating, sucking, rooting activities, and biting.
G. Erikson's Psychosocial Theory of Development
1. The infant is developing a sense of trust versus mistrust.
2. Trust is accomplished if the infant's needs are met consistently.
3. The infant gradually learns that he/she is separate from the mother.
4. The infant is able to tolerate frustration in small doses and to wait for his/her needs to be gratified because he/she has learned that the mother will return.
H. Piaget's Theory of Cognitive Development
1. The infant is in the sensorimotor phase of development.
2. Egocentric thinking predominates.

3. Four substages occur during infancy.
    a. Reflexive reactions (birth to 1 month)
        (1) These are composed entirely of reflexive actions.
        (2) Poor tolerance for frustration and delay of need gratification is shown.
    b. Primary circular reactions (1 to 4 months)
        (1) Simple acts are repeated as the infant recognizes that a consistent stimulus will produce a consistent response.
        (2) Actions are engaged in for the pleasure of the activity rather than the results.
    c. Secondary circular reactions (4 to 8 months)
        (1) These represent the beginning of intentional action.
        (2) The infant repeats actions that produce interesting results.
        (3) The infant is able to imitate activities.
    d. Coordination of secondary schemata and their application to new situations (9 to 12 months)
        (1) Acts are increasingly goal-directed.
        (2) The infant begins to solve simple patterns by utilizing previously mastered responses.
I. Play
1. Predominance of solitary play.
2. Purposes of play during infancy
    a. To practice gross and fine motor skills.
    b. To learn to relate to people and objects.
    c. To express feelings.
3. Suggested toys and activities
    a. Bright objects such as rattles.
    b. Large building blocks.
    c. Floating toys in the bath.
    d. Squeeze toys.
    e. Soft dolls and animals of different textures.
    f. Large rubber balls.
    g. Nesting blocks.
    h. Large strings of beads.
    i. Simple take-apart toys.
    j. Talk, hold, and caress the infant.
    k. Play music.
    l. Place mobiles on the crib.
    m. Initiate simple repetitive games.
    n. Show the infant large picture books.

HEALTH PROMOTION OF THE INFANT

A. Physiological Needs
   1. Daily care
      a. Promote adequate sleep.
      b. Provide fresh air and sunshine.
      c. Provide skin care.
      d. Dress appropriately.
      e. Promote elimination.
   2. Nutrition
      a. Addition of solid foods
         (1) Solid foods are offered in the following sequence, beginning at 4 months: cereals, fruits, vegetables, and meats.
         (2) Finger foods are offered at 6 months.
         (3) Soft table foods are offered at 12 months.
         (4) Egg whites are withheld until 12 months because of the possibility of allergic reactions.
         (5) Whole milk is begun at 12 months. months.
         (6) Dilute fruit juices are offered at 6 months.
         (7) New foods should be offered one at a time at intervals of 1 week in order to observe for allergic reactions.
         (8) Solid foods are offered at the beginning of a meal.
      b. Weaning
         (1) Weaning is a gradual process begun at 6 to 9 months.
         (2) Weaning should never be done during a crisis situation.
B. Safety and Security Needs
   1. Prevention of accidents
      a. Be alert to avoid common accidents: suffocation, falls, poisoning, aspiration of foreign bodies, burns, and motor vehicle accidents.
      b. Assist parents in providing a safe environment.
      c. Assist parents in maintaining age-appropriate limit setting.
   2. Child health conferences
      a. A complete history is recorded.
      b. A physical examination is done every month.
      c. Nutritional counseling is available.
      d. Parents are taught expected patterns of growth and development.
      e. Counseling is available for problems in family relationships.
   3. Immunizations
      a. Diphtheria-tetanus-pertussis immunizations are administered at bimonthly intervals, beginning at age 2 months, for 3 doses.
      b. Oral trivalent polio vaccine is administered at 2 months and at 4 months of age.
      c. HIB vaccine is administered at 2, 4, and 6 months.

THE INFANT AND THE CRISIS OF HOSPITALIZATION

A. Communicating with Parents
   1. Assessment of parental reactions
      a. Assess the anxiety level of the parents.
      b. Identify the parent's fears.
         (1) Responsibility for the child's illness or accident.
         (2) Outcome of the child's illness, both physical and emotional.
         (3) Inability to meet the child's current needs.
         (4) Unfamiliar hospital procedures.
         (5) Spread of illness to other family members.
         (6) Inability to provide optimal medical care due to inadequate financial resources.
      c. Assess for available support systems and coping mechanisms.
   2. Nursing diagnosis/goal/interventions
      Altered family processes related to situational crisis of child's hospitalization
      Goal: Parents will understand the child's condition, the medical treatment plan, and the prognosis.
      Interventions:
      a. Allow the parents to verbalize their feelings.
      b. Provide information concerning the disease process, treatment regimen, and outcome.
      c. Encourage frequent visiting or rooming-in.
      d. Allow the parents to participate in the care of their child.
   3. Evaluation
      a. Parents understand their child's condition, medical treatment plan, and prognosis.
      b. Parents participate in the care of their child as much as possible.
B. The Infant's Response to Hospitalization
   1. Assessment
      a. Early infancy (preattachment)

(1) The young infant does not experience separation anxiety.

(2) Pain and discomfort are experienced as a generalized body response.

(3) The young infant has no memory of past painful experiences; therefore fear and apprehension are absent.

b. Late infancy (postattachment)

(1) Separation anxiety is experienced.

(2) The older infant is able to localize pain.

(3) Response to hospital routines and interventions are based on past experiences.

(4) The older infant is uncooperative and offers resistance to medical and nursing interventions.

2. Nursing diagnosis/goal/interventions

Risk of ineffective coping by the infant related to the situational crisis of hospitalization

Goal: Infant will develop a sense of trust.

Interventions:

a. Encourage parental visiting or rooming-in.

b. Assign one nurse to consistently care for the infant.

c. Meet the child's needs consistently to foster development of a sense of trust.

d. Provide opportunities for sensory stimulation.

3. Evaluation

a. Infant's basic needs are met promptly.

b. Development of a sense of trust is not interrupted.

ALTERATIONS OF HEALTH DURING INFANCY

Cognitive Impairment Significantly below average intellectual functioning, accompanied by deficits in adaptive behavior.

A. Degrees

1. Mild retardation (educable): IQ 51 to 70. Can learn activities of daily living, math and reading skills comparable to a third- to sixth-grade education, and simple vocational skills adequate for self-maintenance in the community.

2. Moderate retardation (trainable): IQ—36 to 50. Shows noticeable delays in development. Can learn simple communication skills, although may have difficulty with speech. Responds to training in various self-help activities. Usually can perform simple jobs under sheltered conditions.

3. Severe retardation: IQ—21 to 35. Shows marked developmental delays. Acquires very poor to no communication skills. May learn a few activities of daily living and is able to conform to repetitive daily routines. Needs continual supervision in a protective environment.

4. Profound retardation: IQ—20 or below. Achieves the mental age of an infant. Shows obvious delays in all aspects of development. Requires complete custodial care.

B. Nursing Care Plan for the Child with a Cognitive Impairment

1. Assessment

a. Determine the child's developmental level.

b. Observe the parent-child relationship.

2. Nursing diagnoses/goals/interventions

a. Altered growth and development related to deficits in cognitive functioning

Goal: Child will function at a level consistent with his/her cognitive skills and adaptive abilities.

Interventions:

(1) Assist in promoting independence in activities of daily living.

(2) Assist in developing communication skills.

(3) Provide a variety of sensory experiences in the environment.

(4) Provide consistency in the environment.

b. Risk for altered parenting related to diagnosis of a child with life-long disability

Goals:

(1) Parents will express an understanding of developmental disabilities.

(2) Family members will express their feelings and concerns.

(3) Parents will interact positively with their child and will facilitate his/her development.

Interventions:

(1) Assure parents that their feelings are normal.

(2) Assist the parents to accept the child's strengths and weaknesses.

(3) Provide information about possible causes, the treatment plan, and prognosis.

(4) Provide the parents with information on available community resources.

3. Evaluation

   a. Child attains optimal developmental level.

   b. Parents accept the child as a unique individual with identified strengths and weaknesses.

C. Specific Alterations Leading to Cognitive Impairment.

1. **Phenylketonuria** A genetic defect in the ability to synthesize phenylalanine, an essential amino acid. Developmental delays occur as a result of the accumulation of phenylalanine derivatives in the brain.

   a. Genetic transmission

      (1) The defect is inherited as an autosomal recessive trait.

      (2) With each pregnancy, there is a 25% probability that the offspring will have the disease if both parents are carriers.

      (3) With each pregnancy, there is a 25% probability that the offspring will be normal if both parents are carriers.

      (4) With each pregnancy, there is a 50% probability that the offspring will be a carrier if both parents are carriers.

   b. Assessment

      (1) Assess the urine and perspiration for a musty odor.

      (2) Inspect the skin for signs of eczema.

      (3) Assess for vomiting and failure to gain weight.

      (4) Observe for hyperactivity and bizarre behavioral patterns.

      (5) Be aware that convulsions may occur.

      (6) Observe for a progressive developmental lag.

      (7) DIAGNOSTIC MEASURES

         (a) The presence of phenylketone bodies in the urine results in a positive ferric chloride test.

         (b) The Guthrie test, done on all newborns, shows elevated serum phenylalanine levels.

c. Patient care management

   (1) A low-phenylalanine diet is given to prevent progression of mental retardation.

   (2) Lofenalac is generally used for infants.

   (3) Phenyl-free is used for older children.

d. Nursing diagnosis/goal/interventions
   Knowledge deficit related to genetic condition and treatment plan
   Goal: Parents will verbalize understanding of home care.
   Interventions:

   (1) Allow the parents to verbalize their feelings and concerns.

   (2) Provide genetic counseling.

   (3) Teach dietary restrictions.

e. Evaluation

   (1) Child shows no signs of a progressive developmental lag.

   (2) Parents understand the genetic implications and dietary management of phenylketonuria.

2. **Hypothyroidism (congenital)** A defect in the fetal development of the thyroid gland, resulting in an inability to synthesize thyroxine.

   a. Assessment

      (1) There is prolonged physiological jaundice in the neonate.

      (2) Feeding difficulties and inactivity are noted in the neonatal period.

      (3) Hypotonic abdominal musculature causes constipation and umbilical hernias.

      (4) There is a characteristic facial expression: eyes are wide set, nose is broad and flat, tongue protrudes, and hairline is low.

      (5) The hair is coarse and brittle.

      (6) A decreased basal metabolism rate results in weight gain, slow pulse, and subnormal temperature.

      (7) Dentition is delayed.

      (8) Anemia is present.

      (9) There is a progressive developmental lag.

      (10) DIAGNOSTIC MEASURES

         (a) A high serum level of thyroid-stimulating factor and a low level of thyroxine are present.

         (b) Retarded bone growth is demonstrated on a skeletal survey.

b. Patient care management
  (1) Life-long replacement therapy with a thyroid hormone preparation is necessary.
  (2) The preparation of choice is synthetic levothyroxine sodium (Synthroid or Levothroid).
c. Nursing diagnoses/goals/interventions
  (1) Altered growth and development related to congenital insufficiency of thyroid hormone
    Goal: Child will show no signs of progressive developmental lag.
    Interventions:
    (a) Administer replacement therapy as prescribed.
    (b) Be on the alert for side effects of levothyroxine sodium: rapid pulse, increased respirations, fever, increased perspiration, vomiting, diarrhea, and weight loss.
    (c) Assess for signs of hypothyroidism, which may indicate that the treatment plan is ineffectual.
  (2) Knowledge deficit related to child's condition and treatment plan
    Goal: Parents will verbalize and demonstrate understanding of home care.
    Interventions:
    (a) Allow the parents to verbalize their feelings and concerns.
    (b) Provide genetic counseling.
    (c) Explain the cause, medical treatment plan, and prognosis.
d. Evaluation
  (1) Child shows no signs of progressive developmental lag.
  (2) Parents understand the importance of the life-long administration of a thyroid hormone preparation.
  (3) Parents recognize the signs of hypo- and hyperthyroidism and the need to seek prompt medical intervention when or if these signs appear.
3. **Down syndrome** A chromosomal abnormality, usually an extra chromosome 21 (trisomy 21), occurring most often in infants born to women over 35 years of age.

a. Assessment
  (1) Assess for typical physical appearance: close-set eyes slanted slightly upward, flat nose, Brushfield's spots on the irises, flat occiput, small ears, and protruding tongue.
  (2) Assess for hypotonicity of the muscles.
  (3) Observe for feeding difficulties.
  (4) Assess for associated abnormalities and complications: congenital heart disease, umbilical hernias, intestinal obstructions, respiratory infections, and leukemia.
  (5) Assess the child's developmental level.
  (6) DIAGNOSTIC MEASURE: Chromosomal analysis demonstrates 47 chromosomes instead of 46.
b. Patient care management
  (1) Early intervention programs followed by special education based on the individual child's developmental assessment.
  (2) Surgery to correct congenital abnormalities.
c. Nursing diagnoses/goals/interventions
  (1) Altered growth and development related to deficits in cognitive functioning
    Goal: Child will attain his/her optimal level of development.
    Interventions:
    (a) Assist in promoting independence in activities of daily living.
    (b) Assist in developing communication skills.
    (c) Provide a variety of sensory experiences in the environment.
    (d) Provide consistency in the environment.
  (2) Risk for altered parenting related to diagnosis of a child with a life-long disability
    Goals:
    (a) Parents will express their feelings and concerns.
    (b) Parents will interact positively with their child and thereby facilitate his/her development.

Interventions:

(a) Encourage parents to express their feelings and concerns.

(b) Provide information about genetic counseling, the medical treatment plan, and the prognosis.

(c) Provide the parents with information on available community resources.

d. Evaluation

(1) Child attains optimal level of development.

(2) Parents accept the child as an unique individual with identified strengths and weaknesses.

Other Alterations of Health

A. **Cystic Fibrosis**   A generalized dysfunction of the exocrine glands; an inherited condition transmitted as an autosomal-recessive trait. The bronchioles are obstructed by thick secretions that prevent normal gas exchange, leading to obstructive emphysema and patchy atelectasis. Stasis of secretions results in bronchopneumonia. Eventually right-sided heart failure (cor pulmonale) may result. The ducts of the pancreas are obstructed by thick secretions that prevent digestive enzymes (trypsin, lipase, and amylase) from reaching the duodenum. As a result fat absorption is impaired. There is an increase in sodium and chloride contents in the saliva and in the sweat. In the liver, biliary cirrhosis may occur because of obstruction of the bile ducts. Meconium ileus may occur in the newborn period.

1. Assessment

a. Determine whether there is a family history of cystic fibrosis.

b. Assess for pulmonary involvement, which is manifested by wheezing respirations and a chronic nonproductive cough. As pulmonary involvement progresses, dyspnea, barrel chest, cyanosis, and clubbing of the fingers result.

c. Assess for pancreatic involvement, which is manifested by bulky, frothy, foul-smelling stools; voracious appetite; weight loss; a progressively emaciated appearance; deficiencies of fat-soluble vitamins A, D, E, and K, and anemia.

d. Assess for sweat gland involvement, which is manifested by hypoelectrolytemia in hot weather.

e. DIAGNOSTIC MEASURES

(1) Chest X-ray: evidence of generalized obstructive emphysema, atelectasis, and bronchopneumonia.

(2) Stool analysis: an absence of trypsin and an increase of fat in the stools.

(3) Quantitative sweat test: an increase in sodium and chloride.

2. Patient care management

a. A pulmonary hygiene regimen is carried out daily.

b. Medications prescribed may include bronchodilators, mucolytic agents, expectorants, and antibiotics.

c. Dietary modifications are an increase in calories and protein, a decrease in fat, a liberal use of salt, and an increase in fluids.

d. Pancreatic enzymes are replaced at each meal.

e. Water-soluble preparations of vitamins A, D, E, and K are administered.

3. Nursing diagnoses/goals/interventions

a. Ineffective airway clearance related to the secretion of thick, tenacious mucus
Goals:

(1) Child will have a patent airway.

(2) Child will have no signs of respiratory infections.
Interventions:

(1) Perform chest physiotherapy before each meal and at bedtime.

(2) Use aerosol therapy and a mist tent as prescribed.

(3) Teach appropriate breathing exercises.

(4) Encourage activity.

(5) Avoid contact with individuals who have respiratory tract infections.

(6) Administer antibiotics as ordered.

b. Altered nutrition: less than body requirements related to inability to digest fats and utilize fat-soluble vitamins
Goal: Child will remain hydrated, gain weight, and ingest a well-balanced diet.
Interventions:

(1) Provide a diet high in calories and protein and low in fat.

(2) Increase salt intake during hot weather and increased exercise.

(3) Encourage intake of fluids.

(4) Administer pancreatic enzymes with all meals and snacks.

(5) Administer synthetic water-soluble vitamins A, D, E, and K.

c. Altered parenting related to situational crisis of nurturing a child with a chronic, life-threatening illness
Goals:

(1) Parents will express feelings, fears, anxieties and guilt.

(2) Parents will verbalize their understanding of the child's physical health and the treatment plan.
Interventions:

(1) Facilitate anticipatory grieving by the parents for the potential loss of their child.

(2) Encourage the parents to verbalize their feelings and concerns.

(3) Refer the parents to appropriate community resources.

(4) Provide genetic counseling.

(5) Teach the parents all aspects of the medical treatment plan.

(6) Encourage the parents to participate in their child's care.

4. Evaluation

a. Child adheres to the recommended pulmonary regime, dietary modifications, and prescribed medication schedule.

b. Child shows no signs of pulmonary infection.

c. Child is free of steatorrhea, and his/her weight and height progressively increase.

d. Parents understand the genetic pattern, medical treatment plan, and prognosis.

B. **Celiac Disease** An inborn error of metabolism that triggers a toxic response to glutens. Damage is done to the mucosa of the intestine, resulting in malabsorption of nutrients. Progressive malnutrition occurs, accompanied by vitamin deficiencies and anemia.

1. Assessment

a. Observe for large, frothy, fatty, foul-smelling stools.

b. Assess for other gastrointestinal manifestations: abdominal distention, abdominal pain, vomiting, and anorexia.

c. Observe for personality changes such as irritability or lethargy.

2. Patient care management

a. A diet absent in wheat, rye, barley, and oat gluten is given.

b. Corn, rice, and soybean flour are substitute grains.

3. Nursing diagnoses/goals/interventions

a. Altered nutrition: less than body requirements related to malabsorption secondary to gluten toxicity
Goal: Child will remain hydrated, gain weight, and ingest a well-balanced diet.
Interventions:

(1) Emphasize the importance of adhering to a lifelong gluten-restricted diet.

(2) Observe for signs of fluid and electrolyte imbalance (celiac crisis).

b. Knowledge deficit related to disease process and dietary treatment plan
Goal: Parents will demonstrate understanding of home-care and follow-up instructions.
Interventions:

(1) Encourage the parents to verbalize their feelings and concerns.

(2) Teach the parents dietary modifications.

(3) Review with the parents the necessity of reading labels to determine the presence of gluten.

4. Evaluation

a. Child adheres to the prescribed diet.

b. Child's weight and height progressively increase.

c. Parents understand the disease process and medical treatment plan.

C. Fluid and Electrolyte Disturbances

1. **Diarrhea** An increased number of stools of reduced consistency. Most often caused by bacterial or viral infections, faulty preparation of formula or food, dietary excesses of fats or carbohydrates, or allergies.

a. Assessment

(1) Determine the number, color, and consistency of stools. Stools are usually green and may contain mucus or blood.

(2) Assess for signs of dehydration: poor skin turgor, dry mucous membranes, decreased saliva, sunken eyes and fontanels, decreased urine output, weight loss, irritability, lethargy, rapid pulse, and rapid respirations.

(3) Observe for deep, rapid respirations that are indicative of metabolic acidosis.

(4) Observe for signs of potassium deficit: muscle weakness, hypotension, cardiac arrhythmias, irritability, and lethargy.

(5) Observe for signs of sodium deficit: weakness, nausea, abdominal cramps, anorexia, and hypotension.

(6) DIAGNOSTIC MEASURES
  (a) Serum electrolyte values.
  (b) Stool culture and sensitivity to identify the causative organism. Bacteria most often involved include *Shigella, Salmonella, Staphylococcus,* and *Escherichia coli.*

b. Patient care management
  (1) Intravenous therapy to replace fluid and electrolyte losses.
  (2) Nothing by mouth, then a progressive diet as the number of stools decreases.
    (a) Glucose water and oral electrolyte solutions.
    (b) Low-fat formulas.
    (c) BRAT diet (bananas, rice, applesauce, and toast) when age-appropriate.

c. Nursing diagnoses/goals/interventions
  (1) Fluid volume deficit related to excessive losses secondary to diarrhea
    Goal: Child will maintain normal hydration, as evidenced by good skin turgor, moist mucous membranes, urine specific gravity within normal limits, and balanced intake and output.
    Interventions:
    (a) Monitor IV fluids.
    (b) Maintain NPO; then provide progressive diet as ordered.
    (c) Measure intake and output.
    (d) Take vital signs.
    (e) Weigh the child daily.
    (f) Monitor urine specific gravity.
  (2) Risk for infection related to presence of infectious organisms
    Goal: Child's infection will not be spread.

Interventions:
  (a) Wash hands frequently.
  (b) Maintain enteric precautions.
  (c) Administer antibiotics as ordered.
(3) Risk for impaired skin integrity related to frequent, loose stools
    Goal: Child's skin and mucous membranes will remain intact.
    Interventions:
    (a) Change the diaper frequently.
    (b) Apply a bland ointment.
    (c) Expose the area to air if excoriation occurs.
    (d) Reposition the child every 2 hours.
    (e) Apply petroleum jelly to lips.
    (f) Use glycerine swabs.

d. Evaluation
  (1) Child shows no signs of dehydration or of electrolyte or acid-base imbalance.
  (2) Number and consistency of stools are within normal limits.
  (3) Child tolerates a progressive diet without recurrence of diarrhea.
  (4) Skin integrity is maintained.

2. **Vomiting**   Emesis due to a wide variety of intrinsic and extrinsic factors: faulty feeding techniques, allergies, infection, intestinal obstruction, increased intracranial pressure, and emotional upset.

a. Assessment
  (1) Observe the frequency, amount, color, and consistency of emesis.
  (2) Note the time of emesis in relationship to feeding.
  (3) Note the force of emesis.
  (4) Observe for signs of dehydration.
  (5) Assess for slow, shallow respirations and muscle hypertonicity, which are indicative of metabolic alkalosis and chloride deficit.
  (6) Assess for signs of sodium and potassium deficit.

b. Patient care management
  (1) Intravenous therapy to replace fluid and electrolyte losses.
  (2) A progressive diet as tolerated.
  (3) Antiemetic medications.

c. Nursing diagnosis/goal/interventions
  Fluid volume deficit related to inability to tolerate oral fluids without vomiting

Goal: Child will have moist mucous membranes, normal skin turgor, and adequate urinary output for age and will gain weight.

Interventions:

(1) Monitor IV fluids.

(2) Maintain NPO; then provide progressive diet as ordered.

(3) Measure intake and output.

(4) Take vital signs.

(5) Weigh the child daily.

(6) Monitor urine specific gravity.

(7) Utilize appropriate feeding techniques.

    (a) Feed the child slowly in an upright position.

    (b) Burp the child frequently.

    (c) Position the child on the right side with the head elevated after feeding to facilitate digestion and prevent aspiration.

    (d) Handle the child as little as possible after feeding.

d. Evaluation

(1) Child shows no signs of dehydration and electrolyte or acid-base imbalance.

(2) Child tolerates a progressive diet without vomiting.

D. Anemias of Childhood

1. **Iron-deficiency anemia**   Anemia due to insufficient supply or poor absorption of iron, resulting in a decrease of hemoglobin synthesis and a reduced oxygen-carrying capacity of the blood.

a. Assessment

(1) Assess dietary intake.

(2) Observe for pallor, irritability, and poor muscle tone.

(3) DIAGNOSTIC MEASURES

    (a) The red blood cell count, hemoglobin and hematocrit are decreased.

    (b) The red blood cell is hypochromic and microcytic.

b. Patient care management

(1) Oral iron supplements.

(2) Vitamin C in diet to enhance the absorption of iron.

(3) Adequate dietary intake of iron.

c. Nursing diagnoses/goals/interventions

(1) Altered nutrition: less than body requirements related to inadequate intake of iron

Goal: Child will experience adequate intake of iron through oral intake.

Interventions:

(a) Teach the parents nutritional modifications.

    1. Provide foods rich in iron: green leafy vegetables, meat, eggs, and fortified cereals and formulas.

    2. Provide foods rich in vitamin C: citrus fruits, tomatoes, and potatoes.

    3. Limit intake of milk.

(b) Administer oral iron preparations to child.

    1. Administer between meals.

    2. Administer with a straw or medicine dropper to prevent staining the teeth.

    3. Brush teeth after administration.

    4. Be aware that stools will become tarry green or black.

    5. Observe for side effects: nausea, vomiting, diarrhea, or constipation.

(2) Risk for infection related to lowered body defenses.

Goal: Child will be free of infection.

Interventions:

(a) Assess temperature.

(b) Wash hands when indicated.

(c) Avoid contact of the child with individuals who have infections.

(3) Activity intolerance related to reduced oxygen-carrying capacity of the blood.

Goal: Child will tolerate increased activity.

Interventions:

(a) Assess motor development and level of activity tolerance.

(b) Anticipate and meet the child's needs.

(c) Provide quiet diversional activities.

d. Evaluation

(1) Child's red blood cell count, hemoglobin, and hematocrit are within normal limits for age.

(2) Child receives adequate dietary sources of iron and vitamin C.

(3) Child receives and tolerates an oral iron preparation without side effects.

(4) Child is free of infection.

(5) Child's level of activity tolerance gradually increases.

2 **Sickle-cell anemia** A hemolytic anemia due to a defect in hemoglobin synthesis that is transmitted by an autosomal-recessive trait; occurs mostly in blacks.

The exact mechanism of the sickling phenomenon is unknown. Under conditions of lowered oxygen tension, the red blood cell sickles and blood viscosity is increased. Stasis of blood results as cells agglutinate. Capillaries are obstructed, and there are anoxic changes in the tissues.

a. Assessment

(1) Individuals with sickle-cell *trait* exhibit no symptoms unless they are exposed to prolonged or extreme conditions of low oxygen tension.

(2) Clinical manifestations of sickle-cell *anemia* include pallor, anorexia, slow weight gain, weakness, nausea and vomiting, fever, joint pain, abdominal pain, and frequent infections.

(3) Clinical manifestations during vaso-occlusive crisis are fever, severe abdominal pain, painful joints, hand-foot syndrome, extreme pallor, and jaundice.

(4) DIAGNOSTIC MEASURES

(a) A sickle-cell prep or Sickledex is used as a screening test. A positive test does not differentiate between sickle-cell trait and sickle-cell anemia.

(b) A hemoglobin electroporesis is done to distinguish between sickle-cell trait and sickle-cell anemia.

b. Patient care management

(1) Bedrest to decrease oxygen consumption.

(2) Oxygenation as necessary.

(3) Analgesics and application of heat to relieve pain.

(4) Increased hydration with IV fluid to decrease blood viscosity.

(5) Antibiotics to control infection.

(6) Folic acid.

(7) Transfusions of packed red blood cells.

c. Nursing diagnoses/goals/interventions

(1) Altered tissue perfusion related to sickling of the red blood cells
Goals:

(a) Child will experience as few sickle cell crises as possible.

(b) Child will have improved peripheral circulation during a sickle cell crisis.

Interventions:

(a) Protect the child from infection and emotional stress.

(b) Avoid strenuous physical activity.

(c) Increase fluids.

(d) Avoid high altitudes.

(e) During a sickle cell crisis, maintain bedrest, administer oxygen as ordered, monitor IV fluid, and measure intake and output.

(2) Pain related to tissue hypoxia
Goal: Child will show evidence that pain is alleviated or controlled.
Interventions:

(a) Administer analgesics as ordered.

(b) Position joints to maintain anatomic alignment.

(c) Handle joints gently.

(d) Use a bed cradle to keep heavy linen off the joints.

(e) Apply warm soaks.

(3) Activity intolerance related to impaired oxygen-carrying capacity of the blood
Goal: Child will tolerate pre-crisis activity level before discharge.
Interventions:

(a) Maintain bedrest.

(b) Anticipate and meet the child's needs promptly.

(c) Provide quiet diversional activities.

(4) **Risk for infection related to decreased body defenses**
Goal: Child will be free of infection.

Interventions:
(a) Avoid contact of the child with individuals who have infections.
(b) Administer antibiotics as ordered.
(5) Altered parenting related to situational crisis of nurturing a child with a chronic, life-threatening illness
Goals:
(a) Parents will express feelings, fears, anxieties, and guilt.
(b) Parents will verbalize their understanding of the child's physical health and the treatment plan.
Interventions:
(a) Facilitate the parents' anticipatory grieving for the potential loss of their child.
(b) Encourage the parents to verbalize their feelings and concerns.
(c) Refer the parents to appropriate community resources.
(d) Provide genetic counseling.
(e) Teach the parents all aspects of the medical treatment plan.
(f) Review measures to prevent sickle cell crisis.
(g) Discuss symptoms of sickle cell crisis and the necessity of seeking prompt medical care.
d. Evaluation
(1) Sickle cell crisis is prevented.
(2) Child's joint pain decreases.
(3) Child participates in activities of daily living as tolerated.
(4) Child is free of infection.
(5) Parents understand the genetic pattern, medical treatment plan, and prognosis.
3. **Thalessemia (Cooley's anemia)** A defect in the ability to synthesize normal adult hemoglobin, inherited as an autosomal-recessive trait. A chronic hemolytic anemia is present because of the abnormal formation and shortened life cycle of the red blood cells.
a. Assessment
(1) Assess for pallor, jaundice, anorexia, and an enlarged liver and spleen.

(2) Be aware that in older children skeletal changes produce a mongoloid facies.
(3) Assess for growth retardation.
(4) DIAGNOSTIC MEASURES
(a) Red blood cells are microcytic and hypochromic.
(b) Red blood cells, hemoglobin, and hematocrit are decreased.
(c) A hemoglobin electroporesis differentiates between thalessemia major and thalessemia minor.
b. Patient care management
(1) Transfusions to maintain hemoglobin levels
(2) Desferioxamine (Desferal) to treat hemosiderosis.
(3) A splenectomy to decrease abdominal pressure.
(4) Antibiotics to treat frequent infections.
c. Nursing diagnoses/goals/interventions
(1) Risk for injury related to complications of transfusion
Goal: Complication of transfusions will be recognized and treated promptly.
Interventions:
(a) Be aware of signs of hemolytic reaction: chills, fever, headache, and backache.
(b) Be aware of signs of allergic reaction: urticaria, wheezing, and laryngeal edema.
(c) Notify physician, stop the transfusion, and keep the IV open with normal saline if any signs of complications occur.
(d) Administer desferioxamine (Desferal) as ordered.
(e) Assess for signs of inflammation at the site of the desferioxamine (Desferal) injection.
(2) Risk for infection related to decreased body defenses
Goal: Child will be free of infection.
Interventions:
(a) Avoid contact of the child with individuals who have infections.
(b) Administer antibiotics as ordered.

(3) Activity intolerance related to impaired oxygen-carrying capacity of the blood

Goal: Child will not experience fatigue.

Interventions:

(a) Maintain bedrest.

(b) Anticipate the child's needs and meet them promptly.

(c) Provide quiet diversional activities.

(4) Altered parenting related to situational crisis of nurturing a child with a chronic, life-threatening illness

Goal: Parents will express understanding of the situational crisis and will interact positively with their child.

Interventions:

(a) Facilitate the parents' anticipatory grieving for the potential loss of their child.

(b) Encourage the parents to verbalize their feelings and concerns.

(c) Refer the parents to appropriate community resources.

(d) Teach the parents about the disease process, the medical treatment plan, and the prognosis.

d. Evaluation

(1) Child's hemoglobin is above 10 grams.

(2) Child does not experience hemosiderosis.

(3) Complications of transfusions are recognized and treated promptly.

(4) Child is free of infection.

(5) Child participates in activities of daily living as tolerated.

(6) Parents understand the genetic pattern, medical treatment plan, and prognosis.

E. **Infantile Eczema (Atopic Dermatitis)** Inflammation of the skin due to an allergic reaction.

1. Assessment

a. Inspect the face, scalp, and flexor surfaces of the body for erythema, papules, vesicles, weeping, and crusts.

b. Assess for secondary skin infections resulting from scratching.

c. Determine whether there is a family history of allergy.

2. Patient care management

a. The specific allergen is eliminated.

(1) A hypoallergenic diet is controversial. If a food allergy is certain, that food is eliminated. Delay solid foods until 6 months.

(2) Exposure to environmental allergens is reduced.

(a) The home must be kept as dust-free as possible.

(b) Exposure to animal dander is avoided.

(c) Toys should be washable, smooth, plastic, or wood.

b. Irritation to the skin is reduced.

(1) The child wears only cotton clothing appropriate for the environmental temperature.

(2) Tepid sponge baths with no soap are given.

(3) Colloid baths with cornstarch or oatmeal relieve itching.

(4) Nonlipid, hydrophilic lotions are prescribed.

(5) Local ointments such as steroids or coal tar preparations are used.

(6) Wet soaks with Burow's solution or potassium permanganate are given.

(7) Systemic medications such as Benadryl or Periactin relieve itching, and antibiotics control infection.

3. Nursing diagnoses/goals/interventions

a. Impaired skin integrity related to lesions

Goal: Child's skin will be free of lesions.

Interventions:

(1) Eliminate known allergens from diet.

(2) Provide skin care as prescribed.

(3) Dress the child in cotton clothing.

(4) Avoid environmental temperature extremes.

(5) Avoid exposure to. potential environmental allergens.

(6) Assess for signs of infection.

(7) Administer antibiotics as ordered.

b. Risk for impaired skin integrity related to pruritus
Goal: Child's skin will remain intact.
Interventions:
(1) Keep the child's fingernails and toenails short and clean.
(2) Place gloves or cotton stockings over the hands.
(3) Administer antihistamines as ordered.
c. Knowledge deficit related to home care of the child with eczema
Goal: Parents will demonstrate and verbalize understanding of home-care and follow-up interventions.
Interventions:
(1) Explain to the parents that eczema is characterized by remissions and exacerbations.
(2) Teach the parents the prescribed skin care regime.
(3) Review the dietary and environmental modifications needed to decrease the child's exposure to allergens.
(4) Suggest strategies to prevent scratching.
(5) Discuss any prescribed systemic medications.
(6) Alert the parents to the possibility of asthma or hay fever in the future.
4. Evaluation
a. Child's skin is free of lesions.
b. Child is not exposed to potential allergens.
c. Child shows no signs of secondary infection.
d. Parents understand and comply with the treatment regime.

F. **Intussusception**   Telescoping of one segment of the intestine into another resulting in an obstruction of the intestines.

1. Assessment
a. The presence of acute paroxysmal abdominal pain is demonstrated by the child's screaming and drawing the legs up to the abdomen.
b. "Current jelly" stools containing blood and mucus may be passed.
c. Emesis of bile-stained vomitus occurs.
d. Abdominal distention is present, and a sausage-shaped mass may be palpated in the right upper quadrant.

2. Patient care management
a. The preferred treatment is hydrostatic reduction of the intussusception by barium enema.
b. If symptoms persist, surgical reduction or intestinal resection of the involved portion is performed.
3. Preoperative nursing diagnoses/goals/interventions
a. Risk for injury related to the presence of an intestinal obstruction
Goal: Child will show no signs of complication of intestinal obstruction.
Interventions:
(1) Assess for the presence or absence of stools.
(2) Assess for complications: perforation, peritonitis, and shock.
(3) Prepare the child for surgery: maintain NPO and monitor IV fluids.
b. Knowledge deficit related to the barium enema and/or surgical procedure to be performed
Goal: Parents will verbalize understanding of the treatment plan.
Interventions:
(1) Encourage the parents to verbalize their feelings and concerns.
(2) Discuss the medical and/or surgical treatment procedures and postoperative care.
4. Evaluation
a. Child shows no signs of complications of intestinal obstructions.
b. Parents understand the medical and/or surgical treatment plan.
5. Postoperative nursing diagnoses/goals/interventions
a. Risk for fluid volume deficit related to surgery and gastric drainage
Goal: Child will remain hydrated and will tolerate sufficient amounts of oral fluids.
Interventions:
(1) Assess for signs of dehydration.
(2) Maintain IV therapy.
(3) Replace fluids lost through the nasogastric tube as ordered.
(4) Monitor intake and output.
(5) Weigh the child daily.
(6) Provide progressive diet for age as ordered.
b. Constipation related to intestinal surgery
Goal: Child will expel a normal, formed stool before discharge.

Interventions:

(1) Assess for the presence of bowel sounds.

(2) Monitor for passage of stools.

(3) Measure and note color of nasogastric drainage.

(4) Irrigate as ordered.

(5) Position in semi-Fowler's position to promote drainage.

c. Risk for infections related to surgical incision and decreased mobility secondary to pain

Goal: Child will remain infection free.

Interventions:

(1) Assess for manifestations of infection.

(2) Use aseptic techniques when changing dressings.

(3) Reposition every 2 hours.

(4) Encourage coughing and deep breathing when age-appropriate.

d. Pain related to incision

Goal: Child will be painfree before discharge.

Interventions:

(1) Decrease environmental stimuli.

(2) Administer analgesics as ordered.

6. Evaluation

a. Child tolerates an age-appropriate diet.

b. Child expels a normal, formed stool.

c. Child is free of wound and respiratory infection.

d. Child is free of postoperative pain.

G. **Wilm's Tumor (Nephroblastoma)** A malignant tumor of the kidney. It is the most common intra-abdominal tumor of childhood.

1. Assessment

a. Usually an abdominal mass is felt by the parents during routine bathing or dressing.

b. Other clinical manifestations are gastrointestinal distress, hematuria, anemia, weight loss, fever, and hypertension.

c. There may be signs of pulmonary metastasis.

2. Patient care management

a. Surgical removal of the tumor, the involved kidney, and the adjacent adrenal gland.

b. Postoperative radiation therapy.

c. Chemotherapy with adriamycin, vincristine, and actinomycin D.

3. Preoperative nursing diagnoses/goals/interventions

a. Risk for injury related to possible rupture of the tumor leading to metastasis

Goal: Child's tumor will not rupture.

Interventions:

(1) Post a sign at the head of the bed stating "Do not palpate the abdomen."

(2) Teach the parents the importance of not placing pressure on the abdomen.

(3) Do not apply the diaper tightly.

b. Anxiety related to the impact of the medical diagnosis on the family

Goal: Parents will verbalize understanding of the disease process, the medical and surgical treatment, and the prognosis.

Interventions:

(1) Encourage the parents to verbalize their feelings and concerns.

(2) Explain all diagnostic tests and surgical procedures to be done.

(3) Discuss the child's postoperative course and the possible need for radiation and/or chemotherapy.

4. Evaluation

a. Tumor does not rupture.

b. Parents understand their child's condition, medical and surgical treatment plan, and prognosis.

5. Postoperative nursing diagnoses/goals/interventions

a. Altered tissue perfusion related to postoperative hemorrhage

Goal: Child's vital signs will be within normal limits.

Interventions:

(1) Monitor vital signs.

(2) Assess dressing, tubes, and catheters for signs of bleeding.

(3) Carefully reposition the child to prevent dislodging any tubes or catheters.

b. Altered urinary elimination related to surgical intervention

Goal: Child's normal urinary pattern will be reestablished.

Interventions:

(1) Measure output from all tubes separately.

(2) Record amount and frequency of urinary output to assess functioning of remaining kidney.

(3) Be sure that all drainage systems are below the level of the child's kidney or bladder as appropriate.

(4) Irrigate drainage systems as ordered.

c. Pain related to postoperative status

Goal: Child will be free of postoperative pain.
Interventions:

(1) Decrease environmental stimuli.

(2) Administer analgesics as ordered.

d. Risk for infection related to surgical incision and decreased mobility secondary to pain

Goal: Child will be afebrile.
Interventions:

(1) Assess for signs of infection.

(2) Use aseptic techniques when changing dressings.

(3) Reposition the child every 2 hours.

(4) Encourage coughing and deep breathing when age-appropriate.

6. Evaluation

a. Child's vital signs are within normal limits.

b. A normal voiding pattern is reestablished.

c. Child shows no signs of wound or respiratory infection.

d. Child is free of postoperative pain.

H. **Abused Child Syndrome** The physical or mental injury, sexual abuse, negligent treatment, or maltreatment of a child under 18 years of age by a parent or other caretaker.

1. Assessment

a. Characteristics of the parents

(1) Be aware that abuse is inflicted by parents of all socioeconomic backgrounds and educational levels. Generally, the parents were abused as children.

(2) Assess parents for immature personalities, poor impulse control, low self-esteem, social isolation.

(3) Since abusers expect the child to meet their needs, assess for unrealistic ideas of child behavior.

(4) Observe the parents' approach to discipline.

(5) Assess for environmental stress and disturbed family relationships.

(6) In the emergency room, assess for discrepencies in the description of the incident or for the appropriateness of the accident in relationship to the child's developmental level.

b. Characteristics of the child

(1) Be aware that the child is usually under 3 years of age. Premature infants and handicapped children are at increased risk.

(2) Assess for burns, cuts, bruises, and fractures in various stages of healing.

(3) Assess for poor hygiene, malnutrition, growth retardation, and developmental delays.

(4) Observe for fearful behavior and for signs of withdrawal or extreme attachment.

2. Nursing diagnoses/goals/interventions

a. Altered parenting related to ineffectual response to stressors leading to child abuse

Goals:

(1) Child will no longer experience abuse from parents.

(2) Parents will acquire adequate coping skills to prevent further abuse of their child.

Interventions:

(1) Identify high-risk families.

(2) Report suspected cases of abuse to appropriate authorities.

(3) Exhibit nonjudgmental behavior toward the parents.

(4) Assist the parents in identifying stressors and effective coping mechanisms.

(5) Teach the parents expected growth and development patterns.

(6) Teach the parents appropriate methods of discipline.

(7) Act as a role model for parenting skills.

(8) Point out positive aspects of the parent-child relationship.

b. Anxiety related to abuse by parents and potential separation from parents
Goal: Child will show evidence of decreased anxiety by increased verbalization, increased interaction with other children, and increased interest in play.
Interventions:
(1) Provide consistency of care to facilitate development of trust.
(2) Implement play therapy.
(3) Reassure the child that he/she was not "bad."
(4) Observe parent-child interactions.
(5) Encourage the parents to visit and participate in care.
3. Evaluation
a. Child is protected from injury.
b. Parents develop effective coping skills to deal with increased stress.

I. **Pervasive Developmental Disorders** According to the *Diagnostic and Statistical Manual of Mental Disorders* (DSM-III-R), these conditions, first seen in infancy or childhood, are characterized by impairment in reciprocal social interaction, verbal and nonverbal communication, and markedly restricted repertoire of activities and interests. (Source: American Psychiatric Association. *Diagnostic and Statistical Manual of Mental Disorders*, Third Edition, Revised. Washington, D.C.: American Psychiatric Association, 1987.)
1. Dynamics/characteristics
a. Many theories have associated these disorders with faulty parenting, organic predisposition, and environmental factors.
b. Hallmark is language development delay.
c. Social interaction is impaired.
d. There are extreme self-isolation and an obsession with the preservation of sameness.
e. Thinking, affect, perception, and verbal communication are disturbed.
f. Patterns of feeding, elimination, and sleep are disturbed.
g. There is difficulty in evaluating reality.
h. Self-mutilative behaviors may occur.

2. Assessment
a. Assess developmental lag.
(1) No system of communication (verbal language is absent).
(2) No communication with the outside world.
(3) Self-stimulation by head banging, rocking, and various gaits.
b. Assess perceptual disturbances.
(1) Avoidance of eye contact and complex visual stimulation such as looking at people.
(2) Changes in visual perception.
c. Assess affect.
(1) Aloofness.
(2) Inappropriate expression of and reaction to fear (child does not fear real danger, but does fear less dangerous objects/situations).
(3) Bizarre thoughts and fantasies.
(4) Preoccupation with morbid thoughts.
(5) Extreme emotional outburst when frustrated, afraid, or subjected to a change.
d. Assess interpersonal relations with others.
(1) Smile response remains a reflex.
(2) Solitary activities are preferred.
(3) There is lack of response to expressions of warmth, such as cuddling and comforting.
(4) Child prefers to relate to inanimate objects.
(5) Child lacks awareness of the feelings of others.
e. Assess play.
(1) Child shows extreme fascination with toys that sparkle or spin, and those that are smooth and shiny.
(2) Child plays with the same toy or object consistently.
3. Patient care management
a. Psychotherapy: individual, group, or family.
b. Selective use of major tranquilizers for agitation.
c. Milieu therapy: environmental manipulation, hospitalization, and residential care.
d. Behavior modification: operant conditioning.

4. Family health promotion
   a. Parenting education programs.
   b. Family counseling.
   c. Genetic counseling.
5. Nursing diagnoses/goals/interventions
   a. Self-care deficit: feeding, bathing and hygiene, dressing and grooming, toileting related to perceptual impairment
      Goals:
      (1) Child will develop self-care abilities needed for daily living.
      (2) Child will maintain self-care abilities as new adaptive skills are added.
      Interventions:
      (1) Determine the child's present functional level of performance in activities of daily living.
      (2) Involve the family in setting goals and planning care.
      (3) Allow the child to participate actively in his/her own care (eating, dressing, toileting).
      (4) Provide a safe environment.
      (5) Provide adequate nutrition and fluid intake.
      (6) Acknowledge any beginning efforts toward self-care.
      (7) Provide emotional support for the family in dealing with their guilt, ambivalence, and other associated feelings concerning the child.
      (8) Move toward the child slowly and gradually. Assist the child to learn skills of activities of daily living at his/her own pace and tolerance.
   b. Impaired verbal communication related to multiple physiological and psychological barriers
      Goal: Child will be able to use verbal language (sounds or words) to reflect interaction with another human being.
      Interventions:
      (1) Repeat the sounds or words that the child attempts to say.
      (2) Start with simple words.
      (3) If no verbal language exists at the time, use sign language to establish beginning communication.
      (4) Make every effort to clarify the message the child conveys.
      (5) Acknowledge any effort toward establishment of verbal communication with another individual.
      (6) Assist family members in all their efforts toward development of verbal communication with the child.
   c. Potential for injury related to visual and perceptual impairment
      Goal: Child will be free from injuries due to self-mutilating patterns of behavior.
      Interventions:
      (1) Determine situations that precipitate self-mutilating patterns of behavior.
      (2) Observe the child for increased restlessness, agitated behavior, and other symptoms.
      (3) Provide a safe environment.
      (4) Use protective devices (such as a helmet to prevent head trauma when there is a tendency for head banging).
      (5) Avoid the use of physical restraints if possible.
      (6) Assist family members in understanding and/or coping with the child's behavior.
      (7) Provide sources of comfort for the child, such as a favorite toy or pillow.
      (8) Provide for adequate rest and sleep.
      (9) Consistently observe the child for any signs of pain or injury (the child may not be able to verbalize feelings associated with them.)
   d. Impaired social interaction related to various dysfunctional patterns of behavior
      Goals:
      (1) Child will be able to establish and tolerate human contact.
      (2) Family will be able to demonstrate ability to interact with the child effectively.
      Interventions:
      (1) Involve the family in setting goals and planning care.
      (2) Help establish meaningful interpersonal relationships (start with brief eye contact with any favorite object).
      (3) Use rewards to reinforce attempts at contact.
      (4) Move toward the child's solitude slowly and gradually.

(5) Use gentle touch when the child is ready and can tolerate it.

(6) Be consistent in approach in order to lessen anxiety-provoking situations.

(7) Have familiar objects and toys around to reduce stress of an unfamiliar environment.

e. Alteration in parenting related to probable inability to accept the autistic child's behavior patterns

Goals:

(1) Family members will be able to identify sources of anger, guilt, and resentment in relation to the child's problem.

(2) Family members will be able to express feelings about the child's condition openly within the family setting.

(3) Family members will be able to accept the treatment plan for the child with the problem.

(4) Family members will be able to assist in the treatment program.

Interventions:

(1) Provide role modeling.

(2) Give supportive counseling to assist family members to accept the child's problem.

(3) Provide the parents with information about the growth and developmental tasks expected of their child at specific ages to help them form realistic expectations.

(4) Explain the treatment plan.

(5) Assist the parents in exploring alternatives open to them in dealing with the problems associated with the autistic child.

(6) Provide genetic counseling.

(7) Assist the parents in expressing their feelings about their child's behavior (e.g., family meetings).

6. Evaluation

a. Child is able to perform activities of daily living consistent with his/her developmental level.

b. Child learns new adaptive skills.

c. Child interacts with other human beings, using verbal language.

d. Child is able to tolerate human contact.

e. Family is able to relate to the child accordingly.

f. Child is free from injury.

g. Family members are able to establish and maintain coping patterns in dealing with the child's problem.

h. Family is able to participate actively in the treatment program.

UNIT THREE

Meeting the Needs of the Toddler

(12 to 36 months)

STUDY GUIDE

DEVELOPMENTAL MILESTONES

A. Physical Growth
B. Gross Motor Development
C. Fine Motor Development
D. Language Development
E. Personal-Social Development
F. Freud's Psychosexual Theory of Development
G. Erikson's Psychosocial Theory of Development
H. Piaget's Theory of Cognitive Development
I. Play

HEALTH PROMOTION OF THE TODDLER

A. Physiological Needs
B. Safety and Security Needs

THE TODDLER AND THE CRISIS OF HOSPITALIZATION

A. Assessment of Separation Anxiety
B. Nursing Care Plan for the Hospitalized Toddler

ALTERATIONS OF HEALTH DURING TODDLERHOOD

Respiratory and Ear Conditions

A. Upper Airway Obstructions
   1. Laryngotracheobronchitis (croup)
   2. Acute epiglottitis

B. Lower Airway Obstructions
   1. Acute bronchiolitis
   2. Asthma
   3. Pneumonia
C. Patient Care Management of Respiratory Conditions
D. Nursing Care Plan for Respiratory Conditions
E. Otitis Media

Accidents

A. Poisoning
   1. Principles of emergency patient care management
   2. Salicylate poisoning
   3. Lead poisoning
B. Burns
C. Fracture of the Femur

Other Alterations of Health

A. Nephrotic Syndrome
B. Cerebral Palsy

DEVELOPMENTAL MILESTONES

A. Physical Growth
  1. Weight gain during this period is 4 to 6 pounds per year.
  2. Height gain during this period is 4 to 5 inches per year.
  3. The average pulse rate is 100 per minute.
  4. The average respiration rate is 26 per minute.
  5. The anterior fontanel closes at 18 months.
  6. Bowel control is achieved at 18 months.
  7. Daytime bladder control is achieved by 24 months.
  8. Nighttime bladder control is achieved by 3 years.

B. Gross Motor Development
  1. Fifteen months
     a. Walks without assistance.
     b. Creeps up stairs.
  2. Eighteen months
     a. Walks up stairs with one hand held.
     b. Runs clumsily.
     c. Jumps in place.
     d. Pulls a toy behind him/her.
  3. Twenty-four months
     a. Climbs up and down stairs alone with both feet on each step.
     b. Walks sideways and backwards.
     c. Runs fairly well.
     d. Can kick a ball.
  4. Thirty months
     a. Stands on one foot momentarily.
     b. Walks on tiptoe.

C. Fine Motor Development
  1. Fifteen months
     a. Builds tower of two blocks.
     b. Scribbles spontaneously.
     c. Opens boxes.
     d. Uses a cup well.
  2. Eighteen months
     a. Turns pages in a book.
     b. Builds tower of three or four blocks.
     c. Manages a spoon.
  3. Twenty-four months
     a. Builds a tower of six to seven blocks.
     b. Copies vertical and circular strokes.
     c. Turns doorknobs.
     d. Unscrews a lid.
     e. Cuts with scissors.
  4. Thirty months
     a. Builds a tower of eight blocks.
     b. Copies a cross.

D. Language Development
  1. Fifteen months
     a. Uses expressive jargon.
     b. Says four to six words.
     c. Indicates needs by pointing.
     d. Uses "no" even if he/she is agreeable (negativism).
  2. Eighteen months
     a. Says ten or more words.
     b. Names one or two body parts.
  3. Twenty-four months
     a. Has a vocabulary of about 300 words.
     b. Uses two- or three-word phrases.
     c. Uses pronouns.
     d. Obeys simple commands.
  4. Thirty months
     a. Gives first and last name.
     b. Uses plurals.
     c. Names one color.

E. Personal-Social Development
  1. Fifteen months
     a. Tolerates some separation from mother.
     b. Imitates parents.
     c. May have temper tantrums.
     d. May give up bottle.
  2. Eighteen months
     a. Beginning awareness of ownership ("mine").
     b. May develop dependency on security objects.
     c. Reaches the thumbsucking peak.
     d. Is beginning to test limits.
  3. Twenty-four months
     a. Shows increased independence from mother.
     b. Has fewer temper tantrums.
     c. May have an imaginary playmate.
     d. Helps to undress self.
     e. Does not know right from wrong.
     f. Considers rituals and consistency in routines important.
  4. Thirty months
     a. Shows a peak in ritualistic behavior.
     b. Displays continuing negativism.
     c. Notices sex differences.

F. Freud's Psychosexual Theory of Development
  1. The toddler is in the anal stage of development.
  2. The reality principle begins to operate.
  3. The id and ego are clear-cut divisions.
  4. The toddler gains control of the environment by mastering his/her own impulses.
  5. The toddler receives pleasure from "holding on" and "letting go."

G. Erikson's Psychosocial Theory of Development
  1. The toddler is developing a sense of autonomy versus shame and doubt.
  2. The toddler learns to accept interferences with his/her wishes as the mother begins to place demands on the child.
    a. Toilet training.
    b. Limit setting.
  3. The toddler becomes very ambivalent toward his/her mother.
  4. Temper tantrums, negativism, and ritualistic behavior help the toddler cope with increasing demands.
  5. The goal of this stage is development of self-control.
H. Piaget's Theory of Cognitive Development
  1. The sensorimotor stage of development continues.
  2. Two substages occur during toddlerhood.
    a. Tertiary circular reactions (13 to 18 months)
      (1) Becomes capable of more complex problem solving.
      (2) Utilizes trial and error.
      (3) Varies an action to observe variation in outcome.
      (4) Begins to be aware of spatial, temporal, and causal relationships.
    b. Invention of new means through mental combinations (19 to 24 months)
      (1) Begins to use mental imagery.
      (2) Achieves object constancy.
      (3) Achieves global organization of thought.
  3. The preconceptual stage of development begins at 2 years of age.
I. Play
  1. Predominance of parallel play.
  2. Purposes of play during toddlerhood
    a. Continued motor development.
    b. Outlet for surplus energy.
    c. Beginning social interaction with other children (plays alongside, not with, another child).
    d. Beginning of the development of moral values.
    e. Learning colors, shapes, sizes, and textures.
  3. Suggested toys and activities
    a. Push and pull toys.
    b. Blocks of different sizes and shapes.
    c. Simple puzzles and take-apart and put-together toys.
    d. Telephones.
    e. Toys that can be pounded.
    f. Dolls and toys to play house, such as dishes and cooking utensils.
    g. Clay, large crayons, and finger paints.
    h. Simple musical instruments.
    i. A low tricycle.
    j. Wagons and trucks.
    k. Listening to stories and looking at picture books.

HEALTH PROMOTION OF THE TODDLER

A. Physiological Needs
  1. Daily care
    a. Be aware that the need for sleep decreases.
    b. Recognize that the toddler is ritualistic in the activities of daily living.
    c. Provide opportunities for fresh air and exercise.
    d. Promote elimination.
      (1) Begin toilet training after voluntary control of anal and urinary sphincters is achieved.
      (2) Realize that the child must be able to communicate the need to void or defecate.
  2. Nutrition
    a. Eats regular table food by 18 months of age.
    b. Has definite likes and dislikes.
    c. Enjoys self-feeding.
    d. Requires less food per unit of body weight.
    e. Is more interested in exploring his/her environment than in eating, so that a "physiological anorexia" results.
B. Safety and Security Needs
  1. Prevention of accidents
    a. Be alert to avoid the major types of accidents during the toddler years: motor vehicle accidents, drowning, burns, poisoning, falls, and aspiration of foreign bodies.
    b. Assist parents in providing age-appropriate discipline and limit setting.
      (1) Protect the child from injury during temper tantrums.
      (2) Ignore attention-seeking behavior.

2. Health maintenance
    a. Physical examinations are done every 2 months during the second year and every 6 months thereafter.
    b. Dental examinations should begin after all 20 deciduous teeth are present.
    c. Measles, rubella, and mumps immunizations are administered at 15 months.
    d. *Hemophilus influenzae* type b vaccine is given at 15 months.
    e. Diphtheria-tetanus-pertussis and oral trivalent polio boosters are given at 18 months.

THE TODDLER AND THE CRISIS OF HOSPITALIZATION

A. Assessment of Separation Anxiety
    1. The toddler perceives separation as punishment and abandonment.
    2. There are three stages of separation anxiety.
        a. Protest
            (1) The toddler is grief stricken.
            (2) The toddler cries constantly for his/her mother and rejects overtures by staff members.
        b. Despair
            (1) The toddler mourns for his/her mother.
            (2) The toddler is depressed, withdrawn, and passive.
            (3) Regressive behaviors may occur.
        c. Denial
            (1) The toddler has repressed the image of his/her mother.
            (2) The toddler interacts superficially with his/her environment, becomes more egocentric, and may become attached to material objects.
B. Nursing Care Plan for the Hospitalized Toddler
    1. Nursing diagnosis/goal/interventions
    Ineffective individual coping related to the situational crisis of hospitalization.
    Goal: Toddler will experience minimal separation anxiety during hospitalization.
    Interventions:
        a. Encourage parents to visit frequently or to room-in.
        b. Assign one nurse to consistently care for the child.
        c. Reassure the child that the parents will return and that he/she will be going home in the future.
        d. Allow the child to have objects from home.
        e. Provide opportunities for play.
        f. Maintain the child's routines and rituals.
        g. Allow the child to participate in activities of daily living.
        h. Give simple explanations just before interventions.
        i. Explain time in relation to ward activities.
        j. Prepare the parents for the possibility of continued regressive behavior after discharge.
    2. Evaluation
        a. Toddler's separation anxiety is minimal.
        b. Development of a sense of autonomy is not interrupted.

ALTERATIONS OF HEALTH DURING TODDLERHOOD

Respiratory and Ear Conditions

A. Upper Airway Obstructions
    1. **Laryngotracheobronchitis (croup)** A viral infection of the larynx, trachea, and bronchi that causes edema, inflammation, and laryngeal obstruction.
    Assessment
        a. Assess for inspiratory stridor, a loose, croupy cough, hoarseness, and aphonia.
        b. Observe for flaring nostrils.
        c. Inspect for retractions in the suprasternal, substernal, and subcostal areas on inspiration.
        d. Observe for increased respiratory distress: increased respiratory and pulse rates, cyanosis, and restlessness.
    2. **Acute epiglottitis** A rapidly progressive inflammation of the epiglottis and surrounding areas, usually attributed to *Hemophilus influenzae*.

    Assessment
        a. Observe for rapidly increasing respiratory distress.
        b. Assess for inspiratory stridor and sternal retractions.
        c. Inspect for difficulty in swallowing, drooling, and the tripod sign.
        d. Assess for high temperature.

B. Lower Airway Obstructions
1. **Acute bronchiolitis** Inflammation and edema of the bronchiole mucosa that obstruct the air passages, preventing normal gaseous exchange; caused primarily by respiratory syncytial virus.
   Assessment
   a. Observe for rapid respirations, wheezing, expiratory stridor, and suprasternum, subcostal, and intercostal retractions.
   b. Assess for a dry, persistent cough.
   c. Inspect for cyanosis.
   d. Assess for a low-grade temperature.
2. **Asthma** Obstruction of the bronchioles by spasms, edema of the mucosa, and tenacious mucus precipitated by an allergic reponse.
   Assessment
   a. Observe for dyspnea, wheezing, and retractions on expiration.
   b. Assess for a productive cough.
   c. Inspect for profuse perspiration and dilated neck veins.
   d. Observe for increased respiratory distress: increased pulse rate, cyanosis, and restlessness.
3. **Pneumonia** An infection of portions of the lung that prevents adequate gaseous exchange because the alveoli are filled with inflammatory exudate. The primary causative agents are respiratory syncytial viruses, *Pneumococcus, Streptococcus,* and *Staphylococcus.*
   Assessment
   a. Assess for high temperature.
   b. In the early stages, assess for a dry, persistent cough.
   c. In the later stages, assess for a loose, productive cough.
   d. Inspect for shallow respirations and retractions in the subcostal and sternal areas.
   e. Determine whether chest pain is present.
   f. Inspect for pallor and cyanosis.
   g. Palpate for increased pulse rate.
   h. Observe for gastrointestinal manifestations: anorexia, abdominal pain, vomiting, constipation, or diarrhea.
   i. Auscultate breath sounds.

C. Patient Care Management of Respiratory Conditions
1. Maintenance of a patent airway and promotion of gaseous exchange.
   a. Nasotracheal intubation or tracheostomy may be needed to alleviate an upper airway obstruction.
   b. Oxygen and increased humidity are needed.
2. Broad-spectrum antibiotics to treat infections.
3. Corticosteroids to reduce inflammation and/or edema.
4. Intravenous therapy to prevent dehydration.
5. Nothing by mouth, to prevent aspiration, progressing to clear liquids as tolerated.
6. Antipyretics to reduce temperature.
7. Bronchodilators to treat asthma.
8. Removal of the offending allergens to prevent future asthma attacks: hypoallergenic diet, environmental modification, desensitization to known allergens.

D. Nursing Care Plan for Respiratory Conditions
1. Nursing diagnoses/goals/interventions
   a. Ineffective airway clearance related to edema, inflammation, and/or increased secretion of mucus
      Goal: Toddler will have a patent airway, clear breath sounds, and age-appropriate respiratory rate before discharge.
      Interventions:
      (1) Assess for signs of increasing respiratory distress.
      (2) Place a cardiorespiratory monitor on the child when appropriate.
      (3) Provide oxygen and humidity as ordered.
      (4) Observe oxygen safety precautions.
      (5) Assess the oxygen concentration level.
      (6) Keep the child warm and dry in the mist tent.
      (7) Provide nasotracheal tube or tracheostomy care when needed.
      (8) Place the child in a semi-Fowler's position.
      (9) Remove retained secretions.
          (a) Encourage coughing and deep breathing.
          (b) Change the child's position every 2 hours.
          (c) Carry out postural drainage with percussion and vibration.
          (d) Suction as necessary.

b. Risk for fluid volume deficit related to increased insensible water loss associated with tachypnea
Goal: Toddler will tolerate age-appropriate fluid volume intake and diet.
Interventions:
(1) Measure intake and output.
(2) Monitor IV therapy.
(3) Maintain NPO or provide fluids by mouth as prescribed.
(4) Monitor urine specific gravity.
(5) Weigh the child daily.

c. Risk for altered body temperature related to infectious processes
Goal: Toddler will be afebrile.
Interventions:
(1) Give tepid sponge baths.
(2) Administer antipyretics as ordered.

d. Anxiety related to respiratory distress and an unfamiliar environment
Goal: Toddler and parents will experience a nonstressful environment.
Interventions:
(1) Stay with the child when he/she is in acute distress.
(2) Provide periods of uninterrupted rest to conserve energy for respirations.
(3) Allow the parents and the child to express their feelings and concerns.
(4) Explain all procedures in simple terms.

2. Evaluation
a. Child has no signs of respiratory distress.
b. Child has no signs of dehydration.
c. Child's temperature is within normal limits.
d. Child's and parents' anxiety is minimized.

E. **Otitis Media** A bacterial infection of the middle ear common in small children because of a shorter, wider, and straighter eustachian tube.
1. Assessment
a. Otoscope examination reveals a red and bulging tympanic membrane, no visible bony landmarks, and an absence of the light reflex.
b. Assess for pain by observing whether the child pulls his/her ear or moves the head continually from side to side.
c. Inspect for purulent drainage in the external auditory canal.

d. Assess for elevated temperature and possible febrile convulsions.
e. Observe for signs of upper respiratory infections and gastrointestinal discomfort, such as vomiting, diarrhea, or anorexia.

2. Patient care management
a. Antibiotics, usually amoxicillin or ampicillin.
b. Tylenol to reduce temperature and alleviate pain.
c. Decongestants to shrink the mucous membranes and provide drainage for the blocked eustachian tube.
d. For some children, a myringotomy to prevent permanent hearing loss.

3. Nursing diagnoses/goals/interventions
a. Pain related to inflammatory process
Goal: Toddler will verbalize a reduction of pain.
Interventions:
(1) Position the child on the affected side.
(2) Apply local heat or cool compresses.
(3) Administer analgesics as ordered.

b. Risk for altered body temperature related to infectious processes
Goal: Toddler will be afebrile.
Interventions:
(1) Encourage fluids.
(2) Administer a tepid sponge bath.
(3) Administer antipyretics and antibiotics as ordered.

c. Risk for impaired skin integrity related to the presence of ear drainage
Goal: Toddler's skin around the ear and pinna will remain intact.
Interventions:
(1) Frequently clean the skin around the ear and pinna.
(2) Apply a bland ointment.
(3) When cleansing the ear, pull the ear lobe down and back in children under 3 years of age and up and back in older children.

4. Evaluation
a. Child is free of pain.
b. Child's temperature is within normal limits.
c. Skin around the ear and pinna is intact.

Accidents

A. Poisoning
  1. Principles of emergency patient care management
     a. Identify the type and quantity of the ingested substance.
     b. Contact the local Poison Control Center for assistance.
     c. Remove the poison from the system.
        (1) Induce vomiting.
            (a) Administer syrup of ipecac.
            (b) Have the child drink milk or water, and then stimulate the posterior pharynx.
        (2) Administer gastric lavage.
     d. Neutralize the poison by administering the appropriate antidote.
     e. Be aware that inducing vomiting is contraindicated when the child is comatose or when corrosive agents have been ingested.
     f. If a corrosive agent has been ingested, neutralize the poison with water.
  2. Salicylate poisoning
     a. Assessment
        (1) Observe for hyperventilation and signs of respiratory alkalosis.
        (2) Assess for hyperpyrexia and profuse perspiration.
        (3) Assess for anorexia and vomiting.
        (4) Observe for signs of dehydration, electrolyte imbalance, and metabolic acidosis.
        (5) Inspect for purpuric manifestations.
     b. Patient care management
        (1) Induce vomiting.
        (2) Administer gastric lavage.
        (3) After lavage, give activated charcoal to decrease salicylate absorption and a cathartic to promote gastrointestinal transit.
        (4) Apply IV therapy to correct fluid and electrolyte disturbances.
        (5) Administer infusion of sodium bicarbonate to facilitate salicylate excretion.
        (6) Reduce temperature with tepid sponge baths or a hypothermia blanket (if ordered).
        (7) Give vitamin K to decrease bleeding tendencies.
     c. Nursing diagnoses/goals/interventions
        (1) Fluid volume deficit related to toxic absorption of salicylate
            Goal: Toddler will show no signs of fluid or electrolyte imbalance.
            Interventions:
            (a) Assess for signs of dehydration.
            (b) Monitor IV fluids.
            (c) Measure intake and output.
            (d) Weigh the child daily.
            (e) Check urine specific gravity.
        (2) Impaired gas exchange related to respiratory alkalosis and metabolic acidosis
            Goal: Toddler will show no signs of acid-base imbalance.
            Interventions:
            (a) Assess for, and report promptly to the physician, signs of acid-base imbalance.
            (b) Take vital signs frequently.
            (c) Monitor blood gases and pH.
        (3) Risk for altered body temperature related to increased metabolic rate
            Goal: Toddler will be afebrile.
            Interventions:
            (a) Administer tepid sponge bath.
            (b) Utilize a hypothermia blanket if prescribed.
            (c) Do not administer antipyretics.
        (4) Knowledge deficit related to prevention of accidental poisoning
            Goal: Parents will understand methods to prevent future accidental poisoning.
            Interventions:
            (a) Review the circumstances of the ingestion and how it can be prevented in the future.
            (b) Discuss the child's developmental characteristics and the ways in which they contribute to increased risk of accidental poisoning.
            (c) Review the appropriate storage of medications.
     d. Evaluation
        (1) Child shows no signs of fluid, electrolyte, or acid-base imbalance.
        (2) Child's temperature is within normal limits.
        (3) Parents understand methods to prevent future accidental poisoning.

3. Lead poisoning
   a. Assessment
      (1) Determine the child's pica pattern.
      (2) Determine possible sources of lead in the child's environment.
      (3) Observe for signs of anemia.
      (4) Observe for signs of central nervous system involvement: peripheral neuritis and convulsions.
      (5) Assess for developmental lag, as mental retardation is a possible outcome of lead poisoning.
      (6) Observe for gastrointestinal complaints: anorexia, vomiting, abdominal pain, and constipation.
      (7) Observe for changes in behavioral patterns: hyperactivity, irritability, lethargy, shortened attention span, and learning difficulties.
      (8) DIAGNOSTIC MEASURES: increased blood lead levels, increased erythrocyte protoporphyrin, and "lead lines" in the long bones.
   b. Patient care management
      (1) Promote urinary excretion of lead by utilizing chelating agents: calcium disodium edetate (EDTA), dimercaprol (BAL), intramuscularly or intravenously.
      (2) Provide IV fluids to promote urinary excretion of lead in conjunction with chelation therapy.
      (3) Restrict fluids if encephalopathy is present.
   c. Nursing diagnoses/goals/interventions
      (1) Altered growth and development related to lead toxicity
          Goal: Toddler's blood lead level will be below toxicity.
          Interventions:
          (a) Administer chelating agents as ordered.
          (b) Assess for nephrotoxicity, which is a side effect of chelation therapy.
          (c) Increase fluid intake.
          (d) Measure intake and output.
      (2) Pain related to repeated injections of chelating agents
          Goal: Toddler will experience minimal discomfort.

          Interventions:
          (a) Administer local anesthetics with chelating agents to decrease pain as prescribed.
          (b) Rotate sites.
          (c) Use warm soaks or baths.
          (d) Provide opportunities for play therapy.
      (3) Risk for injury related to exposure to an environment containing lead
          Goal: Parents verbalize and demonstrate understanding of the prevention of lead poisoning.
          Interventions:
          (a) Discuss the causality and complications of lead poisoning.
          (b) Suggest ways in which the parents can remove lead from the child's environment.
          (c) Teach the parents the importance of follow-up developmental assessments.
   d. Evaluation
      (1) Child's blood lead is below toxic level.
      (2) Child experiences minimal discomfort related to the medical treatment.
      (3) Parents understand how to prevent further exposure to lead.

B. Burns
   1. **Degrees**
      a. A first-degree or superficial burn involves the stratum corneum layer of the epidermis. It appears reddened, blanches with pressure, and is painful.
      b. A second-degree burn is a partial-thickness burn involving all epidermal layers and at times the dermis. It appears blistered, reddened, or pale ivory and is extremely painful.
      c. A third-degree or full-thickness burn involves all skin layers and various underlying structures. It appears dry, pale white, charred, or reddened, and marked edema is present. There is no pain as nerve endings are destroyed.

2. Assessment
   a. Determine the depth of the burn injury and the percentage of body surface involved.
   b. Observe for signs of shock: increased pulse and respirations, decreased blood pressure, restlessness, cool skin, extreme thirst, and decreased urine output.
   c. Observe for signs of dehydration and electrolyte imbalance.
   d. Observe for signs of respiratory distress: hoarseness, dry cough, moist rales, dyspnea, wheezing, and stridor.
   e. Inspect for signs of wound infection.
3. Patient care management
   a. First-aid treatment.
      (1) Put out flames by rolling the child in a blanket.
      (2) Immerse the burned part in cold water.
      (3) Remove burned clothing.
      (4) Cover the burn with a dry sterile dressing.
   b. A booster dose of tetanus toxoid.
   c. Relief of pain with an intravenous analgesic such as morphine sulfate.
   d. Prevention of shock and of fluid and electrolyte imbalance.
      (1) Colloids to expand the blood volume.
      (2) Isotonic saline to replace electrolytes.
      (3) Dextrose and water to provide calories.
   e. Maintenance of a patent airway.
      (1) Oxygen, humidity, and suction as necessary.
      (2) Endotracheal intubation.
      (3) Tracheostomy to relieve upper airway obstruction.
   f. Prevention of wound infection.
      (1) Cleaning and debriding of the wound.
      (2) Open or closed method of wound care.
      (3) Whirlpool therapy.
      (4) Application of topical agents: silver nitrate; mafenide acetate (Sulfamylon); silver sulfadiazine (Silvadene); gentamicin sulfate (Garamycin); povidone-iodine (Betadine).
      (5) Antibiotics.
   g. Skin grafting.
   h. A high-calorie, high-protein diet.

4. Nursing diagnoses/goals/interventions
   a. Ineffective breathing pattern related to upper airway edema secondary to burns of face, neck, or chest and/or smoke inhalation
      Goal: Toddler will maintain a patent airway.
      Interventions:
      (1) Frequently assess for signs of respiratory distress.
      (2) Administer oxygen and humidity as ordered.
      (3) Suction gently as necessary.
      (4) Have tracheostomy and/or intubation equipment present at the bedside.
      (5) Position the child in a semi-Fowler's position.
      (6) Encourage coughing and deep breathing every 2 hours.
   b. Risk for fluid volume deficit related to shift of intravascular fluid to interstitial spaces
      Goal: Toddler will remain hydrated and will show no signs of shock or electrolyte imbalance.
      Interventions:
      (1) Take vital signs frequently.
      (2) Maintain IV therapy.
      (3) Measure intake and output.
      (4) Weigh the child daily.
      (5) Monitor specific gravity of urine.
   c. Risk for infection related to tissue damage
      Goal: Toddler will remain afebrile.
      Interventions:
      (1) Assess for signs of infection.
      (2) Utilize specified isolation techniques.
      (3) Change dressings utilizing strict sterile technique.
      (4) Apply topical antibacterial ointments.
      (5) Assess for side effects of topical ointments.
      (6) Culture wound if infection is suspected.
      (7) Administer prescribed antibiotics.
   d. Pain related to tissue damage
      Goal: Toddler will experience minimal amount of pain.
      Interventions:
      (1) Provide diversional activity.
      (2) Administer analgesics as ordered.

e. Altered nutrition: less than body requirements related to increased need for calories and protein to promote healing
Goal: Toddler's nutritional intake will support healing.
Interventions:
(1) Determine the child's likes and dislikes.
(2) Encourate intake of high-calorie, high-protein meals and snacks.
f. Impaired physical mobility related to contractures and muscle atrophy
Goal: Toddler will not develop contractures.
Interventions:
(1) Position the child in proper anatomical alignment.
(2) Perform active and passive range of motion exercises.
g. Body image disturbance related to burns and scar formation
Goal: Toddler will accept his/her altered body image.
Interventions:
(1) Allow child to express feelings and concerns.
(2) Provide opportunities for play therapy.
(3) Encourage participation in care.
5. Evaluation
a. Child has no signs of respiratory distress.
b. Child has no signs of dehydration, electrolyte imbalance, or shock.
c. Burn shows no evidence of infection.
d. Pain is minimized.
e. Child's weight is stable.
f. Child does not develop contractures.
g. Child accepts his/her altered body image.
C. Fracture of the Femur
1. Assessment
a. Assess the area for swelling, pain, alterations in color, and limited motion.
b. Palpate the pulse in the involved extremity.
2. Patient care management
a. First-aid treatment: immobilization with a splint and application of cold.
b. Analgesics to relieve pain.

c. Realignment of bony fragments.
(1) Skin or skeletal traction: Bryant, Buck extension, Russell, or 90-degree/90-degree traction.
(2) Casting.
d. Physical therapy to restore optimal functioning.
3. Nursing diagnosis/goal/interventions
Impaired physical mobility related to traction
Goal: Toddler's mobility of unaffected extremities will be maintained, and mobility of affected extremity will return to optimal level.
Interventions:
a. Maintain traction.
(1) Position the child in Bryant traction with both legs elevated at a 90-degree angle. The hips are flexed 20 degrees.
(2) Position the child in Buck extension with both legs and hips extended flat in the bed.
(3) Position the child in Russell traction with the hips flexed at a 20-degree angle. There is continuous pull from the knee to an overhead pulley, with weights attached at the foot of the bed.
(4) Position the child in 90-degree/90-degree traction with a 90-degree flexion of both the hip and the knee.
(5) Check for correct positioning of ropes, pulleys, and weights.
(6) Observe the pin sites for signs of infection.
(7) Maintain good anatomical alignment.
(8) Observe for any neurovascular changes in the extremity.
b. Prevent complications of immobility.
(1) Prevent skin breakdown.
(a) Change position every 2 hours.
(b) Massage the skin and bony prominences.
(c) Place a sheep skin or alternating pressure mattress under the child.
(2) Prevent respiratory infections.
(a) Encourage coughing and deep breathing.
(b) Encourage fluids.

(3) Maintain muscle integrity.
   (a) Utilize passive and active range of motion exercises.
   (b) Apply a foot plate to prevent foot drop.
(4) Maintain adequate nutrition.
   (a) Determine the child's likes and dislikes.
   (b) Provide small, frequent feedings.
(5) Promote elimination.
   (a) Increase fluids.
   (b) Increase dietary fiber.
4. Evaluation
   a. Child's fracture heals in proper alignment.
   b. Child experiences no complications of immobility.

Other Alterations of Health

A. **Nephrotic Syndrome** A symptom complex consisting of edema, proteinuria, hypo-albuminemia, and hyperlipidemia of unknown etiology.
There is an increased permeability of the basement membrane, which allows excretion of albumin into the urine. The serum albumin level is decreased. There is a decreased colloidal osmotic pressure in the capillaries, resulting in fluid accumulation in the extracellular spaces. The elevation of serum lipids is unexplained.
1. Assessment
   a. Inspect for periorbital edema, and edema of the extremities, genital area, and ascites.
   b. Assess for decreased urine output.
   c. Be aware that urine appears dark and foamy.
   d. Be aware that anorexia is present.
   e. Observe for signs of concurrent infection.
   f. Observe for respiratory difficulty, which may occur if ascites is present.
   g. DIAGNOSTIC MEASURES
      (1) Urinalysis reveals proteinuria and an increased specific gravity.
      (2) Total serum protein is reduced.
      (3) Serum cholesterol is elevated.
2. Patient care management
   a. Bedrest during the edematous phase.
   b. Corticosteroids, usually prednisone.
   c. Diuretics to decrease edema; increased potassium intake during diuretic therapy.
   d. Antibiotics to prevent infection.
   e. Regular diet with no added salt.

3. Nursing diagnoses/goals/interventions
   a. Risk for infection related to lowered body defenses
      Goal: Toddler will remain free of infection.
      Interventions:
      (1) Monitor temperature.
      (2) Avoid contact of child with individuals who have infections.
      (3) Administer antibiotics as ordered.
   b. Fluid volume excess related to decreased osmotic pressure
      Goal: Toddler will have decreased edema and increased urinary output with decreasing specific gravity, and will show no signs of dehydration.
      Interventions:
      (1) Measure intake and output.
      (2) Take vital signs.
      (3) Weigh the child daily.
      (4) Measure abdominal girth.
      (5) Monitor albumin and specific gravity at each voiding.
      (6) Administer steroids as ordered.
      (7) Observe for the side effects of steroids: Cushing's syndrome, hypertension, gastrointestinal bleeding, infections, bone demineralization, diabetes mellitus, and personality changes.
      (8) Elevate the child's head on a pillow to decrease periorbital edema.
      (9) Assist with parencentesis to remove fluid from the peritoneal cavity.
         (a) Have the child void before the procedure.
         (b) Monitor vital signs after the procedure.
   c. Altered nutrition: less than body requirements related to anorexia
      Goal: Toddler will consume adequate caloric intake to meet metabolic requirements.
      Interventions:
      (1) Assess the child's likes and dislikes.
      (2) Provide small, frequent feedings of the prescribed diet.
   d. Risk for impaired skin integrity related to edema
      Goal: Toddler's skin will remain intact.
      Interventions:
      (1) Reposition the child every 2 hours.
      (2) Gently massage the skin frequently.
      (3) Prevent skin surfaces from touching.

(4) Provide scrotal support for a male child.

(5) Place on a sheepskin and alternating air mattress.

e. Body image disturbance related to edema

Goal: Toddler's self-image will be maintained.

Interventions:

(1) Encourage the child to express his/her feelings and concerns.

(2) Provide opportunities for play therapy.

4. Evaluation
a. Child is free of infection.
b. Child's edema is reduced.
c. Child's weight remains constant.
d. Child's skin remains intact.
e. An optimal body image is maintained.

B. **Cerebral Palsy A nonprogressive disorder due to an abnormality in the pyramidal motor system, which results in an inability to control voluntary muscles.**

1. Types
a. Spastic: characterized by increased muscle tone. The child assumes a typical position with the legs scissored, the forearms flexed and held against the chest, and the fists clenched.
b. Dyskinetic: characterized by involuntary athetoid movements.
c. Ataxic: characterized by muscle incoordination and poor posture.

2. Assessment
a. Assess muscle tone, coordination, and posture.
b. Determine whether infantile reflexes are present.
c. Observe for delayed motor development.
d. Determine whether additional disabilities are present: seizures, mental retardation, and sensory deficits.

3. Patient care management
a. Promotion of optimal habilitation in the areas of locomotion, communication, and the activities of daily living.
b. Correction of associated disabilities.

4. Nursing diagnosis/goals/interventions
a. Impaired physical mobility related to lack of control of voluntary muscles

Goal: Toddler will participate in activities of daily living at an optimal level.

Interventions:

(1) Implement the prescribed exercise program.

(2) Apply brace when indicated.

(3) Provide daily skin care under the brace.

(4) Provide frequent rest periods, especially before exercises and meals.

(5) Avoid stress.

(6) Provide massage, warm baths, or soothing music.

b. Altered nutrition: less than body requirements related to increased energy expenditure

Goal: Toddler will ingest adequate nutrients to promote steady growth.

Interventions:

(1) Provide high-calorie meals and snacks.

(2) Be aware that, because of reversed wave motion of the tongue, food must be placed on the back of the tongue.

(3) Obtain special feeding implements when necessary.

c. Self-care deficit related to inability to carry out activities of daily living

Goal: Toddler will participate in activities of daily living.

Interventions:

(1) Maintain consistency in the child's habilitation program.

(2) Encourage participation in care as early as possible.

(3) Set realistic goals.

(4) Promote opportunities for play and for peer interaction.

d. Impaired communication: verbal related to neuromuscular impairment

Goal: Toddler will be able to communicate needs.

Interventions:

(1) Talk to the child slowly.

(2) Refer the child to a speech therapist.

e. Risk for altered parenting related to situational crisis of diagnosis of a child with a lifelong disability

Goal: Parents will demonstrate understanding of toddler's condition, and home care and follow-up.

Interventions:

(1) Allow the parents to verbalize feelings and concerns.

(2) Provide information on the treatment plan.

(3) Refer the parents to appropriate community resources.

5. Evaluation

a. Child participates in all activities of daily living at an optimal level.

b. Child ingests adequate nutrients to promote steady growth.

c. Child communicates his/her needs.

d. Parents understand their child's condition and habilitation program.

Meeting the Needs of the Preschooler

(3 to 5 years)

DEVELOPMENTAL MILESTONES

A. Physical Growth
   1. Weight gain is 4 to 5 pounds per year.
   2. Height gain is 2 to 3 inches per year.
   3. Average pulse rate is 95 per minute.
   4. Average respiration rate is 25 per minute.
   5. Average blood pressure is 90 systolic and 60 diastolic.
   6. Muscular coordination and strength improve.
   7. Handedness is established by 5 years of age.
B. Gross Motor Development
   1. Three years
      a. Rides a tricycle.
      b. Broad jumps.
      c. Walks backward.
      d. Walks upstairs, alternating the feet.
      e. Tries to dance.
   2. Four years
      a. Jumps and climbs well.
      b. Skips and hops on one foot.
      c. Catches a ball.
      d. Throws a ball overhand.
      e. Walks downstairs, alternating the feet.
   3. Five years
      a. Jumps rope.
      b. Skates with good balance.
C. Fine Motor Development
   1. Three years
      a. Builds a tower of nine to ten blocks.
      b. Copies a circle.
      c. Can string large beads.
      d. Can undress him-/herself.
      e. Helps dress him-/herself.
      f. Can go to the toilet without help.
      g. Can wash his/her hands.
      h. May be able to brush his/her teeth.
      i. Helps to do simple household chores.
   2. Four years
      a. Cuts out pictures.
      b. Copies a square.
      c. Adds three parts to a stick figure.
      d. Can lace shoes.
      e. Buttons front and side of clothes.
   3. Five years
      a. Copies a diamond and a triangle.
      b. Adds seven to nine parts to a stick figure.
      c. Prints a few numbers, letters, or words.
      d. Dresses self.
      e. Washes self without wetting clothes.
D. Language Development
   1. Three years
      a. Has a vocabulary of 900 words.
      b. Uses complete sentences of three to four words.
      c. Uses plurals in speech.
      d. Can repeat three numbers.
      e. Knows his/her family name.
      f. Sings simple songs.
      g. Constantly asks questions.
   2. Four years
      a. Has a 1500-word vocabulary.
      b. Uses sentences of four to five words.
      c. May use profanities or name calling.
      d. Tells exaggerated stories.
      e. Comprehends simple analogies.
      f. Can repeat four numbers.
      g. Is at a peak in regard to questioning.
   3. Five years
      a. Has a 2100-word vocabulary.
      b. Uses sentences of six to eight words.
      c. Uses all parts of speech.
      d. Asks questions that are more relevant.
E. Personal-Social Development
   1. Three years
      a. Knows own sex and the appropriate sex of others.
      b. Is aware of family relationships and sex-role functions.
      c. Plays simple games with others.
      d. Begins to understand what it means to take turns.
      e. May have fears of the dark and animals.
   2. Four years
      a. Is very independent.
      b. Takes pride in accomplishments.
      c. Can go on errands outside the home.
      d. Shows off, tattles, and boasts.
      e. Still has many fears.
      f. Identifies strongly with parent of the opposite sex.
   3. Five years
      a. Takes increased responsibility for actions.
      b. Is eager to please.
      c. Strongly identifies with parent of the same sex.

F. Freud's Psychosexual Theory of Development
1. The preschooler is in the Oedipal stage of development.
2. The focus of libidinal energy shifts to the genital zone.
3. The cathectic object is the parent of the opposite sex.
4. Boys experience the Oepidus complex.
   a. The boy competes with his father for his mother's love.
   b. He is competitive with his father and fears that his father will castrate him.
   c. Castration fear becomes overwhelming.
   d. The boy represses his love for his mother.
   e. He substitutes a strong identification with his father.
5. Girls experience the Electra complex.
   a. The girl concludes that she has been castrated.
   b. She holds her mother responsible.
   c. Hostility develops toward the mother.
   d. The father becomes her love object.
   e. She hopes to produce a baby to replace the lost penis.
   f. Because of guilt over her feelings, she represses her love for her father.
   g. She substitutes a strong identification with her mother.
6. The superego is formed.
7. Sexual curiosity and masturbation are evident.

G. Erikson's Psychosocial Theory of Development
1. The preschooler is developing a sense of initiative versus guilt.
2. The preschooler needs to feel a sense of accomplishment and satisfaction in his/her activities.
3. Preschoolers learn to cooperate with peers.
4. Parents of preschoolers must encourage their plans and the use of their imagination.
5. The preschooler should begin to share in family decision making.
6. Self-care should be encouraged.
7. The preschooler often attends nursery school.

8. Punishment should be limited to behaviors that are morally or socially unacceptable or are harmful.
9. A sense of guilt arises if the preschooler feels that he/she has not acted appropriately.

H. Piaget's Theory of Cognitive Development
1. The child aged 2 to 7 is in the preoperational stage of development.
2. The child is still egocentric and is totally dominated by his/her perceptions.
3. Ideas of cause and effect are rudimentary.
   a. There are three types of reasoning.
      (1) Syncretism: Several ideas are seen as one global mass.
      (2) Juxtaposition: The child states isolated ideas without determining relationships.
      (3) Transduction: The child goes from one idea to another, reaching a faulty conclusion.
   b. The child can think of only one idea at a time (centration).
   c. There are three concepts of the world.
      (1) Realism (sensorimotor): The child feels that he/she causes all things.
      (2) Animism: The child feels that actions are caused by inanimate objects.
      (3) Artificialism: The child feels that actions are controlled by a purposeful agent that controls the world.
4. The concept of conservation has not yet been developed.
5. The concept of time is rudimentary.
   a. The child may know days of the week and seasons of the year.
   b. The child does not fully understand "tomorrow" and "yesterday."

I. Play
1. Cooperative play, in which children share with others, begins.
2. Dramatic play, in which the child imitates the adults in his/her environment, predominates.
3. The rules of the group are loosely established.
4. Preschoolers play very actively, utilizing vivid imaginations.

5. The following is a list of suggested toys and playthings.
    a. Tricycles and wagons.
    b. Backyard gyms.
    c. Household items.
    d. Dress-up clothes.
    e. Transportation toys: cars, boats, trucks, and trains.
    f. Dolls, stuffed animals, and hand puppets.
    g. Doctor and nurse kits.
    h. Store-keeping toys.
    i. Pegboards.
    j. Blocks and simple construction sets.
    k. Farm animals.
    l. Simple carpentry tools.
    m. Puzzles.
    n. Musical toys.

HEALTH PROMOTION OF THE PRESCHOOLER

A. Physiological Needs
    1. Daily care
        a. The preschooler helps in self-care.
        b. Adequate rest should be provided at night.
        c. A daytime nap is no longer needed.
    2. Nutrition
        a. The child continues to require a decreased number of calories per unit of body weight.
        b. Preschoolers are influenced by the food habits of others.
        c. Meals need to be served in a quiet environment to prevent distractions.
        d. Table manners are learned by imitating adults.
        e. The child prefers plain food served attractively.
B. Safety and Security Needs
    1. Prevention of accidents
        a. Major types of accidents are similiar to those in the toddler period.
        b. More accidents occur away from home as the child becomes more independent.
        c. Children should be taught simple safety rules.
    2. Health maintenance
        a. Physical examinations are recommended every 6 months.
        b. Tests of auditory and visual perception are included.
    c. Dental care is important.
    d. Diphtheria-tetanus and polio boosters are given between the ages of 4 and 6 when the child is ready to enter school.

THE PRESCHOOLER AND THE CRISIS OF HOSPITALIZATION

A. Assessment of Behavioral Responses to Hospitalization
    1. Separation anxiety occurs but is less severe than at the toddler stage.
    2. The preschooler is confused as to why the parents cannot protect him/her from pain and discomfort.
    3. The preschooler views hospitalization as punishment.
    4. Fear of pain and of bodily mutilation is of primary concern.
    5. Regressive behaviors may occur.
B. Nursing Care Plan for the Hospitalized Preschooler
    1. Nursing diagnosis/goal/interventions
    Ineffective individual coping related to the situational crisis of hospitalization
    Goal: Child will experience minimum separation anxiety and fear during hospitalization.
    Interventions:
        a. Encourage parental visiting or rooming-in.
        b. Assign one nurse to consistently care for the child.
        c. Maintain the child's routines.
        d. Allow the child to have objects from home.
        e. Reassure the child that he/she is not being punished.
        f. Provide opportunities for the child to verbalize his/her fantasies.
        g. Provide opportunities for play therapy.
            (1) Allows the nurse to assess the child's perceptions of the hospital environment.
            (2) Serves as a method to prepare the child for hospital procedures.
            (3) Allows the child an outlet for his/her feelings after a procedure.
        h. Prepare the child for procedures.
            (1) Use simple terms that the child will understand.

(2) Tell the child what is to occur and how he/she will feel during the procedure.

(3) Promote a sense of initiative by telling the child how he/she can help during the procedure.

2. Evaluation
   a. The preschooler's separation anxiety is minimal.
   b. Development of a sense of initiative is not interrupted.

ALTERATIONS OF HEALTH DURING THE PRESCHOOL YEARS

Disorders of the Urinary Tract and Kidneys

A. **Urinary Tract Infection** A bacterial infection (usually due to *Escherichia coli*) that causes inflammatory changes in one or more areas of the urinary tract.
   1. Assessment
      a. A high fever may be the presenting symptom.
      b. The child may experience urinary frequency, urgency, dysuria, urinary retention, or enuresis.
      c. Pain may occur in the lower abdomen or in the lower back.
      d. DIAGNOSTIC MEASURES
         (1) Culture and sensitivity of urine are done to identify the causative organism.
         (2) A urinalysis will demonstrate cloudy, alkaline urine with a foul odor, a decrease in specific gravity, and an increase in white blood cells.
         (3) Proteinuria or hematuria may be present.
         (4) Ultrasonography, a voiding cystourethrogram, or an intravenous pyelogram may be done to rule out an obstruction of the urinary tract.
   2. Patient care management
      a. Correction of any underlying abnormalities.
      b. Increased fluid intake.
      c. Antibiotics, sulfonamides, or urinary tract antiseptics.
      d. Antipyretics to reduce fever.

3. Nursing diagnoses/goals/interventions
   a. Altered urinary elimination related to presence of infection in the urinary tract
      Goal: Child will exhibit no signs of urinary tract infection.
      Interventions:
      (1) Encourage the child to increase his/her fluid intake.
      (2) Offer the child acidic juices.
      (3) Measure intake and output.
      (4) Continue to note character of urine.
      (5) Promote rest during the febrile stage.
      (6) Administer antibiotics, sulfonamides, or urinary tract antiseptics as ordered.
   b. Knowledge deficit related to the disease process and preventive measures
      Goal: Parents will verbalize an understanding of the disease process and the possibility of recurrence.
      Interventions:
      (1) Review signs of urinary tract infection.
      (2) Teach proper perineal hygiene measures.
      (3) Encourage the child to void every 4 hours.
      (4) Have the child wear cotton underpants.
      (5) Have the child avoid bubblebaths.
      (6) Have the child maintain an adequate fluid intake.
4. Evaluation
   a. Child shows no signs of urinary tract infection.
   b. Urinalysis is within normal limits.
   c. Parents understand strategies for preventing recurrence.

B. **Acute Glomerulonephritis** An antigen-antibody response to group A beta hemolytic *Streptococcus*.
   The child has a streptococcal infection, usually pharyngitis or impetigo. There is a latent period of 10 to 14 days before the onset of symptoms. The antigen-antibody reaction to the organism results in inflammatory changes in the glomerular capillary loops and the basement membrane. Because of capillary damage, the glomerular filtration rate is reduced and there is retention of water and sodium. Vascular and tubular changes are mild. Blood, protein, and cells are excreted in the urine.

1. Assessment
   a. Observe for hematuria and a decreased urine output.
   b. Inspect for periorbital edema and edema of the extremities.
   c. Assess for anorexia, vomiting, malaise, and headache.
   d. Assess for hypertension.
   e. Observe for complications: hypertensive encephalopathy, congestive heart failure, and renal failure.
   f. DIAGNOSTIC MEASURES
      (1) Urinalysis demonstrates hematuria, proteinuria, increased specific gravity, red blood cells, white blood cells, epithelial cells, and casts.
      (2) Blood urea, nitrogen, and creatinine are elevated.
      (3) Antistreptolysin O titer is positive.
      (4) Erythrocyte sedimentation rate is elevated.
2. Patient care management
   a. Bedrest during the acute phase may be recommended.
   b. A regular diet with no added salt is given.
   c. Fluids and protein are restricted if urine output is significantly decreased.
   d. Antibiotics may be prescribed if the child has a persistent streptococcal infection.
   e. Antihypertensive drugs are given.
   f. Diuretics are administered to treat edema.
3. Nursing diagnoses/goals/interventions
   a. Fluid volume excess related to retention of sodium and water
      Goal: Child will maintain fluid balance and edema will disappear.
      Interventions:
      (1) Take vital signs.
      (2) Weigh the child daily.
      (3) Measure intake and output.
      (4) Observe color of urine.
      (5) Administer diuretics as ordered.
   b. Risk for sensory-perceptual alterations related to hypertension
      Goal: Child's neurological status will be within normal limits.

Interventions:
(1) Assess blood pressure frequently.
(2) Monitor level of consciousness.
(3) Maintain bedrest.
(4) Provide quiet diversional activities.
(5) Administer antihypertensive medications as ordered.
   c. Altered nutrition: less than body requirements related to anorexia
      Goal: Child will ingest an adequate nutritional intake to meet metabolic requirements.
      Interventions:
      (1) Assess the child's likes and dislikes.
      (2) Provide small, frequent feedings of the prescribed diet.
4. Evaluation
   a. Urinary output is within normal limits.
   b. Urinalysis and blood studies are within normal limits.
   c. Child's blood pressure is within normal limits.
   d. Edema has resolved.
   e. Child's weight has returned to the pre-illness value.

Disorders of the Blood and Blood-Forming Organs

A. **Acute Lymphoblastic Leukemia** A malignant neoplasm that involves all the blood-forming organs.
   The blood-forming organs produce a large number of immature white blood cells. These proliferating cells depress bone marrow production of normal red blood cells, mature white blood cells, and platelets. The result is anemia, infection, and bleeding tendencies.
   1. Assessment
      a. Assess for signs of infection, especially a persistent low-grade temperature.
      b. Assess for signs of anemia: pallor, malaise, anorexia, weight loss, and enlarged liver and spleen.
      c. Assess for signs of bleeding tendencies: petechiae, purpura, and bleeding from the mucous membranes of the mouth and the rectum.
      d. Assess for bone and joint pain.
      e. Assess for enlarged lymph nodes and vague abdominal pain.
      f. Assess for signs of increased intracranial pressure, which indicates involvement of the central nervous system.

g. DIAGNOSTIC MEASURES
  (1) There is an increased or decreased white blood cell count.
  (2) Bone marrow aspiration reveals an increased number of immature white blood cells.
  (3) Red blood cells and platelets are decreased.

2. Patient care management
  a. Chemotherapeutic agents
    (1) Remission is induced with prednisone, vincristine, and L-asparaginase.
    (2) Maintenance therapy consists of 6-mercaptopurine and methotrexate.
    (3) Allopurine is given to prevent an accumulation of uric acid in the renal tubules.
  b. Radiation therapy and methotrexate, administered intrathecally to prevent or treat central nervous system involvement.
  c. Bone marrow transplants.
  d. Antibiotics to treat infections.
  e. Blood transfusions.

3. Nursing diagnoses/goals/interventions
  a. Risk for infection related to neutropenia
    Goal: Child will be protected from infectious organisms.
    Interventions:
    (1) Monitor temperature.
    (2) Wash hands frequently.
    (3) Assign the child to a private room.
    (4) Avoid contact of the child with individuals who have infections.
    (5) Maintain reverse isolation as ordered.
    (6) Provide meticulous skin care.
    (7) Withhold immunizations when immunosuppression is present.
    (8) Administer antibiotics as ordered.
  b. Activity intolerance related to anemia
    Goal: Child will participate in age-appropriate activity.
    Interventions:
    (1) Allow the child to regulate his/her activity.
    (2) Encourage rest periods throughout the day.
    (3) Anticipate and meet the child's needs promptly.
    (4) Provide quiet diversional activities.
  c. Risk for injury related to decreased platelets
    Goal: Child will not suffer injury.
    Interventions:
    (1) Provide oral hygiene with a soft toothbrush.
    (2) Administer frequent mouthwashes with one-half-strength normal saline or one-half-strength hydrogen peroxide.
    (3) Apply local anesthetics to oral lesions before meals as needed.
    (4) Serve a diet of soft, bland foods when oral lesions are present.
    (5) Do not take a rectal temperature.
    (6) If rectal ulcers occur, position the child to avoid pressure on the area.
    (7) Apply pressure for 5 to 10 minutes after venipuncture.
    (8) Avoid intramuscular injections.
    (9) Hematest all urine and stools.
    (10) Assess for signs of transfusion reactions when the child is receiving blood products.
  d. Altered nutrition: less than body requirements related to anorexia, nausea, and vomiting
    Goal: Child will tolerate adequate nutrition to meet metabolic demands.
    Interventions:
    (1) Weigh the child daily.
    (2) Measure intake and output.
    (3) Assess the child's likes and dislikes.
    (4) Serve small, frequent feedings of the prescribed diet.
  e. Body image disturbance related to alopecia and changes in weight
    Goal: Child will maintain a positive self-image.
    Interventions:
    (1) Discuss the use of a wig or hat before hair loss occurs.
    (2) Stress that alopecia is temporary.
    (3) Encourage the child to express his/her feelings and concerns.
    (4) Provide opportunities for play therapy.
    (5) Promote peer interaction.

   f. Ineffective individual and family coping related to the medical diagnosis and uncertain outcome
Goal: Child and family will have adequate internal and external resources to cope effectively with diagnosis.
Interventions:
(1) Provide consistency in care.
(2) Encourage the child and the family to verbalize their feelings and concerns.
(3) Provide opportunities for play therapy for the child and his/her siblings.
(4) Help the parents in discussing the possible death of their child with other family members.
(5) Provide information on appropriate community resources.
(6) Teach the parents about the child's condition, treatment modalities and associated side effects, supportive measures, and prognosis.
(7) Encourage the parents to participate in the child's care as much as possible.

4. Evaluation
  a. Child experiences a remission.
  b. Child demonstrates no signs of infection, anemia, or hemorrhage.
  c. Child retains adequate nutrients to support age-appropriate growth.
  d. Child and parents demonstrate appropriate coping mechanisms.

B. **Hemophilia** An inherited deficiency in one of the factors required for blood coagulation. It is transmitted as a sex-linked recessive disorder by an unaffected female carrier to her male offspring.
Classic hemophilia or *hemophilia A* is a deficiency in factor VIII (antihemophilic globin) and accounts for 80% of all hemophilic individuals.

1. Assessment
  a. Be aware that spontaneous bleeding from any site in the body may occur in severe hemophilia.
  b. Be alert for prolonged bleeding after injury or surgery.
  c. Since hemarthrosis is the most common type of internal bleeding, assess the joints for warmth, pain, swelling, and limitation of movement.
  d. Soft tissue and intramuscular hemorrhages are common.
  e. DIAGNOSTIC MEASURES
    (1) Partial thromboplastin time is prolonged.
    (2) Prothrombin consumption and thromboplastin generation are decreased.

2. Patient care management
  a. Control bleeding.
    (1) Cleanse the wound.
    (2) Apply pressure and cold.
    (3) Immobilize and/or elevate the involved part.
  b. Replace the missing clotting factor.
    (1) Factor VIII concentrate.
    (2) Cryoprecipitate.
  c. Treat hemarthrosis.
    (1) Analgesics (salicylates are not prescribed).
    (2) Immobilization during the acute phase.
    (3) Progressive exercises to prevent permanent deformity.

3. Nursing diagnoses/goals/interventions
  a. **Risk for injury related to dysfunctional clotting mechanisms**
Goal: Child will not have episodes of acute bleeding.
Interventions:
(1) Monitor vital signs.
(2) Assess for signs of bleeding.
(3) Apply pressure and cold, and immobilize the affected area during the acute phase of bleeding as indicated.
(4) Administer cryoprecipitate as ordered.
(5) Observe for signs of transfusion reactions.
  b. Pain related to trauma and/or hemarthrosis
Goal: Child will be pain free.
Interventions:
(1) Apply local cold compresses.
(2) Immobilize the affected limb.
(3) Give analgesics as ordered, but avoid analgesics containing aspirin.
(4) Perform passive range of motion exercises to affected joints only after bleeding has stopped.
(5) Follow the prescribed exercise regime.

c. Knowledge deficit related to medical management and home care
Goal: Parent will verbalize understanding of home care and disease process.
Interventions:
(1) Allow the child and the parents to verbalize their feelings and concerns.
(2) Provide genetic counseling.
(3) Teach specifics about any home transfusion program.
(4) Discuss first aid to stop bleeding.
4. Evaluation
a. Episodes of acute bleeding are controlled.
b. Child does not experience permanent joint damage.
c. Child is pain free.
d. Parents understand all aspects of home care.

Disorders of Cerebral Function

A. **Meningitis** Inflammation of the meninges lining the brain and the spinal cord, caused by a bacteria or a virus. The most common bacterial agents are *Hemophilus influenzae*, *Streptococcus*, and *Meningococcus*. The disease is transmitted by droplet infection.
1. Assessment
a. Be alert for sudden onset with fever, chills, nausea, vomiting, headache, and possibly seizures.
b. Observe for irritability and possible changes in level of consciousness.
c. Observe for nuchal rigidity and opisthotonos posture.
d. Assess for positive Kernig's and Brudzinski's signs.
e. Observe for signs of increasing intracranial pressure.
f. Observe the skin for petechial and purpuric areas in meningococcal meningitis.
g. DIAGNOSTIC MEASURES
(1) Examination of cerebral spinal fluid reveals the causative organism, an increase in white blood cells and protein, and a decrease in glucose.
(2) Cerebral spinal fluid pressure is elevated.

2. Patient care management
a. Intravenous antibiotics to control infection.
b. Intravenous fluids to maintain hydration.
c. Anticonvulsants to control seizures.
d. Antipyretics to reduce temperature.
3. Nursing diagnoses/goals/interventions
a. Altered tissue perfusion: cerebral related to increased intracranial pressure
Goal: Child will not experience signs and symptoms of increased intracranial pressure.
Interventions:
(1) Assess neurological status frequently: level of consciousness, vital signs, pupil response, and symmetry of movement.
(2) Monitor for specific signs of increased intracranial pressure.
(3) Measure head circumference and palpate fontanels in infants.
(4) Decrease environmental stimuli.
(5) Institute seizure precautions.
(6) Elevate head of the bed 30 degrees.
b. Risk for infection related to the presence of infectious organisms
Goal: Child will be free of superimposed infection.
Interventions:
(1) Maintain respiratory isolation for 24 to 48 hours after initiation of antibiotic therapy.
(2) Wash hands frequently.
(3) Administer antibiotics as ordered.
c. Pain related to meningeal irritation
Goal: Child will be free of pain.
Interventions:
(1) Administer analgesics as ordered.
(2) Place the child in a side-lying position if nuchal rigidity is present.
d. Risk for fluid volume deficit related to decreased intake
Goal: Child will ingest an adequate amount of fluid.
Interventions:
(1) Assess for signs of dehydration.
(2) Monitor IV fluids.
(3) Advance diet as ordered and tolerated.
(4) Weigh the child daily.
(5) Measure intake and output.

e. Hyperthermia related to infectious process
Goal: Child's temperature will maintain age-appropriate range.
Interventions:
(1) Give tepid sponge baths.
(2) Administer antipyretics.

f. Ineffective family coping related to diagnosis of a life-threatening illness
Goal: Family will cope effectively with diagnosis.
Interventions:
(1) Allow the parents to verbalize their feelings and concerns.
(2) Teach the parents about the disease process and treatment modalities.
(3) Encourage parents' participation in child's care.

4. Evaluation
a. Child is alert and oriented.
b. Vital signs are within normal limits.
c. Child experiences no complications of meningitis.
d. Parents understand the child's condition and treatment regime.

B. **Convulsive Disorders** A convulsion is the result of a paroxysmal burst of electrical energy within the central nervous system.
1. Assessment
a. Observe the type of seizure.
(1) Grand mal seizure: alternating clonic and tonic movements with loss of consciousness.
(2) Petit mal seizure: a transitory loss of consciousness.
b. Observe events immediately before a seizure.
c. Note the duration of the seizure.
d. Observe the child's color and respiratory effort.
e. Assess the child's behavior immediately after a seizure.
f. DIAGNOSTIC MEASURE: An electroencephalogram demonstrates abnormal brain waves.
2. Patient care management
a. Anticonvulsant therapy is administered.
(1) Dilantin is the most common medication used to control grand mal seizures.
(2) Zarontin is used to treat petit mal seizures.

b. Optimal dosage is determined by blood levels.
3. Nursing diagnoses/goals/interventions
a. Risk for injury related to seizure activity
Goals:
(1) Child's airway will remain patent during a seizure.
(2) Child will be free from injury during a seizure.
Interventions:
(1) Suction as necessary.
(2) Administer oxygen as necessary.
(3) Do not restrain the child.
(4) Loosen clothing.
(5) Remove objects from the immediate environment.
(6) Do not force a padded tongue blade between the teeth.

b. Knowledge deficit related to seizure management
Goal: Parents will verbalize understanding of child's condition and medical management.
Interventions:
(1) Encourage the parents to verbalize their feelings and concerns.
(2) Discuss seizure recognition and first-aid treatment.
(3) Review the prescribed anticonvulsant medication and its potential side effects.

4. Evaluation
a. Child maintains a patent airway during a seizure.
b. Child is free from injury related to seizure activity.
c. Parents understand the treatment of seizures.

Other Alterations of Health

A. Care of the Patient Undergoing Tonsillectomy and/or Adenoidectomy
1. Indications for surgery
a. A *tonsillectomy* is indicated for children who have had chronic recurrent sore throats and whose tonsils have hypertrophied, causing difficulty with respirations or swallowing.
b. An *adenoidectomy* is indicated for children who have had repeated otitis media and whose adenoids have hypertrophied, causing difficulty with nasal breathing.

2. Assessment
   a. Assess the child's understanding of the surgery and postoperative recovery period.
   b. Check for any signs of acute infection.
   c. Assess for loose teeth.
   d. DIAGNOSTIC MEASURES
      (1) Complete blood count.
      (2) Routine urinalysis.
      (3) Prothrombin time and partial thromboplastin time.
3. Preoperative nursing diagnosis/goal/interventions
   Knowledge deficit related to surgical procedure and postoperative care
   Goal: Child and parents will verbalize understanding of surgical procedure and postoperative course.
   Interventions:
   a. Allow the child/parents to verbalize their feelings and concerns.
   b. Explain the various preoperative and postoperative procedures to the child in terms he/she will understand.
   c. Allow the child to tour the operating room and the recovery room.
   d. Assure the child that only the tonsils and adenoids will be involved.
4. Evaluation
   a. Child's fears are decreased.
   b. Child and parents understand the surgical procedure and the anticipated postoperative interventions.
5. Postoperative nursing diagnoses/goals/interventions
   a. Ineffective airway clearance related to difficulty in swallowing
      Goal: Child will not experience difficulty in swallowing.
      Interventions:
      (1) Monitor vital signs.
      (2) Immediately after surgery, place the child in a prone or side-lying position to prevent aspiration of secretions.
   b. Risk for injury related to surgical procedure
      Goal: Child will not experience injury due to hemorrhage.
      Interventions:
      (1) Observe for signs of hemorrhage: frequent swallowing or clearing of the throat, emesis of bright red blood, increased pulse rate, pallor, and restlessness.

   (2) Discourage the child from coughing and clearing his/her throat.
   (3) If signs of bleeding occur, position the child prone or on side to prevent aspiration, keep NPO, and notify the physician.
   c. Risk for fluid volume deficit related to difficulty in swallowing
      Goal: Child will be hydrated.
      Interventions:
      (1) Encourage fluids such as cool water, synthetic fruit juices, and Jell-o. After clear fluids are tolerated, the child may have milk, ice cream, and puddings.
      (2) Avoid red fluids that may be confused with bleeding if the child vomits.
   d. Pain secondary to the surgical procedure
      Goal: Child will experience minimal pain.
      Interventions:
      (1) Offer an ice collar.
      (2) Administer analgesics as ordered.
   e. Knowledge deficit related to home care
      Goal: Parents will verbalize understanding of home care.
      Interventions:
      (1) Advise the parents to withhold hot, coarse, and spicy foods for a week.
      (2) Teach signs of hemorrhage and infection, and instruct when it is necessary to seek medical care.
      (3) Advise the parents to administer analgesics as recommended by the physician.
6. Evaluation
   a. Child experiences no complications after the surgery.
   b. Child ingests and retains a progressive diet.
   c. Child's pain is minimal.
   d. Parents understand home care.
B. Childhood Schizophrenia
   1. Dynamics/characteristics
      a. This disorder may occur as early as 2 years of age, but usually manifests itself during late childhood.
      b. The onset is gradual, but sudden behavior changes may be precipitated by a crisis situation.
      c. Characteristics include bizarre motor behaviors and disturbed perception, thinking, and affective responses.

d. The hallmark is disturbed thought processes.
e. Intelligence is normal.
f. Language development occurs, but there is inability to communicate clearly.
g. Developmental milestones may not be affected.

2. Assessment
   a. Assess motor behavior disorders: self-mutilating behavior, loss of control, aggressiveness, and impulsivity.
   b. Assess perceptual disturbances: impaired reality testing, visual-motor disturbances, hallucinations, and delusions.
   c. Assess thought disorders: inability to communicate clearly, language problem.
   d. Assess affective responses: lack of affective responses, lack of social responses.
   e. Assess interpersonal relationships: autistic withdrawal, extreme vulnerability to separation.

3. Patient care management
   a. Pharmacotherapy to control delusions, hallucinations, and aggressive-assaultive behaviors. This is used in conjunction with other treatment modalities.
   b. Individual and family counseling.
   c. Milieu therapy: environmental manipulation (educational and psychotherapeutic modalities).

4. Family health promotion
   a. Provide parent education.
   b. Provide counseling to assist the parents in handling their feelings about the child.
   c. Provide role modeling for effective communication within the family.
   d. Provide the family with knowledge about child developmental milestones to establish realistic expectations for the child.

5. Nursing diagnoses/goals/interventions
   a. Impaired verbal communication related to thought disorder
      Goals:
      (1) Child will be able to communicate verbally.
      (2) Child will be able to relate to another person.
      Interventions:
      (1) Start with simple words.
      (2) Make every effort to clarify the message the child conveys.
      (3) Acknowledge any effort toward the establishment of verbal communication with another individual.
      (4) Provide an atmosphere of acceptance.
   b. Impaired interpersonal relationships related to feelings of mistrust
      Goals:
      (1) Child will be able to establish and tolerate human contact and relatedness.
      (2) Child will respond to communication by others.
      (3) Child will be able to initiate communication with another person.
      (4) Family will be able to relate to child.
      Interventions:
      (1) Involve the family in setting goals and in care planning.
      (2) Help establish meaningful interpersonal contact (start with brief eye contact).
      (3) Use gentle touch when the child is ready and can tolerate closeness.
      (4) Accept the child.
      (5) Provide a warm, human environment.
      (6) Be consistent in approach.
      (7) Promote a safe environment where the child can test reality.
      (8) Assist family members in coping with the child's behavior.
      (9) Reinforce desirable behavior by providing opportunities for repetition.
   c. Potential for injury related to perceptual and thought disorders
      Goal: Child will be free from injury.
      Interventions:
      (1) Observe the child for increased restlessness, agitation, and other potentially self-destructive behavior patterns.
      (2) Identify situations that may contribute and/or precipitate self-destructive behaviors such as hallucinations and delusions.

(3) Provide a safe environment.
(4) Avoid the use of physical restraints.
(5) Provide for adequate rest and sleep.
(6) Provide for adequate nutrition and fluid intake.
(7) Support the child during emotional outbursts.
(8) Assist the child to gain control over bizarre behaviors.

6. Evaluation
   a. The child is able to communicate verbally with others.
   b. The child is free from self-destructive behaviors.
   c. The family is able to relate to the child.
   d. The family is able to establish and maintain relationships with other people in the environment.
   e. The child is able to validate objective reality.
   f. The child is able to maintain adequate nutrition and fluid intake.

UNIT FIVE

Meeting the Needs of the School-Age Child (6 to 12 years)

STUDY GUIDE

DEVELOPMENTAL MILESTONES

A. Physical Growth
B. Motor Development
C. Language and Cognitive Development
D. Personal-Social Development
E. Freud's Psychosexual Theory of Development
F. Erikson's Psychosocial Theory of Development
G. Piaget's Theory of Cognitive Development
H. Play

HEALTH PROMOTION OF THE SCHOOL-AGE CHILD

A. Physiological Needs
B. Safety and Security Needs

THE SCHOOL-AGE CHILD AND THE CRISIS OF HOSPITALIZATION

A. Assessment of Behavioral Responses to Hospitalization
B. Nursing Care Plan for the Hospitalized School-Age Child

ALTERATIONS OF HEALTH DURING THE SCHOOL-AGE YEARS

Alterations That May Limit Mobility

A. Supracondylar Fracture of the Humerus
B. Osteomyelitis
C. Rheumatic Fever
D. Juvenile Rheumatoid Arthritis

Alterations of Cerebral Function

A. Head Trauma: Concussion and Skull Fracture
B. Brain Tumors

DEVELOPMENTAL MILESTONES

A. Physical Growth
  1. Usual weight gain during this period is approximately 5 pounds per year.
  2. Usual height gain during this period is approximately 2 inches per year.
  3. Average pulse rate is 90 per minute.
  4. Average respiration rate is 18 to 20 per minute.
  5. Average blood pressure is 95 to 108 systolic and 62 to 67 diastolic.
  6. Eruption of permanent teeth occurs.
  7. The preadolescent growth spurt occurs at approximately 10 years of age in females and at approximately 12 years of age in males.
  8. Secondary sexual characteristics may begin to appear at the end of this age range.

B. Motor Development
  1. Six years
     a. Uses crayons, pencils, scissors, tape, and glue with skill.
     b. Prints letters and numbers.
     c. Runs, jumps, climbs, hops, and skips.
     d. Draws a man, including neck, hands, and clothes.
  2. Seven years
     a. Enjoys bicycling and swimming.
     b. Indulges in quieter play.
  3. Eight years
     a. Produces neater school work.
     b. Enjoys games with gross motor activity and competition.
  4. Nine years
     a. Has fully developed hand-eye coordination.
     b. Shows greater timing and control in play.
  5. Ten years
     a. Displays greater strength and coordination in all motor activities.
     b. Enjoys running, skating, climbing, jumping, and bicycling.
  6. Eleven years
     a. Is less poised.
     b. Becomes clumsy in regard to motor actions.
  7. Twelve years
     a. Still enjoys gross motor activities.
     b. Becomes more refined in regard to fine motor activities.

C. Language and Cognitive Development
  1. Six years
     a. Has a vocabulary of 2500 words.
     b. Can read simple sentences and sound out words.
     c. Counts by ones, fives, and tens.
     d. Differentiates right from left.
     e. Knows seasons of the year.
     f. Distinguishes between morning and afternoon.
     g. Forms religious and death concepts.
  2. Seven years
     a. Can name day, month, and season.
     b. Can tell time.
     c. Uses elementary logic.
     d. Can add and subtract.
  3. Eight years
     a. Has increased memory span.
     b. Improves in spatial concepts.
     c. Has larger vocabulary.
     d. Gives precise definitions of words.
  4. Nine years
     a. Has longer attention span.
     b. Puts learning to practical use.
  5. Ten years
     a. Likes to memorize.
     b. Shows interest in social problems.
     c. Has trouble connecting facts.
  6. Eleven years
     a. Is interested in how things work.
     b. Enjoys reading.
  7. Twelve years
     a. Enjoys science and social studies.
     b. Can define abstract terms.

D. Personal-Social Development
  1. Six years
     a. Fears ghosts, thunder, large animals, and men under the bed.
     b. Can wash and dress with minimal assistance.
     c. Can't bear to lose at games and will cheat to win.
     d. Wants to be best and first.
     e. Projects blame onto others.
     f. Tattles, boasts, and fights.
     g. Has short classroom attention span.
     h. Centers life around school.
  2. Seven years
     a. Responds well to reason.
     b. Is more cooperative.
     c. Is becoming modest.
     d. Displays longer attention span.
     e. Replaces projected blame with alibis.
     f. Complains about parents, but desires their approval.

3. Eight years
   a. Does not like to be alone.
   b. Has a best friend.
   c. Considers secrets important.
4. Nine years
   a. Is peer oriented.
   b. Likes to please others.
   c. Takes responsibility for possessions.
   d. Has good table manners.
   e. Likes clubs.
   f. Accepts blame.
5. Ten years
   a. May become lax about personal hygiene.
   b. Gets along well with many peers.
6. Eleven years
   a. Assumes most responsibility for self.
   b. Strives for conformity with his/her peer group.
7. Twelve years
   a. Enjoys activities involving both sexes.
   b. Is more aware of other's feelings.

E. Freud's Psychosexual Theory of Development
   1. The school-age child is in the latency period of development.
   2. This stage is characterized by a minimum conscious sexual interest.

F. Erikson's Psychosocial Theory of Development
   1. The school-age child is developing a sense of industry versus inferiority.
   2. The child develops a sense of self-worth by engaging in purposeful tasks.
   3. The child is competitive, but learns to compromise, cooperate, and collaborate.
   4. The main relationships at this time center around the peer group.
   5. The child alternately conforms to and rebels against adult authority.
   6. Inferiority develops if the child's accomplishments are not recognized or if the adult's expectations are above the levels of the child's capabilities.

G. Piaget's Theory of Cognitive Development
   1. The child from 7 to 11 is in the concrete operations phase of development.
   2. The child is no longer egocentric.
   3. The school-age child is able to see the viewpoint of others.
   4. Problem solving is evident.
   5. There is an increased ability to deal with hypothetical situations.

6. The child can differentiate between certain, probable, and possible causes.
7. The child can classify objects into classes and subclasses, utilizing both perceptual and abstract qualities.
8. The child is able to arrange objects according to size.
9. The principle of conservation is developed.
10. The child understands present, past, and future.

H. Play
   1. School-age children play most often with peers of the same sex.
   2. Play is competitive and more organized than at the preschool age.
   3. Children enjoy more hobbies and collect a variety of objects.
   4. School-age children participate in household chores.
   5. School-age children enjoy opportunities to earn spending money.
   6. The following is a list of suggested toys and activities:
      a. Indoor board games.
      b. Models.
      c. Scientific toys.
      d. Musical instruments.
      e. Grooming aids.
      f. Bicycles.
      g. Organized sports.
      h. Arts and crafts.

HEALTH PROMOTION OF THE SCHOOL-AGE CHILD

A. Physiological Needs
   1. Daily care
      a. The school-age child sleeps approximately 10 to 12 hours per night.
      b. Opportunities for exercise should be provided to improve muscle strength and coordination.
   2. Nutrition
      a. Caloric requirements per unit of body weight continue to decrease.
      b. A well-balanced diet is necessary to promote growth.
      c. "Empty" calories must be discouraged.
      d. The child's appetite is generally good throughout the school-age period.
      e. Table manners slowly improve.
      f. Likes and dislikes are similar to those of the peer group.

B. Safety and Security Needs
  1. Prevention of accidents
     a. Major types of accidents during the school-age years are motor-vehicle accidents and drowning.
     b. The child should be taught safety rules related to bicycling and sports.
  2. Health maintenance
     a. Physical examinations are recommended once a year.
     b. Dental examinations are recommended twice a year.
     c. Scoliosis screening is begun.
     d. School health programs provide ongoing health maintenance, emergency care, communicable disease control, and safety and health education.

THE SCHOOL-AGE CHILD AND THE CRISIS OF HOSPITALIZATION

A. Assessment of Behavioral Responses to Hospitalization
  1. The school-age child experiences separation anxiety from both parents and peers.
     a. Fears that family relationships will be altered.
     b. Fears that he/she will be replaced in the peer group.
  2. Hospitalization is viewed as a punishment.
  3. The school-age child fears pain, bodily mutilation, and death.
  4. Children constantly ask questions about their bodies and their illness.
  5. Immobilization is particularly difficult for the normally active school-age child.
  6. The school-age child has difficulty expressing his/her feelings. The child is afraid of losing control.
  7. "Magical" words and actions are used to decrease anxiety.

B. Nursing Care Plan for the Hospitalized School-Age Child
  1. Nursing diagnosis/goal/interventions
     Ineffective individual coping related to the situational crisis of hospitalization
     Goal: Child will experience minimal effects of separation, will maintain a secure and trusting relationship with parents, and will react normally and effectively with peers and adults.
     Interventions:
     a. Encourage visiting by parents.

     b. Have the child maintain contact with peers through visiting, telephone calls, and letters.
     c. Introduce the child to peers on the unit.
     d. Reassure the child that he is not being punished.
     e. Encourage the child to express his/her feelings verbally or to use projective techniques such as writing a story and drawing.
     f. Provide opportunities for therapeutic play.
     g. Prepare the child for procedures.
        (1) Provide factual information about the procedure.
        (2) Reassure the child that only the specified body part will be involved.
        (3) Explain the rationale for the procedure.
        (4) Encourage the child to ask questions.
     h. Promote a sense of industry.
        (1) Allow the child to participate in his/her own care.
        (2) Allow the child to make choices.
  2. Evaluation
     a. Separation from parents and peers is minimal.
     b. Child understands hospital routines and procedures.
     c. Development of a sense of industry is not interrupted.

ALTERATIONS OF HEALTH DURING THE SCHOOL-AGE YEARS

Alterations That May Limit Mobility

A. **Supracondylar Fracture of the Humerus** A fracture of the humerus just proximal to the elbow joint.
  1. Assessment
     a. Observe for signs of neurological and circulatory impairment.
     b. Palpate the strength of the radial pulse.
     c. Assess for persistent pain.
     d. Assess for complications: Volkmann's ischemia, peripheral nerve injuries, and angulation deformities.
  2. Patient care management
     a. Dunlop's traction to immobilize the fracture.
     b. After traction is discontinued, a collar and cuff sling.
     c. Analgesics to relieve pain.

d. Physical therapy to restore optimal functioning.

3. Nursing diagnosis/goal/interventions

Impaired physical mobility related to traction

Goal: Child's mobility of unaffected extremities will be maintained, and mobility of affected extremity will return to optimal level.

Interventions:

a. Maintain traction.
   (1) Position the child in Dunlop's traction with the upper arm abducted and the forearm at a 90 degree angle from the plane of the child.
   (2) Check for correct positioning of ropes, pulleys, and weights.
   (3) Observe the pin sites, if present, for signs of infection.
   (4) Maintain good anatomical alignment.
   (5) Observe for any neurovascular changes in the extremity.
b. Prevent complications of immobility.
   (1) Prevent skin breakdown.
      (a) Change the child's position every 2 hours.
      (b) Massage the skin and bony prominences.
      (c) Place a sheep skin or alternating pressure mattress under the child.
   (2) Prevent respiratory infections.
      (a) Encourage coughing and deep breathing.
      (b) Encourage fluids.
   (3) Maintain adequate nutrition.
      (a) Determine the child's likes and dislikes.
      (b) Provide small, frequent feedings.
   (4) Promote elimination.
      (a) Increase fluids.
      (b) Increase dietary fiber.

4. Evaluation

a. Child's fracture heals in proper alignment.
b. Child experiences no complications of immobility.

B. **Osteomyelitis** An infectious process of the bone leading to bone destruction and abscess formation, most often caused by *Staphylococcus aureus*.

1. Assessment
   a. Assess for elevated temperature and rapid pulse.
   b. Inspect the involved area for pain, warmth, swelling, redness, and limited movement.
   c. DIAGNOSTIC MEASURES
      (1) The white blood cells and the erythrocyte sedimentation rate are elevated.
      (2) A blood culture identifies the causative organism.
      (3) X-ray changes occur 10 to 14 days after the onset of symptoms.

2. Patient care management
   a. Intravenous antibiotics.
   b. Immobilization of the involved area by a splint, cast, or traction to prevent the spread of infection.
   c. Surgical drainage and local instillation of antibiotics.
   d. Antipyretics to reduce temperature.
   e. Analgesics for pain.

3. Nursing diagnosis/goals/interventions
   a. Impaired physical mobility related to imflammation
      Goals:
      (1) Child's involved area will become noninfectious.
      (2) Child's mobility will be maintained within limitations of impairment.
      Interventions:
      (1) Maintain strict bedrest.
      (2) Maintain proper anatomical alignment.
      (3) Handle the child carefully to prevent pathological fractures.
      (4) Wash hands frequently.
      (5) If an open wound is present, maintain wound isolation precautions.
      (6) Use aseptic technique when changing dressings.
      (7) Administer antibiotics as prescribed.
      (8) Increase calories and protein in the diet to promote healing.
   b. Hyperthermia related to inflammatory process
      Goal: Child will be afebrile.
      Interventions:
      (1) Monitor temperature.
      (2) Administer tepid sponge baths.

c. Pain related to inflammatory process
Goal: Child will experience minimal pain.
Interventions:
(1) Support limb when moving.
(2) Administer analgesics as ordered.
(3) Apply warm soaks as prescribed.
4. Evaluation
a. Child's limbs show no signs of inflammation.
b. Mobility to the involved area is restored.
c. Child's pain is minimal.

C. **Rheumatic Fever**   A collagen disease resulting from an autoimmune response to group A beta hemolytic streptococci.
The most serious complication is chronic valvular disease.
1. Assessment
a. Observe for major manifestations of rheumatic fever.
(1) Carditis. Manifested by tachycardia that persists during sleep, dyspnea on exertion, fatigue, pain over the pericardial region, and murmurs.
(2) Migratory polyarthritis. Manifested by pain, tenderness, swelling, and limited motion of the large joints. Permanent joint damage does not occur.
(3) Chorea. Central nervous system involvement is manifested by involuntary, purposeless movements of the extremities, facial grimaces, speech difficulties, and mood swings.
(4) Subcutaneous nodules. Manifested by painless nodules over the extensor tendons of the feet, hands, elbows, patella, scapulae, and vertebrae.
(5) Erythema marginatum. A transitory erythematous macular rash with a clear center and wavy border that is found on the trunk and lower extremities.
b. Assess for minor manifestations of rheumatic fever: elevated temperature, arthralgia, positive laboratory tests, and a history of streptococcal infection approximately 1 to 3 weeks before the onset of symptoms of rheumatic fever.

c. DIAGNOSTIC MEASURES
(1) Diagnosis is based on the Jones criteria: The presence of two major manifestations or the presence of one major manifestation and two minor manifestations indicates rheumatic fever.
(2) Positive laboratory tests are as follows.
(a) Increased erythrocyte sedimentation rate.
(b) Positive C-reactive protein.
(c) Positive antistreptolysin-O titer.
(d) Positive throat culture for group A beta hemolytic streptococci.
(e) Prolonged P-R and Q-T intervals, revealed by electrocardiogram.
2. Patient care management
a. Penicillin to eradicate group A beta hemolytic streptococci.
b. Continued prophylactic penicillin to prevent recurrence of rheumatic fever.
c. Bedrest to decrease the cardiac workload.
d. Salicylates to relieve inflammation of the joints.
3. Nursing diagnoses/goals/interventions
a. Activity intolerance related to carditis
Goal: Child will tolerate bedrest with minimal discomfort.
Interventions:
(1) Provide skin care.
(2) Organize nursing care to prevent unnecessary interruptions.
(3) Provide diversional activities.
b. Pain related to inflamed joints
Goal: Child will be free of pain or will experience minimal pain.
Interventions:
(1) Position the child in correct anatomical alignment.
(2) Minimize handling of the joints.
c. Knowledge deficit related to home care
Goal: Parents will verbalize and demonstrate knowledge of disease process and medical treatment plan.
Interventions:
(1) Teach parents the importance of follow-up medical care.
(2) Teach the family the importance of prophylactic penicillin.

4. Evaluation
   a. Child's erythrocyte sedimentation rate is within normal limits.
   b. Child shows no manifestations of carditis.
   c. Child does not exhibit inflamed joints.
   d. Parents understand the home-care management.

D. **Juvenile Rheumatoid Arthritis**   A collagen disease, of unknown etiology, characterized by inflammatory changes of the joints.

There is inflammation of the synovial membrane and joint capsule, resulting in an increased number of synovial cells. The synovium adheres to the articular cartilage, depriving it of nutrition. Fibrosis, then bony ankylosis, result. Complete destruction of the joint may occur.

1. Assessment
   a. Assess for a high temperature and an accompanying pink macular rash on the trunk and extremities.
   b. Inspect the joints for swelling, warmth, pain, and limited motion.
   c. Inspect for symmetrical involvement of the joints.
   d. Inspect the fingers and toes for spindle shape.
   e. Assess for morning stiffness.
   f. Observe for systemic manifestations: anorexia, fatigue, persistent low-grade temperature, anemia, and enlarged lymph glands.
   g. Assess for complications: pericarditis, pneumonitis, and iridocyclitis.
   h. DIAGNOSTIC MEASURES
      (1) The erythrocyte sedimentation rate may be elevated
      (2) Latex fixation occasionally shows the presence of rheumatoid factor.
      (3) Occasionally antinuclear antibodies are present.

2. Patient care management
   a. Reduce inflammation and pain: acetylsalicylic acid, steroids, nonsteroidal anti-inflammatory drugs, slower-acting antirheumatic drugs (gold and antimalarials), application of heat.
   b. Prevent joint deformity: physical therapy, splints.
   c. Prevent blindness by frequent slit lamp examinations.
   d. Treat iridocyclitis with mydriatics and steroid eyedrops.

3. Nursing diagnoses/goals/interventions
   a. Impaired physical mobility related to inflammatory changes
      Goal: Child will demonstrate increasing mobility of joints.
      Interventions:
      (1) Administer anti-inflammatory medications as prescribed.
      (2) Medicate $\frac{1}{2}$ hour before exercise sessions.
      (3) Follow the prescribed program of exercise.
      (4) Encourage participation in activities of daily living.
      (5) Provide periods of rest to prevent excessive fatigue and overexertion.
      (6) Maintain anatomical alignment of joints.
      (7) Apply splints as ordered.
   b. Chronic pain related to inflamed joints
      Goal: Child will experience minimal discomfort or absence of pain.
      Interventions:
      (1) Administer analgesics as ordered.
      (2) Apply heat to involved joints.
      (3) Use a firm mattress.
      (4) Reposition the child in appropriate anatomical alignment every 2 hours.
   c. Knowledge deficit related to diagnosis of a chronic illness
      Goal: Parents will demonstrate understanding of home-care and follow-up instructions.
      Interventions:
      (1) Allow the child and the parents to verbalize their feelings and concerns.
      (2) Review prescribed anti-inflammatory and analgesic medications and their side effects.
      (3) Stress the importance of following the exercise plan in order to prevent decreased joint mobility.
      (4) Refer the parents to appropriate community agencies.

4. Evaluation
   a. Child's joints remain mobile.
   b. Child's pain is relieved.
   c. Parents understand the medication and exercise regime.

Alterations of Cerebral Function

A. **Head Trauma: Concussion and Skull Fracture**
1. Assessment
   a. Determine whether the child lost consciousness.
   b. Assess for memory loss.
   c. Inspect for drainage from the nose, mouth, or auditory canal in children with basal skull fractures.
   d. Test any drainage for the presence of glucose.
   e. Observe for signs of increasing intracranial pressure.
      (1) Early signs: irritability, restlessness, anorexia, and headache.
      (2) Intermediate signs: projectile vomiting; sluggish, unequal pupillary responses; papilledema; blurred or double vision; decreased pulse; increased blood pressure; and seizures.
      (3) Late signs: alterations in level of consciousness, decreased reflexes, decreased respirations, elevated temperature, herniation of the optic disc, and decerebrate rigidity.
   f. Assess for signs of epidural hemorrhage: progressive loss of consciousness, headache, vomiting, hemiparesis, increased deep tendon reflexes, and dilation and (later) fixation of the pupil.
   g. Assess for signs of subdural hemorrhage: drowsiness, irritability, personality changes, headache, vomiting, seizures, unsteady gait, papilledema, retinal hemorrhages, and hemiparesis or quadriplegia.
2. Patient care management
   a. Bedrest and continued observation for 48 hours.
   b. Clear liquid diet; IV therapy if the child is unconscious.
   c. Surgery to decrease pressure and remove bone fragments.
   d. Anticonvulsants to control seizures.
   e. Corticosteroids and hypertonic solutions to decrease intracranial pressure.
3. Nursing diagnoses/goals/interventions
   a. Altered tissue perfusion: cerebral related to trauma
      Goal: Child will show no signs of increased intracranial pressure.

Interventions:
      (1) Monitor neurological status: level of consciousness, pupil response, symmetry of movement and vital signs.
      (2) Assess for signs of increased intracranial pressure.
      (3) Place the child in an environment with decreased stimuli.
      (4) Elevate the head of the bed 30 degrees.
   b. Risk for injury related to seizure activity
      Goals:
      (1) Child's airway will remain patent during a seizure.
      (2) Child will not experience injury during a seizure.
      Interventions:
      (1) Suction as necessary.
      (2) Administer oxygen as needed.
      (3) Do not restrain the child.
      (4) Loosen the child's clothing.
      (5) Remove objects from the immediate environment.
      (6) Do not force a padded tongue blade between the teeth.
   c. Risk for fluid volume deficit related to nausea and vomiting
      Goal: Child will show no signs of dehydration.
      Interventions:
      (1) Assess for signs of dehydration.
      (2) Monitor IV fluids.
      (3) Maintain NPO, followed by a progressive diet as ordered and tolerated.
      (4) Measure intake and output.
      (5) Weigh the child daily.
4. Evaluation
   a. Child shows no clinical manifestations of increased intracranial pressure.
   b. Child is free from injury during seizures.
   c. Child remains hydrated.

B. **Brain Tumors** The majority of tumors during childhood occur beneath the tentorium cerebelli in the cerebellum or brain stem. Others may occur in the ventricles or near the pituitary gland.
1. Types: medulloblastomas, astrocytomas, ependymomas, and brain stem gliomas.

2. Assessment
   a. Observe for signs of increased intracranial pressure.
   b. Assess for motor disturbances: loss of muscle strength, ataxic gait.
   c. Observe for cranial nerve damage: visual defects, facial palsies, inability to swallow.
   d. Assess for behavioral changes.
   e. DIAGNOSTIC MEASURES
      (1) Computerized axial tomography (CAT scan) localizes the site of the tumor.
      (2) Magnetic resonance imaging (MRI) also localizes the site of the tumor.
      (3) A cerebral angiography visualizes the intracranial and extracranial vessels.
3. Patient care management
   a. Surgical removal of the tumor.
   b. Radiation therapy.
   c. Corticosteroids and hypertonic solutions to decrease intracranial pressure.
   d. Chemotherapy with nitrosoureas, vincristine, methotrexate, and cisplatinum.
4. Preoperative nursing diagnoses/goals/interventions
   a. Altered tissue perfusion: cerebral related to an intracranial tumor
      Goal: Child will experience optimal cerebral tissue perfusion.
      Interventions:
      (1) Monitor neurological status: level of consciousness, pupil response, symmetry of movement, and vital signs.
      (2) Assess for signs of increased intracranial pressure.
      (3) Place the child in an environment with decreased stimuli.
      (4) Elevate the head of the bed 30 degrees.
      (5) Maintain seizure precautions.
   b. Ineffective individual and family coping related to the medical diagnosis and uncertain outcome
      Goal: Child and family will have adequate internal and external resources to cope effectively with diagnosis.
      Interventions:
      (1) Provide consistency in care.
      (2) Encourage the child and family to verbalize their feelings and concerns.

      (3) Provide opportunities for play therapy for the child and his/her siblings.
      (4) Help the parents in discussing the possible death of their child with other family members.
      (5) Provide information on appropriate community resources.
      (6) Teach the parents about the child's condition, treatment modalities and associated side effects, supportive measures, and prognosis.
      (7) Encourage the parents to participate in the child's care as much as possible.
5. Evaluation
   a. The child shows less signs of increased intracranial pressure.
   b. The child and the parents demonstrate appropriate coping mechanisms.
6. Postoperative nursing diagnoses/goals/interventions
   a. Altered tissue perfusion: cerebral related to intracranial surgery
      Goal: Child will experience optimal cerebral tissue perfusion.
      Interventions:
      (1) Monitor neurological status: level of consciousness, pupil response, symmetry of movement, and vital signs.
      (2) Assess for signs of increased intracranial pressure.
      (3) Maintain a safe environment.
      (4) Position the child on his/her side with the head flat or elevated as ordered.
      (5) Have suction and nasal oxygen readily available.
   b. Risk for infection related to surgical procedure
      Goal: Child will remain afebrile.
      Interventions:
      (1) Assess temperature.
      (2) Observe the dressing for any drainage.
      (3) Auscultate the lung fields.
      (4) Encourage coughing and deep breathing every 2 hours.
      (5) Administer antibiotics as ordered.

c. Pain related to surgical intervention
    Goal: Child will experience minimal pain.
    Interventions:
    (1) Administer analgesics as ordered.
    (2) Maintain a quiet environment.
    (3) Prevent corneal abrasions.
        (a) Apply cold compresses to relieve edema.
        (b) Irrigate the eyes with normal saline.
d. Risk for fluid volume deficit related to postoperative NPO status
    Goal: Child will not demonstrate signs of dehydration.

Interventions:
(1) Maintain IV therapy.
(2) Monitor intake and output.
(3) Weigh the child daily.
(4) Assess gag and swallowing reflexes before administering fluids by mouth.

7. Evaluation
    a. Child does not demonstrate any manifestations of increased intracranial pressure.
    b. Child does not experience postoperative infection.
    c. Child is free of pain.
    d. Child does not demonstrate any signs of dehydration.

Meeting the Needs of the Adolescent
(13 to 18 years)

STUDY GUIDE

DEVELOPMENTAL MILESTONES

A. Physical Growth
B. Motor Development
C. Language Development
D. Personal-Social Development
E. Freud's Psychosexual Theory of Development
F. Erikson's Psychosocial Theory of Development
G. Paiget's Theory of Cognitive Development
H. Play and Work

HEALTH PROMOTION OF THE ADOLESCENT

A. Physiological Needs
B. Safety and Security Needs

THE ADOLESCENT AND THE CRISIS OF HOSPITALIZATION

A. Assessment of Behaviorial Responses to Hospitalization
B. Nursing Care Plan for the Hospitalized Adolescent

ALTERATIONS OF HEALTH DURING ADOLESCENCE

Adolescent Adjustment Reactions

Eating Disorders

A. Dynamics/Characteristics
B. Types
   1. Anorexia Nervosa
   2. Bulimia Nervosa
C. Assessment
D. Patient Care Management
E. Nursing Diagnosis/Goals/Interventions
F. Evaluation

Alteration in Behavior: Suicide

Alterations Arising from Sexual Activity

A. Adolescent Pregnancy
B. Sexually Transmitted Diseases
   1. Syphilis
   2. Gonorrhea
   3. *Chlamydia trachomatis*
   4. Herpes simplex Type II
   5. Patient care management for sexually transmitted diseases
   6. Nursing care plan for sexually transmitted diseases

Alteration Involving the Skeletal System

A. Scoliosis
B. Bone Tumors

Other Alterations of Health

A. Infectious Mononucleosis
B. Insulin-Dependent Diabetes Mellitus

DEVELOPMENTAL MILESTONES

A. Physical Growth
  1. Weight gain is 15 to 60 pounds.
  2. Height gain is 2 to 8 inches for females and 4 to 12 inches for males.
  3. There is a rapid increase in skeletal size, leading to clumsiness, poor coordination, and poor posture.
  4. The pulse rate, respiration rate, and blood pressure reach adult values by the end of adolescence. Pulse rate is 72 to 80, respiration rate is 16 to 20, and blood pressure is 120/80.
  5. Secondary sexual characteristics in the female begin to develop between the ages of 12 and 14.
  6. The appearance of secondary sexual characteristics in females occurs in the following order:
      a. Growth in the transverse diameter of the pelvis.
      b. Enlargement of the breasts.
      c. Change in vaginal secretions.
      d. Growth of pubic hair.
      e. Menstruation.
      f. Growth of axillary hair.
      g. Ovulation.
  7. Secondary sexual characteristics in the male begin to develop between the ages of 14 and 16.
  8. The appearance of secondary sexual characteristics in males occurs in the following order:
      a. Enlargement of the genitalia.
      b. Swelling of the breasts.
      c. Growth of pubic, axillary, facial, and body hair.
      d. Lowering of the voice.
      e. Production of spermatozoa.
  9. In both sexes, perspiration increases.
  10. The sebaceous glands become more active.
  11. Wisdom teeth erupt between the ages of 17 and 21.
B. Motor Development
  1. Early adolescence (13 to 14 years)
      a. Enjoys sports and dancing.
      b. Shows increased ease of movement, but is usually clumsy.
  2. Late adolescence (15 to 18 years)
      a. Has reached the adult level of motor ability and control.
      b. Moves with grace and poise.

C. Language Development
  1. Period of rapid increase in vocabulary.
  2. Many slang words in the vocabulary.
D. Personal-Social Development
  1. Early adolescence (13 to 14 years)
      a. Is interested in social problems.
      b. Is interested in personal appearance.
      c. May have a part-time job.
      d. Considers sports and school clubs important.
      e. Realizes the differences between his/her own thoughts and feelings and those of others.
  2. Late adolescence (15 to 18 years)
      a. Is making college or vocational plans.
      b. Is independent in areas of personal hygiene.
      c. Is actively engaged in dating.
E. Freud's Psychosexual Theory of Development
  1. The adolescent is in the genital stage of development.
  2. There is a revival of love for the parent of the opposite sex.
  3. The cathectic object is a person of the opposite sex.
F. Erikson's Psychosocial Theory of Development
  1. The *early* adolescent is developing a sense of identity versus identity diffusion.
  2. This is a period of stress for both adolescents and their parents.
  3. Separation from parents, both physical and emotional, is occurring.
  4. The adolescent is concerned with how he/she appears to others.
  5. The adolescent is learning to accept changes in his/her body image.
  6. Decisions are made about future education and vocations.
  7. The *late* adolescent is developing a sense of intimacy versus isolation.
  8. A struggle with sexual feelings occurs at this time.
  9. The adolescent is forming more intimate relationships with the opposite sex.
G. Piaget's Theory of Cognitive Development
  1. The adolescent from 11 to 15 is in the formal operations phase of development.
  2. The ability to solve abstract problems has been developed.
  3. The adolescent is able to consider problems from many points of view.

4. Hypotheses are formulated and tested.
5. Both inductive and deductive reasoning are utilized.

H. Play and Work
   1. Adolescents spend more time with their peers and less time with their parents.
   2. Adolescents enjoy part-time jobs.
   3. The adolescent enjoys games that involve physical skills and team cooperation.
   4. Interest is developed in social functions.
   5. The following is a list of suggested activities:
      a. Clubs.
      b. Sports.
      c. Arts and crafts.
      d. Reading.
      e. Films and television.
      f. Music.

HEALTH PROMOTION OF THE ADOLESCENT

A. Physiological Needs
   1. Daily care
      a. Needs 8 to 9 hours of sleep per night.
      b. Is usually self-sufficient in regard to physical care.
      c. Is interested in good grooming, cleanliness, and general appearance.
   2. Nutrition
      a. Caloric requirements are 2400 per day for females and 3000 per day for males.
      b. Daily protein intake should be 15% of the total calories.
      c. There is an increased need for iron.
      d. Adolescents have problems with overeating and undereating.
      e. Eating habits are influenced by the peer group.
      f. Many between-meal snacks consist of ''empty'' calories.
      g. Adolescents should be encouraged to eat a well-balanced diet.

B. Safety and Security Needs
   1. Prevention of accidents
      a. Major types of accidents are motor vehicle accidents, drowning, sports injuries, and wounds from firearms.
      b. Safety regarding automobiles and sports should be taught.

2. Health maintenance
   a. Physical examinations are recommended once a year.
   b. Dental examinations are recommended twice a year.
   c. Scoliosis screening continues.
   d. Health education should include sex education, safety education, nutritional education, and information about dangerous substances.
   e. The adolescent should be encouraged to take responsibility for his/her own health care.

THE ADOLESCENT AND THE CRISIS OF HOSPITALIZATION

A. Assessment of Behavioral Responses to Hospitalization
   1. The adolescent fears disapproval by parents, peers, and the community.
   2. Illness or injuries are a major threat to the adolescent's developing sense of identity.
   3. The adolescent has difficulty dealing with the dependency that is associated with hospitalization.
   4. The adolescent fears pain, bodily mutilation, death, and losing control.
   5. The adolescent is concerned with how the current illness or injury will affect future plans.

B. Nursing Care Plan for the Hospitalized Adolescent
   1. Nursing diagnosis/goal/interventions
      Methods for coping related to the situational crisis of hospitalization
      Goal: Adolescent will remain as independent as possible and will maintain a positive body image.
      Interventions:
      a. Encourage visiting by parents and peers.
      b. Promote the development of a sense of identity by including the adolescent when planning his/her care.
      c. Encourage the adolescent to verbalize his/her feelings and to ask questions about the illness and treatment regimen.
      d. Prepare the adolescent for procedures.
      e. Provide opportunities for continued cognitive development.
      f. Provide privacy.
      g. Provide grooming aids.

2. Evaluation
   a. Adolescent remains as independent as possible.
   b. Adolescent continues to develop a positive body image.

ALTERATIONS OF HEALTH DURING ADOLESCENCE

Adolescent Adjustment Reactions Emotional and behavioral difficulties experienced by the adolescent in response to psychological and biological changes during this maturational stage of development.

A. Dynamics/Characteristics
   1. Emotional difficulties are triggered by many causes.
   2. Adjustment reaction is expressed in many ways: anxious mood characterized by nervousness, worry, and uneasiness; depressive behavior characterized by feelings of hopelessness; conduct disturbance characterized by acting out, impulsivity, open aggression, and violation of social norms and rules; running away from home with ambivalent feelings toward dependence/independence; physical complaints; social withdrawal; poor work or academic performance.
   3. Adolescents set goals that are idealistic in their search for a comfortable social role. Inability to fulfill this role results in a feeling of defeat, loss of self-confidence, and loss of self-worth.
   4. The primary maturational crisis in this stage is the search for identity.
   5. Family dynamics play a major role in the adolescent's adjustment to all changes during this period.

B. Assessment
   1. Assess the adolescent's perception of what his/her problems are.
   2. Assess the family's values and attitudes about adolescence.
   3. Assess the adolescent's behavioral responses to maturational changes.
      a. Anxious mood: nervousness, worry.
      b. Depressive behavior: feelings of hopelessness.
      c. Impulsivity: unpredictability of behavior.
      d. Acting out: may include sexual responses such as promiscuity and homosexuality.
      e. Conduct disturbance: stealing, open aggression, vandalism, running away.
      f. Poor work/academic functioning: failing grades, truancy, poor concentration, inability to study or complete school work.
      g. Emotional disequilibrium: unpredictable shifts of interest and affection.
      h. Social withdrawal; inability to form loyalty to any group and lack of genuine social involvement.
      i. Physical complaints: various aches and pains.
      j. Constant search for support and identification.
      k. Ambivalent behavior: dependence versus independence.
      l. Substance (drugs or alcohol) abuse to escape from the pain of emotional turmoil. *See* Unit Seven, Alterations in Behavior, Section H: Substance Abuse, page 241.
         (1) Use of substances (drugs or alcohol) to escape from the pain of emotional crises may initially be for experimental purposes, but with continued use the substance becomes a crutch for coping (addiction).
         (2) Manipulative behavior is not uncommon.

C. Patient Care Management
   1. Counseling.
   2. Hospitalization when behavior becomes unmanageable and destructive to self and others.
   3. Family therapy.
   4. Group therapy.

D. Nursing Diagnoses/Goals/Interventions
   1. Ineffective individual/family coping related to perceived inability to deal with maturational changes (psychological and biological)
      Goal: Adolescent and his/her family will state perception of stress situation and develop coping mechanisms.
      Interventions:
      a. Assist the parents to understand that adolescence is a crucial developmental stage.
      b. Assist the family and the adolescent to verbalize their feelings and attitudes.
      c. Help the adolescent to explore his/her own feelings and evaluate the consequences of his/her actions.
      d. Assist the adolescent to deal with problems without the use of drugs or alcohol.
      e. Provide activities that facilitate the

release of energy and aggression in constructive ways.

   f. Set limits in a firm but kind and consistent manner.

   g. Communicate limits and expectations clearly.

   h. Set limits only on behaviors that are clearly destructive to the adolescent and others.

   i. Acknowledge signs of positive changes in the adolescent's behavior.

   j. Encourage the adolescent to talk about, rather than act out, feelings.

   k. Point out specific behaviors that are socially unacceptable, and assist the adolescent to explore alternatives that may modify such behaviors.

   l. Provide a safe environment.

   m. Assist the adolescent to control and modify problematic responses to stressful situations.

2. Knowledge deficit regarding the maturational changes of adolescence
Goal: Parents will identify the maturational changes of adolescence, identify available support, and develop alternative coping methods to solve current problems.
Interventions:

   a. Assist the family to cope with the adolescent in crisis.

     (1) Give counseling.

     (2) Provide information about growth and development and the maturational forces that accompany the adolescent years of adjustment.

   b. Give the parents a resource list of therapists proficient in adolescent and family therapy.

   c. Identify community resources with counseling/information or support groups.

   d. Use role modeling, especially in communicating with the adolescent.

E. Evaluation

1. Adolescent and his/her family appraise the situation realistically.

2. Adolescent and his/her family verbalize their feelings.

3. Adolescent and his/her family identify strategies to cope with problems.

4. Family identifies changes that occur during adolescence.

5. Family seeks professional help.

Eating Disorders   Disorders characterized by severe disturbances in eating behavior resulting in malnutrition and possibly death from starvation.

A. Dynamics/Characteristics

1. The causes are still unknown. Psychological theories center on sexual and social tensions generated by physical and emotional changes associated with puberty.

2. Family interactional patterns play a significant role in these disorders.

3. Regressive behavior is present.

4. Eating behavior may be influenced by society's apparent preoccupation and/or obsession with dieting and "thinness."

5. Individuals with eating disorders have low self-esteem and place strong emphasis on body shape and weight in determining their self-esteem.

6. Individuals with eating disorders frequently lack insight or have considerable denial of the seriousness of their medical condition.

7. Control of food intake is viewed as a form of control over others.

B. Types*

1. Anorexia Nervosa
Essential features:

   a. **Refusal to maintain minimal normal body weight for age and height.**

   b. **Weight loss up to 25% of expected body weight.**

   c. **Intense fear of weight gain though underweight.**

   d. **Disturbed perception of own body shape or size.**

   e. **Absence of at least 3 consecutive menses in post-menarcheal females.**

   f. **Weight loss is viewed as an impressive achievement.**

   g. **Weight loss is accomplished by starvation, purging, and excessive exercise.**

2. Bulimia Nervosa
Essential features:

   a. **Binge eating (eating in a discrete period of time an amount of food that is larger than most individuals would eat under the same circumstances in less than 2 hours in 1 or more seating).**

   b. **A sense of lack of control over eating during the episode.**

   c. **Recurrent compensatory behavior to prevent weight gain by self-induced**

---

*Source: American Psychiatric Association. *Diagnostic and Statistical Manual of Mental Disorders.* 4th ed., Washington, D.C.: American Psychiatric Association, 1994, pp. 539–550.

vomiting, use of laxatives, diuretics, enemas, or other medications; fasting; or excessive exercise.

   d. Binge eating and compensatory behavior both occur at least twice a week for 3 months.

   e. Binge eating is usually triggered by stress, depression, and intense hunger following dietary restraints.

   f. Food typically consumed during binges includes sweets and high-calorie foods.

C. Assessment

  1. Assess the adolescent's physical condition.

  2. Observe the adolescent for purging behaviors and vomiting, which can lead to lower potassium levels and thereby cause cardiac arrhythmias, including cardiac arrest.

  3. Observe for eating binges.

  4. Assess response of the adolescent to treatment.

  5. Assess for signs of endocrine disturbance.

  6. Assess need for sleep (the adolescent may be unable to sleep).

  7. Assess for obsessive-compulsiveness.

D. Patient Care Management

  1. Aim of treatment: restoration of the adolescent's nutritional state.

  2. Medical management.

  3. Personal, behavioral, and family therapies.

  4. Hospitalization.

  5. Drug therapy: chlorpromazine and antidepressants.

E. Nursing diagnosis/goals/interventions

  1. Altered nutrition: less than body requirements related to self-starvation

   Goals:

   a. Adolescent will reestablish a nutritionally adequate eating pattern.

   b. Adolescent will ingest adequate nutrition for growth and development.

   Interventions:

   a. Weigh the adolescent every day at the same time, on the same scale, with the same amount of clothing, after emptying bladder.

   b. Offer support at mealtimes: avoid discussing food or somatic complaints, focus on patient's adaptive interest, praise patient's ability to consume meal within prescribed time period.

   c. Administer tube feedings, hyperalimentation, or IV feedings as ordered.

   d. Observe adolescent for 2 hours after eating to prevent vomiting and regurgitation.

   e. Provide positive reinforcement for weight gain rather than for amount of food eaten.

   f. Demonstrate a nonjudgmental attitude and express concern; avoid threats, pleas, and advice.

   g. Inform entire nursing staff of approaches to take to the adolescent's behavior and also the need to review the therapist-written plan of care.

   h. Ensure that referral to psychiatry and dietary instructions are communicated.

  2. Body image disturbance related to misperception of body size

   Goals:

   a. Adolescent will regain and maintain a realistic body image.

   b. Adolescent will develop realistic attitudes and perception about body size, needs and function.

   Interventions:

   a. Assist the patient in expressing feelings and concerns about self: body size, body function, and physical needs.

   b. Provide support and positive feedback for accurate perception of body size and function.

   c. Assist the adolescent to identify abilities, strengths, and weaknesses.

   d. Teach the adolescent to verbalize and visualize positive affirmations about the body.

  3. Ineffective individual coping related to self-care in activities of daily living (ADL)

   Goals:

   a. Adolescent will participate in treatment plan.

   b. Adolescent will demonstrate effective coping with activities of daily living.

   Interventions:

   a. Assist the adolescent to express feelings and concerns about self and the treatment plan.

   b. Provide opportunities for choices and decision making in the treatment plan and activities of daily living, such as type and time of hygiene, exercise, leisure activities, and hobbies.

   c. Alternate rest with exercise; monitor the amount of exercise.

   d. Assist the adolescent to identify problem areas and to use problem-solving techniques.

e. Set and maintain firm limits in regard to the treatment plan.
4. Knowledge deficit regarding coping with nutrition, activities of daily living, anxiety, and discharge plan
    Goal: Adolescent will discuss the plan to ingest an appropriate diet, make decisions for activities of daily living, and discuss follow-up care and symptoms to report to physician.
    Interventions:
    a. Assess the adolescent's level of knowledge of, and ability to comply with, the diet and treatment plan.
    b. Discuss the schedule for follow-up care.
    c. Instruct the family to give positive reinforcement.
    d. Discuss the plan for activities of daily living after discharge.
    e. Explain medication, treatment plan and follow-up care, and symptoms to report to physician, and have adolescent do return verbalization.
    f. Discuss referral to self-help groups such as American Anorexia/Bulimia Association, Inc.; Anorexia Nervosa and Associated Disorders (ANAD); community resources, such as half-way houses, rehabilitation and vocational training, day care centers.
    g. Include the family and significant other in discharge planning.
    h. Instruct family to give positive reinforcement for weight gain, not for amount of food eaten.
F. Evaluation:
    1. Adolescent:
        a. Demonstrates a nutritionally adequate eating pattern.
        b. Regains and maintains weight within normal range for height and age.
        c. Discuss own body size, needs, and functions in realistic and positive terms.
        d. Participates actively in treatment plan and problem solving for activities of daily living.
        e. Demonstrates self-care in regard to hygiene, exercise, diet and nutrition, rest and sleep, and leisure activities.
        f. Has an appointment for follow-up care with physician/therapist and knows how to contact him/her in an emergency.
        g. Has a plan to ingest appropriate diet.
        h. States symptoms of medical emergency; has telephone number of physician or clinic to call if needed.

i. Makes decisions for activities of daily living.
2. Family: demonstrates positive reinforcement for the adolescent's weight gain.

Alteration in Behavior: Suicide Adolescence is marked by mood swings, depression, loneliness, anger, and other negative feelings, balanced by positive new sensations, experiences and relationships, achievements, independence, and pleasures. These rapid changes cause a sense of loss of control over one's life. A feeling of desperation may lead the adolescent to believe that no other alternative is open but to end life.

A. Assessment   *See* also Unit Nine, Alterations in Behavior, page 383.
    1. Observe for deterioration of hygiene; change in sleeping and elimination patterns; change in usual motor activity; appearance of nervous habits; disorientation to time, place, and person; and the appearance of scratches, bite marks, bruises, lacerations, or burns.
    2. Check background for precipitating factors such as poor school functioning, past patterns of poor management of stress, history of chronic or terminal illness, history of physical/sexual abuse, poor peer/family relations, alcohol/chemical abuse, promiscuity.
B. Patient Care Management
    1. Immediate hospitalization and constant surveillance.
    2. Supportive counseling for patient and family.
    3. Psychotherapy.
C. Nursing Diagnoses/Goals/Interventions. The long-term goal for the adolescent who attempts suicide is the realization that life's frustrations and challenges have possible solutions and that the adolescent will learn effective methods of communicating needs and feelings.
    1. **Risk for injury related to suicidal gestures and/or attempts**
        Goal: Adolescent will not injure self.
        Interventions:
        a. Discuss suicidal ideation; discuss lethality of comments.
        b. Stay with the adolescent at all times if suicidal intent is evident.
        c. Remove potentially lethal objects from the environment.
        d. Place on one-to-one observation.
        e. Remain calm, caring, and supportive.
    2. **Risk for violence: self-directed related to anxiety and/or fear**

Goal: Adolescent will recognize own anxiety and coping pattern and will develop and utilize effective coping skills.
Interventions:
a. Encourage expression of feelings.
b. Assess physical and psychological symptoms that may accompany fear/anxiety/grief.
c. Determine actual or perceived stressors or losses; assist the adolescent in defining precipitating factors, real or imagined.
d. Discuss past and present coping mechanisms; help the adolescent identify effective and ineffective coping mechanisms.
e. Help the adolescent identify alternatives to suicide rather than merely postponing it; help the adolescent find reason to live, something to look forward to.
f. Help the adolescent to recognize behaviors that indicate increased anxiety and to develop mechanisms to manage behavior (e.g., engage in physical activity, practice relaxation techniques, identify factors that can be controlled, make decisions when realistic, seek professional counseling).
g. Instruct the adolescent in the use of relaxation techniques (deep breathing, meditation).
h. Role play adaptive skills.

3. Disturbance in self-concept related to distorted body image; decreased self-esteem
Goal: Adolescent will develop a realistic body image and will increase his/her self-esteem.
Interventions:
a. Note manner of dress and state of hygiene and grooming.
b. Engage in dialogue regarding feelings and opinion about self and personal appearance (e.g., likes/dislikes, strengths/weaknesses).
c. Explore the adolescent's feelings about the changes in his/her body that occur with the onset of puberty.
d. Encourage and reinforce any positive statements about self; discuss ways to highlight good feelings about self (e.g., improving grooming and hygiene).
e. Assist with hygiene and grooming as needed; reinforce attempt toward improvement in hygiene and grooming.

4. Altered family process related to suicidal ideation, gestures

Goal: Family will achieve a productive functional state and will be supportive of the adolescent.
Interventions:
a. Determine level of disruption in family function.
b. Provide opportunities for family members to verbalize their feelings to the nurse and to one another.
c. Encourage the adolescent and the family to listen, hear, and acknowledge one another.
d. Be accepting to the adolescent and the family.
e. Collaborate with the family to establish and facilitate goals and treatment.
f. Encourage the family to seek professional therapy; provide a list of community resources (e.g., mental health clinic, Survivors of Suicide support group, clergy).

5. Knowledge deficit regarding adolescent suicide and early symptoms of suicidal behaviors
Goal: The adolescent and his/her parents will recognize the scope of adolescent suicide; will know warning signs; will seek professional help if these signs appear.
Interventions:
a. Discuss warning signs (e.g., behavior changes, mood swings, change in peer group or loss of peer group, school failure, decreased communication, expressing bad feelings about self, verbalizing suicidal ideation, making suicidal gestures/attempts).
b. Give resource list of therapists proficient in adolescent and family therapy.
c. Educate regarding the scope and seriousness of adolescent suicide.
d. Identify community resources with counseling and information available to those contemplating suicide and their families (e.g., suicide hotline).

D. Evaluation:
1. Adolescent does not injure himself/herself.
2. Adolescent expresses feelings, identifies stressors/losses, develops successful coping mechanisms, and role plays new skills.
3. Adolescent participates in grooming and hygiene and makes positive statement about himself/herself.
4. Family participates in goal-setting and treatment, and in family and individual counseling.

5. Adolescent and parents identify warning signs of suicide, verbalize the scope of the problem, and can name available community resources.

Alterations Arising from Sexual Activity

A. Adolescent Pregnancy
  1. Dynamics/characteristics
    a. The adolescent may not be sure how she got pregnant.
    b. She is at risk for pregnancy-induced hypertension.
    c. She is at risk for premature delivery.
    d. She is at risk for cephalopelvic disproportion.
    e. She may have difficulty with intimate relationships.
    f. She may be concerned with body changes.
  2. Patient care management: The pregnant adolescent needs to be managed as a high-risk patient. *See* Unit Seven, Pregnancy, Section H: High-Risk Pregnancies, page 166.
  3. Nursing diagnosis/goal/interventions
    Knowledge deficit related to unexpected pregnancy
    Goal: Adolescent will participate actively in making a decision about her pregnancy.
    Interventions:
    a. Ascertain whether the adolescent has told her parents that she is pregnant.
    b. If not, allow her to verbalize her fears in regard to telling her parents.
    c. Discuss whether she wants to continue with the pregnancy.
    d. Provide abortion counseling if requested.
    e. Discuss her options if she continues with the pregnancy: foster care, adoption, assistance from parents, marriage to the baby's father, raising the child on her own.
    f. Discuss her plans for her education and her vocational choices.
    g. Discuss sexuality.
      (1) Review the anatomy and physiology of reproduction.
      (2) Discuss how the patient feels about sexual activity.
      (3) Discuss myths she may have heard.
      (4) Discuss birth control.
  4. Evaluation: Adolescent decides how to handle her pregnancy.

B. Sexually Transmitted Diseases*
  1. Syphilis
    Assessment
    a. Primary stage: characterized by the presence of a chancre, usually in the anogenital region. Most often resembles an ulcerated area surrounded by a firm, raised border.
    b. Secondary stage: occurs about 3 weeks after the spontaneous healing of the chancre. Clinical manifestations are generalized skin rash, lesions on the mucous membrane of the oral cavity, low-grade fever, sore throat, and enlarged lymph nodes.
    c. Latent stage: occurs 2 to 6 months after initial infection. No clinical manifestations are present.
    d. Tertiary stage: occurs 4 to 20 years after initial infection. Includes degenerative skin changes and cardiovascular and neurological damage.
    e. Congenital syphilis: may occur in the infants of infected mothers.
    f. DIAGNOSTIC MEASURES
      (1) Identification of the spirochete organism by dark-field microscopic examination of exudate from lesions.
      (2) Serological tests.
  2. Gonorrhea
    Assessment
    a. Many males and females remain asymptomatic.
    b. Early clinical manifestations in males: burning on urination and a purulent urethral discharge.
    c. Early clinical manifestations in females: purulent vaginal discharge, dysuria, urinary frequency, and abdominal discomfort.
    d. Complications in untreated males: scarring of the seminal ducts and sterility.
    e. Complications in untreated females: salpingitis, pelvic inflammatory disease, peritonitis, and sterility.
    f. Arthritis, conjunctivitis, and endocarditis: can occur in untreated individuals of both sexes.
    g. Gonococcal ophthalmia neonatorium: can be transmitted to the newborn by an infected mother.
    h. DIAGNOSTIC MEASURE: microscopic examination of purulent exudate from the male urethra or the female cervical os.
    See also AIDS, page 258.

3. Chlamydia trachomatis
   Assessment
   a. Local edema.
   b. Mucopurulent drainage.
   c. Dyspareunia.
   d. Dysuria and frequency of urination.
   e. Complication in men: urethritis.
   f. Complications in women: pelvic inflammatory disease, sterility, or infertility.
   g. Fetal and/or neonatal effects: stillbirth, prematurity, conjunctivitis, and pneumonia.
   h. DIAGNOSTIC MEASURES
      (1) Positive immunofluorescent test.
      (2) Positive enzyme-linked immunosorbent assay (ELISA).
4. Herpes simplex Type II
   Assessment
   a. Recurrent vesicles in the genital area, surrounded by erythematous tissue.
   b. Local edema.
   c. Pain, often accompanied by a burning sensation.
   d. A thin, white vaginal discharge.
   e. Urinary retention and dysuria.
   f. Dyspareunia.
   g. Elevated temperature, malaise, and anorexia.
   h. Painful inguinal lymphadenopathy.
   i. Complications: disseminated and/or local infection.
   j. Congenital herpes: transmitted during a vaginal delivery or if premature rupture of the membranes occurs when active lesions are present.
   k. DIAGNOSTIC MEASURE: positive tissue culture of the lesion.
5. Patient care management for sexually transmitted diseases
   a. In most states adolescents may be treated without parental permission.
   b. An epidemiological investigation must be conducted to identify sexual contacts during periods of communicability.
   c. Both syphilis and gonorrhea are treated with penicillin.
   d. *Chlamydia trachomatis* is treated with ceftriaxone, tetracycline, or erythromycin.
   e. Herpes simplex Type II is treated with anti-infective agents such as acyclovir and with topical steroids, anesthetics, or antibiotics.
6. Nursing care plan for sexually transmitted diseases

   a. Nursing diagnosis/goals/interventions
      Knowledge deficit related to disease process and complications
      Goals:
      (1) Adolescent will be free of sexually transmitted disease.
      (2) Adolescent understands how to prevent the spread of sexually transmitted disease.
      Interventions:
      (1) Allow the adolescent to verbalize his/her feelings and concerns in a nonjudgmental environment.
      (2) Assess the adolescent's understanding that the disease is most often contracted by sexual contact.
      (3) Explain to the adolescent that the disease is reportable, and encourage him/her to identify sexual contacts.
      (4) Teach the adolescent about the symptoms and possible complications of untreated sexually transmitted diseases.
      (5) When applicable, emphasize the toxic effects to the fetus and/or newborn.
      (6) Encourage compliance with medical treatment and follow-up diagnostic evaluation.
      (7) Discuss the relationship of barrier contraceptives and spermicides to the prevention of sexually transmitted diseases.
      (8) Instruct the adolescent not to resume sexual activity until advised by the physician.
      (9) Teach the adolescent not to engage in sexual activity with untreated previous partners.
   b. Evaluation
      (1) No symptoms of sexually transmitted disease are present.
      (2) Adolescent understands how to prevent the spread of sexually transmitted diseases.

Alterations Involving the Skeletal System

A. **Scoliosis** Lateral curvature of the spine that may be either functional or structural. *Functional* scoliosis shows no abnormality in the shape of the vertebrae and is corrected by bending to the opposite side. *Structural* scoliosis shows permanent changes in the shape of the vertebrae and the thorax and is not correctable by side bending.

1. Assessment
   a. Observe the adolescent in an erect position for unequal shoulder heights, unequal levels of the iliac crests, an uneven waistline, spinal curvature, and shoulder blade prominence.
   b. Observe the adolescent as he/she bends forward at the waist for a convex curve in the upper back and a compensating concave curve in the lower back.

2. Patient care management
   a. Functional scoliosis: improve posture and use exercises.
   b. Structural scoliosis: use exercises and a variety of mechanical devices such as a Milwaukee brace, a Risser localizer cast, or a halo body cast.
   c. Severe structural scoliosis: use spinal fusion with Harrington or Luque rod placement, followed by a body jacket or casting.

3. Preoperative nursing diagnoses/goals/interventions
   a. Body image disturbance related to abnormal curvature of the spine and the treatment regime
      Goals:
      (1) Adolescent will adapt to changes in body image.
      (2) Adolescent will comply with treatment plan.
      Interventions:
      (1) Encourage the adolescent to verbalize his/her concerns.
      (2) Discuss the importance of compliance with the treatment regime.
      (3) Allow the adolescent to participate as much as possible in self-care activities.
      (4) Discuss necessary adjustments in clothing and footwear.
   b. Impaired physical mobility related to the presence of a brace, body jacket, or cast
      Goals:
      (1) Adolescent will participate fully in activities of daily living.
      (2) Adolescent's skin will remain intact.
      Interventions:
      (1) Teach the appropriate application of the brace or jacket.
      (2) Reinforce the importance of wearing the appliance 23 hours a day.
      (3) Encourage participation in the prescribed exercise regime to improve posture and strengthen muscles.
      (4) Check for proper fit of the appliance.
      (5) Remove the appliance twice a day for skin care.
      (6) Massage pressure points every morning and evening.

4. Evaluation
   a. Adolescent develops a positive self-concept.
   b. Adolescent complies with the treatment regime.
   c. Adolescent participates fully in activities of daily living.
   d. Adolescent does not experience any skin breakdown.

5. Postoperative nursing diagnoses/goals/interventions
   a. Ineffective airway clearance related to anesthesia and decreased movement
      Goal: Adolescent's airway will be patent.
      Interventions:
      (1) Monitor vital signs.
      (2) Encourage coughing and deep breathing every 2 hours.
      (3) Reposition the adolescent every 2 hours.
   b. Pain related to surgical intervention
      Goal: Adolescent will be free of pain.
      Interventions:
      (1) Decrease environmental stimuli.
      (2) Administer analgesics as ordered.
   c. Risk for fluid volume deficit related to NPO status
      Goal: Adolescent will be hydrated.
      Interventions:
      (1) Maintain IV therapy.
      (2) Record amount of Hemovac drainage.
      (3) Monitor intake and output.
      (4) Provide progressive diet as ordered.
   d. Impaired physical mobility related to postoperative restrictions
      Goal: Adolescent will gradually ambulate.
      Interventions:
      (1) Change the adolescent's position by logrolling every 2 hours.
      (2) Frequently assess motor and sensory function in the lower extremities.
      (3) Encourage progressive ambulation with the prescribed appliance in place.

e. Risk for infection related to surgical incision
Goal: Adolescent will be free of infection.
Interventions:
(1) Monitor temperature.
(2) Change dressing as ordered, using asceptic technique.
(3) Observe the suture line for redness, odor, or drainage.

f. Constipation related to immobility
Goal: Adolescent will maintain regular bowel elimination.
Interventions:
(1) Ambulate as ordered.
(2) Increase fluid intake.
(3) Include fiber in the diet.

g. Altered urinary elimination related to the presence of the Foley catheter
Goal: Adolescent will return to normal urinary pattern.
Interventions:
(1) Record intake and output.
(2) Encourage fluid intake.
(3) Perform routine Foley catheter care.
(4) After removal of the Foley catheter, offer the bedpan often.

h. Knowledge deficit related to follow-up medical care and home-care management
Goal: Adolescent will comply with home-care management.
Interventions:
(1) Review instructions regarding activity restrictions.
(2) Reinforce continued compliance with the wearing of the prescribed appliance until the healing phase is completed.
(3) Stress the importance of medical follow-up.

6. Evaluation
a. Adolescent's vital signs are within normal limits.
b. Adolescent's postoperative pain gradually decreases.
c. Adolescent maintains an adequate state of hydration.
d. Adolescent progressively ambulates.
e. Adolescent does not demonstrate signs of postoperative infection.
f. Adolescent demonstrates normal patterns of bowel and urinary elimination.
g. Adolescent complies with home-care management.

B. **Bone Tumors**
1. Types
a. **Osteosarcoma** Tumors arising from osteoblasts, occurring most frequently in the shafts of the long bones of the lower extremities.
b. **Ewing sarcoma** Tumors arising from primitive bone marrow cells, occurring most often in the shaft of the femur, the tibia, and the humerus.

2. Assessment
a. Assess for pain and inflammation at the site of the tumor.
b. As the disease progresses, observe for anemia.
c. Assess for signs of pulmonary metastasis.

3. Patient care management
a. Osteosarcoma: excision of tumor, amputation or limb-salvage procedures, and chemotherapy with high-dose methotrexate with citrovorum rescue, doxorubicin, bleomycin, actinomycin-d, cyclophosphamide, or cisplatin.
b. Ewing sarcoma: surgery, radiation, and/or chemotherapy with vincristine, actinomycin-d, cyclophosphamide, or doxorubicin.

4. Preoperative nursing diagnoses/goals/interventions
a. Pain related to tumor growth
Goal: Adolescent will be free of pain.
Interventions:
(1) Administer analgesics as ordered.
(2) Maintain bedrest in correct anatomical alignment if ordered.
(3) When moving the adolescent, handle the involved extremity carefully to prevent pathological fractures.
(4) If the adolescent is ambulatory, prevent weight bearing on the affected limb.

b. Alteration in nutrition: less than body requirements related to anorexia
Goal: Adolescent will ingest a high-calorie, high-protein diet.
Interventions:
(1) Assess the adolescent's likes and dislikes.
(2) Provide small, frequent feedings.
(3) Measure intake and output.
(4) Weigh the adolescent daily.

c. Impaired gas exchange related to pulmonary metastasis

Goal: Adolescent will breathe normally.
Interventions:
(1) Assess respiratory status frequently.
(2) Place the adolescent in a semi-Fowler's position.
(3) Encourage turning, coughing, and deep breathing every 2 hours.
d. Ineffective individual and family coping related to the medical diagnosis and uncertain outcome
Goals:
(1) Adolescent and family will cope with diagnosis.
(2) Adolescent and family will understand the medical and surgical treatment plans.
Interventions:
(1) Provide consistency in care.
(2) Encourage the adolescent and family to verbalize their feelings and concerns.
(3) Provide opportunities for play therapy for siblings.
(4) Help the parents in discussing the possible death of their child with other family members.
(5) Provide information on appropriate community resources.
(6) Teach the parents and the adolescent about the condition, treatment modalities and associated side effects, supportive measures, and prognosis.
(7) Encourage the adolescent to participate in care as much as possible.

5. Evaluation
a. Adolescent experiences a decrease in pain.
b. Adolescent ingests the daily recommended nutrients.
c. No signs of pulmonary metastasis are detected.
d. Parents and adolescent understand the medical and surgical treatment plans.
e. Parents and adolescent demonstrate positive coping mechanisms.

6. Postoperative nursing diagnoses/goals/ interventions
a. Impaired physical mobility related to loss of limb and/or alteration in limb function
Goals:
(1) Adolescent will utilize adaptive devices to maintain maximum mobility.

(2) Skin of the stump will remain intact.
Interventions:
(1) Assist the adolescent to understand and utilize prosthesis and other adaptive devices.
(2) Encourage participation in the prescribed exercise regime.
(3) Check the stump daily for signs of skin breakdown and infection.
(4) Change the dressing and cleanse the stump daily as ordered.
b. Body image disturbance related to loss of limb and/or limb function
Goal: Adolescent will accept alteration in body image.
Interventions:
(1) Encourage the adolescent to verbalize his/her feelings and concerns about the change in body image.
(2) Introduce the adolescent and the parents to another adolescent with a similar disease.
(3) Refer to appropriate community agencies.
c. Pain related to the surgical intervention
Goal: Adolescent will experience diminishing pain.
Interventions:
(1) Reassure the adolescent that phantom pain is normal.
(2) Administer analgesics as ordered.
(3) Provide a quiet environment.

7. Evaluation
a. Adolescent utilizes adaptive devices to maintain maximum mobility.
b. Adolescent accepts his/her alteration in body image.
c. Adolescent is free of postoperative pain.

Other Alterations of Health

A. **Infectious Mononucleosis** An infection, caused by the Epstein-Barr virus, that causes enlargement of lymphoid tissue throughout the body.
1. Assessment
a. Clinical manifestations vary in type, severity, and duration. They are fever, pharyngitis, tonsillitis, enlargement of cervical lymph nodes, enlarged spleen, malaise, anorexia, skin rashes, and headache.

b. Hepatic involvement, often associated with jaundice.

c. DIAGNOSTIC MEASURES

(1) Presence of lymphocytosis with atypical lymphocytes.

(2) A high heterophil antibody titer.

(3) Positive Monospot test.

2. Patient care management

a. Bedrest during the acute phase.

b. Mild analgesics to decrease pain.

c. Antipyretics to lower fever.

3. Nursing diagnoses/goals/interventions

a. Pain related to sore throat, muscle soreness, and low-grade temperature
Goal: Adolescent will be free of pain.
Interventions:

(1) Administer analgesics/antipyretics as ordered.

(2) Encourage prolonged periods of rest and sleep.

(3) Provide quiet diversional activities.

(4) Relieve sore throat with appropriate gargles.

b. Alteration in nutrition: less than body requirements related to anorexia and sore throat
Goal: Adolescent will maintain an adequate intake.
Interventions:

(1) Assess the adolescent's likes and dislikes.

(2) Provide small, frequent feedings.

(3) Encourage increased intake of fluids.

(4) Recommend a bland, soft diet if throat is sore.

4. Evaluation

a. Adolescent no longer experiences any clinical manifestations of infectious mononucleosis.

b. Adolescent maintains an adequate intake.

B. **Insulin-Dependent Diabetes Mellitus** An alteration in the ability to metabolize carbohydrates due to a deficiency of insulin.

Deficient insulin production prevents the breakdown of glucose for energy, the transportation of glucose to muscle and fat cells, and the storage of glycogen in the liver and muscle. An increased glucose concentration occurs in the blood (hyperglycemia). A decrease in osmotic pressure causes body fluid to shift from the intracellular spaces to the extracellular spaces and into the glomerular filtrate.

When the glucose concentration in the glomerular filtrate exceeds the threshold, glucose spills into the urine. Polyuria occurs. The excessive urine output leads to polydipsia. When glucose is unavailable, the body breaks down fats and proteins for energy. The body is in a state of starvation. Polyphagia occurs. Increased food intake further elevates the blood sugar, and more glucose is spilled into the urine. Fat is broken down at a faster rate, and excessive ketone bodies are eliminated via the urine (ketonuria) or the lungs (acetone breath). If this sequence of events is not reversed, dehydration, electrolyte imbalance, acidosis, coma, and eventually death result.

1. Assessment

a. Determine whether there is a family history of diabetes.

b. Assess for the three cardinal symptoms of diabetes: polyuria, polydipsia, and polyphagia.

c. DIAGNOSTIC MEASURES

(1) A glucose tolerance test reveals prolonged high levels of glucose in the blood.

(2) Glucose and acetone are present in the urine.

2. Patient care management

a. Administration of insulin

(1) Short-acting insulins

(a) Regular insulin: Onset of action is 30 minutes to 1 hour, peak of action is 2 to 4 hours, and duration of action is 6 to 8 hours.

(b) Semilente insulin: Onset of action is 1 hour, peak of action is 2 to 6 hours, and duration of action is 12 to 16 hours.

(c) Humulin R insulin: Onset of action is 30 minutes to 1 hour, peak of action is 1 to 3 hours, and duration of action is 6 to 8 hours.

(2) Intermediate-acting insulins

(a) NPH insulin: Onset of action is 3 to 4 hours, peak of action is 8 to 12 hours, and duration of action is 24 hours.

(b) Lente insulin: Onset of action is 1 to 2+ hours, peak of action is 8 to 12 hours, and duration of action is 24 hours.

(c) Humulin N insulin: Onset of action is 2 hours, peak of action is 6 to 10 hours, and duration of action is 18 to 24 hours.

(3) Long-acting Ultralente insulin: Onset of action is 4 to 6 hours, peak of action is 18 to 24 hours, and duration of action is 36+ hours.

b. Dietary modifications

(1) The diet may be based on exchange lists where specific amounts of calories, proteins, carbohydrates, and fats are calculated for daily consumption.

(2) An unrestricted or free diet may be utilized.

(a) The diet is not calculated.

(b) Carbohydrate excesses are avoided.

(c) Meal patterns must be consistent from day to day.

c. Treatment of hypoglycemia

(1) Fruit juice or milk is given when early symptoms are present.

(2) Glucagon is given intramuscularly when the patient is unconscious at home.

(3) If there is no response, the patient is hospitalized and glucose is given intravenously.

d. Treatment of hyperglycemia.

(1) Regular insulin is given intravenously.

(2) Sodium bicarbonate is given intravenously to treat severe acidosis.

(3) Potassium supplement is administered intravenously.

3. Nursing diagnoses/goals/interventions

a. Altered nutrition: less than body requirements related to the body's inability to use available nutrients

Goal: Adolescent's blood glucose level will be within normal limits.

Interventions:

(1) Monitor blood glucose levels with glucometer.

(2) Administer insulin as prescribed.

(3) Encourage adherence to the prescribed diet.

(4) Provide meals and snacks at approximately the same time each day.

(5) Encourage adherence to a daily exercise plan.

b. Risk for infection related to hyperglycemia

Goal: Adolescent will be free of infection.

Interventions:

(1) Teach the adolescent and family proper foot care.

(a) Bathe feet daily, and apply a lotion to soften the skin.

(b) Cut and trim toenails correctly.

(c) Wear properly fitted shoes.

(2) Avoid contact of the adolescent with other persons having infections.

(3) Treat any infections that occur promptly.

c. Knowledge deficit related to medical management

Goal: Adolescent and family will understand and demonstrate the various aspects of diabetic care.

Interventions:

(1) Allow the adolescent and the family to verbalize feelings and ask questions.

(2) Provide teaching according to the adolescent's developmental level.

(3) Teach the principles of diabetic management.

(a) Teach the adolescent and the family urine testing for ketone.

(b) Teach the adolescent and the family to perform capillary blood glucose measurements.

(c) Teach the adolescent and the family insulin administration.
  1. Demonstrate injecting insulin into deep subcutaneous tissue.
  2. Provide the adolescent and his/her family with an opportunity to practice insulin administration.
  3. Emphasize the importance of rotation of sites.
(d) Teach the adolescent and the family dietary modifications.
(e) Teach the adolescent and the family the importance of maintaining a consistent daily exercise program.
(f) Teach the adolescent and the family the signs of hypoglycemia and treatment (see page 150, C.)
  1. Mild to moderate reactions: pallor, weakness, dizziness, sweating, tremors, sudden hunger, emotional lability, double vision, and dilated pupils.
  2. Severe reactions: alterations in levels of consciousness, convulsions, coma and death.
  3. Laboratory findings: low serum glucose and urine negative for glucose and acetone.
(g) Teach the adolescent and the family the factors precipitating hypoglycemia.
  1. Hypoglycemia occurs most often at the time of peak insulin action. A snack should be provided at this time.

  2. Insulin overdose, decreased dietary intake, and increased exercise may cause hypoglycemia.
(h) Teach the adolescent and the family the signs of hyperglycemia.
  1. Early signs: disorientation, lethargy, nausea, vomiting, anorexia, abdominal pain, and extreme thirst.
  2. Later signs: dehydration, acetone breath, hyperpnea, flushed face, cherry red lips, little perspiration, decreased blood pressure, and increased pulse.
  3. Laboratory findings: **high** serum glucose and urine positive for glucose and acetone.
(i) Teach the adolescent and the family the factors precipitating hyperglycemia.
  1. Hyperglycemia occurs most often at the end of the duration of insulin action.
  2. Insufficient insulin, increased dietary intake, infection, and emotional disturbances may cause hyperglycemia.

4. Evaluation
  a. Adolescent metabolizes available nutrients adequately in order to promote normal growth and development.
  b. Adolescent's blood glucose measurements are within normal limits.
  c. Adolescent has no signs of complications of diabetes mellitus.
  d. Adolescent and his/her family understand and demonstrate the various aspects of diabetic care.

UNIT SEVEN

Meeting the Needs of the Young Adult

(19 to 39 years)

Alterations in Blood and Blood-Forming Organs

A. Disorders of the Blood and Blood-Forming Organs
   1. General assessment
   2. General patient care management
   3. Nursing diagnoses/goals/interventions
   4. Evaluation
   5. Aplastic anemia
   6. Iron-deficiency anemia
   7. Hodgkin's disease
   8. Disseminated Intravascular Coagulation (DIC)

Alterations That Interfere with the Meeting of Nutritional Needs

A. General Assessment
B. Alterations in Absorption
   1. Crohn's disease
   2. Ulcerative colitis
   3. Assessment of Crohn's disease and ulcerative colitis
   4. Patient care management of Crohn's disease and ulcerative colitis
   5. Nursing role for Crohn's disease and ulcerative colitis
   6. Management of the patient undergoing colon surgery
   7. Herniorrhaphy
C. Management of patients with intestinal disorders
   1. Herniorrhaphy
   2. Appendicitis

Alterations in Metabolism (Hepatic and Biliary Alterations)

A. General Assessment
B. Liver Disorders
   1. Viral hepatitis (HAV) A
   2. Hepatitis B virus (HBV)
C. Biliary Disorders
   1. Biliary obstruction
   2. Management of the patient undergoing biliary surgery
   3. Other procedures

Alterations in Fluid and Electrolyte Elimination

A. Acute Renal Failure
   1. Causes
   2. Phases

B. Chronic Renal Failure
C. Care of the Patient with Renal Failure
D. Management of the Patient Undergoing Dialysis
   1. Peritoneal dialysis
   2. Hemodialysis

Alterations in Perception and Coordination

A. General Assessment
B. Traumatic Injuries
   1. Fractures in general
   2. Head injuries
   3. Management of the unconscious patient
   4. Management of the patient undergoing intracranial surgery
   5. Spinal cord impairment
   6. Management of the patient undergoing spinal surgery
C. Rheumatoid Arthritis
D. Multiple Sclerosis
E. Systemic Lupus Erythematosus

Alterations in Behavior

A. Anxiety
B. Somatoform Disorders
C. Dissociative Disorders
D. Care of the Patient with Anxiety Disorders, Somatoform Disorders, and Dissociative Disorders
E. Schizophrenia
F. Mood Disorders
G. Personality Disorders
H. Substance-Related Disorders
I. Spousal Abuse
J. Rape
Appendix: Psychotropic Drugs

Alterations That Interfere with the Meeting of Sexual Needs

A. Alterations of Normal Menstruation
B. Vaginitis
C. Alterations of the Pelvis
   1. Endometriosis
   2. Pelvic inflammatory disease
D. Alterations of the Uterus
   1. Retroversion
   2. Fibroid tumors
E. Infertility
F. Acquired Immune Deficiency Syndrome (AIDS)

DEVELOPMENTAL TASKS

According to Erikson, the major developmental tasks of early adulthood are:

1. Intimacy—sharing feelings in heterosexual relations (marriage and parenthood).
2. Firm grasp of identity.
3. Occupational choice.
4. Sense of commitment with others (affiliations and partnerships).

Maladaptation or danger in this stage: isolation due to lack of interpersonal skills, or faulty ones, in developing relationships with others.

HEALTH PROMOTION OF THE YOUNG ADULT

Health Status*

1. Young adults are the healthiest people in the population. Few young adults are seriously sick or incapacitated. Very few have chronic conditions.
2. Women in this age group see physicians more frequently than men do, partially because of routine visits that focus on the reproductive system. They seem to be more sensitive to their bodies, therefore perceiving symptoms and acting upon them sooner, and to have a more elaborate vocabulary for describing symptoms.
3. The most frequent reasons for hospitalization in this age group are childbirth, accidents, and digestive and genitourinary system diseases.
4. The death rate is higher for males than for females.
5. The biggest killer of young men in this society is accidents, particularly automobile accidents. The biggest threat to black men is homicide. Very few young men die of disease.
6. Men in this age group have more heart attacks than women, and those over the age of 35 and in sedentary occupations have more than do active people.
7. Cancer (breast and uterine cancer for women, and lung cancer for men) is the second most frequent cause of death for people over 35.

Routine Health Care of Young Women

1. Physical examination which includes menstrual history, sexual history, pelvic examination, breast examination (women should be taught monthly SBE), Pap smear.

2. Pelvic examination—every year
   a. Inspection of external genitalia.
   b. Speculum exam—visualization.
   c. Bimanual exam—insertion of fingers of one hand into vagina while abdomen is palpated with the other hand.
   d. Rectal exam.
3. Pap smear, diagnostic for cervical cancer—every year
   a. Class I: Normal
   b. Class II: Inflammation
   c. Class III: Mild to moderate dysplasia
   d. Class IV: Probably malignant
   e. Class V: Malignant

Routine Health Care of Young Men

1. Rectal-prostatic and breast examinations should be part of annual routine checkup.
2. Testicular self-examination should be included in health-maintenance patient teaching.

Contraception, Voluntary Interruption of Pregnancy, and Sterilization

A. Contraception
   1. Attitudes toward contraception
      a. Shaped by religious and cultural background.
      b. Influenced by family's attitudes.
      c. Affected by socioeconomic status.
      d. Influenced by both partners' definitions of roles
   2. Influences on effectiveness: intrinsic value of method, acceptability to couple, couple's understanding of method, motivation of couple to use method properly.
   3. Nursing role
      a. Explain all available methods.
      b. Discuss effectiveness, advantages, and disadvantages of each method.
      c. Discuss couple's feelings about contraception.
      d. Once a method is chosen, instruct both partners in the use of the method.
      e. Have the couple return explanation of method chosen.
      f. Clarify any misunderstandings.

---

* Adapted from *Human Development* by Diane Papalia and Sally Olds, pp. 407–408 Copyright © 1981 by McGraw-Hill Book Company. Used with the permission of McGraw-Hill Book Company.

4. Methods of birth control
   a. Rhythm
      (1) Types are as follows.
         (a) Calendar—estimate date of ovulation based on length of cycle (low effectiveness).
         (b) Basal body temperature (BBT)
            1. Identification of ovulation by drop and rise in BBT
            2. Identification of "safe" periods, considering that ova must be fertilized within 24 hours and sperm survives 24 to 48 hours.
      (2) Success depends on motivation of couple.
   b. Chemical agents—creams, foams, jellies, or suppositories.
      (1) Have a spermicidal effect.
      (2) Also act as a mechanical barrier to sperm.
   c. Diaphragm—covers the external os and acts as a mechanical barrier.
      (1) Should be used in conjunction with a chemical agent to increase effectiveness. Leave in place for 6 hours.
      (2) Needs to be fitted; should be refitted after delivery or weight change of more than 15 pounds.
   d. Condom—mechanical barrier that collects sperm and prevents its deposit in vaginal canal
      (1) Decreases penile sensation.
      (2) Can rupture during intercourse.
      (3) Is available without prescription and is inexpensive.
   e. Coitus interruptus—withdrawal of penis before ejaculation.
   f. Oral contraceptives—hormone therapy that suppresses ovulation.
      (1) Single-hormone therapy
         (a) Estrogen given 2 weeks of each month prevents ovulation by suppressing LH and FSH.
         (b) Progesterone given daily makes cervical mucus impervious to sperm and prevents maturation of endometrium. Ovulation occurs, but fertilization and implantation are prevented.
      (2) Combined-hormone therapy
         (a) This is a combination of estrogen and progesterone.
         (b) It is taken from day 5 to day 25 of cycle.
         (c) Bleeding starts 1 to 4 days after the last pill.
      (3) Contraindications: family history of stroke, migraines, hypertension, diabetes, chronic renal disease, thrombophlebitis, heavy smoking (2 packs per day).
      (4) Side effects: nausea and vomiting, edema and weight gain, breakthrough bleeding, thrombophlebitis, pulmonary embolism, stroke.
   g. Intrauterine devices—coil, ring, or loop, made of plastic or metal. Exact action unknown—may prevent implantation.
      (1) Side effects: heavy menstrual bleeding, severe cramping, bleeding between periods.
      (2) Complications: uterine perforation, infections
      (3) Necessary precaution: woman should check for "string" in vagina before intercourse and after period.
   h. Vaginal sponge—polyurethane sponge soaked with spermicide, which is activated by adding water and released continuously for 24 hours; has woven loop for retrieval from vagina.
      (1) Side effects: allergic reaction, irritation.
      (2) Necessary precaution: sponge should not be removed for 6 hours after last intercourse.
   i. Cervical cap—plastic cap that covers cervix. Presized, small, medium, large—should be left in only for 48 hours.
   j. Long-acting methods.
      (1) Norplant—5 years.
      (2) Depo-Provera—3 months.
B. Voluntary Interruption of Pregnancy
   1. Indications
      a. Medical: chronic physical or psychiatric disorder of mother, genetic defects or erythroblastosis of fetus; usually termed "therapeutic."
      b. Nonmedical: financial, social, or personal reasons; usually termed "voluntary."

2. Legality
   a. The U.S. Supreme Court decided in 1973 that the states do not have the right to bar abortion until the fetus is viable (approximately 24 weeks of pregnancy).
   b. In July 1989 the U.S. Supreme Court sent the abortion issue back to the states to decide.
3. Methods
   a. First trimester—
      (1) **Menstrual extraction** Aspiration of endometrium in women who have not yet missed a period.
      (2) **D & C** Cervix is dilated and contents of uterus are removed; endometrium is curretted to assure that all products of conception are removed (up to 12 weeks).
      (3) **Suction aspiration** Cervix is dilated, and products of conception are suctioned out of uterus.
   b. Second trimester—
      (1) **Hysterotomy** Surgical incision into uterus to remove products of conception.
      (2) **Saline injection** Amniocentesis is performed; amniotic fluid is removed and replaced with hypertonic saline solution; onset of contractions occurs between 8 and 48 hours; fetus is delivered vaginally; called "salting out."
      (3) **Prostaglandins** These may be administered vaginally into uterine cavity or abdominally into amniotic sac; contractions usually occur within 30 minutes; abortion takes place within 24 hours.
4. Possible complications
   a. All methods: infection and hemorrhage.
   b. D & C : uterine perforation.
   c. Suction: inversion of uterus.
   d. Saline injection: fluid and electrolyte imbalance and cardiac arrhythmias.
5. Nursing diagnoses/goals/interventions
   a. Knowledge deficit related to abortion procedures (preabortion)
      Goal: Client will verbalize understanding of her options in terminating pregnancy.
      Interventions:
      (1) Discuss the possibility of abortion in an open, nonjudgmental manner.
      (2) Be supportive during decision making.
      (3) Inform the client of available resources for abortion.
      (4) Explain exactly what the procedure will involve.
   b. Risk for injury related to abortion procedure (postabortion)
      Goal: Client will experience no complications of procedure.
      Interventions:
      (1) Check vital signs every 15 minutes for 1 hour.
      (2) Observe for excessive bleeding.
      (3) Observe for electrolyte imbalance in saline injection.
      (4) Provide abdominal postoperative care for hysterotomy.
      (5) Administer RhoGAM to RH-negative women who have been aborted.
      (6) Instruct the client to seek medical assistance for increased bleeding or signs of infection (fever, abdominal pain, foul-smelling vaginal discharge).
      (7) Discuss contraceptive methods.
6. Evaluation
   a. Client makes an informed decision regarding abortion.
   b. Client experiences no complications from abortion.

C. Sterilization
   1. Factors to consider
      a. Sterilization should be considered permanent; there is a low success rate in attempts to reestablish fertility.
      b. Voluntary sterilization is permitted in all states except Utah, which requires a medical condition that threatens the mother's life.
      c. Sterilization of minors or mentally incompetent persons is restricted by most states.
   2. Methods
      a. Male: **vasectomy** Surgical interruption of the vas deferens.
      b. Female
         (1) Removal of ovaries or uterus; rarely done unless pathology exists.
         (2) **Tubal ligation** Surgical interruption of the continuity of the fallopian tubes.

Pregnancy

A. Anatomy
  1. Reproductive organs
     a. External genitalia (vulva): mons veneris, labia majora and labia minora, clitoris, vestibule, hymen, Bartholin's glands, urethral meatus, Skene's glands, perineum.
     b. Internal organs
        (1) Vagina—canal that extends from introitus to cervix; situated between the bladder and the rectum. Functions: passageway for sperm's entrance to uterus, for discharge of menstrual flow, and for fetus emerging from the uterus.
        (2) Cervix—neck of uterus; joins uterus to vagina; consists of internal os, cervical canal, and external os.
        (3) Uterus—muscular cavity situated between bladder and rectum. Fundus—portion of uterus superior to tubal insertion. Corpus—body of uterus. Functions: implantation and growth of fetus; organ from which menstrual discharge flows.
        (4) Fallopian tubes—two small tubular structures that extend from the cornua of the uterus to the ovaries; distal ends of tubes are fimbriated. Functions: fertilization takes place in tubes; peristaltic action propels fertilized ova into the uterus within 3 to 4 days.
        (5) Ovaries—flat, round organs located on either side of uterus; contain ova (female germ cells). Function: expulsion of ova; production of hormones.
  2. Structure of pelvis
     a. Bones of pelvis: right and left innominates, sacrum, coccyx.
     b. Divisions of pelvis
        (1) False pelvis—above the linea terminalis; supports the enlarging uterus.
        (2) True pelvis—below the line of terminalis; consists of pelvic inlet, pelvic cavity, and pelvic outlet; must be "adequate" for delivery.
     c. Types of pelves
        (1) Gynecoid—"normal" female pelvis; well rounded, ideal for delivery.
        (2) Antropoid—narrow transverse diameter; large anteroposterior diameter of inlet.
        (3) Platypelloid—oval inlet; shallow anteroposterior diameter.
        (4) Android pelvis—"male" pelvis; inlet has shallow posterior portion and pointed anterior portion; least suited for vaginal delivery.
     d. Pelvic measurements—done manually early in pregnancy to determine general adequacy of pelvis. X-ray pelvimetry done late in pregnancy or during labor to determine relationship of presenting part to pelvis; done only if disproportion is suspected.
        (1) Diagonal conjugate—most important pelvic measurement; distance between sacral prominence and lower margin of symphysis pubis (diameter of the inlet); must be at least 11.5 cm.
        (2) True conjugate (conjugate vera)—measurement between anterior surface of sacral prominence and posterior surface of symphysis pubis; narrowest portion through which presenting part must pass; can be measured only indirectly or by X-ray; average is 11 cm.
        (3) Ischial tuberosity diameter—transverse diameter of the outlet; measurement between the ischial tuberosities; greater than 8 cm is adequate.
B. Physiology
  1. Menstrual cycle
     a. Cycle usually occurs between ages 12 and 45.
     b. Length of cycle varies from 25 to 35 days; average is 28 days.
     c. Ovulation occurs 14 days before menstruation begins.
     d. There are three phases.
        (1) Proliferative phase (from 5th day to day of ovulation)
           (a) Anterior pituitary secretes FSH (follicle-stimulating hormone).

(b) FSH stimulates growth of the graafian follicle.

(c) Graafian follicle produces estrogen.

(d) Estrogen stimulates proliferation of the endometrium.

(e) Increase of estrogen suppresses FSH and stimulates LH (lutenizing hormone).

(f) LH stimulates ovulation and initiates formation of corpus luteum.

(g) Ovulation occurs.

(2) Secretory phase (from ovulation to 3 days before next menstrual period)

(a) LH stimulates development of corpus luteum, which replaces the ruptured graafian follicle.

(b) Corpus luteum secretes large amount of progesterone and some estrogen.

(c) The lining of the uterus is readied for implantation.

(3) Menstrual phase

(a) Corpus luteum degenerates about 8 days after ovulation unless fertilization occurs.

(b) Progesterone and estrogen drop.

(c) Endometrium degenerates and menstruation begins.

(d) Onset of flow marks the beginning of a new cycle.

2. Fertilization

a. Fertilization occurs when an ovum and a sperm unite.

b. Ovum must be fertilized within 24 hours after ovulation.

c. Fertilization takes place in the distal third of the fallopian tubes.

d. The fertilized ovum take 3 to 4 days to migrate to the uterus.

e. The ovum is free floating in the uterus for another 3 to 4 days.

f. On the 7th or 8th day, the fertilized ovum imbeds in the uterine lining; this is called *implantation* or *nidation*.

3. Fetal development

a. Fertilized ovum is called an *embryo* for the first 2 months of development.

b. There are three primary embryonic layers.

(1) Ectoderm—outer layer: develops into nervous system, skin, hair, nails, sense organs, mucous membrane of anus and mouth.

(2) Mesoderm—middle layer: develops into connective tissue, bones, muscles, cartilage, tendons, kidneys, ureters, reproductive system, heart, circulatory system, blood cells.

(3) Entoderm—inner layer: develops into the lining of the gastrointestinal tract, tonsils, parathyroids, thyroid and thymus glands, bladder, urethra.

c. The first 8 weeks of development constitute the most vulnerable period.

d. Embryo is called a *fetus* from 2 months to delivery.

e. Developmental milestones (1 lunar month = 4 weeks) are as follows.

(1) First lunar month: 30 mm long; weighs 1 gm; does not appear human; heart appears as bulge on anterior surface.

(2) Second lunar month: 4 cm long; weighs 1 gm; organogenesis is complete; heart is beating; facial features are discernible; external genitalia are present but not distinguishable; legs, arms, fingers, toes, elbows, and knees have developed.

(3) Third lunar month: 9 cm long; weighs 30 gm; nail beds are forming; is capable of spontaneous movement; ossification centers are forming in bones; tooth buds are present; male and female features are distinguishable; kidney secretion begins.

(4) Fourth lunar month: 16 cm long; weighs 124 gm; fetal heart beat can be heard; lanugo is forming.

(5) Fifth lunar month: 25 cm long; weighs 248 gm; quickening occurs; age of viability.

(6) Sixth lunar month: 30 cm long; weighs 680 gm; passive antibody transfer occurs; vernix caseosa forms; production of lung surfactant begins; eyebrows and eyelashes are defined.

(7) Seventh lunar month: 35 cm long; weighs 1.1 kg; eyes can open; lung alveoli appear; surfactant can be found in amniotic fluid.

(8) Eighth lunar month: 43 cm long; weighs 1.6 to 1.8 kg; can hear; subcutaneous fat begins to be deposited; assumes delivery position.

(9) Ninth lunar month: 46 cm long; weighs 2.2 to 2.7 kg; stores glycogen, iron, calcium, and carbohydrates; more subcutaneous fat is deposited; testes descend; lanugo begins to diminish; one or two criss-cross creases appear on soles of feet.

4. Placenta
    a. Development
        (1) Placenta is complete by third month.
        (2) It is formed by union of chorionic villi and decidua basalis.
        (3) Fetal surface is smooth (Schultz).
        (4) Maternal surface is rough (Duncan).
        (5) Umbilical cord is implanted in center of fetal surface.
        (6) Umbilical cord contains two arteries and one vein.
        (7) Umbilical cord is covered by Wharton's jelly.
    b. Functions
        (1) Exchange of O_2 and nutrients from mother for CO_2 and waste products from baby.
            (a) There is no direct mixing of maternal and fetal blood.
            (b) There is a placental barrier, and exchange takes place by selective osmosis.
            (c) Drugs, antibodies, and certain viruses can cross the barrier.
            (d) Most bacteria cannot cross the barrier.
        (2) Hormone production: HCG (human chorionic gonadotropin), estrogen and progesterone, HPL (human placental hormone).

5. Fetal circulation
    a. Vein carries oxygenated blood.
    b. Arteries carry unoxygenated blood.
    c. Circulation functions by a series of bypasses.
        (1) Foramen ovale—shunts blood from right to left atria.
        (2) Ductus arteriosus—shunts blood from pulmonary artery to aorta.
        (3) Ductus venosus—bypasses fetal liver.
    d. These bypass structures close at birth.
6. Fetal membranes
    a. Chorion—outer membrane.
    b. Amnion—inner membrane; produces amniotic fluid.
        (1) Fetus swallows amniotic fluid.
        (2) Amniotic fluid is alkaline.
        (3) Quantity usually ranges from 500 to 1000 ml.
        (4) Fetus urinates into fluid.
        (5) Fluid serves as a protective mechanism—cushions fetus and keeps temperature constant.

C. Maternal Changes during Pregnancy
    1. Reproductive organs
        a. Uterus
            (1) The uterus enlarges and thickens.
            (2) There is an increase in fibroelastic tissue.
            (3) Blood vessels increase in size.
            (4) Lower segment softens (Hegar's sign).
        b. Cervix
            (1) Cervix becomes more vascular and edematous.
            (2) A mucous plug (operculum) forms.
            (3) Cervix softens (Goodell's sign).
        c. Vagina
            (1) Vagina shows increased vascularity.
            (2) Secretions increase.
            (3) There is a bluish discoloration (Chadwick's sign).
        d. Ovaries—ovulation ceases.
    2. Breast
        a. Feeling of fullness.
        b. Hyperplasia.
        c. Darkening of areola.
        d. Enlargement of Montgomery's glands.
        e. Increase in vascularity.
        f. Secretion of colostrum by 4th month.

3. Abdomen
   a. Abdomen stretches to accommodate growing uterus.
   b. Umbilicus flattens or protrudes.
   c. Rectus muscles may separate.
4. Skin
   a. Striate gravidarum (stretch marks) on abdomen.
   b. Linea nigra (brown line) on abdomen.
   c. Melasma (chloasma) on face ("mask of pregnancy").
   d. Vascular spiders on thighs.
   e. Increased perspiration.
5. Circulation
   a. Circulating volume increases 30 to 50%.
   b. There is increased cardiac output.
   c. Pseudoanemia is caused by increased volume.
   d. Circulation to lower extremities decreases as uterus enlarges.
   e. Palpitations may occur.
   f. Blood pressure should not increase.
   g. Circulating fibrinogen increases.
6. Respiratory system
   a. Diaphragm is displaced.
   b. Lungs expand horizontally.
   c. Lung capacity increases.
7. Digestive system
   a. Stomach and intestines are displaced.
   b. Peristalsis of intestines slows.
   c. Emptying time of stomach is delayed.
   d. Heartburn and constipation are common.
   e. Nausea and vomiting are common during the first trimester.
   f. Appetite increases after first 3 months.
8. Urinary system
   a. Output increases.
   b. Specific gravity decreases.
   c. Renal threshold for sugar decreases; sugar may spill into urine.
   d. Ureters increase in diameter.
   e. Increase in frequency occurs first 3 months and last 3 weeks.
9. Bones and teeth
   a. Pelvic ligaments and joints soften.
   b. Hypertrophy and bleeding of gums are common.
   c. Teeth should not demineralize.
10. Endocrine system
    a. There is increased estrogen and progesterone from placenta.
    b. FSH and LH are absent.
    c. Thyroid enlarges.
    d. PBI increases.
    e. Parathyroids enlarge.
    f. Adrenal cortex hypertrophies and increases in activity.
11. Metabolism
    a. Pregnancy is a hypermetabolic state.
    b. Basal metabolic rate increases up to 20%.
    c. Normal weight gain is 25 pounds.
    d. There is a tendency to retain fluid.

D. Diagnosis of Pregnancy and Calculation of EDC
   1. Signs and symptoms of pregnancy
      a. *Presumptive:* signs that can be caused by conditions other than pregnancy
         (1) Amenorrhea—absence of menstruation.
         (2) Fatigue—early in pregnancy, even before first missed period.
         (3) Nausea and vomiting—"morning sickness."
         (4) Increased frequency of urination—expanding uterus puts pressure on base of bladder.
         (5) Breast changes: feeling of fullness, darkening of areola, enlargement of Montgomery's glands, secretion of colostrum.
         (6) Vaginal change: bluish discoloration (Chadwick's sign).
         (7) Skin changes: striae gravidarum—"stretch marks," linea nigra, facial melasma (chloasma—"mask of pregnancy").
         (8) Quickening—"fetal movement" felt by mother.
      b. *Probable:* signs that are more reliable than presumptive signs, but can still have other causes
         (1) Uterine changes
             (a) Size: enlarged—must be uterine enlargement, not abdominal.
             (b) Position: anteflexed.
             (c) Consistency
                 1. Hegar's sign—softening of lower uterine segment.
                 2. Goodell's sign—softening of cervix.

(2) Ballottement: rebound of fetus against an examining hand (pedunculated tumors also demonstrate this phenomenon).

(3) Fetal outline: palpated by examiner; tumors can mimic outline.

(4) Braxton-Hicks contractions: painless uterine contractions.

(5) Laboratory tests: based on fact that human chorionic gonadotropin (HCG) is present in urine of pregnant women—95% accurate.

c. *Positive:* signs that prove a fetus is present; not usually determined until 5th month

(1) Fetal heartbeat—can usually be auscultated by 18th week; earlier with electronic devices.

(2) Fetal outline

(a) Ultrasound—accurate after 3rd month

(b) X-ray—should be used only after 5th month and then only if absolutely necessary.

(3) Fetal movements—recognized by examiner.

2. Calculation of EDC (Estimated Date of Confinement)

a. Naegele's rule: Use first day of last menstrual period (LMP). EDC = LMP − 3 months + 7 days.

b. McDonald's rule: Use fundal height. Height of fundus (in cm) × 8/7 = duration of pregnancy in weeks.

c. Naegele's rule is more commonly used. Five percent of pregnancies will deliver on EDC as calculated by Naegele's rule. Ninety percent within 1 week either way.

E. Discomforts of Pregnancy

1. Nausea and vomiting

a. Cause: altered hormone levels; occurs during first trimester.

b. Assessment: Determine what time of day nausea occurs; rule out other causes of GI upset.

c. Patient care management: sedatives or antiemetics if necessary.

d. Nursing role (patient education)

(1) Teach the woman to keep dry crackers at bedside to eat before arising

(2) Modify diet to small, frequent feedings of bland food.

2. Heartburn

a. Cause: regurgitation of gastric secretions into the esophagus due to decreased gastric motility.

b. Patient care management: Maalox or Gelusil may be used.

c. Nursing role (patient education)

(1) Explain the cause of heartburn.

(2) Explain that it has nothing to do with the heart.

(3) Teach the woman to eat small, frequent meals.

(4) Teach the woman not to lie down after meals.

3. Increased frequency of urination

a. Occurrence: during first 3 months until uterus rises out of pelvic cavity, and late in pregnancy after lightening.

b. Assessment: Ask whether urination is accompanied by burning or there is blood in the urine.

4. Constipation

a. Cause: pressure of growing uterus on bowel and decreased peristalsis.

b. Assessment: Ascertain woman's regular bowel habits.

c. Patient care management: stool softeners such as Colace; laxatives and enemas are contraindicated.

d. Nursing role (patient education)

(1) Encourage good bowel habits.

(2) Teach the woman to increase fruits and vegetables in diet.

(3) Increase fluid intake.

(4) Encourage regular exercise.

5. Hemorrhoids

a. Cause: congestion of rectal veins due to pressure of enlarging uterus.

b. Assessment: Determine history of hemorrhoids, size, bleeding if any, burning, pain, thrombosis.

c. Patient care management

(1) Resolution usually follows delivery.

(2) Stool softeners or rectal suppositories may be prescribed.

(3) Excision or injection of hemorrhoids is contraindicated.

d. Nursing role (patient education)

(1) Prevent hemorrhoids by encouraging good bowel habits that decrease straining at stool.

(2) Teach the patient to rest in modified Sims's position.

(3) Teach knee-chest position.

6. Backache
   a. Cause: increased spinal curvature secondary to altered posture.
   b. Assessment: Rule out orthopedic problems.
   c. Nursing role (patient education)
      (1) Teach proper posture and pelvic rocking.
      (2) Teach importance of proper shoes, firm mattress, and sufficient rest.
7. Leg cramps
   a. Cause: pressure on nerves of lower extremities; also decreased calcium absorption due to increased circulating phosphorus.
   b. Patient care management: Amphojel to decrease amount of circulating phosphorus.
   c. Nursing role (patient education)
      (1) Assure the woman that leg cramps are normal occurrence.
      (2) Teach the woman to dorsiflex foot of involved leg while extending leg, keeping her knee straight.
8. Edema of ankles
   a. Cause: impeded venous return due to pressure on lower extremities from enlarging uterus.
   b. Assessment
      (1) Take history of daily activities.
      (2) Examine legs for varicosities.
   c. Nursing role (patient education)
      (1) Teach the woman to take frequent rest periods with legs elevated.
      (2) Teach her to avoid constricting garters or undergarments.
9. Varicose veins (distension of veins)
   a. Cause: pooling of blood in lower extremities.
   b. Assessment
      (1) Examine varicosities.
      (2) Check for signs of thrombophlebitis.
      (3) Take a history of daily activities.
      (4) Assess vitamin C intake.
   c. Patient care management: elastic stockings, vitamin C supplements.
   d. Nursing role (patient education)
      (1) Teach the woman to raise legs against wall for 15 to 20 minutes daily.
      (2) Encourage two short walks a day.
      (3) Teach sources of vitamin C.
10. Increased vaginal discharge
    a. Cause: high estrogen levels and increased blood supply to vagina.
    b. Assessment
       (1) Ask the woman to describe discharge.
       (2) Ask whether pruritus is present.
       (3) Rule out vaginal infection.
    c. Patient care management: none unless infection is present.
    d. Nursing role (patient education)
       (1) Teach the woman that daily bathing should control the problem.
       (2) Teach her not to douche unless prescribed.
       (3) Instruct her not to use bulb-type douche.
       (4) Instruct her not to use tampons.

F. Emotional Needs of Pregnancy
   1. Adjustment to motherhood
      a. Initial reaction—can range from surprise to fear, joy, or anxiety.
      b. Factors that affect perception of pregnancy: the woman's relationship with her own family, her definition of the feminine role, her economic status, her available support systems.
      c. Mood swings—father should be forewarned that these are common.
      d. Acceptance of role of mother
         (1) Role-playing—practice with other children (e.g., babysitting).
         (2) Fantasizing—what will motherhood be like?
         (3) Grieving for present role; woman must grieve for old role before she can accept new one.
      e. Nursing role (patient education)
         (1) Use therapeutic communication to help the woman express her feelings.
         (2) Reassure her that ambivalence is normal.
         (3) Explore new role with her.
   2. Adjustment to fatherhood
      a. Initial reaction—may be ambivalent.
      b. Factors that affect reaction: self-concept, willingness to share woman with child, man's definition of "father," economic status—perhaps concern over added financial responsibility.
      c. Possibility of physiological symptoms such as nausea and vomiting.

d. Acceptance of role of father—must go through same steps as the woman.

e. Nursing role (patient education)
   (1) Explain emotional changes the man should expect in the woman.
   (2) Allow him to express his feelings.
   (3) Inquire as to whether he is having any physical symptoms so he knows that these are a normal occurrence.
   (4) Explore his role with him.

3. Childbirth education
   a. Methods used
      (1) Dick-Read—based on premise that pain in labor is caused by fear and tension; aimed at breaking the fear-tension-pain triad.
      (2) Lamaze—based on the principle of conditioned response; the woman practices responses to contractions.
   b. Components of both methods
      (1) Education—includes labor and delivery process; dispels myths and superstitions.
      (2) Training—to condition the woman to use contolled breathing and exercises in labor.
      (3) Support person—husband or significant other learns method also and acts as coach in labor; presence of the support person decreases feelings of isolation.
   c. Components of each method
      (1) Dick-Read: whole-body relaxation, abdominal breathing.
      (2) Lamaze
         (a) Consciously controlled breathing—four levels of breathing to be used at different times during labor; the woman is trained to switch.
         (b) Relaxation—the woman is taught to relax all other muscle groups while contracting just one.
         (c) Distraction—the woman concentrates on a picture or other object during contractions.
         (d) Effleurage—decreases sensory stimuli to abdominal wall.

d. Nursing role (during labor)
   (1) Cooperate with the parents in the method they have chosen.
   (2) Explain to them that the woman can have medication if she chooses.
   (3) Keep the parents informed of progress of labor.
   (4) Encourage the support person during coaching.
   (5) Assist with coaching as necessary.

4. Education for parenting (based on premise that parenting is a learned skill, not inborn)
   a. Discuss the parents' expectations of parenthood.
   b. Discuss what it is like to have a newborn in the house.
   c. Discuss feeding methods: bottle-feeding and breast-feeding.
   d. Teach skills: holding, feeding and burping, changing the diaper, bathing.
   e. Have the parents practice skills and return demonstrations.
   f. Discuss their feelings about caring for the new baby.
   g. Review growth and development of infant.
   h. Teach safety measures for newborn.

G. Management of Pregnancy
   1. Patient care management
      a. First visit
         (1) History
            (a) Complete family history.
            (b) Complete medical history.
            (c) Gynecologic history: age of menarche, interval between menses and duration of menses, amount of menstrual flow, discomfort with menses, last menstrual period, birth control method used, gynecologic conditions, gynecologic surgery.
            (d) Previous pregnancies: number; dates; outcomes: course of labor, types of deliveries, condition of baby; abortions—spontaneous and voluntary; ectopic pregnancies; number of children living.

(e) Present pregnancy: calculated EDC, nature of pregnancy—planned or unplanned, signs and symptoms.

(f) Review of systems.

(2) Complete general physical examination

    (a) Weight—for baseline.

    (b) Vital signs—for baseline.

    (c) Abdominal examination—height of fundus.

    (d) Pelvic examination

        1. Vaginal—condition of cervix and vagina, position of reproductive organs.

        2. Pap smear and smear for gonorrhea.

        3. Pelvic measurements. *See* Anatomy, page 157.

    (e) Laboratory studies: urinalysis, CBC, VDRL, blood type and RH, antibody titer for rubella.

b. Health maintenance

(1) Schedule of visits: every month through 7th month, every other week in 8th month, every week in 9th month.

(2) Each visit

    (a) Check weight and blood pressure.

    (b) Test urine for sugar, acetone, protein.

    (c) Measure height of fundus.

    (d) Check fetal heart, after 14th week.

    (e) Interval history—any problems, signs or symptoms, complaints.

(3) Midway through pregnancy—repeat vaginal examination to ascertain that all is proceeding normally.

(4) Second trimester—glucose challenge.

(5) Third trimester—repeat hematocrit.

(6) At term—repeat vaginal examination each visit to check for dilatation and effacement.

2. Prenatal teaching

a. Nutrition

(1) Calories—300 additional calories daily (over recommended intake for age).

(2) Protein—should be used to increase calories in diet.

    (a) Increase of 30 gm per day is recommended

    (b) Sources of protein are meat, eggs, cheese, poultry, peanut butter, dried peas and beans, fish, milk.

    (c) Increased protein foods also supply increased iron, B vitamins, calcium, and phosphorus.

    (d) Skim milk provides as much protein as whole milk.

(3) Vitamin A—found in yellow and dark green vegetables.

(4) Vitamin C—occurring in citrus fruits, tomatoes, broccoli, cabbage, brussels sprouts.

(5) Vitamin D—supplied in fortified milk; 1 quart meets daily requirements.

(6) Daily intake of necessary foods

    (a) Meat: 2 to 3 servings.

    (b) Eggs: 1.

    (c) Vegetables: 1 serving dark green or yellow; 2 to 3 servings other vegetables.

    (d) Fruits: 1 serving citrus; 1 serving other fruit.

    (e) Bread: 4 servings.

    (f) Milk: 1 quart (whole, skim, or buttermilk).

    (g) Fluids: 2 glasses (other than milk intake).

(7) Supplementation

    (a) Most doctors order vitamin and iron supplements.

    (b) Woman should be taught to take only what is ordered; overdose of vitamins can cause defects in fetus.

b. Daily activities

(1) Employment. Most pregnant women are able to work at least until their 7th month; rest periods should be arranged during the day.

(2) Exercise
  (a) Exercise such as walking or swimming is necessary to maintain circulatory status.
  (b) Strenuous exercise to point of fatigue should be avoided.
  (c) Any activity the woman is accustomed to may be continued as long as she is comfortable unless the physician specifically advises against it.
  (d) New sports should not be learned at this time.
(3) Alcohol consumption. Occasional consumption in moderation is permited, but abstinence is encouraged.
(4) Smoking. An attempt should be made to cut down or stop during pregnancy.
(5) Drugs. No over-the-counter drugs should be used; only prescribed medication should be taken.

c. Hygiene
  (1) Bathing
    (a) Tub baths may be taken until balance is affected or membranes rupture.
    (b) Showers are permitted throughout pregnancy.
    (c) Daily bathing is encouraged.
  (2) Douching
    (a) Douching should be done only when prescribed.
    (b) A bulb-type syringe should never be used.
  (3) Clothing
    (a) Clothing should be loose and comfortable.
    (b) Garters and panty girdles should be avoided.
  (4) Dental care
    (a) Routine checkups should be done.
    (b) Extractions and fillings may be done.
    (c) Extensive dental surgery should be avoided.

d. Travel
  (1) There are no restrictions on travel early in pregnancy.
  (2) On a prolonged vacation, arrangements must be made for prenatal care while on trip.
  (3) The woman may drive as long as she is comfortable behind the wheel.
  (4) When driving long distances, frequent rest stops should be taken.
  (5) The woman should fly only on planes with well-pressurized cabins (a drop in pressure can cause fetal hypoxia).
  (6) Some airlines do not allow women over 7 months pregnant on board.

e. Sexuality
  (1) Old wives' tales should be debunked.
  (2) Intercourse is contraindicated only if membranes are ruptured or vaginal bleeding is present.
  (3) The couple may need to explore new positions to accommodate the woman's enlarging abdomen.
  (4) The couple should be advised against male oral stimulation of the woman because of the danger of air embolism.
  (5) Some doctors advise restriction of intercourse during the last month to prevent infection once cervical dilatation starts.

f. Danger signs (to be taught at first prenatal visit)
  (1) The woman should be instructed to call the doctor immediately if any of the following signs occur:
    (a) Vaginal bleeding.
    (b) Persistent vomiting.
    (c) Chills and fever.
    (d) Sudden escape of fluid from vagina.
    (e) Abdominal pain.
    (f) Swelling of face or hands.
    (g) Severe, persistent headache.
    (h) Visual disturbances: blurring or flashes of light.
  (2) The woman should be assured that there is no reason to expect any of these things to occur.

3. Assessment of fetal maturity and placental function
   a. Ultrasound.
   b. X-ray—look for presence of distal femoral ossification.
   c. L/S ratio—above 2 shows lung maturity; done by amniocentesis.
   d. Maternal urinary estriol levels—should rise as fetus matures; decrease near term indicates fetal risk.
   e. Nonstress test—measures effect of fetal movement on fetal heart rate.
   f. Biophysical profile.

H. **High-Risk Pregnancies** Pregnancy is "high risk" when there is a significantly increased chance of morbidity or mortality for mother, fetus, or both.

1. Factors to consider:
   a. Age—below 18 and over 35.
   b. Parity—more than five pregnancies.
   c. Social history—alcoholism, drug addiction.
   d. Medical history—diabetes, cardiac disease, RH factor, anemia, infections.

2. Diabetes
   a. Classifications
      Class A: abnormal glucose tolerance test, usually managed by diet, may be gestational.
      Class B: onset over age 20; duration 9 years or less.
      Class C: onset between ages 10 and 19; duration 10 to 19 years.
      Class D: onset under age 10; duration 20 years or more; vascular involvement.
      Class E: no longer used.
      Class F: nephropathy.
   b. Assessment
      (1) Do frequent blood glucose testing.
      (2) Check urine with Testape or Clinistix; they respond to glucose, not lactose (lactose is present in all pregnant women from milk formation).
      (3) Do a glucose tolerance test on any prenatal patient who has a family history of diabetes or a history of large babies.

(4) Monitor blood pressure frequently; toxemia is a possible complication.
(5) Monitor weight frequently; polyhydramnios is a possible complication.
(6) Observe for signs of hypoglycemia or hyperglycemia; insulin needs fluctuate rapidly.

c. Patient care management
   (1) Patient is seen every 2 weeks during first and second trimesters.
   (2) Patient is seen every week during third trimester.
   (3) Labor may be induced early following assessment of fetal maturity.
   (4) Fetal outcome depends on severity of disease and management during pregnancy.

d. Nursing diagnoses/goals/interventions
   (1) Knowledge deficit related to disease process
       Goal: Patient will verbalize understanding of how diabetes affects her pregnancy.
       Interventions:
       (a) Discuss effects of diabetes on pregnancy.
       (b) Explain reason for frequent laboratory tests.
       (c) Discuss the patient's diet.
   (2) Alteration in nutrition: less than body requirements, related to diabetic pregnancy
       Goal: Patient will maintain her blood sugar within normal limits.
       Interventions:
       (a) Monitor the patient in labor for hypoglycemia due to increased energy expenditure.
       (b) Monitor the patient for insulin reaction during first 48 hours postpartum because of rapid drop in insulin needs.

e. Evaluation
   (1) Patient is able to regulate her own diet to maintain blood sugar within normal limits.
   (2) Patient does not develop any complications of diabetes during delivery or postpartum.

3. Cardiac disease
   a. Classifications
      Class I: no limitation of physical activity.
      Class II: slight limitation of physical activity.
      Class III: considerable limitation of physical activity; ordinary activity produces symptoms.
      Class IV: complete limitation of physical activity; any physical activity causes symptoms; symptoms of cardiac failure occur even at rest.
   b. Assessment
      (1) Observe for signs of cardiac decompensation: circulating volume increases up to 50% during pregnancy; peaks in second trimester.
      (2) Assess for factors that increase stress: anemia, infection.
      (3) Assess home situation and daily routine for provision of rest.
      (4) Monitor the woman closely in labor and delivery, as well as postpartum, for signs of heart failure.
   c. Patient care management
      Class I: Limit stress; additional rest; forceps delivery with local anesthesia to shorten second stage.
      Class II: Prophylactic antibiotics in labor; O_2 in labor; forceps delivery.
      Class III
      and Class IV: May be hospitalized; may be induced; may need invasive cardiac monitoring.
   d. Nursing diagnosis/goal/interventions
      Decreased cardiac ouput: related to cardiac disease
      Goal: Patient will not experience cardiac failure.

Interventions:
   (1) Teach the patient her limitations and help her adjust her routines to meet them.
   (2) Refer the patient to social services for homemaker assistance if needed.
   (3) Observe the patient at each visit for signs of decompensation.
   (4) Teach the patient signs of decompensation.
   (5) During labor, keep atmosphere calm to promote rest.
   (6) Minimize discomfort in labor by analgesia and sedation.
   (7) Administer O_2 in labor.
   (8) Monitor the patient carefully in labor for signs of failure.
   (9) Continue close monitoring during postpartal period.
   (10) Arrange for help at home when the patient is discharged.
   (11) Counsel the patient regarding importance of contraception.
   e. Evaluation: Patient delivers without experiencing cardiac failure.

4. Rh blood factor.   A potential for incompatibility exists when an Rh-negative woman is carrying an Rh-positive child.
   a. Assessment: An antibody titer is done early in pregnancy on every Rh-negative mother.
      (1) If positive, repeat every month.
      (2) If negative, repeat at 20 weeks.
      (3) If titer is above 1:16, do an amniocentesis.
   b. Patient care management
      (1) If amniocentesis shows the infant is affected between 26 and 32 weeks, intrauterine transfusion should be considered every 1 or 2 weeks until the fetus is mature enough to be delivered.
      (2) A mature fetus who is affected should be delivered, usually by cesarean section.
      (3) An Rh-negative woman who delivers without developing antibodies should be given RhoGAM; RhoGAM is an Rh immunoglobulin that prevents formation of Rh antibodies in the mother by destroying any fetal red blood cells she may have received at delivery.

c. Nursing diagnosis/goal/interventions
Potential for injury related to Rh status
Goal: Patient will not develop antibodies.
Interventions:
(1) Have the Rh-negative woman crossmatched for RhoGAM immediately after delivery or abortion.
(2) Administer RhoGAM to the mother within 72 hours after delivery of an Rh-positive baby or an abortion.
d. Evaluation: Patient does not develop antibodies.
5. Anemia
a. Type: usually iron deficiency.
b. Patient care management: iron supplements, high-iron diet.
c. Nursing role (patient education): teach high-iron diet.
6. Infections
a. TORCH infectious disease: may cause congenital anomalies if contracted in first trimester
(1) Toxoplasmosis (TO).
(2) Rubella (R).
(3) Cytomegalovirus (C).
(4) Herpesvirus type 2 (H).
b. Urinary tract infections (occur in 10% of all pregnancies)
(1) Predisposing factors: pressure on ureters and bladder, displacement of bladder by uterus.
(2) Increased incidence in those prone to frequent UTI when nonpregnant.
c. Sexually transmitted diseases
(1) Syphilis
(a) Must be treated immediately—passes to fetus after 4th month.
(b) May cause abortion or premature delivery.
(2) Gonorrhea
(a) Must be treated early in pregnancy.
(b) If untreated, causes gonorrheal eye infection in newborn because of contact with organism in birth canal.
(3) Chlamydia—may cause newborn conjunctivitis or pneumonia.
(4) AIDS (*See* page 258.)

I. Alterations of Normal Pregnancy
1. First trimester
a. Spontaneous abortion (miscarriage)
(1) Types
(a) Threatened: bleeding and pain; no cervical dilatation.
(b) Inevitable: bleeding and pain with cervical dilatation.
(c) Complete: all products of conception expelled.
(d) Incomplete: some products of conception, usually placenta, retained.
(e) Habitual: spontaneous abortion in three or more succeeding pregnancies; probably due to incompetent cervix.
(2) Patient care management
(a) Control bleeding.
(b) Do D & C for incomplete abortion.
(c) If incompetent cervix, perform a Shirodkar procedure (suturing the cervix closed after conception) during next pregnancy.
(3) Nursing diagnoses/goals/interventions
(a) Altered tissue perfusion related to vaginal bleeding
Goal: Patient's vital signs will be maintained within normal limits.
Interventions:
1. Use perineal pad count to estimate amount of bleeding.
2. Monitor vital signs as frequently as amount of bleeding indicates.
3. Save any tissue passed for examination.
(b) Anxiety related to situational crisis
Goal: Patient's anxiety will be reduced
1. Let the client express her feelings.
2. Do not offer any false reassurance.
(4) Evaluation
(a) Patient's vital signs are maintained within normal limits.
(b) Patient's anxiety is reduced.

b. **Ectopic pregnancy** Any pregnancy that develops outside the uterus. Fallopian tubes are usual site; tube will rupture within 12 weeks.
  (1) Assessment: sudden, sharp pain in one of lower quadrants; symptoms of shock; vaginal bleeding—may range from spotting to profuse.
  (2) Patient care management
    (a) Replace blood loss.
    (b) Remove ruptured tube.
  (3) Nursing management *See* Unit Eight, Management of the Patient Undergoing Surgery, Section C: Management during the Postoperative Period, page 269.

c. **Hyperemesis gravidarum** Intractable nausea and vomiting that develop in first trimester, but may persist beyond that time.
  (1) Assessment
    (a) Watch for signs of dehydration.
    (b) Watch for signs of fluid and electrolyte imbalance, particularly acidosis.
  (2) Patient care management
    (a) Parental fluids, electrolytes, and vitamins.
    (b) Psychotherapy and sedatives.
    (c) Resumption of diet—six small, dry meals a day.
  (3) Nursing diagnoses/goals/interventions
    (a) Risk for fluid volume deficit related to altered intake
      Goal: Patient will maintain fluid balance.
      Intervention: Observe for signs of acidosis.
    (b) Altered nutrition: less than body requirements related to inability to ingest food
      Goal: Patient will ingest sufficient nutrients.
      Interventions:
      1. Make diet as appealing as possible.
      2. Provide rest.
      3. Decrease environmental stimuli.
    (c) Anxiety related to change in health status
      Goal: Patient's anxiety will be reduced.
      Intervention: Discuss the patient's feelings.

  (4) Evaluation
    (a) Fluid balance is maintained.
    (b) Sufficient nutrients are ingested.
    (c) Patient's anxiety is reduced.

2. Second trimester
  a. **Hydatidiform mole** Proliferation and degeneration of chorionic villi, which become filled with clear fluid. Vesicles form grapelike clusters. Usually there is no fetus.
    (1) Assessment
      (a) Rapid enlargement of uterus.
      (b) Severe nausea and vomiting.
      (c) Absence of fetal heart beat.
      (d) Vaginal passage of vesicles.
      (e) Symptoms of toxemia.
      (f) Vaginal bleeding at 4th month.
      (g) DIAGNOSTIC MEASURE: high levels of urinary HCG.
    (2) Patient care management
      (a) Evacuate uterus, then curettage.
      (b) Provide careful follow-up—mole may lead to carcinoma.
    (3) Nursing diagnosis/goal/interventions
      Anxiety related to threat to self-concept
      Goal: Patient's anxiety will be reduced.
      Interventions:
      (a) Help patient deal with loss. (She thought she was pregnant.)
      (b) Encourage follow-up care.
    (4) Evaluation: Patient's anxiety is reduced.

  b. **Fetal demise** Death of fetus after date of viability.
    (1) Assessment
      (a) Absence of fetal heartbeat and fetal movements.
      (b) Absence of fetal growth.
      (c) DIAGNOSTIC MEASURES: negative pregnancy test, low urinary estriols, ultrasound.
    (2) Patient care management: Induce labor if it does not occur spontaneously.
    (3) Nursing diagnosis/goal/interventions
      Grief related to loss of child
      Goal: Parents will successfully complete grieving process.
      Interventions:
      (a) Encourage the parents to verbalize their feelings.

(b) Allow the parents to see and hold the infant if they wish to do so.

(c) Encourage the parents to join a support group.

(4) Evaluation: Parents' grieving process is experienced and completed.

3. Third trimester

a. **Pregnancy-induced hypertension** Syndrome of pregnancy marked by increased blood pressure, edema, and proteinuria; usually occurs after 24th week.

(1) Types

(a) Mild preeclampsia: rise of 30/15 mm Hg B/P; slight edema; trace of proteinuria.

(b) Severe preeclampsia: B/P above 160/100; marked edema; marked proteinuria; visual disturbances; hyperreflexia (cerebral edema); HELLP syndrome.

(c) Eclampsia: symptoms of severe preeclampsia; urinary output less than 30 cc per hour; convulsions and coma.

(2) Patient care management

(a) Mild preeclampsia: bedrest (at home or in hospital), high-protein diet with moderate sodium restriction.

(b) Severe preeclampsia

1. Bedrest (in hospital).

2. High-protein, low-sodium diet.

3. Sedatives.

4. Magnesium sulfate (given when the patient is hyperreflexive).

a. Loading dose: 4–6 gm IV over 15–20 minutes.

b. Maintenance dose: 1–2 gm IV per hour.

c. Caution: Drug depresses CNS; test deep tendon reflexes before giving.

d. Side effect: respiratory depression.

e. Antidote: calcium gluconate.

(3) Nursing diagnoses/goals/interventions

(a) Decreased cardiac output related to hypertensive syndrome
Goals:

1. Patient's vital signs will be maintained within normal limits.

2. Patient's urinary output will be within normal limits.

3. FHR will be within normal limits.
Interventions:

1. Decrease stimuli in the environment to promote rest.

2. Monitor B/P and FHR every 4 hours in pre-eclampsia; every hour in eclampsia.

3. Record intake and output; hourly output in eclampsia.

4. Monitor daily weight.

5. Assess urine for protein every 4 hours.

6. Assess deep tendon reflexes every 4 hours.

(b) Risk for injury related to seizures
Goals:

1. Patient will sustain no injuries.

2. Infant will not experience injury *in utero*.
Interventions:

1. Maintain seizure precautions.

2. Assess for signs of labor: restlessness, bloody show, contractions.

3. Monitor fetal activity and heart rate when labor begins.

(4) Evaluation

(a) Patient's vital signs and urinary output return to normal.

(b) Patient sustains no injury.

(c) Infant is delivered safely.

b. **Placenta previa** Implanatation of placenta in lower segment of uterus.

(1) Types

(a) Partial: cervical os partially occluded.

(b) Complete: cervical os totally obstructed.

(c) Marginal: implantation along margin of os.

(2) Assessment
   (a) Watch for painless bleeding; may be intermittent or continuous.
   (b) Be aware of increased incidence in multiparas and women with fibroid tumors.
(3) Patient care management
   (a) Localize placenta by ultrasound.
   (b) If at term, deliver baby (usually by cesarean section).
   (c) If not at term, observe carefully; perform cesarean section if bleeding increases.
(4) Nursing diagnosis/goal/interventions
   Altered tissue perfusion related to vaginal bleeding
   Goals:
   (a) Patient's vital signs will be maintained within normal limits.
   (b) FHR will be within normal limits.
   Interventions:
   (a) Estimate amount of blood loss.
   (b) Monitor vital signs as frequently as bleeding indicates.
   (c) Apply external fetal monitor.
   (d) Assess for signs of shock.
   (e) Record intake and output.
   (f) Avoid rectal or vaginal examinations.
(5) Evaluation
   (a) Patient does not experience shock.
   (b) Infant is safely delivered.
c. **Abruptio placenta** Premature separation of placenta.
   (1) Incidence: higher in toxemia or direct trauma to abdomen.
   (2) Types: partial—may be at margins of placenta or in center (concealed bleeding); complete.
   (3) Assessment: sharp abdominal pain (over the fundus); bleeding that may be profuse or concealed; signs of shock; uterine distension or rigidity.
   (4) Patient care management
      (a) If in labor, hasten delivery.
      (b) If bleeding is severe or the patient is not in labor, do cesarean section.
   (5) Nursing diagnosis/goals/interventions

Nursing diagnosis and goals   *See* Placenta previa, above.
Interventions:
   (a)–(f) *See* Placenta previa, above.
   (g) Observe for bleeding in postpartal period; disseminated intravascular coagulation is common.
(6) Evaluation: *See* Placenta previa, above.
d. **Polyhydramnios** Excessive amount of amniotic fluid (more than 1500 cc).
   (1) Occurrence: frequent in fetal anomalies, diabetes, and toxemia.
   (2) Assessment: Observe for uterus enlarged disproportionately to gestation.
   (3) Patient care management
      (a) Amniocentesis can be done for temporary relief.
      (b) Labor should be induced if patient is at term.
e. **Prolonged pregnancy (over 42 weeks)**
   Placental function decreases—may endanger fetus.
   Patient care management
   (1) Labor is induced.
   (2) Cesarean section is performed if induction is not successful.

Labor and Delivery

A. The Process of Labor and Delivery
   1. Presentation, described by the fetal part presenting at the cervix
      a. Cephalic: Head is presenting.
         (1) Vertex—most common, most favorable.
         (2) Brow.
         (3) Chin.
         (4) Face.
      b. Breech
         (1) Complete: Thighs are flexed on abdomen; legs are flexed on thighs.
         (2) Frank: Thighs are flexed, and legs are extended, lying along anterior surface of body.
         (3) Footling: One or both legs are extended downward and become the presenting part.
      c. Shoulder—transverse lie: Fetus is lying horizontally across the mother's abdomen and must be delivered by cesarean section.
   2. Position: relationship of the presenting part to the quadrants of the maternal pelvis

a. Quadrants: right anterior, left anterior, right posterior, left posterior.

b. Landmarks of presenting parts: vertex—occiput, breech—sacrum, shoulder—acromial process, face—mentum (chin).

c. Most common positions (initials usually used)

   (1) LOA (left occiput anterior): Occiput of fetus points to the left anterior quadrant of the mother.

   (2) LOP (left occiput posterior): Occiput of fetus points to the left posterior quadrant of the mother.

   (3) ROA (right occiput anterior): Occiput of fetus points to the right anterior quadrant of the mother.

   (4) ROP (right occiput posterior): Occiput of fetus points to the right posterior quadrant of the mother.

d. Posterior presentations

   (1) These can be responsible for severe back pain during labor—sometimes referred to as "back labor."

   (2) They may slow the progress of labor.

   (3) The head usually rotates and is delivered from an anterior position—may be rotated manually in delivery room.

e. Assessment of fetal position

   (1) Leopold's maneuvers: abdominal palpation of fetal parts.

   (2) Rectal examination.

   (3) Vaginal examination.

3. Engagement: Largest diameter of presenting part has passed the inlet of the maternal pelvis and is at the level of the ischial spines. A presenting part that is not engaged is said to be "floating."

a. Usually occurs 2 weeks before labor in primiparas.

b. May not occur until onset of labor in multiparas.

4. Station: relationship of presenting part to ischial spines of the mother

a. Station 0: level of spines—engagement.

b. Above the spines: −1, −2, −3, −4.

c. Below the spines: +1, +2, +3, +4.

d. At +3 or +4, the presenting part is visible if vulva are separated.

5. Premonitory signs of labor, which indicate labor is impending

a. Lightening—descent of uterus into pelvic cavity as presenting part settles into pelvis (engagement).

b. Weight loss—decrease in water retention.

c. Ripening cervix—becomes softer and shorter, may dilate 1 to 2 cm.

d. Bloody show—blood-tinged, mucous vaginal discharge.

e. Ruptured membranes—may be gush or trickle.

   (1) Patient should go to hospital or doctor.

   (2) Test should be made with nitrazine paper—amniotic fluid is alkaline.

   (3) Patient should be admitted as labor usually occurs within 24 hours.

   (4) Dangers are prolapsed cord and infection.

   (5) If at term, labor will be induced if it does not start in 24 hours.

   (6) If not at term, patient will be kept on bedrest with antibiotic therapy.

   (7) Observations to make of fluid are amount, color, odor if any, meconium staining.

f. Backache—due to descent of fetus.

g. Diarrhea—increased nerve innervation due to descent.

h. Increase in Braxton-Hicks contractions

   (1) May reach uncomfortable level.

   (2) May be confused with labor.

   (3) Will not dilate cervix, but may "ripen" it.

i. Surge of energy—should conserve for labor.

6. False labor versus true labor

FALSE	TRUE
a. Irregular contractions that do not intensify	a. Regular contractions, increasing in intensity
b. Discomfort mainly in abdomen	b. Radiation of discomfort from back to abdomen
c. Discomfort relieved by walking	c. Discomfort intensified by walking
d. No changes visible in cervix	d. Effacement and dilatation of cervix

7. Theories regarding onset of labor
   a. Hormonal: increased prostaglandins, decreased progesterone, increased estrogen, oxytocin from posterior pituitary.
   b. Distended organ—a body organ stretched to capacity will contract and empty.
   c. Aging placenta—starts to degenerate at 38 weeks.
   d. A combination of all three—cause is unknown.
8. Duration of labor
   a. Factors that affect duration
      (1) Parity—once a cervix has dilated, it offers less resistance to dilating again.
      (2) Maternal age—early 20's are when muscles are most efficient.
      (3) Interval between births—if more than 10 years, result is the same as being a primipara.
      (4) Attitude of mother—anxiety retards progress.
      (5) Size of fetus—large baby usually prolongs labor.
      (6) Posterior position—this prolongs second stage.
      (7) Spontaneous rupture of membranes—this usually shortens duration.
   b. Duration for primiparas: up to 18 hours.
   c. Duration for multiparas: usually 8 to 12 hours.
9. Effacement and dilatation
   a. Effacement: shortening and thinning of cervical canal; measured in percentages (100% is full effacement).
   b. Dilatation: enlargement of external cervical os; measured in centimeters (full dilatation is 10 cm).
   c. Assessment of effacement and dilatation: rectal examination, vaginal examination.
10. Changes in uterus during labor
   a. Uterus becomes differentiated into two distinct portions.
      (1) Upper segment becomes thicker and active.
      (2) Lower segment becomes thinner, supple, and passive.
   b. Ridge appears between two portions: physiological retraction ring; cannot be palpated abdominally.
   c. If ridge can be palpated, it is termed a "pathological retraction ring" (Bandl's ring).
11. Stages of labor
   a. First—onset of true labor to full cervical dilatation
      (1) Latent phase (early active): 0 to 4 cm.
      (2) Active phase (midactive): 4 to 8 cm.
      (3) Transition phase (late active): 8 to 10 cm.
   b. Second—full dilatation to birth of baby.
   c. Third—birth of baby to delivery of placenta.
   d. Fourth—first hour after delivery of placenta.
12. Mechanisms of delivery: engagement, descent and flexion, internal rotation, extension, external rotation (restitution), expulsion.
B. Management of Labor and Delivery
   1. First stage
      a. Assessment
         (1) Latent phase—mild contractions, irregular pattern, usually last 20 to 30 seconds; woman usually at home.
         (2) Active phase—moderate contractions, every 3 to 5 minutes, last 40 to 50 seconds; stage at which woman is usually admitted to hospital.
         (3) Transition phase—strong contractions, every 2 minutes, last 60 to 70 seconds; woman has urge to push; increased show; rupture of membranes; cramps and shaking of legs; nausea and vomiting; marked introversion; amnesia between contractions.
      b. Admission to labor and delivery
         (1) Check vital signs: B/P, TPR, FHR.
         (2) Get history of pregnancy.
            (a) Gravida—number of pregnancies.
            (b) Para—number of deliveries at viable term.
            (c) EDC.
            (d) Breast- or bottle-feeding.

(e) Medical history—allergies, blood type and RH, VDRL, Hb, and HCT.

(3) Take labor history.
  (a) Time when contractions started.
  (b) Frequency and strength (mother's perception).
  (c) Time of last meal.
  (d) Presence of bloody show.
  (e) Status of membranes.

(4) Check contractions—frequency, duration, intensity.

(5) Do perineal prep and enema, if ordered.

(6) Check for bloody show.

(7) Check dilatation and effacement.

(8) Assess the mother's emotional reaction to contractions.

(9) Obtain a urine specimen; test for sugar and protein.

(10) Apply external fetal monitor if ordered.

c. Nursing diagnoses/goals/interventions
  (1) Risk for injury related to active labor
    Goals:
    (a) Mother will experience no complications of labor.
    (b) Infant will not experience distress.
    Interventions:
    (a) Active phase
      1. Monitor frequency, intensity, and duration of contractions q 30 minutes.
      2. Monitor mother's blood pressure q 30 minutes.
      3. Check FHR q 15 minutes (either auscultate or check monitor).
      4. Check for bloody show and leakage of membranes q 30 minutes.
      5. Check FHR stat if membranes rupture; observe amount and color of fluid; observe for meconium in fluid.
      6. Monitor IV if started; otherwise provide clear fluids.
      7. Encourage frequent voiding; check q hour for bladder distention.

(b) Transition phase
  1. Monitor contractions, membranes, and bloody show q 15 minutes.
  2. Check FHR q 5 minutes.
  3. Monitor mother's blood pressure q 15 minutes.
  4. Monitor IV (mother will be NPO).
  5. Encourage frequent voiding.

(2) Fear related to active labor
  Goal: Mother will be able to cope with her labor.
  Interventions:
  (a) Active phase
    1. Keep the mother and her support person informed of progress of labor.
    2. Teach the support person comfort measures to be used to assist the laboring woman.
    3. Reduce stimuli to encourage rest.
  (b) Transition phase
    1. Stay with the mother as much as possible.
    2. Make all instructions short and direct. (Mother has difficulty concentrating.)
    3. Encourage the support person in his/her coaching efforts.
    4. Reinforce for the laboring woman and the support person that the transition phase is overwhelming; they need to be reassured that this is normal labor.

(3) Pain related to active labor
  Goals:
  (a) Laboring woman will be as comfortable as possible.
  (b) She will rest between contractions.
  (c) She will not become exhausted.
  Interventions:
  (a) Place the mother in the most comfortable position (not on back).
  (b) Teach or reinforce appropriate breathing techniques.

(c) Use comfort measures such as cool cloth to forehead, frequent mouth care and ice chips, dry linen.

(d) Offer hard candy to keep mouth moist and provide energy.

(e) Rub back during contractions if mother is experiencing back pressure.

(f) Lightly rub abdomen during contractions unless the mother prefers not.

(g) Encourage rest between contractions.

(h) Coach the mother to do pant-blow breathing when she has the urge to push.

(i) Medicate as ordered.

(j) Assist with regional anesthesia.

d. Evaluation

(1) Mother experiences no complications during first stage of labor.

(2) There is no fetal distress.

(3) Mother copes effectively with her labor.

(4) Mother remains as comfortable as possible.

(5) Mother does not suffer exhaustion.

2. Second stage

a. Nursing diagnosis/goals/interventions
Risk for injury related to impending birth
Goals:

(1) Infant will be safely delivered.

(2) Mother will sustain no injury during delivery.

Interventions:

(1) Assist the mother to push with contractions.

(2) Check fetal monitor for decelerations after each contraction.

(3) Check the mother's B/P q 15 minutes.

(4) Transfer the mother to delivery room.

(a) Primipara—when presenting part is visible.

(b) Multipara—when fully dilated.

(5) Position the mother on the delivery table.

(6) Position the support person at the delivery table.

(7) Position the mirror so the mother can observe the progress of delivery.

(8) Encourage the mother to continue pushing with contractions.

(9) Auscultate FHR after each contraction. (Fetal monitor is disconnected in delivery room.)

(10) Administer O_2 if FHR drops.

b. Evaluation

(1) Infant is delivered safely.

(2) Mother sustains no injury during delivery.

3. Third stage
Nursing role

a. Administer immediate care to newborn. *See* Unit One, Immediate Care in the Delivery Room, page 58.

b. Introduce newborn to the mother and father.

c. Observe for lengthening of cord—signals delivery of placenta is imminent.

4. Fourth stage

a. Nursing diagnosis/goals/interventions

(1) Risk for injury related to postpartum status
Goal: Mother will develop no complications during fourth stage.
Interventions:

(a) Check fundus, lochia, and B/P q 15 minutes.

(b) Massage fundus gently if not firm.

(c) Add oxytoxin to IV as ordered, and monitor flow.

(d) Keep the mother warm.

(e) Check voiding and perineum q 30 minutes.

(f) Measure and record first voiding.

(2) Pain related to postpartum status
Goal: Mother will be comfortable during initial postpartum period.
Interventions:

(a) Encourage rest.

(b) Apply ice to perineum.

(c) Offer PO fluids and food.

(d) Offer bath and clean gown.

(e) Teach perineal care.

(3) Knowledge deficit related to parental role
Goal: Mother, father, and baby will bond positively.

Intervention: Allow mother, father, and baby time alone for bonding.

b. Evaluation
   (1) Mother develops no complications.
   (2) Mother remains comfortable.
   (3) Family bonds positively.

5. Assessment of fetus during labor
   a. Fetal heart rate, monitored by auscultation or continuous electronic monitoring (either internal or external)
      (1) Normal rate: 120 to 160 beats per minute.
      (2) Variations seen on fetal monitor
         (a) Early deceleration—occurs at beginning of contraction; returns to normal by end of contraction; no clinical significance.
         (b) Late deceleration—begins late in contraction; continues beyond end of contraction; suggestive of uteroplacental insufficiency.
         (c) Variable pattern—occurs at various times in contraction cycle; indicates cord compression.
   b. Signs of fetal distress
      (1) FHR below 120 or above 160.
      (2) Variations on monitor—late deceleration or variable pattern.
      (3) Meconium staining in amniotic fluid.
      (4) Hyperactivity of fetus after engagement.
   c. Emergency measures
      (1) Turn the mother on her side.
      (2) Administer O₂ via mask.
      (3) Discontinue IV oxytoxin if in progress.
      (4) Increase IV fluids.
   d. Management of fetal distress: immediate cesarean section if none of above measures improves FHR.

6. Induction of labor
   a. Methods: artificial rupture of membranes (amniotomy), use of oxytocin—Pitocin most common.
   b. Pitocin
      (1) Action: produces rhythmic contractions of uterus.
      (2) Indications for use: postmaturity, toxemia, diabetes, uterine dysfunction, membranes ruptured more than 24 hours, Rh incompatability.
      (3) Contraindications for use: multiparity (more than four), previous cesarean section, abnormal presentation, cephalopelvic disproportion, borderline pelvic measurements in a primipara (untested pelvis), heart disease.
      (4) Prerequisites for use: fetus in longitudinal lie, no fetal distress, presenting part engaged, no CPD, ripe cervix, no overdistention of uterus.
      (5) Dosage: 10 U in 1000 ml 5% D/W run at 0.5 mU to 20 mU per minute. Should be run piggyback into mainline, which is plain 5% D/W, to keep vein open; infusion pump should be used to keep rate constant.
      (6) Side effects: water intoxication, fetal distress, tonic uterine contractions.
      (7) Management of Pitocin
         (a) Start Pitocin drip at 3 ml per hour; increase rate gradually until regular contractions are established (never above 20 mU per minute).
         (b) Monitor IV rate on infusion pump.
         (c) Monitor contractions continuously until pattern is established, then q 15 minutes.
         (d) Never leave a patient on Pitocin drip alone; either a nurse or a doctor should be with her at all times (doctor should be in area).
         (e) Use fetal monitor to observe effect of contractions on fetus.
         (f) Auscultate FHR q 10 minutes if not on monitor.
         (g) Stop Pitocin infusion if:
            1. FHR drops below 120 or goes above 160.

2. Contractions last longer than 60 seconds or are closer than q 2 minutes.

    (h) Complications of Pitocin: fetal hypoxia, uterine rupture.

C. Analgesia and Anesthesia
  1. Analgesia
    a. Narcotics
      (1) Demerol has analgesic, sedative, and antispasmodic effects (helps to relax cervix).
        (a) Dose: 50 to 100 mg IM q 3 to 4 hours.
        (b) Onset of action: 20 minutes.
        (c) Peak of action: 1 hour.
        (d) Caution: should not be given if delivery is expected in 1–3 hours
      (2) Morphine has analgesic and sedative effects.
        (a) Dose: 3 to 10 mg IM in labor.
        (b) Use: not as frequent as that of Demerol; used mostly in hypertonic dysfunction for sedative effect.
    b. Sedatives and tranquilizers, used to provide rest and allay anxiety
      (1) Seconal is used early in latent phase to allow the woman to sleep until labor is established.
      (2) Phenergan is used with Demerol to reduce apprehension and enhance the action of the narcotic.
    c. Precautions
      (1) Narcotics should not be administered until labor is well established (regular contractions with 4-cm dilatation) because they can stop contractions in early labor.
      (2) Narcotics should never be administered within 1–3 hours of expected delivery, as they cross the placental barrier.
      (3) If mother has received narcotics, Narcan (narcotic antagonist) should be available at delivery to be administered to infant if he/she has respiratory distress.

      (4) Narcan may be administered to mother immediately before delivery if severe neonatal respiratory distress is anticipated (Narcan crosses the placenta rapidly). Note: Narcan is effective only in narcosis, not in respiratory distress from other causes.
    d. Nursing management
      (1) Check vital signs before administering narcotics (Demerol causes a decrease in B/P).
      (2) Check for allergies before administering any drug.
      (3) Put side rails up and observe safety measures after administering drug.
      (4) Observe for signs of respiratory distress if morphine is used.
      (5) Monitor vital signs and FHR frequently.
      (6) Observe for side effects specific to each drug.
  2. Anesthesia
    a. General anesthesia, usually used only if difficult delivery is anticipated
      (1) Disadvantages: may interfere with maternal-infant bonding, causes respiratory depression in infant.
      (2) Commonly used agents
        (a) Ether—used infrequently; causes severe nausea in mother.
        (b) Nitrous oxide ("laughing gas")—used with contractions after dilatation.
        (c) Cyclopropane — provides rapid induction; used in emergency situations; should not be used with oxytocin or ergot derivatives.
        (d) Trilene — self-administered by mask; patient should never be left alone when using mask.
        (e) Pentothal—IV administration; provides rapid induction.
    b. Regional anesthesia, used to block nerves carrying sensation to uterus and pelvic area

(1) Commonly used agents: Procaine, Pontocaine, Marcaine, Xylocaine, Novacaine.
(2) Nerve root blocks
   (a) Types
      1. Epidural—usually continuous.
      2. Saddle—"low spinal."
   (b) Use: usually administered in latter part of first stage to block sensation of contractions.
   (c) Patient care management
      1. Have the patient void before initiating procedure.
      2. Take a baseline B/P before procedure.
      3. Position the patient on left side with head flexed and knees drawn up or in sitting position.
      4. Check blood pressure as soon as medication is injected.
      5. Thereafter, keep the mother in sidelying position.
      6. Check blood pressure q 5 minutes until stable.
      7. Check for spinal headache, which usually occurs only in saddle block.
      8. Use safety precautions necessary when lower extremities are anesthesized.
(3) Peripheral nerve blocks
   (a) Types
      1. Paracervical — done during transition; anesthesizes lower uterine segment, cervix, vagina.
      2. Pudendal—done at full dilatation; anesthesizes vagina and perineum.
      3. Local infiltration—anesthesizes perineum; used for episiotomy incision and repair.

   (b) Patient care management
      1. Check blood pressure before and after injection; there may be systemic absorption.
      2. Check FHR before and after injection; agents will cross placenta.
      3. Check FHR q 5 minutes × 3 after injection.

D. Operative Obstetrics
  1. **Episiotomy** An incision made into the perineum to facilitate delivery.
    a. Purposes: shorten second stage, enlarge vaginal canal for forceps delivery, decrease pressure on fetal head, prevent tearing of perineum.
    b. Types
      (1) Mediolateral—incision begins in midline but is directed laterally away from rectum.
        (a) If tears, rectum is not involved.
        (b) Healing is painful.
        (c) Postpartum mobility is decreased.
        (d) Dyspareunia (painful intercourse) may result.
      (2) Median—incision is made in midline of perineum
        (a) If tears, tear may extend into rectum.
        (b) There is minimal pain in healing.
        (c) It is easy to repair.
        (d) Blood loss is smaller than with mediolateral.
        (e) Mobility is usually not affected.
  2. **Repair of lacerations** Suturing, as an episiotomy would be repaired (with absorbable sutures).
    a. Types
      (1) First degree—involves vaginal mucosa and perineal skin.
      (2) Second degree—involves perineal body and muscles.
      (3) Third degree—involves entire perineum and anal sphincter.
      (4) Fourth degree—involves rectal mucosa.
  3. **Forceps delivery** Use of instruments to extract the fetal head.

a. Indications for use: regional anesthesia—difficulty with pushing, need to rotate a persistent posterior, maternal exhaustion, fetal distress, prolonged second stage, breech presentation (to deliver the head).

b. Criteria for use: complete dilatation of cervix, ruptured membranes, engagement of presenting part, empty bladder.

c. Types
   (1) Low—head on perineal floor; internal rotation has occurred; also called "outlet forceps."
   (2) Mid—head at station zero; can be used to internally rotate a posterior presentation.

d. Possible complications: ruptured uterus, lacerations, fetal injury—lacerations, facial paralysis.

e. Nursing role: Observe mother and infant for injury.

4. **Cesarean section** Delivery of infant through an incision into the abdominal wall and uterus.

   a. Indications for use: CPD, fetal distress, abruptio placenta, placenta previa, toxemia, diabetes, malpresentations, uterine dysfunction, previous cesarean sections, previous uterine surgery.

   b. Contraindications for use: fetal death, intra-abdominal infection.

   c. Types
      (1) Classical—vertical incision through abdomen and into contractile portion of uterus; fastest to do; used when rapid delivery is necessary; requires repeated cesarean section in subsequent deliveries.
      (2) Lower segment—transverse incision over symphysis pubis and into lower uterine segment; vaginal delivery possible in subsequent deliveries.

   d. Nursing management
      (1) Same as for postoperative abdominal surgery. *See* Unit Eight, Management of the Patient Undergoing Surgery, Section C: Management during the Postoperative Period, page 269.
      (2) Routine postpartum assessment.

E. Alterations of Normal Labor and Delivery
   1. **Preterm labor** Initiation of labor after viability but before 37th week.
      a. Patient care management
         (1) Bedrest.
         (2) Tocolysis.
            (a) Ritodrine.
            (b) Terbutaline.
            (c) Magnesium sulfate.
            (d) Oral magnesium.
            (e) Prostaglandin inhibitors (Indocin).
            (f) Calcium channel blockers (experimental).
         (3) No treatment initiated if:
            (a) Membranes are ruptured.
            (b) Gestation is over 37 weeks.
            (c) Cervix is dilated 4 cm.
            (d) There is fetal distress.
            (e) There is maternal indication for delivery.
   2. **Dystocia** Prolonged (more than 24 hours) or difficult labor and delivery.
      a. Classification of causes
         (1) Forces—subnormal or abnormal uterine forces; uterine dysfunction (inertia).
         (2) Passenger—problem with fetus: faulty presentation, large baby, congenital anomaly (e.g., hydrocephalus).
         (3) Passage—problem with maternal pelvis: pelvic contraction, congenitally small pelvis, nongynecoid pelvis.
      b. Uterine dysfunction
         (1) **Primary inertia (hypertonic)** Ineffective, irregular, extremely painful contractions during latent phase of first stage; hypertonic contractions can cause fetal distress.
            (a) Patient care management
               1. Patient is sedated with morphine and short-acting barbiturate.
               2. When she awakens, effective contractions should begin; if not, they may be induced.

(b) Nursing role: Promote rest, provide hydration.

(2) **Secondary inertia (hypotonic)** Irregular, infrequent, hypotonic contractions occurring near the end of the first stage; well-established labor suddenly ceases to progress. Fetal distress is usually not present.

(a) Contributing factors: maternal exhaustion or dehydration, CPD.

(b) Patient care management: X-ray pelvimetry, artificial rupture of membranes, induction of labor with Pitocin.

(c) Nursing management

 1. Keep the mother informed of progress.
 2. Encourage voiding q 2 hours.
 3. Give the patient sourballs to increase glucose level and provide energy.
 4. Keep the patient well hydrated.

3. **Amniotic fluid embolism** Amniotic fluid escapes into the maternal circulation; solid particles in the fluid reach the lungs as small emboli.

a. Predisposing factors: premature rupture of membranes, premature separation of placenta.

b. Assessment, patient care management, and nursing interventions. *See* Unit Eight, Management of the Patient Undergoing Surgery, Section E4: Pulmonary embolism, page 280.

4. **Inverted uterus** The fundus is forced through the cervix so that the uterus is turned inside out; occurs following third stage.

a. Assessment: Observe for profuse hemorrhage and symptoms of shock.

b. Patient care management: treatment of shock, surgical replacement of uterus, hysterectomy if hemorrhage cannot be controlled.

c. Prevention: To prevent this complication, never pull on umbilical cord.

5. **Prolapsed cord** Loop of umbilical cord slips down in front of presenting fetal part.

a. Causes: rupture of membranes before engagement, breech presentation, premature infant.

b. Assessment: Cord is felt on vaginal examination, or is observed protruding from vagina.

c. Patient care management

(1) If fully dilated, forceps delivery.
(2) If not fully dilated, cesarean section.

d. Emergency measures

(1) Place the patient in exaggerated Trendelenburg position.
(2) Administer O_2 by mask.
(3) Cover exposed cord with wet sterile dressing.
(4) Apply fetal monitor.
(5) Do not attempt to replace cord.
(6) Keep the mother informed about the situation.

The Postpartum Period (also called the "puerperium"; refers to the 6-week period following delivery)

A. Physiology of Involution (return to nonpregnant state)

1. Uterus

a. Contractions of uterus pinch large vessels at placental site and control bleeding.

b. Same contractions reduce the size of the uterus.

c. Immediately after delivery, fundus (uppermost portion of uterus) can be palpated midway between umbilicus and symphysis pubis.

d. Within 12 hours, uterus rises to level of the umbilicus.

e. Uterus descends 1 fingerbreadth per day until the 10th day, when it is no longer palpable.

f. Consistency of uterus should be hard and globular (fundus should feel firm).

g. Drainage from uterus is called *lochia*.

(1) Rubra—mostly blood, red—first 3 days.
(2) Serosa—blood and tissue, pink—4th to 10th days.
(3) Alba—mucus, white or colorless—10th day to 6th week.

h. Uterus never returns to virgin weight, but should weigh 50 gm within 6 weeks.

i. Endometrium is restored by end of 3rd week.

j. Placental site takes 6 weeks to heal.

2. Cervix and vagina

a. By end of first week, cervix is almost completely involuted.

b. Internal os closes; external os never completely returns to prepregnant state.

c. Vagina returns to its prenatal condition by 3rd or 4th week.

d. Most of the vaginal rugae may be permanently flattened.

3. Breasts

a. There is little change in breasts during the first 2 days postpartum.

b. The breasts continue to secrete colostrum as during pregnancy.

c. Breast milk forms as a result of the decrease in estrogen and progesterone.

d. Breasts become distended with milk on the 3rd day (primary engorgement).

e. Breast-feeding will prevent engorgement.

f. Engorgement 48 to 72 hours in non-breast-feeding mothers.

4. Urinary tract

a. Marked diuresis begins within 12 hours of delivery.

b. Pressure on the neck of the bladder may cause a loss of urge to void.

c. These factors may combine to cause urinary retention.

5. Gastrointestinal tract

a. Woman is usually very hungry after delivery.

b. Constipation can occur because decreased muscle tone in the intestines and perineal tenderness.

6. Vascular system

a. Blood clotting factors are activated after delivery.

b. Blood volume is usually back to prenatal level by 3rd week.

7. Vital signs

a. Temperature may be elevated to 100.4° during first 24 hours without any pathology.

b. Blood pressure remains unchanged.

c. Bradycardia is common during 1st week.

8. Menstruation

a. Menstrual flow resumes within 8 weeks in non-breast-feeding mothers.

b. Menstrual flow usually resumes within 3 to 4 months in breast-feeding mothers. However, breast-feeding mothers may experience amenorrhea during the entire period of lactation.

c. A woman may ovulate without menstruating, so breast-feeding should not be considered a form of birth control.

B. Nursing Management for the Postpartum Period

1. Assessment of involution

a. Check fundus (height, consistency) q 4 hours on delivery day, and q 8 hours for remainder of hospital stay.

b. Check vital signs q 4 hours on delivery day, and q day thereafter.

c. Check lochia (color, amount, any clots, any odor) q 4 hours on delivery day, and q 8 hours thereafter.

d. Check breasts each day for engorgement.

e. Check voiding q 4 hours until adequate emptying is established.

f. Check perineum each day for swelling or discoloration.

g. Check episiotomy q 8 hours for healing.

h. Check for BM or flatus each day.

i. Assess bonding with infant at each feeding.

j. Assess emotional status each shift.

l. Assess for pain q 3 to 4 hours.

m. Check dressing for Cesarean section q 4 hours.

2. Comfort measures

a. Afterpains (more common in multiparas)

(1) Encourage ambulation, which makes uterine contractions more effective, less painful.

(2) Encourage frequent voiding.

(3) If woman is experiencing discomfort with breast-feeding, administer analgesic $\frac{1}{2}$ hour before feeding.

b. Perineal discomfort

(1) Apply ice during first 24 hours to reduce swelling.

(2) After first 24 hours, use warmth (sitz baths or perineal light).

c. Discomfort from episiotomy
(1) Teach the patient to administer perineum care after each voiding.
(2) Encourage use of analgesic spray such as Dermoplast.
(3) Encourage use of Tucks (witch hazel compresses); keep in refrigerator for increased analgesic effect.
(4) Administer analgesic only after other measures have not worked.
d. Breast discomfort from engorgement
(1) Encourage wearing of a supporting bra at all times (even when asleep if tolerated).
(2) Use ice packs for comfort. Remove ice pack at least $\frac{1}{2}$ hour before breast-feeding.
(3) Administer analgesic if comfort measures are not effective.
e. Postoperative pain from Cesarean section: managed the same as postoperative pain from any abdominal surgery. *See* Unit Eight, Management of the Patient Undergoing Surgery, Section D1: Pain, page 270.
3. Provision of rest
a. Arrange care to provide rest periods between feedings and visiting hours.
b. Encourage the mother to take naps.
4. Promotion of return to prepregnant state
a. Teach the mother appropriate exercises for postpartum period.
b. Discuss the mother's schedule at home, and stress the importance of adequate rest.
c. Discuss importance of 6-week checkup.
d. Discuss sexual relations.
(1) Can be resumed when episiotomy heals and bleeding stops (3 to 4 weeks).
(2) Should use temporary means of birth control (such as condom or foam) if resumed before 6-week checkup.
(3) Should be discontinued if bleeding occurs.
e. Discuss contraception.
(1) Cannot take pill if breast feeding.
(2) Cannot use old diaphragm; must be refitted.
f. Discuss nutrition: Increase calories by 200 for breast-feeding. Decrease calories by 300 if not nursing.

C. Emotional Reactions of the Puerperium
1. Rubin's postpartum phases
a. Taking-in (first 2 to 3 days). Mother needs to satisfy own needs for rest and support; allows nurse to "take care" of her; needs to verbalize about labor and delivery to integrate the event; not an optimum time to teach baby care.
b. Taking-hold (usually 3rd day). Mother becomes organized and takes command of situation; tasks of mothering take priority; ideal time to teach baby care; nurse must provide ego support—mother very sensitive about "doing it right."
c. Letting-go. Mother lets go of baby as part of herself; may grieve over the loss; time to establish new norms for the family.
2. Postpartum blues
a. Blues may occur between 3rd and 10th days.
b. Reaction varies with individual.
c. Condition is caused by physiological and emotional stress.
d. Verbalization should be encouraged.
e. Blues may progress to postpartum depression if unresolved.
3. Parenting
a. Readiness: Patient must be physically comfortable and emotionally ready.
b. Skills to be taught: feeding, bathing, dressing.
c. Other considerations: growth and development in infancy, safety measures.
4. Bonding
a. Encourage bonding with both parents early in puerperium (in delivery room, if possible).
b. Be aware that bonding process should be continuous.
c. Encourage the parents to make eye contact with the infant.
d. Encourage the parents to explore the infant.
e. Allow the parents time alone with the infant, but periodically assess parent-child interaction.
D. Breast-Feeding
1. Schedule
a. Initially, the infant should feed q 2 or 3 hours during the day and at night.

b. The baby should be left on breast until he/she stops swallowing.

c. The baby will develop his/her own feeding schedule.

d. The baby should not breast-feed more often than q 2 hours; give pacifier between feedings.

2. Procedure to be taught to mother

a. Wash hands and assume a comfortable position.

b. Start with breast the last feeding ended with (baby sucks more vigorously at the beginning of feeding).

c. Stroke baby's cheek with nipple to stimulate rooting.

d. Guide nipple and surrounding areola into baby's mouth.

e. Make a "dimple" in breast to allow room for baby to breathe.

f. When you can no longer hear swallowing, release suction by depressing infant's chin or inserting clean finger into his/her mouth.

g. Burp baby after first breast.

h. Repeat procedure on second breast until baby stops swallowing.

i. Burp baby again.

3. Patient education

a. Breasts should be air dried after each feeding.

b. Breasts may leak; pads should be changed frequently if worn.

c. Bra should be well fitted and supporting.

d. Nipple-rolling exercise should be done.

e. Medications should be avoided unless prescribed.

f. Gassy foods should be avoided.

g. Birth control pills should not be taken.

h. Calories should be increased by 200 including $1\frac{1}{2}$ quarts of milk and 1000 ml additional fluid.

i. Baby's stools will be light yellow, watery, and frequent.

j. At 1 month, baby will nurse 15 to 20 minutes on each breast.

4. Problems and solutions to be taught to mother

a. Retracted nipples.

(1) Do nipple rolling before feeding.

(2) Wear a breast shield, which will act as vacuum when baby sucks and will pull nipple out.

b. Cracked nipples

(1) Use varied positions for baby.

(2) Expose nipples to air for 10 minutes after each feeding.

c. Inadequate milk, manifested by baby's hunger as he/she grows

(1) Increase frequency of feedings to increase milk supply.

(2) Revert to longer intervals once supply increases.

E. Alterations of the Normal Puerperium

1. **Hemorrhage** Blood loss over 500 cc is considered hemorrhage.

a. Occurrence

(1) Usually hemorrhage occurs early in puerperium (first 24 hours most common).

(2) Late postpartum hemorrhage occurs more than 24 hours after delivery.

b. Causes: uterine atony, retained placenta, vaginal or cervical tears.

c. Assessment: assess for boggy fundus, in atony or retained placenta; firm fundus, with bright red bleeding, in lacerations; symptoms of shock regardless of cause.

d. Patient care management (depends on cause)

(1) Treat shock; restore volume of blood.

(2) Repair lacerations.

(3) Administer oxytoxin for atony.

(4) Do D & C for retained placenta.

(5) Perform hysterectomy if bleeding is uncontrollable.

e. Nursing diagnosis/goal/interventions
Altered tissue perfusion related to postpartum hemorrhage
Goal: Vital signs will be maintained within normal limits.
Interventions:

(1) Assess blood loss—weigh perineal pads.

(2) Check vital signs and fundus q 15 minutes.

(3) Massage fundus, being careful not to overmassage.

(4) Monitor intake and output.

(5) Monitor fluid replacement and oxytoxin administration.

(6) Observe for blood reactions if transfused.

(7) Stay with patient; explain what's happening.

(8) Prepare for OR if indicated.

f. Evaluation

(1) Vital signs remain within normal limits.

(2) Shock does not occur.

2. **Puerperal infection**   Any infection of reproductive organs that occurs within 28 days of delivery or abortion.

a. Possible cause: introduction of organisms, or organisms normally resident in vaginal canal.

b. Predisposing factors: prolonged labor, traumatic delivery, premature rupture of membranes, exhaustion and dehydration, anemia or excessive blood loss, retained placenta.

c. Assessment: Assess for temperature above 100.4°, pelvic or abdominal pain, burning on urination, foul-smelling lochia, chills, tachycardia, malaise, and anorexia.

d. Common puerperal infections

(1) Endometritis.

(2) Pelvic thrombophlebitis (may extend to femoral veins—''milk leg'').

(3) Urinary tract infections.

(4) Mastitis.

e. Patient care management

(1) Antibiotics according to organism.

(2) Intravenous therapy.

(3) Bedrest.

f. Nursing diagnosis/goal/interventions
Risk for injury related to infection
Goal: Mother will develop no complications from infection.
Interventions:

(1) Maintain asepsis (isolate from baby).

(2) Monitor temperature q 2 to 4 hours.

(3) Make the patient as comfortable as possible.

(a) Use cool sponges for high fever.

(b) Keep warm if chilled.

(c) Position for comfort.

(d) Use heat and cold as indicated to relieve localized pain.

(e) Administer analgesics prn.

(4) Monitor vital signs q 4 hours.

(5) Monitor intake and output.

(a) Force fluids.

(b) Encourage frequent voiding.

(6) Provide restful environment—patient is usually anxious, exhausted, and very uncomfortable.

g. Evaluation: Infection resolves without complications.

3. **Subinvolution**   Condition that exists when normal involution of the puerperal uterus is retarded.

a. Causes: poor uterine tone, retained placenta, endometritis, fibroids, displacement of uterus.

b. Assessment: Assess for large, boggy uterus, prolonged lochia rubra, backache, and dragging sensation.

c. Patient care management

(1) Methergine or Ergotrate 0.2 mg q 4 hours × 2 or 3 days.

(a) Both are oxytoxins.

(b) Both can cause hypertension.

(2) Antibiotics if subinvolution is caused by endometritis.

(3) Removal of retained placenta by D & C.

d. Nursing role

(1) Encourage ambulation.

(2) Explain condition to patient.

ALTERATIONS OF HEALTH DURING YOUNG ADULTHOOD

Neoplastic Disorders

Cancer   A large group of diseases characterized by uncontrolled growth and spread of abnormal cells. "Cancer" is often used synonymously with "malignant neoplasm."

Cell growth is unregulated, resulting in immature and abnormal cells. Cells tend to reproduce more rapidly than normal cells. Cells are not encapsulated and therefore are capable of invading surrounding tissues. Cellular growth endangers the host by placing pressure on vital organs, eroding blood vessels, and competing with normal cells for nutrients. These cells have the ability to metastasize to distant sites and to grow unrestricted. If metastasis is not controlled or checked, death will ensue.

Causative factors: (1) viruses—a theory; (2) physical causes—exposure to sunlight and chronic irritation; (3) chemical carcinogens—tobacco smoking, diet (i.e., additives, absence of fiber from diet, and high intake of carbohydrates, animal proteins, and fat), air pollutants, industrial waste, and certain drugs; (4) genetics.

A. Metastasis
Cancer cells metastasize via:
1. Direct extension of the tumor into surrounding tissues.
2. The circulating blood.
3. The lymph vessels to regional lymph nodes.
4. Transportation by body fluids from one site in a cavity to another site in the same cavity.

B. Classifications of Cancer
Cancers are classified according to their cellular origins.
1. Carcinomas—arise from epithelial tissues such as skin, lung, gastrointestinal tract lining, breast, and uterus. Carcinomas spread via the lymphatics at first, and through the bloodstream later. These cancers are named for the type of cell involved; for example, adenocarcinoma is cancer of the adrenal gland.
2. Sarcomas and lymphomas—arise from blood vessels, lymphatics, nerve tissue, or connective tissues.
   a. Sarcomas—derived from soft tissue, bone, and muscles. Sarcomas establish huge tumors without nodal metastases. Metastases are blood borne to vascular organs such as the lung and liver.
   b. Lymphomas—arise from lymphoreticular system (e.g., Hodgkin's disease). Disease is localized in Hodgkin's disease but generally disseminated in non-Hodgkin's lymphomas.
   c. Leukemia—involves the blood-forming organs in both acute and chronic forms. Types are named according to the dominant cell involved. There is diffused involvement of the bone marrow.

C. Assessment
1. Assess for the following:
   a. Weight loss and weakness (cachexia).
   b. Pallor (due to anemia).
   c. Fever (due to infection).
   d. Pain (may or may not be present).

2. Observe for the seven danger signals:
   a. A sore that does not heal.
   b. A lump or thickening in the breast or elsewhere.
   c. Indigestion or difficulty in swallowing.
   d. Changes in a wart or mole.
   e. Unusual bleeding or discharge.
   f. Persistent hoarseness or cough.
   g. Change in bowel or bladder habits.
3. DIAGNOSTIC METHODS
   a. Direct examination by biopsy—major diagnostic method to establish tumor classification and stage
      Types: incisional biopsy, needle biopsy, excisional biopsy, exfoliative cytology.
   b. Indirect examination
      Types: X-ray (barium and dye studies), blood and urine examinations.
   c. Staging—establishes the presence and extent of a tumor according to the degree of metastasis. Staging is accomplished before the initiation of treatment to provide for and maintain a systematic and consistent approach to the diagnosis, treatment, and evaluation of intervention.
      TNM system: T—primary tumor, N—regional lymph nodes, M—metastasis by vascular dissemination.
      (1) Tumor: Tx—tumor cannot be adequately assesed.
         To—no evidence of primary tumor.
         Tis—carcinoma *in situ.*
         T1, T2, T3, T4—ascending degrees of increase in tumor size and involvement.
      (2) Nodes: Nx—regional lymph nodes cannot be assessed clinically.
         N0—regional lymph nodes demonstrable.
         N1, N2, N3, N4—ascending degrees of nodal involvement.
      (3) Metastases: Mx—not assessed.
         M0—no evidence of distant metastasis.
         M1—distant metastasis present.

D. Patient Care Management
Methods of treatment: surgery, radiotherapy, chemotherapy, hormones, immunotherapy, adjuvant therapy—using a combination of therapies, bone marrow transplantation.

1. Surgery
   a. Types: diagnostic (biopsy), curative, prophylatic, palliative, reconstructive
   b. Patient care management and nursing interventions. *See* Unit Eight, Alterations That Interfere with the Meeting of Sexual Needs, Section B: Management of the Patient Undergoing Gynecologic Surgery, page 343; and Alterations That Interfere with the Meeting of Nutritional Needs, Section A2: Management of the Patient Undergoing Surgery for Cancer of the Larynx, page 318.
2. Radiotherapy
   a. Categories
      (1) Curative—used primarily for Hodgkin's, some lymphomas, and cancer of the uterine cervix.
      (2) Palliative—used to reduce pain and prevent pathological fracture due to metastases to the bone.
      (3) Adjuvant—used before and/or after surgery and chemotherapy.
   b. Types
      (1) External—gamma rays transmitted by X-rays and radioisotopes.
      (2) Internal—implantation within a cavity, or within tissue (interstitial).
      (3) Combination—the two treatments may be used together.
   c. Side effects
      (1) Radiation sickness—anorexia, nausea, and vomiting.
      (2) Diarrhea.
      (3) Skin reactions—varying degrees of heat burns (erythema) and ulcerations.
      (4) Anemia.
      (5) Systemic reactions that occur when specific areas are irradiated
          (a) Urinary frequency, urgency, dysuria, and hematuria.
          (b) Thick, tenacious sputum, loss of taste, dry mouth, and tooth decay.
          (c) Hair loss (alopecia).
          (d) Pneumonitis.
      (6) Systemic side effects commonly experienced by most patients—fatigue, malaise, headache, nausea and vomiting.
2a. External radiation
   a. Types: linear accelerator (X-ray), cobalt-60.

   b. Nursing diagnoses/goals/nursing interventions
      (1) Knowledge deficit related to administration and side effects of external radiation therapy
      Goals:
          (a) Patient will verbalize an understanding of the side effects of therapy.
          (b) Patient will verbalize an understanding of therapy/treatment.
      Interventions:
          (a) Provide psychological preparation and support.
          (b) Provide patient education.
              1. Explain what to expect before, during, and after treatment.
              2. Explain the radiotherapy room and the role of the radiologist or radiotherapist.
              3. Explain the side effects and means of minimizing them.
          (c) Provide the proper diet: high caloric, high protein, low fat, low residue, with adequate amounts of fluids and B_{12} supplements.
              1. Serve frequent small meals.
              2. Serve appetizing foods in an appealing manner.
              3. Do not give food 2 to 3 hours before or 2 hours after treatment.
          (d) Give appropriate medications. For nausea: Tigan or Compazine. For diarrhea: Lomotil or Kaopectate.
      (2) Impaired skin integrity: erythematous/wet desquamation skin reaction
      Goal: Patient's skin will remain intact.
      Intervention: Provide skin care. (Mild or "dry" skin reaction occurs from 10 to 14 days after treatment.)
          (a) Avoid vigorous washing, keep skin clean, and dry with baby powder or cornstarch. (Avoid washing away dye marks.)
          (b) Avoid creams, lotions, and powders that contain heavy metal or perfume.

(c) Avoid sunlight, and protect skin from extreme temperatures.

(d) If "moist" skin reaction occurs (there is blistering or loss of the epidermis or outer layer of skin), apply the ointments or lotions ordered (use nonadherent dressing and paper tape).

c. Evaluation

(1) Patient understands side effects of treatment and the purpose of therapy.

(2) Patient's skin remains intact.

2b. Internal radiation

a. Types

(1) Radioactive substances sealed in needles, beads, or wires (most commonly used: cesium and cobalt-60 needles).

(2) Radioisotopes administered orally or intravenously, topically and into cavities.

(a) Iodine-131. The patient's body will emit gamma rays. Radioactive contamination occurs via the urine, with lesser hazards from sputum, vomitus, sweat, feces, and blood.

(b) Phosphorus-32. This radioisotope is administered orally, intravenously, and by intracavity insertion. The half-life is 14 days, and the patient's body is not a hazard as this radioisotope emits only beta rays, which are not dangerous. Vomitus, urine, feces, and wound drainage should be handled with special care. Dressings should be handled with long forceps and placed in a lead container. Hands should be washed with soap and water after patient care.

(c) Gold-198. Gamma rays are emitted from the patient's body. The half-life is 2.7 days. Distance, time, and shielding precautions (see below) must be observed. Dressings and drainage should be handled with care.

b. Precautionary measures

(1) Distance

(a) Stay as far as possible from the radioactive source. The further away from the source, the less a person is exposed to radiation.

(b) Stand within 3 feet of the patient only long enough to give basic care.

(2) Time. Spend as little time as possible near the radioactive source. The less time spent close to the source, the less a person is exposed to radiation.

(3) Shielding. Use appropriate materials to halt and absorb the rays from radiant energy.

(a) For X-rays and gamma rays: lead shields.

(b) For beta rays: glass, Lucite, and aluminum shields.

c. Nursing diagnoses/goals/interventions

(1) Knowledge deficit related to administration and side effects of internal radiation

Goals:

(a) Patient will verbalize early signs and symptoms of discomfort during the period when he/she receives radiation.

(b) Patient will verbalize an understanding of the side effects of therapy.

Interventions:

(a) Instruct the patient about potential side effects of internal radiation.

(b) Provide adequate preparation for radiotherapy.

 1. Reinforce the physician's explanations.

 2. Give cleansing enema and insert Foley catheter, if ordered, before bladder, cervical, and uterine radiation.

 3. Give detailed personal care before therapy.

 4. Avoid contact with and properly dispose of all contaminated body discharges.

(2) Risk for injury related to displacement or loss of implant

Goal: Patient will not experience loss of implant.

Interventions:
(a) Limit the patient's activity: enforce bedrest when indicated.
(b) If desired, "logroll" the patient from side to side and lay on back (observe during uterine, cervix, and bladder implantation).
(c) Have the level of the bed no higher than that in a semi-Fowler's position.
(d) Check implant periodically to avoid displacement or loss.
(e) If implant falls out:
    1. Never touch radioactive source with bare hands; pick up with long-handled tongs and place in lead container.
    2. Notify physician and nuclear medicine department.
(f) After removal (uterine, cervical, and bladder implantation):
    1. Observe for bleeding.
    2. Have the patient remain in bed for 1 hour afterward.
    3. Give douche and Fleet enema if ordered.

d. Evaluation
(1) Patient verbalizes understanding of signs and symptoms of discomfort and of side effect of therapy.
(2) Patient is free from adverse effect of internal radiation implant.

3. Chemotherapy (capable of destroying young, rapidly multiplying cells) Two or more drugs are given together or in sequence to prevent resistance of the tumor to any one drug.
a. Uses
(1) Is the primary treatment for patients with leukemia.
(2) Extends the life expectancy of patients with Hodgkin's and other types of lymphomas.
(3) Serves as adjuvant therapy to surgery to prevent recurrence of some cancers.
b. Classification of drugs
(1) Alklyating agents: nitrogen mustard, Thio-Tepa, Cytoxan, Leukeran.
(2) Antimetabolites: 5-fluorouracil, 6-mercaptopurine, methotrexate, cytarabine.
(3) Plant alkaloids: vincristine, vinblastine.
(4) Antibiotics: Adriamycin, bleomycin, dactinomycin, mithramycin, Onovcin.
(5) Miscellaneous drugs: L-asparaginase, procarbazine, interferon.
(6) Hormones: prednisone, diethyl stilbestrol, progestrone, testosterone, Decadron.
c. Methods of administration: orally, IV or IM, intraarterially.
d. Common side effects
(1) Gastrointestinal tract disorders: stomatitis, nausea and vomiting, diarrhea.
(2) Bone marrow depression: anemia, bleeding tendencies (may cause death due to hemorrhage), and decreased resistance to infection.
(3) Hair loss—alopecia occurs with Cytoxan and Adriamycin.
e. Nursing diagnoses/goals/interventions
(1) Knowledge deficit related to the administration and side effects of chemotherapy
    Goals:
    (a) Patient will demonstrate appropriate drug administration.
    (b) Patient will verbalize early signs and symptoms of discomfort.
    (c) Patient will verbalize an understanding of the side effects of therapy, the methods to prevent or control symptoms, and the time to contact the health team.
    Interventions:
    (a) Assess the patient's understanding of the current drug regimen, including drugs, dose, schedule, time of administration, route, and length of treatment.
    (b) Instruct the patient to report to the health-care team any signs and symptoms of adverse reaction to drugs.
    (c) Discuss drug, dietary, and alcohol concerns related to specific drug regimens.
    (d) Provide written information regarding the specific drug regimen.
    (e) Discuss anticipated side effects of drug therapy.

(f) Provide written information about the specific side effects.

(g) Discuss appropriate interventions to prevent or minimize potential side effects.

(2) Risk for infection related to depressed immune system

Goals:

(a) Patient will state the signs and symptoms of infection.

(b) Patient will identify measures to prevent or minimize infection.

Interventions:

(a) Instruct the patient about potential risk of infection.

(b) Assess areas of the body for signs and symptoms of infection: mouth, rectum, GI tract, skin, GU organs, respiratory tract.

(c) Avoid performing invasive procedures (rectal temps, IM injections, enemas, suppositories, tampons, urinary catheters).

(d) Instruct the patient to avoid trauma (use electric razor, wear shoes, avoid straining).

(e) Instruct the patient to report signs and symptoms of infection, including temperature of 101°F at any time, temperature of 100°F on two occasions, temperature of 96°F, and chill or other symptoms noted in (b).

(3) Risk for injury related to thrombocytopenia

Goal: Patient will recognize factors that increase risk of bleeding and will report early signs of bleeding.

Interventions:

(a) Avoid invasive procedures, IM injections, rectal temps, enemas, tampons, prolonged BP cuff pressure, suppositories.

(b) Apply pressure to puncture sites for at least 5 minutes.

(c) Restrict activities if platelet count is <10,000 or active bleeding occurs.

(d) Do not administer aspirin or compounds with aspirins.

(e) Instruct the patient to use a soft toothbrush, use an electric razor, report any bruising or bleeding, and wear shoes when out of bed.

(4) Risk for injury related to decrease in circulating red blood cells

Goal: Patient will verbalize an understanding of the symptoms of anemia, the methods to prevent or control symptoms, and the time to contact the health care team.

Interventions:

(a) Instruct the patient in regard to the risk of anemia.

(b) Explain the signs and symptoms of anemia.

(c) Suggest frequent rest periods during the day.

(d) Discuss the potential need for transfusion.

(e) Administer transfusion if ordered.

(f) Teach the patient to report syncope, palpitations, chest pain, and dizziness to health care provider.

(5) Fluid volume deficit related to nausea and vomiting

Goals:

(a) Patient will state the degree of risk for the development of nausea and vomiting with chemotherapy.

(b) Patient will obtain relief from prescribed antiemetic therapy.

(c) Patient will verbalize an understanding of the undesirable effects of nausea and vomiting, the methods to prevent them, and the time to notify the health care team.

(d) Patient will state recommended strategies to avoid or minimize nausea and vomiting.

Interventions:

(a) Discuss anticipated degree of nausea and vomiting in regard to therapy.

(b) Assess the patient's previous experience with chemotherapy.

(c) Administer antiemetics before therapy as appropriate for anticipated degree of nausea and for vomiting posttreatment.

(d) Teach the patient to monitor actual episodes of nausea, to report inability to maintain adequate hydration, and to report bleeding in vomitus.

(e) Discuss the signs and symptoms of dehydration.

(f) Instruct the patient to drink 2 to 3 liters of noncarbonated beverage daily.

(g) Instruct the patient to avoid fried and greasy food.

(h) Instruct the patient to eat small, frequent meals of bland, high-carbohydrate foods.

(6) Body image disturbances and/or self-concept related to physical changes caused by chemotherapy
Goals:

(a) Patient will verbalize an understanding of the risk for hair loss and a perception of changes in self-image resulting from hair loss.

(b) Patient will identify measures to minimize hair loss during therapy.

Interventions:

(a) Discuss the risk of hair loss.

(b) Discuss potential use of wigs, scarves, or caps.

(c) Reassure the patient that hair will grow back. New growth may be different in color or texture within 1 to 2 months after last treatment.

(d) Implement measures to minimize hair loss.

(e) Instruct the patient to use mild shampoo and to avoid hair dyes and permanent waves.

(f) Instruct the patient to avoid vigorous brushing.

(g) Explore the use of a hypothermia cap or scalp tourniquet.

(h) Identify the written and audiovisual material available.

(7) Altered sexual patterns related to chemotherapy
Goals:

(a) Patient will state the risks to reproductive potential as a result of chemotherapy and will discuss the alternatives available.

(b) Patient will implement the use of effective contraception during treatment.

Interventions:

(a) Obtain a pregnancy test on any woman of child-bearing age before initation of chemotherapy.

(b) Explore the issues related to sperm banking for men before the initiation of chemotherapy.

(c) Discuss the potential for temporary or permanent sterility.

(d) Explore the alternatives for parenthood.

(e) Discuss the need for contraceptive measures during chemotherapy and for 2 years after it for both men and women.

(f) Advise patients who conceive while undergoing chemotherapy to be followed by oncologist. (Normal children have been born to parents who have undergone therapy, but no data exist.)

(8) Altered nutrition: less than body requirements related to anorexia and nausea and vomiting
Goal: Patient will state strategies to minimize the risk of weight loss.
Interventions:

(a) Discuss the potential for weight loss due to change in taste perception, appetite, and GI function.

(b) Discuss the conditions that will affect ability to eat: stomatitis, nausea/vomiting, fatigue, depression.

(c) Encourage small, frequent meals with increased calorie and protein content.

(d) Implement the use of nutritional supplements if the patient is unable to meet calorie requirements.

(e) Monitor the patient's weight (weigh twice a week).

(f) Obtain a dietary consultation if weight loss exceeds 2 pounds per week.

f. Evaluation
  (1) Patient demonstrates understanding of how to take medications.
  (2) Patient verbalizes understanding of home-care management and of signs and symptoms to report to health care team.
  (3) Patient is free of infection.
  (4) Patient recognizes and reports incidents of bleeding and anemia and initiates preventive measures.
  (5) Patient initiates recommended strategies to avoid or minimize nausea and vomiting.
  (6) Patient's weight and nutritional status are maintained.

4. **Bone marrow transplant (BMT)** Replenishing of depleted bone marrow cell reserves. It is performed for leukemia (in remission), aplastic anemia, and lymphoma.
  a. Donor sources
    (1) Allogenic—may be an unrelated person or a sibling.
    (2) Autologous—the patient's own bone marrow, harvested (removed) when maligancy is in remission.
  b. Stages of transplant process
    (1) Admission/preparation
        Preparation procedures are performed. These include procedures for decreasing the amount of bacteria on the body surface as well as inside and diagnostic studies.
        (a) Assessment.
            Response to diagnostic procedures: bone marrow biopsy, lumbar puncture, right atrial catheter insertion, and ability to perform self-care procedures
        (b) DIAGNOSTIC MEASURES:
            Bone marrow studies, CBC, quantitative immunoglobin, total protein, complete red blood cell type, EKG, echocardiogram, pulmonary function test

(c) Patient care management:
  1. Informed consent.
  2. Low bacteria diet.
  3. Nonabsorbable antibiotics.
  4. Bactrim.
  5. Allopurinol (except for aplastic anemia).
  6. Fluconazole (if previous fungal infection).
(d) Nursing diagnoses/goals/interventions:
    Knowledge deficit related to lack of information about transplant and the self-care procedures
    Goal: The patient will gain verbal understanding of self-care procedures.
    Interventions:
    1. Provide information about BMT, outcome, and possible complication.
    2. Explain expected care:
        a. Handwashing technique—before meals, after toileting, before self-care activities.
        b. Mouth care—4 times daily, never use toothbrush; may use sponge cleanser to clean gum and teeth; rinse mouth with alcohol-free mouthwash, 30 ml in sterile water or saline.
        c. Skin care—daily shower with antibacterial soap; dry skin well; avoid vigorous rubbing.
        d. Perineal care—perform after each voiding or bowel movement, periwash with povidone-iodine solution and sterile water, clean perineal area from front to back for female.

USUAL STAGES OF TRANSPLANT PROCESS

Day -10 ▸▸▸▸▸▸▸▸▸▸▸▸▸▸▸▸▸▸▸▸▸▸▸▸ Day 0 ▸▸▸▸▸▸▸▸▸ Day 14 ▸▸▸▸ Day 35

| Admission/ | Conditioning | Bone Marrow | Engraftment/ | Discharge |
| Preparation | | Transplant | Posttransplant | |

e. Maintain strict intake and output—teach patient how to record amount on bedside record.

f. Explain and demonstrate assessment—oral status, skin including perineal area, respiratory, cardiac, hematest for urine and stool; neurological.

g. Explain low bacteria diet—list of foods to avoid, such as fresh fruit and vegetable juices, yogurt, eggnog, cold cuts, raw eggs, cottage cheese, cheese, spices, and herbs added after food has been cooked.

3. Evaluation
Patient and/or significant other follows BMT preparation procedures as taught.

(2) Conditioning—Treating patient with high doses of cytarabine or cyclophosphamide and total body irradiation (TBI)

(a) Assessment:
1. Side effects of medication: stomatitis, diarrhea, hemorrhagic cystitis, liver toxicity, nausea and vomiting, pancytopenia.
2. Side effects of TBI: Nausea and vomiting, anorexia, hepatic veno-occlusive disease (VOD), decreased saliva and tears, erythema, parotid gland swelling.

(b) Diagnostic measures:
A CBC, platelet count, electrolytes, blood culture for temperature spikes, CMV cultures of urine and blood (twice weekly), weekly: PTT, calcium and triglycerides, BUN, weekly ECG.

(c) Patient care management:
1. High-dose cyclophosphamide.
2. Parenteral fluid.
3. Three-way Foley catheter with bladder irrigation.
4. Fractionated TBI for 3 days.
5. Cyclosporin.
6. Antiemetic.
7. Isolation.
8. Antidiarrheals.
9. Antibiotics.
10. Diuretics.
11. Antipyretics.
12. TPN.
13. Irradiated blood products.

(d) Nursing diagnoses/goal/interventions:
Knowledge deficit related to lack of information about medication and TBI procedure
Goal: Patient/significant other will verbalize understanding of medications and TBI
Interventions:
1. Explain the effects of medication and expected care.
2. Explain TBI procedure
   a. Isolation at the completion of procedure.
   b. Must wear mask after completion of TBI while returning to room and whenever leaving room.

(3) Altered tissue perfusion (renal) (bladder) related to local effects of cyclophosphamide
Goal: Patient will not exhibit signs of hemorrhagic cystitis
Interventions:
(a) Force fluids 4000 to 5000 ml/daily unless contraindicated.
(b) Provide fluids of choice for patient.
(c) Administer parenteral fluid as ordered before, during, and after chemotherapy.
(d) Weigh the patient daily at the same time with the same clothing and scale.
(e) Prepare and administer bladder irrigation as ordered.
(f) Check T, P, R, and BP q 4h to 8 h.
(g) Administer osmotic diuretic when ordered.

(4) Altered nutrition: less than body requirement related to nausea and vomiting, and/or inability to ingest nutrients
Goal: Patient will maintain weight or not lose more than 5% of original weight.

Interventions:
(a) Maintain calorie count.
(b) Change eating pattern, serve frequent, light meals.
(c) Provide high-protein drink as supplement.
(d) Administer antiemetic as ordered.
(e) Low bacteria food from home; refrigerate for no longer than 24 hours.

(5) Anxiety related to severity of response to conditioning and possible poor prognosis
Goal: Patient will exhibit less anxiety
Interventions:
(a) Visit frequently or have significant other remain with the patient.
(b) Continue to provide information about condition and procedure.
(c) Be sensitive to needs; listen to verbal clues.

(6) Risk for infection related to neutropenia secondary to TBI and/or chemistry
Goal: Patient will demonstrate the use of preventive measures
Interventions:
(a) Observe strict isolation precautions.
(b) Provide mask when the patient leaves the room.
(c) Never take flowers or plants into the room.
(d) Never use tap water except for bathing.
(e) Assess and record skin condition q 8 h.
(f) Teach the patient signs of infection.
(g) Maintain low-bacteria diet using sterile water for drinking.
(h) Maintain skin integrity; do not give IM injection; observe central line site q 8 h.

(7) Evaluation:
(a) Patient/significant other follows procedure as explained.
(b) The patient is free of signs of hemorrhagic cystitis.
(c) The patient does not lose more than 5% of original body-weight.
(d) No signs of infection are noted.

c. Transplant   Bone marrow is infused to establish a graft and to reinstate production of normal blood cellular components. Autologous transplant—patient's marrow that was previously harvested and preserved and frozen is thawed and infused. Allogenic is infused immediately
(1) Assessment.
Reaction to marrow infusion; allergic reaction to white cell in marrow: chills, fever, hives, chest pain; pulmonary emboli; hematuria; and increase in BUN and creatinine for 24–48 hours after marrow infusion.
(2) Nursing diagnoses/goals/interventions:
Risk for fluid volume excess related to bone marrow infusion
Goal: Patient reaction to infusion will be minimal.
Interventions:
1. Administer marrow infusion at rate ordered through center (must be infused within 4 hours; never infuse through a filter).
2. Autologous transplant— infuse slowly initially; use 80 micron filter; infuse 0.9 saline during procedure; maintain allergic reaction medication at bedside (epinephrine, hydrocortisone, diphenhydramine).
3. Monitor vital signs q 5 min during infusion; then q 15 min to 30 min for 2 hours.
4. Observe for allergic reaction, pulmonary emboli, and volume overload.
5. Never stop infusion; slow if reaction occurs and notify the physician.
(3) Evaluation
(a) Patient's vital signs remain stable.
(b) Patient's lungs are clear on auscultation.

d. Posttransplant   After infusion of bone marrow is a critical time in which many problems can occur.
(1) Assessment.
Hemorrhage-petechiae, bruising, occult blood in urine or feces; infection or graft vs. host disease (GVHD)

a condition that occurs when histocompatible differences exist between bone marrow graft and recipient.

(2) Nursing diagnoses/goal/intervention

(a) Altered protection related to thrombocytopenia
Goal: No bleeding or hemorrhaging will occur
Interventions
  1. Monitor platelet count daily.
  2. Inspect gums and oral cavity for bleeding often.
  3. Assess sensorium and neurological status each shift
  4. Inspect nasal cavity each shift.
  5. Use central line for withdrawal of blood sample and administration of parenteral medications; avoid skin puncture.
  6. Administer mouth care q 2–4 hours using prescribed solutions.
  7. Avoid aspirin and aspirin-containing products.
  8. Administer antacids as ordered.
  9. Test stool for blood.
  10. Administer platelet as ordered.
  11. Monitor Hgb, Hct, and electrolytes as ordered.
  12. Do not take rectal temperature or administer medication rectally.
  13. Avoid using razor blade.

(b) Knowledge deficit related to lack of information about self-care procedures, complications, diet, care of home environment, activities, and continuing health
Goal: Patient will verbalize understanding of home care.
See previous stages' nursing diagnoses, goals, and interventions and evaluations.

(3) Evaluation
Patient is free of signs of hemorrhage or bleeding.

5. Nursing management of the patient with a neoplastic disorder
a. Nursing diagnoses/goals/interventions

(1) Risk for infection related to altered immunologic response
Goal: There will be no incidence of infection.
Interventions:

(a) Assess the patient for infection; check vital signs every 4 hours; monitor WBC count and differential; inspect any site that is a portal for pathogens entering the body (IV sites, wounds, skin folds, bony prominences, perineum, and oral cavity).

(b) Report elevated temperature above 101°F, chills, diaphoresis, swelling, heat, pain, erytherma, exudate on body surface.

(c) Report change in respiratory or mental status, urinary frequency or burning, malaise, muscle ache, arthralagia, rash, or diarrhea.

(d) Obtain culture and sensitivity before initiation of antimicrobial treatment (wound exudate, sputum, urine, stool, blood).

(e) Initiate measures to minimize infection; reverse isolation if WBC count is below 1000/cu mm, avoid contact of patient with persons having known or recent infection; remind personnel to observe strict hand-washing technique, avoid rectal or vaginal procedures (see nursing interventions for patient on chemotherapy); avoid fresh fruits and raw meat, fish, and vegetables; remove fresh flowers and potted plants; change drinking water, denture cleaning fluids, and respiratory equipment containing water daily.

(f) Assess intravenous or central line sites every day for evidence of infection; change IV sites according to hospital policy; cleanse skin with povidone-iodine before arterial puncture or venipuncture; change central venous catheter dressing every other day; change all solutions and infusion set every 24 hours.

   (g) Avoid intramuscular injections.

   (h) *See also* nursing interventions for the patient receiving chemotherapy.

(2) Risk for injury related to bleeding problems

Goal: Patient will be free of injury and bleeding.

Interventions:

   (a) Monitor platelet count.

   (b) Assess for bleeding, petechiae, or ecchymosis; decrease in Hemoglobin/Hematocrit; frank or occult blood in any body excretions; bleeding from orifice.

   (c) Instruct the patient and the family to avoid commercial mouthwashes, use saline solution, avoid foods that are spicy or difficult to chew.

   (d) Administer platelet transfusion as ordered; administer Benadryl (diphenhydramine hydrochloride) or Solu-Cortef (hydrocortisone sodium succinate) to prevent reaction to platelet transfusions.

   (e) Administer pontacine or lidocaine mouthwash to ease dysphagia and/or mild anesthetic lozenges.

   (f) *See also* nursing interventions for the patient receiving chemotherapy.

(3) Impairment of oral mucous membranes; stomatitis *See* goals and nursing interventions for patients receiving chemotherapy, above.

(4) Impaired tissue integrity: alopecia related to radiation and/or chemotherapy

Goal: Patient will cope with hair loss.

Interventions:

   (a) Prevent trauma to scalp: lubricate scalp with vitamin A & D ointment to decrease itching; instruct the patient to wear a hat when in the sun and to use a sunscreen.

   (b) *See also* nursing interventions for patients receiving chemotherapy.

(5) Altered nutrition: less than body requirements related to anorexia/cachexia/malabsorption and nausea and vomiting *See* goals and nursing interventions for patients receiving chemotherapy, above, and Unit Eight, Management of the Patient Undergoing Surgery, Section F, Parenteral nutrition, page 282, and Total parenteral nutrition, page 283.

(6) Pain related to treatment and/or disease process

Goal: Patient will experience relief from pain and discomfort.

Interventions:

   (a) Assess the characteristics of the pain and discomfort: location, quality, frequency, and duration.

   (b) Administer analgesics as ordered. *See* Unit Eight, Management of the Patient Undergoing Surgery, page 267.

   (c) Assess the patient's behavioral response to pain and the pain response.

   (d) Collaborate with the patient, physician, and other members of the health care team when changes in pain management are indicated.

   (e) Teach the patient strategies to relieve pain and discomfort.

(7) Grieving related to anticipatory loss and altered functioning

Goal: Patient and his/her family/significant other will progress through grieving process appropriately.

Interventions:

   (a) Encourage verbalization of fears, concerns, and questions regarding the disease, treatment, and future implications.

   (b) Encourage active participation of the patient and the family in care and treatment decisions.

   (c) Establish a close relationship with the family.

   (d) Allow for ventilation of negative feeling, including projected anger and hostility within acceptable limits.

   (e) Allow for periods of crying and expressions of sadness.

(f) Involve the clergy as desired by the patient and the family.

(g) Arrange for professional counseling for the patient and the family exhibiting signs of dysfunctional grieving.

(8) Body image and self-esteem disturbance related to changes in appearance, function, and roles

Goal: Patient will have improved feeling about body image, and self-esteem will be elevated.

Interventions:

(a) Assess the patient's feeling about body image and level of self-esteem.

(b) Identify potential threats to the patient's self-esteem (e.g., altered appearance, decreased sexual function, hair loss, decreased energy, role change), and validate with the patient.

(c) Encourage the patient to verbalize concerns.

(d) Assist the patient in enhancing personal appearance (e.g., selection of clothing or use of wig).

(e) Encourage the patient and his/her partner to share concerns about altered sexuality/sexual function and to explore alternatives to their usual sexual expression.

b. Evaluation

(1) Patient is free of signs and symptoms of infection.

(2) Patient exhibits no signs or symptoms of bleeding.

(3) Patient verbalizes a decreased level of pain and discomfort.

(4) Patient and his/her family progress through the phase of grief.

(5) Patient demonstrates an elevation in level of self-esteem and of body image.

Alterations in the Blood and Blood-Forming Organs

A. Disorders of the Blood and Blood-Forming Organs

1. General assessment

a. Observe general appearance for **pallor** or jaundice, dizziness, weakness, **dysp**-nea (which may occur upon exertion or at rest), and joint and bone pains.

b. Palpate abdomen for enlarged spleen and/or liver.

c. Inspect skin for petechiae and/or ecchymoses and skin eruptions; and mouth for ulcerative lesions of the tongue, gums, and/or mucous membranes.

d. Measure temperature and vital signs for fever and slight tachycardia on exertion.

e. DIAGNOSTIC MEASURES: complete blood count, reticulocyte count, hemoglobin electrophoresis, Coombs' test, bleeding time, prothrombin time, partial thromboplastin time, bone marrow aspiration, serum albumin, total protein.

2. General patient care management

a. Splenectomy (surgical removal of the spleen).

b. Blood transfusion.

c. Bone marrow transplantation.

3. Nursing diagnoses/goals/interventions

a. Activity intolerance related to weakness, fatigue, and general malaise

Goal: Patient will tolerate normal activity.

Interventions:

(1) Maintain a regular schedule of rest and sleep.

(2) Plan nursing care to conserve the patient's energy.

(3) Encourage ambulation and activities of daily living as tolerated.

(4) Have the patient postpone activities that require undue energy until greater endurance is evident.

(5) Initiate safety precautions to prevent falls due to poor coordination, paresthesias, and weakness.

b. Decreased cardiac output related to increased cardiac workload

Goal: Patient will attain and maintain normal cardiac output.

Interventions:

(1) Avoid situations that precipitate palpitations and dyspnea.

(2) If dyspnea is a problem, elevate head of bed.

(3) Avoid unnecessary exertion for the patient.

(4) Administer oxygen at the rate and by the method ordered.

(5) Measure vital signs every 8 hours.

(6) Assess for fluid retention (e.g., peripheral edema, decreased urinary output, neck vein distention).

c. Alteration in nutrition related to inadequate intake of essential nutrients

Goal: Patient will attain and maintain adequate nutrition.

Interventions:

(1) Provide dietary consultations.

(2) Avoid spicy foods (can cause gastric irritation) and gas-producing foods for the patient.

(3) Provide dietary teaching/reinforcements.

(4) Encourage a diet high in protein and in high-calorie foods, fruits, and vegetables.

(5) Weigh weekly.

(6) Monitor lab values especially serum albumin and protein.

4. Evaluation

a. Patient tolerates normal activity.

b. Patient attains and maintains normal cardiac output.

c. Patient attains and maintains adequate nutrition.

5. **Aplastic anemia**   Deficiency of circulating erythrocytes due to the arrested development of red cells within the bone marrow. It is accompanied by a reduction in leukocytes and platelets.

a. Causes: (1) destruction of erythrocytes by drugs or chemicals: benzene and benzene derivatives; antitumor agents, such as nitrogen mustards, methotrexate, and 6-mercaptopurine; antimicrobials, heavy metals; (2) radiation damage.

b. Assessment. *See* General Assessment.

c. Patient care management

(1) Removal of underlying cause.

(2) Transfusion of red cells and platelets.

(3) Reverse isolation.

(4) Corticosteroid (methyl prednisolone).

(5) Bone marrow transplantation.

(6) Administration of immuno-suppressive therapy with antilymphocyte globulin (ALG) to remove the immunologic function that prolongs aplasia. ALG is given through a central venous catheter for 7–10

days. Patient responds to treatment within 6 weeks to 3 months.

d. Nursing diagnosis/goal/interventions

Risk for injury related to depression of bone marrow

Goal: Patient will be free of injury.

Interventions:

(1) Provide oral hygiene—frequent rinsing of mouth with warm saline or lidocaine.

(2) Protect skin against wounds, abrasions, or ulcerations.

(3) Encourage patient to eat foods high in vitamins and proteins.

(4) Monitor for signs of a beginning cold or infection (e.g., a rise in temperature or sore throat).

(5) If thrombocytopenia is present, avoid IM or SC injections and straining at bowel movement.

e. Evaluation: Patient is free of injury.

6. **Iron-deficiency anemia**   Inadequate absorption or excessive loss of iron.

a. Causes: bleeding (e.g., from ulcer, gastritis, or GI tumors); malabsorption of nutrients (e.g., because of gastric resection); inadequate iron intake.

b. Assessment

(1) Inspect mouth for smooth, sore tongue, and fingernails for thin, flat spoon shape.

(2) Observe for pica (a craving to eat unusual substances such as clay, laundry starch, or ice). These substances may cause this condition.

(3) DIAGNOSTIC MEASURES: serum iron and iron-binding capacity, stool test for occult blood, hemoglobin, and hematocrit.

c. Patient care management

(1) Correction of the underlying cause.

(2) Iron preparation

(a) Oral preparations—ferrous sulfate (Feosol), ferrous gluconate (Fergon), ferrous fumarate (Ircon).

(b) Parenteral preparation—iron dextran (Imferon).

(3) Balanced nutritional diet, high in iron.

(4) Rest periods.

(5) Oxygen therapy for severe iron deficiency.

(6) Blood transfusion.

d. Nursing diagnosis/goal/interventions
Knowledge deficit regarding disease process and treatment
Goal: Patient will verbalize understanding of disease process and treatment.
Interventions:
   (1) Explain purpose and dosages of iron therapy.
   (2) Advise patient to take iron preparation with meals.
   (3) Warn patient that iron salt can change the stool to a darker color.
   (4) Encourage food sources high in iron, including organ and other meats, cooked white beans, leafy vegetables, raisins, and molasses, with foods high in vitamin C to enhance absorption (orange juice, tomatoes).
   (5) Provide dietary consultation.
   (6) Encourage a well-balanced diet.
e. Evaluation
   (1) Patient eats a well-balanced diet.
   (2) Patient verbalizes understanding of disease process and treatment.

7. **Hodgkin's disease**   A malignant disease of unknown cause that originates in the lymphatic system and involves predominately the lymph nodes. There is a proliferation of Reed-Sternberg cells. *See also* Neoplastic Disorders, page 184.
   a. Assessment
      (1) Inspect the body for enlarged, firm, painless lymph nodes. The first nodes to become involved are usually the cervical lymph nodes, followed by the mediastinal, axillary, and inguinal nodes.
      (2) Observe for severe pruritus, edema and cyanosis of the face and neck (due to pressure on superior vena cava), weight loss, nerve pain, and paralgesia.
      (3) Measure temperature for alternating fever and non-febrile period.
      (4) Night sweats.
      (5) DIAGNOSTIC MEASURE: lymph node biopsy, the definitive examination for diagnosing Hodgkin's disease. The lymph tissue is examined for the presence of Reed-Sternberg cells, lymphangiography.
   b. Patient care management
      (1) Radiotherapy.

   (2) Combination chemotherapy— "MOPP" (reduces tumor masses with minimal toxic effects): mechlorethamine (nitrogen mustard), Oncovin, prednisone, procarbazine.
   (3) Surgery, to remove enlarged lymph nodes that are placing undue pressure upon an organ or nerve.
   c. Nursing diagnosis/goal/interventions. *See* External radiation, page 186, and Chemotherapy, page 188.

8. **Disseminated Intravascular Coagulation (DIC)**   Overstimulation of normal coagulation process in such conditions as septicemia, severe hypotension, cancer chemistry, obstetric emergencies, trauma, extensive burns, transplant rejection.
   a. Assessment.
      Abnormal bleeding in all systems and at sites of invasive procedures. Bleeding to hemorrhage—surgical incisions, postpartum uterus, eye fundus with visual changes, invasive procedure sites— injection, IV, arterial catheters, and chest or nasogastric tubes.
   b. DIAGNOSTIC MEASURES:
      Serial studies—PT, fibrinogen, platelets, fibrin, degradation products (FDP).
      Decreased factor assays: V, VII, VIII, X, XIII; PTT, decreases Hct without clinical bleeding; respiratory acidosis.
   c. Patient care management. Treatment of underlying disorder; anticoagulant therapy—heparin IV; fresh frozen plasma, platelets, clotting factors, other blood products, and parenteral fluids; thrombolytic therapy; oxygen therapy.
   d. Nursing diagnoses/goals/interventions:
      Altered tissue perfusion: renal, cerebral, cardiopulmonary, gastrointestinal, or peripheral related to interruption of flow to organs
      Goals: Patient's vital signs will be stable and bleeding will be controlled.
      Interventions:
      (1) Maintain venous access using strict aseptic technique.
      (2) Administer IV heparin and fresh frozen plasma, platelets, and other blood products as ordered; observe for response and/or reaction.
      (3) Observe for bleeding at venipuncture or clotting at end of catheter; apply pressure dressing if needed.

(4) Monitor FDP titers and report to physician for heparin dosage changes. (Lee-White and PTT are prolonged in DIC and are not reliable indicators of heparin therapy.)

(5) Monitor arterial pressure, ECG, BP, T, P, and R, q 30 min to q 60 min; report progressive decrease in BP, increase in heart rate, and elevated temperature.

(6) Assess neurologic status q 30 min to q 60 min, report changes.

(7) Monitor arterial blood gases; report acidostic states immediately.

(8) Monitor effects of oxygen therapy when administered.

(9) Assess for increased bleeding and/or new sites of hemorrhage in all body systems; report changes immediately.

(10) Administer careful skin care as needed; pad heels and elbows and support joints.

(11) Apply Gelfoam or thrombin dressing to areas with frank bleeding or those that continue to bleed.

(12) Provide oral hygiene every q 2 h to 4 h; avoid vigorous tooth-brushing; use soft-bristled toothbrush, cotton swabs, and diluted mouth rinse or saline.

(13) Weigh patient daily.

(14) Protect from trauma; use caution when suctioning or inserting lines or tubes; avoid invasive procedures.

(15) Apply pressure to site for 5 to 10 minutes or until bleeding stops if IM injection is necessary, or when removing catheters; observe q 10 mins to 15 mins; apply pressure dressing if appropriate.

e. Pain related to tissue trauma
Goal: Patient will verbalize relief from pain.
Interventions: (See section of pain management, Unit Eight.)

f. Anxiety related to threat of death
Goal: Patient will understand condition; participates in care; uses positive coping measures.
Interventions:
(1) Assess level of patient's fears and understanding of current condition when appropriate.
(2) Maintain calm, nonstressful environment.

(3) Prepare family/significant other for patient's appearance.

(4) Remain with patient or have significant other stay with patient; use touch and reassure patient.

(5) Provide information about condition, procedures, and diagnostic studies in language understood by patient.

(6) Encourage questions; answer clearly and consistently and clarify when necessary.

(7) Note positive progress in physical condition when appropriate.

(8) Be sensitive to needs; listen to nonverbal cues.

(9) Maintain and assist with coping strategies.

(10) Provide access to others to assist patient: clergy, social worker, psychologist, etc.

g. Evaluation
(1) There is no further evidence of bleeding and past sites of bleeding are resolving.
(2) Patient is free of pain.
(3) Symptoms of anxiety are absent.

Alterations That Interfere with the Meeting of Nutritional Needs

A. General Assessment
1. Observe general appearance.
   a. Nutritional status—body build, fat distribution, and weight.
   b. Skin color—pallor, cyanosis, jaundice.
2. Inspect oral cavity (mucous membrane, lips, gingivae, teeth, and tongue).
3. Observe ability to swallow; note pain or difficulty in swallowing.
4. Observe abdomen.
   a. Inspect skin for color; discoloration or marks due to vascular condition; shape and movement; and umbilicus shape.
   b. Auscultate for bowel sound.
   c. Percuss for the presence of air or fluid.
   d. Palpate for painful or tender areas and muscle tone development.
5. Observe anus and rectum.
   a. Inspect for signs of irritation, abscess, sweating, and itching.
   b. Palpate for tenderness, muscle tone, hemorrhoids, masses, polyps, and any other abnormalities.
6. Observe for nausea, vomiting, loss of appetite, change in bowel habits (constipa-

tion, diarrhea), and frequency of elimination.

7. Measure and note quality of vital signs—elevation of temperature, change in pulse or respiration (observe for shock).

8. Assess for pain, indigestion, intestinal "gas" (belching and flatulence), vomiting, and hematemesis.

9. DIAGNOSTIC MEASURES

    a. Roentgenography of the gastrointestinal tract.

      (1) Upper gastrointestinal tract

        (a) Procedure: Barium is swallowed under direct fluoroscopic examination. X-rays are taken for permanent records. Additional X-rays may be taken at intervals.

        (b) Patient preparation

          1. Give nothing by mouth (NPO) after midnight.

          2. Explain procedure to the patient.

      (2) Lower gastrointestinal tract

        (a) Procedure: Barium enema is given to reveal the presence of polyps, tumors, and other lesions of the large intestine and to demonstrate any abnormal anatomy or malfunction of the bowel.

        (b) Patient preparation

          1. Administer GoLYTELY to cleanse tract.

          2. Give nothing by mouth after midnight.

          3. Explain procedure to patient.

    b. Upper gastrointestinal fiberoscopy (allows for direct visualization of the gastric mucosa through a lighted endoscope)

      (1) Patient preparation

        (a) Have the patient fast for 6–8 hours before examination.

        (b) Administer the ordered narcotic analgesic a half-hour before procedure.

        (c) Have the patient gargle with a local anesthetic, along with IV administration of diazepam (Valium), before scoping.

        (d) Administer atropine to reduce secretions and glucagon to relax the smooth muscle if ordered.

      (2) Procedure: The patient's lips, oral cavity, and pharynx are sprayed with tetracaine (Pontacaine), after which the scope is passed.

      (3) Aftercare

        (a) Give nothing by mouth until gag reflex returns in 3 to 4 hours.

        (b) Observe for signs of perforation (pain and elevated temperature).

        (c) Relieve minor throat discomfort with lozenges, cool saline gargle, and oral analgesic medications.

    c. Endoscopy

      (1) Procedure: visualization of the inside of a body cavity—esophagus, stomach, duodenum, rectum, or sigmoid colon—by means of a lighted tube.

      (2) Purposes

        (a) To directly visualize mucosa to observe pathological lesions.

        (b) To obtain a biopsy specimen.

        (c) To secure a specimen for cytological examination.

      (3) Special procedure for viewing the lower bowel by means of a tubular instrument incorporating small electric lights that allow the lumen of the bowel to be viewed directly

        (a) Anoscopy—used to examine the anal canal.

        Proctoscopy and sigmidoscopy—used to inspect the rectum and the sigmoid. The flexible sigmoidscope permits examination of up to 16–20 inches from the anus.

        Patient preparation

          1. Give clear liquid the day before.

          2. Give cleansing enema or Fleet's enema until clear return.

        (b) Fiberoscopy colonoscopy—used for direct visualization of the colon. The procedure is used as a diagnostic aid; instrument can remove foreign bodies,

polyps, or tissue for biopsy.
Patient preparation

1. Give liquids only for 3 days before.
2. Cleanse tract with GoLYTELY (polyethylene glycol electrolyte) lavage solution, which works in about 4 hours.
3. Administer Demerol (meperidine) a half hour before test. Valium may also be administered during the examination.

d. Hematological studies: complete blood count, electrolyte determination, prothrombin time, partial thromboplastin time.
e. Ultrasonography: Sound waves are passed into internal body structure. Procedure is useful in studying the liver, pancreas, spleen, gallbladder, and retroperitoneal tissues.
f. Computer tomography (CT scanning).
g. Magnetic resonance imaging (MRI).

B. Alterations in Absorption

1. **Crohn's disease (regional enteritis, regional ileitis)** A chronic, inflammatory disease that may involve any portion of the intestinal tract; characterized by spontaneous remissions and exacerbations.
Cause is unknown. The disease affects both sexes equally. There is a high incidence in persons of Jewish origin. A familial tendency is present. The disease occurs most often between the second and third decades of life.
The inflamed areas in the bowel are scattered and clearly demarcated from the normal portions. Thickening of the mesentery and bowel wall and enlarged lymph nodes may occur. Scarring may narrow the lumen of the intestines.

2. **Ulcerative colitis** An inflammatory disease of the colon and rectum of unknown origin. It is characterized by periods of exacerbation and remission.

3. Assessment of Crohn's disease and ulcerative colitis
   a. Assess health history for family history of the disease and for diarrhea.
   b. Inspect the general appearance for weight loss and dehydration.
   c. Auscultate the abdomen for increased peristalsis.
   d. Inspect stool for consistency, frequency, and the presence of blood.
   e. Observe for abdominal pain (note frequency, duration, precipitating factors) and for straining upon defecation.
   f. DIAGNOSTIC MEASURES: stool examination, proctoscopy, sigmoidoscopy, barium enema X-ray examination.

4. Patient care management of Crohn's disease and ulcerative colitis
   a. Medical measures
      (1) Low-residue, high-protein diet with supplemental vitamin therapy and iron replacement.
      (2) Intravenous therapy to correct fluid and electrolyte imbalance.
      (3) Sedatives and antidiarrheal medications to reduce colonic peristalsis.
      (4) Nonabsorbable sulfonamides (Azulfidine or Gantrisin) as anti-infectives.
      (5) Antibiotics for secondary infections such as abscesses, perforations, and peritonitis.
      (6) ACTH and corticosteroids, early in the disease, to relieve inflammation.
   b. Psychotherapeutic treatment.
   c. Surgical intervention (colostomy and ileostomy).

5. Nursing role for Crohn's disease and ulcerative colitis
   a. Encourage the patient to rest after meals and to maintain activity within physical capacity.
   b. Maintain fluid and electrolyte balance.
      (1) Observe IV drip rate.
      (2) Measure and record intake and output.
      (3) Add potassium chloride.
   c. Teach the patient proper diet.
      (1) Avoid foods that exacerbate diarrhea (e.g., bovine milk products).
      (2) Avoid cold food (increases intestinal motility).
   d. Tell the patient to stop smoking (increases intestinal motility).
   e. Note the number of stools and inspect for blood.
   f. Observe for constipation (measure abdominal girth daily).

g. Observe for corticosteroid side effects (hypertension, fluid retention, and hirsutism).
h. Record patient responses to all medications.
i. Encourage the patient to talk and ventilate feelings.
j. Try to direct the patient's attention to self and not the intestinal tract.
k. Help the patient to accept and learn to live with the disease.
l. Educate both the patient and his/her family about the pathology and treatment of the disease.

6. Management of the patient undergoing colon surgery
   a. Types of surgery
      (1) **Ileostomy**   Surgical opening of the ileum onto the abdominal wall, used in treatment for Crohn's disease and ulcerative colitis.
      (2) **Colostomy**   Opening of some portion of the colon onto the abdominal surface. Causes: cancer of the colon, diverticulitis (temporary double-barrel colostomy is used for this condition—see diagram), mechanical disruption (intestinal obstruction).
      (3) **Primary resection and end-to-end anastomosis**   Diseased colon is removed, and ends of remaining bowel are joined.
         (a) Cause: chronic diverticulitis.
         (b) Nursing role   *See* Unit Eight, Alterations That Interfere with the Meeting of Nutritional Needs, Section B2: Management of the patient undergoing gastric surgery, page 324.
   b. Preoperative management
      (1) Ileostomy
         (a) Low-residue diet in small feedings.
         (b) Replace fluids: administer blood and protein.
         (c) Give steroids and antibiotics.
         (d) If the patient is on steroid therapy, assess adrenal function by measuring pulse and blood pressure, and observe urinary output, general appearance, and reactions.
      (2) Colostomy
         (a) Present information about surgery by means of literature, models, and discussion.
         (b) Have another patient who has had colostomy visit.
         (c) Offer high-caloric and low-residue diet for several days.
         (d) Administer intestinal antiseptics of the sulfur group and neomycin PO. These reduce the bacterial content of the colon and soften and decrease the bulk of its contents.
         (e) Record intake and output.
         (f) Insert nasogastric tube to minimize postoperative distention.
         (g) Insert indwelling catheter to ensure an empty bladder during surgery.
   c. Preoperative nursing diagnosis/goal/interventions for ileostomy and colostomy
      Knowledge deficit regarding the surgical procedure and preoperative preparation
      Goal: Patient will verbalize understanding of the surgical procedure and the necessary preoperative preparation.
      Interventions:
      (1) Reinforce information given by the surgeon.
      (2) Use pictures or drawings to illustrate the location and appearance of the wounds and the stoma if the patient is interested.
      (3) Explain that an oral/parenteral antimicrobial will be administered to cleanse the bowel preoperatively; mechanical cleansing may also be required.
      (4) Assist the patient during nasogastric intubation.
   d. Preoperative evaluation: Patient demonstrates understanding of the surgical procedure and preoperative preparation.
   e. Postoperative nursing diagnoses/goals/interventions for ileostomy and colostomy
      (1) Body image disturbance
          Goal: Patient will attain a positive self-concept.

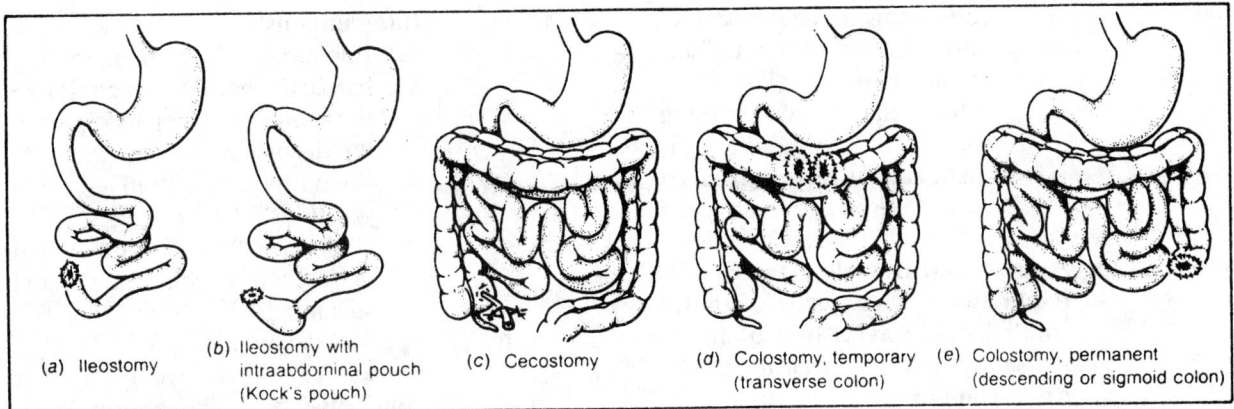

(a) Ileostomy

(b) Ileostomy with intraabdominal pouch (Kock's pouch)

(c) Cecostomy

(d) Colostomy, temporary (transverse colon)

(e) Colostomy, permanent (descending or sigmoid colon)

Surgical Interventions of the Bowel Which Alter Elimination. (From *Medical-Surgical Nursing—A Conceptual Approach*, Second Edition by D. Jones et al. Copyright © 1982 by McGraw-Hill Book Company. Used with the permission of McGraw-Hill Book Company.)

Interventions:
(a) Encourage the patient to verbalize his/her feelings about the stoma.
(b) Be present with the patient when he/she views the stoma for the first time.
(c) Suggest that spouse or significant other view the stoma.
(d) Encourage the patient to care for the stoma.
(e) Encourage the patient to care for the colostomy from the first irrigation (done on 4th or 5th day). All colostomies must be irrigated at least once.
(2) Anxiety related to the loss of bowel control
Goal: Patient will experience reduction in anxiety.
Intervention:
Provide information about expected bowel function
(a) Colostomy—*ascending colostomy* drains fluid feces, therefore is difficult to train, and needs daily irrigation. *Descending colostomy* drains solid feces and is easier to control. The purpose of irrigation (300 to 1000 ml of fluid may be used) is to distend the bowel sufficiently to stimulate peristalsis. Rectal tube or catheter is inserted about 3 inches. Irrigation catheter passes through a cone to hold the fluid within the bowel during irrigation. The bag may be held in place with a karaya gum ring. Colostomy is opened on 2nd or 3rd day after surgery.
1. Instruct the patient with a descending colostomy that irrigation may be done according to his/her preference (daily, every other day, or every 3 days).
2. Cleanse the appliance properly. (Aspirin, baking soda, or charcoal in the bag controls odor.)
(b) Ileostomy
1. Place temporary plastic bag over ileostomy (content will always be liquid) immediately after surgery.
2. Control odor (small doses of bismuth subcarbonate orally, proper cleansing of appliance, and ventilation and deordorizers in room).
(3) Risk for impaired skin integrity related to irritation of periostomal skin by effluent
Goal: Patient's skin will remain intact.
Interventions:
(a) Demonstrate how to apply skin barrier.
1. Ileostomy: Dust skin around ileostomy with nystatin powder to prevent irritation and yeast growth.

2. Colostomy: Keep skin around stoma free of irritation, clean, and dry. (Use Kenalog spray and nystatin powder, or Maalox, Gelusil, and milk of magnesia.)
   (b) Demonstrate how to remove the pouch.
(4) Altered nutrition: less than body requirement, inadequacy of nutrients related to avoidance of foods secondary to a fear of gastrointestinal discomfort
   Goal: Patient will achieve optimal nutritional intake.
   Interventions:
   (a) Colostomy
      1. Discover what foods have laxative effect. Avoid gas-forming foods.
      2. Control diarrhea by means of Lomotil, Kaopectate, or paregoric.
      3. Drink prune juice or apple juice to relieve constipation.
   (b) Ileostomy
      1. Measure and record fluid intake, urinary output, and fecal discharge.
      2. Offer large amounts of fluid.
      3. Give a low-residue, high-caloric diet.
(5) Fluid volume deficit related to anorexia and vomiting
   Goal: Patient will attain fluid and electrolyte balance.
   Interventions:
   (a) Maintain strict intake and output.
   (b) Weigh the patient daily, using the same scale and same amount of clothing.
   (c) Monitor serum and urinary values of sodium and potassium.
   (d) Observe and record skin turgor and the appearance of the tongue.
(6) There is an altered sexuality pattern related to altered body image
   Goal: Patient will attain/regain satisfactory sexual performance.
   Interventions:
   (a) Encourage the patient to verbalize his/her fear. Suggest that the sexual partner participate in the discussion.
   (b) Recommend alternative sexual positions.
   (c) Seek assistance from a sexual therapist or psychiatric clinical specialist.
f. Postoperative evaluation
   (1) Patient expresses freely his/her concerns about the alteration in body image.
   (2) Patient expresses interest in learning about bowel function, handles equipment correctly, and cares for ostomy correctly.
   (3) Patient's skin around the stoma is intact.
   (4) Patient modifies his/her diet and ingests an adequate amount of nutrients.
   (5) Patient expresses fears and concerns about sexual function, discusses alternative sexual positions, and accepts the services of a professional counselor.
   (6) Patient maintains fluid and electrolyte balance.

C. Management of Patients with Intestinal Disorders
   1. **Herniorrhaphy**   Removal of the hernial sac after it has been dissected free from surrounding structures, then suturing and/or reinforcing muscle and fascial layer to prevent recurrence.
      a. Types of hernias
         (1) Inguinal, due to weakness of the abdominal wall at the point through which the spermatic cord emerges in the male and the round ligament in the female.
         (2) Umbilical, due to failure of the umbilical cord orifice to close.
         (3) Incisional, due to weakness of the incisional site after surgery.
         (4) Femoral, occurring below the inguinal (i.e., below the groin).
      b. Patient care management
         (1) Reduction of hernia via mechanical means (i.e., application of a truss).

(2) Surgical intervention—herniorrhaphy. Hospitalized patient may go home the day following surgery or may stay 3 to 5 days or longer. Patient may have same-day surgery with local anesthesia.

c. Nursing diagnoses/goals/interventions

(1) Knowledge deficit in regard to surgical treatment

Goal: Patient will demonstrate understanding of surgical treatment. Intervention: *See* Unit Eight, Management during the Preoperative Period, page 267. (Note: Notify physician immediately, if patient has upper respiratory infection, sneezing, allergy, or chronic cough from smoking. Surgery may be postponed.)

(2) Potential alteration in urinary elimination related to discomfort

Goal: Patient will void and will not develop retention.

Interventions:

(a) Ambulate the patient on the day of or after surgery.

(b) Check voiding; institute nursing measures to stimulate urination if urinary retention occurs.

(c) Apply ice bag and scrotal support for males after inguinal repair.

(d) Instruct the patient to splint incision site when coughing or sneezing to lessen pain and protect the site.

(3) Knowledge deficit regarding home-care needs

Goal: Patient will demonstrate understanding of home-care and follow-up instructions.

Interventions:

(a) Instruct patient to limit activities for 5 to 7 days, avoid heavy lifting for 4 to 6 weeks, and use correct body mechanics at all times.

(b) Teach patient which signs and symptoms to report to the physician: drainage from incision, painful urination or difficulty with urination.

(c) Caution patient to avoid straining during defecation by diet modification, bulk cathartics or stool softeners, and a daily fluid intake of 2000 ml.

d. Evaluation

(1) Patient understands surgical treatment.

(2) Patient has adequate urinary output.

(3) Patient has decrease in scrotal swelling.

(4) Patient avoids straining during defecation.

2. **Appendicitis** Acute inflammation of the appendix.

a. Assessment

(1) Palpate abdomen for tenderness around the umbilicus and mid-epigastrum. Observe for Rovsing's sign (upon palpation of left lower quadrant, pain is felt in right lower quadrant) and muscular rigidity.

(2) Observe for pain in the anterior abdominal wall, occurring upon coughing.

(3) Observe general appearance for right hip flexion (protective maneuver).

(4) Measure temperature and vital signs, and note temperature elevation.

b. Preoperative nursing role: Administer aspirin (to lower temperature) and antibiotic as ordered.

c. Postoperative nursing role

(1) Place the patient in Fowler's position to relieve abdominal strain.

(2) Medicate for pain as ordered.

(3) Give fluids as soon as bowel sounds return.

(4) Ambulate the patient on the day of surgery.

(5) Advise the patient to avoid heavy lifting for several months.

Alterations in Metabolism (Hepatic and Biliary Alterations)

A. General Assessment

1. Inspect skin and sclera for jaundice.

2. Percuss abdomen for shifting dullness or fluid wave as ascites.

3. Palpate upper right quadrant of abdomen for tenderness or heptomegaly.

4. Observe mental state for disorientation.
5. Observe general appearance for weight loss, enlarged abdomen, edema of the legs, ecchymotic areas, and spider nevi of face, neck, and arms.
6. Obtain health history.
7. DIAGNOSTIC MEASURES
  a. Laboratory tests
     (1) Liver function studies, i.e., pigment studies—abnormal in liver and biliary diseases that cause jaundice.
         (a) Serum bilirubin (direct)—normal, 0 to 0.3 mg.
         (b) Serum bilirubin (total)—normal, 0 to 0.9 mg.
         (c) Urine bilirubin—normal, 0.
         (d) Urine urobilinogen—normal, 0 to 16 for 24 hours.
     (2) Protein studies
         (a) Total serum protein—7.0 to 7.5 gm %.
         (b) Serum albumin—3.5 to 5.5 gm %.
         (c) Serum globulin—1.5 to 3.0 gm %. (Albumin is elevated in cirrhosis and chronic hepatitis; globulin is elevated in cirrhosis, liver disease, viral hepatitis, and obstructive jaundice.)
         (d) Albumin/globulin (A/G) ratio—A>G or 1.5:1–2.5:1.
     (3) Prothrombin time—prolonged in liver disease.
     (4) Serum alkaline phosphatase—a sensitive measure of biliary tract obstruction (2 to 3 Bodansky units).
     (5) Serum transaminase studies—SGOT, SGPT, and LDH. *See* Unit Eight, Section A: General Assessment of Cardiac Function, page 304.
     (6) Blood ammonia—level rises with liver failure.
     (7) Indocyanine green—replacing Bromsulfalein excretion (BSP). Its clearance depends on functioning liver cells and absence of obstruction.
     (8) Cholesterol (150 to 250 mg)—elevated in biliary obstruction, decrease in liver disease.

  b. **Liver biopsy** Sampling of liver tissue by needle aspiration.
     (1) Nursing role
         (a) Measure and record vital signs before biopsy.
         (b) Ascertain that prothombin time and blood typing have been done before biopsy.
         (c) Explain procedure to the patient. Give support during this procedure.
         (d) Position the patient on his/her back; expose the right upper abdomen.
         (e) Instruct the patient when to inhale and exhale.
         (f) After procedure, position the patient on the right side to prevent hemorrhage.
         (g) Measure and record vital signs.
         (h) Observe for shock.
  c. Roentgenographic examinations
     (1) Liver scan, done to evaluate biliary patency or anatomical changes.
         (a) Colloid gold or other radioactive substance is injected intravenously.
         (b) Scan is done 1 hour after injection.
     (2) **Cholecystogram** (Chronic cholecysititis only) Visualization of the gallbladder to detect gallstones and to estimate the ability of the gallbladder to fill, concentrate its contents, contract, and empty normally. Nursing role
         (a) Give nothing by mouth after ingestion of contrast-medium tablets.
         (b) Administer a saline enema in the morning.
     (3) **Ultrasonography** Has replaced oral cholecystography in many areas of the country. The patient is not exposed to ionizing radiation. Ultrasound detect calculi in the gallbladder or dilated common bile duct.

(4) **Cholangiography** Injection of dye directly into the biliary tree, to distinguish jaundice caused by liver disease from that due to biliary obstruction. The liver, hepatic ducts, common hepatic duct, cystic duct, and gallbladder are delineated with clarity.

B. Liver Disorders
1. **Viral hepatitis A (HAV) (infectious hepatitis)** Inflammation of the liver; the disease is endemic in some areas of the world, especially those with poor sanitation, but epidemics occur elsewhere as well.
   a. Transmission: fecal-oral contact; water, milk, or shellfish from contaminated water; (rarely) blood transfusion.
   b. Incubation period: 1 to 7 weeks (usually 30 days).
   c. Assessment
      (1) Inspect skin and sclera for jaundice, and urine for color change (dark color).
      (2) Observe and note complaints of epigastric distress, anorexia, heartburn, and flatulence.
      (3) Measure temperature and vital signs, and note any temperature elevation.
      (4) Palpate abdomen for enlarged liver and spleen.
   d. Patient care management: bedrest, frequent small feedings supplemented with IV infusions of glucose.
   e. Control and prevention
      (1) Administer immune serum globulin (ISG) to all individuals exposed to persons with type A viral hepatitis.
      (2) Instruct the patient to avoid alcohol and all drugs except those prescribed.
      (3) Teach measures to prevent the spread of disease: safe hand-washing techniques; universal precautions.
2. **Hepatitis B virus (HBV)** Inflammation of the liver.
   a. Transmission: oral via saliva (even during breast feeding); blood transfusion, skin prick, sexual intercourse; contaminated equipment.

   b. Cause: Australian antigen.
   c. Incubation period: 50 to 150 days.
   d. Assessment
      (1) Obtain health history. Question the patient concerning blood transfusion, drug addiction, recent surgery or cuts, ear piercing, acupuncture, or tattooing.
      (2) Inspect for rash and bruising.
      (3) Note complaints of arthralgia and pharyngitis.
   e. Control and prevention. *See* Hepatitis A, above. Also:
      (1) Obtain blood from paid donors instead of volunteers.
      (2) Use disposable syringes and needles.
      (3) Use gloves when handling positive specimens.

C. Biliary Disorders
1. **Biliary obstruction**
   a. Definitions
      (1) **Cholecystitis** Inflammation of the gallbladder.
      (2) **Cholelithiasis** Presence of gallstones.
   b. Assessment
      (1) Observe and note pain in upper right abdomen that radiates to the back and shoulder (biliary colic), nausea, and vomiting.
      (2) Palpate abdomen for a mass in the right upper quadrant.
      (3) Inspect the skin and sclera for jaundice.
      (4) Obtain health history; do symptoms occur most often after a meal of fatty or fried foods?
      (5) DIAGNOSTIC MEASURE: cholecystography.
   c. Patient care management
      (1) Drug therapy
         (a) Papaverine or Demerol.
         (b) Broad-spectrum antibiotics.
      (2) Nasogastric tube to relieve distension and vomiting.
      (3) Maintenance of fluid and electrolyte balance.
      (4) Low-fat diet; non-gas-forming vegetables; no alcohol.
   d. Preoperative nursing role
      (1) If nasogastric tube is in place, at-

tach it to suction, monitor drainage, and provide nasal and oral care.

(2) Monitor IV fluids; record intake and output; observe serum electrolyte levels.

(3) Observe for biliary obstruction (jaundice, dark urine, clay-covered stools).

(4) Observe for bleeding (ecchymosis, melena, or hematemesis).

2. Management of the patient undergoing biliary surgery

  a. Surgical interventions

    (1) **Cholecystectomy** Removal of gallbladder after ligation of the cystic duct and artery. A Penrose drain is inserted.

    (2) **Cholecystostomy** Opening and drainage of the gallbladder.

    (3) **Choledocholithotomy** (Usually done with a cholecystectomy). Incision into the common duct for the removal of stones. A T-tube is inserted into the duct for drainage.

    (4) **Choledochostomy** Incision into the common duct for removal of stone.

  b. Postoperative nursing diagnoses/goals/interventions

    (1) Pain related to surgical intervention
    Goal: Patient will have relief from pain.

    (2) Ineffective breathing pattern and pain related to high abdominal surgical incision
    Goal: Patient will not experience respiratory complications.
    Interventions:

      (a) Place the patient in low Fowler's position.

      (b) Monitor IV fluids.

      (c) Irrigate nasogastric tube every 4 hours.

      (d) Encourage the patient to cough, turn, and deep-breathe at frequent intervals.

      (e) Assist the patient in splinting the operative site when coughing or deep breathing.

      (f) Ambulate the patient as soon as permissible.

    (3) Risk for impaired skin integrity related to altered biliary drainage following surgical interventions
    Goal: There will be an absence of complication from altered biliary drainage
    Interventions:

      (a) Connect T-tube to closed gravity drainage and place well below level of the incision.

        1. Measure and record bile drainage every 24 hours (normal—300 to 500 cc). Report to physician drainage over 500 cc.

        2. Clamp tube for 1 hour before and after meals.

        3. Protect skin from irritation due to bile drainage. Apply petroleum jelly, gauze or skin prep as needed.

        4. Apply Montgomery straps.

      (b) Carefully monitor urine, feces, and skin for biliary obstruction (change in color).

    (4) Altered nutrition: less than body requirements related to inadequate bile secretions
    Goal: Patient will ingest adequate nutrients.
    Interventions:

      (a) Provide a low-fat diet, high in carbohydrates and proteins.

      (b) Administer vitamin K.

    (5) Knowledge deficit regarding home-care management
    Goal: Patient will understand home-care routine.
    Interventions:

      (a) Explain medications: vitamins, anticholingerics, antispasmodics—name, dosage, purpose, time schedule, and side effects.

      (b) Explain signs and symptoms to report to physician: jaundice, dark urine, pale-color stool, pruritus, and signs of inflammation, such as elevated temperature or pain.

      (c) Explain that fat restriction will be lifted in 4–6 weeks.

c. Evaluation
  (1) Patient achieves relief from pain.
  (2) Patient is free of respiratory complications.
  (3) Patient's skin remains intact around site of biliary drainage.
  (4) Patient ingests adequate amounts of nutrients.
3. Other procedures
  a. Biliary lithotripsy—a noninvasive procedure performed under analgesia using high-energy shock waves to disintegrate gallstones, allowing them to pass through the common bile duct into the intestine.
  b. Laparoscopic, endoscropic laser cholectomy—removal of the gallbladder with surgical incision; 4 small punctures are made in the abdominal wall, and with the use of a laparoscopic laser, the gallbladder is removed.
  Intervention   *See* Postoperative nursing diagnoses.

Alterations in Fluid and Electrolyte Elimination

A. **Acute Renal Failure**   Sudden and almost complete loss of kidney function caused by failure of renal circulation or by glomerular or tubular damage.
  1. Causes
    a. Prerenal: hypotension, due to burn, hemorrhage, septic shock, or cardiac insufficiency; renal artery obstruction.
    b. Renal: infections, nephrotoxic drugs, severe tranfusion reaction.
    c. Postrenal: obstruction due to stones, tumors, or trauma, resulting in blockage of ureteral and/or urethral drainage.
  2. Phases
    a. Period of oliguria. Urinary output is less than 400 to 600 mL in 24 hours, lasting about 10 days.
    b. Period of diuresis. Urinary output increases, signaling that glomerular filtration has returned, combined with the leveling of blood urea nitrogen (BUN).
    c. Period of recovery. BUN stabilizes and returns to normal (full recovery takes 3 to 12 months).

B. **Chronic Renal Failure**   An irreversible disease of the kidney, characterized by a progressive loss of renal function, leading to end-stage renal disease and death. Most common causes include glomerulonephritis, pyelonephritis, diabetes, hypertension, lupus erythematosis and polycystic kidney disease.

C. Care of the Patient with Renal Failure
  1. Assessment
    a. Obtain health history. Assess for:
      (1) Decrease in urinary output in spite of an increase in fluid intake.
      (2) Recent drugs, including recent diagnostic test using contrast medium.
      (3) Handling of chemical at place of employment.
    b. Observe general appearance for edema of the eyes, distended neck vein, weight gain, and weakness.
    c. Measure and note vital signs for elevation of blood pressure; increased, bounding pulse; and shortness of breath.
    d. Auscultate heart for bradycardia.
    e. Observe mental status for confusion.
    f. Auscultate lungs for moist rales and frothy sputum (if fluid overload is severe).
    g. DIAGNOSTIC MEASURES: routine urinalysis; urine specific gravity; serum electrolytes; serum blood urea nitrogen; serum creatinine; urine electrolytes; urine osmolality; creatinine clearance; uric acid serum and urine; X-ray of kidney, ureters, and bladder (KUB); renal ultrasound; renal computer tomography (CT); intravenous pyelography (IVP); renal biopsy
  2. Patient care management
    a. Removal or control of cause.
    b. Dialysis, peritoneal or hemodialysis.
    c. Daily weights.
    d. Sodium bicarbonate to correct acidosis.
    e. Medications: Diuretics, antihypertensives, aluminum hydroxide, antacids, kayexalate, diphrenhydramine, multivitamins.
    f. Dietary management.
    g. Blood transfusion.
    h. Renal transplant.
    i. Treatment of complications.

3. Nursing diagnoses/goals/interventions
   a. Fluid volume excess related to decreased kidney function
      Goals:
      (1) Patient will receive a fluid intake adjusted to body need during the acute phase of illness.
      (2) Patient will maintain fluid and electrolyte balance and normal blood pressure.
      Interventions:
      (1) Maintain fluid balance.
         (a) Weigh the patient daily.
         (b) Observe skin for turgor and mucous membranes for dehydration.
         (c) Monitor for elevated blood pressure.
         (d) Maintain strict intake and output and weigh daily.
         (e) Administer IV fluids as ordered to avoid fluid overload.
      (2) Maintain electrolyte balance.
         (a) Provide electrocardiogram monitoring.
         (b) Restrict potassium-containing foods and medications.
         (c) Avoid magnesium-containing antacids (because of phosphatemia).
      (3) Observe for cardiac overload (increase in blood pressure, respiratory rate, and pulse rate).
      (4) Observe for electrolyte complications.
      (5) Administer antihypertensive medication as ordered.
      (6) Monitor serum electrolyte levels, ammonia, creatinine, and BUN; report abnormal values.
      (7) Auscultate breath and heart sounds every shift.
      (8) Assess peripheral pulses, and check for peripheral edema or distended neck vein every 4 hours; note skin turgor every 8 hours.
      (9) Administer diuretics, carefully monitoring for toxic effects and urinary output after administration.
      (10) Encourage diet low in sodium, potassium, and protein; high in carbohydrates; restrict oral intake of fluids as ordered.
      (11) Prepare the patient for dialysis.
   b. Pain related to effect of pericarditis (increased levels of ammonia present in renal failure are toxic to the pericardial sac and may produce pericarditis with possible tamponade)
      Goal: Patient will experience relief from pain.
      Interventions:
      (1) Assess for chest pain, percardial rub, narrowing pulse pressure, distended neck vein, peripheral edema, rales, cardiac dysrhythmias.
      (2) Administer analgesics as prescribed, and monitor effect.
      (3) Maintain bed in semi-Fowler's position.
      (4) Administer oxygen as prescribed.
   c. Risk for infection related to decreased functioning of immune system
      Goal: Patient will be free of infection.
      Interventions:
      (1) Monitor for signs and symptoms of infection (elevated temperature, decreased WBC, redness or inflammation).
      (2) Have the patient cough and do deep breathing exercises; use incentive spirometer.
      (3) Change IV site dressing every 24 hours; change IV tubing according to hospital policy.
      (4) Administer prophylactic antibiotic in a timely manner to ensure maintenance of therapeutic blood levels; monitor for signs of toxicity.
   d. Altered nutrition: less than body requirement related to anorexia, stomatitis, or dislike of dietary restriction
   e. Impaired skin integrity related to poor nutritional status and immobility
      Goal: Patient will ingest adequate amounts of prescribed diet, and will maintain positive nitrogen balance.
      Interventions:
      (1) Encourage the patient to eat prescribed diet, high in carbohydrates, vitamins, and fat and low in sodium, potassium, and protein.
      (2) Provide dietary consultation.
      (3) Record food intake.
      (4) Administer tube feeding, total parenteral nutrition, and Intralipids as ordered.

(5) Change in the patient's position every hour; place the patient on alternating air mattress overlay.

f. Anxiety related to unexpected serious illness and uncertain prognosis
Goal: Patient and his/her family will experience a lessening of anxiety, and will understand the condition and treatments as necessary.
Interventions:
(1) Give explanation of treatment and condition appropriate to family anxiety level.
(2) Encourage the patient to verbalize his/her feelings.
(3) Keep the family informed of the patient's condition and progress.
(4) Answer all questions as honestly as possible.

g. Knowledge deficit regarding care after acute episode
Goal: Patient and his/her family will understand the prescribed convalescent regimen
Interventions:
(1) Assess the specific learning needs of the family and the patient; modify the teaching plan accordingly.
(2) Teach about normal kidney function, and explain the alteration the patient has experienced.
(3) Provide the patient with written guidelines for prescribed medications and diet and fluid restrictions.
(4) Review signs and symptoms to report to the physician: elevated temperature, malaise.
(5) Instruct the patient to keep appointments with the physician/clinic.

4. Evaluation
a. Patient's serum electrolyte is normal.
b. Patient has balanced intake and output.
c. Patient's vital signs are within normal limits.
d. Patient is afebrile.
e. Patient maintains body weight.
f. Patient's skin is intact.
g. Patient and family display decreased anxiety.
h. Patient and family can describe acute renal failure and the prescribed treatment during the convalescent phase.

D. Management of the Patient Undergoing Dialysis

1. **Peritoneal dialysis** (PD)   Use of the peritoneum as a semipermeable membrane in which to diffuse substances when there is failure of the kidney.
An appropriate sterile dialyzing fluid is introduced into the peritoneal cavity at intervals. Urea is cleared at a rate of approximately 15 to 20 mL per minute; creatinine, at a slower rate. The dialysate is selected according to the serum electrolyte level. The exchange is repeated until blood chemistries are near normal, usually within 36 to 48 hours.
a. Procedure
(1) Before dialysis, a catheter is inserted into the peritoneal cavity. A Teflon catheter is used in intermittent PD and removed after treatment; for continuous PD, the catheter is made of silastic with a Dacron felt cuff (bacterial barrier) and has an average life of 9 months.
(2) Dialysis is accomplished by repeating a three-phase cycle. Each cycle includes (1) *inflow*—the time required for the dialysate to flow into the peritoneal cavity by gravity (usually 10–15 minutes); (2) *diffusion* or *dialysis*—the time that the dialysate is in contact with the peritoneal cavity (30–40 minutes); and (3) *outflow*—the time required for the dialysate to drain from the peritoneal cavity by gravity.
(3) Four common methods are available:
(a) Manual single-bag/bottle method: 1–2 liters of sterile dialysing solution warmed to body temperature is run in by gravity.
(b) Automatic PD system (multiple cycler/reverse osmosis machine): this machine composes, sterilizes, and cycles the dialysate through three phases; a monitor and alarms are incorporated into the system. Done for 30–40 exchanges as often as 3 times per week.
(c) Continuous ambulatory peritoneal dialysis (CAPD): a prescribed amount of dialysate is connected to a permanent

catheter to flow into the abdomen, dwell for 4–5 hours, then empty. The process is then repeated with a new dialysate for 3–5 cycles a day, 7 days a week. During the night allowed to dwell for 7–8 hours.

    (d) Continuous cycling peritoneal dialysis (CCPD): a simple cycle machine does cycles during the night, with long dwells during the day, thereby affording the patient much more personal freedom for daytime activity.

  (4) Peritoneal dialysis requires no sophisticated equipment, and the technique is simple. However, it does take longer than hemodialysis.

b. Nursing diagnoses/goals/interventions

  (1) Anxiety related to fear of procedure
Goal: Patient will experience decreased anxiety.
Interventions:

    (a) Explain the steps of the procedure; answer all questions honestly.

    (b) Assess emotional and mental status beforehand.

    (c) If the patient has been dialyzed before, inquire what can be done to enhance comfort.

    (d) Consult social worker, clergy, or mental health worker as needed.

  (2) Pain related to dialysate in abdomen
Goal: Patient will verbalize relative comfort during procedure.
Interventions:

    (a) Assess for pain or discomfort during inflow and diffusion phases; have the patient describe the pain on a 0 to 10 scale.

    (b) Administer frequent back rubs, massage pressure areas, and change the patient's position as needed. (During infusion, patient is usually supine with head slightly elevated to decrease discomfort from the abdominal organs pushing against the diaphram.)

    (c) Warm dialysate to core temperature before instilling into peritonum.

    (d) Assure the patient that a feeling of fullness will lessen after the first few exchanges.

    (e) Administer analgesics when indicated; monitor for effectiveness and side effects; notify the physician if pain continues.

    (f) Inspect to ensure that complete drainage is occurring.

  (3) Risk for injury (bowel, bladder, vessel perforation) related to catheter insertion
Goal: Patient will remain free from injury or will be promptly treated for complication of peritoneal catheter insertion.
Interventions:

    (a) Have patient void before catheter insertions; monitor for bladder perforation.

    (b) Assess for bowel perforation (e.g., fecal material in returning dialysate fluid, strong urge to move bowels, sudden decrease in blood pressure, tachycardia); notify the physician.

    (c) Monitor vital signs before treatment and then every 4 hours.

  (4) Fluid volume deficit related to rapid removal of intravascular fluid

  (5) Altered fluid volume excess or deficit related to fluid retention
Goal: Patient will maintain fluid balance.
Interventions:

    (a) Record baseline assessment of weight and vital signs; weigh the patient after dialysis.

    (b) Check vital signs at the beginning and ending of each outflow.

    (c) Hold antihypertensive drugs during dialysis.

    (d) Check urinary output hourly.

    (e) If the patient is slightly hypotensive, turn on side to increase pressure on vena cava.

    (f) Assess and record the patient's hydration status before each dialysis.

(g) Assist with insertion of the peritoneal catheter, using strict asepsis.
1. Attach warm dialysis solution to catheter.
2. Permit dialysis solution to flow unrestricted into the peritoneal cavity (usually takes 5 to 10 minutes for completion); inflow should be approximately 100 to 200 ml.
3. Allow fluid to remain in the peritoneal cavity for prescribed time; then drain out of the cavity.
4. After outflow ceases, clamp; then infuse the exchange solution.
5. Repeat the procedure until blood chemistry level improves.
(h) Keep accurate record of patient's fluid exchange balance; for each exchange, record exchange time on flow sheet (time infusion started and ended, time outflow began and ended, amount of solution infused and returned, computer balanced—usually a plus or minus amount).
(i) Describe and record dialysate color and clarity; report any cloudy outflow.
(j) If outflow is not steady, have the patient turn from side to side or apply firm pressure to lower abdomen.
(k) Check with the physician about the amount of oral fluids permitted; adequately record intake and output.
(6) Risk for infection related to contamination through direct access of peritoneal cavity
Goal: Patient will remain free from infection.
Interventions:
(a) Maintain strict sterile technique while caring for peritoneal catheter and changing dressing.

(b) Monitor for signs and symptoms of infection (e.g., fever, increased WBC, cloudy dialysate, persistent abdominal pain).
(c) Check site for redness and drainage.
(d) Administer antibiotics as ordered; monitor effectiveness and side effects.
(7) Constipation related to decreased peristalsis secondary to abdominal distension during dwell time
(a) Assess for bowel sounds, bowel movements, bowel distension.
(b) Have the patient ambulate and/or change position to decrease distension.
(c) Keep NPO if ileus occurs.
(8) Altered nutrition: less than body requirements related to excessive protein loss through dialysis outflow, anorexia secondary to abdominal distension, or vomiting after too rapid instillation of dialysate
Goal: Patient will maintain adequate nutrition.
Interventions:
(a) Monitor serum albumin levels daily or as ordered.
(b) Administer salt-poor albumin as ordered.
(c) Provide protein supplements to diet.
(d) Plan meal to allow for approximately 2 hours by absorption time before instillation of dialysate.
(e) Review foods allowed on diet; instruct the patient as needed.
(9) Knowledge deficit regarding treatment, procedure, and care of catheter
Goal: Patient will verbalize understanding of treatment and possible complications, and will demonstrate proper care of catheter if it is permanent.
Interventions:
(a) Instruct the patient of all possible complications; give

telephone number of person to reach in an emergency.

    (b) Teach aseptic catheter care to patient with permanent catheter and dialysis procedure; have the patient return demonstration.

c. Evaluation

    (1) Patient verbalizes reduced anxiety about treatment.

    (2) Patient tolerates procedure comfortably.

    (3) Patient states absence of or decrease in discomfort.

    (4) Patient's hydration status is balanced and vital signs are normal.

    (5) Patient has normal temperature, dialysate return is clear, and patient is free from infection.

    (6) Patient moves bowels at least 3 to 4 times a week.

    (7) Patient has normal serum albumin.

    (8) Patient ingests an adequate amount of nutrients.

2. **Hemodialysis** Use of a synthetic semipermeable membrane to cleanse the blood of accumulated waste products.

Requirements for hemodialysis are (a) access to the circulation: external arteriovenous access, and fistula (internal) anastomosis of an artery to a vein; (b) dialyzer; (c) appropriate dialysate bath.

a. Procedure

    (1) Toxic nitrogenous substances are extracted from the blood, and excess water is removed.

    (2) Heparinized blood passes through a semipermeable membrane by dialysis to the dialysate fluid.

    (3) Through appropriate adjustment of the composition of the dialysate bath, noxious substances are transferred from the blood to the dialysate so that they can be discarded.

    (4) Purified blood is returned to the body through one of the patient's veins.

    (5) At the end of dialysis the majority of the nitrogenous substances should have been removed, electrolytes and water balances restored, and the buffer system replenished.

b. Nursing diagnoses/goals/interventions

    (1) Anxiety related to limited understanding of hemodialysis procedure and expected outcome of renal dysfunction

    (2) Powerlessness related to perceived lack of control over the disease and treatment

    (3) Body image disturbance related to loss of renal function and use of external device to achieve bodily function

Goal: Patient and his/her family will indicate a decreased level of anxiety, will identify the aspects of the disease process/treatment regimen she/he can control, and will incorporate new body image into self-concept.

Interventions:

    (a) Assess the patient's level of anxiety before dialysis begins; validate your observation with the patient.

    (b) Encourage questions by the patient and the family regarding disease process and treatment.

    (c) Make referral to counselor (clinical nurse specialist, social worker).

    (d) Allow the patient to plan and manage some aspects of care.

    (4) Fluid volume deficit related to rapid volume depletion

    (5) Alteration in cardiac output: decrease related to dysrhythmias, effects of congestive heart failure

    (6) Impaired gas exchange related to decreased cardiac output, effects of chronic renal failure (anemia), the dialysis procedure

Goal: Patient will maintain fluid and electrolyte balance and a cardiac output sufficient to promote normal gas exchange.

Interventions:

    (a) Review laboratory tests before treatment (serum electrolytes, BUN, hematocrit/hemogloblin) for instructions concerning composition of dialysate and administration of medication/blood products.

(b) Monitor blood pressure, pulse, and respiration every 5–10 minutes during the first half-hour of dialysis and then every 15–30 minutes; be alert for complications: hypotension or hypertension, loss of kidney endocrine, serum iron, removal of testosterone, and mental confusion.

(c) Auscultate for moist rales, and observe for other signs of pulmonary edema.

(d) Observe for seizure.

(7) Risk for injury (hemorrhage) related to heparinization

(8) Risk for injury (air embolism) related to air entering hemodialysis tubing

(9) Risk for infection related to impaired skin integrity at vascular access site and increased susceptibility to hepatitis and AIDS through frequent blood transfusions

(10) Risk for injury related to seizures, secondary to fluid volume excess, related to electrolyte imbalances
Goal: Patient will remain free of injury and infection.
Interventions:

(a) Inspect site every 15–30 minutes during dialysis for patency and signs of bleeding and infection.

(b) Check patency of shunt or fistula by ascultating for bruit and palpating for thrill every 4 hours while the patient is not being dialyzed.

(c) Monitor coagulation and hematology studies.

(d) Ensure that no punctures are made in external shunt; do not take blood pressure or withdraw blood from access extremity (post a sign at bedside or by door of patient's room); explain reason to the patient.

(e) Be alert for signs of air embolism (chest pain, cyanosis, drop in blood pressure, rapid pulse, coughing, loss of consciousness); if present, turn patient onto left side, place in Trendelenburg position to isolate air embolus in right atrium, discontinue dialysis, administer oxygen, and notify physician.

(f) Monitor for signs of systemic infection.

(g) Administer antibiotic as ordered.

(h) Monitor liver function for indication of hepatitis.

(i) Monitor hematology studies for indication of AIDS.

(j) Maintain seizure precautions.

(k) Monitor serum electrolytes before and after dialysis; inform physician of abnormal values.

(11) Knowledge deficit regarding shunt or fistula care and home care
Goal: Patient and his/her family will demonstrate proper shunt care, will describe dialysis schedule, and will discuss evaluative procedure for renal transplanation.
Interventions:

(a) Assess the patient's knowledge of, and ability to carry out, skin cleansing at fistula site, using aseptic technique.

(b) Provide continued emotional support to the patient and his/her family. (Patients often die because of noncompliance with treatment regimen. Consuming forbidden food and fluid is the area of noncompliance.)

(c) Instruct the patient concerning diet—low sodium, low protein, high carbohydrate, and low potassium.

(d) Teach the patient to check the external shunt site for swelling, coolness, redness, or discoloration of skin and to report to dialysis team.

(e) Teach the patient necessary restrictions for bathing and swimming when external shunt is used; ensure that the patient has two bulldog clamps available at all times in case of accidental separation of cannulae and that the patient and the family know how to use the clamps.

(f) Teach the patient to protect the shunt from injury, and to avoid pressure, weight, or constrictions on the arm (e.g., blood pressure cuff, tourniquet, tight clothing), carrying a purse or package on the affected arm, or sleeping on the arm.

(g) Reinforce what the physician has told the patient concerning anticipated dialysis sessions after discharge.

(h) Refer the patient to the local chapter of the National Kidney Foundation for additional information.

c. Evaluation

(1) Patient participates in decision making regarding treatment plan.

(2) Patient expresses acceptance of the need for dialysis.

(3) Patient verbalizes decreased anxiety concerning the dialysis and prognosis.

(4) Patient has stable blood pressure and pulse.

(5) Patient has normal respirations and breath sounds.

(6) Patient is afebrile and has stable vital signs.

(7) Patient is free from seizure activity.

(8) Patient has normal laboratory values.

(9) Patient expresses relief from headache and/or angina.

(10) Patient demonstrates proper shunt care.

(11) Patient verbalizes home-care-management regimen.

Alterations in Perception and Coordination

A. General Assessment

1. Observe for appearance of pain, change in muscle strength, and disturbance of sensation.

2. Observe mental status for depression, euphoria, and mood swings (irritability, apprehension, anger, elation).

3. Check cranial nerves for disturbance in vision, hearing, speech, taste, and touch.

4. DIAGNOSTIC MEASURES

a. Computerized axial tomography.

b. **Air studies**   Cerebrospinal fluid in and around the brain is replaced with a gas; then X-rays are taken.
Types: pneumoencephalography, ventriculography.

c. Cerebral angiography

(1) Pretest nursing intervention: Give nothing by mouth.

(2) Posttest nursing interventions

(a) Observe for weakness on one side of body.

(b) Observe for hematoma over the injection site.

(c) Apply ice bag over puncture site.

d. **Myelography**   X-ray of the spinal subarachnoid space, taken after an opaque medium or air is injected into the space.

e. **Lumbar puncture**   Insertion of a needle into the lumbar subarachnoid space in order to withdraw cerebrospinal fluid for diagnostic and therapeutic purposes.

f. **Electroencephalography (EEG)**   Recording of the electrical activity generated in the brain.

g. **Electromyography (EMG)**   Introduction of a needle electrode into the skeletal muscles in order to study changes in the electrical potential of the muscles and the nerves leading to them.

h. Radioisotope brain scanning.

i. **Echoencephalography**   Recording of echoes from deep structures within the skull be means of ultrasound.

j. Magnetic resonance imaging (MRI).

k. Brain scan (radionuclide imaging studies, based on the principle that radiopharmaceuticals diffuse through the blood and into the brain where there is pathology).

B. Traumatic Injuries

1. **Fractures in general**   A fracture is an interruption and/or disruption in the normal

continuity of a bone due to the exertion of excessive force or stress.

a. Common types
  (1) Closed. There is no trauma to skin integrity.
  (2) Comminuted. Bone is broken into many fragments.
  (3) Compound. Bone tears through the soft tissue as it fractures.
  (4) Compressed. One bony surface is forced against an adjacent one, as in the vertebrae.
  (5) Greenstick. Fracture is incomplete; only one side of the periosteum is disturbed.

b. Assessment
  (1) Obtain health history.
    (a) Description of injury.
    (b) Events leading up to injury.
  (2) Measure blood pressure and pulse for shock.
  (3) Palpate peripheral pulse, and check skin temperature near site of bleeding.
  (4) Observe for pain and tenderness over the involved area, swelling, loss of function of extremity, deformation, and muscle spasm.
  (5) Inspect area for overriding, crepitation, false motion, and shortening.
  (6) DIAGNOSTIC MEASURE: X-ray studies.

c. Patient care management
  (1) Traction
    (a) Types
      1. Skin traction is accomplished by a pulley and weights attached to the skin by Ace bandages. Types: Buck's extension—may be bilateral or unilateral, Russell's, cervical (used for cervical spasm), pelvic (used for low-back pain).
      2. Balanced suspension traction consists of two systems: traction and balanced suspension, accomplished with a Thomas splint and Pearson attachment.
      3. Skeleton traction is applied to the bone by means of a metal pin or wire inserted distally to the fracture. It is used with balanced suspension (the most reliable type of traction).
  (2) Manual manipulation.
  (3) Cast. The traditional cast consists of a *plaster bandage* molded smoothly to the body's contours. When dry, the cast is odorless, resonant when percussed, white, and shiny. The cast requires 24–72 hours to dry, depending on the thickness and the environmental drying conditions. *Nonplaster/fiberglass casts* are lighter in weight and stronger than plaster casts. They are also water resistant and durable. When wet, they are dried with a hair dryer on a cool setting. Thorough drying prevents skin breakdown.
  (4) Surgical intervention.

d. Nursing diagnoses/goals/interventions for the patient in a cast
  (1) Pain related to cast pressure
  (2) Altered tissue perfusion (peripheral) related to cast pressure
  (3) Risk for impaired skin integrity related to cast pressure
  Goal: Patient will achieve comfort, will attain tissue perfusion, and, will maintain skin integrity.
  Interventions:
    (a) Elevate wet cast on pillows to prevent flattening. Elevate above level of heart to promote drainage, reduce edema, and stimulate circulation.
    (b) Handle wet cast with palms of hands to prevent dents and flat spots (never use fingers).
    (c) Reposition the patient every 3 hours to allow the cast to dry faster.
    (d) Cover rough edges with adhesive to prevent pieces of cast from getting into the cast.
    (e) Do a neurovascular check every 30 minutes during the first 8 hours, then every 3 hours. Check for color (pale-

ness or blueness), motion (have patient wiggle toes or fingers), temperature (coldness), and sensation of toes and fingers. Symptoms of nerve damage are numbness and tingling. Do capillary filling response: press lightly the nail bed and the fleshy pulp of toes or fingers, and release to check how quickly blood returns (blood should return quickly).

(f) Observe cast for drainage every 3 hours.

(g) Administer care to skin near and under cast edges. (Apply lotion to pressure areas, i.e., elbows, heels, iliac crest, buttocks, and back.) Pain is the main symptom of circulation impairment from a cast.

(h) Investigate complaints of pain, but do not give analgesics until the cause is defined; report unrelieved pain, excessive swelling, poor capillary filling response, or inability to move fingers or toes immediately (to avoid paralysis and necrosis) to physician.

(4) Impaired physical mobility related to presence of cast
Goal: Patient will achieve mobility.
Interventions:

(a) Have the patient perform isometric exercises.

(b) Encourage the patient to exercise fingers and toes actively.

(5) Knowledge deficit concerning cast management
Goal: Patient will verbalize understanding of cast care.
Interventions:

(a) Instruct the patient to:
   1. Keep cast dry;
   2. Report to the physician if cast breaks;
   3. Clean cast with a damp cloth, and touch up stained areas with a thin layer of white shoe polish;
   4. Note any odor about the cast, cast staining areas, warm spots, and pressure areas, and report to physician;
   5. Report to the physician: persistent pain, swelling that does not respond to elevation, changes in sensation, decreased ability to move exposed fingers or toes, and changes in skin color and temperature.

(b) Explain to the patient that a large amount of dead skin will adhere to the skin area after the cast is removed. (The skin is then washed and blotted dry, and an emollient lotion is applied. The part will appear atrophied, but this will disappear after the return of muscle function.)

e. Evaluation for the patient in a cast
   (1) Patient maintains adequate circulation to extremity.
   (2) Patient shows no signs of necrosis, pressure sores, or nerve paralysis.
   (3) Patient verbalizes understanding of home-care management.

f. Nursing role for traction and crutch walking
   (1) General traction care
      (a) Make sure ropes and pulleys are in straight alignment.
      (b) Make sure the weights hang free and the rope is unobstructed.
      (c) Make sure the knot in the rope is not touching the pulley or the foot of the bed.
      (d) Raise the bed in such a manner as to add countertraction.
      (e) Encourage motion of unaffected joints.
   (2) Skin traction (straight/running)
      (a) Remove wrapping daily; inspect and wash skin.
      (b) Check for pressure points.
      (c) Give special care to back at regular intervals.
      (d) Prevent foot drop.
      (e) Check peripheral pulses.
      (f) Check for calf tenderness and Homan's sign (thrombophlebitis).
   (3) Balanced suspension/skeletal traction

(a) Observe for skin irration around traction bandage.

(b) Check area around pin or wire for odor or other signs of infection.

(c) Observe for pressure under sling at the popliteal space.

(d) Use foot support to prevent foot drop.

(e) Check traction.

(f) Cleanse around insertion site with betadine.

(g) Cover ends of pin and wire with cork or rubber stopper.

(4) Crutch walking

(a) The patient should keep the crutches 4 to 6 inches in front and slightly to the side of either foot.

(b) The patient's weight should be on the palms of the hands, with the wrists extended and the elbows flexed. This position prevents nerve damage to the brachial plexus.

(c) The top bar should be pressed against the chest, 2 inches below the axilla.

(d) The gaits are as follows:

1. Swing-through: Feet swing through the crutches and are usually placed ahead of crutches. Crutches are used concurrently for non-weight-bearing.

2. Two-point: This involves the concurrent advancement of the left foot and right crutch, then the right foot and left crutch.

3. Three-point: Weight is placed on the unaffected leg; then both crutches are placed forward, and the patient swings through, using the hand for weight bearing (used when weight must be kept off the affected limb).

4. Four-point: The left crutch is advanced, then the right leg, then the right crutch, and finally the left leg (allows for partial weight bearing on both legs).

(e) Crutches should be measured with shoes on. Two methods for measurements are (a) from anterior fold of axilla down to the heel and add 2 inches (used when patient is bedridden), and (b) from anterior fold of axilla diagonally out to a point 6 inches from the heel.

2. Head injuries

Injuries set up an inflammatory response that leads to cerebral edema. This in turn produces increasing intracranial pressure.

a. Types

(1) Fractures

(2) Hemorrhages

(a) **Epidural hematoma** Accumulation of blood between the outer meningeal layer and the skull. (This is a surgical emergency; cessation of breathing may occur within minutes.) URGENT

(b) **Subdural hematoma** Collection of venous blood between the outer and middle meningeal layers. (Symptoms may occur several weeks after the injury.)

(c) **Intracerebral hematoma** Compression or penetration of the cerebral tissues by a foreign body.

(3) **Contusion** Bruises of the brain tissues.

(4) **Concussion** Temporary disarrangement of normal nervous activity.

b. Assessment of increased intracranial pressure

(1) Obtain health history.

(a) Nature of the injury and time when it occurred.

(b) Presence of diplopia and headaches.

(c) Dizziness.

(2) Measure and note vital signs for temperature elevation, slowing of pulse or widening of pulse pressure, change in respiration rate, and increase in systolic blood pressure.

(3) Inspect eye for nystagmus and hemianopia, and eye field for papilledema. RApid eye movement

blindness in ½ th visual field

(4) Elicit deep tendon reflex, and note absence of reflexes, hyperreflexia, or a positive Babinski sign.

(5) Observe muscles for motor deficits such as weakness or paralysis of part of the body.

(6) Observe behavior changes such as lethargy or drowsiness and belligerence.

(7) Observe for seizures.

(8) DIAGNOSTIC MEASURES. *See also* General Assessment—Diagnostic measures, page 216.

  (a) Visual field examination.

  (b) Skull X-ray.

c. Patient care management

(1) Surgical removal of cause

  (a) Insertion of shunt for drainage

  (b) Decompressive surgery (removal of some brain tissues)

(2) Nonsurgical intervention

  (a) Osmotic diuretics

  (b) Steroids

  (c) Mechanical ventilation

d. Nursing role. *See also* the Management of unconscious patient, below.

(1) Institute nursing measures for elevated temperature.

(2) Observe the patient for changes in level of consciousness.

(3) Monitor temperature, vital signs, and pupillary response.

(4) Administer medications.

  (a) Osmotic diuretics—mannitol, Urevert, glycerol solution (dehydrate).

  (b) Steroids—Decadron (reduce cerebral edema). Side effects: formation of peptic ulcer (give antacid to reduce gastric bleeding).

  (c) Antibiotics—ampicillin (given prophylactically for open injury).

  (d) Anticonvulsants—Valium, Dilantin, phenobarbital.

(5) Turn and position the patient every 2 hours.

(6) Observe for seizure (keep padded tongue blade at bedside).

(7) Maintain a quiet environment.

(8) Maintain a patent airway.

(9) Administer oxygen as necessary.

(10) Monitor IV, and maintain intake and output record.

(11) Observe for signs of shock.

3. Management of the unconscious patient
Unconsciousness   A condition in which there is a depression of cerebral function, ranging from stupor to coma.

a. Assessment

(1) Observe the level of responsiveness or consciousness for any change.

(2) Measure and note any change in temperature or vital signs, such as increased respiration or alteration of pulse rate.

(3) Check pupillary response, eye movements, and corneal reflexes for changes. (Eye movements are absent in lesions of brain stem or pons; corneal reflex is absent in deep coma.)

(4) Observe movement of the extremities and overall posture for pathological posturing (decerebrate rigidity or decorticate rigidity).

(5) Observe face for symmetry. (Asymmetry is a sign of paralysis.)

(6) Elicit reflexes.

  (a) Tap patellar and biceps tendons—hyperactive reflexes suggest upper motor neuron disease (deep tendon reflexes).

  (b) Check plantar response for dorsiflexion of toes (positive Babinski).

  (c) Check corneal reflex (absent in coma).

  (d) Check swallowing reflex (absent in coma).

b. Nursing diagnoses/goals/interventions

(1) Ineffective breathing related to unconscious state
Goal: Patient will breathe normally.
Interventions:

  (a) Insert oral airway if tongue is paralyzed or is obstructing airway. Prepare for insertion of cuffed endotracheal tube if patient's condition requires.

  (b) Suction as necessary.

  (c) Administer oxygen if needed (humidified).

(d) Position the patient properly.
  1. Place in a lateral, recumbent position with face dependent.
  2. Use foot board to prevent foot drop.
  3. Use trochanter roll to prevent external rotation of hip.
  4. Keep arm abducted and hands slightly flexed.

(2) Altered tissue perfusion: cerebral related to unconscious state
Goal: Patient will achieve cerebral perfusion.
Interventions:
  (a) Assess level of consciousness and progression of vital signs at specified intervals.
  (b) Assess movement of extremities in response to verbal command or painful stimuli.
  (c) Examine pupil for size, shape, and reaction to light.
  (d) Record the patient's exact reactions, eye opening, and verbal response; describe the stimuli required to elicit.

(3) Altered nutrition: less than body requirements related to unconscious state
Goal: Patient will receive adequate nutrition.
Interventions:
  (a) Give nasogastric feedings. *See* Unit Eight, Management of the Patient Undergoing Surgery, Section F4: Nasogastric and nasoenteric tube feeding, page 287.
    1. Give 2000 to 2500 ml of fluids daily through the tube.
    2. Initially, give 100 to 150 ml of blenderized formula, then increase to 400 to 500 ml at each feeding.
    3. Maintain intake and output record.
  (b) Give IV fluids as indicated.
  (c) Give oral care.

(4) Risk for injury related to occurrence of seizures and restlessness

(5) Risk for impaired skin integrity related to immobility and restlessness
Goal: Patient's skin will remain intact and will be free of injury.
Interventions:
  (a) Prevent injury.
    1. Avoid restraints if possible.
    2. Pad side rails, and keep in upright position when care is not being given.
    3. Keep skin clean, dry, and free of pressure.
  (b) Put extremities through range of motion exercises 4 times daily.
  (c) Give catheter care.
  (d) Turn and position the patient every 2 hours.
  (e) Protect eye from corneal irritations.
    1. Instill ophthalmic solution and/or antibiotic drops.
    2. Apply gauze pads or eye shields.
  (f) Protect the patient during convulsive seizures.
  (g) Prevent fecal impaction.
  (h) Initiate cooling measures for elevated temperature.

c. Evaluation
  (1) Patient breathes normally.
  (2) Cerebral hemeostasis returns, as evinced by pupils returning to normal size and alertness of patient: opens eyes to commands, moves extremities appropriately.
  (3) Patient receives adequate nutrition.
  (4) Patient is free from injury.
  (5) Patient's skin is intact.

4. Management of the patient undergoing intracranial surgery
  a. Causes: aneurysm, abscess, hematoma (epidural, subdural, and intracerebral), tumor.
  b. Surgical procedures
    (1) **Supratentorial craniotomy** Surgery above the tentorium into the supratentorial compartment. (The tentorium divides the cerebrum from the cerebellum.)
    (2) **Infratentorial craniotomy** Surgery below the tentorium into the posterior fossa.

(3) **Craniectomy** Excision of a portion of the skull.

(4) **Cranioplasty** Repair of a defect by means of a plastic or metal plate.

c. Preoperative nursing role

(1) Observe and record neurological assessment and symptoms.

(2) Shave the patient's head (save hair).

(3) Administer enema only if it is ordered (intracranial pressure increases when the fluid is expelled).

(4) Administer steroids and Dilantin.

(5) Insert indwelling catheter and/or nasogastric tube.

d. Postoperative nursing diagnoses/goals/interventions

(1) Altered cerebral tissue perfusion related to cerebral edema

(2) Ineffective thermoregulation related to damage to the hypothalamus, dehydration, and infection

(3) Decreased intracranial adaptive capacity related to decreased cerebral perfusion pressure equal to or greater than 50 to 60 mm Hg.

Goal: Patient will achieve cerebral homeostasis to improve tissue perfusion and will achieve thermoregulation.

Interventions:

(a) Assess the level of responsiveness: response to command, spinal motor reflexes, orientation to time and place.

(b) Evaluate neurological and vital signs every 15 minutes until stable, then every 30 minutes.

(c) Monitor temperature.

1. Take rectal temperature at specified intervals.

2. Employ measures to reduce elevated temperature (aspirin, ice bags to groin and axillae, hypothermia blanket if ordered, tepid or alcohol sponge).

(d) Maintain patent airway.

1. Suction prn through mouth (avoid nasal suctioning, which may increase the intracranial pressure).

2. Carry out arterial gas studies.

3. Observe the patient for respiratory distress.

(e) Maintain positioning.

1. Supratentorial

a. Place the patient on his/her side with one pillow under the head.

b. Elevate the head of the bed as ordered (usually no more than 45 degrees).

2. Infratentorial

a. Keep the patient flat on his/her side (off back) with the head on a small, firm pillow.

b. In turning patient on either side, never allow the head to flex on the chest.

(f) Change position every 2 hours.

(g) Reinforce dressing. If heavily soiled with blood and/or cerebrospinal fluid, immediately notify the physician.

(h) Administer drugs.

1. Dehydratory agents, used to reduce cerebral edema—mannitol, dexamethasone, oral glycerol.

2. Antacids, given with steroids to protect the gastric mucosa.

3. Antiseizure agents—Dilantin, phenobarbital, and Valium.

4. Anti-infectives

(i) Observe for complications: intracranial bleeding, cerebral edema, postoperative meningitis, seizures, wound infection.

(4) Fluid volume deficit related to dehydration

Goal: Patient will achieve and maintain fluid and electrolyte balance.

Interventions:

(a) Monitor intake and output.

(b) Monitor serum and urine electrolytes (sodium retention often occurs).

(c) Check urine for glucose every 4 hours (because of large doses of corticosteroid).

e. Postoperative evaluation
   (1) Patient achieves neurologic homeostatis and improved cerebral tissue perfusion.
   (2) Patient attains thermoregulation.
   (3) Patient attains fluid and electrolyte balance.
   (4) Patient experiences no complications.

5. Spinal cord impairment
   When the spinal cord is impaired, there are abnormalities in the conduction of nervous impulses between the body and the brain. The changes that occur are concerned with motion and sensation.
   a. Causes
      (1) Trauma—vertebral fracture or dislocation, herniation.
      (2) Diseases or conditions—myelomeningocele, multiple sclerosis, lupus erythematosus, poliomyelitis.
   b. Types
      (1) Lower motor neuron (LMN)
         (a) This arises from the anterior horn of the spinal cord and terminates in a muscle fiber.
         (b) The LMN must be intact for motion to occur.
         (c) In the presence of an LMN lesion there will be hypotonicity (flaccidity), indicating that no reflex activity at that spinal cord level is present.
         (d) The muscle fiber will atrophy.
      (2) Upper motor neuron (UMN)
         (a) This lies entirely within the central nervous system and extends from the brain to some segmental level within the spinal cord.
         (b) In the presence of a UMN lesion there will be hypertonicity (spasticity).
   c. Extent of injury: partial destruction, hemisection—lesion that affects one fifth of the cord, complete transection.
   d. Classification of injury: quadriplegia—cervical injury; paraplegia—thoracic or lumbar injury.

e. **Spinal shock**   An immediate, complete loss of motor, reflex, sensory, and autonomic activity below the level of a spinal lesion. (Perspiration is absent and vasodilation or flushing of the skin occurs. Initially there are flaccid paralysis and absences of reflexes.)

f. Assessment. *See also* Section A: General Assessment, page 216.
   (1) Follow assessment guide below (findings are dependent on the level of the lesion).
      (a) L5, S1, and S2. Request patient to bend and straighten toes. Observe: toes.
      (b) L2–L4. Request patient to straighten legs. Observe: knees.
      (c) L1–L3. Request patient to bend (flex) hips. Observe: hips.
      (d) T5–T12. Request patient to tighten abdomen. Observe: abdomen, pubis, navel, and nipple.
      (e) C3–C5. Request patient to shrug shoulders and take a deep breath. (Diaphragm descends causing abdomen to bulge, and upper chest moves.) Observe: shoulders, chest, and abdomen.
   (2) Measure temperature and vital signs for elevations.
   (3) Observe breathing pattern.
   (4) Observe bladder for distension.
   (5) Obtain health history, including patient's account of symptoms.
   (6) DIAGNOSTIC MEASURES: radiographic examination of the spine, myelogram.

g. Patient care management
   (1) Skeletal traction
      (a) Crutchfield, Roto-Rest, Stryker frame—used to reduce the fracture/dislocation and maintain alignment of the cervical spine.
      (b) Halo vest—used for cervical spine injuries.
   (2) Surgical intervention—laminectomy.

h. Nursing diagnoses/goals/interventions
   (1) Impaired physical mobility related to motor and/or sensory impairment
   (2) Risk for impaired skin integrity related to immobility and/or sensory loss

Goal: Patient will experience improvement of mobility and achievement of skin integrity.
Interventions:
(a) Transfer the patient to bed.
  1. Maintain the patient in an extended position; avoid twisting or turning any part of the body.
  2. Place the patient on a Stryker frame Roto-Rest bed.
(b) Turn the patient every 2 hours.
(c) Prevent foot drop by attaching a foot board to the bed.
(d) Perform passive range of motion exercises, as prescribed.
(e) Do neurological check and note changes.
(f) Apply antiembolic stocking.
(g) Apply hydrocolloid to sacrum.
(h) Use a heel protector.
(3) Urinary retention related to inability to void spontaneously
Goal: Patient will experience relief from urinary retention.
Interventions:
(a) Give catheter care.
(b) Observe for autonomic hyperreflexia, caused by full bladder or bowel.
  1. Signs and symptoms: extreme hyptertension (as high as 260/140), severe pulsating headache, bradycardia, red blotches on face and trunk, diaphoresis, and "goose bumps."
  2. Treatment
    a. Drain the bladder or manually evacuate the bowel. Apply dibucaine ointment before any rectal stimulation.
    b. Place the patient in sitting position, if allowed.
    c. Administer ganglionic blocking agents such as Apresoline.
(c) Bladder retraining
  1. Encourage fluids. A urine output of approximately 3 liters ensures adequate dilution of urine.
  2. Avoid citrus juices. They produce an alkaline residue in the urine.
  3. Change Foley catheter at least every 7 days. In the presence of dilute urine and acid urine the catheter will remain patent.
(4) Constipation related to presence of atonic bowel as a result of autonomic disruption
Goal: Patient will experience improvement in bowel function.
Interventions:
(a) Offer diet high in bulk.
(b) Encourage fluids (3000 to 4000 ml per day).
(c) Provide stool softeners or bulk formers.
(d) Administer suppository (Dulcolax).
i. Evaluation
  (1) Patient is able to move within limits of dysfunction.
  (2) Patient's skin remains intact.
  (3) Patient regains bladder control.
  (4) Patient regains bowel elimination capacity.
6. Management of the patient undergoing spinal surgery
  a. Surgical procedures
    (1) **Laminectomy** Removal of the laminae to expose the neural element of the spinal canal.
    (2) **Spinal fusion** A stabilizing procedure in which bone chips from the iliac crest are used to fuse the spinous process.
    (3) **Discectomy** Removal of herniated or extruded fragments of an intervertebral disc.
    (4) **Laminotomy** Division of the lamina of a vertebra.
    (5) **Microdiscectomy** Procedure that incorporates the use of an operating microscope to visualize the discs. It generally involves a shorter hospital stay, and patient makes a more rapid recovery.
  b. Preoperative nursing role
    (1) Instruct the patient in the turning procedure ("logrolling").
    (2) Have the patient practice deep

breathing, coughing, and muscle setting exercises.

c. Nursing diagnoses/goals/interventions
   (1) Pain related to the surgical procedure
   (2) Altered mobility related to the postoperative surgical regimen

   Goal: Patient will achieve comfort and will attain improved mobility.

   Interventions:

   See also Unit Eight, Management of the Patient Undergoing Surgery, Section C: Management during the Postoperative Period, page 269.

   (a) Cervical surgery
      1. Check vital signs frequently to detect any signs of respiratory difficulty.
      2. Observe for recurrent laryngeal nerve damage (e.g., hoarseness).
      3. Relieve sore throat with spray.
      4. Offer a blenderized diet (dysphagia).

   (b) Lumbar surgery
      1. Inspect wound for evidence of hemorrhage and leakage of spinal fluid.
      2. Evaluate sensation and motor power of the lower extremity, along with color and temperature of both legs and sensation in the toes at specified intervals.
      3. Check for urinary retention.
      4. Monitor vital signs.
      5. Place pillow under the patient's head, and elevate knee rest slightly to relax back muscles.
      6. Change the patient's position by "logrolling" with a pillow placed between his/her legs.
      7. Administer analgesic and sedative as necessary.
      8. Assist the patient to ambulate either from a side-lying or a semi-Fowler's position.

   (c) Spinal fusion
      1. Check hemovac; measure every 8 hours.
      2. Observe dressing at bone graft site.
      3. Assist patient to ambulate.
      4. Check vital signs until stable, then every 3 hours.
      5. Ambulate with a back brace.
      6. Turn and position the patient every 3 hours ("logrolling"); avoid twisting.

   (3) Knowledge deficit about postoperative course and home-care management

   Goal: Patient will verbalize understanding of home-care management.

   Interventions:

   (a) Advise that it will take 6 weeks for muscle to heal.
   (b) Instruct the patient to:
      1. Avoid activities that place flexion strain on the spine (i.e., automobile riding) until healing occurs.
      2. Apply heat to soothe and relax muscle spasm.
      3 Avoid overexertion, and schedule rest periods.
      4. Avoid heavy work for 2 to 3 months after surgery.
      5. Follow prescribed exercise program.
      6. Wear back brace or corset if back pain persists.

d. Evaluation
   (1) Patient experiences minimal discomfort.
   (2) Patient is mobile.
   (3) Patient verbalizes home-care management.

C. **Rheumatoid Arthritis**   A chronic systemic disease of unknown cause, characterized by recurrent inflammation involving the synovium or lining of the joints. *See also* Unit Five, Alterations That May Limit Mobility, Section D: Juvenile Rheumatoid Arthritis, page 132.

1. Assessment
   a. Inspect joints for swelling, stiffness, loss of flexibility, subcutaneous nodules, and deformities.
   b. Note complaint of joint pain that occurs in the morning, and fatigue and weakness.
   c. Measure temperature and note elevations.

2. Patient care management
   a. Drug therapy to reduce inflammation and relieve pain

(1) Acetylsalicylic acid (aspirin).
(2) Nonsteroidal drugs: Motrin, Nalfon Indocin, Naprosyn, Clinoril.
(3) Gold therapy (chryostherapy)
   (a) Used when nonsteroid drugs do not control symptoms.
   (b) Takes several months to work.
   (c) Given deep IM.
(4) Steroids (prednisone)
   (a) Given in low dosages.
   (b) Used during flare-up only.
b. Maintenance of joint mobility and muscle strength.
c. Surgical interventions—joint replacement and synovectomy.

3. Nursing role
  a. Provide for rest periods.
  b. Apply warm compresses to joints as prescribed.
  c. Administer medication as prescribed.
  d. Assist with exercise and paraffin bath.
  e. Educate the patient about the nature of the disease and its treatment.

D. **Multiple Sclerosis (MS)**   A chronic, progressive disease of the central nervous system, characterized by the occurrence of small patches of demyelination in the brain and spinal cord, and by long remissions and exacerbations.

Demyelination is scattered irregularly throughout the central nervous system except for the axons. Eventually the myelin peels off the axis cylinders, and the axons themselves degenerate. The patches in the involved areas become sclerosed, interrupting the flow of nerve impulses. The areas most often affected are the optic nerve and chiasm; the margins of the lateral, third, and fourth ventricles; the pons, medulla, and cerebellar peduncles; and the spinal cord.

1. Causes
  a. Causes are unknown; research suggests that the disease is precipitated by an autoimmune response.
  b. The condition is aggravated by exposure to cold, damp weather and improves in a mild, dry climate.
  c. Relapses are often associated with periods of emotional and physical stress (illness, injuries, inoculations).

2. Assessment
  a. Examine the eye for nystagmus.
  b. Observe for vertigo with nausea and vomiting, spastic paraplegia with speech disturbance, and intention tremor.
  c. Observe mental status for euphoria and hyperexcitability.
  d. Elicit reflexes and note whether they are hyperactive or depressed.
    (1) Depression or absence of abdominal reflexes.
    (2) Hyperactive deep tendon reflexes.
    (3) Positive Babinski.
  e. Evaluate muscle strength for weakness (bilateral weakness can occur).
  f. DIAGNOSTIC MEASURES
    (1) Electrophoresis: used to study cerebrospinal fluids (CSF) for the presence of IqG. Abnormal IqG appears in the CSF of 95 percent of patients with MS.
    (2) CT Scan.
    (3) MRI: used to evaluate the course of the disease.
    (4) Urodynamic studies for bladder dysfunction.
    (5) Neuropsychological testing for cognitive impairment.

3. Nursing role (rehabilitation)
  a. Avoid emotional and physical stress (cold, infection).
  b. Administer medication as prescribed.
  c. Combat muscle dysfunction: exercise, walking exercise to improve gait.
  d. Instruct the patient in bowel and bladder training.
  e. Provide psychological and educational support to the patient and his/her family.
  f. See that the patient has speech therapy (allow the patient to communicate).

E. **Systemic Lupus Erythematosus (SLE)**   A chronic autoimmune, inflammatory disease of the connective tissue that produces structural changes in skin, joints, and muscles, usually with multiple-organ involvement; the number of organs involved makes the disease an imitator of many other diagnoses.

The etiology is unknown, although there is a familial association. Certain drugs, such as Apresoline, Pronestyl, and some anticonvulsants, have been thought to trigger the onset of symptoms. Other risk factors are hormonal abnormality and ultraviolet radiation.

There is an immune system defect that produces inflammation and local tissue damage. A reduction in T-lymphocytes causes the body to synthesize immunoglobulin and autoantibodies, which then form immune complexes. The onset of SLE may be acute or insidious. If insidious, weight loss, fatigue, rash, and joint inflammation may be the earliest signs; a characteristic "butterfly" rash appears around the eyes in 50 percent of patients, and other cutaneous lesions may be present on the trunk or extremities. The rash either shows a diffuse, flat pattern or is a raised, scaly patch. Other common manifestations are polymyositis (skeletal muscle inflammation), alopecia (hair loss), and photosensitivity (sensitivity to light); vasculitis (vessel wall inflammation) is life threatening because it decreases the blood supply to major organs, causing necrosis and dysfunction. Other organs are also affected. Acute glomerular nephritis and renal failure occur.

1. Assessment
   a. Assess for fever, malaise, weakness, anorexia, nausea and vomiting, diarrhea, abdominal pain, and weight loss.
   b. Assess for edema, hematuria and proteinuria (keep 24-hour urinary output), and serum creatinine.
   c. Palpate peripheral pulses for rate and volume.
   d. Assess heart for size, rate, and rhythm (valvular damage can occur); pericaditis and heart murmurs may be present.
   e. Palpate spleen for size and tenderness; splenomegaly may occur.
   f. Inspect joints for swelling and pain; paralysis and paraesthesia may be present.
   g. Do neurological assessment; note neuritis, headache, seizures, behavioral changes, neuroses, or psychoses.
   h. Assess respiratory system for insufficiency; pleura effusion or infiltration may be present.
   i. Inspect skin and mucous membranes for rash or erythema ("butterfly" over cheeks and bridge of nose), partial alopecia, and oral or nasal ulcerations.
   j. DIAGNOSTIC MEASURES   LE prep (positive); antinuclear antibodies, ANA (positive); false positive serology: fluorescent treponemal antibody absorption, FTA-ABS (negative); complements: C3 and C4; creatinine clearance test; chest radiological study; skin and kidney biopsies; CBC, thrombocytopenia; C-reactive protein; ESR, coagulation profile; rheumatoid factor; urinalysis.

2. Patient care management
   a. Nonsteroid anti-inflammatory agents.
   b. Corticosteroid therapy.
   c. Anti-infective agents.
   d. Antineoplastic agents.
   e. Medications related to system(s) affected.
   f. Plasmopheresis, dialysis.
   g. Joint arthroplasty.
   h. Appropriate diet, activity, rest.

3. Nursing diagnoses/goals/interventions
   a. Altered tissue perfusion related to multi-system involvements (renal, cardiopulmonary, cerebral, musculoskeletal)
      Goal: Patient's condition will stabilize, and complications will be managed or minimized.
      Interventions. *See* Assessment, above.
   b. Pain related to restricted joint movement
      Goal: Patient will experience relief from pain and discomfort.
      Interventions:
      (1) Administer anti-inflammatory or other prescribed drugs as ordered for joint and muscle pains.
      (2) Assist the patient in establishing a therapeutic life-style.
      (3) Decrease stress (it exacerbates pain) and encourage the patient to express his/her feelings.
      (4) Initiate pain relief such as muscle relaxation techniques, guided imagery and other forms of distraction, and self hypnosis. *See* Unit Eight, Section D: Management of Postoperative Discomfort, page 270.
   c. Body image disturbance related to physical appearance
      Goal: Patient will attain a positive image of self.
      Interventions:
      (1) Encourage the patient to verbalize his/her feelings and concerns; listen carefully.
      (2) Reinforce the physician's explanation of the disease process—its chronicity, treatment, remission, and exacerbations; clarify misconceptions.
      (3) Provide a supportive environment,

praising positive ideas and accomplishments.

(4) Identify present coping patterns and strengths that were successful in the past.

(5) Promote communication with significant other.

(6) Advise the patient to visit a cosmetologist who specializes in skin disorders for help in covering the rash and making it less noticeable.

d. Altered nutrition: less than body requirements related to anorexia, fatigue, and/or electrolyte imbalance
Goal: Patient's nutritional status will improve.
Interventions:

(1) Assess nutritional status and monitor caloric intake.

(2) Provide well-balanced, small, frequent meals.

(3) Determine any weight gain related to steroid therapy; sodium may be restricted.

(4) Weigh the patient daily at the same time, and with the same clothing.

e. Risk for activity intolerance related to fatigue and arthralgia
Goal: Patient will increase activities to tolerance within limitations of impairment.
Interventions:

(1) Provide bedrest during periods of exacerbation.

(2) Increase activity slowly.

(3) Support affected joint(s); assist the patient with chair when sitting.

(4) Increase ambulation as tolerated; have the patient use crutches, walker, or cane as needed.

f. Risk for infection related to steroid therapy
Goal: Patient will remain afebrile without signs of infection.
Interventions:

(1) Monitor WBC and differential ESR, C-reactive protein, urinalysis, and cultures for signs of sepsis.

(2) Culture drainage from skin rashes, breaks, and injection sites, and also sputum and urine.

(3) Monitor temperature for elevations.

(4) Maintain clean environment and good physical hygiene.

(5) Provide planned rest periods.

(6) Administer antipyretics, antimicrobials, and analgesics as ordered.

g. Knowledge deficit regarding home-care management
Goal: Patient and/or significant other will demonstrate understanding of home-care and follow-up instruction.
Interventions:

(1) Provide written diet and activity restrictions as prescribed.

(2) Instruct patient in proper skin and hair care: use nonallergic skin and hair products; avoid exposure to sun or use sunscreen with a minimum protection factor of 15; and avoid hair spray and hair dyes.

(3) Provide instructions for medications: give names, dosages, schedules, and side effects, especially for steroids; explain that medications must be taken uninterruptedly; explain the need to avoid penicillin, sulfa, phenytoin, and oral contraceptives.

(4) Discuss signs and symptoms of exacerbation to report to physician: fever, rash, cough, joint pain.

(5) Encourage the patient to wear Medic-Alert tag indicating dose of steroid and name and number of his/her physician.

(6) Give community resources, such as the Lupus Erythematosus Foundation.

(7) Instruct the patient to keep follow-up appointments with his/her physician.

4. Evaluation

a. Complications are prevented or controlled.

b. Patient is afebrile.

c. Patient's nutritional status is adequate.

d. Patient's pain is manageable.

e. Patient complies with treatment and understands home-care management.

f. Patient demonstrates adaptive behaviors toward body-image change.

Alterations in Behavior

A. **Anxiety** A heightened degree of tension manifested both physiologically and psychologically in response to a perceived danger to oneself.

1. Dynamics/characteristics
   a. Anxiety is a purposeful, motivating force that alerts the individual to danger that threatens the self.
   b. It arises when ideas, wishes, feelings, and impulses that are unacceptable to the ego come into one's conscious awareness.
   c. A variety of adaptive mechanisms are called upon by the ego for the purpose of controlling anxiety to a tolerable level.
   d. If ego defenses fail to serve the purpose of controlling anxiety, physical symptoms of anxiety are developed to release tension.
   e. Anxiety symbolizes the individual's unconscious conflicts.
   f. Adaptive patterns of adjustment are created by the ego to channel off anxieties caused by aspects of a person's environment or his/her own feelings that are unacceptable and threatening to the self. These coping mechanisms are also referred to as *defense mechanisms*. The dynamics and characteristics of defense mechanisms are as follows:
      (1) All persons utilize defense mechanisms to a certain degree to relieve tension and anxiety.
      (2) The purpose of defense mechanisms is to reduce anxiety to a manageable level for effective coping.
      (3) Most defense mechanisms are unconscious, but some of them operate on a conscious level.
      (4) Defense mechanisms are constructive if they help the person to reevaluate the problem from a positive viewpoint.
      (5) Excessive and exaggerated use of defense mechanisms does not foster emotional growth.
      (6) Defense mechanisms do not resolve underlying conflicts. They merely provide temporary relief of the problem by controlling the anxiety to a manageable level.
      (7) The most commonly used defense mechanisms are shown in the following table.

MECHANISM	EXAMPLE
1. *Denial*—unconscious refusal to acknowledge the presence of painful and anxiety-provoking thoughts, feelings, memories, or experiences.	A middle-aged man, after being admitted to the coronary care unit because of an acute myocardial infarction, insists that he is in the hospital for a diagnostic work-up.
2. *Suppression*—conscious refusal to acknowledge the presence of painful, threatening, or unwelcome ideas, feelings, or experiences.	A student fails the midterm examination and says to a friend, "I'd rather not discuss the test today."
3. *Repression*—unconscious pushing away from one's conscious awareness unbearable and unacceptable thoughts, feelings, or memories. They are buried in the unconscious, not to be recalled.	A young girl does not remember having been sexually abused 3 months after her engagement.
4. *Rationalization*—an attempt to find a justifiable cause and/or excuse for one's wishes, feelings, or actions. A guilt-ridden person may find temporary relief from his/her anxiety through this process, which is a frequently used coping mechanism.	A professional tennis player claims that he lost because there were many distractions during the game that affected his concentration.
5. *Identification*—integration of certain aspects of someone else's personality into one's own. It can mean achievement through another person or group of persons (e.g., clubs or associations). Most early learning is achieved through this process.	A new, young school teacher adopts her former mentor's teaching style when conducting class sessions.

(Continued)

MECHANISM	EXAMPLE
6. *Compensation*—development of certain personality traits that make up for one's inadequacies or lack of ability.	A person lacking the physical stature to engage in competitive sports excels in scholastic works.
7. *Regression*—return to an earlier coping pattern of behavior, proven to be less threatening or more gratifying, when faced with stressful situations. This is a normal reaction to intensified stress. When utilized consistently and exaggeratedly, however, it can result in personality disintegration.	A 5-year-old child becomes unable to control his bowels immediately after the arrival of a new baby brother.
8. *Conversion*—expression of an underlying emotional conflict as a physical symptom.	A young mother suddenly develops paralysis of her right arm after birth of her first child.
9. *Displacement*—transfer of one's thoughts, ideas, or feelings about one object or situation to another. Expression of these feelings, ideas, or thoughts to the appropriate object is not perceived by the person as safe. This mechanism is involved in most phobic-neurotic patterns of behavior.	An adolescent boy, after an argument with his father, goes to the gym and hits a punching bag.
10. *Sublimation*—channeling off a strong but socially undesirable impulse or drive into something socially acceptable.	A strong drive to expose oneself in public is socially unacceptable. A person having this drive becomes a nude model for an artist.
11. *Withdrawal*—refusal to invest energy in anything outside the person's self. This is a protective mechanism to avoid noxious situations or further experience of anxiety and trauma to one's security.	A woman refuses to see anyone after being diagnosed as having a malignant breast cancer. A man refuses to go out of his house after the tragic death of his wife, for which he blames himself because he was driving the car at the time of the accident. He suffered only minor injuries.
12. *Projection*—blaming another object or person, or the environment for one's own inadequacies, unacceptable thoughts, impulses, or actions in order to escape self-reproach and feelings of shame and guilt. Everyone uses this mechanism to some extent to relieve anxiety. It is extensively used by persons whose behaviors are characterized by paranoid patterns of responses.	A person unable to accept his ill feelings towards his parents says, "My parents hate me." A suspicious patient unable to express her hostility directly toward others refused to sit in a chair during a ward meeting because "The chair has been charged with electricity to kill me."

2. Types of anxiety disorders
   a. **Generalized anxiety disorder.** This disorder is characterized by:
      (1) Unrealistic worry about certain life circumstances for no apparent identifiable reason.
      (2) Motor tension: muscular tension, restlessness, tremulousness, feeling of tiredness, body aches and pains.
      (3) Autonomic reactions: sweating, dry mouth, palpitations, dizziness, light headedness, bladder and bowel disturbances, shortness of breath, cold, clammy hands, "choking" feeling.

(4) Hypervigilance: extreme suspiciousness and insecurity, insomnia, irritability, inability to concentrate.

b. **Obsessive-compulsive disorder**

(1) Anxiety is associated with persistent undesirable and uncontrollable thoughts (obsessiveness) and repetitive, irresistible, and stereotyped acts (compulsiveness).

(2) The person is aware of the irrationality of his/her behavior but is not able to control it.

(3) The obsessive-compulsive person is overcontrolled, rigid, task-oriented, unable to relax, meticulous, moralistic, and unable to tolerate change.

(4) Attempts to stop the obsessive-compulsive behavior result in extreme anxiety that may reach panic proportions.

(5) The obsessive-compulsive behavior is distressing to the patient. These behaviors are time-consuming and interfere with the person's life functions.

c. **Phobic disorders**

(1) There is intense fear of a situation or object characterized by feelings of apprehension, insecurity, and physical symptoms such as palpitations, faintness, fatigue, nausea, sweating, and tremors.

(2) The phobic person uses defense mechanisms of displacement, repression, and avoidance.

(3) Phobia may paralyze a person's normal functioning. (Normal fear reaction may help a person to devise adaptive protective responses.)

(4) Types of phobic disorders*

(a) **Agoraphobia** A fear of being in places or situations that the phobic person perceives as unsafe, with "no escape," or help might be unavailable, in the event that he/she develops distressing symptoms. Examples of commonly feared situations include being in open places alone, traveling in a train, car, or bus, and passing over a bridge.

(b) **Social phobia** A persistent fear of public exposure. The phobic person fears public scrutiny. Examples include fear of eating in public, of writing in the presence of other people, and of using a public lavatory.

(c) **Specific phobia** (formerly **Simple phobia**) Excessive marked and persistent fear of clearly discernible objects or situations. Exposure to the phobic stimulus provokes an immediate anxiety response. The phobic person recognizes that his/her fear is unreasonable. Avoidance, fear, or anxious anticipation of encountering the phobic stimulus may interfere with the person's normal functioning.

(d) **Panic attack** A discrete period of intense fear or discomfort accompanied by motor tension, autonomic reactions, hypervigilance, fear of losing control or "going crazy," feelings of unreality, depersonalization, fear of dying, and paresthesias.

(e) **Panic disorder**

1. There is a presence of recurrent, unexpected panic attack.

2. There may be a presence or absence of agoraphobia.

3. Symptoms not associated with direct physiological effects of substance abuse, medication, or a medical condition.

(f) **Posttraumatic stress disorder**

1. A stressor or catastrophic event or events a person experienced, witnessed, or was confronted with involved an actual or threatened death, serious injury, or a threat to the physical integrity of self and others.

2. Responses involve intense fear, helplessness, or horror.

3. The person experiences recurrent recollections of the traumatic event.

*Source: American Psychiatric Association. *Diagnostic and Statistical Manual of Mental Disorders,* 4th ed., Washington, D.C.: American Psychiatric Association, 1994.

4. The person feels that the traumatic event is happening again.
5. The person may manifest social and emotional detachment from others.
6. The person experiences insomnia, guilt, memory impairment, suspiciousness, or phobic reactions when exposed to situations that may resemble the traumatic event experienced.
7. Other symptoms include depression, restlessness, labile emotions, emotional outbursts, vertigo, headaches, substance abuse.

B. **Somatoform Disorders**
 1. Dynamics/characteristics
  a. There is a presence of physical symptoms with no general medical pathology.
  b. Physical symptoms experienced by the person are real and cause distress and impairment of normal life functioning.
 2. Types
  a. **Conversion disorder**
   (1) The underlying conflict is expressed as a physical symptom.
   (2) It involves unexplained symptoms or deficits suggesting neurological or other general medical conditions.
   (3) Mental functioning is intact.
   (4) The person often shows an unusual lack of concern over the symptom(s) (*la belle indifférence*).
   (5) The symptoms serve various purposes:
    (a) The person is removed from the stressful situation (primary gain).
    (b) The person elicits attention and nurturing from others (secondary gain).
    (c) The person may achieve a need for self-punishment to relieve feelings of guilt.
  b. **Hypochondriasis**
   (1) The person is preoccupied with the fear of having a serious disease based on his/her interpretation of own bodily symptoms or functions. This becomes the center of the individual's self-image.
   (2) The person does not recognize that the concern about the illness is excessive and unreasonable.
   (3) Negative medical findings do not reassure the person regarding the perceived disease.
   (4) Preoccupation with the perceived illness may cause impaired life functioning.
   (5) This condition can begin at any age; the most common age at onset is early adulthood.
   (6) The person utilizes the fear of serious illness as a response to life stresses.
   (7) Defense mechanisms used by the person to cope with the situation include regression and/or denial.
  c. **Somatization disorder**
   (1) There is a pattern of recurring, multiple, somatic responses to stress.
   (2) Intensified psychosocial stress predisposes the person to the progression and recurrence of physical illness.
   (3) Defense mechanisms used by the person to cope with the situation include repression, introjection, and/or denial.
   (4) Common somatic conditions include migraine, body pains and aches, gastrointestinal (peptic ulcer, ulcerative colitis), sexual dysfunctions, pseudoneurological symptoms or deficit.
   (5) The person's physical condition can be life-threatening. Medical treatment is a priority.

C. **Dissociative Disorders**
 1. Dynamics/characteristics
  a. There is a disruption of integrated functions of consciousness, memory, identity, and perception of the environment.
  b. The disorder may be sudden or gradual, transitory or chronic.
 2. The disorder is manifested in the following forms:
  a. **Dissociative amnesia**   Sudden inability to recall significant personal information.
  b. **Dissociative fugue**   Sudden, unexpected travel away from one's home with inability to recall one's identity.
  c. **Multiple personality**   The presence within one person of two or more differ-

ent personalities, each possessing its own patterns of behavior.

   d. **Depersonalization disorder** A feeling of being detached from oneself (observing one's own body and one's own mental processes).

D. Care of the patient with anxiety disorders, somatoform disorders, and dissociative disorders

  1. Assessment

    a. Observe behavior and physical manifestations of anxiety.

    b. Determine how the individual perceives events and circumstances that may have precipitated and/or contributed to his/her anxiety (e.g., recent bereavement and other traumatic events).

    c. Identify the individual's strengths and weaknesses in handling anxiety.

    d. Determine the individual's relationship with his/her family and other significant persons.

    e. Determine the person's ability to cope with anxiety.

  2. Patient care management

    a. Supportive psychotherapy.

    b. Psychoanalysis.

    c. Antianxiety agents.

    d. Hypnosis.

    e. Behavior modification (for phobias).

    f. Health promotion

      (1) Parenting programs (parent education classes on normal growth and development, anticipatory guidance for new parents, etc.).

      (2) Role modeling (demonstration by the health-care giver that, when feelings are recognized and verbalized, they become less threatening and more manageable).

      (3) Assisting the family to develop an effective system of communication among its members.

  3. Nursing diagnosis/goals/interventions
Ineffective coping related to situational crises
Goals:

    a. Individual will identify own anxiety.

    b. Individual will express feelings appropriately.

    c. Individual will utilize growth-promoting coping mechanisms.

    d. Individual will recognize own strengths and weaknesses in handling anxiety.

    e. Individual will be able to problem-solve in order to meet life's demands and role expectations.

Interventions:

  a. Generalized anxiety disorder

    (1) Accept the patient.

    (2) Encourage the patient to verbalize feelings.

    (3) Reassure the patient.

    (4) Have a nonjudgmental attitude.

  b. Obsessive-compulsive disorder

    (1) Accept the patient's compulsion.

    (2) Do not force the patient to end obsessive-compulsive behavior abruptly.

    (3) Avoid a confrontation with the patient regarding obsessive-compulsive behavior.

    (4) Limit ritualistic behavior that endangers the safety of the patient.

    (5) Provide a consistent approach and routines to promote a feeling of security.

    (6) Acknowledge any improvement that the patient demonstrates.

    (7) Avoid lengthy discussions and arguments with the patient.

    (8) Empathize with the patient.

  c. Phobic disorders

    (1) Divert the patient's attention away from his/her phobia.

    (2) Be consistent in your attitude toward the patient.

    (3) Reduce the patient's decision-making activities.

    (4) Be supportive during behavior modification therapy.

    (5) Move toward the patient slowly when attempting to establish a trusting relationship.

  d. Dissociative disorders

    (1) Provide reassurance.

    (2) Deemphasize the patient's symptoms.

    (3) Provide a supportive environment.

    (4) Accept the patient's reactions as meaningful and purposeful.

    (5) Direct the patient's attention away from self.

    (6) Avoid expressions of sympathy.

  e. Conversion disorder

    (1) Provide reassurance.

    (2) Assist the patient to be aware of his/her feelings and to accept them.

(3) Remember that the patient's symptoms are real to him/her.

(4) Deemphasize the physical symptoms.

(5) Do not confront the patient with his/her symptoms.

(6) Avoid criticizing the patient.

(7) Reduce decision-making tasks.

(8) Provide social and recreational activities to divert the patient's attention away from the physical symptoms.

f. Hypochondriasis

(1) Accept the patient's symptoms.

(2) Provide appropriate physical evaluation of the patient's physical complaints.

(3) Divert the patient's attention away from his/her symptoms.

(4) Do not challenge the validity of the patient's physical symptoms and sensations.

(5) Limit the patient's decision-making tasks.

(6) Provide a safe environment.

g. Posttraumatic stress disorder

(1) Reassure the patient.

(2) Encourage the patient to verbalize his/her feelings freely.

(3) Provide relaxation activities.

(4) Provide a safe environment.

(5) Provide physical care.

(6) Protect the patient from self-destructive tendencies.

h. Somatoform disorders

(1) Provide appropriate physical evaluation of the patient's physical complaints.

(2) Treatment of the patient's medical condition is a priority. Provide physical care.

(3) Encourage verbalization of feelings.

(4) Accept the patient's symptoms.

(5) Do not challenge the validity of the patient's perception regarding his/her illness.

(6) Assist the patient in learning new sets of problem-solving techniques in order to gain control over own feelings and impulses.

(7) Provide relaxation activities.

(8) Use of biofeedback.

(9) Encourage the patient to make necessary life style changes.

4. Evaluation

a. Patient identifies own anxiety.

b. Patient verbalizes feelings freely.

c. Patient utilizes coping mechanisms that are growth promoting.

d. Patient utilizes own inner resources and support systems in solving problems.

e. Patient expresses feelings appropriately.

E. **Schizophrenia** A psychotic reaction characterized by severe impairment in mental and emotional processes, regression, and impoverished interpersonal relationships.

1. Dynamics/characteristics

a. Etiological basis

(1) Genetic or hereditary predisposition.

(2) Biochemical theory—imbalance in the biochemical system.

(3) Environmental or social theory—unhealthy family dynamics and interpersonal relationships and faulty communication system.

b. Manifestations of profound withdrawal: increased self-preoccupation, autistic thinking, depersonalization, increased somatization (hypochondriasis), social isolation, regression.

c. Major areas of malfunction

(1) Disturbed thinking processes: flights of ideas, "magical" thinking that is wish-fulfilling, looseness of association, inability to deal with abstractions, fusion and condensation of ideas to form neologisms—"word salad."

(2) Disturbed perception of reality: interpretation of events in terms of autistic thinking, rather than reality; delusions, hallucinations, illusions.

(3) Disturbed affectivity: inappropriate or flat affect, apathy, ambivalence.

(4) Grossly disorganized behavior: silliness to unpredictable agitation; difficulties in performing activities of daily living; disheveled appearance; unusual manner of dress; decreased reactivity to the environment; catatonic stupor; bizarre posturing (waxy flexibility); unstimulated excessive motor activity (catatonic excitement).

    (5) Dysfunction in interpersonal relations, self-care, work, education, and other areas of functioning.

2. Subtypes*

  a. Paranoid type
    Essential features:

    (1) The patient has prominent delusions or auditory hallucinations.

    (2) Delusions are persecutory or grandiose or both. These delusions may predispose the person to suicidal behavior and violence.

    (3) Other delusional themes such as jealousy, religiosity, or somatization may occur.

    (4) Onset tends to be in later life.

    (5) The patient shows little or no neuropsychological impairment.

    (6) The prognosis may be better than other types with regard to occupational functioning and capacity for independent living.

  b. Disorganized type (also termed Hebephrenic type)
    Essential features:

    (1) The patient has disorganized speech, disorganized behavior, and flat or inappropriate affect.

    (2) Associated features include grimacing, mannerisms, and other odd behavior.

    (3) Behavior disorganization causes severe disruption in performing activities of daily living.

    (4) Onset is early and insidious, and continuous with no remissions.

  c. Catatonic type
    Essential features:

    (1) The patient has a marked psychomotor disturbance with motor immobility (catalepsy, waxy flexibility, or stupor).

    (2) There is excessive motor activity that is purposeless and not influenced by external stimuli.

    (3) There are peculiar voluntary movements (posturing, stereotyped movements, prominent mannerisms, or grimacing).

    (4) Echolalia or echopraxia are present.

    (5) There are potential risks for malnutrition, exhaustion, hyperpyrexia, dehydration, self-injury or harm to others during severe catatonic stupor or excitement.

  d. Undifferentiated type
    Essential features—presence of 2 or more of the following symptoms:

    (1) Delusions, hallucinations.

    (2) Disorganized speech.

    (3) Grossly disorganized or catatonic behavior.

    (4) Flat affect, avolition, alogia.

  e. Residual type
    Essential features:

    (1) There is a presence of at least one episode of schizophrenia but the current clinical picture is without psychotic symptoms such as delusions, hallucinations, disorganized speech, and grossly disorganized or catatonic behavior.

    (2) The course of this disturbance may be time limited and may represent a transition between a full-blown episode and complete remission.

    (3) Symptoms may be present for many years with no acute exacerbations.

3. Assessment

  a. Assess the patient's perception of objective reality.

  b. Assess the patient's thinking pattern.

  c. Assess the patient's environment and his/her relationships with significant persons in it.

  d. Assess how the patient's family perceives the problem.

4. Patient care management

  a. Psychotropic drugs. *See* Appendix: Psychotropic Drugs, page 253.

  b. Family therapy.

  c. Psychotherapy.

  d. Milieu therapy.

  e. Group therapy.

  f. Health promotion

    (1) Provide anticipatory guidance for new parents because there is increasing, though still limited, evidence that family dynamics are an important etiologic factor in schizophrenia.

    (2) Assist in developing an effective communication system within the family milieu.

*Source: American Psychiatric Association. *Diagnostic and Statistical Manual of Mental Disorders,* 4th ed., Washington, D.C.: American Psychiatric Association, 1994.

  (3) Provide crisis intervention.

  (4) Provide learning experiences that will assist the patient to readjust when he/she returns to the community (half-way house, group therapy, foster home).

  (5) Instruct the patient and his/her family about medications to be taken at home and the importance of regular follow-up visits to the physician.

5. Nursing diagnoses/goals/interventions

 a. Body image, self-esteem, role performance, and/or personal identity disturbance related to inability to develop trust and withdrawal from interpersonal relationships

  Goal: Patient will develop a sense of trust.

  Interventions:

  (1) Provide an accepting environment.

  (2) Provide a consistent environment.

  (3) Listen actively.

  (4) Observe the patient's nonverbal behavior.

  (5) Encourage the patient to identify his/her own perceptions, feelings, and behaviors in order to be able to express them.

  (6) Acknowledge any indication of positive behavior change in the patient.

  (7) State your observations verbally to the patient so that the issue or the behavior can be dealt with openly.

  (8) Set an external limit on the patient's behavior; protect the patient from possible consequences of self-destructive behavior.

 b. Altered thought processes related to inability to evaluate objective reality

  Goals:

  (1) Patient will test reality.

  (2) Patient will learn socially acceptable ways of controlling behaviors that are harmful to the self and others.

  Interventions:

  (1) Help the patient to recognize his/her distorted perception of reality.

  (2) Provide an environment wherein the patient can safely validate reality.

  (3) Provide reality-oriented activities that will result in successful experience.

  (4) When the patient is delusional, respond to the theme of the delusion rather than to the verbal component.

  (5) Remove harmful objects because of the patient's faulty reality orientation, faulty judgment, and impulsiveness.

  (6) Observe the patient's nonverbal behavior.

 c. Impaired social interaction related to alteration in thought processes that results in faulty communication and inaccurate interpretation of the environment

  Goal: Patient will be able to communicate his/her thoughts and feelings in an appropriate manner.

  Interventions:

  (1) Listen actively to what the patient is saying.

  (2) Acknowledge any indication of positive change in the patient's communication pattern.

  (3) Encourage the patient toward participation in social activities.

  (4) Do not try to invalidate the patient's disturbed thought processes; this will only reinforce the distorted perception.

  (5) Provide for reality-oriented activities that will result in successful experience in communication.

  (6) Prevent regressive behavior.

  (7) Recognize that clear communication is important.

 d. Self-care deficit: feeding, bathing and hygiene, dressing, grooming related to poor self-concept and perceptual and cognitive impairment

  Goal: Patient will regain ability to perform activities of daily living for him-/herself.

  Interventions:

  (1) Provide for physical needs.

  (2) Provide for dietary adjustments needed, especially when the patient is delusional.

  (3) Monitor the patient's response to the therapy, including side and toxic effects of medications.

  (4) Teach the patient and his/her family about drug therapy and follow-up care.

(5) Acknowledge any indication of positive behavior toward self-care.

6. Evaluation
   a. Patient demonstrates some degree of tolerance for closeness with another person (e.g., the nurse).
   b. Patient verbalizes feelings.
   c. Patient tests reality.
   d. Patient controls own behavior.
   e. Patient discusses with the nurse adaptive behaviors in dealing with anxiety.
   f. Patient demonstrates interest in personal appearance and good hygiene.
   g. Patient demonstrates interest in own nutrition by eating meals served.
   h. Patient demonstrates understanding of own treatment regime (medications, follow-up care).
   i. Patient discusses plans for discharge.

F. **Mood Disorders** Major affective disturbances in mood characterized by an increase or a decrease of psychomotor activity and thought disorder expressive of elation or depression.
1. Dynamics/characteristics
   a. Significant factors considered in the cause of these disorders include inconsistent emotional environment with faulty communication system.
   b. Types
      (1) Depressive disorders (Unipolar depression)—disorders characterized by major depressive episodes with no history of manic, mixed, or hypomanic reactions. *See* Unit Eight, Alterations in Behavior, Section A: Depression, page 338.
      (2) Bipolar disorders—disorders characterized by presence of manic, mixed, or hypomanic episodes, with history of major depressive episodes. These disturbances are thought to represent an adjustment to avoid consciously recognizing and experiencing feelings of depression; a massive form of denial characterized by:
         (a) Elation that stimulates grandiose ideas.
         (b) Mood swings.
         (c) Manipulative behavior, diminished inhibition, verbal abuse, unreasonable demands.
         (d) Flights of ideas, delusions of grandeur, rapid association of ideas.
         (e) Pressured speech, excessive physical activity that seems purposeless (this can lead to exhaustion).
         (f) Loss of weight due to excessive activity and poor nutrition.
         (g) Dehydration.
         (h) Loss of sleep.
         (i) Poor concentration and easy distractibility by environmental stimuli.
         (j) Violent motor excitement.
         (k) Inability to sustain close meaningful relationships with others.

2. Assessment
   a. Determine factors that may have contributed to the patient's current situation.
   b. Determine previous patterns of elated behavior.
   c. Assess the family dynamics and the role of the patient in the family.
   d. Assess the patient's physiological functioning state.
   e. Assess the patient's patterns of handling anxiety and their effects.
   f. Determine the patient's safety needs.
   g. Assess the patient's ability to learn and adopt new sets of coping behaviors.

3. Patient care management
   a. Drug therapy—lithium carbonate, chlorpromazine, Haldol, antidepressants, minor tranquilizers.
   b. Electroconvulsive therapy (ECT) *See* Unit Eight, Alterations in Behavior, Appendix: Electroconvulsive Therapy, page 340, for the depressive phase.
   c. Psychotherapy.
   d. Health promotion
      (1) Family counseling.
      (2) Parenting education programs.
      (3) Advising the patient and family about drug therapy. (Lag of 1 week to 10 days between the initial treatment and the control of symptoms may discourage the patient.)
      (4) Informing the family of the nature of the manic reaction. The family must recognize the patient's need for safety.
      (5) Assisting the patient as he/she tests new sets of problem-solving methods.

(6) Role modeling by the health-care giver.

4. Nursing diagnoses/goals/interventions

   a. Risk for injury related to excessive activity, violent motor excitement, and faulty environmental perception

   Goals:

   (1) Patient will recognize unsafe behavior and its precipitating causes.

   (2) Patient will utilize his/her energy toward constructive activities to improve self-esteem.

   Interventions:

   (1) Set limits on the patient's behavior, and convey them clearly to the patient.

   (2) Protect the patient from his/her self-destructive tendencies. Anticipate unsafe behavior and its possible precipitants.

   (3) Assist the patient toward constructive use of his/her energy by providing activities and tasks that are noncompetitive in nature, short term and attainable, and geared toward constructive discharge of tension (e.g., walking, house cleaning, finger painting, linen folding). Activities must be simple and must not require concentration.

   (4) Observe the patient for suicidal behavior/ideation.

   (5) Encourage the patient to discuss feelings of fear and frustrations openly.

   (6) Support the patient during expression of his/her feelings.

   (7) Adopt a nonjudgmental attitude.

   (8) Accept the patient as a unique human being.

   (9) Be consistent in your approach.

   (10) Monitor the patient's response to drug therapy, such as lithium carbonate and chlorpromazine.

   b. Self-care deficit: feeding, hygiene, and grooming related to perceptual/cognitive impairment and hyperactivity

   Goals:

   (1) Patient will resume performance of own activities of daily living.

(2) Patient will resume adequate food and fluid intake in order to maintain adequate nutrition and fluid balance.

(3) Patient will have adequate number of hours of rest and sleep.

Interventions:

(1) Provide for self-care activities that are flexible and unhurried.

(2) Provide for physical care with special attention to:

   (a) Nutrition—high-caloric diet, adequate fluid intake, finger foods.

   (b) Rest and sleep—quiet environment, sedation as needed, short naps, soft light at night, nonstimulating room decor, warm bath, loose, comfortable sleepwear.

(3) Acknowledge any positive sign of progress in the patient's behavior.

c. Altered thought processes related to inaccurate interpretation of the environment and faulty perception of reality; impaired environmental interpretation syndrome

Goal: Patient will have reality-based thinking.

Interventions:

(1) Accept the patient as a unique human being.

(2) Establish a sense of trust.

(3) Provide the patient with experiences wherein he/she can safely examine reality.

(4) Encourage the patient to validate his/her own thoughts and perception of his/her environment by verbalizing them.

(5) Set limits on the patient's behavior, and convey these limits to the patient clearly.

(6) Listen for themes in the patient's conversation in order to identify possible origins of faulty perception of his/her environment.

(7) Do not challenge the patient's faulty perception of reality. Present objective reality to the patient.

(8) Protect the patient from his/her destructive delusional thinking.

d. Self-esteem, role performance disturbance related to maladaptive individual coping patterns and poor self-perception

Goals:
(1) Patient will identify own strengths and weaknesses.
(2) Patient will utilize adaptive patterns of behavior in dealing with his/her problems.
Interventions:
(1) Adopt a nonjudgmental attitude.
(2) Encourage the patient to verbalize both negative and positive thoughts and feelings so that he/she may be able to identify and sort them.
(3) Assist the patient to identify healthy coping patterns that he/she has utilized before.
(4) Set limits in dealing with the patient's demands.
(5) Acknowledge positive signs in the patient's behavior.
(6) Identify to the patient socially unacceptable behaviors and their effects on him-/herself and others.
(7) Allow the patient to test new sets of patterns of behavior without fear of ridicule.

5. Evaluation
   a. Patient recognizes unsafe behavior and its possible causes.
   b. Patient utilizes his/her energy toward constructive activities.
   c. Patient manages activities of daily living with minimal assistance from the staff.
   d. Patient resumes normal eating, rest, and sleep patterns.
   e. Patient is well nourished and hydrated.
   f. Patient is free from injury.
   g. Patient is able to distinguish between subjective and objective reality.
   h. Patient is able to make reality-based plans.
   i. Patient is able to utilize adaptive, growth-promoting patterns of coping behavior.
   j. Patient and his/her family have a good understanding of the patient's treatment plan and follow-up care.
   k. Patient and his/her family are able to recognize side effects of drug therapy and to report them as early as possible.

G. **Personality Disorders** Personality trait disturbances characterized by "an enduring pattern of inner experience and behavior that deviates markedly from the expectations of the individual's culture." (American Psychiatric Association: DSM-IV, American Psychiatric Association, 4th ed., 1994, p. 630.)

1. Dynamics/characteristics
   The person with a personality disorder is characterized by:
   a. Failure to establish an identity with constructive patterns of adaptation.
   b. Failure to develop a socialized super-ego.
   c. Inability to delay gratification of needs and desires.
   d. Behavior that often results in conflict with the law.
   e. Absence of remorse over his/her offensive and destructive behaviors.
   f. Antisocial behavior that often appears in the midteens.
   g. Limited socialized ways of coping with frustrations.
   h. Deceptive social facades (superficial sincerity and maturity) and appears charming in initial social encounters.
   i. Inability to learn from punishment. Change is difficult for this person because habits are deeply rooted and highly resistant to reasoning.
   j. Impulsivity.
   k. Insensitivity to the feelings of others.
   l. "Acting-out" behavior when faced with anxiety-provoking situations.

2. Assessment
   a. Assess the patient's coping patterns of behavior.
   b. Assess the patient's interpersonal relationships.
   c. Assess the patient's behavior themes.
   d. Assess the patient's attitude toward the rules and regulations of the health facility.
   e. Assess the patient's attitude toward authority.
   f. Assess the patient's judgment.
   g. Assess the patient for possible substance abuse.
   h. Assess the patient's school and employment status/history.
   i. Assess the patient's ability to handle frustration and delay in gratification of his/her needs.

3. Patient care management
   a. Psychotherapy.
   b. Group therapy.
   c. A therapeutic community (placement in

group homes, firm surrogate parental figures).

d. Hospitalization for control of impulsivity, evaluation of suicidal and homicidal tendencies, treatment of a psychotic episode, drug or alcohol abuse, and other psychiatric emergencies.

e. Health promotion
   (1) Family counseling.
   (2) Parenting programs.
   (3) Community mental health services.
   (4) Crisis intervention.
   (5) School guidance and counseling programs.

4. Nursing diagnoses/goals/interventions
   a. Self-esteem, personal identity disturbance related to inability to establish an identity with constructive patterns of adaptation, and to fragmented and conflicting perception of others (view of the world as split into two extremes of "goodness" and "badness")
   Goals:
   (1) Patient will recognize and express feelings in socially acceptable patterns of behavior.
   (2) Patient will recognize self-damaging effects of his/her impulsivity.
   (3) Patient will have realistic view of his/her own situation (therapy and hospitalization).
   (4) Patient will be able to experience both love and hate toward another person.
   Interventions:
   (1) Assist the patient to recognize his/her own strengths and limitations.
   (2) Assist the patient to use positive attributes within him-/herself.
   (3) Provide the patient with opportunities to learn new sets of socially acceptable behaviors.
   (4) Assist the patient to recognize the destructive aspects of his/her behavior.
   (5) Convey a nonjudgmental attitude toward the patient.
   (6) Avoid making empty promises or threats.
   (7) Set firm, consistent, clear limits.
   (8) Communicate expectations clearly.

   (9) Point out reality to the patient in making plans.
   (10) Be honest and be a role model.
   (11) Help the patient to learn that a loving and caring person can also frustrate him/her and arouse anger.
   (12) Assist the patient to understand that other people have both good and bad qualities.
   (13) Provide a warm, human experience wherein the patient is able to experience closeness to another human being in a gradual, consistent, and nonthreatening manner.

   b. Ineffective coping related to maturational crises
   Goals:
   (1) Patient will be able to use socially acceptable methods of coping.
   (2) Patient will be able to identify and control his/her behaviors that are destructive to self and others.
   (3) Patient will be able to handle delay of gratification and frustration.
   (4) Patient will be able to express anger verbally instead of acting-out and regressive behavior.
   (5) Patient will learn that there are consequences to one's actions.
   (6) Patient will learn to act within limits.
   Interventions:
   (1) Set limits in a consistent manner.
   (2) Encourage verbal expressions of anger instead of acting it out.
   (3) Be supportive and empathetic in a firm and direct manner.
   (4) Acknowledge the patient's behavior, and point out its effect on other people so that the patient may be able to examine his/her own behavior.

   c. Risk for injury related to severe impulsivity, self-destructive acting out, and distortion of reality.
   Goals:
   (1) Patient will be able to perceive the environment as real.
   (2) Patient will be able to express feelings of alienation, anger, and frustration appropriately.
   (3) Patient will recognize self-damaging effects of his/her behavior.

Interventions:

(1) Observe the patient for both suicidal and homicidal thoughts and ideations.

(2) Set limits; tell the patient what is and what is not acceptable, and what the expectations are, in a clear, consistent manner.

(3) Encourage the patient to express both positive and negative feelings.

(4) Assist the patient to identify situations that provoke anger and frustration.

5. Evaluation
   a. Patient is free from self-injury.
   b. Patient verbalizes anger and feelings of frustration appropriately.
   c. Patient does not utilize acting out to express feelings.
   d. Patient identifies situations that provoke feelings of anger and frustration.
   e. Patient is able to tolerate closeness with other people.
   f. Patient is able to control impulsive behavior.
   g. Patient is able to test new sets of coping behaviors.
   h. Patient is able to delay gratification of needs and to handle frustrations appropriately.
   i. Patient is able to make realistic plans.

H. **Substance-Related Disorders** Disorders resulting from the use of a drug of abuse, from alcohol, from the side effects of a medication, and from exposure to a toxic substance.

1. Definitions*
   a. Substance—A drug of abuse, a medication, or a toxin.
   b. Dependence—Continued use of a substance despite significant physical and mental distress and impairment upon withdrawal from the substance.
   c. Tolerance—The need for increased amounts of the substance to achieve desired effects.
   d. Addiction—Chronic and compulsive use of a substance resulting in physical and psychological dependence and increasing tolerance for the substance.

2. Psychosocial Effects:
   a. Legal problems (e.g., arrests for disorderly conduct while impaired, theft, or other unlawful acts to support substance abuse).
   b. Interpersonal consequences (e.g., marital/family problems, domestic violence).
   c. Loss of productivity (e.g., occupational/work performance problems, absenteeism).

3. Physical Effects: (Refer to Drug Abuse and Alcohol sections below.)

4. Dynamics/characteristics
   a. Significant factors involved are as follows:
      (1) Failure of the individual to develop trust in him/herself and others.
      (2) Failure of the individual to develop internal controls (unable to delay gratification of needs and desires).
      (3) Low threshold for tension and anxiety.
      (4) Overdependent, passive personality.
      (5) Underlying guilt and anger.
   b. Prevalence has increased among the adolescents and the young adults of the world. Drug abuse affects all levels of the American social structure.
   c. Drug abusers continue drug use because:
      (1) Drugs offer a sense of pleasure, euphoria, and freedom from pain.
      (2) Drugs are used to escape from reality, tension, and anxiety.
      (3) Drugs can be utilized to express anger and rebellion against society.
      (4) Physical dependence on the drug has become established.
   d. Related physical problems are nutritional disturbances, skin problems, hepatitis, menstrual irregularities, impotence, and constipation.
   e. Withdrawal syndrome (from opium alkaloids and derivatives) has various phases.
      (1) Yawning, lacrimation, rhinorrhea, sneezing, sweating, anorexia, dilated pupils, tremors, and

*Source: American Psychiatric Association. *Diagnostic and Statistical Manual of Mental Disorders,* 4th ed., Washington, D.C.: American Psychiatric Association, 1994. pp. 285–290.

gooseflesh—12 to 14 hours after the last dose.

(2) Muscle twitching; cramps in the leg, abdomen, and back; restlessness; insomnia; increased pulse and blood pressure; vomiting; and diarrhea—36 hours after the last dose. These symptoms become marked about 48 hours after the last dose and persist at the same peak for 72 hours.

(3) Duration: Symptoms subside slowly in 5 to 10 days.

(4) Other symptoms of withdrawal: irritability, increased psychomotor activity, verbal abuse, crying, impulsiveness, suicidal behaviors, and feeling of general body weakness.

f. Behavior problems include manipulativeness, impulsiveness, withdrawal, and grandiosity.

g. Drugs commonly abused are as follows:

(1) Narcotics: morphine, heroin, Dilaudid, and codeine. Large doses produce lessened physical energy and ambition, and mental lethargy. The pleasurable feeling produced makes the drug abuser repeat the drug use.

(2) Central nervous system stimulants: cocaine, amphetamines, and amyl nitrate. Psychological dependence may develop with countinued use, even on therapeutic doses. These drugs bring about a sense of well-being.

(3) Hallucinogens: LSD, mescaline, psilocybin, marijuana, and hashish. These drugs do not result in physical dependence but can produce psychological dependence and mild tolerance. They cause kaleidoscopic visual hallucinations of vivid colors and forms. Illusions, auditory hallucinations and distorted perceptions of body image are common. Chronic use produces panic episodes and intellectual changes.

(4) Sedative-hypnotics: meprobamate, Doriden, barbiturates, and minor tranquilizers. These drugs

are potentially addictive and can produce tolerance. Sudden withdrawal can cause convulsions. Overdoses can lead to coma and death.

5. Assessment

a. Assess the patient's need for medical management.

b. Assess the circumstances or events that may have precipitated the drug use.

c. Assess the patient's life-style, health habits, and practices.

d. Assess the patient's potential sources of support, both internal and external resources.

e. Assess the patient's present coping patterns.

f. Assess the impact of the patient's behavior on his/her role in the family.

g. Determine the availability of the drug in the patient's environment.

h. Determine what drug (or drugs) is being used, and the amount and frequency.

6. Patient care management

a. Therapeutic communities.

b. Group therapy.

c. Detoxification.

d. Supportive therapy.

e. Psychotherapy.

f. Drug therapy (psychotropics, sedatives) used with caution.

g. Health promotion

(1) Early parent counseling.

(2) Community programs (Narcotics Anonymous, Cocaine Anonymous).

(3) Assessment of family dynamics.

(4) Family therapy.

(5) Case-finding activities to identify potential abusers and chronic users of drugs.

(6) Drug-free school campaign.

(7) Health education—information about drug abuse, community health resources in the community and in the schools.

(8) Crisis intervention.

7. Nursing diagnoses/goals/interventions

a. Risk for injury: poisoning and trauma related to chemical (drug) use and the physiological effects of drugs when ingested in high dosages during a period of time

Goal: Patient will be free from life-

threatening effects of the drug.
Interventions:
(1) Provide for physical care.
(2) Avoid making judgmental remarks on the patient's condition.
(3) Make every effort to identify the abused drug.
(4) Gear patient care toward the patient's symptoms.
(5) Assess the patient's level of consciousness.
(6) Report any changes in the patient's condition promptly.
(7) Assess the patient's vital signs.
(8) Check the patient's airway for patency.
(9) Make sure that all emergency equipment, drugs, and supplies are available.
(10) Observe the patient for withdrawal signs and symptoms and response to treatment.
(11) Assess the patient's respiratory status (watch for signs of respiratory distress).
(12) Monitor fluid intake and output.
(13) Provide for adequate nutrition.
(14) Be supportive and accepting.
b. Ineffective individual coping related to situational and maturational crisis and to personal vulnerability
Goals:
(1) Patient will use growth-promoting defense mechanisms in dealing with his/her life situation.
(2) Patient will be able to channel his/her anxiety toward constructive activities.
(3) Patient will be able to express his/her feelings appropriately.
(4) Patient will be able to identify potential sources of stress so that he/she may be able to anticipate coping patterns that are adaptive.
(5) Patient will be able to identify coping resources that he/she has used in the past that may prove helpful in his/her present life situation.
(6) Patient will be able to handle stressful life situations without using drugs.
(7) Patient will be able to develop patterns of communication that

will assist him/her in establishing and maintaining meaningful relationships with other people.
Interventions:
(1) Assist the patient to recognize that substituting another chemical for the drug abused does not resolve the underlying emotional conflicts leading to substance abuse.
(2) Communicate expectations clearly and consistently.
(3) Assist the patient to identify his/her own behavior in order to be able to control it.
(4) Avoid value judgments on the patient's behavior and capabilities.
(5) Assist the patient to recognize and develop his/her strengths so that they can be used constructively.
(6) Provide the patient with learning experiences that facilitate growth.
(7) Support the patient as he/she tests new patterns of coping behavior.
(8) Provide role modeling.
(9) Be patient.
(10) Identify behaviors that are clearly unacceptable.
(11) Acknowledge positive coping behaviors.
(12) Do not enter into lengthy discussions or arguments with the patient.
(13) Set firm, consistent limits.
(14) Encourage the patient to make realistic plans for the future by reinforcing his/her reality-based thoughts and concerns.
(15) Listen to the patient.
(16) Encourage self-care.
8. Evaluation
a. Patient is free from life-threatening effects of drug use.
b. Patient uses adaptive coping mechanisms instead of drugs.
c. Patient is able to channel his/her energies into constructive activities that promote self-esteem.
d. Patient is able to identify potential stressful situations and to devise adaptive coping patterns of behavior.
e. Patient is able to develop meaningful

interpersonal relationships with other people.

f. Patient takes responsibility for reality-based plans for the future (return to work, family living, etc.).

Substance Abuse: Alcohol *Alcoholism* is defined by the World Health Organization as chronic, excessive use of alcohol that causes a major problem by interfering in the person's life functions. *Alcohol addiction* is present when there is direct evidence that the person is dependent on alcohol. The best evidence is the appearance of withdrawal symptoms.

1. Dynamics/characteristics
   a. Alcoholism is a major health problem in America.
   b. It is estimated that there are over 9 million alcoholics in the United States.
   c. The cost exceeds 20 billion dollars in lost productivity, property damages, and medical costs each year in the United States.
   d. Seventy percent of alcoholics are male, but the number of female alcoholics is increasing.
   e. Theories on the causes of alcoholism include the following:
      (1) Strong oral tendencies, influences in childhood, regression, and escape from reality.
      (2) Inconsistent gratification of dependency needs.
      (3) Confused self-image and poor self-esteem.
      (4) Genetic factors, allergic reactions to food and chemical substances, endocrine imbalance, and nutritional deficiencies.
      (5) Sociocultural viewpoint—ritualization of alcohol use in traditional and social customs; drinking as socially accepted behavior.
   f. Interpersonal forces include: rigid, unrewarding relationships; hostility; unsatisfactory sex life; feelings of inferiority and insecurity, fear or rejection, and anxiety.
   g. The effects of alcohol are as follows:
      (1) Sedative, anesthetic effect.
      (2) Depression of cortical centers.
      (3) Stimulant in small doses.
      (4) Lessening of inhibitions. Re-pressed feelings surface under the influence of alcohol.
      (5) Impaired intellectual alertness.
      (6) As blood level increases, effect on motor areas → impaired motor coordination → effect on lower brain centers → coma → death.
   h. Clinical features are chronic use, preoccupation with alcohol intake, inability to control drinking behavior, use of alcohol to escape tension and anxiety, and deterioration of physical and psychological health due to chronic use.
   i. Intoxication is considered to be 0.1% concentration of alcohol in the blood after 2 ounces of alcohol is ingested.
   j. Alcohol absorption is rapid on an empty stomach. After ingestion of food, especially fatty foods, absorption is gradual. Ninety percent of alcohol is metabolized by the liver.
   k. Physical problems related to chronic alcoholism are peripheral neuritis, malnutrition, organic brain disease (Korsakoff's disease), lipid deposition, malnutrition, liver cirrhosis, fluid and electrolyte imbalance, and esophageal varices.
   l. Withdrawal symptoms (delirium tremens) include:
      (1) Restlessness, apprehension, psychomotor agitation hallucinations, and illusions.
      (2) Tremors, motor impairment, and convulsions.
      (3) Anxiety and excessive perspiration.
      (4) Nausea and vomiting.
      (5) Sleep disturbances.
      (6) Self-destructive behaviors.
2. Assessment
   a. Assess the patient's physical status.
   b. Assess the events or situations that may have precipitated the drinking behavior.
   c. Know the factors that usually precipitate alcohol use.
   d. Assess how the drinking behavior affects other members of the family.
   e. Determine the patient's position within the family structure.
   f. Assess the family dynamics.

g. Assess the patient's patterns of coping with stressful life situations.

h. Assess the patient's occupational functioning.

i. Assess the patient's environmental support systems and their potential for assisting the patient with his/her problems with alcohol.

j. Assess the patient's drinking pattern.

k. Assess the patient's strengths and weaknesses.

3. Patient care management

a. Detoxification—the process of removing alcohol from the body. This is ideally done in a hospital setting. The environment must be quiet and supportive.

b. Group therapy.

c. Family therapy.

d. Psychotherapy.

e. Behavior modification—use of Antabuse (disulfiram) to block action of enzyme required for the metabolism of alcohol.

Effects of Antabuse after alcohol intake: nausea and vomiting, palpitation, general prostration. Patient becomes violently ill and therefore avoids alcohol thereafter.

Encouragement of the patient during the treatment is important.

f. Alcoholics Anonymous (Twelve Step Program)—composed of former alcoholics. This lay organization operates on principles of group therapy and is the primary source of rehabilitation for the alcoholic.

g. Al-Anon and Alateen—organizations to assist family members to cope with the problem of alcoholism.

(1) Al-Anon—organization of spouses and other family members of alcoholics.

(2) Alateen—organization of teenaged children of alcoholics.

These groups treat alcoholism as a family problem.

h. Health Promotion

(1) Health education of the public about alcoholism.

(2) Crisis interventions.

(3) Vocational rehabilitation—informs the public about available community resources and facilities.

(4) Family counseling.

4. Nursing diagnoses/goals/interventions

a. Risk for injury related to the toxic effects of alcohol, such as delirium tremens

Goal: Patient will be free from the toxic effects of alcohol (e.g., delirium tremens).

Interventions:

(1) Reassure the patient.

(2) Attend to the patient's physical comfort and safety.

(3) Provide for proper care of the patient during delirium tremens:

(a) Provide a nonstimulating environment (speak calmly), minimize noise, adjust room lighting, keep procedures at a minimum.

(b) Avoid physical restraints if possible.

(c) Force fluids, and monitor intake and output.

(d) Give vitamin supplements (B-complex and C).

(e) Provide proper diet (high carbohydrate, high protein, low fat).

(f) Take seizure precautions; give anticonvulsants.

(g) Observe for agitation and increasing restlessness; do not leave the patient alone.

(h) Interpret the surroundings clearly to the patient to reduce fear.

(i) Explain that the hallucinations and illusions are part of his/her condition and will disappear as this condition improves.

(j) Use side rails as necessary.

(k) Explain all procedures to the patient clearly.

(4) Document and report changes in the patient's condition and his/her response to symptomatic treatment.

b. Ineffective individual coping related to situational and maturational crises and personal vulnerability

Goals:

(1) Patient will be able to handle stressful life situations without using alcohol as a means of coping.

(2) Patient will identify coping resources that proved to be adaptive in the past.

(3) Patient will be able to verbalize his/her feelings appropriately.

(4) Patient will be able to channel his/her anxiety into constructive activities.

Interventions:

(1) Be nonjudgmental.

(2) Be firm and consistent in setting limits to the patient's behavior.

(3) Assist the patient to identify coping patterns that are self-damaging, such as the use of alcohol and other psychoactive substances.

(4) Assist the patient in developing patterns of communication that will be conducive to effective and meaningful interpersonal relationships.

(5) Assist the patient in recognizing his/her strengths and vulnerabilities.

(6) Acknowledge positive signs of the use of adaptive behaviors in handling stress.

(7) Listen to the patient.

(8) Encourage the patient to make realistic plans for the future.

(9) Provide support for the patient as he/she tests out the new patterns of behavior.

(10) Provide the patient with learning experiences that facilitate growth and feelings of self-worth.

5. Evaluation

a. Patient is free from the toxic effects of alcohol.

b. Patient is able to substitute adaptive coping mechanisms for alcohol use.

c. Patient is able to identify own response to stress and utilizes healthy coping mechanisms.

d. Patient is well nourished and hydrated.

e. Patient is able to make realistic plans for the future.

f. Patient is able to demonstrate understanding of the treatment regime.

g. Patient is able to establish meaningful relationships.

I. **Spousal Abuse**   Marital or spousal abuse is a major type of domestic violence. The major problem is wife abuse, though husband abuse is also reported.

1. Dynamics/characteristics

a. Researchers have encountered difficulties in determining the accuracy of the data on the incidence and prevalence of marital abuse because of unreported cases. It is believed that this failure to report may be due to the stigmatizing effect of this type of violent experience.

b. It is estimated that spousal abuse occurs in 3 to 65 million families in the United States.

c. Marital or spousal abuse does not appear to be limited to any specific group of individuals. It is known to occur in all socioeconomic classes. However, although clear evidence is lacking, there is a very strong assumption that marital abuse, as well as other types of family violence, is more common among lower socioeconomic groups.

d. Spousal abuse is most frequent in families where there are drug use problems and also alcoholism.

e. Violence in families has been sanctioned and even reinforced by society. "In a survey of a representative national sample of adult men and women, 20 percent approved of husband and wife hitting. The right of a husband to beat his wife was part of the written law of the United States until 1874."*

f. Marital murder is considered to be the most frequent form of murder within the family.

g. Women are more likely to be victimized by marital abuse than are men.

h. Women are often blamed by society for their experience as victims of violence from their spouses. This attitude frequently reinforces the victimized woman's diminished sense of self-worth and her feelings of self-defeat.

---

*Virginia A. Sadock, "Normal Human Sexuality and Psychosexual Disorders," *Comprehensive Textbook of Psychiatry,* 4th ed., eds. H.I. Kaplan, A.M. Freedman, B.J. Sadock (Baltimore, Maryland: Williams and Wilkins, 1985) 1092.

i. Adults considered to be particularly prone to commit violent acts against their families are those who were themselves abused as children; who had unstable family lives; who were products of broken homes; who were considered "problem children" because of physical, psychological, or developmental difficulties; who were children of substance abusers; and who were exposed to acts of family violence at an early age.

j. The spouse abuser is usually characterized as immature, dependent, insecure, demanding, manipulative, hostile, and distrustful, with low frustration and stress tolerance and poor self-image.

2. Assessment
   a. Assess for possible physical signs of abuse, such as bruises or lacerations, especially on unexposed areas of the body.
   b. Assess the victim's ability and willingness to verbalize feelings about his/her predicament.
   c. Determine the possibilities of child abuse in conjunction with spouse abuse.
   d. Assess the family dynamics.
   e. Assess role functions within the family.
   f. Assess the victim's family environment and living conditions.
   g. Assess the marital couple's present coping abilities.
   h. Determine the victim's current economic situation.

3. Patient care management
   a. Physical care and medical management of injuries.
   b. Crisis intervention.
   c. Family therapy.
   d. Counseling.
   e. Referral to Human Abuse Services Program.
   f. Health promotion
      (1) Educational program for public awareness of the prevalence, effects, and prevention of human abuse in general.
      (2) Marital encounter programs.

4. Nursing diagnoses/goals/interventions
   a. Risk for violence (self-directed or directed at others) related to spousal abuse
   Goals:
      (1) Patient will recognize increasing anxiety levels, anger, provocative behavior, hostile or threatening verbalizations, and other overt and aggressive acts that may precipitate spouse abuse.
      (2) Patient will verbalize own feelings about the experience.
   Interventions:
      (1) Encourage the patient to verbalize feelings about own experience of violence.
      (2) Adopt a nonjudgmental attitude in dealing with the victim and the family.
      (3) Communicate empathic understanding to convey acceptance of the victim.
      (4) Convey genuine interest and willingness to listen to the victim.
      (5) Avoid making critical statements about the marital partner. These may reinforce the victim's ambivalence toward the abusive spouse and prompt the victim to defend him/her.
      (6) If abuse is suspected, ask the victim directly.
   b. Risk for trauma related to dangerous home situation (family violence)
   Goals:
      (1) Patient's family will resolve the violence in the marriage.
      (2) There will be no evidence of spousal abuse, either physically or psychologically.
      (3) Marital couple will enter therapy to resolve the violence in the family.
   Interventions:
      (1) Observe for physical signs of abuse.
      (2) If abuse is suspected, ask the victim directly.
      (3) Assess the extent of the injury.
      (4) Provide for physical care as needed.
      (5) Be nonjudgmental.
      (6) Encourage the patient to seek professional help in resolving violence in the family.
      (7) Encourage verbalization of the

patient's feelings without fear of ridicule.

    (8) Assess the patient's home situation.

    (9) Refer to Human Abuse Services Program as needed.

    (10) Assess the patient for self-destructive ideations.

  c. Ineffective individual coping related to situational crisis

    Goals:

    (1) Patient will be able to verbalize feelings about his/her situation.

    (2) Patient will be able to identify own inner strengths and resources to deal with his/her family situation.

    (3) Patient will be able to seek help as abuse occurs.

    (4) Patient will be able to make realistic plans for his/her future.

    Interventions:

    (1) Be nonjudgmental.

    (2) Listen to the patient.

    (3) Assess the patient's coping abilities.

    (4) Encourage the patient to express both positive and negative feelings about his/her marital partner.

    (5) Assist the patient in making realistic plans about his/her situation.

    (6) Encourage the patient to utilize community resources available for battered spouses.

  5. Evaluation

    a. Patient verbalizes feelings about his/her experience.

    b. Patient seeks assistance regarding violence in his/her family as needed.

    c. There is no evidence of marital abuse.

    d. The marital partners enter therapy as needed.

    e. The patient makes realistic plans about his/her situation.

J. **Rape**   Any forced sexual activity. The legal definition refers to forced vaginal or anal penetration without the consent of the individual. *Sexual assault* refers to other forced sexual acts. Victims of rape may be male or female; male victims rarely seek treatment.

1. Dynamics/characteristics

  a. The actual number of rapes is estimated to be higher than reported.

  b. The typical victims of rape are individuals between 15 and 24 years of age.

  c. Most often the offender lives within the victim's neighborhood and is usually known to the victim.

  d. Victims of rape often suffer from societal moral judgments and certain myths about rape ("women ask for it" and "only bad girls get raped").

  e. It is very common for women who have been raped to feel guilty, as if the sexual assault were their fault.

  f. The patient's reaction to rape is termed the "rape trauma syndrome" and is seen as an acute stress reaction to a life-threatening situation. Rape trauma syndrome includes two phases:

    (1) Acute phase (disorganization of life-style)—manifested in either of two ways: *expressed state,* in which shock, disbelief, fear, guilt, humiliation, anger, etc., are encountered; or *controlled state,* in which feelings are masked or hidden and the victim appears composed. There is a period of denial or unwillingness to talk about the incident, followed by a phase of heightened anxiety, fear, flashbacks, sleep disturbances, hyperalterness and psychosomatic reaction.*

    (2) Long-term phase (reorganization of life-style)—manifested by an attempt to put the incident into perspective. Some victims never fully recover and develop chronic stress disorders and phobias.

2. Assessment

  a. Assess the extent of physical trauma.

  b. Assess the victim's specific concern or immediate needs.

  c. Assess the victim's response to the crisis and injury.

  d. Assess the victim's psychological status.

  e. Assess the victim's coping potential.

  f. Assess the patient's source of support system.

  g. Assess the victim's family and/or significant other's attitude and response to the trauma.

---

*Burgess and Holmstrom identified three phases; the second phase was characterized by denial: A.W. Burgess and L. Holmstrom, "The Rape Victim in the Emergency Ward," *The American Journal of Nursing,* Vol. 73, pp. 1740–1745 (October 1973).

h. Assess the family's and/or significant other's need for support.

3. Patient care management
   a. Immediate action in the emergency room.
   b. Medical care.
   c. Crisis intervention.
   d. Pregnancy prevention alternatives.
   e. Follow-up for venereal disease and pregnancy testing.
   f. Follow-up counseling.
   g. Health promotion through rape prevention programs for the public.

4. Nursing management
   a. Emergency management. The goals of management are to give sympathetic support to reduce the emotional trauma of the patient, and to gather available evidence for possible legal proceedings.
      (1) Assist with physical exam; secure written, witnessed, informed consent from the patient (or parent/ guardian if the patient is a minor) for examination, for taking of photograph if necessary, and for release of findings to police.
      (2) Take a history only if the patient has not already talked to a police officer, social worker, or crisis intervention worker. Do not have the patient repeat the history. If you take the history, record it in the patient's own words.
      (3) Ask whether the patient has bathed, douched, brushed teeth, changed clothes, urinated, or defecated since the attack; any of these actions may alter the interpretation of subsequent findings.
      (4) Record the time of admission, time of examination, date and time of alleged rape, and general appearance of patient; document any evidence of trauma: discoloration, bruises, lacerations, secretions, torn and bloody clothing; record emotional state.
      (5) Assist patient to undress, drape properly; place each item of clothing in a separate *paper bag* (plastic bags retain moisture, which may lead to mildew that can destroy evidence); label bags and give them to appropriate law enforcement authorities.
      (6) Examine the patient from head to toe for injuries, especially to the head, neck, breasts, thighs, back, and buttocks; assess for external evidence of trauma (bruises, contusion, lacerations, stab wounds); assess for dried semen stains (appear as crusted, flaking areas) on the patient's body; inspect fingers for broken nails and for tissue and foreign material under nails; assist in conducting oral examination; secure a specimen of saliva; if ordered, take cultures of gum and tooth areas.
      (7) Document evidence of trauma with body diagrams and photographs.
      (8) Assist with examination of the pelvic and rectal areas; use light that facilitates identification of semen stains (ultraviolet filtered light); note color and consistency of any discharge present; use a water-moistened vaginal speculum for examination (lubricant contains a chemical that will interfere with forensic testing of specimen).
      (9) Assist with securing laboratory specimens; collect vaginal aspiration (for sperms mobile and nonmobile); collect with a sterile swab a specimen for acid phosphatase, blood group antigen, and precipitin test against human sperm and blood; obtain smears from the oral, vaginal, and anal areas; obtain cultures of body orifices for gonorrhea; obtain blood specimen for syphilis; conduct pregnancy test if there is a possibility the patient may be pregnant; place foreign material collected (leaves, grass, dirt) in a clean envelope; comb the pubic hair with a prepackaged clean comb; trim areas of pubic hair suspected of containing semen and also collect hair with follicles; place samples in separate container and note that specimen

is from patient; examine rectum for signs of trauma, blood, semen stain; *label each specimen with name of patient, date, time of collection, body areas from which specimen was collected, and name of person collecting specimen; give to designated person; obtain an itemized receipt.*

(10) Administer prophylaxis against sexually transmitted disease—usually probenecid orally followed by penicillin IM if patient is not allergic; serology test should be done in 6 weeks.

(11) Administer antipregnancy regimen as prescribed; after pregnancy test administer estradiol or conjugated estrogens (Premarin); administer antiemetic to decrease discomfort from side effects; inform the patient that, if she misses a menstrual period, she has the option of having a menstrual extraction or an abortion.

(12) Offer cleansing douche, mouthwash, and fresh clothing.

(13) Provide for follow-up services; make appointment for follow-up in regard to pregnancy and sexually transmitted disease; inform patient of counseling services and services for family; ensure that patient is accompanied by family member or friend when leaving the health care facility.

b. Nursing diagnoses/goals/interventions

(1) Rape-trauma syndrome (acute phase)
Goal: Patient will acknowledge situational support from her/his family, will begin adaptive coping with the situation in her/his own way, will seek appropriate medical treatment, and will regain a measure of control over her/his life.
Interventions:

(a) Provide a private examining room, and stay with the patient or arrange for another support person to stay with her/him.

(b) Explain hospital procedure in advance; help the patient to see that the physical examination is important to well-being and not an intrusion.

(c) Explain police procedure.

(d) Approach the victim in a non-judgmental manner.

(e) Explain the process of gathering evidence for law enforcement personnel, as this is often humiliating for the victim.

(f) Provide support for the victim as physical evidence of the violence is collected (physical examination, interview, etc.).

(g) Provide the victim with information and assistance concerning treatment options and procedures.

(2) Rape trauma syndrome (long-term phase)
Goal: Patient will return to the pre-crisis level of functioning, and will experience optimal physical, psychologic, social, and sexual adjustment to the rape-trauma events.
Interventions:

(a) Assist the victim toward mastery of the crisis situation.

(b) Provide emotional support and reassurance.

(c) Provide for verbalization of feelings. Consider the victim's readiness to talk about the experience.

(d) Acknowledge that the victim is in a state of disequilibrium because of the physical and psychological trauma.

(e) Assist the patient to develop specific actions to overcome feelings (e.g., change telephone number, take trips, engage in diversional activities).

(f) Discuss relationship with the patient's partner and help to identify positive responses and support from partner/family.

(g) Explain that the period of reorganization takes time and that gradually the experience will integrate and become less painful.

(h) Assist the patient to verbalize her/his fear and anxiety about sexual relationships and intercourse; discuss partner's response and concerns.

(i) Educate the patient and partner about the grief process; grieving takes time and involves a variety of emotions, which need to be expressed.

(j) Give specific, written instructions regarding follow-up medical appointments, crisis and rape counseling phone numbers, and symptoms to report.

(3) Altered family process related to rape crisis

Goal: Family will verbalize an understanding of the victim's experience and will give the victim situational support.

Interventions:

(a) Assess the family's reaction to the victim's situation (the family is often nonsupportive, tends to blame the victim, and isolates her/him).

(b) Assist the victim's family and/ or significant others in understanding the psychological impact of the violence to the victim.

(c) Support the family and significant others as they may verbalize guilt over the incident for not protecting the victim.

(d) Assist the family and significant others as they support the victim.

(e) Explain to the family that it is typical for rape victims to have increased fears and anxiety during the initial 48 hours and to want to talk at length about the experience.

(f) Instruct the family to work out with the victim ways to feel safe (e.g., put locks on windows, install new lights, do not walk alone at night).

(4) Knowledge deficit regarding potential physiologic and psychologic difficulties

Goal: Patient and family will demonstrate understanding of potential psychologic and physiologic symptoms, and will use adaptive coping

mechanisms in dealing with feelings regarding the rape.

Interventions:

(a) Educate the patient and family to behaviors that would indicate poor coping:

1. Increase use of alcohol and drugs.
2. Continued somatic complaints (e.g., migraine headache, GI disturbances, GU discomfort, skeletal muscle ache).
3. Persistent phobic reaction (fear of being alone, going out at night).
4. Extreme changes in sexual behavior, and avoidance of members of the opposite sex.
5. Increased feelings of guilt, anxiety, and lowered self-esteem.
6. Recurrence of rape trauma symptoms in response to minor events (e.g., anniversary date).
7. Negative behavior toward family and friends.
8. More frequent nightmares.
9. Withdrawal, lack of verbalization of rape, silence.

(b) Educate the patient and family to the fact that recovery may be delayed and prolonged if any of the below is true:

1. The rape was the victim's first sexual experience.
2. The victim is young.
3. Prior victimization occurred within 2 years.
4. The victim lacks social support.
5. The victim is a chronic life stressor.

(c) Instruct the patient to seek long-term counseling to prevent dysfunctional reactions if she/he is at risk for delayed reaction.

(d) Identify community resource centers available to the victim and family.

c. Evaluation

(1) Patient experiences decreased

symptoms of anxiety, fear, and guilt.

(2) Patient leaves the emergency room with someone.

(3) Patient has written instructions for follow-up medical care and a rape counseling telephone number.

(4) Patient discusses her/his feelings about the event.

(5) Patient engages in precrisis activities on the job and in the home and community.

(6) Patient discusses her/his perception of the event with the therapist, family, and partner.

(7) Family offers acceptance and emotional support to victim.

(8) Family expresses feelings and reactions to the rape.

(9) Patient has an appointment for follow-up care with the physician or clinic and knows that she/he should contact this source of help if needed.

(10) Patient has an appointment with rape crisis center or counselor.

(11) Patient and family discuss emotional and physiologic responses to rape and treatment plan.

(12) Patient and family have a list of community resources and support groups, including sexual counseling.

Appendix

Psychotropic Drugs   Drugs that influence a person's mental processes. They may elevate a low mood or calm agitated patients, enabling them to better direct their activity. The primary action of psychotropic drugs is on the central nervous system.

Classification

Antipsychotic agents.

Antidepressants.

Antianxiety agents.

Lithium carbonate.

Antipsychotic agents   Generally safe compounds primarily used in the management of schizophrenia, affective illnesses with psychotic features, and various organic psychoses.

Table 1.   Antipsychotic Agents

Types	Generic Name	Trade Name	Average Oral Dosage/Day
Phenothiazines	Chlorpromazine	Thorazine	100–1000 mg
	Promazine	Sparine	25–1000 mg
	Triflupromazine	Vesprin	20–150 mg
	Thioridazine	Mellaril	30–80 mg
	Mesoridazine	Serentil	20–30 mg
	Piperacitazine	Quide	20–160 mg
	Trifluoperazine	Stelazine	2–60 mg
	Fluphenazine	Prolixin	5–40 mg
	Perphenazine	Trilafon	2–60 mg
	Acetophenazine	Tindal	40–80 mg
	Prochlorperazine	Compazine	15–125 mg
Thioxanthines	Thiothixene	Navane	6–60 mg
	Chlorprothixene	Taractan	10–600 mg
Dibenzoxazepines	Loxapine	Loxitane	20–25 mg
Dibenzodiazepines	Clozapine	Clozaril	100–900 mg
Butyrophenes	Haloperiodol	Haldol	3–50 mg
Dihydroindolenes	Molindone	Moban	15–225 mg

Side effects
A. Extrapyramidal.
B. Autonomic.
C. Allergic.
D. Other.

A. Extrapyramidal side effects. These subside within 6 months after the drug is discontinued.
1. Dystonias—generally occur within the first 2 days or weeks of treatment. Characterized by bizarre, involuntary movements of the arms, legs, face, and neck; difficulty in talking and excessive salivation; and muscle spasms.
   Treatment: anti-Parkinsonian drugs such as Akineton, Artane, and Cogentin.
2. Parkinsonian-like syndrome, characterized by masklike facies, tremor, rigidity, and shuffling gait.
   Treatment: anti-Parkinsonian drugs.
3. Akathisia, characterized by restlessness, inability to sit still, pacing, and fidgeting.
   Treatment: anti-Parkinsonian drugs.
4. Tardive dyskinesia—occurs after long-term treatment with phenothiazines at high doses. Characterized by a dystonia with bizarre facial and tongue movements.
B. Autonomic side effects: postural hypotension, dry mouth, constipation, urinary retention.
   Treatment
   a. Postural hypotension. To prevent postural hypotension, teach the patient to sit up gradually, dangle the legs over the bed, and make a gradual change from a prone to an upright position. If postural hypotension occurs, ask the patient to lie down in bed.
   b. Dry mouth. Have the patient rinse mouth with water; chewing gum, candy, and other sweets are not recommended.
   c. Constipation. Instruct the patient to eat proper diet, with adequate liquids, and to use laxatives if necessary.
   d. Urinary retention. Reduce dosage; use antispasmotics.
C. Allergic side effects
1. Agranulocytosis—rare but most dangerous of the phenothiazine side effects; generally occurs during the first 6 to 8 weeks of treatment.
   Signs and symptoms: sore throat and high fever.
   Treatment
   a. Prevent exposure to infection.
   b. Discontinue drug.
2. Jaundice—generally occurs during the first 6 to 8 weeks of treatment.
   Signs and symptoms
   a. Initial flulike syndrome such as fever, general malaise, occasional vomiting, diarrhea, and abdominal pain.
   b. Obstructive jaundice after 1 to 7 days. Jaundice is mild, lasts several weeks, and disappears without sequelae.
   Treatment: discontinue drug.
3. Contact dermatitis in personnel who handle the drugs.
4. Photosensitivity.
5. Blue-gray or purple discoloration of the skin, which occurs after long-term treatment with high doses of chlorpromazine.
D. Other side effects: opacities in the anterior lens and posterior cornea.

Antidepressant agents Primarily used in the management of mood disorders, some unclassified psychotic disorders, and organic mental disorders with depressive reactions.

Table 2. Antidepressant Agents

Types	Generic Name	Trade Name	Average Oral Dosage/Day
Tricyclic antidepressants	Imipramine	Tofranil	50–300 mg
	Desipramine	Norpramin	75–300 mg
	Amitriptyline	Elavil	50–300 mg
	Nortriptyline	Pamelor/Aventyl	20–150 mg
	Doxepin	Sinequan	75–300 mg
New (second generation antidepressants)	Maproptiline	Ludiomil	75–300 mg
	Amoxapine	Asendin	150–300 mg
	Trazodone	Desyrel	50–600 mg
	Fluxethine	Prozac	20–80 mg
	Bupropion HCL	Wellbutrin	300–450 mg
MAOIs (Monoamine Oxidase Inhibitors)	Phenelzine	Nardil	45–90 mg
	Isocarboxazid	Marplan	10–30 mg
	Tranylcypromine	Parnate	20–30 mg

A. Tricyclic compounds—for treatment of depression and phobic symptoms associated with severe anxiety attack, also enuresis in children. The lag period between start of treatment and effect can be as long as 4 weeks.
   Side effects
   1. Palpitation, tachycardia, postural hypotension, dizziness, fainting, loss of visual accommodation, nausea and vomiting, profuse sweating, constipation, urinary retention, and aggravation of glucoma. These side effects are mild, and patient develops tolerance after the first few days or weeks.
   2. CNS effects: rapid tremor of upper extremities, convulsions, paresthesias, twitching, ataxis. These are minor and are controlled by decreasing the dose.
   3. Sedation—most common side effect.
B. Monoamine oxidase inhibitors (MAOI)—for patients who do not respond to tricyclics or are allergic to them.

Side effects
1. "Parnate cheese" reaction is a severe reaction occurring when a MAOI is combined with tyramine or tyrosine and causing an increase in blood pressure and acute hypertensive crisis.
2. MAOIs may not be used with tricyclic compounds. Interaction causes restlessness, convulsions, muscle twitching, hypereflexia, and hyperpyrexia, which may lead to death.

Treatment
a. Instruct the patient to avoid cheese, wine, yeast products, yogurt, broad beans, chicken liver, pickled herring, and other foods rich in tyramine or tyrosine.
b. Instruct the patient to avoid taking over-the-counter drugs such as cold remedies, psychomotor stimulants, and diet pills without a doctor's approval.
c. Reduce the dose of MAOI.
d. Maintain careful surveillance of the patient.

Antianxiety agents   Primarily used to provide symptomatic relief of anxiety and to enable the patient to participate in the therapeutic process.

Table 3.   Antianxiety Agents

Types	Generic Name	Trade Name	Average Oral Dosage/Day
Benzodiazepines	Chlordiazipoxide HCL	Librium	5–100 mg
	Oxazepam	Serax	30–120 mg
	Alprazolam	Xanax	0.25–4 mg (divided doses)
	Lorazepam	Ativan	2–6 mg
	Diazepam	Valium	6–40 mg
	Chloraxepate dipotassium	Tranxene	15–60 mg
	Meprobamate	Equanil Miltown	1.2–1.6 g
Antihistamines	Hydroxyzine HCL	Vistaril	75–400 mg
	Hydroxyzine pamoate	Atarax	75–400 mg
Barbiturates	Amobarbital	—	30–50 mg
	Aprobarbital	—	40 mg
	Butabarbital Sodium	—	15–30 mg
	Pentobarbital	—	20–40 mg
	Phenobarbital	—	30–120 mg
	Secobarbital	—	100–300 mg
	Talbutal	—	30–60 mg
Miscellanous	Buspirone	Buspar	30–30 mg

Side effects: drowsiness and physical addiction.

Precaution: Advise the patient not to operate dangerous machinery.

Lithium carbonate—considered most useful in the treatment of mania associated with manic-depressive illness. It is fairly safe when used under medical supervision and control. Usually it is combined with Haldol or with phenothiazines to cover the lag period until the lithium works. Its therapeutic effect is not evident until 1 to 3 weeks after the first dosage. It is also used as a prophylactic or as a maintenance treatment to prevent recurrence of cyclic manic and depressive phases, recurrent depression, and certain types of periodic disorders in children.

Side effects

1. Temporary coarse tremor, not helped by anti-Parkinsonian drugs.
2. Transient nausea.
3. Rare polyuria and polydipsia.
4. Nausea, vomiting, and diarrhea.
5. Severe signs of myoclonus and twitching.
6. Marked drowsiness, slurred speech, confusion, chorea, convulsions, and even light coma.

Treatment

a. Discontinue the drug.
b. Use with care for patients on diuretics or those with disturbed electrolyte balance.
c. Use with caution for patients who have a history of thyroid enlargement or are taking thyroid extracts.
d. Use with caution for patients with renal or cardiac pathology.

Alterations That Interfere with the Meeting of Sexual Needs

A. Alterations of Normal Menstruation
1. **Dysmenorrhea** Painful menstruation.
2. **Amenorrhea** Absence of menstruation.
3. **Menorrhagia** Excessive bleeding at the time of a normal period.
4. **Metrorrhagia** Bleeding between periods.
B. **Vaginitis** Infection of the vagina that occurs when there is a change in normal flora or pH, or invasion by a virulent organism.
1. Types
   a. Leukorrhea: normal vaginal discharge that is considered pathological when it increases in amount, becomes foul smelling, or changes color or character.
   b. Simple vaginitis
      (1) Organisms: *Escherichia coli, Streptococcus, Staphylococcus.*
      (2) Discharge: profuse, yellowish, pruritic.
      (3) Patient care management: vinegar douches, sulfonamide creams.
   c. *Trichomonas* infection
      (1) Organism: *Trichomonas vaginalis.*
      (2) Discharge: white or yellow, frothy, foul smelling.
      (3) Patient care management: vinegar douches, Flagyl (for both partners).
   d. *Moniliasis* infection
      (1) Organism: *Candida albicans.*
      (2) Discharge: watery with white curds (sometimes described as ''cottage cheese''); white patches on vaginal mucosa.
      (3) Patient care management: Mycostatin, gentian violet applications.
2. Patient education
   a. Explain what is happening, and review anatomy with the patient.
   b. Explain proper douching technique.
   c. Explain use of prescribed medication.
   d. Review perineal hygiene.
C. Alterations of the Pelvis
1. **Endometriosis** Growth of endometrial tissue outside the uterus, usually in the pelvic cavity, commonly on ovaries and tubes.
   a. Assessment: Assess for dysmenorrhea, backache, rectal pain, dyspareunia, menstrual irregularities, infertility.
   b. Patient care management: oral contraceptives in large doses, total hysterectomy in severe cases.
2. **Pelvic inflammatory disease (PID)** Infection that involves the entire genital tract; may be caused by staphylococci, streptococci, gonococci, or tubercle bacilli.
   a. Assessment: Assess for chills and fever, anorexia, nausea and vomiting, abdominal and pelvic pain, purulent, foul vaginal drainage.
   b. Patient care management: antibiotics according to organism, heat to lower back or abdomen, sitz baths, analgesics.
   c. Nursing diagnosis/goal/interventions
      Risk for injury related to infection
      Goal: Patient will experience no complications of infection.
      Interventions:
      (1) Maintain the patient in semi-Fowler's position to promote drainage.
      (2) Check vital signs and temperature every 4 hours.
      (3) Assess amount, color, character, and odor of vaginal discharge every 4 hours.
      (4) Administer perineal care frequently.
      (5) Teach the patient to do perineal care.
      (6) Administer antibiotics as ordered.
      (7) Administer analgesics as ordered.
      (8) Teach the patient perineal hygiene and avoidance of tampons, douches, and intercourse until drainage disappears and physician says it is safe to resume sexual activity.
   d. Evaluation: Patient experiences no complications of infection.
D. Alterations of the Uterus
1. **Retroversion** Posterior displacement of uterus.
   a. Assessment: Assess for backache, pelvic pressure, dyspareunia, amenorrhea, infertility.
   b. Patient care management: knee-chest exercises, surgical correction (''uterine suspension'').
   c. Nursing role: Teach knee-chest exercises.
2. **Fibroid tumors** Benign tumors of the uterus.
   a. Assessment: Assess for pelvic heaviness, menorrhagia, anemia.

b. Patient care management: D & C for bleeding, myomectomy (removal of tumor), hysterectomy (vaginal or abdominal) if tumor is large or bleeding is excessive.

c. Nursing management: Provide routine postoperative care for abdominal or vaginal surgery (*see* Unit Eight, Alterations That Interfere with the Meeting of Sexual Needs, Section B: Management of the Patient Undergoing Gynecologic Surgery, page 343).

E. **Infertility**   Inability to conceive after at least 1 year of adequate exposure to the possibility of pregnancy.

1. Causes of male infertility: coital difficulties, spermatazoal abnormalities, testicular abnormalities, abnormalities of penis or urethra, inadequate production of sperm, nutritional deficiencies, emotional problems.

2. Diagnosis of male infertility: complete history and physical examination, analysis of semen, testicular biopsy.

3. Causes of female infertility: nutritional deficiencies, endocrine abnormalities, vaginal disorders, cervical abnormalities, uterine anomalies, ovarian abnormalities, tubal disorders, emotional factors, coital difficulties, chronic disease states, immunologic reactions to sperm.

4. Diagnosis of female infertility: complete history and physical examination, endocrine workup, endometrial biopsy, Huhner test (cervical aspiration), Rubin's test (tubal insufflation), hysterosalpingogram, culdoscopy.

5. Nursing role
   a. Explain all diagnostic procedures.
   b. Discuss couple's feelings about tests.

F. **Acquired immunodeficiency syndrome (AIDS)**   The severest form of a continuum of illness associated with human immunodeficiency virus (HIV) infection. HIV has previously been referred to as lymphadenopathy-associated virus (LAV) and human T-cell lymphotropic virus type III (HTLVIII). HIV is a retrovirus (retroviruses carry their genetic material in the RNA rather than the DNA) and selectively infects T-cell lymphocytes. HIV reprograms the genetic material of the infected T_4 cell and as a result can use the T_4 cell to reproduce the virus itself. Consequently, whenever the infected T_4 cell is stimulated to reproduce by an invading organism, HIV is reproduced instead of T_4 lymphocytes. Then the newly produced virus can infect other T_4 lymphocytes. *When T_4-cell function is impaired, organisms that do not usually cause disease are given the opportunity to invade and cause serious illness.*

Incidence: Seventy percent of AIDS victims are male homosexuals and bisexuals. Users of intravenous drugs comprise 25 percent of AIDS victims. Other groups at risk include sexual partners of those infected with HIV, persons who have received blood products and transfusions infected with HIV (before blood and blood products were screened), and children born to mothers infected with HIV. The urban areas with the most cases of AIDS (because they have proportionately greater numbers of homosexuals and intravenous drug abusers) are New York, San Francisco, Los Angeles, and Newark. AIDS has reached epidemic proportions in other parts of the world.

Age: Most often affected are men between 20 and 49 years.

Transmission: (1) Sexual intercourse. In male homosexuals, anal intercourse or manipulation causes trauma to the rectal mucosa and increases the chance of the virus entering the body through body secretions. Increased frequency of this practice and multiple partners increase the incidence of infection. Heterosexual intercourse with an individual infected with HIV is a means of transmission in this population. (2) Among intravenous drug users transmission occurs through direct exposure via contaminated needles and syringes. (3) Contaminated blood products are a means of transmitting HIV to a recipient. (4) The virus may be transmitted *in utero* from mother to child.

Blood products are screened for evidence of HIV by ELISA (enzyme-linked-immunosorbent assay) to determine the presence of antibodies directed specifically against HIV. ELISA does not establish the diagnosis of AIDS, but rather indicates that an individual has been exposed to or infected with HIV. Persons whose blood contains antibodies for HIV are said to be *seropositive.* To identify the HIV antibodies the western blot assay is used.

1. Assessment
   a. Inspect the body for the presence of at least two enlarged lymph nodes in areas

other than the inguinal that remain enlarged for 3 months or longer.

b. Assess for shortness of breath, dyspnea, cough, chest pain, and fever.

c. Assess for unexplained diarrhea, fatigue/malaise, night sweats.

DIAGNOSTIC MEASURES: CBC, hemoglobin/hematocrit, platelet count, stool tests, bronchoscopy, CT scan, MRI, antibody for HIV: ELISA, HIV antigen, T-cell assessment.

d. Assess for opportunistic diseases (see the following table).

TYPE	SIGNS AND SYMPTOMS (S/S)

Protozoan infections
Toxoplasma gondii
    encephalitis or disseminated
    infection
	Causes serious nervous system infection. The parasitic cyst penetrates the GI tract and is carried via the bloodstream to the brain, heart, and muscles. S/S: neurologic, systemic, ophthalmological.

Chronic *Cryptosporidium* enteritis (longer than 1 month)	S/S: loss of appetite, nausea, vomiting, and diarrhea, systemic, neurological, gastrointestinal.
Pneumocysis carinii pneumonia (PCP)	Has a mortality rate of approximately 60 percent; causes disease only in immunocompromised hosts. It invades and proliferates within the pulmonary alveoli, causing pulmonary parenchyma consolidation. The most common method of diagnosis is transbronchial biopsy obtained by using a fiberoptic bronchoscope. S/S: shortness of breath, fever, cough, chest pain, and dyspnea. *Not transmitted from person to person.*
Giadiasis	S/S: gastrointestinal.
Fungal infections *Candidiasis* (esophageal, bronchial, or pulmonary)	Is universal in all AIDS and AIDS-related conditions. The development of oral candidiasis often precedes other life-threatening infections. S/S: creamy white patches in the oral cavity (if untreated, they progress to the esophagus), difficult and painful swallowing, and retrosternal pain; ulcerating oral lesions may be present.

Chronic *Cryptococcosis*
    (meningitis or disseminated)
    neoformans
	S/S: high fevers, severe headaches, and decreased mental status. Like PCP, it is *not transmitted from person to person.*

Bacterial infections Disseminated *Myobacterium* *avium intracellulare* (MAI)	Is seen most often in patients with AIDS. It is isolated from blood, lymph nodes, liver, spleen, and lung. S/S: fevers, weakness, and cachexia.
Mycobacterium tuberculous (MTB)	Is marked by classic symptoms (fever, productive cough, systemic wasting). Isolation is discontinued after a few days of treatment.
Salmonella	Affects the GI tract, gallbladder, and blood, causing severe diarrhea, fluid and electrolyte imbalance, perianal skin excoriation, weakness, and profound weight loss.
Viral infections Cytomegalovirus (CMV)	Is a common cause of infection in AIDS patients. CMV is transmitted sexually and via blood and blood products. S/S: fever, malaise, weight loss, and lymphadenopathy. CMV causes major damage in retina, lung, and small intestine. Diagnosis is by biopsy and histopathologic evidence. *CMV seems to be the leading cause of death in AIDS.*

TYPE	SIGNS AND SYMPTOMS (S/S)
Chronic mucocutaneous or disseminated herpes simplex virus (HSV)	Is a common occurrence in patients with AIDS. Perirectal mucocutaneous disease causes perirectal ulcers (severe rectal pain, bleeding, tenesmus, rectal discharge).
Varicella-zoster virus (VZV) Multidermatomal herpes zoster	S/S: unilateral eruptions characterized by itching or a tingling sensation and sometimes severe pain. VZV is the cause of common childhood chickenpox.
Epstein-Barr virus (EBV)	Is found frequently in AIDS patients. S/S: low-grade fever, malaise, pharyngitis, and lymphadenopathy.
Jakob-Creutzfeldt papovavirus (causing progressive multifocal leukoencephalopathy, PML)	Is a central nervous system demyelinating disorder. S/S: mental confusion and rapid progress to blindness, aphasias, paresis, and death.
Neoplasm Kaposi's sarcoma	Is the most common neoplasm in AIDS, occurring in approximately 30 percent of patients and accounting for 20 percent of newly diagnosed cases. It is almost never seen in heterosexuals. It appears as raised purplish spots, most often painless and nonpruritic, scattered over the trunk, arms, and face (tip of ears or nose). Diagnosis is by biopsy of suspicious cutaneous lesion or lymph nodes.
Primary brain lymphoma	Is a neoplasm that arises in the central nervous system. S/S: similar to those of toxoplasmosis; focal neurologic deficits and seizures.
Non-Hodgkin's lymphomas (NHL)	Are solid tumors that involve the lymphatic tissues, typically found in axillary, cervical, and inguinal nodes, as well as deeper nodes. Diagnosis is by biopsy of enlarged nodes, bone marrow, or liver. S/S: obstruction of a vital structure by tumor mass, fatigue, fever, night sweating, anorexia, weight loss, and hemolytic anemia and lowered platelet count.
Idiopathic thrombocytopenia purpura (ITP)	Hematological, systemic petechiae, ecchymosis, gum bleeding, heavy menses, hematemesis, hematuria, nose bleeds.

2. Patient care management
Drug therapy for HIV infections and secondary diseases
   a. HIV infections—Retrovir (formerly AZT, azidothymidine). Administered IV. Blocks the replication of viral RNA and DNA.
   b. Kaposi's sarcoma—Adriamycin (doxorubicin), Blenoxane (bleomycin), Oncovin (vincristine), Velban (vinblastine), Ve Pesid (Etoposide). Administered IV.
   c. Herpes simplex, herpes zoster, Varicella—Zovirax (acyclovir).
   d. *Pneumocystis carinii* pneumonia—Bactrim (sulfamethoxazole), Septra (trimethoprim), known as TMP/SMZ; Pentam 300 (pentamidine isethionate).
   e. Candidiasis—oropharyngeal: Mycelex (clotrimazole), Mycostatin (nystatin), oral-local use; cutaneous, disseminated: Nizoral (ketaconazole), administered IV.
   f. Cryptococcosis—Funizone (amphotericin-B), Ancobon (flucytosine).
   g. Toxoplasmosis—Microsulfon (sulfadiazine). Administered IV with Daraprim (pyrimethamine).
   h. Cytomegalovir—DHPG.
3. Nursing diagnoses/goals/interventions
   a. Risk for infection related to immunosupression
   Goal: Patient will be monitored for early signs of infection, and staff, other patients, and visitors will be free from contagion.

Interventions:

Institute universal precautions, including:

(1) Using gloves whenever in contact with body secretions, fluid, or excretions.

(2) Wearing a gown if the patient has copious secretions or excretions.

(3) Wearing a mask when splattering of secretions or excretions may occur.

(4) Concurrent cleaning of patient-care surface with disinfectants.

(5) Avoiding recapping needle.

(6) Avoiding self-wounds with sharp instruments contaminated with infectious material.

(7) Monitoring closely the patient's vital signs and doing laboratory tests for signs of infection.

(8) Administering antimicrobial therapy as ordered; monitor for side-effects.

(9) Instructing visitors about universal precaution procedures, especially handwashing before entering and leaving the room.

(10) Advising pregnant women to avoid contact with the patient because of possibly contracting CMV.

b. Impaired skin integrity (anal) related to immunosuppression

c. Altered oral mucous membranes related to immunosuppression

Goals:

(1) Patient will maintain maximum possible comfort.

(2) Patient will maintain skin integrity.

Interventions:

(1) Cleanse rectal area after each bowel movement with warm, soapy water, and pat dry.

(2) Change bed linen frequently, and give sponge bath when fever is present.

(3) Position the patient every 2 hours, and provide skin care.

(4) Instruct the patient to brush teeth with a soft toothbrush and non-abrasive toothpaste.

(5) Place air mattress on bed to prevent skin breakdown.

(6) Assess oral mucous membrane q 8 hours.

(7) Institute oral hygiene q 2 hours.

(8) Use nondilute nonalcohol mouthwash q 2 hours.

d. Impaired gas exchange related to *Pneumocystis* pneumonia, increased bronchial secretions, and decreased ability to cough related to weakness and fatigue

Goal: Patient will experience improved airway clearance.

Interventions:

(1) Monitor use and effectiveness of ordered therapies, such as oxygen, medical ventilation, humidification, chest tubes, and pharmaceuticals.

(2) Reassess respiratory status every 2–4 hours or as necessary for signs of respiratory failure.

(3) Monitor arterial blood gas; report changes to physician.

(4) Administer medications as ordered; expectorants, antimicrobial, antipyretics.

(5) Instruct patient to deep-breathe and cough every hour.

(6) Suction as needed.

e. Altered nutrition: less than body requirements related to catabolic state, anorexia, difficulty in swallowing

f. Impaired swallowing related to esophagitis

Goal: Patient will receive adequate intake to meet nutritional needs.

Interventions:

(1) Weigh patient daily, do calorie count × 3, and record oral intake.

(2) Provide dietary consultation.

(3) Provide low-volume, high-protein supplement, and encourage family to bring in patient's favorite foods.

(4) Administer supplemental vitamins and minerals.

(5) Encourage intake of food to increase calories.

(6) Monitor electrolyte, serum albumin, total protein.

(7) Administer TPN.

(8) *See* Unit Eight, Management of the Patient Undergoing Surgery, Section F: Common Postoperative Nursing Modalities, Nasogastric and Nasoenteric tube feedings, page 287.

g. Diarrhea related to G.I. infection, Kaposi's sarcoma, or chemotherapy.

Goal: Patient will experience control of bowels.

Interventions:
(1) Encourage electrolyte-containing fluids to 2000 cc daily.
(2) Administer antidiarrheal agents as ordered (opiates, etc.).
(3) Obtain stool cultures as ordered.
(4) Offer small, frequent meals.
(5) Monitor intake and output.
(6) Perform perineal care after each stool.
(7) Instruct the patient to avoid raw fruits and vegetables, nuts, foods high in fat, fried foods, onions, popcorn, carbonated beverages, spicy foods, and foods at extreme temperatures.

h. Altered thought processes related to shortened attention span, impaired memory, confusion, restlessness, and disorientation associated with AIDS encephalitis

Goal: Patient will experience improved thought processes.

Interventions:
(1) Reorient the patient to person, place, and time as necessary; keep calendar within the patient's view; leave light on at night.
(2) Repeat instructions slowly, using simple language.
(3) Implement measures to keep the patient free from injury.
(4) Assess the patient for evidence of impaired thought processes, and record.

i. Dysfunctional grieving related to diagnosis and loss of healthy state

j. Ineffective individual and family coping related to diagnosis and life-style choices

k. Impaired social interaction related to isolation precautions and to grieving over diagnosis

l. Social isolation related to societal non-acceptance of disease

Goals:
(1) Patient will experience decreased feeling of social isolation.
(2) Patient and family will be able to express feelings, concerns, and fears, and support system will remain intact.

Interventions:
(1) Assess the patient and his/her family for stage of grieving.
(2) Support adaptive responses.
(3) Provide information, answer questions, and be gentle in telling the truth.
(4) Encourage family, friends, and staff to visit the patient; avoid unnecessary exaggeration of precautions.
(5) Recognize the need for privacy when sexual partner is visiting, honor wish for confidentiality, and assist others (family, friends, staff) to cope with the patient's preference.
(6) Educate the patient's friends and family about the disease.
(7) Initiate referral to mental health nurse or clinical specialist.

m. Altered sexuality pattern related to physiologic limitations and life-style changes imposed by disease

Goal: Patient will explore and use alternative ways to meet sexual needs.

Interventions:
(1) Support the patient's partner; encourage him/her to be tested.
(2) Educate the patient and partner regarding transmission of the disease and safe sex activity (use condom during sex from beginning to end, avoid combination of oral and anal sex, abstain from sex with a partner having a known infection).

n. Powerlessness related to grave prognosis

Goal: Patient will be able to identify the aspects of AIDS and its treatment that can be controlled and will participate in decision making concerning treatment.

Interventions:
(1) Identify the patient's usual coping style.
(2) Allow the patient to express fears and concerns; listen attentively and offer suggestions.
(3) Keep the patient informed about his/her condition.
(4) Provide opportunities for the patient to control as many decisions as possible.

(5) Record the patient's preferences on the care plan to ensure that they are acknowledged.

o. Knowledge deficit regarding safe hygiene practices in the home and indications for seeking medical attention
Goal: Patient will receive safe, adequate care at home, posing minimal risk to healthy family members and significant others.
Interventions:

(1) Teach the patient, family and significant other good handwashing techniques.

(2) Advise disinfecting the patient's bathroom and toilet with a 1:10 solution of household bleach and water.

(3) Instruct the patient, family and significant other to wash soiled linen in a washing machine with hot water, detergent, and bleach.

(4) Demonstrate how to dispose of soiled tissues, dressing, and gloves in plastic bags, closing tightly before discarding; ask for returned demonstration.

(5) Instruct the patient, family and significant other to restrict visitors who are ill or susceptible to illness.

(6) Instruct the patient, family and significant other about the signs of AIDS and encourage them to seek medical attention as needed.

(7) Ensure that the patient has a written list of prescribed medications with times, dosages, and possible side effects; explain measures to minimize toxic effects and ask the patient to repeat this information at another time.

(8) Explain cross-infection and the signs of infection; stress the need to contact the physican when these signs occur.

(9) Provide information about community resources; give social service referral and referral to visiting nurses/public health nurse.

p. Pain related to neoplasm or sites of infection
Goal: Patient will have a decrease in pain.

(1) Assess pain level.

(2) Provide non-pharmacological comfort measure.

(3) Observe for desired effects and side-effect of medication.

4. Evaluation

a. Patient maintains isolation precautions.

b. Patient is protected from cross-infection.

c. Patient is free from skin breakdown and oral pain or lesions.

d. Patient has decreased dyspnea on exertion.

e. Patient demonstrates improved respiratory functioning.

f. Patient's blood gases are within normal limits.

g. Patient's weight is stabilized or increases.

h. Patient has a balanced intake and output.

i. Patient has a decrease in the number of stools per day.

j. Patient maintains social interaction with family, friends, and staff.

k. Patient verbalizes satisfaction with emotional support provided by staff, family and friends.

l. Patient is oriented to time, place, and person.

m. Patient expresses satisfaction with close relationship and methods of sexual expressions.

n. Patient has a feeling of control over some aspects of his/her life.

o. Patient participates in decision-making process regarding treatment.

p. Patient verbalizes plans to receive continuing care at home from family or significant other.

q. Patient will verbalize a decrease in pain.

UNIT EIGHT

Meeting the Needs of the Middle-Aged Adult (40 to 64 years)

STUDY GUIDE

DEVELOPMENTAL TASKS

HEALTH PROMOTION OF THE MIDDLE-AGED ADULT

A. Health Status
B. Physiological Needs
C. Sexual Changes
D. Health Maintenance

ALTERATIONS OF HEALTH DURING MIDDLE AGE

Management of the Patient Undergoing Surgery

A. Management during the Preoperative Period
   1. Assessment
   2. Preoperative nursing diagnoses/ goals/interventions
   3. Preoperative evaluation
B. Management during the Period of Anesthesia
   1. Objectives of anesthesia
   2. Preoperative medications
   3. Types of anesthesia
   4. Adverse effects of anesthesia

C. Management during the Postoperative Period
   1. Immediate postoperative care in the Recovery Room
   2. Postoperative care in the surgical unit
D. Management of Postoperative Discomfort
   1. Pain
   2. Vomiting
   3. Abdominal distension
   4. Urinary retention
   5. Postoperative nursing diagnoses/ goals/interventions
   6. Postoperative evaluation
E. Management of Postoperative Complications
   1. Hemorrhage
   2. Shock
   3. Thrombophlebitis
   4. Pulmonary embolism
   5. Respiratory complications
   6. Atelectasis
   7. Pneumonia
   8. Wound infections
   9. Wound disruptions

F. Common Postoperative Nursing Modalities
   1. Intravenous infusion
   2. Total parenteral nutrition
   3. Administration of blood and blood products
   4. Enteral feedings
   5. Suctioning

Alterations in Respiration and Carbon Dioxide Exchange

A. General Assessment
B. General Patient Care Management
C. Pneumonia
D. Pulmonary Tuberculosis
E. Pleural Effusion
F. Pulmonary Tumors
G. Traumatic Injuries of the Chest
H. Management of the Patient Undergoing Chest Surgery
I. Management of the Patient Undergoing Closed Chest Drainage

Alterations in Cardiovascular Organs, Blood, and Blood-Forming Organs

A. General Assessment of Cardiac Function
B. General Patient Care Management
C. Coronary Artery Disease
D. Angina Pectoris
E. Myocardial Infarction
F. Management of the Patient Undergoing Cardiovascular Surgery
   1. Cardiovascular surgery
   2. Preoperative nursing diagnoses/ goals/interventions
   3. Preoperative evaluation
   4. Postoperative nursing diagnoses/ goals/interventions
   5. Postoperative evaluation
G. Diseases of the Blood and Blood-Forming Organs
   1. Pernicious anemia
   2. Leukemias
H. Disorders of the Cardiovascular Organs
   1. Hypertensive vascular disease (hypertension)
   2. Varicose veins

Alterations That Interfere with the Meeting of Nutritional Needs

A. Alterations in Ingestion
   1. Cancer of the larynx
   2. Management of the patient undergoing surgery for cancer of the larynx
   3. Hiatus hernia
B. Alterations in Digestion
   1. Peptic ulcer
   2. Management of the patient undergoing gastric surgery
C. Alterations in Absorption
   1. Intestinal obstruction
D. Alterations in Metabolism
   1. Postnecrotic, biliary cirrhosis/portal hypertension
   2. Esophageal varices
   3. Hepatitis coma
   4. Diabetes mellitus
   5. Diabetic ketoacidosis
   6. Hyperosmolar hyperglycemic nonketotic coma (HHNC)
   7. Adrenal crisis
   8. Myxedema (hypothyroidism)
   9. Graves's disease (hyperthyroidism)
   10. Management of the patient undergoing thyroidectomy
   11. Thyroid crisis
   12. Management of the patient undergoing parathyroidectomy

Alterations in Perception and Coordination

A. Management of the Patient Undergoing Surgery for Retinal Detachment
B. Management of the Patient Undergoing Musculoskeletal Surgery
   1. Amputation
   2. Knee surgery
   3. Arthroscopic surgery

Alteration in Behavior

Depression
Electroconvulsive Therapy

Alterations That Interfere with the Meeting of Sexual Needs

A. Management of the Patient with a Gynecologic Condition
  1. Menopause
  2. Prolapsed uterus
  3. Vulvitis

B. Management of the Patient Undergoing Gynecologic Surgery
  1. Anterior and posterior colporrhaphy
  2. Hysterectomy
  3. Vulvectomy

C. Management of the Patient Undergoing Breast Surgery

DEVELOPMENTAL TASKS

According to Erikson, the major developmental tasks of the middle adult years are:

1. Generativity, centered on productivity and creativity; nurturing the next generation.
2. Maintenance of occupational adjustment.
3. Concern with the number of years one has left.

Maladaptations or dangers in this stage are:

1. Stagnation and self-absorption.
2. Inability to accept changes in one's role in society, resulting in feeling sorry for oneself, preoccupation with many real or imagined physical ailments, and dependency.

HEALTH PROMOTION OF THE MIDDLE-AGED ADULT

A. Health Status*
  1. Many of the health changes from young adulthood to middle age are minor.
  2. A major change is the loss of reserve capacity, which provides a backup in times of stress or of dysfunction of one of the body's systems.
  3. The most common chronic ailments of middle age are asthma, bronchitis, diabetes, nervous and mental disorders, arthritis, impairment of sight and hearing and malfunction due to diseases of the circulatory, respiratory, digestive, and genitourinary systems.
  4. People in this age group see their physicians up to six times a year on the average, and from the age of 45 they are more likely to miss work because of illness.
  5. Habits from earlier years show striking effects on health.
     a. Smoke-related illness, such as cancer of the mouth, throat, and lungs, and emphysema, are likely to appear.
     b. Other lifestyle-related ailments that emerge in middle age are heart disease (linked to inactivity, high cholesterol levels, smoking, drinking, and overweight), cirrhosis of the liver (overuse of alcohol), and cancer of the cervix (early multiple sexual contacts).
     c. Obesity due to too much food and too little exercise is a critical health problem. It contributes to hypertension, digestive disorders, and complications of diabetes.
  6. The main causes of death during middle age are heart disease, cancer, stroke, and respiratory disease.

B. Physiological Needs
  1. Sleep. There is an increase in the need for sleep.
  2. Nutrition. Weight gain is common because of a more sedentary life style and a decreased metabolic rate.

C. Sexual Changes
  a. Women. Menopause occurs as a result of a decreased level of hormones from the ovaries.
  b. Men. Physical changes do not occur. There are periods of anxiety, irritability, confusion, depression, and hypochondria.

D. Health Maintenance
  1. Annual physical examination (includes dental, eye, and genitourinary or gynecological exams).
  2. Exercise program to maintain muscle tone and endurance.

---

* Adapted from *Human Development* by Diane Papalia and Sally Olds, pp. 463–465. Copyright © 1981 by McGraw-Hill Book Company. Used with the permission of McGraw-Hill Book Company.

3. Increase in rest (perhaps naps) and some decrease in activity.
4. Decrease in caloric consumption.

ALTERATIONS OF HEALTH DURING MIDDLE AGE

Management of the Patient Undergoing Surgery

A. Management during the Preoperative Period
  1. Assessment
     a. Psychosocial assessment
        (1) Assess for anxiety exhibited as fears (unknown, death, pain, anesthesia, cancer) or worries about financial problems, family responsibilities, or employment obligations.
        (2) Assess for denial of anxiety.
        (3) Assess mental/emotional status.
     b. Physical assessment and health history
        (1) Obtain baseline data—height, weight, temperature, pulse, respiration, blood pressure.
        (2) Observe for use of prosetheses or assistance devices.
        (3) Obtain health history, including:
           (a) Allergies.
           (b) Life-style.
           (c) Medications.
           (d) Personal habits, including intake of alcohol and smoking.
           (e) Patterns of hygiene, rest/sleep, meals/diet, activity status, and elimination (bowel and bladder).
        (4) DIAGNOSTIC MEASURES
           (a) Blood count—WBC, RBC, hematocrit, and/or hemoglobin determination.
           (b) Chest X-ray.
           (c) Electrocardiogram, done on all middle-aged and elderly clients.
           (d) Blood studies—fasting blood sugar, BUN, or NPH.
           (e) Urinalysis.
  2. Preoperative nursing diagnoses/goals/interventions
     a. Anxiety related to surgical experience and the outcome of surgery
     b. Knowledge deficit regarding preoperative procedures and protocols and postoperative expectations

Goal: Patient will experience relief from preoperative anxiety and increased knowledge of preoperative preparations and postoperative expectations.
Interventions:
  (1) Provide patient education.
     (a) Deep breathing and coughing to prevent pneumonia.
     (b) Leg exercises to prevent thrombophlebitis.
     (c) Turning from side to side to prevent pneumonia.
     (d) Medication and pain control.
     (e) Explanation of special equipment.
     (f) Visiting information and spiritual resources.
  (2) Provide proper nutrition as ordered by physician.
     (a) Surgery scheduled in early morning—no solid food after evening meal; water may be given up to 4 hours before operation.
     (b) Surgery scheduled in afternoon—a liquid diet for breakfast, then NPO.
  (3) Give cleansing enema, if ordered.
  (4) Perform preoperative shave and skin preparation; before surgery, have the patient shower with antibacterial soap (Betadine most often used).
  (5) Remove jewelry, hairpins, dentures, and nail polish.
  (6) Apply elastic stocking, if ordered.
  (7) See that consent is signed.
  (8) Complete preoperative checklist.
  (9) Check the chart for results of diagnostic tests and the presence of a complete history and physical examination. Notify physician of abnormal findings.
  (10) Check identification band.
  (11) Administer preanesthetic medication as ordered; then place side rails up and provide a quiet environment.
  3. Preoperative evaluation
     a. Patient is free from anxiety during the preoperative period.
     b. Patient demonstrates understanding of the preoperative procedures and protocols and is prepared for the postoperative period.

B. Management during the Period of Anesthesia
1. Objectives of anesthesia
   a. To render the patient free of pain during the operative procedure.
   b. To promote a relaxed state of mind and sense of security in the patient.
2. Preoperative medications
   a. Anticholenergic drugs—atropine, scopolamine. Sedatives; dry bronchial secretions.
   b. Antianxiety agents—Librium, Valium. Alleviate anxiety and induce hypnosis. May be used as an induction adjunct.
   c. Narcotic analgesics—Demerol, morphine. Sedative analgesics. (Demerol is used with scopolamine to produce twilight sleep.)
   d. Barbiturates—Seconal,   Nembutal. Sedatives; used the night before surgery to alloy insomnia. Nembutal may be given the morning of surgery.
   e. Antihistamines — Vistaril, Atarax (hydroxyine).   Mild antisecretory and skeletal muscle relaxant activity.
3. Types of anesthesia
3a. General anesthesia—administered IV or by inhalation.
   a. **Balanced anesthesia** The use of multiple agents during the anesthetic process. Agents used: general anesthetic, IV anesthetics, neuroleptics, tranquilizers, narcotics, and skeletal muscle relaxants.
   b. Objectives: analgesia (loss of pain sensation), narcosis (loss of consciousness), amnesia (loss of memory), and skeletal muscle relaxation (loss of voluntary and some involuntary muscle activity).
   c. Types of anesthetics
      (1) Inhalation anesthetics
         (a) Liquids—ether, halothane, methoxyflurane, enflurane, isoflurane.
         (b) Gases—nitrous oxide, cyclopropane.
      (2) Intravenous anesthetics (used to induce or maintain surgical anesthesia and hypnosis): Brevital, Surital, Pentothal (cause rapid and smooth induction of anesthetic).
      (3) Miscellaneous general anesthetics
         (a) Dissociative anesthesic—ketamine.

   1. Is used for short diagnostic procedures or in combination with other anesthetics.
   2. Has no analgesic or muscle-relaxing properties.
   (b) Neuroleptic agent—Innovar (a combination of a short-acting synthetic narcotic and droperidol, an antiemetic), sufentanil.
      1. Causes psychological apathy and tranquilization without inducing sleep or analgesia.
      2. Is used for patients undergoing surgery or diagnostic procedures when cooperation and responsiveness are necessary.
      3. May be used alone or in combination with other anesthetic agents (adjuncts: muscle relaxants; drugs used—Anectine, Pavulon, Flaxedil).
   d. Stages of anesthesia (These stages may not be apparent when balanced anesthesia is used.)
      (1) Stage I: stage of analgesia
         (a) This stage is characterized by tranquilization in which consciousness is maintained.
         (b) Noises are exaggerated; therefore a quiet environment is needed.
      (2) Stage II: excitement
         (a) Patient experiences a progressive loss of consciousness and uncontrolled movement.
         (b) Shouting, crying, laughing, and singing may be experienced.
      (3) Stage III: surgical anesthesia
         (a) Unconsciousness is achieved, and surgery is permitted.
         (b) Respiration is regular, pulse rate is normal, and the skin is pink.
         (c) This stage is divided into four planes.
      (4) Stage IV: respiratory paralysis (This toxic stage should be prevented at all costs.)

3b. Local anesthesia—administered topically or regionally.
  a. Objective: loss of pain and voluntary muscle activity without loss of consciousness.
  b. Action: blocks nerve conductions when applied in sufficiently high concentration either to tissue containing nerve fibers or around nerve fibers.
  c. Types of anesthetics
    (1) Topical
      (a) May be applied to the skin, mucous membrane, or eye.
      (b) Is used for the relief of pain or irritation, or to prevent pain (e.g., in eye procedures such as tonometry and removal of foreign objects).
      (c) Common drugs used: lidocaine, Pontocaine, Nupercaine, benzocaine.
    (2) Peripheral nerve block
      (a) May be injected around peripheral nerve terminal (infiltration anesthesia) or into the sheaths of peripheral nerves.
      (b) Is used in dental procedures and minor surgical procedures.
      (c) May be injected alone or with other drugs (e.g., cortisone) intraarticularly or intrabursally.
      (d) Common drugs used: lidocaine, Novocain, carbocaine.
    (3) Regional anesthetics
      (a) Types: spinal, caudal saddle, and epidural.
      (b) Spinal and epidural anesthesia: Anesthetic is administered into the subarachnoid space or the epidural space surrounding the spinal cord.
        1. Drugs used: Novocain, Pontacaine, Nupercaine, lidocaine. They are mixed with glucose, thereby making the anesthetic heavier than the spinal fluid. This controls the level of the spinal anesthesia. Pontacaine, 10 times as potent as procaine, is most often used; it is usually given with epinephrine.

        2. Dangers
          a. Respiratory failure—may occur if the drug reaches the cervical cord.
          b. Postoperative nausea and vomiting.
          c. Hypotension.
          d. Postoperative complications: headaches, paralysis, and bacterial contamination (meningitis).
        3. Postspinal-anesthesia nursing interventions
          a. Monitor blood pressure.
          b. Keep the patient flat and quiet.
          c. Increase fluids to prevent headaches.
          d. Apply tight abdominal binder to prevent loss of spinal fluids (by applying pressure).
          e. Observe closely, and record the time when motion and sensation returns to legs and toes.
    4. Adverse effects of anesthesia
      a. Toxic effects
        (1) Central nervous system—restlessness, confusion, tremors, convulsions, and respiratory depression or paralysis.
        (2) Cardiovascular system—hypotension and arrhythmias.
      b. Allergic responses—rashes, bronchospasm, and possibly anaphylaxis.
      c. Countermeasure: Administration of histamine and epinephrine reduces the incidence of these adverse effects.
C. Management during the Postoperative Period
  1. Immediate postoperative care in the Recovery Room
    a. Assessment
      (1) Assess for level of consciousness.
      (2) Assess respiratory function—rate, rhythm, and depth; presence of an airway: endotracheal tube or tracheostomy tube; signs of anoxia.
      (3) Measure temperature, pulse, and blood pressure.
      (4) Observe condition and color of skin, nail beds, and lips.

(5) Observe amount and type of drainage (if any) on dressing.

(6) Assess for pain or discomfort.

(7) Observe amount and type of intravenous infusion, and site of needle or intracatheter.

(8) Measure total urine output.

b. Nursing role

(1) Provide respiratory care first.

    (a) Administer oxygen via mask or nasal cannula.

    (b) Turn head to side, or position the patient on his/her side.

    (c) Keep airway in place until gag reflex returns.

    (d) Suction prn.

    (e) Encourage deep breathing and coughing when indicated.

(2) Provide cardiovascular care.

    (a) Monitor vital signs every 15 minutes for 2 hours; then every $\frac{1}{2}$ hour for the next hour.

        1. Pulse—check rate, rhythm, volume.

        2. Respiration—check rate, rhythm, depth.

        3. Blood pressure—report a fall of 5 to 10 mm Hg at each reading to the physician or anesthesiologist.

    (b) Check temperature every 1 to 4 hours.

    (c) Maintain body warmth with blanket.

    (d) Encourage leg exercise.

(3) Provide comfort and safety care.

    (a) Turn and position the patient every 2 hours.

    (b) Keep the side rails up.

    (c) Give pain medication only if vital signs are stable. Drugs commonly used: morphine and meperidine (Demerol).

(4) Maintain fluid balance.

    (a) Offer small quantities of tepid water or cracked ice if nausea is not present.

    (b) Observe IV for correct drip rate and signs of infiltration.

    (c) Monitor transfusion for untoward reaction and correct drip rate.

(5) Inspect and reinforce dressing if necessary.

(6) Monitor and record urinary output.

(7) Position the patient to promote comfort and adequate ventilation.

(8) Connect drainage tube to appropriate gravity or suction apparatus.

(9) Assess the patient for discharge from Recovery Room.

    (a) Level of consciousness—the patient is awake; spinal anesthesia—feeling and motion have returned.

    (b) Urinary output—adequate (at least 30 cc per hour).

    (c) Vital signs—stable.

    (d) Drainage or bleeding—absence of excessive amount from any site or body cavity.

(10) Transfer the patient to the surgical floor.

    (a) Notify the nurse of the patient's return to the floor.

    (b) After transferring the patient, make him/her comfortable in bed.

    (c) Place side rails in upmost position and bed in lowest.

    (d) Check functioning of tubes and drainage equipment (reconnect to appropriate receptacles).

2. Postoperative care in the surgical unit

Assessment

a. Monitor blood pressure, pulse, respiration, and temperature every 4 hours, if stable.

b. Monitor respiratory function.

c. Assess pain.

d. Check dressing.

e. Monitor intake and output.

f. Check skin color.

g. Check IV site for infiltration and thrombophlebitis.

D. Management of Postoperative Discomfort

1. **Pain** A feeling of distress, suffering, or agony that is often disabling.

a. Neurophysiology

(1) Three current theories of the neurological mechanism of pain

    (a) *Specificity theory* proposes that the pain mechanism can be initiated only by painful stimuli.

(b) *Pattern theory* assumes that stimulation is sent to receptors in the spinal cord, which initiate a mechanism that results in perception of pain in the brain, and muscle response in the striated muscles.

(c) *Gate control theory* suggests that along nerve pathways (including the spinal cord, brain stem, and cerebral cortex) pain impulses can be altered or regulated. This theory also explains how present and past experiences influence pain perception.

(2) Other physiological factors

(a) A lack of cells, in the brain, that attract narcotics, or of the chemicals, enkepholins, that bind these cells to the brain, thereby explaining why some people are more sensitive to pain than others.

(b) The presence of chemical mediators that initiate the pain impulse.

(c) The presence of prostaglandin, which produces some pain but also plays a role in sensitizing tissue to other pain- and fever-producing substances.

(3) Origins of pain

(a) Visceral pain originates in the viscera; causes are spasm, overdistension, obstruction of blood supply to the viscera, and chemical stimuli.

(b) Referred pain is felt in an area distant from the point of tissue stimulation.

(c) Muscle contraction pain is felt as muscle spasm, with an established self-perpetuating circle.

b. Sociocultural influences

(1) Membership in various cultural and social groups shapes the attitude and responses to pain and suffering.

(2) Religious views concerning the reasons for or the causes of pain influence a person's responses to pain.

(3) Taboos concerning the discussion or display of certain parts of the anatomy may prevent a person from complaining of pain in such an area or seeking medical attention when pain is present.

(4) Research suggests that pain is better tolerated as people grow older, and is better tolerated by men than by women.

(5) Previous experience with pain influences a person's response to pain.

c. Types of pain

(1) Acute—episode of pain that lasts from a second to about 6 months.

(2) Chronic—pain lasting for 6 months or longer. It may be limited, intermittent, or persistent.

d. Phases of pain experience

(1) Anticipation: This is often more difficult for the patient to bear than the actual sensation of pain.

(2) Sensation.

(3) Aftermath: A feeling of fear, embarrassment, or guilt may last for a long period after the pain has ended.

e. Assessment

(1) Differentiate between acute and chronic pain.

(2) Identify the phases of the pain experience and reassess at regular intervals (2–4 hours).

(3) Identify the characteristics of the sensation of pain.

(a) Nature (sharp, prickling, dull, etc.).

(b) Intensity (mild, moderate, severe).

(c) Location and origin.

(d) Onset (sudden, slow build up in intensity, etc.)

(e) Duration.

(f) Progression and severity.

(g) Aggravating factors.

(h) Relief mechanism (pain diminishes when sitting, lying still, etc.).

f. Patient care management

(1) Nonsteroidal anti-inflammatory drugs (NSAIDs)

(a) Salicylates (aspirins, Dolobid, Doan's pills)

1. Action: decrease the perception of pain without drowsiness; reduce fever—anti-inflammatory action.

2. Indications: headaches, muscle aches, arthralgia, and other somatic pain.
3. Side effects
   a. Gastrointestinal effects: epigastric distress, nausea, vomiting, bleeding.
   b. Hypersensitivity: urticaria, asthma.
   c. Anemia, due to GI bleeding.
   d. Postoperative bleeding.
   e. Ototoxic effects: tinnitus, vertigo, deafness.
   f. Thrombocytopenia.
4. Dosage: 600 to 900 mg every 4 hours.
5. Nursing diagnosis/goal/interventions
   Knowledge deficit related to side effects of aspirin (salicylates)
   Goal: Patient will verbalize side effects of aspirin.
   Interventions:
   a. Notify the physician if there are signs of bleeding (dark stool), hives, ear manifestations such as ringing sensation, dizziness, confusion, or hyperventilation.
   b. Increase total fluid intake to 2 to 3 liters to prevent urinary crystal formation.
   c. Keep salicylates in a tightly closed container out of the reach of children.
   d. Reduce gastric irritation by taking the drug with milk, food, or a large amount of water.
   e. Instruct patient to wear Medic Alert device if hypersensitivity is known.
6. Evaluation: Patient experiences minimal, or is free of, side effects.
   (b) Acetaminophen (Datril, Tylenol)
   1. Action: similar to that of aspirin (anti-inflammatory action—reduce fever).

2. Side effects: similar to those of aspirin. Does not affect platelet function
3. Usual dosage 600 to 900 mg every 4 hours.
   (c) Ibuprofen (Motrin)
(2) Narcotic analgesics
   (a) Actions: reduce pain and produce feelings of peace and tranquility.
   (b) Indications: severe pain of visceral origin, postoperative pain, intractable pain of carcinoma, myocardial infarction, severe trauma.
   (c) Side effects: nausea and vomiting; constipation; urinary retention; depression of respiration and coughing; allergic reaction—urticaria, skin rash, itching; behavioral changes—restlessness, euphoria, delerium.
   (d) Types
      1. Narcotics/opiates
         a. Morphine—potent analgesia. Cornerstone for the management of moderate to severe acute pain. Should be administered on a regular time schedule initially (every 4 hours around the clock). Primary side effects: pinpoint pupil (miosis), constipation, respiratory and cough depression, bradycardia (similar for all narcotic analgesics). Usual dosage: 10 mg every 3 to 4 hours prn.
         b. Codeine
            Primary side effect: constipation.
            Usual dosage: 60 mg every 3 to 4 hours, subcutaneously or orally.
      2. Synthetic narcotics
         Prescribed for patients with a demonstrated allergy and intolerance to opioids such as morphine or codeine.

a. Meperidine (Demerol)
Primary side effects: hypertension, sweating, dilated pupils.
Usual dosage: 100 mg every 3 to 4 hours prn and parenteral; oral—300 mg every 2–3 hours; commonly used for postoperative pain.

b. Oxycodone hydrochloride
Action: is more potent than codeine, but less so than morphine.
Preparation and usual dosage: available in combination with aspirin, Percodan, Percocet (combined with acetaminophen). Usual dosage: 1 tablet (5 mg) every 6 hours prn.

c. Hydromorphine (Dilaudid). Usual dosage: PO—8 mg; SC, IM—1–2 mg every 3–4 hours.

d. Oxymorphone (Numorphan). Usual dosage: PO—6 mg; SC, IM—1 mg every 3–4 hours.

e. Talwin (pentazocine)
(1) Action: is potent analgesic, equivalent to codeine.
(2) Indication: moderate pain.
(3) Side effects: sedation, sweating, dizziness, lightheadedness, euphoria.
(4) Dosage and preparation: 50 mg—oral route; 60 mg—subcutaneous or intramuscular injections every 3–4 hours.

(e) Nursing diagnosis/goal/interventions
Knowledge deficit related to side effects of narcotic analgesia
Goal: Patient will be free of, or will experience minimal, side effects.
Interventions:
1. Check vital signs before administering drug.

2. Withhold drug if respiratory rate is below 10 per minute.
3. Encourage patient to exercise, turn, cough, and breathe deeply.
4. Use side rails if patient exhibits signs of drowsiness or confusion.
5. Administer laxative such as milk of magnesia to prevent constipation.
6. Assess intake and output.
7. Administer medication before pain becomes severe.
8. Administer medication before ambulation or coughing to increase patient participation.
9. Provide patient education.
   a. Keep medication out of the reach of children.
   b. Avoid driving after taking a narcotic.
   c. Avoid simultaneously taking alcohol or any other drugs that depress the central nervous system, and a narcotic.

(3) Pain control options
(a) Patient controlled analgesia (PCA)—medication delivered by pump. This route is suitable for bolus administration and continuous infusion. It can be administered by subcutaneous or intramuscular. Once the patient is able to take oral opioids, codeine-acetaminophen combination is provided on an around-the-clock schedule.
(b) Spinal analgesia, usually by means of an epidural opioid and/or local anesthetic injected intermittently or infused continuously.
(c) Intermittent or continuous local neural blockade.
(d) Physical agents such as massage or application of heat or cold.
(e) Electroanalgesia such as transcutaneous electrical nerve stimulation (TENS).

2. Vomiting
   a. Causes: accumulation of fluid in stomach, ingestion of food and fluid before peristalsis returns, psychological factors.
   b. Antiemetic agents
      (1) Actions: prevent impulses from stimulating the chemoreceptor trigger zones, CTZ (found in the uterus, ears, heart, intestines, pharynx, stomach, and kidney), and depress the vomiting center.
      (2) Side effects: drowsiness, dry mouth, nervous system manifestations.
      (3) Common drugs
         (a) Phenothiazines—Compazine, Phenergan, Torecan
            1. Primary side effects: hypertension, urinary retension, constipation, blurred vision.
            2. Dosages
               a. Compazine—5 to 10 mg q.i.d.
               b. Phenergran—25 to 50 mg q.i.d.
               c. Torecan—10 to 30 mg daily in divided doses.
         (b) Antihistamines—Vistaril, Atarax, Dramamine
            1. Specific action: have potent sedative properties without inducing drowsiness (side effects are rare).
            2. Dosage: 25 mg t.i.d.
         (c) Miscellaneous agent—trimethobenzamide (Tigan), benzquinamide (Emete-Con), diphenidol (Vontrol)
            1. Action: depress the chemoreceptor trigger zone in the medulla rather than the vomiting center; long acting with little or no sedative effect.
            2. Side effects (incidence rate): dizziness, irritation after rectal administration, diarrhea.
3. Abdominal distension
   a. Causes: trauma due to manipulation of the intestine during surgery, swallowing large quantities of air, immobility following surgery, frequent use of narcotics suppressing peristalsis.
   b. Patient care management
      (1) Rectal intubation to dilate the anal sphincter and release the accumulated rectal gas.
      (2) Massage of the lower abdomen in the direction of the rectum, if not contraindicated.
4. Urinary retention
   a. Cause: spasm of the bladder sphincter.
5. Postoperative nursing diagnoses/goals/interventions
   a. Ineffective airway clearance related to depressant effects of medications and anesthetic agent
      Goal: Patient will experience optimum respiratory function.
      Interventions:
      (1) Promote lung expansion.
         (a) Encourage deep breathing and coughing.
         (b) Ambulate the patient within 24 to 48 hours after surgery (dangle first).
         (c) Provide mechanical measures — incentive spirometry and IPPB.
      (2) Turn and position the patient every 2 hours.
      (3) Provide back care every 2 hours.
      (4) Provide mouth care every 2 hours, especially if NPO.
      (5) Encourage bed exercises when ambulation is not feasible: deep breathing; arm exercises through full range of motion; hand, finger, and foot exercises.
   b. Alteration in comfort: pain and other postoperative discomfort related to surgical incision, muscle tension/contraction/spasm and immobility
      Goal: Patient will experience relief of pain, nausea and vomiting, abdominal distension, and urinary retention.
      Interventions:
      (1) Pain
         (a) Establish a relationship with the patient by letting him/her know that you believe what is being said about the pain experience.
         (b) Teach the patient about pain and its relief. This activity is most often used in the preoperative period.
         (c) Use the principle of small-group therapy to teach the patient and his/her family about the patient's pain experience.

(d) Assist other people who come in contact with the patient to help him/her with the pain experience.

(e) Use cutaneous stimulation such as pressure, vibration, heat, and cold.

(f) Provide distraction—for example, breathing exercises.

(g) Promote relaxation—for example, show rhythmic breathing.

(h) Use guided imagery; for example, assist the patient to imagine a pleasant event.

(i) Administer pharmacological agents. Give medication before the pain becomes severe. Place side rails in upright position after administration of narcotics or mind-altering medications.

(j) Decrease noxious stimuli; for example, splint the wound during coughing and deep breathing.

(k) Inform the patient that the source of noxious stimuli has been removed or decreased.

(l) Utilize the assistance of professionals such as clergymen.

(m) Spend time with the patient; have the family or a volunteer sit at the patient's bedside.

(n) Assist with the assimiliation of the painful experience through discussion of it.

(2) Nausea and vomiting

(a) Give nothing by mouth.

(b) Begin oral solids with small amounts of dry foods such as crackers.

(c) Give carbonated beverage to relieve nausea.

(d) Give frequent small feedings to prevent GI distension.

(e) After episode of vomiting, provide adequate oral hydration and nutrition.

(f) If patient is receiving parenteral fluids and electrolytes, observe for signs of infiltration. Maintain correct infusion flow rate and accurate intake and output record.

(g) Evaluate the patient's emotional status.

(3) Abdominal distension (Mild symptoms may be relieved by nursing measures.)

(a) Assist the patient with ambulation.

(b) Encourage turning and exercise in bed.

(c) Give hot liquid (tea or coffee).

(4) Urinary retention

(a) Observe the patient for signs of retention (i.e., restlessness, distension of area above the pubis or presence of a palpable bladder, frequent voiding of small amounts of urine).

(b) Allow the patient to stand or sit to void.

(c) Provide the patient with warm bedpan or urinal.

(d) Pour warm water over perineum.

(e) Have the patient hear or see running water.

(f) Catheterize the patient if ordered (should not be delayed longer than 12 hours).

c. Altered nutrition: less than body requirements related to decreased appetite, and nausea and vomiting

d. Risk for fluid volume deficit related to nausea and vomiting
Goals:

(1) Patient will maintain normal nutrition.

(2) Patient will maintain adequate fluid volume.

Interventions:

(1) Determine return of bowel sounds before initiating diet modification.

(2) Encourage liberal amounts of fluids, if tolerated. (Parenteral fluids are discontinued.) Offer water, fruit juices, and tea with lemon (helps dissolve mucus better than cold water).

(3) As soon as soft foods are tolerated well, give solid food.

e. Impaired physical mobility related to depressant effects of anesthesia, decreased activity tolerance, and activity restriction required by therapeutic plan
Goal: Patient will be mobile within limitations of postoperative and rehabilitative plan.

Interventions:

(1) Ambulate as ordered; check pulse rate beforehand. If patient feels faint, return to bed and have him/her move legs in bed before attempting to ambulate.

(2) Assist patient with bed exercises when early ambulation is not feasible: deep breathing exercises, arms through range of motion, hand and finger exercises, foot exercises (to prevent foot drop and toe deformities), abdominal and guteal contraction exercises.

(3) Reposition patient, or have patient move, every 2 hours.

f. Impaired skin integrity related to surgical incision

g. Risk for infection: wound related to susceptibility to bacterial invasion

Goals:

(1) Integrity of patient's skin will remain intact.

(2) Patient will avoid infection.

Interventions:

(1) Administer antibiotics as ordered.

(2) Observe strict handwashing.

(3) Inspect dressing periodically for hemorrhage or abnormal drainage; check drainage tube also every 4 hours. Reinforce dressing as needed. If incision is on the anterior part of the body, the posterior area should be checked for signs of bleeding (due to gravity drainage accumulating in an area other than around incision).

(4) Monitor temperature every 8 hours, and notify the physician of elevations after 3rd day postoperative.

6. Postoperative evaluation

a. Patient maintains optimum respiratory function.

b. Patient experiences relief of pain and postoperative discomfort.

c. Patient maintains fluid balance.

d. Patient maintains nutritional balance.

e. Patient avoids infection and maintains skin integrity.

f. Patient resumes mobility within the limitations of the postoperative and rehabilitation plan.

E. Management of Postoperative Complications

1. **Hemorrhage** The discharge of blood from a ruptured blood vessel.

a. Classifications

(1) Occurrence

(a) Primary—occurring at the time of an operation.

(b) Intermediary—occurring within the first 5 hours after an operation.

(c) Secondary—occurring some time after an operation.

(2) Kind of vessel

(a) Capillary. Bleeding is characterized by a slow, general oozing.

(b) Venous. Blood bubbles out quickly and is dark in color.

(c) Arterial. Blood appears in spurts with each heartbeat and is bright in color.

(3) Site of bleeding

(a) External/evident—on the surface and can be seen.

(b) Internal/concealed—cannot be seen (e.g., is in peritoneal cavity).

b. Assessment. *See* Shock (hypovolemic), page 277.

c. Nursing role. *See* Shock (hypovolemic), page 277.

2. **Shock** Inadequate cellular metabolism due to poor tissue perfusion.

a. Classic clinical signs: hypertension; weak, rapid, thready pulse; cold, clammy skin; mental confusion; reduction of urine output to less than 20 cc per hour; rapid breathing; thirst; tachycardia.

b. Classification of shock

(1) **Hypovolemic** Decrease in fluid volume.

(a) Causes

1. Blood loss—hemorrhage.

2. Plasma and/or protein loss—burns, exfoliative "weeping" dermatitis, nephrotic syndrome, cirrhosis.

3. Fluid and electrolyte loss—excessive sweating, diarrhea, vigorous diuretic therapy, diabetes.

(b) Classification of symptoms
  1. Mild—up to 20% of blood volume loss.
  2. Moderate—20 to 40% of blood volume loss.
  3. Severe—40% of more of blood volume loss.

(2) **Cardiogenic** Decrease in ability of the heart to pump blood due to poor perfusion of the coronary vessels.
Causes: myocardial infarction, congestive heart failure, arrhythmias.

(3) **Neurogenic** Increase in the size of the vascular bed, resulting in the pooling of venous blood, decreased venous return to the heart, and decreased cardiac output.
Causes: deep general anesthesia, central nervous system injury, barbiturate intoxication, spinal anesthesia, fainting.

(4) **Septic** Action on blood vessels and other cells of toxic substances produced by bacteria, often causing hypovolemia and depressed cardiac function.
Causes: gram-positive organisms (pneumococci, staphylococci, streptococci), peritonitis, trauma.

c. Assessment
  (1) Skin: Check color, temperature, and moisture level.
    (a) Hypovolemic shock—cold, clammy, moist skin.
    (b) Septic and neurogenic shock—warm, red skin.
    (c) Cardiogenic shock—cold, clammy, moist skin.
  (2) Respiration
    (a) Check respiratory rate and character.
    (b) Check lungs for quality and intensity of breath sounds and the presence of abnormal sounds (rales, rhonchi, or friction rub).
  (3) Pulse and blood pressure
    (a) Check every 5 to 15 minutes.
    (b) Report diastolic pressure under 70 mm Hg and/or systolic pressure under 90 mm Hg.

(c) Check pulse rate, rhythm, and quality.
(d) Determine pulse pressure.
(4) Central venous pressure
  (a) Take readings every 5 minutes or 100 ml of fluids.
  (b) Check site of insertion for bleeding, infection, inflammation, or infiltration.
(5) Urinary output: Check hourly.
(6) Sensorium: Assess orientation to time, place, persons, and mood.
(7) Blood studies
  (a) Arterial blood gases—pCO_2, carbon dioxide; pO_2, oxygen.
  (b) Hemoglobin—men: 14 to 18 gm %; women: 12 to 16 gm %.
  (c) Hematocrit—men: 45%; women: 40%.
  (d) Serum lactate.
  (e) Serum electrolytes.
  (f) Prothrombin time—70 to 110% of control value.
  (g) pH—5.3 to 7.8 per 100 cc of serum.

d. Patient care management
  (1) Ensure adequacy of airway.
  (2) Restore blood/fluid volume.
    (a) Crystalloids—electrolyte solutions that diffuse into interstitial spaces (e.g., lactated Ringer's) and aid in microcirculation.
    (b) Colloids—blood, blood substitutes, artificial blood, plasma, serum albumin, and plasma substitutes such as dextran.
  (3) Drug therapy
    (a) Cardiotonics, diuretics, vasoactive medications.
    (b) Vasodilators to reduce peripheral resistance, decrease the work of the heart, and increase cardiac output and tissue perfusion. Sodium nitroprusside (Nipride) is commonly used.

e. Nursing role
  (1) Hypovolemic shock
    (a) Administer oxygen.
    (b) Prepare intravenous fluids for administration. (Intravenous fluid commonly used is lactated Ringer's solution, dextrose 5%, blood plasma or albumin.)

(c) Monitor flow rate of IV infusion to prevent circulatory overload. (IV is infused at a rapid rate until CVP rises to a satisfactory rate.)

(d) Place the patient flat in bed with legs elevated. (Avoid Trendelenburg position because of pressure on respiratory structures.)

(e) Monitor vital signs every 5 to 15 minutes.

(f) Measure and record urine output hourly.

(g) Monitor skin temperature and color.

(h) Monitor central venous pressure.

    1. A normal reading is 5 to 10 cm/water.

    2. A reading above 15 cm/water indicates congestive heart failure.

    3. A low reading indicates hypovolemic shock.

(i) Carry out rapid assessment to determine the cause of shock.

(j) Administer drugs (dopamine, sodium bicarbonate, etc.).

(k) Keep the patient warm but avoid overheating.

(2) Cardiogenic shock. *See also* Nursing role for hypovolemic shock, above, and patient care management, above.

(a) Administer digitalis and antiarrhythmic drugs (lidocaine, Pronestyl, quinidine).

(b) Administer a vasopressor (Isuprel, Aramine, Levophed, norepinephrine).

    1. Monitor blood pressure every 2 to 5 minutes.

    2. Keep the patient flat during administration.

    3. Discontinue drug and increase flow rate of IV fluids if systolic blood pressure falls below 70 mm Hg.

    4. Discontinue IV infusion of Levophed if infiltration occurs.

(c) Take serial electrocardiograph recordings if the patient is not attached to a cardiac monitor.

(d) Monitor arterial blood gases and serum electrolytes.

(3) Neurogenic shock. *See also* Nursing role for hypovolemic shock, above.

(a) Administer vasopressor (Levophed, Aramine, Isuprel, Neo-Synephrine).

(b) Monitor blood pressure for undesirable elevation.

(4) Septic shock. *See also* Nursing role (a) to (j) for hypovolemic shock, above.

(a) Administer antibiotic (Keflin, Kantrex, ampicillin, gentamicin, streptomycin).

(b) Check culture and sensitivity test to determine whether the patient is receiving the correct antibiotic.

(c) Keep the patient cool (high fever will increase the cellular metabolism effect of shock).

3. **Thrombophlebitis** Formation of clots within the vein, accompanied by inflammatory changes in the vessel wall. It may occur in the superficial veins (upper arm and saphenous) or deep veins (left lower leg; the soleal veins of the calf are most often affected).

a. Causes

(1) Injury to the blood vessel during surgery.

(2) Venous stasis or slowing of blood flow (most often due to obesity, bedrest, prolonged sitting, pregnancy, congestive heart failure, as a complication of abdominal or pelvic surgery, or fraction of an extremity or the pelvis.

(3) Advanded age.

(4) Rapid blood coagulation secondary to dehydration, use of oral contraceptives, cancer, or blood dyscrasias.

b. Assessment

(1) Physical assessment (The focus of the assessment is the lower extremity.)

(a) Size and symmetry
  1. Inspect the leg from groin to feet for edema.
    a. Detect ankle edema by observing from behind while the patient is standing.
    b. Palpate the swollen area. (Edematous tissue will pit if compressed by the thumb.)
  2. Measure the circumference of the calf. (Unilateral edema results from thrombophlebitis.)
  3. Inquire about the presence of leg pains, functional impairment, or thromboses.
    a. Palpate the leg to detect areas that are tender, bumpy, or knotty.
    b. Have the patient put the extremity through the range of motion. (A positive Homan's sign is present in only 50% of patients.)
(b) Skin
  1. Inspect the skin for shininess and tautness.
  2. Palpate the skin to determine temperature.
(2) Diagnostic measures: fibrogen labeled with ^{125}I, ultrasound, phlebography, plethysmography.
c. Patient care management
  (1) Bedrest and elevation of the affected part.
  (2) Application of heat.
  (3) Medications: agents for relief of pain; anticoagulants; antibiotics if necessary; dextran 70 to decrease blood viscosity; fibrinolytic drugs to dissolve thrombi—streptokinase, urokinase.
  (4) Elastic stockings.
  (5) Surgical interventions.
d. Nursing management role
  (1) Implement preventive measures.
    (a) Encourage early postoperative ambulation.
    (b) Encourage leg exercise while on bedrest.
    (c) Apply elastic stocking if ordered.
    (d) Elevate lower extremities 6 inches to increase venous return.
    (e) Provide patient education.
      1. Avoid wearing constricting clothing.
      2. Avoid a standing or sitting position for long periods of time.
      3. Discontinue cigarette smoking.
      4. Wear support hose if prescribed.
      5. Exercise the extremity for 5 minutes out of every hour.
      6. Control weight.
      7. Avoid crossing legs.
      8. If using oral contraceptives, be aware of their potential thrombus-formation side effect.
  (2) Maintain bedrest for 7 to 10 days.
  (3) Elevate the bed by raising the foot on blocks, if ordered.
  (4) Do not use pillows or elevate the bed under the knee.
  (5) Avoid massaging the legs.
  (6) Put the unaffected limb through passive range of motion exercises.
  (7) Avoid dangling; have the patient stand at bedside.
  (8) Apply an antiembolic stocking to the unaffected leg.
  (9) Apply hot pack, if ordered, for 2 to 3 days.
  (10) Apply a layer of petroleum jelly to protect the skin from the moisture of the hot packs.
  (11) Medicate with acetaminophen, since salicylates also inhibit or delay clotting.
  (12) Administer anticoagulant if ordered. A single or combined administration of a heparin or coumarin derivative is used.
    (a) Actions: delays the clotting time of the blood, prevents the formation of a thrombus, prevents the extension of a thrombus.

(b) Administration
   1. Heparin: continuous pump infusion; intermittent IV injection every 4 hours; subcutaneous injections (8- to 42-hour intervals).
   2. Coumadin (warfarin): orally.
(c) Nursing role
   1. Observe for blood in the urine or stool, bleeding from gum or nose, and bruises.
   2. Check PTT (partial thromboplastic time) or clotting time before administering heparin. Norm: PTT—60 to 85 seconds.
   3. Check prothrombin time before administering Coumadin (therapeutic range: 25 to 30 seconds; normal: 12 to 14 seconds).
   4. Check vital signs every 4 hours for signs of shock.
   5. Have antagonist available (heparin—protamine sulfate; Coumadin—vitamin K).
(13) Administer antibiotic as ordered.
(14) Patient education
   (a) Take anticoagulant at the same time each day.
   (b) Obtain a Medic-Alert bracelet or carry ID card.
   (c) Use electric razor for shaving.
   (d) Keep appointments for blood work.
   (e) Avoid alcohol.
   (f) Do not begin or discontinue drug without physician's consent.
   (g) Avoid changes in diet (coumadin–avoid foods high in vitamin K, leafy vegetables).
   (h) Inform all health professionals consulted that you are on anticoagulant therapy.
   (i) Report illness or side effects.
   (j) Avoid activities that may cause injury.
(15) Observe the patient for signs of thrombus extension.
(16) Check the potency of IV infusion of dextran and fibrinolytic drugs.

4. **Pulmonary embolism** Obstruction of one or more pulmonary arteries by a thrombus. Most cases of pulmonary embolism occur secondary to venous thrombosis.
   a. Assessment
      (1) Observe for gasping, swallowing, rapid breathing, coughing, anxiety, substernal pain, dizziness, and weakness.
      (2) Auscultate lungs for pulmonary rales and increased respiratory rate.
      (3) Auscultate heart for increased intensity of pulmonic component of second heart sound and increased heart rate.
      (4) Inspect sputum for presence of blood. Measure vital signs.
      (5) DIAGNOSTIC MEASURES: lung scanning, pulmonary arteriography, chest X-ray, electrocardiogram, arterial blood gases, ultrasound.
   b. Patient care management
      (1) Bedrest.
      (2) Anticoagulant and fibrinolytic therapy.
      (3) Treatment for shock.
      (4) Oxygen therapy.
      (5) Surgical interventions: ligation of the inferior vena cava, ligation of the femoral artery, pulmonary embolectomy.
      (6) Prevention: aspirin daily to prevent platelet aggregation; liberal intake of fluids to prevent dehydration, which predisposes to thrombus formation.
   c. Nursing role
      (1) Administer oxygen via mask or nasal cannula.
      (2) Position the patient in semi-Fowler's position if shock is not present.
      (3) Prepare IV solution for infusion.
      (4) Monitor vital signs every 15 minutes until stable, then every 1 to 4 hours.
      (5) Provide emotional support.
      (6) Administer narcotic analgesic. (Morphine is most often given; observe for respiratory depression.)
      (7) Administer anticoagulant and fibrinolytic agents.
      (8) Observe for signs of shock.

(9) Auscultate breath and heart sounds every 1 to 2 hours.

(10) Maintain bedrest, and advise the patient to avoid sudden movements or exertion.

5. **Respiratory complications** These develop within the first 48 hours after surgery (bronchitis, bronchopneumonia, lobar pneumonia, pleurisy, hypostatic pulmonary congestion).

a. Causes

(1) Respiratory infections that are not controlled before surgery.

(2) Exposure to respiratory infection after surgery.

(3) Irritation from anesthetics, endotracheal tube, and oxygen.

(4) Prolonged immobilization during and after surgery.

(5) Patient reluctance to turn, cough, or deep-breathe after surgery because of severe pain.

(6) Depressive effect of narcotics on the cough reflex.

(7) Aspiration of vomitus.

b. Assessment

(1) Measure temperature, pulse, respiration, and blood pressure the first 72 hours.

(2) Auscultate breath sounds.

(3) Observe for coughing, chest pain, difficulty in breathing, and restlessness.

c. Nursing role (preventive measures)

(1) Give preoperative instructions concerning turning, coughing, and breathing exercises.

(2) Encourage the patient to turn, cough, and deep-breathe every 2 hours in the postoperative period.

(3) Promote lung expansion by mechanical means: spirometer, IPPB, rebreathing carbon dioxide.

(4) Maintain a patent airway.

(5) Provide early postoperative mobilization.

(6) Encourage warm fluids to thin mucous secretions.

(7) Administer the liquefying agent to aid in the expectoration of secretions: Alevaire or Mycomyst.

(8) Medicate for pain to allow for ambulation, coughing, and deep breathing.

6. **Atelectasis** Condition in which an area of lung tissue (lobe) or a lung has collapsed.

a. Causes: mucous plug, tumor, bronchospasm, pneumothorax.

b. Assessment

(1) Observe for painful respiration, anxiety, cyanosis, and weakness.

(2) Inspect chest for asymmetrical movement. (Ventilatory movement is observed on the affected side.)

(3) Auscultate chest for reduction or absence of breath sound on the affected side.

(4) Percuss over the affected side to delineate areas of dullness.

(5) Measure temperature, pulse, respiration, and blood pressure. (Elevated temperature, decreased blood pressure, and increase in heart rate are seen when infection accompanies atelectasis.)

(6) DIAGNOSTIC MEASURES: chest X-ray, bronchoscopy.

c. Nursing role

(1) Administer oxygen if necessary.

(2) Suction as necessary.

(3) Turn the patient frequently, and position with the involved side elevated to facilitate drainage of the affected area.

(4) Administer a detergent aerosol with a nebulizer (Alevaire).

(5) Administer antibiotics, expectorants, and other medications as ordered.

(6) Auscultate breath sounds every 2 to 4 hours.

(7) Encourage fluids to thin mucous secretions.

(8) Perform percussion, vibration, and postural drainage at times ordered. *See* Alterations in Respiration and Carbon Dioxide Exchange Section B: General Patient Care Management, page 292.

7. **Pneumonia.** *See* Section C: Pneumonia, page 298.

8. **Wound infections** These occur around the 5th postoperative day. Initial symptoms may be evident 36 to 48 hours after surgery.

a. Causative organisms: *Staphylococcus aureus, Escherichia coli, Pseudomonas aeruginosa, Proteus vulgaris, Aerobacter aerogenes.*

b. Assessment
  (1) Measure temperature, pulse, respiration, and blood pressure every 4 hours within the first 72 hours.
  (2) Observe the wound for swelling and the presence of drainage.
  (3) Inquire whether the patient is experiencing pain, tenderness, and/or warmth around the wound site.
c. Nursing role
  (1) Take a wound culture before starting antibiotics.
  (2) Administer a specific antibiotic at the times ordered.
  (3) Use sterile technique when changing the dressing.
  (4) Apply wet dressings, if ordered.
  (5) Use prescribed solution (Betadine solution or hydrogen peroxide) to irrigate or cleanse the wound.

9. **Wound disruptions** These occur on the 4th to 7th postoperative day.
a. Types
  (1) Dehiscence—separation of wound edges.
  (2) Evisceration — separation of wound edges with the protrusion of loops of bowel and drainage of pinkish fluid.
  b. Predisposing factors: malnutrition (insufficient protein A), obesity, defective suturing, wound infection, unusual strain on the wound (coughing, sneezing, or vomiting).
c. Nursing role
  (1) To prevent, apply an abdominal (Scultetus) binder when the patient is ambulatory.
  (2) Give the patient emotional support and assurance.
  (3) Place the patient in the position that places least strain on the operated site.
  (4) Notify the physician.
  (5) Cover exposed intestine with sterile towels or dressing moistened with normal saline.
  (6) Take vital signs, and observe for shock.
  (7) Notify operating room that the patient will be returning for wound closure.
  (8) Set up IV equipment, and prepare IV fluid.

F. Common Postoperative Nursing Modalities
1. Intravenous infusion
  a. Goals of fluid therapy
    (1) To repair preexisting deficits of water and electrolytes.
    (2) To provide water and electrolytes to meet the patient's maintenance requirements.
    (3) To replace water and electrolytes lost through vomiting, diarrhea, tubal drainage, wound drainage, burn drainage, or diuresis.
  b. Calculation of the drip rate
    (1) Variations in drop size
      (a) Regular drops usually depend on the commercial administration set (10, 15, or 20 gtt/cc fluid).
      (b) Microdrop = 60 gtt/cc fluid.
    (2) Formula:

$$\frac{\text{Total volume infused} \times \text{drops/cc}}{\text{Total time of infusion in minutes}}$$
$$= \text{drops/min.}$$

    (3) Sample problem: The order is to administer 1000 cc of 5% D/W in 8 hours, using an administration set that delivers 10 gtt/cc. What should the drip rate be?
Solution:

$$\frac{1000 \times 10}{480} = 20.8 \text{ or } 21 \text{ gtt/min.}$$

  c. Factors that may alter the drip rate
    (1) Change in needle position. (An adequate flow rate diminishes when needle pushes against vein wall, increases when needle moves away.)
    (2) Change in the height of the solution bottle.
    (3) Occlusion of the lumen of the needle.
    (4) Kink in the tubing.
  d. Parenteral nutrition
    (1) From 150 to 200 gm of carbohydrates daily is required to minimize ketosis and protein catabolism.
    (2) To provide 150 gm of dextrose and 600 calories, 3000 cc of 5% D/W must be administered daily.

(a) 5% D/W is the solution most commonly used for fluid replacement.

(b) 1000 cc of 5% D/W provides 200 calories and 50 gm of carbohydrates/dextrose.

(3) A daily intake of 1500 to 3000 cc of fluids is required by the body.

(4) Water-soluble vitamins (vitamin C and B complexes) are administered parenterally when the patient is to receive NPO and is on parenteral therapy longer than 3 days.

e. Types of IV solutions

(1) Carbohydrate solutions—provide calories and fluid.

Common types of solution: 5 and 10% in water or saline.

(2) Electrolyte solutions

(a) Sodium chloride—used in the treatment of dehydration, shock, and hydrogen ion imbalance.

Common types of solution— normal saline (0.9%), 0.45% (half-strength), 3%, and 5% (also available in dextrose solution).

(b) Lactated Ringer's (Hartmann's) —has an electrolyte concentration closely resembling that of extracellular fluid.

(3) Protein hydrolysate solution— supplies protein.

Common types of solution: Amigen, Aminosol.

(4) Plasma volume expander—a glucose solution that draws interstitial fluid into the bloodstream to restore blood volume.

Common types of solution: dextran 70, Gentran 75.

f. Nursing role

(1) Maintain the rate of infusion as ordered.

(2) Check the circulation of the extremity that is being immobilized with an armboard.

(3) Check the doctor's orders against label of IV solution.

(4) Check IV solution for damage to the container and the fluid for discoloration.

(5) Inspect the infusion site for infiltration or thrombophlebitis.

(6) Observe temperature, pulse respiration, and blood pressure.

2. **Total parenteral nutrition (TPN)** A method of supplying all necessary nutrients via a central vein (subclavian). Also known as hyperalimentation and parenteral feeding.

a. Purposes of TPN

(1) To provide calories.

(2) To maintain a positive nitrogen balance (provide protein).

(3) To supply or replace needed electrolytes, vitamins, and minerals.

b. Adult postoperative caloric requirements

(1) Approximately 1500 calories a day is required to preserve body proteins.

(2) Complications such as fever and trauma require additional calories daily.

c. Types of patients requiring TPN

(1) Patients who are unable to digest any food given by mouth or by tube.

(2) Patients who cannot digest enough food to maintain an anabolic state (those with burns, multiple injuries, or Crohn's disease).

(3) Patients who are able to ingest food but refuse to do so (those with anorexia nervosa or psychiatric depressions).

(4) Patients who should not be fed by mouth or by tube (those with acute pancreatitis).

d. Composition of TPN mixture

(1) A hypertonic solution of glucose is the main source of calories in the solution. (Equal amounts of dextrose and amino acids are mixed. The final solution contains 25% dextrose and 6% amino acids and provides 1240 calories per liter.)

(2) Potassium is added to the solution to provide proper electrolyte balance and to transport the glucose and amino acids across the cell membrane. Other electrolytes (sodium, magnesium, chlorine, calcium, phosphorus) may be given in varying amounts according to patient's serum electrolytes.

(3) Multiple vitamin preparation and trace elements (copper, zinc, cobalt, manganese, iodine) are added to the solution.

(4) Fat emulsion (intralipid) can be administered simultaneously with intravenous hyperalimentation. Usually 500 ml of 10 percent emulsion is administered over 6 hours, 1 to 3 times a week. This can provide up to 30 percent of the total calorie intake.

(5) Partial nutrition, administered by peripheral vein, may be used to supplement oral intake. The usual length of therapy is less than 2 weeks.

e. Method of administration and catheter care

(1) A double-lumen Hickman/Broviac catheter or an atrial catheter may be used.

(2) The transparent dressing covering the catheter is changed q 48 hours.

   (a) Place the patient in supine position.

   (b) Mask yourself and the patient. Turn the patient's head from dressing site. Put on sterile gloves.

   (c) Remove old dressing, and inspect area around the catheter site for infection. Using a circular motion apply alcohol and cleanse with a Betadine swabstick. Cover with an occlusive, transparent, waterproof dressing. Write the date applied on the dressing.

f. Nursing diagnoses/goals/interventions

(1) Altered nutrition: less than body requirements related to inability to absorb nutrients via GI tract, inability to digest sufficient nutrients
Goal: Patient will receive adequate nutrition to restore and maintain health.
Interventions:

   (a) Assist with assessment of nutrition needs by maintaining accurate records of daily weights and intake and output.

   (b) Check drip rate every hour. Use electronic infusion pump.

   (c) Monitor blood and urine chemistries and complete blood count.

   (d) Monitor blood sugar according to method ordered (serum glucose or finger-prick glucose monitoring) every 4 hours during therapy.

   (e) Administer intralipids as ordered. Maintain an even flow rate with an electronic control device to prevent fatty acid overload; take daily blood studies to determine the level of free-floating triglycerides; perform hepatic function tests to monitor liver function; observe for complications.

      1. Immediate adverse reactions (up to $2^1/_2$ hours): rise in temperature, flushing, sweating, pressure sensation over the eyes, nausea, vomiting, headache, chest and back pains, dyspnea, cyanosis.

      2. Delayed adverse reactions (within 10 days): hepatomegaly, gastroduodenal ulcer, hepatic damage, hyperlipemia, splenomegaly, jaundice.

   If the patient experiences any of these reactions after fat emulsion therapy, notify the physician.
(Intralipids may be given via a peripheral vein because the solution is isotonic; they are occasionally piggybacked into TPN solution, sometimes given simultaneously via a second IV access site, sometimes given while TPN is turned off.)

   (f) Regularly measure the patient's fluid intake and output, caloric intake, and temperature.

(2) Risk for injury (air embolism, glucose imbalance, impaired catheter integrity) related to infusion of TPN via a central line.

(3) Risk for infection related to central-line TPN
Goal: Patient will be free from complications associated with parenteral nutrition.
Interventions:
(a) Prevent sepsis.

1. Refrigerate the solution at 4°C until 1 hour before administration.

2. Use aseptic technique when changing the dressing bottle or administration set. (Change every 24 hours.) Use administration set with 0.22-micron in-line filter to remove impurities.

3. Inspect the catheter site for inflammation and infection at each dressing change.

4. Take temperature and vital signs every 4 hours. Notify physician of temperature elevation.

(b) Do not allow bottle to run dry or to hang for more than 12 hours.

(c) Check for leak in catheter line or kinks in IV tubing. Tape all catheter connections securely.

(d) Do not use central venous line for drawing or giving blood or medications, or piggybacking other solutions.

(e) Ambulate the patient, using a rolling IV pole.

(f) Administer insulin coverage as ordered after finger-stick blood glucose or urine sugar; observe for hypoglycemia (sweating, pallor, palpitation, nausea, headache, hunger, shakiness, blurred vision) or hyperglycemia (nausea, weakness, thirst, headache, polyuria).

(g) Flush catheter with heparin solution between infusions if treatment is intermittent rather than continuous; clamp catheter with specially designed toothless, nontraumatic clamp between infusions; clamp tubing at a different place each time to prevent clot formation within catheter and breaks in catheter.

(4) Altered health maintenance related to digestive dysfunction

(5) Social isolation related to fear of being different

(6) Dysfunctional grieving related to loss of body function and inability to eat normally

(7) Ineffective individual coping related to altered health status
Goal: Patient will develop effective coping behavior to deal with a new method of nutritional support.
Interventions:

(a) Be an attentive, supportive listener during the patient's grief stage.

(b) Assess for fluid and electrolyte imbalance, sepsis, and protein imbalance if the patient demonstrates delirium.

(c) Assess for signs of depression and hopelessness; provide support and clarify facts as needed.

(d) Educate the patient regarding treatment and long-term needs.

(e) If the family is overprotective, work with members to encourage the patient to progress toward an independent lifestyle.

(f) Encourage the patient to participate in family meals. (Patient can tolerate small amounts of clear liquids during usual mealtimes.)

(g) Encourage the patient to resume normal work and leisure activities.

(h) Supply the name of a community resource, such as Lifeline Foundation, Inc., in order for the patient to obtain support and ideas for adaptation to condition.

(8) Knowledge deficit regarding new method of nutritional support
Goal: Patient will verbalize need for parenteral nutrition and will cooperate with treatment.
Interventions:

(a) Explain the treatment as the patient is interested. Keep explanation brief but include the need to keep head turned away from insertion site during dressing change, and to avoid turning suddenly or pulling at the dressing and thereby dislodging the catheter.

(b) Teach the patient how to monitor blood/urine glucose at home and to administer insulin if needed.

(c) Teach the patient to weigh him-/herself every day.

(d) Include the family/significant other in the instruction.

(e) Refer the patient/family/significant other to a support group.

(f) Provide referral for visiting nurse.

g. Evaluation

(1) Patient receives adequate nutrition.

(2) Patient is afebrile and free from injury.

(3) Patient progresses through the grief response appropriately.

(4) Patient resumes pre-illness work and leisure activities.

(5) Patient verbalizes home management regimen.

3. Administration of blood and blood products

a. Preparation

(1) Obtain blood from blood bank when transfusion is to begin. (If it must be held before administration, refrigerate. Do not allow blood to stand at room temperature for several hours.)

(2) Never warm blood. (This promotes the growth of organisms.)

(3) Use a blood administration set with a filter. (Strain precipitates of fibrin, platelets, or leukocytes.)

(4) Check and double-check the label on the blood container against the transfusion form for the patient's name, the hospital number, the bottle number, the patient's blood group and Rh status, and the donor blood group and Rh status. (Two people should do this checking.)

(5) Before administering blood, check for signs of contamination (discoloration, bubbles).

(6) Start the transfusion with an isotonic saline solution. (Glucose solution causes red cell hemolysis.)

b. Administration of blood

(1) Whole blood (used to treat massive hemorrhage or hypovolemic shock): Use standard blood filter. Administer blood at a rate of 20 to 40 drops per minute for the first 15 minutes. If no symptoms occur, administer between 80 and 100 drops per minute. Monitor vital signs every 15 minutes.

(2) Packed cells (red cells separated from whole blood; used in transfusion of anemic patient and surgical patient before and after surgery): Use standard blood filter. Administer 1 unit (250 cc) over 1 to 2 hours. Squeeze bag to mix cells every 20 to 30 minutes during administration.

(3) Platelets (removed from fresh blood or single-donor platelet apheresis; administered within 48 hours of collection): Use special nonwettable filter, and administer as rapidly as possible, usually within 4 hours. Each unit raises the recipient's platelet count by 10,000/cu ml.

(4) Granulocytes (normal white cells): Use standard blood filter. Do not use microaggregate filter. Administer over 2 to 4 hours.

(5) Plasma (fresh frozen, contains all the coagulation factors and can be stored for 12 months; used for patient who is hemorrhaging and being massively transfused with whole blood): Use straight line set. Administer as rapidly as tolerated.

(6) Factor VIII (used in treatment of hemophilia A, Von Willeband's disease, DIC, and uremic bleeding): Use standard syringe or component drip set.

(7) Factor IX concentrate (used in treatment of hemophilia B— Christmas disease): Administer same as Factor VIII.

(8) Prothrombin complex (contains Factors VII, IX, and X; used in treatment of acquired or congenital defect in these factors): Use straight line set.

c. Management of possible complications

(1) Observe for hemolytic transfusion reaction, caused by the administration of mismatched blood.

(a) Clinical manifestations: chills, fever, hematuria, oliguria, jaundice, headache, backaches, dyspnea, cyanosis, chest pain.

(b) Nursing role if manifestations occur

1. Disconnect transfusion set. Keep intravenous line open with saline solution in case intravenous medication should be needed rapidly.
2. Notify the physician and laboratory or blood bank.
3. Administer oxygen and other ordered drugs.
4. Take vital signs every 15 minutes.
5. Save the blood bag and tubing. They should be sent to blood bank for repeat typing and culture.
6. Insert Foley catheter, measure urine hourly, and record intake and output.
7. Observe for oliguria.
8. Alleviate the patient's anxiety.
9. Notify blood bank that a suspected transfusion reaction has occurred.

(2) Observe for bacterial reaction, most frequently caused by the administration of contaminated blood.
  (a) Clinical manifestations: fever, chills, peripheral vasodilation (warm, dry, pink skin), weakness, lumbar pain, diarrhea.
  (b) Nursing role if manifestations occur
    1. Discontinue blood immediately.
    2. Notify the physician.
    3. Change the administration set, and start an IV of dextrose in water.
    4. Return donor blood and sample of patient's blood to laboratory for culture and sensitivity tests.
    5. Take temperature and vital signs every 15 to 30 minutes.
    6. Insert Foley catheter and record intake and output.
    7. Initiate cooling measures ordered (sponge baths, antipyretics, hypothermic blanket) if temperature is above 101°F.

(3) Observe for signs of allergic reactions, caused by recipient's allergy to foods or drugs that the donor consumed. These reactions are common and usually mild.
  (a) Clinical manifestations: hives, wheezing, urticaria.
  (b) Nursing role if manifestations occur
    1. Slow blood if reaction is mild; discontinue if severe and connect IV fluids.
    2. Notify the physician.
    3. Administer antihistamine (Benadryl) to control itching and relieve edema.
(4) Observe for circulatory overload, caused by too rapid administration of transfusion, or quantity of fluid that is too great for circulatory system.
  (a) Clinical manifestations: respiratory distress (cough, dyspnea, rales), tachycardia, hemoptysis, and pink-tinged sputum.
  (b) Nursing role if manifestations occur
    1. Discontinue transfusion.
    2. Administer oxygen.
    3. Place the patient in Fowler's position to facilitate breathing.
    4. Administer medications as ordered (digitalis, Lasix).

4. Enteral feedings. Nasogastric tube is passed through the nose into the stomach; nasoenteric tube is passed into the stomach and through the pylorus into the duodenum or proximal jejunum with a weighted-tip catheter.
  a. Preparation
    (1) Formula and/or medication (commercially prepared feedings include Compleat B, Ensure)
      (a) Refrigerate formula prepared by dietary department.
      (b) Check dietary-prepared formula for spoilage. (Formulas are dated; discard day-old formulas.)

(c) Warm container with blenderized meal in a bowl of hot water. (Heating can destroy vitamins and proteins; canned formulas are kept at room temperature.)

(d) Crush dry medications and mix with a small amount of water.

(e) Administer medication separately, just before feeding.

(2) Feeding schedule

(a) Intermittent feeding—every 4 to 6 hours (by suspended container).

(b) Continuous controlled pump.

(3) Patient position

(a) Place the patient in semi-Fowler's or left-side position with head elevated (30 degrees).

(b) Have the patient remain in this position for a minimum of 30 minutes after feeding.

b. Nursing diagnoses/goals/interventions

(1) Altered nutrition: less than body requirement related to inadequate intake of nutrition

Goal: Patient will attain/maintain nutritional balance.

Interventions:

(a) Check the position and patency of the tube.

(b) Aspirate and measure stomach content. If more than 150 ml, delay feeding.

(c) If aspirated amount is one half or less of total to be fed, return to stomach.

(d) Give feeding slowly by gravity flow: 200 to 350 ml in 15 minutes; 50 to 100 ml at a time if intermittent, 40 to 60 ml/per hour if continuous fluid, for a total of 2,400 to 3,600 calories per day.

(e) Give 50 ml of water before and after feeding (intermittent).

(f) Give 250 cc of free water every 4 hours.

(2) Diarrhea related to the dumping syndrome

Goal: Patient will maintain a normal bowel pattern.

Interventions:

(a) Decrease the instillation rate to provide for carbohydrate and electrolytes to be diluted.

(b) Give feedings at room temperature to prevent stimulation of peristalsis.

(c) Administer feeding by continuous drip rather than bolus.

(d) Advise the patient to stay in semi-Fowler's position for 30 minutes after each feeding.

(e) Instill minimal amount of water needed to flush the tubing before and after feeding.

(3) Risk for ineffective airway clearance related to aspiration of tube feeding

Goal: Patient will maintain a patent airway.

Interventions:

(a) Check tube placement before administering feeding.

(b) Administer feeding with the patient in semi-Fowler's position and his/her head elevated at least 30 degrees for nasoenteric feedings.

(c) If aspiration is suspected, remove the nasogastric tube and notify the physician.

(4) Ineffective coping related to discomfort imposed by the presence of the nasogastric/nasoenteric tube

Goal: Patient will improve in individual coping.

Interventions:

(a) Praise the patient when he/she adheres to medical plan of care.

(b) Encourage self-care within parameters of activity level.

(c) Reinforce an optimistic approach by mentioning signs and symptoms that indicate progress (daily weight gain, electrolyte balance, absence of diarrhea and nausea).

(5) Knowledge deficit regarding home-care management

Goal: Patient will verbalize understanding of home-care management.

Interventions:

(a) Teach the procedure, and reinforce the mechanics, while administering feedings.

(b) Before discharge, give information about the equipment, formula purchase and storage, and administration of feedings (frequency, quantity, rate of instillation).

(c) Include in teaching sessions family members who will participate in patient's home care.

(d) Give available printed information about the delivery system and formula after reviewing it.

(e) Monitor a return demonstration by the patient and a family member.

(f) Refer to Community Nurse Service.

c. Evaluation

(1) Patient attains/maintains nutritional balance.

(2) Patient is free from episodes of diarrhea.

(3) Patient's airway is patent.

(4) Patient copes with the tube-feeding regimen.

(5) Patient understands the home-care regimen.

d. Management of the patient with a gastrostomy

This is similar to the care of the patient with a nasogastric/nasoenteric tube with the addition of one nursing diagnosis: Potential for skin integrity impairment related to enteral feeding.

5. Suctioning

a. Nasotracheal suctioning

(1) Equipment: sterile catheters (adult size No. 14 and No. 16 French), sterile gloves, sterile saline, suction machine (in absence of wall suction), small Y-tube if catheters do not have suction control.

(2) Procedure

(a) Turn on suction; then put on sterile gloves.

(b) Lubricate catheter with saline and check for patency.

(c) Do not create suction when introducing catheter.

(d) Advance catheter into nares as far as possible; create suction intermittently while withdrawing catheter. (Period of suction should last for 15 seconds.)

(e) Withdraw catheter with a rotary movement.

(f) If the patient appears anoxic, administer oxygen.

b. Tracheostomy suctioning

(1) Equipment

(a) This is the same as for nasotracheal suctioning (catheter size should be smaller than trach tube).

(b) Sterile normal saline (3 to 5 ml) is inserted into the tube before suctioning if the secretion is thick.

(c) Hand resuscitator (ambu bag) is provided for the patient's use only and is changed daily.

(2) Procedure

(a) Auscultate chest before and after suctioning. Wash hands; fill basin with sterile normal saline.

(b) Preoxygenate the patient with a ventilation bag for 1 to 2 minutes. Instill normal saline if needed.

(c) Position the patient's head to the appropriate side to reach the desired bronchus (e.g., right side for left bronchus).

(d) Turn on suction; put on sterile gloves; pick up suction catheter with gloved hand.

(e) Lubricate catheter with saline, and check catheter patency.

(f) Insert catheter 6 to 8 inches or until an obstruction is felt, then pull catheter back slightly. (Catheter will enter right bronchus if head is turned to left side, left bronchus if head is turned to right side.)

(g) AVOID APPLYING SUCTION DURING INSERTION.

(h) Slowly withdraw catheter, rotating and intermittently applying suction.

(i) Suction for no longer than 5 seconds.

(j) Oxygenate the patient, using ventilation bag; then suction again if necessary.

(k) Repeat suctioning procedure on opposite bronchus.

(3) Precaution: Keep clamp at bedside, to be used to keep trachea wound open if the inner cannula is completely expelled.

Alterations in Respiration and Carbon Dioxide Exchange

A. General Assessment
  1. General factors
     a. Age. Aging causes a decrease in ventilatory capacity.
     b. Body size. Body size affects metabolic needs, which in turn affect respirations.
     c. Posture. The posture assumed determines the extent, severity, and type of breathing disorder.
     d. Respiratory movements. These are observable signs of a breathing struggle.
     e. Speech. Mannerisms and characteristics are affected by breathing.
     f. Skin. Texture reflects hydration status; color indicates oxygen status.
     g. Sensorium. Orientation, degree of alertness, and emotional expression are affected by oxygen status.
     h. Vital signs and temperature. These are indicators of the condition of body processes.
     i. Health history. Smoking, occupation, allergies, and family history are relevant.
  2. Chest
     a. Inspect for deformities and abnormalities in rate and rhythm of breathing.
     b. Palpate to identify areas of tenderness and abnormality, to obtain more data on respiratory movements, and to elicit vocal or tactile fremitus.
     c. Percuss to determine whether tissues are air filled, fluid filled, or solid.
     d. Auscultate to identify, describe, and locate abnormal breath sounds.
  3. Respiratory symptoms
     a. Cough—presence, character, onset.
     b. Sputum—amount, color, consistency, odor.
     c. Dyspnea—onset, type of wheezing (inspiration, expiration), precipitating factors.
     d. Chest pain—location, intensity, quality, precipitating factors.
     e. Hemoptysis—location of source, color.
     f. Pneumothorax—onset of dyspnea, presence and location of pain.
     g. Hemothorax—onset of dyspnea, presence and location of pain.
     h. Hydrothorox—onset of dyspnea, presence and location of pain.
     i. Atelectasis. *See* Section G6, Atelectasis, page 281.
  4. Systemic signs and symptoms: fever, cyanosis, clubbing of fingers and toes.
  5. Diagnostic measures
     a. Radiology examinations
        (1) Chest X-ray.
        (2) Fluoroscopy.
        (3) **Tomography** Visualization of the lung at different planes.
        (4) **Bronchogram** An outline of the bronchial tree after introduction of an opaque medium.
           (a) The patient receives NPO for 6 to 12 hours before the test.
           (b) After the test the patient is not allowed oral intake until cough reflex returns.
        (5) **Angiographic studies of pulmonary vessels** Examination of the outline of the chest vasculature after injection of a radiopaque medium.
     b. **Perfusion lung scan (gallium scan, bronchial brushing, ventilation scan)** Measurement of the perfusion of blood through the lung after the injection of a radioactive isotope.
     c. **Bronchoscopy** Examination of the interior of the tracheobronchial tree through a lighted tube containing mirrors; also used to remove foreign objects. Anesthetic, local or general, may be used. Diazepam (Valium) may be prescribed before examination.
        (1) Nursing role
           (a) Before the test, have the patient remove contact lenses, dentures, and other prostheses.
           (b) Assist the patient to maintain hyperextended position during the test.

(c) After the test, observe the patient for impaired respiration and bleeding.

(d) Maintain NPO until gag reflex returns.

d. **Sputum studies** Examination of sputum to identify the pathogenic organism and determine the presence of malignant cells.

(1) Nursing role

(a) Obtain a morning specimen.

(b) Instruct the patient to clear nose and throat, rinse mouth, and take a few deep breaths; then have him/her cough up specimen from lung and tracheobronchial tree.

(c) Send the specimen to the laboratory immediately, or refrigerate to prevent overgrowth of organism.

(d) Obtain specimen for culture before initiating anti-infectives.

e. **Thoracentesis** Aspiration of pleural fluid for diagnostic or therapeutic purposes.

(1) Nursing role

(a) Support and reassure the patient during the procedure.

(b) Observe the patient after the procedure for faintness, hemoptysis, coughing, and rapid pulse.

f. **Biopsy** Microscopic examination of tissue, obtained by needle or surgical exposure, from any of various sites, such as the pleura, lung, scalene, and mediastinal nodes.

(1) Nursing role. After needle aspiration, inspect the patient's sputum for blood, and observe the patient for respiratory distress.

g. Pulmonary function tests

(1) Purposes

(a) To follow the course of a patient with established respiratory disease and assess his/her response to therapy.

(b) To serve for screening in potentially hazardous industries (coal mining, asbestos).

(2) Factors measured: lung volume and capacity, flow, compliance and resistance, diffusion characteristics, oxygen consumption, respiratory quotient, ventilation, and perfusion.

h. Arterial blood gas studies

(1) Factors measured

(a) Oxygen (pO_2); normal values: 93–98%

(b) Carbon dioxide (pCO_2); normal values: 36–42 mm Hg (39)

(c) pH; normal values: 7.38–7.44 (7.41)

(d) Bicarbonate (HCO_3) concentration; normal values: 25–28 meq/L (26.5)

(2) Factors evaluated: rate of cellular metabolism, tissue perfusion, ventiliation efficiency, ability of hemoglobin to transport oxygen and carbon dioxide, buffer system. Blood is obtained from radial, brachial, or femoral artery.

i. Skin tests

Types commonly used

(1) Tests for allergies.

(2) Schick test—measures immunity to diphtheria.

(3) Fungal tests—employ coccidioidin and histoplasmin.

(4) Tuberculin tests—identify tuberculosis infection.

(a) Mantoux (intradermal; the method of choice)

1. Five tuberculin units of intermediate-strength purified protein (PPD) is commonly used.

2. The test is read 48 to 72 hours after injection.

3. The injected area is inspected for the presence of induration (hardening or thickening of tissues).

4. An area of induration 10 mm or more in diameter is interpreted as a positive reaction.

(b) Tine (multiple-puncture; used for surveying and screening large groups. Less accurate than the Mantoux but has the advantages of being easy to apply and using disposable equipment).

1. The test is read on the 3rd day after administration.

2. The presence of vesiculation is interpreted as a positive reaction.

3. All positive reactors should be retested with the Mantoux test and should have a chest X-ray.

B. General Patient Care Management
1. Drug therapy
   a. Antihistamines to block the effects of histamines; used to treat disorders caused by allergic reaction.
      (1) Side effects: drowsiness, dry mouth, blurred vision
      (2) Drugs used: Chlor-Trimeton, Benadryl, Pyribenzamines, Dimetane.
   b. Antimicrobials
      Types used to combat pulmonary infections: tetracycline, penicillin, cephalosporin antibiotics (Keflin), amoxicillin, sulfonamides, erythromycin.
   c. Bronchodilators, administered via IV, orally, and subcutaneously, and via hand-held inhalation routes, and IPPB device.
      (1) Sympathomimetic medications
         (a) Side effects: headaches, nausea, anxiety, palpitations, tachycardia.
         (b) Drugs used: epinephrine hydrochloride (adrenalin), Isuprel, Brethine, Alupent, Bronkosol.
      (2) Theophylline preparations
         (a) Side effects: gastrointestinal upset, nervousness, insomnia, headache, tachycardia, hypotension.
         (b) Drugs used: aminophylline, theophylline.
   d. Cough medications
      (1) Antitussive agents to inhibit the cough reflex in the cough center. Drugs used: Tessalon, codeine phosphate, Romilar, Hycodan, Robitussin DM. Side effects: very rare; usually limited to gastrointestinal upset.
      (2) Mucolytics Agents used: Mucomyst, which reduces the viscosity of secretions and water.
   e. Corticosteroid to control the symptoms of asthma; used when conventional therapy is unsuccessful
      Drugs used: Solu-Cortef, Medrol, prednisone, Vanceril (metered dose inhaler).
   f. Antiallergenic
      Drug used: cromolyn sodium (Intal).
   g. Narcotic antagonists to overcome respiratory depression caused by narcotic drugs
      Drugs used: Nalline, Lorfan.
   h. Vasoconstrictors and decongestants, used to treat allergic reactions; administered topically, parenterally, or orally
      Drugs used: ephedrine, Isuprel, Neo-Synephrine.
2. Chest physiotherapy
   a. Breathing exercises
      (1) Purposes
         (a) To promote muscle relaxation.
         (b) To relieve anxiety.
         (c) To assist the patient in energy conservation.
         (d) To slow the respiratory rate.
      (2) Types
         (a) Diaphragmatic
            1. Serves to increase the use of the diaphragm during breathing.
            2. Can become automatic with sufficient practice.
         (b) Pursed-lip (positive pressure breathing). Patient breathes through nose while counting to 3. Exhales slowly and evenly against pursed lip while tightening the abdominal muscle, and counts to 7 while prolonging expiration.
            1. Improves oxygen transport and helps to induce a slow, deep breathing pattern.
            2. May be used to cope with shortness of breath while walking or climbing stairs.
      (3) Nursing role (patient education)
         (a) Breathe slowly and rhythmically in a relaxed manner to permit complete exhalation and emptying of lung.
         (b) Inhale through the nose. (The nose filters, humidifies, and warms the air.)
         (c) Schedule sessions 2 to 4 times daily.
         (d) Discontinue breathing exercises if shortness of breath occurs.

(e) Exercises may be practiced in several positions but are often performed lying flat on a firm surface.

b. Postural drainage

(1) Purpose: to clear the lungs of secretions by using gravity to move the secretions to the main bronchi and trachea, where they are removed by coughing.

(2) Schedule: usually done 4 times daily (before meals and at bedtime).

(3) Methods

(a) Patient remains for 10 to 15 minutes in one position.

(b) Patient changes to several different positions, remaining in any one for a few seconds.

(4) Nursing role

(a) Give bronchodilator aerosol medications, if ordered, before procedure.

(b) Make the patient comfortable in each position.

(c) Instruct the patient to cough when position is changed.

(d) After procedure, note the amount, color, viscosity, and character of ejected sputum.

(e) If necessary, administer oxygen during procedure.

(f) Evaluate the patient's color and pulse the first few times the exercise is performed.

c. Percussion and vibration

(1) Purpose is to aid in loosening and removing thicker secretions.

(2) Physiotherapy is performed while the patient is in postural drainage position(s).

(3) Percussion is continued for 1 to 2 minutes over the involved area and is followed by vibration.

(4) Vibration is performed only while the patient exhales.

(5) After vibration the patient is encouraged to cough, using the abdominal muscles.

(6) Secretions can be moved by the patient by making tapping movements on the chest.

(7) Breath sounds are evaluated after percussion and vibration.

3. Respiratory therapy

a. Oxygen therapy

(1) Goal: to treat hypoxemia while decreasing the work of breathing and the stress on the myocardium.

(2) Assessment

(a) Observe the patient for a change in his/her respiration, which is often evidence of the need for oxygen therapy.

(b) Observe the patient for other signs of hypoxia: change in mental status, dyspnea, increase in blood pressure, change in heart rate, arrhythmias, cyanosis (late sign), cool extremities.

(3) Precautions

(a) Excessive oxygen may produce toxic effects on the lungs and central nervous system and/or result in depression of ventilation in certain conditions.

(b) Oxygen supports combustion; therefore oxygen equipment should be handled carefully, and a "NO SMOKING" sign posted when oxygen is in use.

(c) Breathing circuits (masks and tubings) should be changed and sterilized daily to prevent bacterial cross-infection.

(d) Oxygen should be humidified before it is supplied to the patient to prevent drying and irritation of the mucous membranes.

(4) Common methods of administration

(a) Nasal cannula—used to administer between 3 and 5 liters of oxygen.

(b) Face mask—used to deliver high concentrations (3 to 5 liters) of oxygen.

(c) Venturi mask—administers precisely controlled oxygen concentrations (4 to 6 liters).

b. Intermittent positive pressure breathing (IPPB)

(1) Actions: delivers aerosols to the lung that mobilize secretions and promote coughing; assists in ventilation in order to decrease the work of breathing; prevents atelectasia.

    (2) Precaution: Nebulizer devices should be changed and sterilized to prevent pulmonary infection and possible superinfection.

    (3) Nursing role

      (a) Calm the anxious dyspneic patient.

      (b) Reinforce the teaching concerning the use of the machine.

  c. Incentive spirometer—maximizes voluntary lung inflation. Should be used 10 to 20 times every hour.

4. General nursing role for drug therapy, chest physiotherapy, and respiratory therapy

  a. Encourage the patient to maintain correct posture (head and chest elevated) to ease breathing.

  b. Provide frequent oral hygiene to remove the unpleasant taste and odor of sputum.

  c. Provide small, frequent meals served in a pleasant environment.

  d. Provide a supportive, nonthreatening environment.

  e. Observe a patient receiving corticosteroids or antimetabolites for signs of infection.

  f. Administer antibiotics as prescribed.

  g. Protect the patient from persons with upper respiratory or other infections.

  h. Provide patient education.

    (1) Avoid irritants (i.e., cigarette smoke, dust, fumes, and known allergenics).

    (2) Avoid gas-forming foods (restrict ventilation by producing abdominal distension).

    (3) Have an ample fluid intake (3000 to 4000 ml daily) to liquefy bronchopulmonary secretions.

    (4) Avoid extremely cold or hot fluids.

    (5) Adequately humidify the air to prevent the drying of secretions.

    (6) Use an air conditioner to filter, cool, and recirculate air.

    (7) Prevent the development of new infections.

      (a) Dress appropriately ̠during cold or damp weather.

      (b) Avoid excessive exertion in very cold or humid environments.

      (c) Avoid crowds during periods when respiratory infections are prevalent.

      (d) Follow the doctor's advice concerning influenza shots and antibiotics.

5. **Tracheostomy** A *tracheotomy* is an operation in which an opening is made into the trachea. When an indwelling tube is inserted into the trachea, the term *tracheostomy* is used. A tracheostomy, which may be either temporary or permanent, is done to bypass an upper airway obstruction, to remove tracheobronchial secretions, to permit the use of mechanical ventilation, to prevent aspiration of oral or gastric secretions in an unconscious or paralyzed patient by closing off the trachea from the esophagus, and to replace an endotracheal tube.

The procedure is usually done in an area where respiration can be well controlled, that is, the operating room or intensive care unit. The tracheostomy is held in place by tape fastened around the patient's neck.

The cuff on a tracheostomy tube should be *deflated* except in the following situations: during and after eating, or during and 1 hour after tube feeding; during IPPB treatment; at any time when there is increased risk of aspiration. The cuff is *inflated* until a seal (contact with the tracheal wall) is established. The optimal cuff pressure is 15 to 25 cm H_2O.

  a. Nursing diagnoses/goals/interventions

    (1) Ineffective airway clearance related to inability to expel excess secretions

    Goal: Patient will maintain a patent airway.

    Interventions:

      (a) Record respiratory rate and characteristics every 4 hours; auscultate chest.

      (b) Suction every 2 to 4 hours as needed; record color, consistency, and amount of secretions.

      (c) Observe for restlessness, anxiety, stridor, tachycardia, cyanosis; monitor blood gases if ordered, especially pCO_2.

      (d) Assess for tactile fremitus.

      (e) Provide humidification.

      (f) Administer a fluid intake of 2,000 cc daily.

      (g) Elevate head of bed, or place patient in semi-Fowler's position.

(h) Keep obstructive material such as sheet or cotton away from stoma.

(i) Tape obstructor to head of bed; maintain an extra tracheostomy set/hemotat at bedside.

(j) Provide tracheostomy care every 8 hours or as necessary. Keep ties/tape securely knotted; tie tape on the side, instead of the back, of the neck for comfort; do not remove old ties until new tapes are in place or unless a second person holds the flange in place.

(k) Flex the patient's neck and thrust chin downward to facilitate swallowing of food and fluids; inflate cuff during and 30 minutes after each feeding.

(2) Risk for infection related to altered pattern of ventilation, ineffective airway clearance
Goal: Patient will remain free from infection.
Interventions:

(a) Inspect skin around the stoma for signs of inflammation every 2 to 4 hours during the first few days postoperatively, then at least every 8 to 12 hours.

(b) Use sterile technique in suctioning the patient and in performing tracheostomy care.

(c) Change the external dressing and ties when wet or soiled.

(d) Administer prophylactic antibiotics if prescribed, carefully monitoring for effectiveness.

(e) Apply providone-iodine ointment around the stoma, and cover with a sterile dressing.

(3) Impaired communication: verbal related to effects of tracheostomy
Goal: Patient will establish an effective communication method.
Interventions:

(a) Provide pad and pencil or erasable slate for writing.

(b) Arrange signal for bells or buzzer.

(c) Work out an alternative method of communication for common needs (e.g., tongue clicks, eye blinks, finger taps).

(4) Anxiety related to weaning process
Goal: Patient and significant other will express decreasing anxiety; patient will ventilate through nose, pharynx, larynx, and trachea.
Interventions:

(a) Explain the process to the patient and significant other carefully, showing a fenestrated tracheostomy tube.

(b) Begin by suctioning the tracheostomy thoroughly.

(c) Deflate the cuff; remove inner cannula; clean and store in hydrogen peroxide.

(d) Insert the plug in outer cannula for 5 to 10 minutes; monitor the patient constantly for any signs of respiratory distress.

(e) Do not leave the patient unattended while tube is plugged.

(f) At the end of 10 minutes, remove the plug; rinse inner cannula in saline solution and reinsert.

(g) Over a period of days, gradually increase the time the outer cannula is plugged.

(h) Decrease the size of the tube, or remove tube, as ordered by physician; cover stoma with light dressing until edges are closed.

(5) Knowledge deficit related to tracheostomy care
Goal: Patient and significant other will suction the airway, will provide routine care, and will know how to manage problems related to the care of the tracheostomy.
Interventions:

(a) Implement the teaching plan with the patient and/or significant other.

(b) Allow the patient to increase the amount of self-care while hospitalized.

(c) Advise the patient to avoid swimming; a shower may be taken, if directed, below the stoma or if the patient uses a water-mask.

(d) Review the physician's instructions with the patient regarding what to do for dislodged tube.

(e) Suggest using a porous covering for the stoma to filter out dust and foreign objects.

(f) Recommend wearing a Medic-Alert bracelet to advise of tracheostomy.

b. Evaluation

(1) Patient breathes easily with a respiration rate between 8 and 20.

(2) Patient remains afebrile, and stoma skin is clean and dry.

(3) Patient expresses decreased anxiety about the weaning process and breathes through normal passages.

(4) Patient and significant other demonstrate ability to care for tracheostomy, and can describe the process for reinserting the outer cannula and avoiding aspiration.

6. **Mechanical ventilation**   A positive/negative pressure breathing device that can maintain respiration automatically for an extended period of time. The indication for mechanical ventilation is acute respiratory failure (elevated pCO_2 and pH). The mechanical ventilator delivers oxygen to the lungs, but gas exchange occurs within the alevoli.

a. Types of positive pressure ventilators.

(1) Volume-cycled ventilators (most commonly used) deliver a preset volume of air. Popular models are Servo 900, OHIO 560, Bennett MA-2, and Bourns Bear 1 and 2.

(2) Pressure-cycled ventilators (often used for a short period of time—24 hours or less) force air into the lungs until a predetermined airway pressure is reached. Common models are Bennett PR-1 and PR-2, Monaghan 300, and bird Mark 7 and 8.

(3) Time-cycled ventilators (used primarily for children) terminate or control inspiration after a preset time. Common models are Baby Bennett, Monaghan 225, and Bennett PR-2.

b. Features and setting of volume-cycled ventilators

(1) MA-2, FIO_2 40%, VT 800 cc, SIMV 8

(a) MA-2   gives a preset volume of air with the breaths it delivers.

(b) FIO_2 40%   40% is the fraction of inspired air or the concentration delivered (the concentration can vary from 21% to 100%).

(c) VT 800 cc   tidal volume; 800 the amount of air the machine has been set to deliver with each ventilator breath.

(d) SIMV 8   indicates the mode of ventilation, the way the patient receives breaths from the ventilator, and the number of breaths he/she gets per minute.

(2) Setting

(a) SMVT stands for synchronized intermittent mandatory ventilation. This setting is used to wean a patient from the ventilator; the number of ventilation breaths are gradually decreased.

(b) Other modes of ventilation

1. Controlled: The ventilator delivers a predetermined volume at a fixed rate. The breaths are not synchronized with the patient's breaths. The patient may need a sedative or paralyzing agent to diminish or eliminate his/her own respiratory efforts.

2. Assisted: The ventilator augments the patient's own breaths with an additional preset volume.

3. Assist-controlled: The ventilator assists the patient unless he/she stops breathing. Then the ventilator delivers automatically a predetermined volume.

c. Endotracheal care

(1) A tube is inserted through the nose or mouth, and then passed between the larynx and into the trachea.

(2) After intubation, the patient is checked for bilateral breath sounds and the tube is marked at the point where it exits from the nose or mouth and is secured with tape.

(3) A chest X-ray should be taken to verify placement. (*See* Management of Cuff under Tracheostomy, above.)

d. Dealing with ventilator problems
   (1) Primary concern   When a ventilator alarm sounds, the primary concern is to maintain the patient's respiratory status; therefore the first and last measure is the assessment of the patient.
   (2) Causes for ventilator alarm to sound and management approaches
      (a) Patient is in respiratory distress. Management: Disconnect the patient from the machine and manually ventilate. Check for bilateral breath sounds: if coarse, suction ET tube; if absent, check ET placement; if displaced or pneumothorax or bronchospasm is suspected, notify physician.
      (b) Patient is disconnected from the machine.
         Management: Reconnect the patient to the machine.
      (c) Patient shows no sign of respiratory distress.
         Management: Determine which alarm is sounding. *High-pressure alarm:* check bilateral breath sounds for equal expansion (see Management in (a) above); check to see if the patient is biting ET tubes—apply bite block; check for kinks in tubing—straighten tubing; check for water in tubing—drain water. *Low-pressure alarm:* Check for leaks in the system: tighten or reconnect tubing, deflate the ET tube cuff, reinflate to check for leaks; if cuff leak is found, notify physician.
e. Nursing diagnoses/goals/interventions
   (1) Ineffective breathing pattern related to bronchospasm, mucosal edema, hypoxemia, hypercapnea
   (2) Ineffective airway clearance related to bronchospasm, inability to expectorate excessively thick secretions, mucosal edema
   (3) Impaired gas exchange related to hyperinflation of alevoli, ventilator/perfusion mismatch

Goal: Patient will maintain optimal ventilation with mechanical assistance, will maintain a clear airway, and will resume normal breathing patterns after removal of ventilator.
Interventions:
   (a) Monitor respiratory status every 1 to 2 hours, auscultate and document breath sounds, and inspect and record chest movements and use of accessory muscles.
   (b) Verify that endotracheal or tracheal tube is secured in place and that ventilator settings and cuff pressure, when applicable, are as ordered; record every 8 hours or whenever changes are made.
   (c) Administer humidified air; monitor level of water in reservoir every 8 hours; validate patency of all tubing; remove pooled liquids; reconnect tubing securely.
   (d) Check ventilator alarm system every 8 hours to ensure that it is in the "ON" position at all times.
   (e) Monitor the patient's response to mechanical ventilation.
   (f) Suction every 2 hours as necessary (*see* Suctioning, page 285).
   (g) Monitor arterial blood gases, and notify the physician of changes.
   (h) Observe the patient for signs of "fighting" the ventilator; if necessary, initiate appropriate action to correct the situation; note results of nursing action.
   (i) Observe the patient carefully if Pavulon (to paralyze the respiratory muscles) is prescribed to correct "fighting" the ventilator.
(4) Risk for infection related to inability to expel accumulated secretions
Goal: Patient will be free of infection.
Interventions: *See* Tracheostomy, above.

(5) Altered nutrition: less than body requirements related to increased metabolic demands secondary to illness

Goal: Patient will maintain or regain nutritional balance.

Interventions:

(a) Monitor skin turgor, inspect oral mucous membrane, check laboratory studies as ordered; report significant findings.

(b) Provide appropriate feeding as ordered (*see* Nasogastric and nasoenteric tube feeding, page 287, and Total parenteral nutrition, page 283).

(c) Encourage patient with tracheostomy to eat slowly; inflate cuff while eating and for 30 minutes after.

(d) Provide oral hygiene every 8 hours.

(e) Check stool for presence of occult/overt bleeding.

(f) Weigh daily or every other day; report a loss of more than 3 pounds.

(6) Impaired verbal communication related to intubation (*see* Tracheostomy, above)

(7) Dysfunctional ventilatory weaning response

Goal for diagnoses (6) and (7): Patient will experience decreased anxiety and/or relief from fear.

Interventions:

(a) Provide explanation for all nursing actions; repeat if necessary.

(b) Explain function of equipment in use at bedside and diagnostic procedure.

(c) Respond quickly to the patient's call for help.

(d) Medicate with prescribed bronchodilators, analgesics, sedatives, and hypnotics; observe patient's response, and notify physician.

(e) Decrease weaning procedure if blood pressure increases 20 mm and heart rate 20 beats and notify physician.

(f) Provide social service referral, and collaborate with discharge planner.

f. Evaluation

(1) Patient maintains optimal ventilation.

(2) Patient is afebrile.

(3) Patient has optimal nutritional status.

(4) Patient states that fear and/or anxiety has decreased and expresses understanding of equipment and procedures.

C. **Pneumonia** Acute inflammation of the alveolar spaces causing consolidation of the lung tissues; this results in the alveoli filling with exudates, disrupting oxygen and carbon dioxide exchange.

1. Causative agents

a. Bacterial: *Streptococcus pneumoniae* (pneumonococcus), *Staphylococcus aureus*, *Klebsiella*, *Pseudomonas aeruginosa*.

b. Nonbacterial: *Mycoplasma pneumoniae*, viruses (i.e., influenza, adenovirus, etc.), fungus.

2. Location

a. Lobar pneumonia—involves one or more lobes of the lung.

b. Bronchopneumonia—originates in one or more localized areas within the bronchi and extends to the surrounding lung tissues.

3. Types

a. *Streptococcus* pneumonia (pneumonococcal pneumonia).

b. *Mycoplasma* pneumonia (primary atypical pneumonia).

4. Assessment

a. Bacterial infection (*Streptococcus* pneumonia)

(1) Observe for sudden onset of shaking chills, stabbing chest pain that is aggravated by respiration and coughing, profuse sweating, flaring nares during inspiration, cyanosis of lips and nailbeds.

(2) Inspect sputum (rusty color during earlier stages, then becomes yellow and mucopurulent during resolution).

(3) Measure temperature and vital signs for rapidly rising temperature (101 to 105°F); rapid, bounding pulse; and increase in respiration.

(4) Auscultate chest for respiratory grunts, bronchial breathing, rales, and pleuritic friction rub; and abdomen for the presence of bowel sounds.

(5) Percuss lung and abdomen for dullness.

(6) Observe cough (initially dry and hacking, later becomes productive).

b. Nonbacterial infection (*Mycoplasma* pneumonia)

(1) Observe for severe frontal headache aggravated by coughing; harassing, nonproductive cough; tightness in the chest; and generalized aching.

(2) Inspect sputum (mucoid or mucopurulent sputum is expectorated).

(3) Measure temperature for elevation, and vital signs.

c. DIAGNOSTIC MEASURES: chest X-ray, sputum smear and culture, blood culture.

5. Nursing diagnoses/goals/interventions (*See also* General nursing role, page 294)

a. Ineffective airway clearance related to increased tracheobronchial secretions secondary to infectious process

b. Impaired gas exchange related to tracheobronchial secretions and lung consolidation with decreased ineffective lung surface

Goals:

(1) Patient will have adequate gas exchange.

(2) Patient will maintain a patent airway.

Interventions:

(1) Elevate head of bed 45 to 60 degrees.

(2) Initiate isolation precautions if ordered.

(3) Administer IPPB as ordered.

(4) Assist during coughing episodes: have patient sit upright, splint with pillow.

(5) Assist and teach the patient to turn and deep-breathe.

(6) Administer medications as ordered: antibiotics, analgesics, antipyretics, sedatives (avoid respiratory depressants), expectorants.

(7) Observe the patient for allergic reaction to penicillin. (Erythromycin, cephalothin, and clindamycin are alternative drugs.)

Monitor temperature for recurring fever from drug resistance, inappropriate antimicrobial therapy, or superinfection.

(8) Collect sputum for bacteriological study before initiating antibiotic therapy.

(9) Administer prescribed antibiotic at correct time intervals (penicillin and drug of choice for *Streptococcus* pneumonia; tetracycline or erythromysin drugs for *Mycoplasma* pneumonia).

c. Risk for alteration in body temperature regulation related to bacterial or viral infection

Goal: Patient's temperature will be in normal range.

Interventions:

(1) Monitor temperature and vital signs every 4 hours.

(2) Check sputum cultures as ordered.

(3) Administer antimicrobials and antipyretics.

(4) Encourage oral fluids as ordered.

(5) Administer cooling procedure as ordered.

(6) Isolate if ordered.

d. Pain related to respiratory distress and coughing

Goal: Patient will experience diminished pain.

Interventions:

(1) Encourage the patient to verbalize pain.

(2) Administer medication to treat cough.

(3) Administer analgesic as ordered; assess for depressed respiration; evaluate effectiveness of medications.

(4) Keep the patient warm and dry.

(5) Maintain planned rest periods.

(6) Discourage smoking.

(7) Administer oral hygiene every 2 to 4 hours after meals and prn; assess for lesions and dry mouth (keep ice chips at bedside).

e. Knowledge deficit regarding self-care management
Goal: Patient and/or significant other will demonstrate understanding of home-care and follow-up instructions.
Interventions:
(1) Explain the importance of avoiding transmission of disease: turn head away when coughing and cover mouth with tissues; use tissue once; dispose of tissues in waste container.
(2) Explain the importance of gradual convalesence: limit exercise and activity to tolerance; plan rest periods during the day.
(3) Explain the need to maintain diet as tolerated; force fluids up to 3000 cc daily.
(4) Explain the need to prevent recurrence of disease: keep warm; avoid chilling; avoid persons with infections, especially of the upper respiratory system; receive influenza vaccine as ordered.
(5) Explain the importance of ongoing outpatient care.
(6) Teach the patient the symptoms to report to the physician: elevated temperature, diaphoresis, difficulty in breathing, persistent coughing, and cold or flu.
(7) Explain the importance of postural drainage and deep-breathing exercises for 6 to 8 weeks; have patient and/or significant other return demonstration.

6. Evaluation
a. Patient maintains adequate gas exchange.
b. Patient maintains an effective breathing pattern.
c. Patient experiences decreased pain.
d. Infection is minimized.
e. Patient demonstrates knowledge of self-care management.

D. **Pulmonary Tuberculosis**   An infectious, communicable, inflammatory, chronic disease caused by *Mycobacterium tuberculosis*. It may occur in almost any part of the body, but the lungs are most frequently infected.
Mycobaterium tuberculosis is a rod-shaped, aerobic, nonmotile, acid-fast microorganism that reproduces very slowly. When the tubercle bacilli invade the lung, the body's defense mechanism (white blood cells and macro-phages) attempts to isolate and destroy the organism. If the organism continues to survive and multiply, a tubercle is formed. The central portion of the tubercle undergoes caseation (a process of degeneration). The lesion may then heal by resolution, or the center may soften and liquefy, spilling into the tracheobronchial tree, and be expectorated as sputum, leaving an air-filled cavity. Three to ten weeks after the first infection, cellular immunity develops. (This hypersensitivity is detected by tuberculin skin test and is usually successful in arresting the infection.)

1. Assessment
a. Observe for weight loss, dyspnea, fatigue, indigestion, pallor, cough, and sputum production.
b. Auscultate the lungs for rales and bronchial breath sounds.
c. Percuss the chest for dullness and bilateral, unequal lung expansion in chronic tuberculosis.
d. Inspect the sputum (yellow mucoid to blood tinged).
e. Observe the temperature for a pattern of elevation in the afternoon.
f. DIAGNOSTIC MEASURES: chest X-ray, tuberculin skin test, sputum examination.

2. Patient care management
a. Chemotherapy
(1) Two or more drugs are administered simultaneously to minimize the emergence of drug-resistant organisms.
(2) Choice of drug depends on the results of sputum studies and the extent of the disease.
(3) Treatment is continued until X-ray demonstrates improvement and negative sputum cultures are obtained.
(4) Drugs are bacteriostatic; therefore the therapy may continue for 2 years to allow the body defenses to contain the organism.
(5) Drugs are more effective when administered in a single daily dose.
(6) Two main types of drugs are used.
(a) Primary drugs
1. Isoniazid (INH)—300 mg daily
a. Pyridoxine is given to prevent neuritis.

b. Chemoprophylaxis users are as follows:

Tuberculin converters without the active disease.

Persons who have been in close contact with an individual with active tuberculosis.

Persons with silicosis.

Persons receiving long-term corticosteroid therapy.

2. Ethambutol—15 mg/kg of body weight daily.

3. Rifampin—600 mg, used with Isoniazid.

4. Streptomycin—1 gm IM, 2 to 3 times a week.

(b) Secondary drugs—used if patient is resistant to primary drugs. Examples: para-aminosalicylic, capreomycin, ethionamide, viomycin, kanamycin, cycloserine, pyrazinamide. (Note: Pyrazinamide, 3 gm daily, is used only in combination with primary drugs—INH, ethanbutol, rifampin, streptomycin—in resistant patients.)

(c) BCG (Bacille Calmette-Guerin)—used in areas of high tuberculosis outside the United States.

b. Surgical resection—performed when cancer coexists or the disease does not respond to chemotherapy.

c. Isolation—continued until symptoms have declined and there is absence of bacilli in sputum smear (usually achieved within 2 weeks after drug therapy starts).

d. Corticosteroids—used with antituberculosis drugs to alleviate symptoms.

3. Nursing diagnoses/goals/interventions

a. Ineffective breathing pattern related to decreased total lung capacity

Goal: Patient will achieve full lung expansion with adequate ventilation within limits of the disease.

Interventions:

(1) Check quality and depth of respiration.

(2) Provide frequent rest periods, avoid fatigue, and exercise to tolerance.

(3) Measure temperature and vital signs every 4 hours.

(4) Administer medication as prescribed, and observe for toxic effects.

(5) Perform cooling measures for high temperature, and provide dry linen when necessary.

(6) Offer frequent oral hygiene.

b. Risk for infection transmission related to noncompliance with medical regimen

Goal: Potential for infection transmission will be decreased.

Interventions:

(1) Prepare the patient for and assist with diagnostic and investigatory procedures.

(2) Maintain respiratory isolation.

(a) Any person entering the room must wear a mask.

(b) Hands must be washed on entering and leaving the room.

(c) All articles contaminated must be disinfected.

(3) Teach the patient to cough into tissues.

(4) Collect sputum for culture as ordered; avoid direct contact with sputum.

(5) See Interventions for diagnosis e, below.

c. Altered nutrition: less than body requirements related to chronic infection

Goal: Patient will attain/maintain optimal nutrition status.

Interventions:

(1) Obtain admission weight, and monitor weight daily.

(2) Maintain high-protein, high-carbohydrate diet with small, frequent feedings.

(3) Administer stool softeners, laxatives, or enemas as ordered.

(4) Provide dietary consultation.

(5) Monitor percentage of food eaten.

(6) Place the patient in semi-Fowler's position at meals to reduce dyspnea.

(7) Encourage the family/significant other to bring in patient's favorite food.

(8) Measure intake and output.

d. Noncompliance with treatment regimen related to alteration in perception and/or lack of motivation
Goal: Patient will follow recommended diet and medication regimen as ordered.
Interventions:
(1) Assess for evidence of noncompliance behavior (change in weight, alcohol or drug abuse).
(2) Evaluate the patient's health belief system, including spiritual and cultural factors.
(3) Arrange for social service and visiting nurse referral.
(4) Re-educate the patient to the importance of following the prescribed regimen.
(5) Discuss with the family or significant other possible reasons for noncompliant behavior.

e. Knowledge deficit regarding disease, medications, and self-care techniques
Goal: Patient will verbalize understanding of disease, medication and self-care technique.
Interventions:
(1) Provide patient education to prevent the spread of the disease.
(a) Take antituberculosis medication regularly as instructed.
(b) Cover nose and mouth with several layers of disposable tissue when coughing, sneezing, or laughing.
(c) Expectorate sputum into a disposable container or tissue.
(d) Avoid close contact with others until advised that such contact is safe.
(2) Instruct the patient and his/her family as to the nature of the disease and its treatment.

4. Evaluation
a. Patient maintains an effective breathing pattern.
b. Patient has a decreased potential for transmission of disease.
c. Patient maintains an adequate nutritional status.
d. Patient follows medical regimen as ordered.
e. Patient demonstrates increased level of knowledge regarding diet, treatment, and the disease process.

E. **Pleural Effusion**   Collection of fluid in the pleural space that is usually secondary to other disease (i.e., tuberculosis, pneumonia, neoplastic tumor).
1. Assessment
a. Observe for dry cough, dyspnea, pallor, and pleural pain.
b. Inspect the chest for distension and absence of movement during breathing.
c. Percuss chest for dullness or flatness over the area of the fluid.
d. Auscultate lungs for minimal breath sounds or their absence.
e. Measure temperature and vital signs for increased pulse rate and elevated temperature.
2. Patient care management
a. Thoracentesis to remove fluid, collect a specimen for analysis, and relieve dyspnea.
b. Treatment of underlying disease.
3. Nursing role. *See* General nursing role, page 294.

F. **Pulmonary Tumors**   A pulmonary tumor may be primary or represent metastasis from a primary tumor site. It usually arises in a segmented bronchus and then extends to surrounding areas.
Histologic types: epidermoid carcinoma (squamous cell, the most common type)—develops in the main bronchi or larger bronchial branches, metastasizes slowly, occurs most often in males and is associated with cigarette smoking; adenocarcinoma—develops in the small bronchi, is confined to one lobe of the lung, metastasizes by all routes, and occurs more often in women than in men; bronchiolar carcinoma (a rare, multinodular tumor)—involves the bronchiolar or alveolar lining and occurs more often in women; anaplastic or undifferentiated carcinoma— metastasizes early and occurs in males.
1. Assessment
a. Observe for persistent cough—initially a hacking, nonproductive cough, progressing to produce thick, purulent sputum.
b. Inspect sputum for blood.
c. Observe for signs of pulmonary infection (chill and fever), chest pain, dyspnea, and wheezing.
d. Observe the general appearance for weight loss, fatigue, and anorexia (occur late in the disease).

e. Inspect extremities for clubbing of fingers and toes and arthralgias.

f. Observe for central nervous manifestations (headache, diplopia).

g. DIAGNOSTIC MEASURES. *See* General Assessment, page 290.

2. Patient care management. *See also* Unit Seven, Neoplastic Disorders, Section D: Patient Care Management, page 185.

a. Surgery. *See* Section H, Management of the Patient Undergoing Chest Surgery, page 304.

b. Radiation.

c. Chemotherapy.

G. Traumatic Injuries of the Chest

Air enters the plural cavity, destroying the negative intrapleural pressure and resulting in collapse of the lung. Trauma to the parenchyma of the lung results in inadequate oxygenation of the blood, which leads to hypoxia.

1. Causes

a. Penetrating injuries (e.g., bullets, knives).

b. Nonpenetrating injuries (e.g., forceful contact with a blunt object, blast injury, radiation burn of the lung tissue, alteration in atmospheric pressure).

2. Assessment

a. Inspect and observe:

(1) Level of consciousness and emotional state.

(2) Presence and degree of pallor.

(3) Respiratory rate, rhythm, and quality.

(4) Character and amount of sputum.

(5) Wound for entrance and exit.

b. Palpate and percuss to:

(1) Determine equality and amplitude of pulse.

(2) Determine cardiac size and location of apical pulse.

(3) Evaluate chest expansion, and chest for area of hyperresonance or dullness.

(4) Determine areas of tenderness or pain, abnormal mobility of ribs or sternum, tracheal shifts, or crepitation.

c. Auscultate to:

(1) Evaluate breath sounds.

(2) Assess cardiac sounds.

d. Determine blood pressure in both arms and legs when indicated.

3. Nursing role

a. Maintain patent airway.

(1) Clear airway of obstructions.

(2) Suction.

(3) Position the patient to prevent aspiration.

(4) Turn the patient and encourage to cough every hour.

b. Maintain adequate ventilation.

(1) Administer oxygen as necessary.

(2) Monitor blood gas and the patient's general respiratory status.

(3) Maintain the head in an elevated position.

c. Maintain fluid and electrolytes.

(1) Monitor fluid/body drip rate.

(2) Observe for complications.

(3) Record intake and output.

d. Monitor vital signs every 15 minutes until stable, then every 1 to 2 hours.

e. Cautiously administer analgesic as indicated.

(1) Atropine, morphine, and barbituates are contraindicated.

(2) Small doses of meperidine (Demerol) should be given so that central nervous system depression will not occur.

f. Reassure the patient and enlist his/her cooperation.

g. Observe for signals of complications.

h. Assist with treatments (i.e., closed chest drainage, thoracotomy, nerve block).

4. Common types of injuries

a. Rib fractures (most commonly broken are the fifth and ninth ribs)

(1) Assessment

(a) Observe for pain over the affected area that is aggravated by coughing or deep breathing.

(b) Auscultate for rales.

(2) Nursing role

(a) Observe patient closely after administration of narcotic analgesics.

(b) Encourage deep breathing and coughing.

b. **Flail chest**   Loss of stability of the chest as the result of multiple rib fractures.

During inspiration the detached part of the chest (the flail segment) moves paradoxically (pulls inward instead of pushing outward), thus causing the mediastinum to shift to the normal side. On expiration the flail segment bulges outward, impairing the patient's ability to exhale and causing the mediastinum to shift to the injured side. This paradoxical action results in increased dead-space ventilation, retained airway secretions, and reduced alveolar ventilation.

(1) Assessment

    (a) Inspect the entire chest for paradoxical movement.

    (b) Palpate the entire throax.

(2) Nursing role

    (a) Prepare for and assist with tracheostomy. *See* Tracheostomy, page 294.

    (b) Attach patient to mechanical ventilator. *See* Mechanical ventilator, page 296.

5. Complications

  a. Hemothorax and pneumothorax

    (1) Definitions

      (a) **Hemothorax**   Collection of blood in the pleural cavity.

      (b) **Pneumothorax**   Air in the pleural cavity.

    (2) Assessment

      (a) Auscultate for diminished breath sounds.

      (b) Percuss for hyperresonance.

      (c) Inspect the patient for dyspnea and cyanosis.

    (3) Nursing role. *See also* General patient care management, page 292.

      (a) Prepare for and assist with thoracentesis and insertion of chest tube.

      (b) Monitor vital signs for shock.

  b. **Cardiac tamponade**   Compression of the heart as a result of fluid within the pericardial sac.

    (1) Assessment

      (a) Auscultate heart for distant or muffled sounds.

      (b) Monitor vital signs for a drop in blood pressure, fluctuating with respiration; narrowing pulse pressure; dyspnea; and tachypnea.

      (c) Inspect the patient for distended neck veins, cyanosis, and precardial pain.

    (2) Nursing role

      (a) Prepare and assist with pericardiocentesis.

      (b) Connect the patient to cardiac monitor, and observe for arrhythmias.

      (c) Monitor central venous pressure.

      (d) After periocardiocentesis, monitor blood pressure, venous pressure, and heart sounds for recurrence of cardiac tamponade.

  c. Adult respiratory distress syndrome (ARDS; traumatic wet lung; may also occur after hemorrhagic shock, pneumonia, and fat embolism).

The capillary bed of the lung becomes hemorrhagic and edematous. Surfactant is lost, causing deflation and collapse of the alveoli. Lung compliance decreases, causing profound hypoxia.

    (1) Assessment

      (a) Observe for cyanosis, anxiety, and mental confusion.

      (b) Auscultate for noisy respiration.

      (c) Monitor vital signs for tachycardia, hypertension, and dyspnea.

      (d) Monitor arterial blood gases.

    (2) Nursing role

      (a) Restrict fluid intake.

      (b) Record intake and output.

      (c) Attach the patient to mechanical ventilator.

      (d) Prepare for and assist with tracheostomy.

H. Management of the Patient Undergoing Chest Surgery

1. Preoperative management. *See also* Section A: Management during the Preoperative Period, page 267.

  a. Assessment. *See* General Assessment, page 290.

  b. Nursing role (patient education)

    (1) Inform the patient of what to expect in the postoperative period [i.e., possible presence of chest tube(s), drainage bottles, and ventilator].

(2) Instruct the patient in the technique of coughing and the "huffing" technique (expulsion of air through an open glottis).

2. Operative procedures
   a. **Lobectomy** Removal of a lobe of the lung. (Closed chest drainage is used for several days postoperatively.)
   b. **Pneumonectomy** Removal of an entire lung. (Removal of the right lung is more dangerous because of its large vascular bed; no drain is used so that the accumulation of fluid consolidates, preventing extensive mediastinal shift.)
   c. **Segmental resection** Removal of one or more segments of the lung.
   d. **Wedge resection** Removal of a small triangular area of localized diseased tissue near the surface of the lung.
   e. **Exploratory thoracotomy** Surgery performed to locate the source of injury or bleeding, or a tumor in the thorax.
   f. **Bronchoplastic or sleeve resection** Excision of only one lobar bronchus together with a part of the right or left bronchus. The distal bronchus is reanastomosed to the proximal bronchus or trachea.

3. Postoperative nursing diagnoses/goals/interventions
   a. Ineffective airway clearance related to lung impairment and anesthesia
      Goal: Patient will experience improvement of airway clearance and achieve a patent airway.
   b. Pain related to incision and surgical procedure
      Goal: Patient will experience relief of pain and discomfort.
      Interventions:
      (1) Maintain a patent airway.
          (a) Suction, using sterile technique.
          (b) Administer humidified oxygen.
          (c) Attach the patient to mechanical ventilator.
          (d) Administer IPPB treatment as directed.
      (2) Encourage and promote an effective cough routine.
          (a) Assist the patient to sitting position and support incision while the patient coughs (anteriorly and posteriorly).
          (b) Assist the patient to cough at least every 1 to 2 hours during the first 24 hours and when necessary thereafter.
          (c) Auscultate chest for rales after cough routine.
          (d) Administer small, frequent doses of narcotic to enable the patient to deep-breathe and cough more effectively.
      (3) Position the patient as ordered.
          (a) Lobectomy. The patient is turned alternately on either side to permit expansion of the lung tissue on both sides.
          (b) Segmental resection. Lying on the operated side is contraindicated.
          (c) Pneumonectomy
              1. The patient is positioned on the operated side long enough to perform back care. Placing on unoperative side should be avoided during early period.
              2. The patient may be turned on either side 24 hours after surgery. (Some physicians permit the patient to be positioned only on the back or operated side.)
              3. The patient is assisted to change position from horizontal to semi-Fowler's (this allows residual air to rise to the upper portion of the pleural space and to be removed via the upper chest catheter) every 1 to 2 hours.
      (4) Assist the patient with exercises.
          (a) Range of motion exercises of the shoulder and arm (prevent shoulder ankylosis and contractures of the arm).
              1. Exercise is performed every 4 to 6 hours through the first 24 hours.
              2. Thereafter arm and shoulder are put through full range of motion approximately 20 times every 2 hours.
          (b) Breathing exercises. *See* General Patient Care Management, page 292.

(5) Assist the patient with ambulation as soon as vital signs are stable postoperatively (usually the evening of surgery or the morning of the 1st postoperative day).

c. Impaired gas exchange related to lung impairment and surgery
Goal: Patient will experience improvement in gas exchange and breathing.
Interventions:
(1) Monitor chest drainage system. *See* Management of the Patient Undergoing Closed Chest Drainage, below.
(2) Observe the patient for complications (hermorrhage, atelectasis, cardiac arrhythmias, pulmonary edema, respiratory acidosis, renal failure).
(3) Support chest tube when the patient moves or changes position.
(4) Monitor vital signs every 15 minutes.
(5) Monitor heart rate and rhythm by auscultation and electrocardiography.
(6) Monitor blood gases, serum electrolytes, hemoglobin, and hematocrit.

d. Fluid volume deficit related to the surgical procedure
Goal: Adequate fluid volume will be maintained.
Interventions:
(1) Measure and record hourly urinary output. (The patient should excrete at least 30 ml of urine hourly after surgery.)
(2) Maintain drip rate of blood and parenteral fluid at rate ordered (drip rate is slowed to prevent pulmonary edema).

e. Knowledge deficit related to care procedures at home
Goal: Patient will demonstrate the ability to carry out care procedures at home.
Interventions:
(1) Encourage the patient to practice arm and shoulder exercises five times daily.
(2) Instruct the patient to practice assuming a functionally erect position in front of a full-length mirror.

(3) Instruct the patient in following aspects of home care.
(a) Relieve intercoastal pain by local heat or oral analgesia.
(b) Alternate activities with frequent rest periods.
(c) Practice the breathing exercises at home.
(d) Avoid heavy lifting until complete healing has occurred.
(e) Avoid undue fatigue, increased shortness of breath, or chest pain.
(f) Avoid bronchial irritants.
(g) Prevent colds or lung infections.
(h) Get annual influenza vaccine.
(i) Keep follow-up appointments.
(j) Stop smoking.

4. Postoperative evaluation
a. Patient's lungs are clear on auscultation, and respiratory rate is within normal range and with no episodes of dyspnea.
b. Patient's airway is patent.
c. Patient is free of pain or experiences minimal pain.
d. Patient is adequately hydrated.
e. Patient verbalizes understanding of home-care procedures.

I. **Management of the Patient Undergoing Closed Chest Drainage**
1. Purposes
a. To remove solids, liquids, and gases from the pleural space or thoracic cavity.
b. To restore pleural negative pressure, thereby facilitating reexpansion of the lung after surgery or trauma.
2. Types of closed chest drainage; water seal, pleura-EVAC.
3. Water seal drainage
a. General principles
(1) Chest tubes from the pleural space drain under water. (Water acts as a seal and keeps the air from being drawn into the pleural space.)
(2) Sterile drainage bottle(s) with sterile water or saline is used as water seal.
(3) The original fluid level is marked on the outside of the drainage bottle (enables correct measurement of drainage from the chest).

b. Types
   (1) One-bottle system

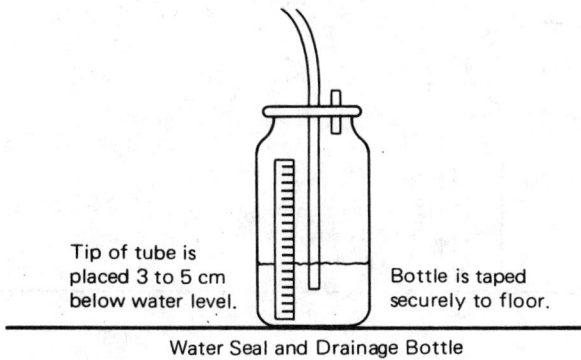

Tip of tube is placed 3 to 5 cm below water level.

Bottle is taped securely to floor.

Water Seal and Drainage Bottle

   (a) This system provides no suction; the drainage is effected by gravity.
   (b) The short tube is an air vent (allows air escaping from the chest to escape out of the bottle).
   (c) The longer tube acts as a water seal.
   (2) Two-bottle system

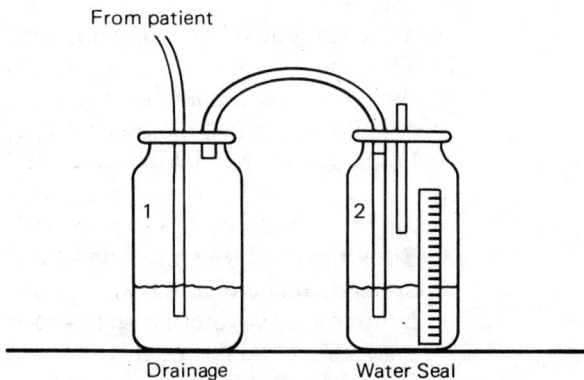

From patient

Drainage   Water Seal

   (a) The first bottle is for drainage.
      1. The chest drainage tube is attached to a short tube.
      2. The second, short tube is attached, via tubing, to the underwater seal in bottle 2.
      3. The tape is marked to indicate the amount of drainage.

   (b) The second bottle is for the water seal.
      1. The long tube extends under water.
      2. The short tube is an air vent.
      3. The strip of tape on the outside of the bottle is marked to indicate the initial level of the sterile solution.
      4. The fluid in the underwater tube fluctuates with inspiration and expiration.
      5. If suction is desired, it is achieved by connecting a suction source at the vent stem of the water-seal bottle.
   (3) Three-bottle system
   (a) This system provides a third bottle to control the amount of suction applied.
   (b) Suction is attached to bottle 3.
   (c) This bottle contains three tubes.
      1. A short tube extends from the water-seal bottle to bottle 3.
      2. A long tube extends below the water level (20 cm) and is open to the atmosphere. The amount of suction is determined by the depth to which this tube is submerged.
      3. A short tube leads to the suction source of the control bottle.
   (d) Proper functioning of the control bottle is indicated by periodic emptying of the fluid in the control tube and the bubbling of air through the water being drawn into the tube.
   (e) Whenever mechanical suction is removed, tubing is detached from the suction port to provide an air vent.
4. Pleura-EVAC
   a. This disposable plastic apparatus duplicates the principle of the three-bottle water-seal drainage system.

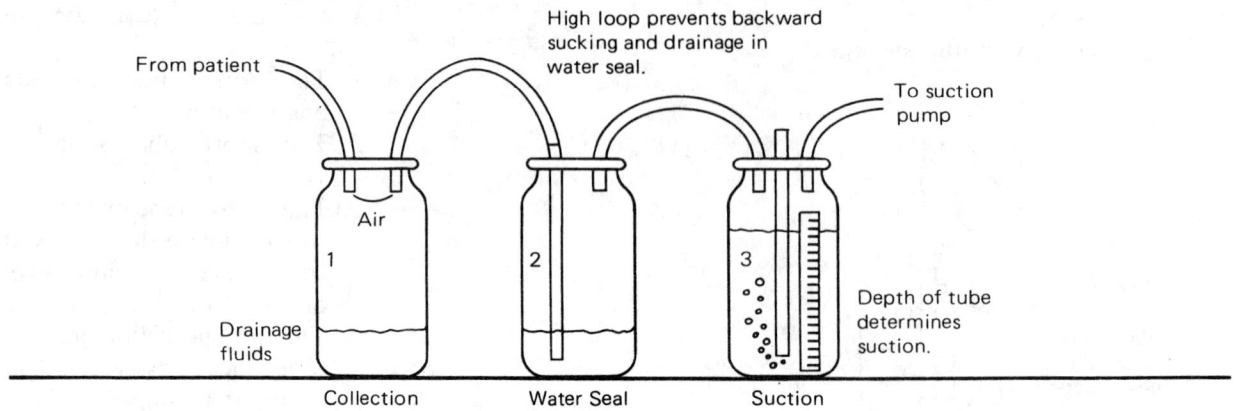

From patient

High loop prevents backward sucking and drainage in water seal.

To suction pump

Air

1   2   3

Drainage fluids

Depth of tube determines suction.

Collection   Water Seal   Suction

b. It contains three separate chambers.
   (1) Drainage collection. (Tubing from the patient connects to this chamber.)
   (2) Water seal.
   (3) Suction control (tubing attached from suction chamber to suction source).
c. It is attached to the bedside or placed in a floor stand.
5. Nursing role
   a. Fill the water chamber with sterile water to the level equaling 2 cm H_2O.
      (1) If suction is used, fill the suction control chamber with sterile water to the 20-cm level or as prescribed.
      (2) Tape the connecting points of the tubing to maintain airtightness of the system.
   b. Prevent kinking, looping, or pressure on tubing.
   c. Keep bottles below chest level.
   d. Stabilize drainage bottle on the floor, or place it in a special holder.
   e. Keep a rubber-tip hemostat at the bedside, in a place where it can easily be seen, in case of a break in the airtight system.
   f. Record color, consistency, and amount of drainage every 8 hours. Mark the original fluid level with tape outside of drainage unit.
   g. Encourage coughing and deep breathing.
   h. Clamp chest tube, if ordered, for a few minutes during transportation of the patient to another area of the hospital (e.g., for X-ray).

   i. Put the patient's arm and shoulder through range of motion exercises several times daily; some pain medication may be offered.
   j. Monitor fluid level in the water-seal chamber for fluctuation ("tidaling"). Fluctuations of fluids in the tubing will stop when (1) the lung has re-expanded; (2) the tubing is obstructed by blood clots or fibrin or by kinking; (3) a dependent loop develops; (4) the suction motor or wall suction is not working properly.
   k. Assist the surgeon in removing the tube.
      (1) The patient is instructed to perform the valsalva maneuver (forcible exhalation against a closed glottis, holding one's breath).
      (2) The chest tube is clamped and quickly removed.
      (3) Simultaneously, a small bandage is applied, made airtight with petrolatum gauze covered by a 4x4-inch gauze pad, and thoroughly covered and sealed with adhesive tape.

Alterations in Cardiovascular Organs, Blood, and Blood-Forming Organs

A. General Assessment of Cardiac Function
   1. Auscultate the heart to identify first or second heart sounds; note the appearance of abnormal heart sounds and nonpathological heart sounds.
   2. Auscultate the lung for wheezing rales.
   3. Measure vital signs.

a. Pulse
   (1) Take apical and radial pulses.
   (2) Examine radial, brachial, carotid, femoral, popliteal, posterior tibial, and dorsalis pedis pulses.
   (3) Examine venous pulse. (Arterial and venous pulsations are visible in the neck.)
b. Respirations. Examine rate, depth, and character.
c. Blood pressure. Take on both arms and leg initially; measure in both supine and standing positions.

4. Note the presence of chest pain (*see* Section D1: Pain, page 270), nonproductive cough occurring at night, headache, and palpitations.
5. Inspect sputum for hemoptysis.
6. Inspect extremities for edema and clubbing of the fingers, and neck veins for engorgement.
7. Observe for fatigue, syncope or fainting, abdominal pain or discomfort, position assumed (e.g., orthopnea), and dyspnea (exertional, paroxysmal, nocturnal).
8. Observe skin color and temperature—pallor, flushing, cyanosis (observe the mucous membrane of the mouth, since color variation is less; examine nailbeds and palms), jaundice, petechiae; sweating, cold, clammy, warm, or dry skin.
9. Obtain health history.
10. DIAGNOSTIC MEASURES
   a. Chest X-ray—is used to determine the size, contour, and position of the heart.
   b. Fluoroscopy—provides visual observation of the heart on a luminescent X-ray screen.
   c. Electrocardiogram—provides visual representation of the electrical activity (depolarization and repolarization) of the myocardium, as reflected by changes in electrical potential at the skin surface.
      (1) Clinical uses: to diagnose disturbances of rate and rhythm, disorder of conduction, enlargement of heart chamber, and the presence of myocardial infarction.
      (2) Normal cardiac cycle
         P waves—depolarization of the atria.
         P-R interval—the time required for impulses to spread from atria to ventricle.

QRS complex—ventricular contraction.
T wave—repolarization of the ventricle.
S-T segment—completion of ventricular depolarization and the beginning of ventricular repolarization.
      (3) Nursing role
         (a) Reassure the patient that the machine is safe.
         (b) Explain the purpose and the procedure to the patient.
   d. Angiocardiography—outlines the heart and blood vessels by means of dye injected into the vascular system. Cineangiography (rapidly changing films on a fluoroscopic screen) records the passage of the dye.
      (1) Types
         (a) **Selective angiocardiography** Injection of dye directly into the heart chamber, coronary arteries, or great vessels.
         (b) **Aortography** Outlining of the lumen of the aorta and the major arteries arising from it.
         (c) **Coronary arteriography** Passage of a radiopaque catheter into the ascending aorta and into one of the coronary arteries via the right brachial artery or femoral artery: this is done under fluoroscopic controls.
      (2) Nursing role
         (a) Report history of allergic reactions to the physician before the procedure.
         (b) Give nothing by mouth to minimize the danger of pulmonary aspiration if emesis occurs.
         (c) After the procedure measure vital signs every 15 minutes until stable.
         (d) Check puncture or cutdown site for bleeding and the extremity for numbness and loss of pulse.
   e. Echocardiography—is used to diagnose and differentiate heart murmurs. High-frequency waves are sent into the chest wall and are recorded as they return. An electrocardiogram is recorded simultaneously to time events within the cardiac cycle.

f. Phonocardiography—provides electronic measurement, amplification, and graphic recording of low-frequency cardiac sounds.

g. Exercise stress testing—assesses cardiac function after the performance of some type of exercise (walking a treadmill, pedaling a stationary bicycle, or climbing stairs). Electrocardiograms are taken before, during, and after the exercise test; also, blood pressure, skin temperature, physical appearance, and the occurrence or worsening of chest pain are monitored.

Patient education

(1) Avoid smoking, eating, and drinking for 4 hours before test.

(2) After the test, rest and avoid stimulants, eating, or extreme temperature changes.

h. Cardiac catheterization

(1) Purposes

    (a) To measure oxygen concentration and pressure in the various chambers of the heart.

    (b) To detect congenital abnormalities.

    (c) To obtain blood samples for analysis.

    (d) To determine cardiac output and pulmonary blood flow.

(2) Types

    (a) Right-heart catheterization—passage of a radiopaque catheter via the antecubital or femoral vein into the right atrium, right ventricle, and pulmonary vasculature under direct visualization with a fluoroscope.

    (b) Left-heart catheterization

        1. Retrograde advancement of a catheter under direct vision via the right brachial or femoral artery into the ascending aorta and the left ventricle.

        2. Transseptal approach: passage of a catheter from the right femoral vein into the right atrium through the septum separating the right and left atria. (The septum is punctured by a long needle passed through the catheter.)

(3) Nursing role

    (a) Determine whether the patient has any allergies.

    (b) Give nothing by mouth for 6 hours before the procedure.

    (c) Explain to the patient what to expect during the procedure (i.e., procedure will last more than 2 hours; different sensations will be experienced during the injection of the dye and when the catheter touches the myocardium).

    (d) Check the puncture site for hematoma formation and the extremities for numbness, loss of pulse, and temperature or color change.

    (e) Monitor apical and radial pulses every 10 to 15 minutes.

    (f) Allow the patient to rest for 24 hours after the procedure.

    (g) Report any complaint of chest pain to the physician immediately.

    (h) Check temperature every 5 hours.

i. Central venous pressure (CVP) measurement—measures the pressure within the superior vena cava.

(1) Normal CVP reading is 4 to 10 cm H_2O, measured by the height of a column of water in a manometer.

(2) Decreased CVP (values below 5 cm H_2O) indicates hemorrhage or fluid loss from other causes.

(3) Increased CVP (values above 10 cm H_2O) indicates congestive heart failure or circulatory overload.

(4) Procedure

    (a) Place the patient in supine position.

    (b) Place the zero mark on the manometer at the phlebostatic axis.

(c) Make an ink mark on the patient's chest to indicate the location.
(5) Possible complications
   (a) Infection.
   (b) Air embolism.
j. Laboratory studies
  (1) Blood electrolyte studies to provide an evaluation of potassium, sodium, and calcium.
  (2) Blood chemistries—blood urea nitrogen, glucose, blood lipids, and lipoprotein.
  (3) Enzyme and isoenzyme tests (Enzymes are also present in a variety of tissues.)
   (a) Creatinine phosphokinase (CPK). Normal level is 0 to 200 sigma units. Levels are greatly elevated in myocardial infarction. Test is most useful in early diagnosis of MI. Isoenzyme CPK-MB.
   (b) Lactic acid dehydrogenase (LDH) and its isoenzyme. Normal level is 165 to 300 units. Elevated levels follow MI and many other conditions.

B. General Patient Care Management

1. **Rest (physical and emotional). Rest reduces the work of the heart, increases heart reserves, reduces blood pressure, and decreases the work of the respiratory muscles and oxygen utilization.**
2. Pharmacological therapy
  a. Digitalis
   (1) Actions: increases cardiac output by enhancing the contraction of the ventricles, slows heart rate, slows ventricular rate in the setting of supraventricular arrhythmias, promotes diuresis, reduces heart size.
   (2) Uses: for congestive heart failure, atrial fibrillation, atrial flutter, and supraventricular tachyarrhythmia; before cardiac surgery.
   (3) Preparations
    (a) Digoxin—daily dose: 0.25 to 0.5 mg PO, IM, or IV.
    (b) Digitoxin—daily dose: 0.1 mg PO, IM, or IV.

(4) Nursing role
  (a) Observe for toxic effects:
   1. Gastrointestinal: anorexia, nausea and vomiting, diarrhea.
   2. Neurological: fatigue, headache, malaise.
   3. Visual: loss of visual acuity and color perception (usually green and yellow), with colored halos around lights.
   4. Others: allergic reaction, gastrointestinal hemorrhage, gynecomastia.
  (b) Assess clinical response of the patient by relief of symptoms (dyspnea, orthopnea, rales, peripheral edema).
  (c) Monitor serum potassium level, especially in a patient receiving both digitalis and diuretics. (A potassium deficiency predisposes a person to arrhythmias and digitalis toxicity.)
  (d) Check pulse, preferably apical, before giving each dose to detect any marked change in rate or rhythm. Record and report a pulse below 60 in an adult. A decision may be made to withhold the drug.
  (e) Observe for symptoms of electrolyte depletion: lassitude, apathy, mental confusion, decreasing urinary output.
b. Antiarrhythmic agents
  (1) Actions: depress myocardial excitability, slow conduction time in atria and ventricles, depress myocardial contractibility (except lidocaine), decrease automaticity.
  (2) Specific drugs and their uses
   (a) Quinidine—for atrial tachycardia, atrial flutter, and atrial fibrillation; ventricular tachycardia; premature systoles.
   (b) Pronestyl—for premature ventricular contractions; ventricular tachycardia (Procan-SR, Pronestyl-SR, sustained release).
   (c) Lidocaine—for premature ventricular contraction and arrhythmias that occur during surgery or cardiac diagnostic procedures.

(d) Disopyramide (Norpace, Napamide)—for chronic ventricular arrhythmias.

(3) Side and toxic effects

(a) Quinidine: hypersensitivity, cinchonism (nausea, vomiting, diarrhea, tinnitus, vertigo), thrombocytopenia purpura, hypotension, ventricular fibrillation.

(b) Pronestyl: gastrointestinal disturbance (anorexia, nausea, vomiting, diarrhea), hypotension, systemic lupus erythematosus.

(c) Lidocaine (used cautiously in patients with congestive heart failure or liver disease, since cumulative effect can occur because of slowed metabolism): central nervous system disturbance (drowsiness, disorientation, dizziness, blurred or double vision, paresthesias), cardiac depression.

(4) Other antiarrhythmic agents

(a) Propranolol (Inderal) (beta adrenergic block agent)

1. Actions: decreases heart rate and ventricular volume, decreases A-V node conduction and ventricular irritability.

2. Uses: for angina, premature ventricular contractions, atrial and ventricular tachycardias.

3. Side and toxic effects: bradycardia, hypotension, acute heart failure.

(b) Phenytoin sodium (Dilantin)

1. Actions: decreases the excitability of the myocardial tissue, reduces ventricular automaticity.

2. Uses: for patient with digitalis-induced arrhythmias and patients unable to tolerate quinidine or procainamide.

3. Side effects: transient hypotension due to peripheral vasodilation, respiratory or cardiac arrest.

c. Other agents

(1) Isoproterenol (Isuprel)

(a) Actions: increases heart rate, stroke volume, and coronary blood flow; decreases diastolic blood pressure.

(b) Uses: for A-V block (Stokes-Adams syndrome); sinus bradycardia, sinus arrest; heart block.

(c) Side effects: tachycardia; palpitations, anginal pain; weakness, sweating, nausea, headache, skin flushing.

(2) Verapamil

(a) Actions: is calcium channel blocker. Inhibits the influx of calcium through the slow membrane channel (calcium channel) into cells of the cardiac conductile system. AV conduction is slowed, SA and AV nodes suppressed; restores normal sinus rhythm.

(b) Side effects: IV dose—transient hypotension, dizziness, bradycardia; oral dose—palpitation, heartburn, fatigue.

(3) Atropine

(a) Actions: is anticholinergic. Inhibits the vagal nerves, thereby increasing the heart rate.

(b) Uses: for sinus bradycardia and second-degree A-V block.

(c) Side effects: dry mouth, blurred vision, flushing, difficult voiding.

(4) Nitrites

(a) Actions: relax vascular smooth muscles, reduce peripheral resistance, decrease myocardial oxygen consumption.

(b) Side effects: severe headaches, flushing, nausea and vomiting, hypotension, vertigo.

(c) Preparations

1. Nitroglycerin (short-acting)

a. Sublingual dose. Usual dose is 0.4 mg (may be repeated several times during the day). Drug appears in the blood in 2 minutes. Repeat every 5 to 10 minutes until relief is obtained. (Also available as oral spray and controlled-release buccal tablets.)

Nursing teaching
  (1) Keep drug in a dark, airtight container.
  (2) Store a supply of the drug in the refrigerator. Obtain a fresh supply every 3 months.
  b. Nitroglycerin ointment. Squeeze ¹/₂-inch layer on chest, abdomen, or anterior thighs; apply every 3 to 4 hours.
  c. Nitroglycerin transdermal system. Apply one patch to a nonhairy area once every 24 hours. Side effects: headache, hypotension.
2. Isordil (long-acting). Usual sublingual dose ranges from 5 to 30 mg four times daily. Onset of action is 2 minutes; duration is 3 to 4 hours.
3. Peritrate (long-acting). Usual oral dose is 10 mg t.i.d. Onset of action is 1 hour; duration is 3 to 4 hours.
4. Cardilate (long-acting). Usual sublingual dose is 5 to 30 mg t.i.d. Onset of action is 5 to 10 minutes; duration is 2 to 4 hours.

d. Diuretics
  (1) Action: decrease the reabsorption of electrolytes (principally sodium) by the kidneys, promoting water loss as a secondary action. Some increase glomerular action.
  (2) Drugs
    (a) Thiazides [chlorothiazide (Diuril), hydrochlorothiazide (HydroDiuril, Esidrix), chlorthalidone (Hygroton)]
      1. Action: antihypertensive (they cause a decrease in extracellular and plasma volume).
      2. Side effects: hypokalemia, hyperglycemia, hyperuricemia, hyponatremia, hematologic complications.

3. Nursing interventions
  a. Monitor for electrolyte depletion.
  b. Provide diet supplement of potassium (e.g., fresh nuts, vegetables, and fruits—bananas, orange juice).
  c. Give other potassium supplements [e.g., potassium chloride (liquid) slow-K (potassium in a slow resin), K-LOR].
  (b) Potassium-sparing diuretics
    1. Actions: inhibit the action of aldosterone in distal tubules, reduce the reabsorption of sodium and chloride and retention of potassium.
    2. Drugs: spironolactone (Aldactone); triamterene (Dyrenium), which potentiates the action of antihypertensive drugs.
    3. Side effects: nausea and vomiting, gynecomastia, skin rash.
  (c) Potent diuretics—have immediate action (within 5 minutes) when given IV.
    1. Drugs: furosemide (Lasix), ethacrynic acid (Edecrin)
    2. Uses: congestive heart failure, cirrhosis of the liver.
    3. Side effects: hyponatremia, hypokalemia, nausea and vomiting, allergic reaction (skin rash, pruritus).
e. Antihypertensive drugs
  (1) Action: lower blood pressure within normal range (less than 90 mm Hg diastolic) with the fewest side effects.
  (2) Stepped-care approach
    (a) Step-1 drugs (mild hypertension): diuretics, beta blockers.
    (b) Step-2 drugs: beta blockers, Catapres, labetalol, Aldomet, prazosin (Minipress), captopril (Capoten), Vasotec, lisinopril (Prinivil), reserpine (Serpasil).
    (c) Step-3 drugs: hydralazine.
    (d) Step-4 drugs: guanethidine, minoxidil.

(3) Drugs
  (a) Diuretics (thiazides, furosemide, Edecrin, Aldactone, Dyrenium), often used in combination with other antihypertensive drugs.
  (b) Resperine (hydralazine)
    1. Action: decreases peripheral vasoconstriction (hypotensive).
    2. Side effects: depression, sodium retention, nasal stuffiness.
  (c) Hydralazine (Apresoline)
    1. Action: dilates peripheral blood vessels (hypotensive).
    2. Side effects: tachycardia, gastric irritation, headaches, palpitation, angina pectoris.
  (d) Methyldopa (Aldomet)
    1. Action: is hypotensive.
    2. Side effects: drowsiness, skin rash, dry mouth, erection difficulties.
  (e) Guanethidine (Ismelin)
    1. Action: is a postganglionic blocking agent.
    2. Side effect: postural hypotension.
  (f) Clonidine hydrochloride (Catapres)
    1. Action: is hypotensive.
    2. Side effects: sedation, dry mouth, postural hypotension.
  (g) Sodium nitroprusside (Nipride)
    1. Action: is a powerful vasodilator and decreases peripheral resistance.
    2. Side effects: postural hypotension, headaches, nausea and vomiting, sweating.
  (h) Diazoxide (Hyperstat)
    1. Action: has a direct vasodilating effect on the peripheral arterioles.
    2. Side effects: hyperglycemia, sodium retention, postural hypotension.

(4) Drugs for hypertensive emergencies
  (a) Nitropress/Nipride.
  (b) Hyperstat.
3. Sodium-restricted diet. See table.

Dietary Substances Generally to be Avoided in Sodium Restriction

1. Smoked, processed or cured meats and fish, such as ham, bacon, corned beef, cold cuts, frankfurter, sausage, tongue, salt pork, chipped beef and anchovies.
2. Meat extracts, bouillon cubes and meat sauces.
3. Salted foods, such as potato chips, nuts and popcorn.
4. Prepared condiments, relishes, Worcestershire sauce, catsup, pickles, mustard and olives.
5. Vegetable salts and flakes, such as onion, garlic or celery salt; celery and parsley flakes.
6. Sodium in any form, such as sodium benzoate as a preservative and monosodium glutamate as a flavoring aid.
7. Bread or bakery products unless prepared without salt and other sources of sodium.
8. Frozen fish fillets and shellfish, except oysters.
9. Prepared flours, flour mixes, baking powder and baking soda.
10. Frozen peas and lima beans; sauerkraut in any form.
11. All canned meat and vegetable products unless prepared without salt (dietetic pack).
12. Butter, cheese and peanut butter unless prepared without salt.

From *Food, Nutrition, and Diet Therapy,* 6th ed., by Marie Krause and Kathleen Mahan. Copyright © 1981 by W. B. Saunders Company. Used with permission.

4. Patient education. *See* Hypertensive vascular disease, page 320.
C. **Coronary Artery Disease** Abnormal accumulation of lipid substances and fibrous tissue in the vessel wall, which leads to changes in arterial structure and function and an insufficient blood supply to the myocardium. Major disorders resulting are angina pectoris and myocardial infarction.
  1. Precipitating factors
    a. Diet: high-caloric, high-fat (the most significant factor)—intake of large amounts of cholesterol and saturated fat.
    b. Other diseases: hypertension, gout, diabetes mellitus.

c. Obesity.

d. Physical inactivity.

e. Genetic predisposition.

f. Stress: type A behavior (competitive striving for achievement, exaggerated sense of time urgency, aggressiveness, hostility).

g. Cigarette smoking.

h. Age: Pathological changes appear predominately in persons over 40.

i. Sex: Males are more prone than women.

D. **Angina Pectoris**   A temporary state of myocardial hypoxia characterized by transient paroxysmal attacks of substernal or precordial pain.

1. Cause: insufficient coronary blood flow and/or inadequate oxygen supply to the myocardial muscle.

2. Precipitating factors

   a. Physiological: physical exertion, exposure to cold, digestion of heavy meal, stress, strong emotion.

   b. Pathological: anemia, polycythemia, aortic insufficiency, thyrotoxicosis.

3. Assessment

   a. Observe and note the characteristics of the pain. (Weakness or numbness in the arm, wrist, and hand may accompany the pain.)

      (1) Location—deep in the chest behind the upper or middle third of the sternum to the left side.

      (2) Radiation—to neck, jaw, shoulder, and inner aspects of the upper extremities.

      (3) Intensity—tightness, a choking or strangling sensation of viselike, insistent quality.

      (4) Duration—usually no more than 3 to 5 minutes.

      (5) Mode of relief—cessation of the precipitating factor, or the use of nitroglycerin.

   b. Measure vital signs for increased heart rate and/or elevated blood pressure caused by increased sympathetic nervous system activity.

   c. Observe patient for apprehension, increased perspiration, and complaint of inability to breathe.

   d. DIAGNOSTIC MEASURES: nitroglycerin test, electrocardiographic monitoring, exercise stress test.

4. Patient care management

   a. Decrease oxygen demand of the myocardium.

   b. Give pharmacological therapy: nitroglycerin—sublingual tablet and ointment; long-acting nitrites—Cardilate, Isordil, Peritrate; Inderal.

   c. Increase oxygen supply to the myocardium.

   d. If necessary, provide surgical treatment—coronary artery revascularization.

5. Nursing role (patient education)

   a. Use moderation in all activities.

   b. Avoid situations that are emotionally stressful.

   c. Avoid overeating.

   d. Stop smoking, since smoking increases the heart rate, blood pressure, and blood carbon monoxide levels.

   e. Try to avoid going out in cold weather. If not possible, dress warmly.

   f. Carry nitroglycerin at all times.

   g. Place nitroglycerin under tongue at the first sign of chest discomfort.

   h. Take nitroglycerin prophylatically to avoid pain known to occur with certain activities (climbing stairs, sexual intercourse).

E. **Myocardial Infarction**   The process by which myocardial tissue is destroyed in regions of the heart that are deprived of an adequate blood supply because of reduced coronary blood flow.

1. Causes: atherosclerosis, coronary artery embolus or thrombus, decreased coronary blood flow due to shock or hemorrhage.

2. Assessment

   a. Observe and note the characteristics of the patient's pain.

      (1) Location—at the start, over the lower sternal region and upper abdomen.

      (2) Precipitating factors—none; begins spontaneously (not following effort, emotional upset, etc.).

      (3) Radiation—to the shoulder and down the arm, usually the left arm.

      (4) Intensity—heavy and viselike, increasing steadily in severity.

      (5) Duration—hours or days; is relieved neither by rest nor by nitroglycerin.

b. Measure vital signs. Pulse may become rapid, irregular, and imperceptible; elevated temperature and decreased blood pressure may occur with severe occlusion; respiration may be rapid and shallow; orthopnea may occur.

c. Auscultate the heart for accentuated third heart sounds (gallop rhythm), and the lung for moist rales.

d. Observe the general appearance for ashen color, clammy sweat, and apprehension; belching and vomiting may also be experienced.

e. Obtain health history.

f. DIAGNOSTIC MEASURES

(1) Electrocardiogram: abnormal Q waves, elevation of S-T segment, inversion of T wave.

Silent myocardial infarction—a significant percentage of cases are diagnosed on the basis of ECGs, and the patient denies experiencing any pain or discomfort.

(2) Laboratory studies

(a) CPK (the first enzyme to reach peak value, in particular CPK-MB). Maximal serum values are achieved 12 to 24 hours after the onset of symptoms.

(b) LDH. Levels may remain elevated for 5 to 7 days.

(c) SGOT. Levels rise within 6 to 12 hours after infarction. (This is the second enzyme to be elevated.)

(d) Increased white blood cells.

(e) Elevated sedimentation rate.

3. Patient care management

a. Detect and treat arrhythmias by continuous ECG monitoring.

b. Thrombolytic therapy—Infusion of thrombolytic agents to promote clot lysis, restore coronary blood flow, and limit myocardial ischemia.

(1) Preprocedure teaching.

(2) Explanations:

(a) Explain and review intraprocedure and postprocedure routines.

(b) Explain need for bedrest during and after administration.

(3) Preparation:

(a) Obtain informed consent for therapy.

(b) DIAGNOSTIC MEASURES: CBC with platelets, PT, fibrinogen, fibrin split, product labels, CPK-MB, blood type and cross-match, electrolytes, BUN and creatinine, 12 lead ECG.

(4) Assessment/observations:

(a) Abrupt cessation of chest pain.

(b) Return of S-T elevation to baseline.

(c) Dysrhythmias—Sinus bradycardia, A-V Block with hypotension, ventricular tachycardia

(d) Isoenzyme—Early peaking of CPK-MB within 12 hours of onset of symptoms

(e) Bleeding/hemorrhage—Surface bleeding and GI bleeding.

(f) Coronary artery reocclusion—Chest pain, ECG changes, dysrhythmias.

(g) Skin—Pale, clammy, diaphoretic.

(h) Tachycardia.

(i) Anxiety.

(5) Medical management
Thrombolytic agents, Streptokinase (SK), Urokinase (UK), tissue plasminogen activator (t-PA), anisoylated plasminogen-SK activator complex (APSA, diphenhydramine, heparin).

c. Relieve pain with analgesic (IM or IV)—morphine, Demerol, or Dilaudid.

d. Percutaneous transluminal coronary angioplasty (PTCA).

e. Prevent complications: arrhythmias, congestive heart failure.

f. Promote physiological and functional rehabilitation.

4. Nursing diagnoses/goals/interventions

a. Chest pain related to blocked coronary blood flow
Goal: Patient will experience relief from chest pain.

b. Inadequate tissue perfusion related to cardiac output
Goal: Patient will attain/maintain adequate tissue perfusion.
Interventions:

(1) Place the patient in semi-Fowler's position (promotes better ventilation).

(2) Maintain complete bedrest for 24 hours; then sitting in chair.

(3) Provide bedside commode for bowel movement (less fatiguing than bedpan or urinal in bed).

(4) Give stool softener (prevents constipation and straining).

(5) Give mild sedatives—Librium, phenobarbital, Valium—as ordered.

(6) Give clear liquid diet for 48 hours; then 1500-calorie, low-cholesterol, soft, 2000-mg sodium diet.

(7) Measure and record central venous pressure.

(8) Monitor temperature every 4 hours and vital signs every 1 to 2 hours.

(9) Measure urine output every 2 hours.

(10) Monitor IV drip rate, and record intake and output.

(11) Administer oxygen (humidified).

c. Anxiety related to fear of death
Goal: Patient will experience reduced anxiety.
Interventions:

(1) Assess, document, and report to the physician the patient's and family's level of anxiety and coping mechanisms.

(2) Assess the need for spiritual counseling and refer as appropriate.

(3) Allow the patient and family to express anxiety and fear.

(4) Permit flexible visiting hours to allow supportive family to assist in reducing the patient's level of anxiety.

(5) Teach stress-reduction techniques.

d. Nonadherence to self-care program related to denial of diagnosis of myocardial infarction
Goal: Patient will adhere to home-health program.
Interventions:

(1) Teach modification of lifestyle:

(a) Avoid activity that produces chest pain, dyspnea, or undue fatigue.

(b) Avoid extreme heat and cold.

(c) Take off weight as directed.

(d) Stop smoking.

(e) Alternate activity with rest periods.

(f) Eat three or four small meals a day.

(g) Stay within prescribed diet, modifying calories, fat, and sodiums as prescribed.

(h) Comply with medical regimen, especially in regard to taking medications (antiarrhythmias, anticoagulants, antihypertensive drugs).

(i) Pursue a hobby that affords release of tension.

(2) Teach regimen of physical conditioning with a gradual increase in activity levels.

(a) Walk daily, increasing distance and time as prescribed.

(b) Avoid activities that tense the muscles (isometric exercises, weight lifting, etc.).

(c) Avoid physical exercise immediately after a meal.

5. Evaluation

a. Patient reports relief of chest discomfort.

b. Patient experiences no episodes of respiratory difficulty.

c. Patient maintains/attains adequate tissue perfusion.

d. Patient reports less anxiety.

e. Patient adheres to home health-care program.

F. Management of the Patient Undergoing Cardiovascular Surgery

1. Cardiovascular surgery

a. Types

(1) Closed heart—performed without benefit of extracorporeal circulation (ECC: cardiopulmonary bypass).
Examples: mitral commissurotomy (valvulotomy), coronary revascularization.

(2) Open heart—performed with the aid of ECC because of length and complexity.
Example: heart valve replacement.

(3) Coronary artery revascularization. This is indicated when there is evidence of incapacitating angina.
Types of surgical procedures

1. In the Vineburg procedure the internal mammary artery is implanted into the myocardium.

2. The saphenous vein coronary artery bypass graft procedure (CABG) provides for prompt myocardial perfusion. The saphenous vein is removed, reversed, and anastomosed end to end with the distal end of the vein sutured to the ascending aorta below the point of blockage.

3. The internal mammary artery is used as a bypass graft.

2. Preoperative nursing diagnoses/goals/interventions

   See also Management during the Preoperative Period, page 267.

   a. Fear related to the surgical procedure, its questionable outcome, and the threat to well-being

   b. Knowledge deficit regarding the surgical procedure and postoperative course

      Goal: Patient will experience reduction of fear and will learn about the surgical procedure and postoperative course.

      Interventions:

      (1) Reduce anxiety.
         (a) Introduce the patient to another person who has undergone the same operation.
         (b) Give details about equipment, machines, chest tubes, and monitors a day or two before surgery.
         (c) Answer any questions the patient or his/her family may have.
         (d) Use diagrams, models, or prosthetic devices for demonstration purposes.

      (2) Prepare the inguinal area along with the thoracic if a cardiopulmonary bypass is to be done.

      (3) Insert a nasogastric tube and a Foley catheter the morning of surgery.

3. Preoperative evaluation
   a. Patient experiences reduction in fear.
   b. Patient acquires knowledge about the surgical procedure and postoperative course.

4. Postoperative nursing diagnoses/goals/interventions

   a. Decreased cardiac output related to blood loss and compromised myocardial function

      Goal: Patient's normal cardiac output will be restored.

   b. Risk for impaired gas exchange related to trauma and extensive chest surgery

      Goal: Patient will have adequate gas exchange.

      Interventions:

      (1) Place the patient on ventilator assistance (usually left intact from 8 to 48 hours), assisted or controlled. (*See* Mechanical ventilator, page 296).

      (2) Ventilate with 100% oxygen before and after suctioning.

      (3) Suction at frequent intervals (at least every hour).

      (4) Observe blood gas determination.

      (5) Change position every 1 to 2 hours.

      (6) Observe respiration, rate, depth, and pattern.

      (7) Auscultate lungs for wheezing or rales.

      (8) Check and milk chest tubes hourly. *See* water-seal drainage, page 306.

      (9) Check cardiac enzymes daily.

      (10) Monitor central venous pressure.

      (11) Assess all peripheral pulses (pedal, tibial, popliteal, radial, brachial, carotid).

      (12) Monitor ECG pattern for dysrhythmias.

      (13) Observe for postoperative complications: hemorrhage, cardiac tamponade, cardiogenic shock, cardiac failure, myocardial infarction, renal failure, embolization, psychosis, hypotension.

      (14) Monitor arterial blood gas and tidal volume findings.

      (15) Check neck vein for distension.

      (16) Measure vital signs, heart rate, CVP, and arterial pressure.

      (17) Measure and record urinary output.

      (18) Observe nailbeds, buccal mucosa, lips, and ear lobes for signs of cyanosis or duskiness.

(19) Check skin for coldness and/or clamminess.

(20) Elevate the patient's head to semi-Fowler's position to facilitate chest drainage and lung re-expansion.

(21) Administer morphine sulfate to alleviate anxiety and pain.

c. Risk for fluid volume deficit and electrolytic balance related to alteration in blood volume

Goal: Patient's fluids and electrolytes will be balanced.

Interventions:

(1) Observe daily electrolyte studies.

(2) Observe for signs of paralytic ileus and abdominal distension.

(3) Offer water 12 hours postoperatively; if well tolerated, give clear liquids, followed by a full diet, low in sodium.

(4) Observe hematocrit, hemoglobin, prothrombin time, and pO_2.

(5) Weigh daily.

d. Risk for sensory-perceptual alterations related to sensory overload

Goal: Patient will experience a reduction of symptoms of sensory overload and will have no symptoms of postcardiotomy syndrome. (**Postcardiotomy syndrome/psychosis** A group of abnormal behaviors due to anxiety, sleep deprivation, increased sensory input, and disorientation to night and day when patient loses track of time; patient may have lucid periods.)

Interventions:

(1) Check that the patient awakens 1 to 2 hours after surgery.

(2) Check pupillary response for size, equality, and reaction to light.

(3) Check hourly for orientation to time, place, and person; response to verbal command and painful stimuli; signs of denial, hallucinations, or paranoid delusions.

(4) Check movement of extremities and hand-grasp ability.

(5) Explain all procedures and the need for patient cooperation.

(6) Plan nursing care to provide for periods of uninterrupted sleep with day/night pattern.

(7) Orient the patient frequently to time and place.

(8) Encourage the family to visit at regular times.

e. Risk for hyperthermia related to infection or postpericardiotomy syndrome

Goal: Patient will maintain normal temperature.

Interventions:

(1) Maintain systolic blood pressure between 20 mm above and 20 mm below baseline.

(2) Check apical and radial pulse.

(3) Monitor temperature. Treat elevations with aspirins, ice bag, or hypothermia blanket on physician's orders.

(4) Report elevation of 102° or higher and abnormally low temperature of 94 to 96.8°. Treat with electric pad or blanket to raise temperature.

f. Risk for alteration in renal perfusion related to decreased cardiac output, hemolysis, or vasopressor drug therapy

Goal: Patient will maintain adequate renal perfusion.

Interventions:

(1) Measure urine hourly, and report an output of less than 20 mL for 2 consecutive hours.

(2) Observe patient for bladder distension.

(3) Measure urine specific gravity.

(4) Report laboratory results: BUN, serum creatine, urine and serum electrolytes.

(5) Prepare to administer rapid-acting diuretics or inotropic drugs (dopamine).

(6) Prepare the patient for peritoneal dialysis or hemodialysis if indicated.

5. Postoperative evaluation

a. Cardiac output is restored.

b. Gas exchange is adequate.

c. Fluid intake and output is balanced.

d. Normal serum electrolyte is attained.

e. No perceptual distortions, hallucinations, disorientation, or delusions are experienced.

f. Body temperature is normal.

g. Renal perfusion is adequate.

G. Diseases of the Blood and Blood-Forming Organs
1. **Pernicious anemia** Vitamin B_{12} deficiency due to lack of the intrinsic factor in the gastric juice.
   a. Causes: hereditary factors; secondary to total gastrectomy, strictly vegetarian diet, and inflammatory disease of the ileum; autoimmune disorder.
   b. Pathophysiology
      (1) The gastric mucus atrophies and fails to secrete the intrinsic factor.
      (2) Dietary vitamin B_{12}, which can be absorbed only in the presence of the intrinsic factor, cannot enter the body.
      (3) Eventually the body store of B_{12} is used up, and the patient begins to show signs of anemia.
   c. Assessment
      (1) Inspect mouth for smooth, sore, red tongue and extremities for paresthesias.
      (2) Note complaints of mild diarrhea and difficulty in maintaining balance.
      (3) DIAGNOSTIC MEASURES: gastric analysis, Schilling test.
   d. Patient care management: IM injections of vitamin B_{12}; nutritious diet—foods high in iron, protein, and vitamins; bedrest.
2. **Leukemias** Neoplastic disorders of the blood-forming tissues (spleen, lymphatic system, and bone marrow). *See also* Unit Four, Disorders of the Blood and Blood-Forming Organs, Section A: Acute Lymphoblastic Leukemia, page 118. *See* Unit Seven, Neoplastic Disorders, page 184.

H. Disorders of the Cardiovascular Organs
1. **Hypertensive vascular disease (hypertension)** Persistent levels of blood pressure in which the systolic pressure is above 150 mm Hg and the diastolic pressure is above 90 mm Hg; in the elderly, 160 mm Hg systolic pressure and 90 mm Hg diastolic pressure.
   a. Types
      (1) Primary (essential) hypertension.
      (2) Secondary, occurring in thyrotoxicosis, preeclampsia, Cushing's syndrome, renal disease, tumor of the adrenal cortex (aldosteronism), coarctation of the aorta.
   b. Assessment
      (1) Obtain health history.
         (a) Age—primarily begins in the late 30's to early 50's.
         (b) Sex—more prevalent in men than women.
         (c) Race—occurs most often in black males.
      (2) Note morning headaches, fatigability, nervousness, dizziness, blackouts, and palpitation.
      (3) Note blood pressure for elevations.
      (4) Inspect retina for hemorrhage, exudates, narrowed arterioles, and papilledema.
      (5) Auscultate heart for enlargement and arrhythmias.
      (6) DIAGNOSTIC MEASURES: intravenous pyelogram, fasting blood glucose, serum cholesterol and triglyceride, urinalysis, electrocardiogram, chest X-ray.
   c. Patient care management, *See also* General Patient Care Management, page 311.
      (1) Antihypertensive drugs: diuretics (Dyazide, Diuril, HydroDiuril, Hygroton, Lasix); resperine; hydralazine (Apresoline); prazosin (Minipress); Inderal; methyldopa (Aldomet); guanethidine (Ismelin); minoxidil.
      (2) Diet—sodium and cholesterol restricted.
      (3) Weight reduction.
      (4) Treatment of disease state.
   d. Nursing role (patient education)
      (1) Teach patient to measure blood pressure at home.
      (2) Advise patient to:
         (a) Remain on salt-restricted diet.
         (b) Reduce calories and lose weight.
         (c) Practice moderation in the us of coffee and alcohol.
         (c) Avoid smoking.
         (e) Elevate the head of the bed to avoid orthostatic hypertension.
         (f) Avoid orthostatic hypertension by moving slowly from a lying to a sitting position and from a sitting to a standing position. This allows for physiological adjustment of the vascular system.

(g) Avoid omission of medications.
2. **Varicose veins**   Abnormally dilated veins caused by a deficiency of the venous valve.
  a. Assessment
    (1) Inspect lower extremities or lower trunk for darkened, tortuous, swollen veins.
    (2) Note the characteristic leg pain (night cramps, pain during menstrual period, easy fatigue, and a heavy feeling in the leg).
    (3) Observe the skin for breakdown.
    (4) Diagnostic measures (to demonstrate competence of the deep vein valves):   Brodie-Trendelenburg test, Perthes test, and flow studies (thermography and Doppler)
  b. Patient care management
    (1) Avoidance of practices that cause venous stasis (e.g., wearing circular tight garters or a constricting panty girdle, crossing legs at the thighs, sitting or standing for long periods of time).
    (2) Weight reduction if overweight.
    (3) Support hose or elastic stockings.
    (4) Surgical treatment if needed:
      (a) Ligation. The saphenous vein is tied off at its juncture with the femoral vein.
      (b) Stripping. The dilated saphenous vein with its incompetent valves may be removed with a metal or plastic stripper.
  c. Postoperative nursing role
    (1) Elevate the leg above the level of the heart.
    (2) Check the leg circulation (i.e., monitor pedal pulses, check and compare leg for warmth and color).
    (3) Encourage walking (standing or sitting is to be avoided).
    (4) Ambulate the patient at least every hour.

Alterations That Interfere with the Meeting of Nutritional Needs

A. Alterations in Ingestion
  1. **Cancer of the larynx**   Cancer may develop within the larynx on the true vocal cord (intrinsic cancer) or in some other part of the larynx (extrinsic cancer). This occurs in white males at the age of 60.

Prognosis for intrinsic cancer is very good, and treatment not seriously disabling.
  a. Assessment
    (1) Assess health history for complaints of hoarseness, dyspnea, cough, pain radiating to the neck, and pain and burning of the throat when drinking hot liquids or orange juice.
    (2) Palpate the cervical lymph nodes for enlargement.
    (3) Diagnostic measures: direct laryngectomy, biopsy, tomography, barium esophagograms.
  b. Patient care management
    (1) Surgery—most effective treatment in advanced cancer. Preoperative irradiation may slightly increase the cure rate.
    Types: laryngectomy, radical neck dissection.
    (2) Chemotherapy—intra-arterial infusion with methotrexate or vinblastine, followed by X-ray therapy.
2. Management of the patient undergoing surgery for cancer of the larynx
  a. Surgical procedures
    (1) **Laryngectomy**   Surgical treatment of cancer of the larynx.
    Types
      (a) Total laryngectomy, used for advanced lesions. The entire larynx is removed. Speech is not possible. The pharyngeal opening of the trachea is closed, and the distal portion is formed into a permanent tracheostomy. A radical neck dissection may also be performed.
      (b) Conservation laryngectomy. Enough of the larynx remains to function. The voice is preserved. The diseased part is removed, and a radical neck dissection may be performed on the involved side.
      (c) Partial laryngectomy, used to remove a lesion of the true cord on one side. The lesion is removed along with a wide margin of normal tissue. After surgery the patient is able to talk and has a normal airway.

(2) **Radical neck dissection** Treatment for regional lymph node metastases. The lymph channel from the neck, sternocleidomastoid muscle, omohyoid muscle, spinal accessory nerve, internal and external jugular vein, and subcutaneous tissue are removed. A total laryngectomy may also be performed at this time.

b. Nursing diagnoses/goals/interventions *See also* Section A: Management during the Preoperative Period, page 267, and Section C: Management during the Postoperative Period, page 269.

(1) Ineffective airway clearance related to obstruction secondary to edema, hemorrhage, or inadequate wound drainage
Goal: Patient will maintain normal respiratory function.
Interventions:

(a) Place the patient in Fowler's position.
(b) Observe for dyspnea and cyanosis, and auscultate the trachea for the presence of stridor.
(c) Encourage coughing.
(d) Suction PRN.
(e) Observe dressing for hemorrhage and hematoma formation.
(f) Administer oxygen (humidified).

(2) Risk for injury: infection related to improper wound healing
Goal: Patient will be free from infection.
Interventions:

(a) Reinforce dressing as needed.
  1. Observe dressing for hemorrhage and constrictions.
  2. Measure and record drainage from portable wound suction drainage hemovac.
  3. Use strict aseptic technique when in direct contact with the surgical site.
(b) Care for laryngectomy tube if present.
  1. Clean tube as often as necessary.

  2. Suction PRN.
  3. Use mist mask.

(3) Altered nutrition: less than body requirements related to anorexia and dysphagia
Goal: Patient will attain an optimal level of nutrition.
Interventions:

(a) Weigh 3 × a week.
(b) Maintain fluid and electrolyte balance.
(c) Observe for difficulty in swallowing if liquids are allowed.
(d) Provide mouth care every 2 to 4 hours.
(e) Seek a dietary consultation.
(f) Administer enteral feeding as ordered.

(4) Self-concept and body image disturbance related to changes in appearance and alterations in communication
Goal: Patient will attain a positive self-image.
Interventions:

(a) If total laryngectomy was performed, maintain communication by providing paper and pencil. Magic Slate, flash cards, or flip chart.
(b) Make sure that call bell is readily accessible.
(c) Develop nonverbal methods of communication.
(d) Encourage verbalization of fears.
(e) Observe for lower facial paralysis.
(f) Start rehabilitation before hospital discharge: speech therapy; esophageal training (similar to controlled belching); and artificial larynx (use of mechanical and electronic instruments).

c. Evaluation

(1) Patient maintains normal respiratory function.
(2) Patient is free of infection.
(3) Patient attains optimal level of nutrition.
(4) Patient attains positive self-image.

3. **Hiatus hernia** Opening in the diaphragm becomes enlarged, and part of the upper stomach tends to herniate into the lower position of the thorax.
   a. Causes: congenital weakness; acquired weakness due to increased intra-abdominal pressure (e.g., obesity, pregnancy, ascites).
   b. Assessment
      (1) Observe for epigastric pain occurring after meals and becoming worse upon lying, bending forward, or exertion.
      (2) Note substernal heartburn, belching, nausea, and vomiting, disappearing within 1 hour after meal.
      (3) Note if pain radiates to the back, jaws, shoulders, and arms.
   c. Patient care management
      (1) Bland diet of small, frequent feedings.
      (2) Antacids.
      (3) Surgery (to reduce the hernia through an abdominal or thoracic approach).
   d. Nursing role (patient education)
      (1) Avoid lying down after meals.
      (2) Avoid tight garments and heavy lifting.
      (3) Elevate head of bed.
      (4) If obese, reduce.
      (5) Avoid activities that involve bending forward.

B. Alterations in Digestion
   1. **Peptic ulcer** An ulceration in the mucosal wall of the stomach, the duodenum, or the esophagus.
   Erosion is due to an increase in the concentration or activity of acid pepsin, and/or a decrease in normal resistance of the mucosa. Risk factors are as follows: familial tendency, emotional stress, caffeine-containing beverages (coffee, tea, cola), certain drugs (e.g., salicylates, steroids, indomethacin, alcohol).
   a. Assessment
      (1) Obtain health history. *See* Risk factors, above.
      (2) Observe for the presence of pain that is relieved by food or antacids.
      (3) Inspect stool for melena, and vomitus for blood.

   (4) DIAGNOSTIC MEASURES: gastric analysis, gastroscopy—fiberoptic endoscopy, upper GI series, hematologic and stool examinations.
   b. Patient care management
      (1) Duodenal ulcer is treated with a medical regimen; gastric ulcer, with surgical intervention.
      (2) Antacids are used for both duodenal and gastric ulcers.
         (a) Actions: neutralize the acid content of the stomach, inactivate pepsins.
         (b) Common antacids: Amphojel, Gelusil, Maalox, Mylanta.
         (c) Side effects: diarrhea, constipation.
         (d) Nursing role
         Administer antacids, 15 to 30 ml, 1 to 3 hours after meal and at bedtime to enhance the duration of the buffering effect.
      (3) Anticholinergic drugs are used for duodenal ulcers. Their effectiveness is limited because undesirable side effects may occur at therapeutic doses. They are not used for patients with glaucoma, urinary retention, or pyloric obstruction.
      (4) Histamine receptor antagonist—cimetidine (Tagament); ranitidine (Zantac); famotidine (Pepcid)—is used for duodenal ulcers.
         (a) Actions: reduces acid secretion to an almost unmeasurable level, relieves ulcer pain. (When drug is discontinued, ulcer tends to recur.)
         (b) Nursing role: Administer with each meal and at bedtime.
      (5) Carafate (Sycralfate) is used orally for the short-term treatment of duodenal ulcers.
         (a) Actions: Exerts a local action on the GI tract and may form an ulcer-adherent complex at ulcer site, thus protecting the ulcer from further irritation by acid, pepsin, and bile salts. Does not neutralize gastric acid.

(b) Side effects: Constipation, nausea, gastric upset, diarrhea, indigestion, dry mouth, rash, pruritus, sleepiness, and dizziness.

(6) Diet should consist of small, frequent feedings, using buffering foods such as milk. Coffee, alcohol, and seasonings (pepper and mustard) must be avoided.

(7) Proper rest is essential.

   (a) Sedatives and tranquilizers may be given (phenobarbital, Librium, Valium).

   (b) Hospitalization may be required if bleeding, perforation, or severe nocturnal pain is present.

   (c) Bedrest is required until the patient is free of pain and eating normally.

   (d) Visitors and business activities must be limited.

c. Nursing role

   (1) Promote mental and physical rest.

      (a) Maintain bedrest.

      (b) Administer sedatives to promote relaxation.

      (c) Give medication and dietary feedings on time.

   (2) Provide patient and family education.

      (a) Assist in the development of insight into the causes of tension and frustration.

      (b) Reinforce the physician's instructions.

      (c) Encourage the elimination of smoking.

      (d) Encourage moderation in all activities.

      (e) Instruct the patient to take prescribed medication and diet on time.

      (f) Instruct the patient in the recognition of complications.

d. Complications

   (1) Hemorrhage

      (a) Assessment

         1. Inspect stool and vomitus for blood.

         2. Observe the patient for faintness, dyspepsia, nausea.

      (b) Patient care management

         1. Blood and/or plasma transfusions.

         2. Gastric lavage with ice cold saline.

         3. Surgery if bleeding recurs in 48 hours.

      (c) Nursing role

         1. Monitor vital signs every 15 to 30 minutes.

         2. Prepare IV fluid.

         3. Insert indwelling urinary catheter.

         4. Measure and record urinary output every hour.

         5. Observe and record the color, consistency, and volume of stools and vomitus.

   (2) Perforation

      (a) Assessment

         1. Observe for sudden, severe upper abdominal pain that radiates to shoulder.

         2. Palpate abdomen, and note tenderness and boardlike rigidity.

         3. Measure and note vital signs for hypotension, tachycardia, and increased respiration.

      (b) Patient care management: surgical intervention.

   (3) Pyloric obstruction

      (a) Causes: scar tissue formation or edema.

      (b) Assessment

         1. Observe for nausea, vomiting, anorexia, constipation, and epigastric fullness.

         2. Observe general appearance for weight loss.

      (c) Patient care management

         1. Gastric decompression.

         2. Intravenous therapy for correction of electrolyte and fluid imbalance.

         3. Surgical interventions.

2. Management of the patient undergoing gastric surgery

   a. Postoperative nursing role

(1) Place the patient in modified Fowler's position, after recovery from anesthesia, for comfort and easy drainage of the stomach.

(2) Medicate for pain before deep breathing or coughing.

(3) Observe drainage from the nasogastric tube—initially bright red, changing to dark red within 12 hours and back to normal within 36 hours.

(4) Irrigate tube with sodium chloride as ordered.

(5) Administer mouth care every 2 to 4 hours.

(6) Maintain fluid and electrolyte balance.

    (a) Measure and record intake and output.

    (b) Give nothing by mouth until peristalsis returns (auscultate for bowel sounds).

    (c) Give small amount of water initially, then other types of clear fluids).

(7) Give diet of bland food until patient is able to eat six small meals a day.

(8) Encourage ambulation on first postoperative day.

(9) Check drainage tube and reinforce dressing if necessary (serosanguinous drainage is normal).

(10) For total gastrectomy:

    (a) Observe nasogastric drainage (small amount of drainage is normal).

    (b) Offer clear fluids hourly and small feeding after 2 or 3 days.

    (c) Observe for temperature elevation (anastomosis leakage).

b. Postoperative complications

    (1) Hemorrhage.

    (2) Shock (from hemorrhage).

    (3) Pulmonary complications.

    (4) Steatorrhea (unabsorbed fat in stool due to rapid gastric emptying).

    (5) Dumping syndrome, due to rapid emptying of the gastric contents into the small intestine. Hypertonic content draws extra cellular fluid from the plasma, causing symptoms of shock.

    (a) Assessment: Assess for a feeling of fullness and nausea, pallor, sweating, palpitation, weakness, and fainting, which begin 5 to 30 minutes after a meal.

    (b) Nursing role

      1. Explain to the patient that sedatives and antispasmodics may help to delay emptying of the stomach.

      2. Instruct the patient to:

        a. Lie down for 20 to 30 minutes after meals (eat in a semirecumbent position).

        b. Avoid taking fluids with meals.

        c. Keep carbohydrate intake low (avoid sucrose and glucose). A high-protein, high-fat diet is recommended.

        d. Eat small, frequent meals.

    (6) Vitamin B_{12} deficiency. Production of intrinsic factor (gastric secretion that is required for absorption of B_{12}) is halted. Vitamin B_{12} is administered parenterally throughout life.

C. Alterations in Absorption

   1. **Intestinal obstruction** Inability of the intestinal contents to move forward because of partial or complete stoppage. Proximal to the obstruction there is an accumulation of intestinal contents, fluid, and gas. A temporary increase in peristalsis occurs as the bowel attempts to force the intestinal contents through the obstructed area. The peristalsis ends, and the bowels become flaccid. The absorption of fluids in the small intestine is reduced. Pressure on the intestines causes reduction in the circulation of blood, and shock may develop.

   a. Types of obstruction

    (1) Mechanical obstruction. There is an intraluminal obstruction or an obstruction from pressure on the intestinal wall (dynamic ileus, organic ileus, spastic ileus).

(2) Paralytic ileus (adynamic ileus). The intestinal musculature is unable to propel the contents along the bowel because of laparotomy trauma, infection, metabolic disorder, or mesenteric schemia.

b. Assessment
(1) Inspect abdomen for distension and visible peristalsis.
(2) Percuss abdomen for tympany and ascites.
(3) Palpate abdomen for tenderness.
(4) Auscultate abdomen for audible peristalsis and gas movement.
(5) Measure abdominal girth.
(6) Observe and inspect stool for the presence of blood.
(7) Observe the patient's general appearance for weight loss.
(8) Palpate rectum for obstruction.
(9) Measure vital signs, and note increase in pulse and respiration and decrease in blood pressure (shock).
(10) Observe and note pain (location, frequency).
(11) Obtain health history for clues about site involved and underlying cause.
(12) DIAGNOSTIC MEASURES: X-ray of abdomen, sigmoidoscopy, colonoscopy.

c. Patient care management
(1) Decompression of the small intestine by nasogastric suction.
(2) Parenteral therapy for fluid and electrolyte replacement.
(3) Surgical intervention—depends on the cause of the obstruction.

d. Nursing role
(1) Send stool specimen to laboratory.
(2) Measure vital signs and intake and output.
(3) Give oral and nasal care if nasogastric tube is inserted.
(4) Measure and record abdominal girth daily.
(5) Prepare for surgery, if indicated.

D. Alterations in Metabolism
1. **Postnecrotic biliary cirrhosis/portal hypertension** Disruption of the normal configuration of the hepatic lobules, leading to cell death and regeneration with scarring.

Destroyed liver cells are replaced by scar tissue, eventually causing the liver to contract—hence the term "hobnail liver." Obstruction of portal circulation occurs because blood is not allowed to circulate freely through the scarred tissue; therefore blood dams back into the spleen and gastrointestinal tract. Esophageal, gastric, and hemorrhoidal varicosities, which are prone to rupture, form. Fluid accumulates in the abdominal cavity (ascites), resulting in increased aldosterone.

a. Types:
(1) Laennec's portal cirrhosis (alcoholic/nutritional). Scar tissue surrounds the portal areas because of chronic alcoholism.
(2) Postnecrotic cirrhosis. This results from acute viral hepatitis; there are broad bands of scar tissue.
(3) Biliary cirrhosis. This results from chronic biliary obstruction and infections; there is pericholangitic scarring.

b. Causes: alcoholism, exposure to certain chemicals, viral disease.
c. Incidence: occurs most often in men between the ages of 40 and 60 years.
d. Assessment. *See* Unit Seven, Alterations in Metabolism, Section A: General Assessment, page 205.
e. Patient care management
(1) Portal hypertension
(a) Diet—200 mg sodium.
(b) Diuretics—Diuril, Aldactone, Lasix, Edecrin.
(c) Restriction of fluids.
(d) Paracentesis.
(e) Portacaval shunt.
(2) Cirrhosis
(a) Bedrest.
(b) High-protein diet with vitamin supplements (vitamins A, B, and K and folic acid).
(c) No intake of alcohol.
f. Nursing interventions
(1) Provide high-protein, high-caloric diet, offered in small, frequent feedings; provide oral hygiene.
(2) Offer supplementary feedings.
(3) Administer supplementary vitamins.
(4) Maintain intake and output record.

(5) Weigh the patient daily.

(6) Relieve pruritus with good skin care: bathing without soap and massage with emollient lotions; protect bony prominence.

(7) Observe for signs of complications.

(8) Record vital signs every 4 hours.

(9) Observe for increasing stupor (mental change, lethargy, hallucinations).

(10) Administer antibiotics.

(11) Turn and position the patient, or have the patient reposition him-/ herself every 2 hours.

2. **Esophageal varices** Dilated tortuous veins, usually found in the submucosa of the lower esophagus and caused by portal hypertension due to cirrhosis of the liver. They may extend up into the esophagus and the stomach.

a. Assessment (The focus is on detection of bleeding.)

(1) Observe skin for pallor and coolness.

(2) Measure and note vital signs for decreased blood pressure and increased respiration and pulse.

(3) Observe for hematemesis, melena, and restlessness.

(4) Inspect abdomen and anus for dilated veins.

(5) Assess health history for alcoholism and poor nutritional status.

b. Patient care management

(1) Administration of Pitressin IV to lower portal hypertension.

(2) Gastric lavage with ice-cold saline until returns are clear.

(3) Administration of fresh blood or plasma.

(4) Insertion of a Sengstaken-Blakemore tube (see diagram) to stop bleeding by applying pressure to the esophageal varices.

(a) The tube has three openings: for gastric aspiration, inflation of the gastric balloon, inflation of the esophageal balloon.

(b) The appropriate tube opening is connected to gastric suction.

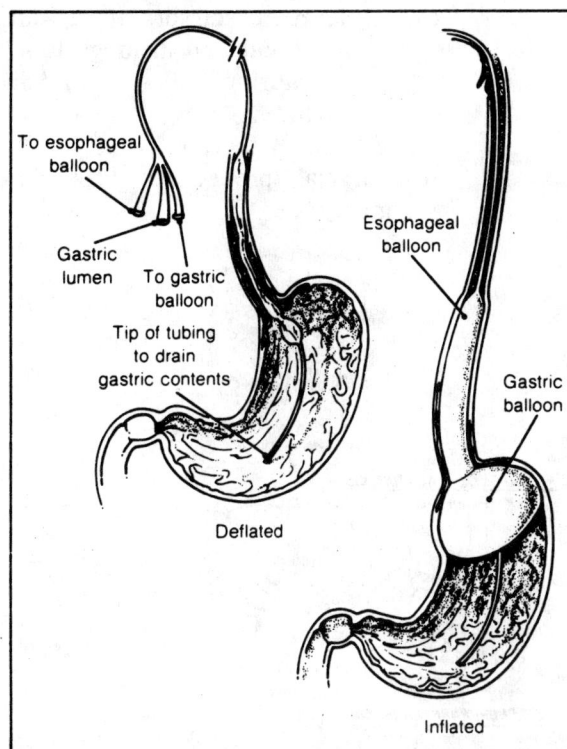

Diagram of Properly Placed Sengstaken-Blakemore Tube. (From *Medical-Surgical Nursing—A Conceptual Approach,* Second Edition by D. Jones et al. Copyright © 1982 by McGraw-Hill Book Company. Used with the permission of McGraw-Hill Book Company.)

(c) Ice water may be circulated in and out of the stomach balloon to constrict the gastric vessel.

(d) Nursing role

1. Observe gastric suction.

2. Provide comfort measures to avoid chilling as ice water is circulating in the gastric balloon.

3. Monitor vital signs every 15 minutes until stable, then every hour.

4. Irrigate tube to detect bleeding.

5. Check pressure on both balloons (25 to 30 mm Hg).

6. Deflate tube for 5 minutes at 8- to 12-hour intervals.

7. Offer frequent mouth and nasal care.

8. Provide a quiet environment and calm reassurance.

9. Keep scissors at bedside to cut and dislodge tube, causing deflation of balloon.

(5) Vitamin K therapy.

(6) Surgical procedures (see diagram)

NORMAL

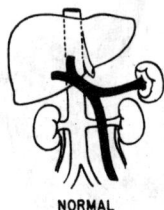

PORTA-CAVAL ANASTOMOSIS

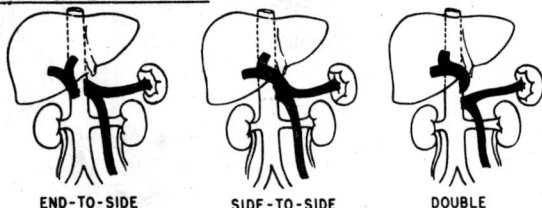

END-TO-SIDE   SIDE-TO-SIDE   DOUBLE

SPLENO-RENAL ANASTOMOSIS

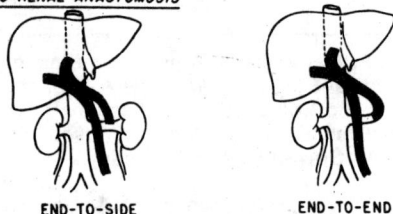

END-TO-SIDE   END-TO-END

CAVAL-SUPERIOR MESENTERIC ANASTOMOSIS

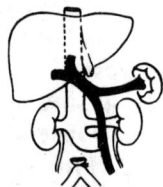

Diagrammatic Representation of Major Portosystemic Shunts. (From *Principles of Surgery* by S. I. Schwartz et al. (eds.). Copyright © 1974 by McGraw-Hill Book Company. Used with the permission of McGraw-Hill Book Company.)

(a) Direct surgical ligation of varices.

(b) Bypass procedures to lower the pressure in the portal system

1. **Portacaval anastomosis** Portal blood is shunted into the vena cava.

2. **Splenorenal shunt** A shunt is inserted between the splenic vein and the left renal vein.

3. **Mesocaval shunt** The inferior vena cava is severed, and the proximal end of the cava is anastomosed to the side of the superior mesenteric vein.

c. Nursing role. *See* Section C: Management during the Postoperative Period, page 269.

3. **Hepatitis coma**   A complication of liver disease in which there is an accumulation of ammonia in the blood, leading to hepatic failure.

a. Causes:

(1) Enzymatic and bacterial digestion of protein (including dietary and blood proteins) in the gastrointestinal tract.

(2) Ammonia from gastrointestinal bleeding, a high-protein diet, or bacterial growth in small and large intestines.

(3) Other factors that cause high ammonia levels: alkalosis and hypoxalemia, overdiuresis, surgery, central nervous system depressants (sedatives, tranquilizers, and narcotics), infection.

b. Assessment

(1) Observe closely for disorientation (time and place), confusion, difficult speech, and altered moods.

(2) Observe hands for flapping tremors (asterixis) and difficulty in handwriting.

(3) Observe for fetor hepaticus (odor of fresh-mowed grass, acetone, or old wine).

c. Patient care management

(1) Cleansing enema—reduces ammonia absorption from GI tract.

(2) Antibiotic drug (neomycin)—destroys intestinal bacteria; therefore reduces the amount of ammonia formed.

(3) Lactulose—promotes the excretion of ammonia in the stool.

(4) Correction of fluid and electrolyte imbalance.

(5) Elimination of precipitating cause.

d. Nursing role

(1) Observe and evaluate neurological status several times each day.

(2) Measure and record vital signs every 4 hours.

(3) Weigh the patient daily.

(4) Administer sedatives and analgesics sparingly.

(5) Monitor electrolyte status.

(6) Give supportive nursing care to unconscious patient.

4. **Diabetes mellitus**   A condition characterized by hyperglycemia, insulin insufficiency due to failure of the beta cells of the islet of Langerhans. *See also* Unit Six, Other Alterations of Health, Section B: Insulin-Dependent Diabetes Mellitus, page 149.

a. Types

(1) Type I: Insulin-dependent diabetes mellitus (IDDM). Usually begins in childhood, but can occur at any age, not uncommon in adult. Measurable insulin may still be present. The onset is abrupt. Management includes subcutaneous injection of insulin, and diet and exercise are essential parts of the therapy. Mortality and morbidity result from acute and chronic complication. Retinopathy, nephropathy, neuropathy, and cardiovascular effect will not occur if blood glucose levels are maintained within the normal range.

(2) Type II: Non-insulin-dependent diabetes mellitus (NIDDM). Usually occurs after the age of 40, but can occur in younger persons who do not require insulin and are not prone to developing ketosis. This type is referred to as *maturity onset diabetes of the young (MODY)*. In general, these patients may never require insulin and are managed adequately by diet alone. The majority of NIDDM's are overweight when the condition is first diagnosed. The symptoms are so minor that they may go undetected for years. The diagnosis may be suspected as the result of a urinalysis or the patient's seeking medical treatment for complications such as deteriorating vision, pain in the leg, or impotence. Management consists of diet and exercise; medications (insulin and/or an oral agent) may be added if diet and exercise

alone are unsuccessful after a reasonable trial period. The goals of management are to achieve normal glucose levels and to prevent vascular complications. The vascular problem accounts for most of the morbidity and mortality.

b. Assessment

(1) Observe general appearance for weight loss, skin break or changes, or poor skin turgor.

(2) Inspect lower extremities for dryness, thickened toenails, shiny skin, and numbness and tingling.

(3) Palpate peripheral pulse.

(4) Measure vital signs and note elevation of blood pressure.

(5) Inspect the fundus of the eye for retinal exudates or hemorrhage.

(6) Obtain health history. Note and record complaints of the following, commonly seen in Type I:

(a) Feeling of nervousness or irritability, tremors.

(b) Polyuria.

(c) Polydipsia (thirst).

(d) Polyphagia (hunger).

(e) Weight loss.

(7) DIAGNOSTIC MEASURES

(a) Blood glucose

1. Postprandial test (following meals)

a. Blood sample is taken every 2 hours after meals.

b. Value over 150 mg is diagnostic of diabetes.

2. Glucose tolerance test.

3. Urine testing for glucose and acetone

a. Glucose Tes-tape (Clinistix and Diastrix).

b. Ketone (Acetest and Ketostix).

c. Keto-Diastrix for glucose and ketone. (Glucose is present in the urine: ketone may or may not be present.)

c. Patient care management

(1) Diet (based on concern for total caloric intake and complex carbohydrates in diet)

(a) Overweight patient must attain normal weight.

(b) Total caloric intake is controlled—20% to 30% fat, 12% to 20% protein, 50% complex carbohydrates.

(c) ADA exchange diet consists of milk, vegetables, fruits, bread (includes starchy vegetables), meat, and fat exchange, and is high in fiber.

(d) Sweeteners include nutritive (about 4 calories per gram—sorbitol, fructose, aspartame) and nonnutritive (no calories) — cyclamates, saccharin.

(e) Glycemic index measures the ability of selected foods to raise the blood glucose level. Glucose is assigned a value of 100%. Other foods are assigned percentages based on glucose:

Glucose	100%
Carrot	92%
Cornflakes	92%
Rice	72%
Banana	66%
Raisin	64%
Corn	59%
Sponge cake	46%
Apple (golden delicious)	39%
Ice cream	36%
Peanut	13%

(2) Exercise to lower the blood sugar level (regular pattern to be done daily is prescribed).

(a) Patient with blood glucose over 300 mg/dl or with ketones in urine should not exercise until blood glucose is within normal range. (Exercise increases hormone and catecholamine levels; this will, in turn, cause the liver to release more glucose and thereby raise the blood glucose.)

(b) Insulin-dependent patients should exercise (moderately) after meals or take a 15-gram carbohydrate snack (a fruit exchange) beforehand.

(3) Drug therapy. *See also* Unit Six, Other Alterations of Health, Section B: Insulin-Dependent Diabetes, page 149.

(a) Insulin, prescribed in units and available in two strengths that correspond to the number of units of insulin per milliliter of solution: U.40 (40 units/ml) and U-100 (100 units/ml). The insulin syringe must correlate with the strength of insulin used.

1. Dosage of insulin

a. The dosage of insulin is adjusted according to the levels of blood glucose, the degree to which glucose is present, and the time when high glucose levels appear in relation to insulin administration and meals. (Meals are planned to conform with the insulin peaks and exercise pattern of the patient receiving one or more insulin injections per day.)

b. In the absence of complications, treatment may be started with 10 to 20 units of intermediate-acting insulin combined with a shorter-acting insulin given subcutaneously before breakfast. This dose is gradually increased until the urine is free of glucose and the blood glucose level before each meal is near the normal level.

2. Insulin preparations available in the United States *See also* Unit Six, Other Alterations of Health, Section B: Insulin-Dependent diabetes mellitus, page 149.

a. Short acting—regular (may be administered subcutaneously, IM or IV)

b. Intermediate acting—NPH and lente.

c. Long acting—ultra-lente.

d. Other (insulin may be of human, beef, or pork origin)—mixed insulin, NPH (70%) and regular (30%) (should be administered within 5 minutes after being mixed or after a period of 24 hours because different ratios are delivered depending on when administered).

3. Side effects of insulin
   a. Local allergic reaction: redness, swelling, tenderness, and induration; a wheal may appear at the site of injection. Occurs at the beginning stage of therapy.
   b. Systemic allergic reaction: Symptoms ranging from hives to general edema and anaphylaxis. Give small doses of insulin to desensitize.
   c. Insulin lipodystrophy: reaction at the site of injection; dimpling of fat has disappeared with the use of purified U-100 insulin.
   d. Insulin edema: occurs in patient with prolonged hyperglycemia.
   e. Insulin resistance: is common is obese patients. Overcome by weight loss. Patient may need 200 to 500 units or more.

4. Monitoring of glucose and ketones
   a. Self-monitoring of blood glucose: use of a commercial meter that measures electronically the amount of glucose in the blood.
   b. Hemoglobin A1C (glycosylated hemoglobin A1C): Blood test that shows the pattern of blood glucose level over a period of approximately 3 months; normal value is 6 to 8.
   c. Urine test for glucose and ketones (*See* Unit Six, page 149).

5. Hypoglycemic reactions (insulin shock)
   a. Causes: excessive amount of insulin, too little food, excessive physical activity.
   b. Clinical manifestations: headache, lightheadedness, confusion, and emotional changes; sweating, tremors, tachycardia, and palpitation; cold, clammy skin, numbness, or tingling.
   c. Treatment: oral (4 oz of orange juice with 2 packages of sugar) or IV administration of glucose (IV 50% glucose in water); subcutaneous administration of glucagon.
   d. Prevention: following a regular pattern and timetable for eating, administering insulin, and engaging in daily exercise; eating a snack during peak activity.

(b) Oral hypoglycemia agents (sulfonylureas)
   1. Primary action is direct stimulation of pancreatic insulin secretion.
   2. For successful treatment, diet must be restricted in regard to total calories and carbohydrates.
   3. Agents used
      a. First generation: tolbutamide (Orinase), chlorpropamide (Diabinese), acetohexamide (Dymelor), tolazamide (Tolinase).
      b. Second generation: Glucotrol-XL, Diabeta, Micronase, Glynase. Last up to 24 hours.

d. Nursing diagnoses/goals/interventions
   (1) Deficit in knowledge concerning the maintenance of near-normal blood glucose level

(2) Altered nutrition related to dietary regulations to combat abnormal metabolism of carbohydrates, proteins, and fats

Goal: Patient will have a normal glucose level and improved metabolism of carbohydrates, proteins, and fats.

Interventions:

(a) Teach the patient the proper dietary regimen.
   1. Eat three or more regularly spaced meals a day.
   2. Become thoroughly familiar with food exchange lists.
   3. Avoid concentrated carbohydrates.
   4. If taking insulin, eat extra calories when unusual activity is anticipated.

(b) Teach the patient about exercise.
   1. Exercise regularly and consistently.
   2. Keep a form of carbohydrate available.

(c) Teach the patient proper insulin usage.
   1. Rotate the sites of injection.
   2. Keep a reserve of insulin refrigerated; check the expiration date on the bottle.
   3. Watch for signs of insulin reactions or diabetic coma.
   4. Wear Medic-Alert band or carry diabetic identification card.

(d) Teach the patient to perform capillary glucose test
   1. Test glucose level before meals and at bedtime.
   2. Keep a record of blood glucose test.

(e) Provide emotional support to the patient and his/her family.

(f) Teach the patient to take oral hypoglycemic medication as prescribed.

(g) Teach the patient about diabetic control.
   1. Notify the physician when any unusual symptoms occur.
   2. Watch for signs of diabetic acidosis.
   3. Take only prescribed medication.

(3) Impairment of skin integrity related to neuropathy

Goal: Patient will maintain skin integrity.

Interventions:

Teach the patient about foot care.

(a) Wear well-fitted, non-compressive shoes and socks.

(b) Provide proper daily foot care: bathe feet in warm water (avoid soaking for prolonged period); dry feet carefully, especially between toes; massage feet with lubricating lotion, except between toes; prevent moisture between toes to avert maceration of skin.

(c) Inspect feet routinely for corns, calluses, and skin breakdown.

(d) Have corns and calluses cared for by a podiatrist.

(e) Report any foot injury to the physician.

e. Evaluation

(1) Patient describes diabetes and how it effects the body.

(2) Patient maintains health at optimal level.

(3) Patient follows the prescribed dietary regimen.

(4) Patient utilizes proper practices of insulin therapy.

(5) Patient utilizes measures to determine the degree of diabetic control.

(6) Patient takes prescribed oral hypoglycemia medication.

(7) Patient practices proper foot care to prevent infection.

(8) Patient maintains diabetic control during periods of illness.

f. Potential complications of diabetic mellitus

(1) Development of hypoglycemia related to imbalance between insulin need and insulin dose.

(2) Development of ketosis/ketoacidosis related to insulin deficiency and faulty fat metabolism.

(3) Development of long-term complications related to persistent hyperglycemia and accelerated vascular disease.

5. Diabetic ketoacidosis (DKA)

Insulin deficiency affects the metabolism of carbohydrates. The amount of glucose entering the cell is reduced, and fat is metabolized instead of carbohydrates. Free fatty acids are mobilized from adipose tissue. Liver oxidase acts upon these fatty acids to produce ketone bodies. The ketone bodies escape into the blood and metabolic acidosis results, with lowering of serum bicarbonate, pCO_2, and pH. If acidosis is allowed to become severe, coma results.

a. Causes
   (1) Failure to take insulin.
   (2) Insufficient insulin intake.
   (3) Resistance to insulin because of infection or physiological stresses.
b. Incidence: more common in insulin-dependent diabetes.
c. Assessment
   (1) Obtain health history (a complaint of few days' duration). Assess for:
      (a) Polyuria, polydipsia, polyphagia, weakness, and abdominal pain.
      (b) Glucosuria and ketonuria.
      (c) Muscular aches and headaches.
   (2) Inspect the patient's general appearance for poor skin turgor; flushing of the face; warm, dry skin: odor of acetone on breath.
   (3) Measure and note vital signs for temperature elevation and deep breathing (Kussmaul breathing).
   (4) Inspect extremities for paresthesia and diminished deep tendon reflexes.
   (5) DIAGNOSTIC MEASURES: elevated blood glucose, decreased serum bicarbonate and pH, postive plasma ketone, postive urine sugar and acetone.
d. Nursing role
   (1) Prepare for IV infusion of saline and potassium.
   (2) Administer insulin as ordered (regular insulin may be given IV, subcutaneously, or IM).
   (3) Test urine for sugar and acetone hourly.
   (4) Frequently monitor electrolytes, serum glucose, CO_2-combining power, and pH.
   (5) Observe neurological status.
   (6) Give personal hygienic care.

6. Hyperosmolar hyperglycemic nonketotic coma (HHNC) Metabolic disorder in which the blood sugar level is extremely elevated, increasing the serum osmolality and resulting in hypertonic deydration. Serum ketosis is usually not present.
   a. Medical management
      (1) IV insulin administration.
      (2) IV fluid administration; plasma expanders as needed.
      (3) Electrolyte replacement as needed (blood glucose, electrolyte, and bicarbonate levels; ABG; monitor ECG, CVP).
   b. Nursing diagnoses/interventions/evaluation See DKA for Nursing Diagnoses, Goals, and Interventions.
7. **Adrenal crisis** A life-threatening situation resulting from inadequate amounts of aldosterone and cortisol.
   a. Assessment
      (1) Observe for fatigue, hypotension, epigastric pain, nausea, hyperthermia, petechiae, or ecchymosis.
      (2) DIAGNOSTIC MEASURES: serum electrolytes (hyperkalemia), normal or lowered sodium, CBC (eosinophil count is elevated), plasma cortisol (normal or decreased).
   b. Patient care management
      (1) Start IV; hand 5% dextrose normal saline and allow to drip rapidly (1 liter per hour).
      (2) Administer steroids—hydrocortisone succinate (SoluCortef), 100 to 200 mg IV stat, and 50 to 100 mg every 2 to 4 hours.
      (3) Give pressor agents (e.g. Dopamine, Neo-Synephrine).
      (4) Monitor CVP.
      (5) Use cardiac monitor.
      (6) Insert Foley catheter; measure output at least every hour.
      (7) Ensure adequate airway.
8. **Myxedema (hypothyroidism)** A severe degree of long-standing hypothyroidism in adulthood.
   a. Assessment
      (1) Assess health history for the following:
         (a) Past history of thyroid disease and/or goiter, thyroid surgery, or hormone therapy.

(b) Complaints of fatigue, increased need for sleep, muscle weakness, hypersensitivity to cold, and inability to concentrate.

(c) Changes in voice quality.

(d) Menstrual disturbances, as well as a loss of libido.

(e) Changes in appetite or bowel habits.

(f) Forgetfulness and personality changes.

(2) Inspect skin for dryness, roughness, scaliness, and brittle nails and hair.

(3) Inspect eyelids, hands, and feet for swelling.

(4) Palpate the thyroid for enlargement.

(5) Auscultate the abdomen for diminished bowel sounds.

(6) Measure and note temperature and vital signs for lowered temperature, heart rate, and blood pressure.

(7) Observe for slowness of speech, deafness, and shortening of attention span.

(8) DIAGNOSTIC MEASURES: low thyroxine concentration, radioactive iodine uptake (RAI), elevated serum cholesterol, scanning of thyroid gland.

b. Nursing role

(1) Provide a warm environment; advise patient to dress adequately and provide extra blankets.

(2) Recommend a diet high in cellulose and fiber, and increase fluid intake to relieve constipation.

(3) Apply lanolin and lotion to relieve skin dryness.

(4) Monitor the effect of thyroid hormone replacement.

(5) Monitor intake and output.

(6) Weigh the patient daily.

9. **Graves's disease (hyperthyroidism)** An excess of thyroid hormone.

a. Assessment

(1) Assess health history for the following:

(a) Complaints of weight loss, weakness, dyspnea, palpitation, increased thirst or appetite, irritability, profuse sweating, prominence of the eyes (exophthalmos), diplopia, and presence of a goiter.

(b) Past history of thyroid problem and/or goiter in the family.

(c) Female: scanty menstruation; male: gynecomastia and increased sexual desire.

(2) Measure and note changes in temperature and vital signs such as increased pulse rate (over 90 beats per minutes) and widening pulse pressure.

(3) Auscultate abdomen for an increase in bowel sounds.

(4) Weigh the patient and compare previous record (weight loss is observed).

(5) Palpate thyroid gland for enlargement.

(6) Observe general appearance for excessive perspiration, patchy hyperpigmentation, separation of nail from nailbed (especially fourth and fifth fingers), and tremor.

(7) Inspect and palpate eyes for periorbital edema, and lower leg and toes for edema.

(8) DIAGNOSTIC MEASURES

(a) Elevated T_4 and T_3 resin uptake and ^{131}I uptake test.

(b) Scanning of thyroid gland.

b. Patient care management

(1) Antithyroid agents: propylthiouracil, methimazole (Tapazole).
Side effects: skin rash, pruritus, fever, and agranulocytosis.

(2) Adjunctive therapy

(a) Propranolol—rapidly alleviates the toxic symptoms.

(b) Lugol's solution (concentrated iodine solution)—reduces the release of thyroid hormones and the vascularity and size of the thyroid.

(3) Radioactive iodine—destroys the cells in the thyroid gland that make thyroxine by ingestion of radioactive iodine.

(4) Surgical intervention—thyroidectomy. *See* Management of the patient undergoing thyroidectomy, below.

10. **Management of the patient undergoing thyroidectomy** Removal of the thyroid gland (may be total or partial).
    a. Surgical procedures
       (1) Total thyroidectomy, performed for thyroid cancer. Patient must take thyroid hormone on a permanent basis.
       (2) Subtotal thyroidectomy, performed to correct hyperthyroidism and some cases of simple goiter. One sixth of the thyroid tissue is left intact; therefore hormonal replacements are not necessary.
    b. Preoperative nursing role
       (1) Administer antithyroid drug (propylthiouracil) as ordered until hyperthyroidism disappears.
       (2) Administer iodine (Lugol's solution, potassium iodide) to reduce the size and vascularity of the goiter.
       (3) Administer general preoperative care.
    c. Postoperative nursing role
       (1) Place the patient in semi-Fowler's position to prevent stain or suture line.
       (2) Check dressing periodically, and reinforce when necessary.
       (3) Monitor vital signs every 30 minutes for first 12 hours; take temperature rectally every hour for 24 hours, then orally.
       (4) Observe neck and pillow carefully for bleeding.
       (5) Observe recurrent laryngeal nerve damage (dyspnea, noisy breathing, voice changes, and stridor).
       (6) Assist with ambulation the 1st postoperative day by supporting the patient's head and neck.
       (7) Observe for signs of injury or removal of parathyroid (spasm of hands and feet and twitching of facial muscles).
       (8) Observe for thyroid crisis (*see* below).

(9) Keep tracheostomy set at bedside.
    d. Complication
11. **Thyroid crisis** An acute, sometimes fatal episode of thyroid overactivity.
    (1) Causes: infection, trauma, acute cardiovascular disease, emotional stress, abrupt withdrawal of antithyroid drug.
    (2) Assessment: tachycardia (over 30); elevated temperature; exaggerated symptoms of thyrotoxicosis; gastrointestinal symptoms (diarrhea, abdominal pain, nausea, and vomiting); neurological symptoms (psychosis, coma).
    (3) Patient care management
        (a) Administer Lugol's solution or SSKI (saturated solution of potassium iodide).
        (b) Administer dextrose-containing parenteral fluids to replace liver glycogen.
        (c) Administer hydrocortisone to treat shock.
        (d) Administer antithyroid drugs.
    (4) Nursing role
        (a) Administer aspirin or acetaminophen, and initiate other measures to reduce temperature.
        (b) Administer oxygen.
        (c) Monitor vital signs and temperature.
        (d) Monitor IV infusion.
12. **Management of the patient undergoing parathyroidectomy** Removal of one or more of the parathyroids. It may occur accidentally during a thyroidectomy.
    a. Preoperative nursing role
       (1) Feed fluids up to 3000 ml daily.
       (2) Encourage low-calcium, low-phosphate diet.
       (3) Strain urine, and send calculi to the laboratory for analysis.
       (4) Encourage mobility. (When bone is under stress, there is less calcium excretion.)
    b. Postoperative nursing role
       (Immediate care is similar to that for thyroidectomy, above.)
       (1) Observe for tetany and treat with IV calcium gluconate (as ordered).

(2) Monitor intravenous infusion of phosphorus and fluids (reverses hyperparathyroid crisis).

Alterations in Perception and Coordination

A. Management of the Patient Undergoing Surgery for Retinal Detachment.

The retina receives visual images and transmits them to the brain via the optic nerve. The sensory retina (rod and cone layer) separates from the pigment epithelium of the retina. Fluid from the vitreous cavity seeps through the opening and elevates the retina away from the pigment epithelium, producing a sensation of floating spots, blurred vision, and loss of vision.

1. Causes of retinal detachment: trauma, degeneration, hemorrhage, tumor.

2. Assessment
   a. Assess health history for complaints of flashing light, floating spots before the eyes, and progressively blurred vision. (Because the retina contains no fiber, there is no pain, redness, or inflammation.)
   b. DIAGNOSTIC MEASURES: testing of visual acuity, ophthalmoscopy, testing of visual field.

3. Patient care management (surgery)
   a. **Electrodiathermy** An electrode is passed through the sclera, allowing the collected fluid to escape.
   b. **Retinal surgery** Retinal tears are sealed by the production of localized chorioretinal adhesions. After exudative choroiditis is produced, the retina must be brought back into place. Draining the fluid from the subretinal space (by perforating the sclera and choroid) helps make it possible for the sclera to return to its normal position. In addition, other mechanical procedures may be performed.
      (1) **Cryosurgery** Use of a supercooled probe (causes minimal damage) on the sclera to produce scarring.
      (2) **Photocoagulation** Use of a strong beam of light directed through the dilated pupil to form a scar. A laser beam can be used in photocoagulation.

(3) **Scleral buckling** Shortening the sclera to enhance contact between the choroid and the retina (this is the most common procedure). After the subretinal fluid is withdrawn, the detachment is treated by one of the retinal surgery methods (e.g., cryosurgery). The treated area is then indented, to "buckle" inward toward the vitreous humor.

(4) **Circling procedure** Application of a strip encircling the eye and indented over the retinal defect.

4. Preoperative nursing role
   a. Maintain bedrest.
   b. Cover both eyes with patches to promote the return of the retina into place.
   c. Position the patient's head as ordered. (The detached area should be in a dependent position; most common position is superior temporal detachment.)
   d. Administer sedation and tranquilizer as ordered.
   e. Caution against straining, sudden movement (e.g., sneezing, coughing, sitting up in bed, combing hair), bending over, or touching or rubbing the eye.
   f. Keep side rails up; assist the patient with meals, feeding if necessary.
   g. Minimize sensory deprivation; speak to the patient when approaching, visit frequently, place call bell within reach.
   h. Administer stool softeners.
   i. Before surgery, dilate the pupils with mydriatics; 10% phenylephrine (Neo-Synephrine), cycloplegics (1% Cyclogyl), and $\frac{1}{4}$% scopolamine eyedrops.

5. Postoperative nursing role
   a. Maintain bedrest.
   b. Observe for hemorrhage (only the operated eye is patched).
   c. Place the patient on his/her back or on operated side.
   d. Provide patient education.
      (1) Reading should be avoided for 2 to 3 weeks.
      (2) Television watching is permitted.
      (3) Care must be taken not to bump the head.
      (4) Light work is allowed after 3 weeks. (Before then, bending or lifting heavy objects must be avoided.)

e. Provide proper care after scleral buckling.

   (1) Antibiotic ointment is instilled and a pressure dressing is applied, using an eye pad and plastic tape.

   (2) Antiemetic (e.g., Tigan, Compazine) is ordered to prevent soiling the eye dressing and strain on the eye.

   (3) Medication for pain (Demerol) is given.

   (4) The patient is allowed out of bed to go to the bathroom after recovery from anesthesia; the 2nd day, resumes all activities of daily living; is discharged on the 4th to 5th day after surgery.

B. Management of the Patient Undergoing Musculoskeletal Surgery

1. **Amputation** Surgical removal of all or part of an extremity.

  a. Preoperative nursing role

   (1) Reinforce information given by the physician concerning the postoperative period.

   (2) Arrange for a visit from a rehabilitated amputee.

   (3) Inform the patient about phantom limb sensation.

   (4) Have the patient practice arm pushing-up and sit-ups to strengthen the tricep.

   (5) Teach the patient to crutch-walk.

  b. Postoperative nursing role

   (1) Observe stump dressing for hemorrhage every 30 minutes until vital signs are stable, then every 3 hours thereafter.

   (2) Keep tourniquet in plain view at bedside (apply if hemorrhage occurs).

   (3) Reinforce dressing as required, using aseptic technique.

   (4) Elevate the foot of the bed to lessen edema of the stump and hasten venous return. (Avoid elevating stump on pillows.)

   (5) Turn the patient to prone position 2 to 3 times daily to prevent hip contracture.

   (6) Observe for signs of infection (e.g., foul odor) and neuroma (e.g., severe pain).

   (7) Encourage exercise while on bedrest (e.g., range of motion of unaffected leg, arm push-ups).

   (8) Provide stump care several times daily.

    (a) Wrap with clean Ace bandage.

    (b) Wash stump with mild soap and water.

    (c) Apply petrolatum-based lotion if skin is dry.

    (d) Apply stockinette sock if ordered.

    (e) Massage stump to stimulate circulation.

   (9) Provide patient education.

    (a) Instruct the patient and his/her family on correct method of bandaging.

    (b) Provide clear directions for stump care and exercise.

2. Knee surgery

3. Arthroscopic surgery Arthroscope introduced into knee joint and surgery is performed.

  a. Causes: torn cartilage or meniscus, advanced destruction of joint.

  b. Surgical procedures

   (1) **Arthrotomy** Incision into a joint for exploration or removal of diseased tissue.

   (2) **Total knee replacement** Replacement of the tibial and femoral joint.

  c. Nursing role

   (1) Have the patient do quadricep setting exercise, straight leg raising, and flexion and extension of foot.

   (2) Elevate operated leg above the heart.

   (3) Elevate head of bed only at meals.

   (4) Apply ice pack to operated site.

   (5) Check dressing for excessive drainage.

   (6) Observe hemovac and measure drainage (should not exceed 300 ml).

   (7) If cast is in place, observe for pressure areas and pain.

   (8) Watch for knee flexion, which should occur by 14 days postoperative.

   (9) Encourage bed exercise.

  (10) Ambulate the patient with crutches when he/she can raise leg and flex knee adequately.

Alteration in Behavior

Depression A subjective response to threat, loss, or failure—tangible or intangible, actual or imagined.
1. Dynamics/characteristics
   a. It is a mood state that may be experienced by any person in response to a loss (loneliness, feelings of hopelessness, helplessness, apathy).
   b. Depression may be viewed as a cluster of symptoms that may persist and impair the functional abilities of a person, such as:
      (1) Loss of interest in surroundings.
      (2) Sleep disturbance.
      (3) Fatigue.
      (4) Disturbed appetite.
      (5) Increased pessimism.
      (6) Self-reproach.
      (7) Feelings of inadequacy.
      (8) Loss of self-esteem.
      (9) Crying spells with or without apparent cause.
      (10) Decreased motivation.
      (11) Gastrointestinal disturbances.
      (12) Vague complaints of pain, dizziness, lightheadedness.
   c. A recent theory of the cause of depression is deficiency in certain brain bioamines such as norepinephrine.
   d. Depression is often masked as a physical symptom and therefore may persist unrecognized and thus untreated.
   e. Depression affects others in the patient's environment.
   f. Depressive reactions may be classified as:
      (1) Reactive (exogenous) or mild depression
         (a) It is precipitated by a tangible or identifiable loss.
         (b) There is sleep disturbance.
         (c) The patient feels worse as the day progresses.
         (d) The individual responds to environmental stimuli.
         (e) It is self-limiting when the loss is accepted, feelings associated with it are expressed and understood, and new relationships are formed to replace the loss.
         (f) It does not persist continually and does not impair functioning.
         (g) This type of depression is an adaptive response to the realities of life.
      (2) Endogenous depression
         (a) There is no clear-cut (tangible) precipitating event.
         (b) Psychomotor retardation occurs.
         (c) The individual feels worse in the morning and better as the day progresses.
         (d) The individual does not respond to environmental stimuli appropriately because of self-absorption.
         (e) Obsessional thoughts are present.
         (f) Marked weight loss (more than 10 pounds) occurs.
         (g) There is a feeling of worthlessness.
         (h) There is inability to maintain and perform the basic activities of daily living.
         (i) Disturbances in urinary and digestive functions are common.
2. Assessment
   a. Assess the patient's depressive behavior, based on observation while interacting with the patient, his/her family, or significant others.
   b. Be alert to affects, somatic complaints, psychomotor activity, thought content, and communication patterns.
   c. Assess the patient's strengths and weaknesses.
   d. Assess the patient for suicidal behavior.
   e. Assess the patient's environmental support system (family, friends, significant others) and their potential for meeting the patient's needs.
   f. Assess the patient's physiological functioning.
   g. Assess the patient's ability to communicate his/her thoughts, feelings, and needs.
3. Patient care management
   (1) Electroconvulsive therapy (ECT). *See* Appendix, page 340.

(2) Psychotherapy.
(3) Drug therapy—antidepressants, lithium carbonate.
(4) Supportive counseling and family therapy.
(5) Health promotion
  (a) Provide family counseling.
  (b) Assist the patient to explore ways of coping with stress.
  (c) Assist the patient in promoting a healthful lifestyle (good health habits and practices).

4. Nursing diagnoses/goals/interventions
  a. Ineffective (individual) coping related to feelings of ambivalence, anxiety, helplessness, and hopelessness associated with depression
  Goal: Patient will identify feelings of ambivalence, anxiety, helplessness, and hopelessness and will develop new, effective techniques for their management.
  Interventions:
  (1) Assist the patient to feel accepted.
  (2) Encourage appropriate verbalization of feelings.
  (3) Discuss unreasonable demands openly with the patient.
  (4) Do not foster dependency. Provide help only when warranted.
  (5) Use simple, direct, clear explanations.
  (6) Help the patient to develop new sets of social skills in order to form important relationships with others.
  b. Self-care deficit: feeding and bathing/hygiene/dressing/grooming/toileting related to depression
  Goal: Patient will resume self-care and will achieve an adequate sleep/rest/activity pattern.
  Intervention: Provide physical care that includes nutrition; skin care, appearance, hygiene; maintenance of fluid and electrolyte balance; and prevention of contractures and other circulatory problems, especially during the acute stage.
  c. Self-esteem disturbance related to real or threatened losses
  Goal: Patient will improve his/her level of self-esteem.

Interventions:
(1) Support the patient as he/she develops an awareness of his/her illness.
(2) Listen to the patient.
(3) Be honest.
(4) Be nonjudgmental (acknowledge the patient's perceptions as personal and meaningful).
(5) Acknowledge and support the patient as dislikes and likes are expressed. Help the patient to perceive that his/her emotional expressions are a positive learning experience.
(6) Be aware of your own attitudes and nonverbal communications, and the way they affect the patient.
(7) Assist the patient to reevaluate what he/she wants to accomplish and to readjust to these goals.
(8) Gradually move the patient from a one-to-one relationship into participation in group experience at his/her own pace.

d. Risk for violence related to feelings of anger, hostility, or suicidal ideation
Goal: Patient will be safe from injury and will channel destructive impulses into constructive expression.
Interventions:
(1) Protect the patient from self-destructive tendencies. Be alert for suicidal cues.
(2) Provide nonthreatening, noncompetitive but productive activities.
(3) Tasks must be short, simple, and attainable, with a high probability of successful experience for the patient.
(4) Avoid direct provocation.
(5) Provide privacy, with consideration for safety.

5. Evaluation
  a. Patient verbalizes feelings more readily and makes small daily decisions regarding care assistance.
  b. Patient maintains activities of daily living.
  c. Patient's level of self-esteem improves.
  d. Patient is safe from injury.

Appendix

Electroconvulsive Therapy   A measured amount of electric current is administered to produce a grand mal seizure. This treatment has been available for certain mental and emotional illnesses since 1938.

A. Amount of electric current administered: 105 to 125 volts at 700 to 800 milliamperes for 0.7 to 1.5 seconds.

B. Indications: patients with severe affective illnesses (endogenous or bipolar depression); schizophrenic patients (acute or chronic, not responsive to high doses of antipsychotic drugs); suicidal patients (actively psychotic, highly impulsive patients).

C. Contraindications: brain tumor, recent myocardial infarction, heart failure, cerebral aneurysm, cardiac arrhythmias, severe hypertension.

D. Preparation of the patient for ECT
   1. Obtain EKG, skull films, spinal films.
   2. Obtain consent.
   3. Give nothing by mouth.
   4. Check vital signs record; have emergency equipment ready.
   5. Check the patient for glaucoma (atropine sulfate is used as a preanesthetic medication).
   6. Check for dentures.
   7. Assist the patient and his/her family to deal with anxiety about ECT by explaining the treatment to them, providing active listening, and showing them the room and equipment where ECT is given.
   8. Assess the patient's memory, ability to function, and behavior before ECT to have baseline data for post-ECT assessment.
   9. Give atropine sulfate, a short-acting IV anesthetic agent (Brevital or Thiopental),

and a curare-like muscle relaxant such as succinylcholine (Anectine) to decrease muscle spasm during the procedure.

E. Method of ECT administration: unilaterally or bilaterally in the temporal area.

F. Care of the patient during ECT
   1. Monitor the patient during the procedure.
   2. Support the patient's jaw and extremities.
   3. Time the seizure.

G. Care of the patient after ECT
   1. Check vital signs until stable.
   2. Administer oxygen to the patient for 1 to 2 minutes for apnea.
   3. When the patient responds verbally, assist him/her to return to own room to rest.
   4. Reorient the patient as to time, place, and person. (Temporary loss of memory is distressing.)
   5. Help the patient to structure his/her time and activities throughout the treatment series.
   6. Provide memory aids—calendar, written schedule, and certain reminders.
   7. Provide safety.

H. Some problems associated with the treatment series: memory loss, loss of sense of control, anxiety.

I. Nursing role to alleviate the patient's and his/her family's anxiety about the treatment
   1. Explain the procedure.
   2. Encourage the patient and his/her family to express their concerns about the ECT.
   3. Encourage the patient to participate in planning his/her care according to own abilities.
   4. Monitor the patient's behavior and his/her response to the treatment series.

Alterations That Interfere with the Meeting of Sexual Needs

A. Management of the Patient with a Gynecologic Condition
1. **Menopause** Cessation of menstrual periods. Marks end of reproductive life.
   a. Characteristics
      (1) Starts with the "climacteric"— irregular, less frequent, and diminished menstrual flow.
      (2) Usually occurs between ages 45 and 52.
      (3) During the climacteric, both ovulatory and anovulatory periods occur.
      (4) Menopause is considered complete when there have been no periods for 1 year.
   b. Assessment: Observe for hot flashes, palpitations, headaches, insomnia, anxiety, and depression.
   c. Patient care management: estrogen replacement; sedatives and tranquilizers.
   d. Nursing role
      (1) Explain to the patient what is happening physiologically.
      (2) Let her express her feelings about this time of her life.
      (3) Inform the patient that contraception should be continued until menses have been absent for at least 6 months.
2. **Prolapsed uterus** Downward displacement of the uterus into the vagina.
   a. Types
      (1) First degree: Uterus descends into vaginal canal.
      (2) Second degree: Uterus and cervix descend into the vaginal canal.
      (3) Third degree: Entire uterus and cervix protrude through introitus with inversion of vaginal canal.
   b. Patient care management: vaginal hysterectomy with anterior and posterior repair; pessary (mechanical aid to keep uterus in place).
   c. Nursing role
      (1) Prevent by teaching Kegel's exercise to postpartum patients.
      (2) Teach patients with pessary to douche frequently.

      (3) Observe for urinary retention after anterior and posterior (A & P) repair.
      (4) Catheterize A & P repair patients for residual after first voiding.
      (5) Catheterize for residual until return is below 100 cc.
3. **Vulvitis** Inflammation of vulva, caused by direct irritation from vagina.
   a. Common causes: senile atrophy, diabetes, vaginitis, allergies.
   b. Assessment: note complaints of pruritus, burning on urination, redness, and edema.
   c. Patient care management: sitz baths, cornstarch, steroid creams, weak acid douche (15 ml of vinegar to one liter of water), B-lactose suppository, hydrocortisone cream/ointment, intravaginal antibiotics.
   d. Nursing role: teach perineal hygiene (cleanse area after voiding and defecation; use tampons during menstrual period).

B. Management of the Patient Undergoing Gynecologic Surgery
1. Anterior and posterior colporrhaphy
   a. Definitions
      (1) **Anterior colporrhaphy** Repair of the anterior vaginal wall.
      (2) **Posterior colporrhaphy** Repair of the posterior vaginal wall.
   b. Causes
      (1) **Cystocele** Downward displacement of the bladder, treated with an anterior colporrhaphy.
      (2) **Rectocele and laceration of the perineum** Injuries to the muscles and tissues of the pelvic floor, causing the vaginal wall to push upward by the rectum.
   c. Assessment: Assess health history for urinary frequency and urgency, stress incontinence, and complaints of pelvic pressure.
   d. Nursing role
      (1) Administer perineal care (irrigate the perineum with warm sterile saline) after urination or bowel movement.
      (2) Keep perineal suture line clean. Two methods are available.
         (a) Daily vaginal douches with sterile saline are given 5 to 10 days postsurgery.

(b) Small douches of sterile saline are given twice daily, starting on day after surgery.

(c) Heat lamp may be used to keep area dry and enhance the healing process.

(3) Observe for urinary retention and catheterize as ordered.

(4) Teach perineal (Kegel's) exercise to strengthen muscles. (Tell the patient to tense the perineal muscles by pressing the buttocks together, hold this position, then relax. This exercise should be done 10 to 20 times each hour while sitting or standing.)

2. **Hysterectomy**   Currently the most common type of surgery performed. Conditions commonly treated with surgical removal of the uterus are cancer of the uterine endometrium or ovary, severe cervical dysplasia in women who do not want further pregnancies, (lieomyomas) uterine fibroids, persistent bleeding, endometrosis (if future pregnancies are not desired) with menorrhagia and severe dysmenorrhea, chronic pelvic infections, uterine prolapse with pelvic relaxation. (Note: A second opinion is desirable before having a hysterectomy.) Hysterectomy may be performed through either the vaginal or the abdominal wall. An abdominal approach (ABD) is used in the presence of large tumors, if the ovaries and fallopian tubes are removed in addition to the uterus, and if a vaginal approach is contraindicated. Although ABD are most common, vaginal hysterectomy is increasing and advocated for women of reproductive age. The advantages of vaginal hysterectomy over abdominal hysterectomy are: the vaginal procedure can be done quickly with little anesthesia, minimal respiratory complications occur, fewer postoperative bowel problems occur because early ambulation is possible, and there is less overall postoperative discomfort, recovery is faster than with ABD, and vaginal sexual activity can usually be resumed after about three to four weeks. There is a greater risk of postoperative infection with a vaginal hysterectomy, therefore prophylactic antibiotics are often prescribed. Contraindications to vaginal hysterectomy are: pelvic inflammatory disease (PID) or any condition that limits uterine mobility and vascular or orthopedic conditions because the surgery requires suspension in stirrups.

a. Types

(1) Total hysterectomy   Removal of uterus including cervix.

(2) Subtotal (partial) hysterectomy   Removal of the uterus, leaving the cervix in place.

(3) Radical hysterectomy   An abdominal approach with the removal of the uterus, adnexa, proximal vagina, and bilateral lymph nodes en mass, along with extensive areas of the parametrial, uterosacral, and paracervical tissues.

(4) Radical vaginal hysterectomy   A vaginal approach with the removal of the uterus, adnexa and proximal vagina, along with extensive areas of the parametrial, uterosacral, and paracervical tissues.

(5) Pelvic extenteration   Removal of the pelvic organ.

(6) Salpingo-Oophorectomy   Removal of the uterine tube and ovary.

b. Preoperative nursing role (*See* Management of Patient Undergoing Surgery, page 267).

(1) Administer an enema the night before surgery.

(2) For a vaginal hysterectomy, in addition to the above, administer prophylactic antibiotic and antibacterial douche.

c. Nursing diagnoses/goals/interventions

(1) Preoperative

(a) Body image disturbance, sexuality, fertility, and relationships with family and partner
Goal: Patient will be accepting of alteration.

(b) Knowledge deficit regarding aspects of hysterectomy as well as adjustment to postoperative recovery and convalescence
Goal: Patient will acquire knowledge and understanding of what a hysterectomy means.

(c) Grieving related to loss of significant reproductive organs
Goal: Patient will experience reduction in grief.
Interventions:
1. Provide a description in simple terms of what a hysterectomy is, of the surgical procedure, and of what the effects will be.
2. Provide group instruction if indicated.
3. Provide time to explore individual feelings and to answer questions.
4. Prepare the patient for surgical menopause following surgery (no menstrual period after removal of the uterus, experience menopausal symptoms such as hot flashes, and reduction in vaginal lubrication). Application of estrogen patch after surgery.
5. Provide information to patient and partner about sexual activities after surgery.

(2) Postoperative (*See* Management of Patient Undergoing Surgery, page 267).
(a) Pain related to surgery
Goal: Patient will experience absence of or minimal pain and discomfort.
Interventions:
1. Administer narcotic and sedation as ordered (usually ordered liberally for the first 24 hours).
2. Administer comfort measures such as back rub, early ambulation, application of heat (heating pad), or other nursing measures.
(b) Knowledge deficit regarding home-care management
Goal: Patient will acquire the information necessary to care for herself at home.

Interventions:
Teach the patient to:
1. Do abdominal strengthening exercises.
2. Avoid lifting anything heavy for two months.
3. Avoid activities that increase pelvic congestion (dancing, horseback riding, prolonged standing) until the surgeon says it is safe to do them.
4. Avoid vaginal and rectal sexual activity and douching until the surgeon informs the patient that they may be safely performed.
5. Avoid constrictive clothing for several months.
6. Report bleeding or any other abnormal vaginal discharge.
7. Keep her appointment with the physician.
c. Vaginal hysterectomy—specific postoperative nursing care
(1) Replace sterile perineal pad put on after surgery with a clean pad.
(2) Observe for heavy vaginal bleeding, expected after 4th, 9th, 14th and 21st day postoperatively, due to dissolving of sutures (true also for ABD hysterectomy).
(3) Vaginal packing and/or drain removed by surgeon within 24–48 hours.
(4) Administer sitz bath as ordered.
(5) Observe for urinary tract infection (especially if an indwelling catheter is left in place) and urinary retention.
d. Abdominal hysterectomy—specific postoperative nursing care
(1) Administer catheter care. If catheter is not in place, catheterize as ordered (usually after each voiding for residual urine).
(2) Observe dressings (abdominal and perineal pads) for excessive drainage, and reinforce as needed.
(3) Monitor vital signs frequently.
(4) Encourage early ambulation to relieve pain.
(5) Avoid high Fowler's position.

(6) Apply antiembolic stockings.

(7) Encourage leg exercises.

(8) Allow the patient to ventilate her feelings.

(9) Observe for depression due to change in hormonal level and psychological reaction to surgery.

e. Evaluation

(1) Preoperative

(a) Patient accepts altered body image.

(b) Patient understands what a hysterectomy is, how the surgery will be done, and what the postoperative effects will be.

(2) Postoperative

(a) Patient experiences absence of, or minimal, pain and discomfort.

(b) Patient is able to care for herself at home.

3. Vulvectomy

a. Cause: malignancy of the vulva.

b. Nursing role

(1) Apply T-binder to hold dressing in place. Apply dry heat from heating lamp while stitches are in place.

(2) Attach tubes draining the area to suction.

(3) Place the patient in low Fowler's position with small pillow under the knee.

(4) Turn with pillow placed between the legs.

(5) Ambulate the second day.

(6) Give catheter care.

(7) Give routine postoperative care.

C. **Management of the Patient Undergoing Breast Surgery**

1. Cause: malignancy. *See also* Unit Seven, Neoplastic Disorders, page 184.

2. Management

a. **Simple excision**   Tumorectomy/lumpectomy, followed by radiation of unremoved breast tissue and axillary nodes.

b. **Simple mastectomy**   Removal of breast. Axillary lymph nodes are not removed. Followed by irradiation of unremoved axillary nodes plus radiation boost to scar area.

c. **Quadrantectomy**   Resection of the involved breast quadrant (usually upper outer quadrant), dissection of axillary lymph nodes, and irradiation to the residual breast tissue.

d. **Modified radical mastectomy**   Removal of entire breast and axillary nodes with or without pectoral muscle.

e. **Radical mastectomy**   Removal of entire breast, axillary lymph nodes, and both pectoral muscles.

f. **Adjuvant chemotherapy**   Cytotoxic drugs may be given combined with or as supplement to surgery. Drugs are started immediately following surgery to eliminate hidden or micrometastatic spread of disease. Three or more chemotherapeutic drugs are used in combination (e.g., CMF: cyclophosphamide, methotrexate, 5-fluorduracil; or CMF-VP: cyclophosphamide, methotrexate, 5-fluorduracil, plus vincristine and prednisone; or CAF: cyclophosphamide, adriamycin, 5-fluorduracil; or PAM: melphalan or phenylsamine mustard).

3. Assessment

a. Obtain health history and assess for family history of breast cancer, other breast problems, menstrual patterns, pregnancies and lactations, and the use of oral contraceptives.

b. Palpate breast for hard, circumscribed mass that is not freely movable.

c. Inspect breast for fixation of the skin to the tumor, causing nipple retraction and skin edema.

d. DIAGNOSTIC MEASURES: mammography, thermography, biopsy, MRI, ultrasound.

4. Nursing diagnoses/goals/interventions

a. Preoperative

Fear and ineffective coping related to diagnosis, treatment, and prognosis of cancer

Goal: Patient will experience a reduction of emotional stress, fear and anxiety, and will improve in her ability to cope with the diagnosis and treatment.

Interventions:

(1) Alleviate stress and enhance the coping abilities of the patient and her family.

(2) Reinforce the information given by the physician, such as dressing and catheter attached to wound.

(3) If skin graft is to be done, prepare donor site.

(4) Explain arm exercise and position after surgery.

b. Postoperative
   (1) Body image disturbance related to extensiveness of surgery and side-effects of radiation and/or chemotherapy
   Goal: Patient will retain a positive self-image.
   (2) Pain related to tissue trauma
   Goal: Patient will experience minimal amount of pain.
   (3) Self-care deficit related to partial immobility of upper extremity on the side of the breast surgery
   Goal: Patient will avoid using area of impaired mobility and will be able to provide self-care.
   (4) Possible sexual dysfunction related to loss of body part and fear of partner's reaction to this loss
   Goal: Patient will identify satisfying/acceptable sexual experiences.
   Interventions:
      (a) Observe vital signs for hemorrhage and shock.
      (b) Inspect dressing, and especially under dressing near the axilla and the area where the patient is lying; reinforce if necessary.
      (c) Monitor for hemorrhage; measure hemovac output.
      (d) Place the patient in semi-Fowler's position; elevate arm if free, with each joint positioned higher than the proximal joint.
      (e) Turn the patient and have her cough and deep-breathe every 2 hours.
      (f) Administer medication for pain.
      (g) Observe for acute edema, which is due to trauma to axillary vessel during surgery.
      (h) Engage arm in active bed exercise after 24 hours.
         1. Patient is instructed in hand and wrist movement and in flexion and extension of the elbow at hourly intervals.
         2. Patient is encouraged to feed herself, comb her hair, and wash her face; arm is not to be abducted.
         3. Exercises frequently started before the patient leaves the hospital are hair brushing, hand wall-climbing, and rope turning (rod and broom and pulley are used as devices to aid in exercising).
      (i) When wound healing is well established, begin abduction and external rotation of the upper arm in the recumbent position (10th to 12th day). Exercise such as the pendulum swing (to improve shoulder function) is performed.
      (j) Apply a custom-fitted pressure-gradient elastic sleeve after the elastic bandage is removed. This sleeve prevents changes in edema during the period needed for regrowth of lymphatic pathways. If wound healing is normal, adequate collateral lymphatic circulation usually develops within a month.
      (k) Assist with ambulation.
      (l) Introduce the patient to mastectomy support groups (upon authorization of the doctor). Volunteers from "Reach to Recovery" will visit the hospital and give the patient information and assistance.
      (m) Teach breast self-examination, to be done monthly for the remaining breast a week after conclusion of the menstrual period.
5. Evaluation
   a. Patient demonstrates willingness to deal with the anxiety caused by the diagnosis and with the impact of surgery on sexual functioning and self-image.
   b. Patient experiences little or no discomfort.
   c. Patient participates actively in self-care activities.
   d. Patient experiences no complications.

UNIT NINE

Meeting the Needs of the Older Adult
(65 years and older)

STUDY GUIDE

DEVELOPMENTAL TASKS

HEALTH PROMOTION OF THE OLDER ADULT

A. Health Status
B. Changes That Occur in the Older Adult
C. Population of the Older Adult (over 65)

ALTERATIONS OF HEALTH DURING THE LATER YEARS

Alterations in Cardiovascular Organs

A. Dysrhythmias (cardiac arrhythmia)
B. Management of the Patient Undergoing Pacemaker Therapy
C. Management of the Patient Undergoing Surgery for an Aortic Aneurysm
D. Congestive Heart Failure
E. Acute Pulmonary Edema
F. Peripheral Vascular Problems

Alterations in Perception and Coordination

A. Management of the Patient with Cataract
B. Glaucoma: Adult Onset
C. Parkinson's Disease
D. Cerebrovascular Accident
E. Osteoporosis
F. Osteoarthritis
G. Fall Prevention
H. Management of the Patient Undergoing Hip Surgery

Alterations in Respiration and Carbon Dioxide Exchange

A. Chronic Obstructive Pulmonary Disease
B. Chronic Bronchitis
C. Bronchiectasis
D. Bronchial Asthma
E. Pulmonary Emphysema
F. Pulmonary Heart Disease

Alterations in Behavior

A. Dementia
   1. Multi-infarct dementia
   2. Alzheimer's disease
B. Delirium
C. Depression in the Elderly
D. Suicide
E. Sundowner Syndrome
F. Physical Restraint

Alterations That Interfere with the Meeting of Sexual Needs

A. Urinary Incontinence
B. Management of the Patient Undergoing Prostatectomy

Other Alterations of Health
A. Pressure Ulcers

DEVELOPMENTAL TASKS

According to Erikson, the major developmental tasks of the older adult are:

1. Ego integrity. Maintenance of identity is the immediate concern.
2. Adjustment to new situations—economic, social, family, and sexual changes; fear of invalidism; fear of approaching death.

Maladaptations or dangers during this period are:

1. Feeling of despair.
2. Apprehension regarding threats to body image.
3. Feeling of worthlessness; threat to self-esteem; feeling of being rejected.

HEALTH PROMOTION OF THE OLDER ADULT

A. Health Status*
1. The majority of elderly persons are reasonably healthy, although the rate of illness in the elderly is higher than that for younger age groups.
2. Chronic conditions increase with age and cause disability.
3. The most common ailments that limit the activities of older persons are heart conditions, high blood pressure, arthritis, orthopedic impairments, and mental and nervous conditions.
4. Other chronic conditions frequent among the elderly include obesity, abdominal-cavity hernias, cataracts, varicose veins, hemorrhoids, and prostate disorders.
5. Persons over 65 have one health advantage over younger people—they have fewer colds, flu infections, and digestive problems. They may have become immune to many of the causative organisms; also, they are less exposed to them because they go out less.
6. People over 65 average fewer than 10 sick days a year. When acute illness strikes, however, it leads to more days of restricted activity.
7. At least one out of five older persons spends some time in a long-term health facility, such as a mental hospital, a nursing home, or a convalescent home.
8. As a rule, women outlive their husbands. Therefore they are more likely to be alone and to need outside help when they get sick.

B. Changes That Occur in the Older Adult
1. Physical changes
   a. Cardiovascular changes
      (1) Valves become thick and rigid.
      (2) Endocardium thickens and scleroses.
      (3) Contraction and dilation of cardiac muscle become difficult because of decreased elasticity and increased rigidity.
      (4) There is increased prevalence of arrhythmias.
      (5) The incidence of lower hemoglobin is high.
      (6) Heart rate is slower (rate can range from 44 to 108 beats per minute).
      (7) Cardiac oxygen usage becomes less efficient.
      (8) Systolic blood pressure is higher because of loss of elasticity in peripheral vessels and increased peripheral resitance.
      (9) Baroreceptor sensitivity decreases.
      (10) EKG changes occur.
   b. Respiratory changes
      (1) Various connective tissues responsible for respiration and ventilation are weaker.
      (2) Decreased body fluid and drier mucous membranes impede removal of mucus and create greater risk of infection.
      (3) Loss of resilient force which holds thorax in lightly contracted position and decreased muscle strength in thorax and diaphragm occur, both promoting barrel chest.
      (4) Expiration requires active use of accessory muscles.
      (5) Alveoli are less elastic and contain fewer functional capillaries.
      (6) Arterial oxyhemoglobin saturation is reduced to 93% to 94%.

---

* Adapted from *Human Development* by Diane Papalia and Sally Olds, pp. 506–507. Copyright © 1981 by McGraw-Hill Book Company. Used with the permission of McGraw-Hill Book Company.

c. Gastrointestinal changes
  (1) Decreased salivary gland activity; dried oral mucosa.
  (2) Loss of taste buds, especially for sweet and salty flavors.
  (3) Weakening of pharyngeal muscle in some older adults.
  (4) Slight dilation of esophagus, with a decrease in esophageal mobility.
  (5) Decreased peristalsis.
  (6) Fewer digestive enzymes produced by pancreas.
  (7) Altered rates of insulin release.
d. Nervous system changes
  (1) Dilation of the ventricles.
  (2) Loss of neurons.
  (3) Decrease in brain weight by 5% to 7%.
  (4) Impaired vision: less transparent lens, decreased pupil size, changes in vitreous humor.
  (5) Impaired hearing: decreased ability to hear high-frequency sounds.
  (6) Reduced olfaction.
  (7) Decreased tactile sensation.
  (8) Slower conduction of impulses; delayed reaction time.
  (9) Poor short-term memory; long-term memory relatively unchanged.
e. Urinary system changes
  (1) Decreased bladder capacity: frequency of urination, nocturia.
  (2) Weakened bladder muscles: poorer retention of urine, stress incontinence, dribbling.
  (3) Decreased tubular function: lower specific gravity (proteinuria of 1 + may be normal).
  (4) Lower renal threshold for glucose; may be little correlation between blood glucose level and level spilled in urine.
f. Sexual function changes
  (1) Female
    (a) Atrophic appearance of vulva.
    (b) Loss of pubic hair.
    (c) Vaginal environment more alkaline, drier, altered in type and flora.
    (d) Shrinkage of cervix and uterus.
    (e) Atrophy of fallopian tubes and ovaries.
    (f) Cessation of ovulation and estrogen production.
    (g) Dyspareunia.
    (h) Sagging breasts.
  (2) Male
    (a) Decreased size and firmness of testes, but no cessation in testosterone production.
    (b) More time needed to obtain erection.
    (c) Slower, less forceful ejaculations.
    (d) Some degree of prostatic enlargement.
g. Musculoskeletal changes
  (1) Weakening bone.
  (2) Decreased muscle strength.
  (3) Poorer coordination.
  (4) Increased muscle fatigability.
2. Psychological changes due to:
  a. Altered body image.
  b. Loss of spouse, other family members, and friends.
  c. Loss of sense of identity.
  d. Loss of feeling of security due to decreased income and productivity.
  e. Concern about health, loss of status, loss of physical ability, loss of peer relationships.
3. Socioeconomic changes
  a. Reduced income due to retirement and/or economic reversals.
  b. Loss of opportunity to be productive.
  c. Narrowing social relationships.
  d. Need for more extensive leisure-time activities.
4. Mental status
  a. Personality consistent throughout life.
  b. Intelligence unaltered.
  c. Short-term memory poorer; long-term memory relatively unchanged.
  d. Learning ability unaltered although other factors may interfere with learning.
  e. Decline in mental status not a normal consequence of aging process.
C. Population of the Older Adult (over 65)
1. Graying of America
  1990—12.7% of population 31.5 (in millions).
  2030—20% of population 64.6 (in millions).
2. Categorization by age:
  a. "Young old": older adults 65–74 years.
  b. "Middle old": older adults 75–84 years.
  c. "Old old"/Frail elderly: 85 years and up.

ALTERATIONS OF HEALTH DURING THE LATER YEARS

Alterations in Cardiovascular Organs

A. **Dysrhythmias (cardiac arrhythmia)**   A dysrhythmia is a disorder of the heartbeat that may include a disturbance of rate, rhythm, or both. Dysrhythmias are derangements of the heart's conduction system, not of the heart structure. They are identified by analyzing the electro cardiogram waveform and are named according to the site of impulse origin and the mechanism of conduction involved.

1. Common types in older adults
   a. Premature ventricular contraction (due to caffeine, alcohol, nicotine).
   b. Atrial frillation.
   c. Bundle branch block (BBB).
   d. Sick sinus syndrome, characterized either by instances of a very slow heart rate or by sudden occurrences of a very rapid heart rate alternating with a slow rate, accompanied by dizziness or syncope. It may be caused by drugs such as digoxin, proprandol, quinidine, and lithium, and by most sympathetic drugs. It is treated by removing the underlying cause.
2. Risk factors precipitating dysrhythmias
   a. Myocardial ischemia (congestive heart failure).
   b. Hypokalemia.
   c. Systemic infections.
   d. Blood loss.
   e. Digitalis toxicity.
3. Assessment
   a. Changes in mental status, personality, and behavior.
   b. Decreased blood pressure.
   c. Chest pain.
   d. Dizziness.
   e. Dyspnea.
   f. Tachypnea.
   g. Pale, clammy skin.
   h. Pulse—may be rapid, slow, or irregular, depending on the type of dysrhythmia.
   i. DIAGNOSTIC MEASURES
      (1) Electrocardiogram.
      (2) Holter monitoring.
4. Patient care management
   a. Treatment of the underlying health problems that precipitate the dysrhythmias, such as infection and cardiac or pulmonary disorders.
   b. Administration of anti-arrhythmia drugs based on the specific dysrhythmia.
      (1) Premature ventricular contractions: acute care, lidocaine; long-term therapy, procainamide (Pronestyl).
      (2) Atrial fibrillation: digitalis preparation to slow the heart rate and an antidysrhythmic such as quinidine to correct the dysrhythmia.
   c. Use of elective cardioversion, defibrillation, and pacemaker when drugs alone are not adequate.

B. **Management of the Patient Undergoing Pacemaker Therapy**   A pacemaker is an electronic device that provides repetitive electrical stimuli to the heart muscle for control of the heart rate.
1. Uses: in bradycardias, heart blocks, arrhythmias, and conduction conditions following open heart surgery.
2. Methods of pacing
   a. Demand. Pacemaker is set for a specific rate and stimulates the heart when normal ventricular depolarization does not occur or if the heart drops below the specified rate.
   b. Fixed. Pacemaker stimulates the ventricles at a preset constant rate that is independent of patient rhythm (used in heart block).
3. Placement
   a. Endocardial (used for either temporary or permanent pacing). Electrodes are passed through the neck vein into the right ventricle. The generator is placed in the subcutaneous tissues beneath the clavicle or axilla.
   b. Epicardial (used for permanent pacing). Electrodes are implanted in the myocardium, and the pulse generator is implanted in the abdominal wall.
4. Assessment (after insertion of a temporary or permanent pacemaker)
   a. Monitor electrocardiogram.
   b. Assess pacemaker rate, which may vary as much as 5 beats above or below preset rate.
   c. Assess the incision site for evidence of bleeding or hematoma formation.
5. Nursing diagnoses/goals/interventions
   a. **Risk for injury: trauma related to electrical hazards**
      Goal: Patient will be free of injury.

Interventions:

(1) Check all electrical equipment in the vicinity of the patient for three-prong grounded plug inserted into proper outlet.

(2) Have biomedical engineer, electrician, or other qualified person check the area for leakage of current, which can produce ventricular fibrillation.

(3) Observe for potential sources of electrical hazards, such as exposed metal parts of output terminal or pacemaker wires.

(4) Cover bare metal with nonconductive tape to prevent accidental ventricular fibrillation from stray currents.

b. Risk for infection related to catheter or generator insertion
Goal: Patient will be free of infection.
Interventions:

(1) Inspect the incision site for redness, edema, pain, unusual bleeding, or hematoma formation.

(2) Take the patient's temperature every 4 to 8 hours.

(3) Change the dressing as the physician has ordered.

c. Knowledge deficit regarding self-care program
Goal: Patient will adhere to self-care program.
Interventions:

(1) Instruct the patient to:

(a) Report to the physician periodically as prescribed so that the rate of the pacemaker and its function can be checked.

(b) Adhere to a weekly monitoring schedule (especially the first month).

(c) Check his/her pulse daily, and report immediately any sudden slowing or increase of the pulse rate.

(d) Resume weekly monitoring when battery depletion is anticipated.

(e) Wear loose-fitting clothing around the area of the pacemaker and notify the physician if the area becomes reddened or painful.

(f) Avoid trauma to the area of the pacemaker.

(g) Study the manufacturer's instructions and become familiar with the pacemaker.

(h) Avoid heavy-contact sports.

(i) Carry an identification card or bracelet indicating the physician's name, the type, model number, and rate of the pacemaker, the manufacturer's name, and the hospital where the pacemaker was inserted.

(j) Avoid coming close to microwave ovens, welder's arcs, large electric generators, and electric cautery and diathermy equipment.

(k) Show identification card, and request scanning by a hand scanner, when going through a weapon detector.

(2) Remind the patient that hospitalization is necessary for a battery or unit change.

6. Evaluation

a. Patient is free of injury.

b. Patient is afebrile.

c. Patient verbalizes the times to seek medical attention and the signs and symptoms of infection.

C. **Management of the Patient Undergoing Surgery for an Aortic Aneurysm** A sac formed by the dilatation of an artery as a result of localized weakness and stretching of the arterial wall.

Aneurysms commonly affect males over the age of 60. An aneurysm may be saccular (balloons out to one side), fusiform (encircles the vessel), or dissecting (is a bilateral outpouching in which the lining of the vessel separates, creating a cavity).

1. Causes: arteriosclerosis, syphilis, congenital defects, trauma, infection.

2. Types: thoracic aortic aneurysm, abdominal aortic aneurysm.

3. Assessment

a. Abdominal aortic aneurysm

(1) Back, flank, and abdominal pain from increasing pressure on lumbar nerves and adjacent struc-

tures such as the duodenum or inferior vena cava.

(2) Nausea and vomiting.

(3) Bloody stools and postprandial abdominal pain.

(4) Enlarging abdominal girth.

(5) Palpation of a pulsating mass approximately 3.6 cm across.

(6) Leg numbness; tingling, loss of motor function.

(7) Mottled cyanosis of the area below the level of the aneurysm.

(8) Blood in, and reduced output of, urine.

(9) Profound drop in blood pressure.

(10) Apprehension, anxiety, and restlessness.

(11) Rupture: observe for constant back pain, falling blood pressure, and decreased red and white count, plus soft abdomen.

b. Thoracic aortic

(1) Pain of a constant, boring character when the person is lying in a supine position.

(2) Dyspnea (pressure of the sac against the trachea).

(3) Cough.

(4) Hoarseness.

(5) Stridor.

(6) Weakness of the voice or aphonia (due to pressure on the laryngeal nerve).

(7) Dysphagia (due to impingement on the esophagus).

4. Patient care management: resection and insertion of bypass graft, either synthetic or vascular.

5. Preoperative nursing diagnoses/goals/interventions

a. Anxiety related to condition, impending surgery, and knowledge deficit regarding surgery and postoperative course
Goals:

(1) Patient and family will experience a decrease in anxiety and will express realistic expectations of the postoperative regimen.

(2) Patient will be able to carry out postoperative deep breathing, coughing, and exercise routines.
Interventions:

(1) Take time to listen to the feelings and concerns of the patient and family, to answer questions, and to try to calm fears.

(2) Explain the preoperative procedure.

(3) Explain to the patient what to expect during the postoperative period (e.g., ventilator, central venous pressure, arterial pressure; nasogastric tube).

(4) Instruct the patient in the postoperative routine and the importance of coughing; demonstrate leg exercises and have the patient return the demonstration.

(5) Assure the patient that pain medication will be available.

(6) Assess coping strategies, and assist the patient and family.

(7) Assess the need for referral to clergy or social worker.

b. Decrease in cardiac output related to effects of untreated aneurysm
Goal: Patient will maintain hemodynamic stability.
Interventions:

(1) Monitor and record vital signs every 4 hours; monitor for widening of pulse pressure.

(2) Check peripheral pulse in both legs.

(3) Monitor for peripheral vasoconstriction (cold clammy skin, or weak absent peripheral pulse and impaired renal tissue perfusion—decreased urinary output); report finding to physician.

(4) Administer vasodilator if systolic blood pressure exceeds parameter set by physician; obtain blood pressure every 15 minutes, and titrate medication to achieve systolic blood pressure indicated by physician; monitor for toxicity and effectiveness.

6. Preoperative evaluation

a. Patient expresses decreased anxiety.

b. Patient describes immediate postoperative regimen.

c. Patient demonstrates coughing and leg exercises.

d. Patient's circulation is stable.

7. Postoperative nursing diagnoses/goals/interventions
See also Unit Eight, Section F: Management of the Patient Undergoing Cardiovascular Surgery, page 317.

a. Altered tissue perfusion: peripheral

related to low circulating blood volume and hypotension

b. Fluid volume deficit related to blood loss during aortic aneurysm repair

Goal: Patient will maintain normal vital signs, demonstrate adequate tissue perfusion, and maintain adequate intake of fluid and electrolytes.

Interventions:

(1) Check dressing for blood or drainage every 4 hours; use abdominal binder to give support and comfort for moving.

(2) Take vital signs every 4 hours or as physician orders; report changes; monitor and record dorsalis pedis pulses in both legs at the same time (use Doppler if pulse is not palpable).

(3) Record warmth, color, sensation, and movement of extremities.

(4) Record intake and output; report urinary output of 30 cc or less.

(5) Maintain the patient in flat position for a week; avoid extreme flexion that increases abdominal pressure or impedes leg circulation.

(6) Report back pain (retroperitoneal hemorrhage or thrombus).

(7) Encourage and monitor leg exercise every 2 hours.

(8) Remove and then reapply elastic stocking every 8 hours.

(9) Give ice chips while NPO; assess for return of bowel sounds; advance from fluids to soft diet; observe tolerance and amount taken.

(10) Administer medications as ordered: analgesics, antibiotics, anticoagulant; observe for side effects and effectiveness.

c. Knowledge deficit regarding care of operative site, length of convalescence, diet, medication

Goal: Patient will verbalize risk factors that can increase blood pressure and decrease circulation; and will demonstrate the ability to manage the home care regimen.

Interventions:

(1) Explain to the patient the importance of keeping the follow-up appointment with the surgeon.

(2) Instruct the patient on care of the operative site; have him/her return demonstration.

(3) Teach the patient about the prescribed diet; arrange a dietary consultation for a sodium-restricted diet and nonconstipating foods.

(4) Instruct the patient to avoid constipation and straining.

(5) Instruct the patient about prescribed medications: explain expected action, administration schedule, side effects.

(6) Discuss ways of maintaining normal blood pressure; if needed, initiate referral to psychologist.

8. Postoperative evaluation

a. Patient has stable cardiopulmonary status, vital signs, and circulation.

b. Patient has balanced intake and output and stable electrolytes.

c. Patient demonstrates understanding of home care management, and verbalizes accurate information in relationship to medication, diet, activity, and follow-up care.

D. **Congestive Heart Failure (CHF)**   Inability of the heart to pump a sufficient amount of blood to meet the needs of the tissues for oxygen and nutrients.

Atrial and venous pressures increase because of decreased ventricular ejection fraction in the failing heart. Increased pulmonary venous pressure leads to transudation of fluid from pulmonary capillaries (pulmonary edema). Increased systemic venous pressure results in generalized peripheral edema and weight gain.

The right and left ventricles can fail separately. Right-sided failure usually follows left-sided failure. Pulmonary congestion predominates when the left ventricle fails, whereas congestion of the viscera and peripheral tissues predominates when the right ventricle fails.

1. Causes: coronary atherosclerosis, arterial hypertension, myocardial infarction, valvular disease, pericarditis.

2. Assessment

a. Observe breathing for dyspnea, orthopnea, paroxysmal nocturnal dyspnea (PND), and Cheyne-Stokes respiration.

b. Auscultate lungs for moist rales and wheezing, and heart for third heart sound (gallop rhythm).

c. Observe cough for the production of large amounts of frothy, blood-tinged sputum.

d. Observe general appearance for cyanosis, pallor, distended neck veins, and muscular weakness.

e. Inspect extremities for edema and abdomen for ascites.

f. Observe behavior for anxiety, irritability, and a shortened attention span.

3. Patient care management. *See also* Unit Eight, Alterations in Cardiovascular Organs, Blood, and Blood-Forming Organs, Section B: General Patient Care Management, page 307.

a. Pharmacologic therapy

(1) Digitalis preparation to decrease the force of myocardial contraction and slow the heart rate. Also increases cardiac output; decreases heart size, venous pressure, and blood volume; and promotes diuresis.

(2) Diuretic therapy to promote the excretion of sodium and water through the kidneys. Observe for side effects such as hyponatremia (deficiency of serum sodium) and hypokalemia (potassium depletion).

(3) Vasodilator therapy to reduce resistance to left ventricular ejection of blood. Sodium nitroprusside is given IV or nitroglycerin is given.

b. Dietary support. Restriction of sodium is indicated for the prevention, elimination, and control of edema.
Dietary restriction: low-calorie diet, 1000 to 2000 mg sodium.

c. Oxygen therapy.

d. Physical and mental rest (morphine reduces anxiety).

e. Mechanical removal of pleural and peritoneal effusions (paracentesis and thoracentesis).

4. Nursing diagnoses/goals/interventions

a. Decrease in cardiac output related to inefficient heart action

b. Altered tissue perfusion: peripheral related to decreased cardiac output
Goal: Patient will maintain a cardiac output adequate to circulate blood to the body's tissues.
Interventions:
(1) Maintain complete bedrest.

(2) Place in a semirecumbent position with pillows under the arms and behind the back.

(3) Avoid fatiguing the patient; give partial bath and mouth care.

(4) Turn and position the patient every 2 hours, and massage pressure points.

(5) Monitor cardiac rhythms continuously; record a rhythm strip every 4 hours or more if irregular; administer antidysrhythmic agents; assess for expected response and untoward effects.

(6) Assess cardiac functioning (blood pressure and pulse as ordered).

(7) Observe the quality of peripheral pulses and skin appearance.

(8) Administer medications as ordered: inotropic agents, vasodilators, alpha-adrenergic agents, digitalis preparation; assess response to digitalis preparation, especially electrolyte levels.

(9) Administer sedative/hypnotic as ordered; assess respiration for shallowness, irregular rate.

c. Impaired gas exchange related to effects of altered pulmonary circulation

d. Ineffective breathing pattern related to pain anxiety, impaired circulation
Goal: Patient will maintain respiratory functioning adequate to oxygenate all body tissues.
Interventions:
(1) Administer oxygen as prescribed (usually 4 to 6 liters per minute unless contraindicated; then 2 liters if chronic hypoxic) via nasal cannula.

(2) Medicate for pain; monitor for expected results or untoward effects.

(3) Assess respiratory status (rate, depth, quality, breath sounds, productiveness of cough) every 2 to 4 hours; observe for orthopnea, increased rate, decreased depth, rales, frothy sputum. *See also* Section E: Acute Pulmonary Edema, page 355.

(4) Prepare the patient for intubation and assisted ventilation. *See* Section D: Bronchial Asthma, page 380.

(5) Monitor arterial blood gas.

(6) Position the patient in semi-Fowler's position.

(7) Monitor mental status for alterations (decreased consciousness, restlessness, and agitation).

(8) Explain procedures and treatments to the patient before initiating them.

e. Excess fluid volume related to effects of right-sided failure and decreased renal perfusion pressure with left-sided heart failure

Goal: Patient will maintain or regain fluid and electrolyte balance.

Interventions:

(1) Weigh the patient on admission and daily at the same time on same scale and with same clothing; report daily gains or losses of more than 3 pounds.

(2) Inspect extremities, sacrum, and periorbital areas for edema, and assess jugular vein for distension every 4 to 8 hours.

(3) Monitor central venous pressure/hemodynamic reading as ordered; adjust IV intake to physician's order.

(4) Restrict fluids as ordered.

(5) Maintain strict intake and output.

(6) Provide sodium-restricted diet as ordered; order dietary consultation.

(7) Administer diuretic as ordered; monitor electrolyte values, especially sodium and potassium.

f. Risk for infection related to invasive catheters (IV's, hemodynamic monitoring, Foley)

Goal: Patient will remain free of infection.

Interventions:

(1) Inspect catheter sites every 4 to 8 hours; observe for signs of inflammation (redness, swelling, elevated temperature).

(2) Cleanse meatus around urinary catheter every 8 hours.

(3) Change IV tubing and dressing according to hospital policy.

(4) Monitor temperature every 4 to 8 hours for elevations.

(5) Administer prophylactic antibiotics on time to ensure proper blood level; monitor for desired and toxic effects.

g. Anxiety related to pain, dyspnea, unfamiliar surroundings, procedures, and fear of dying related to severity of condition

h. Knowledge deficit regarding disease process, diagnostic procedures, and proposed treatments

Goal: Patient and family will experience and express reduced feelings of anxiety or fear, and will indicate understanding of proposed procedures and treatments.

Interventions:

(1) Explain the physical setting (e.g., ICU or CCU), monitoring equipment, and unit routines to the patient and his/her family; stress that continuing assessment by the nursing staff does not necessarily reflect a deteriorating status.

(2) Keep the patient and his/her family informed of progress and procedures.

(3) Stay with the patient during acute episodes of anxiety or fear, or permit the family to stay as much as possible without tiring the patient.

(4) Explain to family members the effect of their anxiety on the patient.

(5) Point out improvement in the patient's status.

(6) Offer to contact spiritual advisor if patient/family desire.

(7) Initiate referral to social worker.

i. Knowledge deficit regarding prescribed treatment and home management

Goal: Patient and family will demonstrate understanding of prescribed treatment and home management.

Interventions:

(1) Explain the need for adequate rest: shorter work hours and daily rest period and avoidance of emotional upset.

(2) Instruct the patient to take digitalis as ordered, to check pulse rate daily, and to take diuretic as prescribed.

(3) Instruct the patient to weigh himherself daily at the same time with the same amount of clothing and the same scale, report a gain of more

than 2 to 3 pounds in a few days; and to know the signs of potassium depletion.

    (4) Instruct the patient to take vasodilator as prescribed, to take his/her blood pressure, and to recognize and prevent signs of orthostatic hypotension.

    (5) Review the written diet plan and list of permitted and restricted foods; instruct the patient to restrict sodium as directed: avoid salt, examine labels (laxatives, cough remedies, antacids, and the like) to ascertain sodium content.

    (6) Review the activity program; instruct the patient to avoid causing dyspnea and to start walking gradually, avoid extremes of heat and cold, and use air conditioning on hot, humid days.

    (7) Instruct the patient in signs of recurring heart failure: gain in weight; loss of appetite; shortness of breath on activity; swelling of ankles, feet, or abdomen; persistent cough; frequent urination at night.

5. Evaluation
   a. Patient has improved, stable vital signs and hemodynamic readings.
   b. Patient is free of dysrhythmias.
   c. Patient has normal respiratory rate, depth, effort, and breath sounds.
   d. Patient has normal arterial blood gases.
   e. Patient and family indicate decreased anxiety and fear.
   f. Patient is free from dyspnea at rest and from pain.
   g. Patient maintains or regains mental alertness.
   h. Patient is afebrile.
   i. Patient is free of inflammation at catheter insertion sites.
   j. Patient verbalizes understanding of disease process and home management.

E. **Acute Pulmonary Edema** Abnormal accumulation of fluid in the lungs, either in the interstitial space or in the alveoli.

The pulmonary vascular bed receives more blood from the right ventricles than the left ventricles can accommodate and remove. Stagnated fluid leaks through the capillary wall and permeates the airway, giving rise to dyspnea.

1. Assessment
   a. Observe breathing for severe dyspnea, orthopnea, noisy breathing, and paroxysmal nocturnal dyspnea.
   b. Auscultate lungs for moist rales, rhonchi, and wheezing; and heart for third heart sound (gallop rhythm) and tachycardia.
   c. Observe cough for the production of a large amount of frothy, blood-tinged sputum.
   d. Observe the general apperance for cyanosis, pallor, distended neck veins, and anxiety.

2. Patient care management. *See also* Unit Eight, Alterations in Respiration and Carbon Dioxide Exchange, Section B: General Patient Care Management, page 292.
   a. Positioning—to reduce venous return to the heart.
   b. Oxygenation—high concentration by face mask; IPPB therapy.
   c. Pharmacological therapy
       (1) Morphine—reduces anxiety and dyspnea.
       (2) Diuretics (furosemide or Edecrin acid).
       (3) Aminophylline—relaxes bronchospasm.
       (4) Digitalis—improves the contractile force of the heart.
       (5) Vasodilator (sodium nitroprusside).
   d. Rotating tourniquets. The application of rotating tourniquets to the extremities decreases venous return and right ventricular output, thus helping to decongest the lung.
   e. Phlebotomy—withdrawal of 250 to 500 ml of blood from a peripheral vein to reduce the venous return to the heart.

3. Nursing diagnoses/goals/interventions
   a. Impaired gas exchange related to accumulation of fluid in alveoli
   b. Ineffective breathing pattern related to hypoxia and/or anxiety
   c. Ineffective airway clearance related to inability to cough up frothy secretions
   Goal: Patient will be oxygenated adequately, will maintain a patent airway, and will resume a normal breathing pattern.
   Interventions:
       (1) Place the patient in an upright sitting position, with feet and legs

down to prevent lung engorgement and to increase pooling of blood in the dependent area of the body.

(2) Administer oxygen as ordered (usually in a high concentration by nasal cannula or mask, unless contraindicated — COPD).

(3) Auscultate lungs as ordered (a minimum of every 30 minutes).

(4) Monitor arterial blood gases.

(5) Check blood pressure every 15 to 30 minutes; assess and record quality of pulse, respiration, orthopnea, wheezing, cough, skin appearance (turgor, color, moistness) every 2 to 4 hours.

(6) Assess mental status for signs and symptoms of confusion, anxiety, restlessness, stupor, and coma every 8 hours or less.

(7) Administer medications as ordered: morphine, diuretics, digoxins, aminophylline.

(8) Prepare to assist with phlebotomy if indicated.

d. Anxiety related to knowledge deficit regarding treatment modalities and fear of inability to breathe
Goal: Patient and family will express decreased feeling of anxiety.
Interventions:

(1) Stay with the patient, giving assurance.

(2) Explain procedures and treatments including medications: how they work, what the expected outcomes are, and when relief can be expected.

(3) Administer morphine sulfate IV as ordered to relieve anxiety; monitor respiration for depression and for expected relief.

(4) Decrease environmental stimuli.

(5) Provide comfort measures (e.g., positioning with pillow, light covering, mouth wash, clean cloth for diaphoretic patients).

e. Knowledge deficit regarding illness and health maintenance plan
Goals:

(1) Patient will express understanding regarding the importance of compliance with the treatment of pul-

monary edema during the acute phase.

(2) On discharge, patient will verbalize information necessary for compliance regarding activity, medications, diet, warning signs, and symptoms of pulmonary edema.
Interventions:

(1) Explain to the patient and his/her family the disease process, signs and symptoms, and treatment; provide appropriate literature.

(2) Explain activity regulations and special diet instructions.

(3) Instruct the patient as to prescribed medications: name of drugs, dosage, frequency, and side effects; have patient repeat information.

(4) Explain the warning signs and symptoms of pulmonary edema (e.g., paroxysmal nocturnal dyspnea, cough, restlessness, anxiety) that should be reported to the physician.

(5) Explain the need to restrict fluids and sodium.

(6) Instruct the patient to weigh him-/ herself daily and to report excess weight gain to the physician.

4. Evaluation

a. Patient maintains a patent airway.

b. Patient's arterial blood gases are within normal limits.

c. Patient's lungs are clear.

d. Patient and family verbalize feelings of reduced anxiety.

e. Patient demonstrates decreased fear of treatment and cooperates with treatment plan.

f. Patient verbalizes understanding of prescribed treatment and home-care management.

F. Peripheral Vascular Problems

1. Assessment of peripheral circulation (This assessment is limited to the lower extremities.)

a. Observe and note the characteristics of the pain. (This pain is called "intermittent claudication.")

(1) Precipitating factor: exercise.

(2) Location: thigh and limb.

(3) Intensity: crampy.

(4) Mode of relief: rest (Later, pain will occur even upon rest.)

b. Observe skin for coldness, pallor, numbness, dryness, tautness, hair loss, and thickening of nails. If circulation is severely damaged the limb will develop an intense reddish hue (rubor). Cyanosis occurs when there is a concentration of deoxygenated hemoglobin.

c. Palpate peripheral pulse bilaterally. (The most common sites are femoral popliteal, dorsalis pedis, and dorsal tibialis.)

d. Auscultate over the artery for bruit (a high-pitched sound occurring during systole as blood flows through the constricted arterial vessel).

e. Inspect joints for mobility. Mobility may be limited because of decreased joint use and increased pain upon movement.

f. Assess
   (1) Sex—males experience claudication more frequently than females. (After menopause, females are affected to a greater degree.)
   (2) Age—most peripheral vascular disease occurs after age 50.

g. Diagnostic measures
   (1) Exercise stress tests. These are used to determine when the functional capacity of impaired circulation is exceeded.
   (2) Oscillometry. This serves to locate sites of arterial occlusion not heard through manual palpation of arterial pulses.
   (3) Plethysmography. This monitors changes in pulse and leg size with each heartbeat.
   (4) Digital subtraction angiography (DSA). This is radiologic visualization of arterial vessels, utilizing computer technology.
   (5) Peripheral arteriography. Contrast medium is injected into specific arteries to demonstrate stenosis, obstruction, thrombi, or aneurysm.
       Nursing role
       (a) Give nothing by mouth for 6 hours before test.
       (b) Report history of allergic reactions to physician before the procedure.
       (c) Explain to the patient what to expect during the procedure.
   (6) Serum cholesterol level. Level over 220 per 100 ml is considered elevated.
   (7) Serum lipid level. Triglyceride level above 150 per 100 ml is considered elevated.
   (8) Doppler ultrasound. This serves to detect peripheral flow.

2. Patient care management
   a. Buerger-Allen exercises (to promote blood flow by muscular exercise and to encourage the formation of collateral circulation to substitute for the primary vessels that are occluded).
   b. Promotion of vasodilation
      (1) Nerve blocks—epidural block.
      (2) Sympathectomy.
      (3) Replacement of occluded arteries by grafts.
      (4) Endarterectomy.

3. Nursing diagnoses/goals/interventions
   a. Altered peripheral tissue perfusion related to compromised circulation
      Goal: Patient's extremities will have increased arterial circulation.
      Interventions:
      (1) Instruct the patient to keep extremities below the level of the heart, thereby enhancing arterial blood supply.
      (2) Encourage moderate amount of walking or extremity exercises.
      (3) Encourage the patient to perform Buerger-Allen exercises.
      Goal: Patient will have decreased venous congestion.
      Interventions:
      (1) Elevate the patient's extremities above the heart (promotes venous return).
      (2) Discourage standing still or sitting for a prolonged period.
      (3) Encourage walking (promotes venous return).
      Goal: Patient will have adequate vasodilitation and absence of vascular compression.
      Interventions:
      (1) Provide counsel to avoid emotional upset; aid in stress management.
      (2) Maintain warm temperature and avoid chilling.

(3) Administer vasodilator drugs and adrenergic blocking agents as prescribed.

b. Pain related to impaired ability of peripheral vessel to supply tissue with oxygen

Goal: Patient's pain will be relieved.

Interventions:

(1) Promote circulation (*See* Interventions for diagnosis a).

(2) Administer analgesics as ordered.

c. Risk for impaired skin integrity related to compromised circulation

Goal: Patient's skin will remain intact.

Interventions:

(1) Instruct the patient in ways to avoid trauma to extremities.

(2) Encourage the patient to wear protective shoes and padding for pressure areas.

(3) Provide patient education.

(a) Wear adequate clothing to avoid chilling.

(b) Avoid using hot-water bottle or electric pad.

(c) Bathe with superfatted soap; dry with gentle rubbing or patting, and apply a softening lotion or cream.

(d) Take proper care of the feet.

1. Avoid going barefoot or in stocking feet.

2. Wash feet daily with neutral soap and warm water.

3. Use lanolin or petrolatum to prevent the skin from drying and cracking.

4. Wear clean socks.

5. Avoid using strong antiseptics.

6. Do not cut corns or calluses; seek expert care.

7. Avoid crossing legs or wearing tight garters, belts, or girdles.

(e) Avoid prolonged standing.

(f) Eat a proper diet—low fat, high protein, with a good selection of fruits and vegetables.

(g) Avoid the use of tobacco.

d. Knowledge deficit regarding the self-care program

Goal: Patient will adhere to self-care program.

Interventions:

(1) Include family and significant other in teaching program.

(2) Provide written instruction about foot and leg care.

(3) Refer to self-help groups such as Smoke-Enders, Stress Management.

4. Evaluation

a. Patient has increased arterial blood supply to extremities.

b. Patient experiences decreased venous congestion.

c. Patient is free of pain.

d. Patient experiences no incidence of vascular compression.

e. Extremities have proper arterial flow.

f. Skin of the extremities is intact.

g. Patient performs self-care activities.

Alterations in Perception and Coordination

A. Management of the Patient with Cataract

Opacity of the crystalline lens that causes, or is accompanied by, loss of visual acuity.

1. Causes: Congenital factors, ultraviolet radiation, drugs, diabetes, smoking, and alcohol

A cataract is a cloudy area in the lens of the eye.

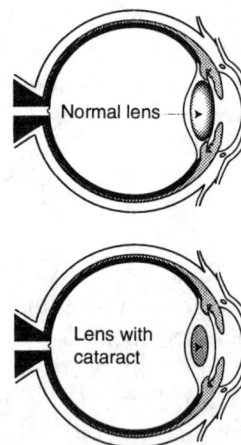

Side view of eye

A normal lens is clear. It lets light pass to the back of the eye. A cataract blocks some of the light. As a cataract develops, it becomes harder for a person to see.

Cataract is a normal part of aging. About half of Americans ages 65 to 74 have cataract. About 70% of those age 75 and over have this condition.

Most people with cataract have a cataract in both eyes. However, one eye may be worse then the other because each cataract develops at a different rate.

Source: "Cataract in Adults: A Patient's Guide," U.S. Department of Health and Human Services, Public Health Services AHCPR: Inside cover.

2. Symptoms:
   a. Cloudy, fuzzy, foggy, or filmy vision.
   b. Changes in the way you see colors.
   c. Problems driving at night because headlights seem too bright.
   d. Problems with glare from lamps or the sun.
   e. Frequent changes in your eyeglass prescription.
   f. Double vision.
   g. Better near vision for a while only in farsighted people.

   These symptoms also can be signs of other eye problems.

3. Patient care management
   a. Nonsurgical management
      (1) Change to distance spectacle lens prescription.
      (2) Use of strong bifocals.
      (3) Use of magnifications or other aids.
      (4) Use of appropriate illumination.
   b. Surgical management—Outpatient surgery in a hospital or independent surgery center. Anesthesia can be general or local.
      (1) Indications for surgery:
         (a) Visual disability with a Snellen acuity of 20/50 or worse.
         (b) Visual disability with a Snellen acuity of 20/40 or better, such as diplopia or polyopia; visual disparity between the 2 eyes; visual function that fluctuates because of glare or dim illumination.
         (c) Visual disability of a one-eyed patient.
         (d) Lens-induced disease.
         (e) Concomitant ocular disease that requires clear media.

         The widespread use of local anesthetic instead of general anesthetic, better wound closure activities, and earlier visual rehabilitation with intraocular lens (IOL) implants have led to an earlier return to everyday activities.
      (2) Surgical procedures (An enzyme, alphachymotrypsin, is injected into the anterior chamber to free the capsule of the zonular fibers that hold it in place, thereby making lens extraction easier.)
         (a) **Extracapsular** An incision is made in the lens capsule, and the lens is removed. The back half of the capsule is left (the outer covering of the lens).
         (b) **Phacoemulsification** Extracapsular surgery; the lens is softened with sound waves and removed through a needle. The back half of the lens is left behind.
         (c) **Intracapsular** Both lens and capsule are removed. Cryosurgery is used in this procedure, but it is rare.
         (d) **Intraocular lens implant (IOL)** A prosthetic lens is slipped into the vacated pocket and attached to surrounding tissues in an anatomically correct position. The chief advantage of this 1-hour procedure is that there is minimal distortion in shape or shape of image.

Replacing the Lens

A person who has cataract surgery usually gets an artificial lens at the same time. A plastic disc, called an intraocular lens, is placed in the lens capsule inside the eye. Other choices are contact lenses and cataract glasses.

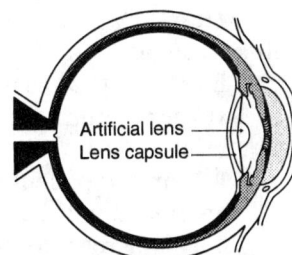

Artificial lens
Lens capsule

Side view of eye with artificial lens

Source: "Cataract in Adults: A Patient's Guide," U.S. Department of Health and Human Services, Public Health Serivce, AHCPR, 1993, p.7.

4. Postoperative care (for ambulatory patient)
   a. Criteria for discharge after ambulatory surgery include: stable vital signs; return to preoperative mental state; absence of nausea; absence of significant pain; availability of an escort; review with patient or escort postsurgical care until the first postoperative visit on the day following surgery, including relief of pain, activity level permitted, and access to emergency care if needed; prearranged follow-up appointment; written postoperative instructions; suitable home environment; adequate home care support.

b. Unplanned postoperative hospitalization.
  (1) Operative complication of an ocular or medical nature.
  (2) Ocular complications can include infection, severe pain, retrobulbar hemorrhage, wound dehiscence, endophthalmitis, uncontrolled elevated intraocular pressure.

5. Planned postoperative hospitalization
  a. Medical conditions that require prolonged postoperative observation by a nurse or skilled personnel.
  b. Best correctable vision in the unoperated eye is 20/200 or worse.
  c. Patient is mentally debilitated, diagnosed as mentally ill, or functionally incapacitated so that risk of injury exists in the immediate postoperative period.
  d. Physical disability prevents satisfactory immediate postoperative care.
    (1) Preoperative nursing diagnosis/goal/interventions
      Fear and/or depression related to sensory impairment and lack of understanding of procedure
      Goal: Patient will experience diminished fear.
      Interventions:
      (a) Explain the nature of the surgery and the expected results.
      (b) Inform the patient that a local anesthetic will be given in the operating room. (Local anesthesia prevents operative complications such as vomiting.)
      (c) Scrub the face before surgery to reduce pathogens.
      (d) Give medications topically.
        1. Mydriatic—facilitates removal of the cataract because the pupil is dilated.
        2. Cycloplegic—paralyzes the muscle of accommodation.
        3. Antimicrobial—may be given.
      (e) Preoperative evaluation. Patient's anxiety is lessened.
    (2) Postoperative nursing diagnoses/goals/interventions
      Goals:
      (a) Patient will be free of complications.

      (b) Patient will adjust to altered visual status.
      Interventions:
      (a) Instruct the patient not to cough, sneeze, or move too rapidly.
      (b) Maintain dressing and eye shield to prevent injury. (Only the operated eye is covered. The dressing is changed by the physician.)
      (c) Observe for complications such as hemmorrhage from the eye and sudden eye pain.
      (d) Elevate the head of the bed 30 to 45 degrees; a firm pillow is allowed.
      (e) Position the patient on his/her back or the unoperated side.
      (f) Unless otherwise instructed, allow the patient out of bed on the day of surgery.
      (g) Instruct the patient not to stoop. (Slip-on slippers and shoes eliminate the need to bend.)
      (h) Provide the patient with diversional activities.
      (i) Provide patient education.
        1. Instill eyedrops as prescribed, and use a metal eye shield at night for 3 weeks.
        2. Use eyeglasses properly (for patients without lens transplants).
          a. Glasses must be worn at all times (decrease in peripheral vision)
          b. Patient must look in the center of the glasses for clear vision, and turn head to bring objects into central vision. (Magnify objects 20% to 30%.)
          c. Distance perception has changed; therefore objects appear one-third larger than they really are.
          d. Permanent glasses are ordered 2 to 12 weeks after surgery.
          e. They allow patients to focus.
          f. Explain contact lens use:
            (1) Fitted after surgery and worn 2 to 12 weeks after.

(2) They allow patients to focus; glasses needed for close vision.

(3) Explain that ocular lens implant aids in focusing, but glasses will be fitted for close vision in 8 to 12 weeks and does not alter depth perception loss.

3. Wash hair in about 2 weeks; do not bend over sink or tub; tilt head slightly backward.

4. Avoid the following: rubbing eyes; squeezing eyelids; straining at bowel movement; getting soap in eyes; lifting over 15 to 20 pounds; driving, if possible; bending head down below the waist—bend knees only and keep back straight when picking up something from the floor.

5. Wash hands before and after instilling eye medications; cleanse around eye with sterile cotton balls or gauze sponges moistened with sterile water; instill drugs while seated with head tilted back, and gently pull down lower lid margin.

6. Bring all eye medications to follow-up visit.

7. Report to the physician eye pain, changes in visual acuity, headache, or inflammation.

8. Postoperative evaluation
   a. Patient is free of complications.
   b. Patient has adjusted to altered visual status.

9. Postoperative visit for patients without complications—The day following surgery; approximately 1 week, 3 weeks, and 6–8 weeks following surgery. If a complication occurs, more frequent visits are needed.

6. Complications
   In about half of all people who have extracapsular surgery or phacoemulsification,
   the lens capsule becomes cloudy. If it occurs, it usually develops a year or more after surgery. It causes the same vision problems as a cataract does.

   The treatment for this condition is a procedure called YAG capsulotomy, in which a laser (light) beam is used to make a tiny hole in the capsule to let light pass. This surgery is painless and does not require a hospital stay.

   Most people see better after YAG capsulotomy, but, as with cataract surgery, complications can occur.

7. Benefits and Risks
   a. Improvements in activities.
      (1) Everyday activities.
      (2) Driving.
      (3) Reading.
      (4) Working.
      (5) Moving around.
      (6) Social activities.
      (7) Hobbies.
      (8) Safety.
      (9) Self-confidence.
      (10) Independence.
   b. Possible complications.
      (1) High pressure in the eye.
      (2) Blood collection inside the eye.
      (3) Infection inside the eye.
      (4) Artificial lens damage or dislocate.
      (5) Drooping eyelid.
      (6) Retinal detachment.
      (7) Severe bleeding inside the eye.
      (8) Swelling or clouding of the cornea.
      (9) Blindness.
      (10) Loss of the eye.

B. **Glaucoma: Adult Onset**   A condition characterized by increased tension or pressure within the eye, causing progressive structural or functional damage.
   1. Types
      a. **Acute (narrow-angle/closed-angle)** Disease characterized by sudden impaired vision due to intraocular tension caused by imbalance in production and excretion of aqueous humor. This build-up can occur within $1/2$ to 1 hour and is an emergency. It may be precipitated in patients who have a narrow anterior-chamber angle by administering anticholinergic drugs such as atropine and scopolamine.
      b. **Chronic (wide-angle/open-angle)** Disease characterized by impaired

vision due to intraocular tension caused by actual obstruction in the excretion of aqueous humor. This disorder, which is believed to be inherited, is the second most common cause of blindness in the United States.

2. Assessment
   a. Acute (narrow-angle/closed-angle)
      (1) Rapid onset of severe pain in eye(s).
      (2) Blurred vision.
      (3) Headaches.
      (4) "Rainbows" in artificial light.
      (5) Halos around lights.
      (6) Nausea, vomiting.
      (7) Dilated pupil(s).
   b. Chronic (wide-angle/open-angle)
      (1) Insidious onset: patient may have mild discomfort such as tired eyes, trouble in focusing, and headache.
      (2) Gradual loss of peripheral vision.
      (3) Detection during annual eye examination or physical examinations; patient is rarely admitted into hospital.
   c. DIAGNOSTIC MEASURES
      (1) Tonometry—normal reading is 11 to 22 mm Hg.
      (2) Electronic tonometry.
      (3) Gonioscopy.
      (4) Visual field examination.

3. Patient care management
   a. Pharmacotherapy
      (1) Miotics, such as pilocarpine, to increase the outflow of aqueous humor.
      (2) Timolol maleate (Timoptic), a beta adrenergic receptor blocking agent. Topically applied, it decreases production of aqueous humor and reduces intraocular pressure for as long as 24 hours. It does not change vision because it does not affect pupillary size or cila body. It may cause palpitation and tachycardia.
      (3) Carbonic anhydrase inhibitors, such as Diamox, to decrease the production of aqueous humor.
      (4) Anticholinesterase, such as echothiophate iodide (Phospholine Iodide) or demecarium bromide (Humorsol) to facilitate the outflow of aqueous humor.
      (5) Epinephrine drops to decrease the production of aqueous humor and promote its outflow from the eye.

   b. Surgical management
      (1) Acute (closed-angle) glaucoma is treated surgically.
         (a) **Peripheral iridectomy** An incision is made through the cornea so that a portion of the iris may be drawn out and excised. Thus, it prevents the iris from bulging forward to crowd the chamber angle and permits drainage from the anterior chamber.
         (b) **Argon laser surgery** The laser beam burns the iris, with the same effect as an iridectomy. After the treatment there may be headaches and blurring of vision, which disappear within 24 hours. Topical steroids may be prescribed to decrease inflammation. An eye patch may be used for a few hours. This treatment may be repeated in 1 or 2 weeks.
      (2) Chronic (open-angle) glaucoma is treated pharmacotherapeutically and surgically.
         (a) **Corneal trephining and trabeculectomy** An opening is made at the junction of the cornea and the sclera through which the aqueous humor can drain. The opening is permanent and is usually covered by a flap of conjunctiva. In trabeculectomy, a small fistula or opening is made into the anterior chamber at the junction of the cornea and the sclera, allowing the aqueous humor to flow into the subconjunctiva space.

            After a trabeculectomy, the patient's head is elevated or the patient is placed in a sitting position to prevent blood from entering the anterior chamber. An eye shield is used for 3 to 4 weeks.
         (b) **Laser or argon laser trabeculoplasty** A narrow beam of laser is focused on the trabecular network of the open angle, resulting in an nonpenetrating

burn that changes the mesh-work pattern and facilitates drainage of the aqueous humor. It is a painless outpatient procedure. The patient continues to use prescribed eye drops and possibly steroid eye drops to control inflammation. The success rate is 80%.

4. Nonsurgical nursing diagnoses/goals/interventions
   a. Pain related to the disease process
      Goal: Patient will indicate that pain is reduced or alleviated.
      Interventions:
      (1) Maintain bedrest in a darkened room with head of bed elevated 30 degrees or in position of comfort.
      (2) Administer analgesic and other medications as ordered.
      (3) Administer antiemetics to prevent nausea and vomiting.
      (4) Assess visual acuity.
      (5) Assess type and location of pain; observe for increase in intraocular pressure.
   b. Anxiety related to hospitalization and loss of vision
      Goal: Patient will verbalize anxieties and demonstrate understanding of the disease and disease process.
      Interventions:
      (1) Answer questions honestly.
      (2) Explain all procedures.
      (3) Reinforce the physician's explanation of the disease process and the surgery if indicated.
      (4) Discuss visual limitation, and explain nursing care plan.
      (5) Place all needed articles within the patient's reach, and try to keep them in the same place at all times.
      (6) Assist with self-care and teach altered activities of daily living as needed.
      (7) Assist with meals.
   c. Knowledge deficit regarding self-care and the disease process
      Goal: Patient and/or significant other will demonstrate understanding of the disease process, home-care management, and follow-up.
      Interventions:
      (1) Instruct the patient and significant

other to instill eye drops.
      (2) Instruct the patient to count drops and not to miss any dose, to keep an extra bottle, to wear Medic-Alert band and carry card, and never to take over the counter drugs or atropine-containing drugs.
      (3) Explain the signs and symptoms to report to the physician: severe eye pain, blurred vision, nausea, headache, halo or "rainbow."
      (4) Explain the importance of keeping appointments with the physician/clinic.

5. Nonsurgical evaluation
   a. There are no complications.
   b. Intraocular pressure is stabilized.
   c. Patient and significant other demonstrate ability to instill eye drops.
   d. Patient and significant other understand the disease process and prescribed medical regimen, and anxiety is reduced.

6. Postoperative nursing diagnoses/goals/interventions
   a. Risk for infection related to invasive surgical procedure
      Goal: Patient will exhibit no signs of wound dehiscence or symptoms of intraocular pressure or infection.
      Interventions:
      (1) Check dressing every 2 hours for 12 hours, then every 4 hours.
      (2) Observe for bleeding, drainage, and/or pain; if present, report immediately.
      (3) Apply eye shield or patch as ordered.
      (4) Caution the patient not to touch, squeeze, or rub eye.
      (5) Monitor vital signs every 4 hours, then every shift.
   b. Risk for injury related to altered visual acuity
      Goal: Patient will be free from injury.
      Interventions:
      (1) Keep side rails up at all times.
      (2) Explain routine to the patient; plan care with the patient.
      (3) Assist with deep breathing exercise; avoid coughing.
      (4) Elevate head of bed 30 degrees or as ordered.
      (5) Administer antiemetic; avoid vomiting.

(6) Assist with ambulation as needed.

(7) Teach self-care; assist as needed.

c. Sensory perception alterations related to impaired vision

Goal: Patient will express positive feelings and show no untoward reactions due to limited visual acuity.

Interventions:

(1) Visit frequently to determine needs; anticipate needs if possible.

(2) Keep articles in same place at bedside.

(3) Place call bell within reach.

(4) Encourage self-care with assistance.

(5) Assist with meals.

d. Knowledge deficit regarding home care and complications

Goal: Patient and/or significant other will demonstrate understanding of home care, follow-up, and possible complications.

Interventions:

(1) Instruct patient and significant other in care of the eye: change dressing using aseptic technique; use eye patch or shield at night; avoid rubbing, squeezing, or touching eyes; use eyeglasses as ordered; use eye as ordered by physician (*see* Nonsurgical nursing diagnoses/ goals/interventions, above).

(2) Caution patient to avoid constipation, bending, straining, and lifting heavy objects.

(3) Give information about community resources for the visually impaired.

(4) Discuss home-care arrangements with family/significant other: arrange furniture for safety; allow the patient to do self-care; avoid emotional stress and upset.

(5) Discuss symptoms to report to the physician: increased eye pain, redness, drainage, decreased visual acuity, floater, halos, sparks.

(6) See also nursing intervention for non-surgical patient, above.

7. Postoperative evaluation

a. There are no complications.

b. Patient performs self-care with assistance as needed.

c. Patient demonstrates understanding of change in life-style.

d. Patient understands signs and symptoms to report to physician and the need for follow-up care.

C. **Parkinson's Disease** A progressive neurological disorder affecting the brain centers responsible for control and regulation of movement. It is characterized by slowness of movement, tremor, and muscle stiffness or rigidity. There is loss of pigmentation of neurons, particularly in the substantia nigra of the brain. Dopamine, a major transmitter, is depleted in the substantia nigra and the corpus striatum. Depletion of dopamine in the basal ganglia is associated with the major symptoms of this condition.

1. Assessment

a. Observe for cognitive, perceptual, and memory deficits.

b. Observe walking and gait for stiffness and dragging, or a shuffling and propulsive gait.

c. Observe general appearance for posture change (head bent forward, stoop posture, rigidity); tremors of hands and arms (unilateral); a slow pronation-supination (pill-rolling of thumb against fingers), which decreases upon performance of a delicate act; masklike appearance of face; and weight loss.

2. Patient care management

a. Medications

(1) Levodopa—reduces tremor and rigidity. Side effects; anorexia, nausea, and vomiting; dyskinesias; postural hypotension; mental changes such as hallucination.

(2) Sinemet (a combination of levodopa and carbidopa)—allows levodopa to reach the brain.

(3) Anticholinergic drugs (Artane, Cogentin)—inhibit acetylcholine.

(4) Antihistaminic drug (Benedryl)— reduces tremors.

(5) Symmetrel—is similar to levodopa in action except that there is less side effect.

(6) Disipal and Benadryl (antiparkinson and antihistamine)

b. Surgical intervention—stereotactic thalomotomy.

c. Nutrition therapy.

d. Speech therapy.

e. Occupational therapy.

3. Nursing diagnoses/goals/interventions
   a. Impaired physical mobility related to muscle rigidity and weakness
   Goal: Patient will experience improved mobility.
   Interventions:
   (1) Reinforce progressive exercise program such as:
       (a) Walking and using stationary bike. Special walking technique: use broad-based gait, swing arms and raise the feet while walking, and use heel-toe, heel-toe gait in long stride; advise patient to practice walking to marching music, and to practice breathing exercises while walking to help move the rib cage.
       (b) Stretching exercise (stretch-hold-relax).
       (c) Frequent rest periods between periods of exercise.
   (2) Assist with warm baths and massage.
   (3) Assist with passive and active exercises to help relax muscles and relieve painful muscle spasms that accompany rigidity.
   b. Self-care deficits (eating, drinking, dressing, hygiene) related to tremors and motor disturbances
   Goal: Patient will attain independence in the activities of daily living.
   Interventions:
   (1) Teach and supervise the patient during the activities of daily living.
   (2) Advise the patient regarding environmental modifications that may enhance self-care abilities such as: bedside rails on the bed at home or tieing a rope at the foot of the bed to assist in pulling up without help.
   c. Constipation related to medications and reduced activity
   Goal: Patient will achieve adequate bowel elimination.
   (1) Increase the patient's fluid oral intake to 3000 cc daily.
   (2) Provide a dietary consultation.
   (3) Assist the patient in selecting foods with a moderate fiber content.
   (4) Assist the patient in establishing a bowel routine.
   (5) Advise the patient regarding environmental modifications such as a raised toilet seat to facilitate moving from a sitting to standing position.
   d. Altered nutrition: less than body requirements related to tremors, slowness in eating, and difficulty in chewing and swallowing
   Goals:
   (1) Patient will maintain his/her weight and/or gain 0.5 to 1.0 pound per week.
   (2) Patient will not experience choking or aspiration of food.
   Interventions:
   (1) Place the patient in an upright position for meals and for 1 hour afterward.
   (2) Provide a dietary consultation.
   (3) Avoid solids and thin liquids; a semi-solid diet with thick liquids is easiest to swallow.
   (4) Teach the patient to place food on the tongue, close the lips and teeth, lift the tongue up and then back, and swallow; and to chew first on one side of the mouth and then on the other.
   (5) Instruct the patient to hold the head upright and make a conscious effort to swallow and to control saliva.
   (6) Massage the facial and neck muscles before meals; this may be beneficial, and massaging or stroking the throat may aid in swallowing.
   (7) Monitor the patient's weight weekly.
   (8) Administer high-calorie protein and low-volume supplements.
   (9) Advise the patient regarding environmental modifications such as an electric warming tray to keep food hot and to allow for rest during the prolonged time it takes to eat and special utensils such as a stabilized plate, nonspill cup, and specially constructed eating utensils.
   e. Impaired verbal communication related to decreased speech volume, slowness

of speech, and inability to move facial muscles

Goal: Patient will adequately communicate with others.

Interventions:

(1) Remind the patient to face the listener, exaggerate the pronunciation of words, and speak in short sentences.

(2) Instruct the patient to take a few deep breaths before speaking.

(3) Reinforce the speech improvement exercises prescribed by speech pathologists.

f. Impaired social interaction related to depression and dysfunction due to progression of disease

Goal: Patient will develop positive coping mechanisms.

Interventions:

(1) Encourage and reassure the patient by praising perseverance and pointing out activities that are being maintained through active participation in self-care.

(2) Encourage full participation in the planned program of activity during the day to prevent sleeping, apathy, and disinterest.

(3) Encourage the patient to carry out the activities of daily living.

(4) Administer antidepressant drugs (tricyclic) as ordered.

g. Knowledge deficit regarding the disease progression, treatment, and home management

Goal: Patient and care giver will verbalize understanding of disease progression, treatment, and home-care management.

(1) Explain the nature of the disease and its progression, the treatment, and home management to the patient, family, and caregiver.

(2) Refer the patient to the American Parkinson's Disease Foundation, and distribute literature from the foundation on patient education.

(3) Allow the family members and caregiver to express feelings of frustration, anger, and guilt.

4. Evaluation

a. Patient strives toward improved mobility.

b. Patient progresses toward self-care.

c. Patient achieves and maintains adequate nutritional status.

d. Patient communicates with others effectively.

e. Patient and family cope with Parkinson's disease.

f. Patient and family understand the disease progression, treatment, and home management.

D. **Cerebrovascular Accident** A sudden loss of brain function resulting from a disruption of the blood supply to a part of the brain; commonly called "stroke."

Changes that occur are (1) absence of oxygen to the brain tissue for more than 5 to 6 minutes, which leads to irreversible cerebral changes and tissue necrosis; (2) cerebral edema, caused by the extravasation of blood into the brain tissue, which in turn causes pressure on the ventricular system; (3) lack of glucose, which causes irritability of the neurons and disrupts nerve transmission; seizure may occur.

1. Causes: thrombosis, cerebral embolism, hemorrhage, compression or spasm.

2. Types of CVA's may be classified according to severity.

a. **Transient ischemic attack (TIA)** Involves loss of neurologic function that is abrupt in onset; lasts less than 24 hours without residual signs.

b. **Reversible ischemic neurologic disability** Resembles TIA but neurologic deficit lasts longer (up to 2 days before neurologic signs remit).

c. **Stroke-in-evolution** Begins as a relatively small neurologic deficit that increases over a period of several hours or days.

d. **Complete stroke** Produces neurologic deficits that remain stable for a long period of time and do not regress.

The clinical features of a CVA vary with the artery affected, the severity of the damage, and the extent of collateral circulation.

If the CVA occurs in the left hemisphere, it produces symptoms on the right side of the body; if it occurs in the right hemisphere, it produces symptoms on the left side of the body. *See* table.

3. Assessment. *See also* Unit Seven, Alterations in Perception and Coordination,

Section A: General Assessment, page 216.

a. Assess health history for past history of hypertension, transient ishemic attacks, or transient aphasia.

b. Observe for TIA signs and symptoms:
   (1) Paresis or paralysis of the face or extremities.
   (2) Aphasia.
   (3) Vision loss in one eye or hemianopia.
   (4) Areas of anesthesia.
   (5) Behavioral or mental changes, including confusion.
   (6) Loss of postural tone.
   (7) Vertigo.
   (8) Vomiting.
   (9) Dysarthia.
   (10) Perioral numbness.
   (11) Visual blurring.
   (12) Diplopia.

c. Assess for the following at the onset of CVA:
   (1) The patient is unconscious with stertorous respiration or Cheyne-Stokes rhythm.

Deficits That May Occur After a Cerebrovascular Accident

FUNCTION	RIGHT-SIDED HEMIPLEGIA	LEFT-SIDED HEMIPLEGIA
Language	Varying degrees of receptive and expressive aphasia are experienced	Language abilities are usually intact.
Speech	There is difficulty in finding the correct word, as well as in speaking.	There is difficulty in speaking clearly, but not in choosing words or understanding speech.
	Dysarthia may be present because of impaired coordination, usually from nerve damage.	
Sensation	In both right-sided and left-sided hemiplegia, awareness of painful stimuli and temperature may decrease; deep pain sensation remains the same; proprioception may diminish; vision may also be affected—homonymous hemianopia may occur on the same side as hemiplegia, or patient may not be able to see out of either eye in the direction of the paralyzed side.	
Perception	Awareness of body and spatial orientation are normal.	Awareness of the left side of the body and the envrionment to the left are lacking, with or without visual deficit; stimuli from the left side of the body may be ignored (unilateral neglect); difficulty in correctly judging depth and vertical and horizontal orientation in the environment may be experienced.
Movement	There is less apraxia, but typically it is bilateral.	Apraxia develops on the affected side.
	Paralysis on one side of the body occurs; immediately following a stroke, the affected side may become flaccid or limp; if paralysis does not remit, the affected side becomes spastic or stiff; facial asymmetry may result; if vocalization muscles are involved, unclear speech and dysphasia may result; loss of ability to carry out purposeful, learned motor activity (apraxia) may occur.	
Behavioral style	The patient does not have impaired judgment and underestimates his/her abilities.	The patient tends to overestimate his/her abilities and reacts quickly and impulsively; attention span is impaired with poor concentration; there is concern about disabilities and future developments.
	In both right-sided and left-sided hemiplegic patients, increased emotional lability occurs, characterized by inappropriate laughter or crying.	
Memory	Difficulty with new language information may be experienced, such as remembering names.	Difficulty in remembering new information about the environment is experienced.
Rehabilitation	The patient may be able to live independently afterwards.	The patient may not be able to maintain an independent life-style because of spatial and perceptual deficits.

(2) Pulse rate slows with elevated blood pressure.

(3) If facial paralysis occurs, one cheek blows out rhythmically with respiration.

(4) Hands and eyes may turn toward injured side of brain.

(5) Swallowing reflex may be absent.

(6) Deep reflex may be absent in paralyzed limb.

d. Observe for other signs and symptoms of CVA:

(1) Hemiplegia.

(2) Quadriplegia.

(3) Hemianopia.

(4) Urinary and fecal incontinence.

(5) Sensory loss or alteration.

(6) Dysphasia.

(7) Dysphagia.

e. DIAGNOSTIC MEASURES

(1) Magnetic resonance imaging (MRI).

(2) Computed tomography scan (CT).

(3) Brain scan.

(4) Lumbar puncture.

(5) Angiography.

(6) Electroencephalography (EEG).

f. Assess for **homonymous hemianopia** Loss of half of visual field, temporary or permanent. The affected side of vision corresponds to the paralyzed side of the body.

(1) Observe whether the patient's head turns away from the affected side of the body, and tends to neglect that side and the space on that side.

(2) Assess for hemianopia (have patient look at your face while you move finger from patient's ears on the unaffected side toward affected line of vision; inability to see the moving finger indicates hemianopia).

Nursing diagnosis/goal/interventions˙
Unilateral neglect related to disturbed perceptual ability
Goal: Patient will compensate for visual deficit.
Interventions:

(1) Approach the patient on the side where visual perception is intact.

(2) Place all visual stimuli (clock, calendar, television) on this side.

(3) Instruct the patient to turn head in the direction of the defective visual field to compensate for this loss.

(4) Draw the patient's attention to the affected side by encouraging him/her to move the head.

(5) Increase the amount of natural or artificial lighting in the room; provide glasses.

4. Patient care management

a. Acute phase—first 48 to 72 hours

(1) Endotracheal intubation and mechanical ventilation to prevent respiratory arrest.

(2) Medications

(a) Steroids to reduce cerebral edema.

(b) Antibiotics to prevent or control infection.

(c) Dilantin to control seizures.

(d) Anticoagulants if CVA was caused by cerebral infarct.

(e) Stool softener to prevent straining.

(f) Diuretics and antihypertensive to control blood pressure.

(g) Acetaminophen and codeine for pain.

(3) Parenteral fluids for hydration.

(4) Humidified oxygen therapy.

(5) Hypothermia blanket for increased temperature.

b. Rehabilitation phase—begins on day after stroke, intensifies during the convalescent phase.

c. Transient ischemic accident (TIA)

(1) Vascular surgery for extracranial lesion.

(a) Anastomosis of superior artery.

(b) Endartectomy (carotid most common).

(2) Antiplatelet medications: aspirin and Persantine.

5. Nursing diagnoses/goals/interventions for acute phase

a. Altered tissue perfusion: cerebral related to inadequate cerebral blood supply, increased intracranial pressure (ICP), decreased cerebral oxygenation
Goal: Patient will demonstrate adequate cerebral perfusion.
Interventions:

(1) Assess neurologic status, includ-

ing level of consciousness and mental status, pupil and eye movements, motor and sensory functions, verbal response every 1 to 4 hours.

(2) Monitor vital signs every 1 to 4 hours.

(3) Administer hypertensive medication, and monitor effect.

(4) Maintain a patent airway and adequate ventilation.

(5) Elevate the head, and align head and neck.

(6) Use restraint as necessary (get a physician's order; release and massage areas according to hospital policy). Do not use a vest restraint.

(7) Administer medications as ordered.

(8) Monitor intake and output.

(9) Monitor laboratory tests (e.g., PTT, PT, electrolytes) to determine therapeutic drug level or electrolyte imbalances that may alter patient's sensorium.

(10) *See* Unit Seven, Alterations in Perception and Coordination, Section B3: Management of the unconscious patient, page 220.

b. Ineffective breathing pattern related to obstructed airway, increased intracranial pressure, and alteration in level of consciousness

c. Ineffective airway clearance related to obstructed airway, poor cough reflex, and alteration in level of consciousness

Goals:

(1) Patient will maintain a patent airway.

(2) Patient will be free of accumulated bronchial secretions.

Interventions:

(1) Place patient in semi-Fowler's position, and suction as necessary.

(2) Monitor respiratory rate, rhythm, and depth every 1 to 4 hours.

(3) Encourage cough and deep breathing.

(4) Assess amount, color, and consistency of sputum; send specimen to laboratory for culture and sensitivity to determine the need for antibiotic therapy.

(5) Monitor arterial blood gases.

(6) Administer humidified oxygen at the rate and by the method ordered.

(7) Administer bronchiodilator and pulmonary expectorant as ordered.

(8) Notify the physician of significant findings.

d. Impaired physical mobility related to decreased level of consciousness and paresis/plegia

Goal: Patient will maintain muscle strength.

Interventions:

(1) Assess motor function, sensation, and reflexes in all extremities.

(2) Maintain body alignment with head, shoulders, and hips level on a firm mattress.

(3) Utilize footboard: heels off mattress and protected to prevent skin breakdown.

(4) Utilize trochanter roll to prevent external rotation of hip and pain and discomfort.

(5) Support arms and hands in function positions: elbow slightly flexed, wrist extended, a hard handball or rubber ball to keep fingers in "grasp" position and to control spasm; hands elevated to prevent dependent edema.

(6) Reposition the patient every 2 hours.

(7) Perform passive range of motion exercises every 2 to 4 hours.

(8) Coordinate efforts with physical and occupational therapists.

(9) To prevent hip-flexion contracture, keep bed flat except when the patient is engaged in activities of daily living.

(10) Remove footboard as soon as spasticity occurs (use only during flaccid period).

6. Evaluation for acute phase

a. Patient demonstrates unchanged or improved neurologic status.

b. Patient's blood pressure is maintained within specified parameters.

c. Patient has adequate bilateral lung aeration.

d. Patient's blood gases are within normal limits.

e. Patient's respiratory rate is within normal limits.

f. Patient is free of pressure sores, muscle atrophy, and contractures.

g. Patient is ambulated and repositioned on a regular basis.

7. Nursing diagnoses/goals/interventions for rehabilitation phase

a. Altered nutrition: less than body requirements related to difficulty in swallowing, chewing, and loss of appetite

b. Impaired swallowing related to the loss of motor function

Goal: Patient will maintain adequate nutritional status, fluid intake, and electrolyte balance.

Interventions:

(1) Assess patient's gag reflex, ability to swallow, presence of facial paralysis, motor and sensory functions of upper extremities, evidence of perceptual deficit to determine eating ability.

(2) Monitor intake and output and percentage of meal eaten.

(3) Provide dietary consultation.

(4) Monitor electrolytes.

(5) Administer parenteral fluids as ordered; change IV site, tubing, and site dressing according to hospital policy.

(6) Administer nasogastric feeding and water as ordered; maintain the patient in upright position during feeding and for 1 hour afterward.

(7) Administer hyperalimentation therapy as ordered. *See* Unit Eight, Section H2: Total parenteral nutrition, page 283.

(8) Assist with oral feeding; avoid thin fluids—use only semisolid fluids.

(9) Assess patient's likes and dislikes.

(10) Advance diet as tolerated (full liquid—soft/pureed—regular) (*see* feeding under nursing interventions for Parkinson's Disease, page 364).

(11) Weigh the patient weekly.

(12) Provide oral hygiene before and after meals.

c. Risk for disuse syndrome, painful shoulder, related to hemiplegia and disuse

Goal: Patient will be free of shoulder pain.

Interventions:

(1) Avoid lifting the patient by the flaccid shoulder or pulling on the affected arm.

(2) Position the flaccid arm on a table or pillow while the patient is seated.

(3) Use arm sling, if ordered, when patient is ambulatory to prevent dangling of arm.

(4) Place the arm through range of motion exercises.

(5) Elevate the arm and hands to prevent dependent edema of hands.

d. Self-care deficits: total (hygiene, toileting, feeding, transfers) related to stroke sequelae

Goal: Patient will achieve optimal self-care.

Interventions:

(1) Encourage the patient to assist with personal hygiene as soon as he/she is able to sit up.

(2) Have the patient carry out all self-care activities on the unaffected side (combing hair, brushing teeth, shaving with an electric shaver, bathing, eating).

(3) Encourage the patient to wear clothing while performing ambulatory activities; instruct the family to bring in clothing one size larger than normally worn and fitted with velcro closures.

(4) Instruct the patient to dress seated; clothing is placed on affected side, in order in which the garments are to be worn, in front of a large mirror.

e. Functional incontinence related to sensory/motor impairment, immobility, and impaired communication

Goals:

(1) Patient will remain continent of urine.

(2) Patient will be protected from complications of incontinence.

Interventions:

(1) Observe for incontinence; note type and pattern.

(2) Assess whether the patient is aware of need to void or able to communicate need (observe for nonverbal

clues such as restlessness).

(3) Establish a regular voiding schedule.

(4) Offer bedpan/urinal frequently.

(5) Stimulate voiding, utilizing privacy (running water, comfortable position, Crede maneuver), as needed.

(6) Palpate bladder for distension as needed.

(7) Perform catheter care twice daily if Foley is in place (perineal washing, application of bacteriostatic ointment to urinary meatus, taping of catheter to prevent traction).

(8) Assess character/appearance of urine to determine concentration and possible urinary infection; obtain urine specimen as indicated.

f. Constipation, diarrhea, or incontinence of feces related to fluid and dietary intake, loss of voluntary control, impaired communication, peristaltic changes, intolerance to tube feedings, immobility.
Goal: Patient will evacuate bowel on regular basis.
Interventions:

(1) Assess whether patient is aware of, and able to communicate, need to defecate.

(2) Assess patient's previous bowel habits.

(3) Assist with mobilization and increase activity as needed to stimulate peristalsis.

(4) Administer stool softeners, bulk-forming laxatives, suppositories, enemas.

(5) Assess the patient's nutritional status; encourage high-fiber foods and roughage.

(6) Offer extra fluids if the patient is able to tolerate them.

(7) Observe for incontinence.

(8) Assess and record character and frequency of bowel movements.

(9) Stimulate evacuation by providing privacy and comfortable position.

g. Impaired communication: verbal related to expressive/receptive aphasia, dysarthria, altered thought processes
Goal: Patient will establish or re-establish an effective means of communication.
Interventions:

(1) Assess the patient's ability to express him/herself, understand others, and remain oriented.

(2) Address the patient in a slow and unhurried manner.

(3) Ask questions that may be answered with "yes" or "no" or with gestures.

(4) Respond to the patient's nonverbal behavior.

(5) Reinforce interventions recommended by speech therapist.

(6) Give one instruction at a time, allowing the patient time to process the information.

(7) Keep extraneous noises and sounds at a minimum to avoid distraction.

(8) Maintain eye contact when talking to the patient.

h. Sensory-perceptual alterations: visual, tactile, or kinesthetic related to visual defects, impaired sensations

i. Unilateral neglect related to disturbed perceptual abilities

j. Risk for injury related to impaired self-protective mechanisms
Goals:

(1) Patient will adapt to visual deficit.

(2) Patient will compensate for sensory disturbances.

(3) Patient will be free of injury.
Interventions:

(1) Assess the patient's visual sensory functions.

(2) Position call light, food tray, and other objects within reach of unaffected side.

(3) Cover affected eye with eye patch or shield if diplopia is present.

(4) Assist the patient in gauging the distances of objects.

(5) Assist with activities of daily living and mobility as needed.

(6) Monitor temperature of food and bath water to prevent accidental injury; teach the patient and family to do the same.

k. Grieving related to actual or perceived loss of function

l. Ineffective individual coping related to loss of well-being

m. Body image, self-esteem, role performance, or personal identity disturbance related to loss of body functions, physical changes, role changes, dependences

Goal: Patient will effectively adapt to altered appearance, abilities, and roles.
Interventions:
(1) Explore with the patient and family fears of dying, loss of dependence, loss of control of body functions, crippling and permanent disability, and loss of speech.
(2) Encourage verbalization and expression of feelings (anger, depression, frustration, anxiety, helplessness, hopelessness).
(3) Determine the impact of altered health status on the patient and family on an ongoing basis.
(4) Remind the patient and family that progress will be slow, but possible; reinforce all positive gains.
n. Risk for caregiver strain related to catastropic illness.
Goals: Family functioning will be restored.
Interventions:
(1) Facilitate family coping by involving members in the patient's care.
(2) Explain the expected outcome of the patient's stroke, and counsel the family to allow the patient to do what he/she can for self.
(3) Explain that rehabilitation takes many months, progress will be slow, and they should approach the patient with a supportive and optimistic attitude, focusing on the abilities remaining.
(4) Prepare the family for occasional episodes of emotional lability (the patient may laugh or cry easily, may be irritable and demanding or depressed and confused), and state that emotional lability usually improves with time.
o. Knowledge deficit regarding disease process, treatment, prognosis, and home management
Goal: Patient and family will demonstrate adequate knowledge of disease process, treatment, prognosis, and home management.
Interventions:
(1) Explain all treatments, procedures, and aspects of home-care management.
(2) Utilize resources to aid in teaching (written materials, movies).

(3) Coordinate occupational therapist consultation.
(4) Review medications: names, dosages, time schedules, and side effects.
(5) Instruct the patient to keep appointments with physician or clinic.
(6) Explain signs and symptoms to report to the physician.
8. Evaluation for rehabilitation phase
a. Patient achieves improved mobility.
b. Patient has no complaints of shoulder pain.
c. Patient achieves self-care.
d. Patient is continent, communicates need to void, and is free from evidence of urinary infection.
e. Patient has soft, formed bowel movements on a regular basis.
f. Patient communicates the need to defecate.
g. Patient establishes an effective method of communication with verbal and nonverbal cues.
h. Patient is free from injury.
i. Patient adapts to sensory impairment.
j. Patient demonstrates increased independence.
k. Patient verbalizes concerns and fears.
l. Patient and family demonstrate adequate knowledge of the disease process, treatment, prognosis, and home management.
m. Patient maintains weight within 10% of admission weight.
n. Patient tolerates parenteral feedings or tube feedings with no diarrhea and balanced electrolyte.
o. Caregiver is able to cope with illness and responsibility.

E. **Osteoporosis** A disorder in which there is a reduction of total bone mass. There is a change in normal homeostatic bone turnover; the rate of bone resorption is greater than the rate of bone formation, resulting in a reduced total bone bass. The bones become porous, brittle, and fragile; they fracture easily under stresses that would not normally break bones. Osteoporosis frequently results in compression fractures of the neck and intertrochanteric region of the femur and in multiple fractures of the vertebrae, resulting in kyphosis.
Women develop osteoporosis more frequently than men. Black women have greater bone

mass than white women and therefore experience less osteoporosis. The prevalence of osteoporosis in women over 75 is 90%. The withdrawal of estrogen at menopause accelerates bone resorption.

1. Causes
   a. Excessive use of corticosteroids, Cushing's syndrome, hyperthyroidism and hyperparathyroidism, immobility (bone formation is enhanced by the stress of weight bearing).
   b. Nutritional factors. Dietary calcium and vitamin D must be adequate—800 mg of calcium. Postmenopausal women need 1500 mg of calcium daily.
   c. Coexisting medical conditions (malabsorption syndrome, lactose intolerance, alcohol abuse, renal failure, endocrine disorders).
   d. Medications (isoniazid, heparin, tetracycline, aluminum-containing antacids, furosemide, anticonvulsants, corticosteroids, and thyroid supplements) that affect calcium utilization and metabolism.
2. Assessment
   a. DIAGNOSTIC MEASURES
      (1) Laboratory studies—serum calcium and phosphate, alkaline phosphatase, urine calcium excretion, hemocrit, erythrocyte sedimentation rate.
      (2) X-rays.
      (3) Computer tomography of hip and spine.
   b. Identification of high-risk individuals.
3. Patient care management
   a. Maintain bone mass (weight-bearing exercise, adequate dietary and/or supplemental calcium, modification of lifestyle, e.g., reduce caffeine, cigarettes, and alcohol).
   b. At menopause, utilize estrogen/progesterone replacement therapy to retard bone loss and prevent the occurrence of fractures, especially for women who have undergone premature menopause. These women must examine their breasts monthly since estrogen therapy has been linked with increase in breast cancer. Also, a Papanicolaou smear and endometrial smear should be done 1 to 2 times a year.

F. **Osteoarthritis**   Degeneration of the articular cartilage in the joints.

1. Assessment
   a. Observe for joint stiffness and Heberden's nodes (appear on the distal joints of the finger).
   b. Note whether joint pain (knee, fingers, toes, and lower spine) is worse after inactivity but continues with increased use of joints and is improved by rest.
2. Patient care management
   a. Pharmacology: analgesics and anti-inflammatory agents. Acetaminophen (Tylenol) is prescribed most often to avoid the side effects of aspirin (*see* Unit Seven, Section C: Analgesia, page 177). Nonsteroidal anti-inflammatory agents are recommended during flare-ups.
   b. Conservative measures: heat, weight reduction, joint rest and avoidance of joint overuse, orthotic device to support inflamed joints (splints, braces), isometric and postural exercises.
   c. Occupational and physical therapy.
   d. Transcutaneous electrical nerve stimulation (TENS) for spinal stenosis.
   e. Surgery   When conservative measures are ineffective, arthrodesis (fusion), osteotomy (transection of the bone), or arthroplasty (replacement) may be performed.
3. Nursing diagnosis/goal/interventions
   Acute pain related to joint degeneration and muscle spasm
   Goal: Patient will experience relief from pain.
   Interventions:
   a. Apply hot pack and warm soaks, assist with tub bath and paraffin dip.
   b. Give anti-inflammatory agents, analgesics, and muscle relaxants.
   c. Rest the involved part with splints, braces, or cervical collars.
   d. Instruct the patient in postural exercises.
   e. Provide rest periods.
   f. Provide psychological support.
4. Evaluation: Patient experiences relief from pain and discomfort.

G. Fall Prevention
   1. Definitions
      a. Fall—An event that results in a person coming to rest inadvertently on the ground or other lower level other than a consequence of sustaining a violent blow, loss of consciousness, sudden

onset of paralysis as in a stroke, or an epileptic seizure.

b. Trip—An accidental encounter with a low-lying object.

c. Slip—A change in the pattern of walking because of something on the floor or ground.

d. Stumble—A quick series of steps to correct a temporary change in balance.

e. Stagger—Irregular steps with feet wide apart.

f. Sway—Moving from one side to another when standing.

2. Causes/risk factors

a. Medications
  (1) Psychotropics
    (a) Antidepressants.
    (b) Antipsychotics.
    (c) Benzodiazepines.
    (d) Phenothiazines.
    (e) Sedatives.
    (f) Tranquilizers.
  (2) Other medications
    (a) Diuretics, thiazides.
    (b) Antihypertensives.
    (c) Antiarrhythmics.
    (d) Substance abuse.
    (e) Alcohol.

b. Cognitive impairment.
  (1) Memory problem.
  (2) Confusion.
  (3) Alzheimer's.
  (4) Parkinson's.
  (5) Multi-infarct dementia.
  (6) Delirium.
  (7) Alcoholic dementia.

c. Balance-gait.
  (1) Rising.
  (2) Transferring.
  (3) Walking.
  (4) Difficulties due to:
    (a) Poor vision.
    (b) Reduced hearing.
    (c) Syncope.
    (d) Dizziness.
    (e) Musculoskeletal disorders.
    (f) Neurological diagnosis.
    (g) Orthopedic diagnosis.
    (h) Vestibular dysfunction.

d. Lower extremity disability (decreased knee or leg strength).
  (1) Metastasis to the bone.
  (2) Debilitation secondary to acute illness such as congestive heart failure, pneumonia, or urinary tract infection.

e. Foot problems.
  (1) Bunions.
  (2) Calluses (severe).
  (3) Grossly long toenails.
  (4) Toe deformities.
  (5) Vascular or pressure ulcers.

3. Inappropriate patterns of care
a. Excessive use of restraints.
b. Prolonged immobilization, leading to muscular weakness, loss of bone mass, and lack of practice of ambulatory skills.

4. Assessment for cause of a fall.
a. A systematic search for the cause of the fall is made after stabilization of injuries.
b. The history is directed toward identifying the circumstances surrounding the fall, such as:
  (1) Sequence of events.
  (2) Symptoms experienced.
  (3) Associated activities and stresses.
  (4) Potential predisposing factors in the environment.
c. Physical examination, assessment of mental status, and neurologic examination are done.
d. Laboratory work includes a complete blood count, chemistries, electrocardiogram, and a thyroid function test.
e. Ambulatory cardiac Holter monitoring is performed. The client must keep a diary of activities and symptoms during Holter monitoring to evaluate for a relationship between syncope and suspected arrhythimas.

5. Patient care management after a fall
a. Treatment is directed toward specific etiologic or predisposing factors believed to be present.
b. Reversible physiologic problems, such as arrhythmias, dehydration, and TIA's are treated.
c. Careful evaluation for other contributing factors, such as visual and hearing problems, is completed.
d. The client's drug regimen is reviewed, and dosages are adjusted to minimize their contribution to falling. Drugs more likely to predispose clients to falls are those that include:
  (1) Somnolence, such as hypnotics.
  (2) Postural hypotension, such as diuretics, nitrates, antihypertensive agents, and tricyclic antidepressants.

(3) Confusion, such as cimetidine and digitalis.

6. Nursing diagnoses/goals/interventions
Risk for injury (*see* risk factors)
Goal: The patient will remain free of injury during hospital stay.
Interventions:

a. Assess previous pattern of falling and establish safety guidelines with patient and family.

b. Orient to environment.
   (1) Free environment from obstacles.
   (2) Demonstrate nurse call system.
   (3) Explain use of bathroom.

c. Mental status assessment.

d. Repeatedly reinforce activity limits and safety needs to patient/family.

e. Involve family as much as possible.

f. Move patient closer to nurses' station.

g. Assess need for sitter supervision.

h. Instruct sitter in individualized patient needs.

i. Assess patient's ambulatory status (have patient walk for you).

j. Provide for safe environment:
   (1) Put bed in low position, brakes locked.
   (2) Have no unnecessary furniture in the room.
   (3) Provide nightlights—at bedside and in bathroom.
   (4) See that patient has nonskid footwear.
   (5) See that call light (communication system) is within easy reach and working.
   (6) See that assistive device is in reach.

k. Communication deficit:
   (1) Assess patient's communication pattern.
   (2) Establish effective communication system with patient. Use visual aids, bells, etc.
   (3) Make frequent patient rounds.
   (4) Provide interpreter for foreign language patients.

l. Vision deficit:
   (1) Assess vision in nonaffected eye.
   (2) Check effectiveness of eyeglasses.
   (3) Put a poster in the room indicating a sensory deficit.

m. Medications monitor:
   (1) Evaluate patient's medications—appropriate dosages.
   (2) Assess risk of side effects, particularly drug-associated hypotensive episodes; alert patients to side effects.
   (3) Check for use of laxatives and diuretics.
   (4) Be particularly aware of drug side effects in elderly or post-op patients.
   (5) Observe mobility patterns post-anesthesia.

n. Urinary patterns:
   (1) Assess usual pattern of urination.
   (2) Plan individualized toileting schedule.
   (3) Assess need for bedside commode, Texas catheter, bedpan.

o. Hearing ability:
   (1) Check effectiveness of hearing aid; batteries available.
   (2) Speak as loudly as necessary to communicate.
   (3) Put a poster in the room indicating a sensory deficit.

p. Check patient's slippers for fit, safety, nonskid.

q. Assess mental status.
   (1) Evaluate patient's ability to interpret information given to him/her.
   (2) Determine the history of the problem.

r. Teach patient to ambulate in stages.

s. Provide elastic stockings.

t. Teach patient to make position changes slowly.

7. Evaluation: Patient does not sustain injury.

8. Home Safety*
Recommend that patient/significant other:

a. Discard small sliding mats and frayed rugs.

b. Eliminate trailing electrical cords.

c. Tack down carpeting on stairs and use nonskid treads.

d. Remove throw rugs that tend to slide.

e. Tack down ends of rugs.

f. Rearrange furniture to provide supports rather than obstacles.

g. Use a raised toilet seat.

h. Have the top and bottom steps of stairways painted a bright color that shows contrast with the other stairs, flooring, and carpet.

i. Be sure both sides of stairways have sturdy handrails.

*From U.S. Consumer Product Safety Commission: *Safety for Older Consumers: Home Safety Checklist.* Washington, D.C. 20207.

j. Check that handrails are sturdy and optimally contoured for a good grasp with the ends shaped so that the patient will know by touch alone when the top and bottom steps have been reached.

k. Keep outdoor steps and walkways in good repair.

l. Use rubber-backed nonskid rugs and nonskid floor waxes.

m. Wear corrugated or rubber soles on slippery surfaces.

n. Use grab bars on bathroom walls and nonskid mats or strips in the bathtub (*see* figure below).

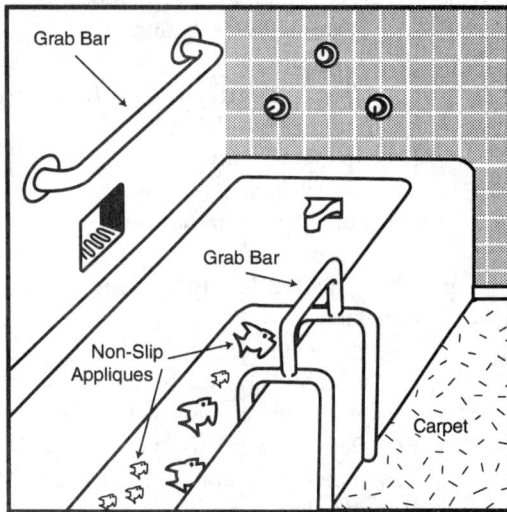

o. Watch out for grandchildren, toys, and pets.

p. Provide adequate illumination by:

(1) Lighting all stairways and landings.

(2) Providing light switches at both the bottom and the top of stairways.

(3) Installing baseboard lights and adequate lighting at the bedside and from bed to bathroom at night.

(4) Making switches easily accessible.

(6) Having flashlights available for emergencies.

H. Management of the Patient Undergoing Hip Surgery

1. Causes

a. Fractures

(1) **Intracapsular** Fracture occurring within the hip joint (neck and head of the femur).

(2) **Extracapsular** Fracture of the trochanteric region of the femur.

b. Other conditions—arthritis and congenital disease.

2. Patient care management

a. Temporary skin traction (Buck's extensions) to reduce muscle spasm, immobilize the extremity, and relieve pain.

b. Surgical procedures

(1) Reduction of fracture and internal fixation with nail plate, screws, and wires.

(2) Replacement of the femoral head with a prosthesis (e.g., Austin-Moore prosthesis).

(3) Total hip replacement, in which the acetabulum and femur are replaced.

3. Nursing diagnoses/goals/interventions

a. Pain related to fracture, soft tissue damage, muscle spasm, and surgery

Goal: Patient will experience relief from pain.

Interventions:

(1) Administer pain medication as ordered.

(2) Handle affected extremity with care.

(3) Maintain traction (Buck's) on affected extremity.

(4) Evaluate and record the patient's response to medication.

(5) Maintain the patient's body in alignment.

b. Risk for altered thought processes related to age, stress of trauma, surgery, drug therapy, and unfamiliar surroundings

Goal: Patient will remain oriented and will participate in care.

Interventions:

(1) Assess the patient's mental status.

(2) Assess the patient for auditory and visual deficits.

(3) Interview the family and/or significant other regarding orientation and cognitive abilities before injury.

(4) Orient the patient to the environment; minimize the number of staff working with the patient.

(5) Explain all procedures and treatments beforehand.

(6) Assess the patient's mental response to medication, especially sedatives and analgesics.

c. Risk for injury related to altered mental status and surgery

Goal: Patient will be free of injury.

Interventions:

(1) Keep side rails up while the patient is in bed.

(2) Use vest restraints (get a physician's order).

(3) Keep light on at night to avoid confusion.

(4) Have call bell available.

(5) For *total hip replacement*, do the following:

    (a) Position the patient flat in bed with the leg held in abduction with a pillow.

    (b) Elevate the bed 45 degrees only during meals.

    (c) Turn the patient on the unoperated side only, with legs kept in abduction with pillows, or *keep flat if ordered*.

    (d) Avoid hip flexion.

    (e) See that there is no weight bearing during ambulation.

(6) Provide patient education.

    (a) Avoid crossing legs.

    (b) Avoid sleeping on the operated side.

    (c) Avoid sitting for more than 30 minutes.

    (d) Avoid sitting on low-back chair or side of bed.

    (e) Keep leg extended when sitting.

d. Altered tissue perfusion: peripheral related to surgical intervention and anesthesia

Goal: Patient's circulation will be maintained to fulfill body requirements.

Interventions:

(1) Monitor vital signs every 2 to 4 hours.

(2) Assess neurovascular status of the affected extremity; every hour observe color, temperature, pulse, sensation, mobility; observe for signs of thrombophlebitis.

(3) Apply antiembolic stocking as ordered.

(4) Monitor CBC, electrolytes, and PT.

(5) Administer parenteral fluids as ordered; monitor intake and output.

(6) Administer anticoagulants as ordered.

(7) Assess lung status; promote coughing and deep breathing; encourage use of incentive spirometer.

(8) Monitor body temperature.

(9) Assess for Homan's sign every shift; supervise ankle exercise.

e. Risk for infection related to surgical intervention and immobility

Goal: Patient will remain afebrile.

Interventions:

(1) Monitor incision and dressing for drainage: monitor hemovac output for color and amount every 4 hours; reinforce dressing as needed.

(2) Assess respiratory status every shift; observe for tachycardia, pain, and dyspnea.

(3) Monitor temperature every 4 to 8 hours, and report any elevation.

(4) Administer antipyretics and/or antibiotics as ordered.

f. Impaired physical mobility related to surgical procedures and pain

Goal: Patient will regain optimal mobility of hip.

Interventions:

(1) Maintain bedrest with the patient's hip in neutral position.

(2) Place a pillow between the leg when turning the patient.

(3) Administer skin care.

(4) Encourage the patient to use trapeze.

(5) Ambulate the patient with assistance.

(6) Observe weight-bearing restrictions.

(7) Monitor for vertigo, weakness, and nausea.

g. Knowledge deficit regarding rehabilitation plan and home-care management

Goal: Patient and significant other will demonstrate understanding of rehabilitation plan, home care, and follow-up.

Interventions:

(1) Discuss the need for a safe environment.

(2) Explain the signs and symptoms of wound infection to report to the physician immediately: fever, pain, inflammation.

(3) Explain the signs and symptoms of thrombophlebitis to report to physician immediately: pain in calf, tenderness, warmth.

(4) Instruct the patient to keep follow-up appointments with the physician.

(5) Provide medication schedule: names, purposes, dosages, and side effects of drugs; if the patient is on anticoagulant, explain the need to have PT checked regularly and to observe urine and feces for bleeding.

(6) Review activity limitations and exercises; provide written instructions.

(7) Teach the care giver the home health-care regimen.

(8) Assess availability of physical assistance for health-care activity.

(9) Provide social service referral.

(10) Reinforce instruction in use of ambulatory aids.

4. Evaluation
   a. There are no complications.
   b. Patient's pain is managed.
   c. The incision is clean, dry, and intact.
   d. Mobility is restored to optimal level.
   e. Rehabilitation program and home-care management are understood.

Alterations in Respiration and Carbon Dioxide Exchange

A. **Chronic Obstructive Pulmonary Disease (COPD)** A functional category for diseases characterized by persistent obstruction of the bronchial air flow.

1. Causes: asthma, bronchiectasis, chronic bronchitis, pulmonary emphysema, cigarette smoking, air pollution, occupational pollutants, the aging process, hereditary factors.

2. Assessment. *See* Unit Eight, Alterations in Respiration and Carbon Dioxide Exchange, Section A: General Assessment, page 290.

3. Patient care management. *See* Unit Eight, Alterations in Respiration and Carbon Dioxide Exchange, Section B: General Patient Care Management, page 292.

4. Nursing diagnoses/goals/interventions. *See* Unit Eight, Alterations in Respiration and Carbon Dioxide Exchange, Nursing diagnoses/goals/interventions, page 297, for goals and interventions for the following nursing diagnoses:
   a. Impaired gas exchange related to ventilation-perfusion inequality

   b. Ineffective airway clearance related to bronchoconstriction, increased mucus production, ineffective cough, and bronchopulmonary infection

   c. Ineffective breathing pattern related to shortness of breath, mucus, bronchoconstriction, and airway irritants.

   d. Activity intolerance related to imbalance between oxygen supply and demand
   Goal: Patient will demonstrate an increased tolerance for activity.
   Interventions:
      (1) Plan care to provide optimum rest.
      (2) Assist and teach the patient to perform active and passive exercises.
      (3) Instruct the patient on methods to conserve energy.
      (4) Instruct the patient in pursed-lip breathing.
      (5) Provide oxygen as prescribed (no more than 1 to 2 liters per minute).
      (6) Observe for signs for chest pain, diaphoresis, or fatigue.

   e. Ineffective individual coping related to chronic illness
   Goal: Patient will attain an optimal level of coping.

   f. Anxiety and/or fear related to change in health status
   Goal: Patient will experience a reduction in anxiety and/or fear.
   Interventions:
      (1) Remain with the patient when he/she is experiencing difficulty in breathing.
      (2) Limit visitors as necessary.
      (3) Provide a nonstressful environment.
      (4) Plan care to provide ample rest periods.
      (5) Explain to the patient that the condition can be stabilized if treatment plan is followed.
      (6) Assess the patient's coping skills.
      (7) Explain all procedures and treatments beforehand.

   g. Altered nutrition: less than body requirements related to decreased oral intake associated with dyspnea, anorexia, and fatigue
   Goal: Patient will maintain adequate nutritional status.
   Interventions:

(1) Administer high-calorie-protein, low-volume supplementary feedings between or with meals.

(2) Maintain liquid to soft high-protein diet.

(3) Provide a dietary consultation.

(4) Monitor the percentage of meal that is eaten.

(5) Implement methods to relieve dyspnea.

(6) Place the patient in high-Fowler's position at meal times to reduce dyspnea.

(7) Schedule rest periods before and after meals.

(8) Provide frequent, small feedings.

(9) Encourage the family and significant other to bring in favorite foods.

(10) Weigh the patient daily with the same clothing at the same time.

(11) Administer stool softeners, laxatives, and enemas as ordered to prevent straining at bowel movements.

h. Knowledge deficit regarding disease process and home management
Goal: Patient, family, and significant other will demonstrate understanding of disease process, home-care management, and follow-up care.
Interventions:

(1) Explain the importance of maintaining respiratory functioning.

(2) Instruct the patient to avoid respiratory irritants such as aerosol sprays, fumes, smoke, dust, perfumes, cold temperatures, lint, talcum.

(3) Explain the importance of not smoking (cigarette smoke depresses the activity of scavenger cells and affects the ciliary cleaning mechanism of the respiratory tract).

(4) Explain the need to avoid contact with persons with infections, especially upper respiratory infections.

(5) Discuss the symptoms to report to the physician immediately: sore throat, elevated temperature, increased sputum production, increased difficulty in breathing, decreased tolerance of activity, upper respiratory infection, decreased appetite, change in color of sputum, increase in use of oxygen, nebulizer, or IPPB.

(6) Explain the need to avoid chilling and to keep warm.

(7) Encourage the patient to get yearly influenza immunization.

(8) Explain the need to avoid emotional stress.

(9) Explain the need for environmental control: use a humidifier but avoid high humidity; maintain home environment between 75 and 80°F.

(10) Instruct the patient to schedule rest periods and to limit activity on high-pollution, cold, and high-humidity days, and to rest before and after meals if shortness of breath increases at mealtimes.

(11) Instruct and review medications: names, dosages, times of administration, purposes, and side effects.

(12) Explain the need to avoid over-the-counter drugs and medications without checking with the physician.

(13) Demonstrate the use of bronchodilator nebulizers: use three or four times daily, take one or two inhalations, watch for side effects such as tachycardia, avoid overuse.

(14) Instruct the patient to drink 2000 to 3000 mL of fluids daily and to eat a high-calorie diet.

(15) Explain the need to avoid constipation and straining.

(16) Have the patient and significant other demonstrate pursed-lip breathing, the position for postural drainage, the use of oxygen equipment, and the cleansing and proper use of the humidifier.

5. Evaluation

a. Patient maintains an adequate nutritional status.

b. Patient demonstrates increased tolerance for activity.

c. Patient experiences decreased anxiety and/or fear.

d. Patient demonstrates an understanding of the disease process, home-care management, and follow-up.

B. **Chronic Bronchitis** A chronic inflammation characterized by hypersecretion of bronchial mucus and accompanied by a chronic or recurrent productive cough for a minimum of 3 months a year for at least 2 consecutive years. There is abundant production of inflammatory exudate that fills and obstructs the bronchioles and is responsible for a persistent, productive cough and shortness of breath. Constant irritation leads to hypertrophy of mucus-secreting glands and increased mucus production, causing bronchial plugging and narrowing. Cilia are destroyed; therefore sputum and bacteria are not removed effectively. Alveoli adjacent to the bronchioles may become damaged and fibrosed, causing further narrowing of bronchi. (Narrowing produces dyspnea, wheezing, and impaired gas exchange.)

1. Assessment
   a. Observe for cough that may be loose, rattling, and constant or paroxysmal (worse in morning).
   b. Inspect sputum (tenacious mucoid, purulent, or blood tinged).
   c. Auscultate for moist rales and wheezing.
   d. Observe for general appearance (overweight and cyanotic).
2. Patient care management
   a. Bronchodilators, to relieve bronchospasm and reduce airway obstruction, thus improving gas distribution and alveolar ventilation.
   b. Postural drainage and chest percussion after treatment.
   c. Water for hydration and as an aid to the patient in coughing up secretions.
   d. Antibiotic therapy after culture and sensitivity.
   e. Steroid therapy if patient does not respond to conservative measures.
3. Nursing diagnoses/goals/interventions.
   See Chronic Obstructive Pulmonary Disease, above, and Unit Eight, Alteration in Respiration and Carbon Dioxide Exchange, Section C, page 298.

C. **Bronchiectasis** Persistent dilation of the bronchi, resulting from a variety of causes (i.e., obstruction of the bronchi, pulmonary infection, atelectasis).
Infection damages the bronchial wall, causing loss of its supporting structure and producing thick sputum. The walls become permanently distended by severe coughing. Inflammatory scarring or fibrosis replaces functioning lung tissues, resulting in respiratory insufficiency. The retention of secretion and the obstruction ultimately lead to atelectasis.

1. Assessment
   a. Observe for persistent cough and the production of copious amounts of purulent sputum.
   b. Inspect fingers for clubbing.
   c. Inspect sputum for hemoptysis.
   d. Auscultate for moist rales and rhonchi over the lower lobes.
2. Patient care management. *See also* Unit Eight, Alterations in Respiration and Carbon Dioxide Exchange, Section B: General Patient Care Management, page 292.
   a. Postural drainage (e.g., the first drainage upon awakening, and the last at bedtime).
   b. Chemotherapy: bronchodilators, mucolytic agents, and antimicrobials to suppress bacteria in the pockets of infection and reduce cough sputum and other symptoms.
   c. Bronchoscopic removal of bronchial obstruction and/or dilation of a stenosed bronchus.
   d. Bedrest.
3. *See* Unit Eight, Alterations in Respiration and Carbon Dioxide Exchange, Nursing diagnoses/goals/interventions, page 297.

D. **Bronchial Asthma** An intermittent or reversible type of obstructive lung disease in which narrowing of the bronchial lumina changes in severity either spontaneously or as a result of treatment.
The mucosal lining swells and secretes thick, tenacious mucus. The smooth muscles of the bronchi and larger bronchioles constrict (bronchospasm). Air movement is impaired during expiration, causing wheezing and prolongation of this phase of respiration. The alveoli become greatly distended, trapping air and weakening the alveoli walls.

1. Precipitating factors: emotional stress, exercise; endocrine changes (menopause, pregnancy, puberty, menstruation); atmospheric changes (humidity and temperature); inhalation of irritant; family history of hypersensitivity.
2. Types

a. Extrinsic asthma
(1) This is caused by dust, lint, insecticides, mold spores, pollens, food items, synthetic drugs (e.g., aspirin), animal dander, and feathers.
(2) It develops before age 40; attacks increase in frequency and duration.
(3) Adolescents may recover completely, whereas adults often do not.
b. Intrinsic asthma
(1) The specific cause frequently cannot be identified.
(2) The precipitating cause is infection in the upper and lower respiratory tracts.
(3) This type develops most commonly after age 40 and often merges into asthmatic bronchitis.

3. Assessment
a. Observe for severe dyspnea, prolonged expiration, pallor or cyanosis, apprehension, tightness or pain in the chest, and profuse sweating.
b. Measure temperature and vital signs for a drop in blood pressure and pulse, and for elevated temperature.
c. Auscultate lungs for rales, rhonchi, wheezing, and the presence of breath sounds.
d. Observe cough and sputum production. (Initially, there is cough with a minimal amount of sputum; as the attack increases, the cough becomes more pronounced with a large amount of sputum produced.)
e. Inspect skin turgor and mucous membrane hydration status.
f. Observe chest. (The chest appears fixed in the inspiratory position, and accessory muscles are used.)
g. DIAGNOSTIC MEASURES. *See also* Unit Eight, Alterations in Respiration and Carbon Dioxide Exchange, Section A: General Assessment, page 290.
(1) Health history.
(2) Skin test to identify specific allergens.

4. Patient care management. *See also* Unit Eight, Alterations in Respiration and Carbon Dioxide Exchange, Section B: General Patient Care Management, page 292.
a. Drug therapy: epinephrine; theophylline preparations; Brethine, corticosteroids; antibiotics; mild sedatives and tranquilizer, administered with caution; Mucomyst and expectorant.
b. Respiratory therapy.

5. Nursing diagnoses/goals/interventions
a. Anxiety related to difficulty in breathing, fear of suffocation, and/or fear of recurrent attacks
Goal: Patient will exhibit reduced anxiety and/or fear.
Interventions:
(1) Provide emotional support.
(a) Remain with the patient when he/she is anxious.
(b) Anticipate the patient's needs.
(c) Maintain bedrest in a quiet environment.
(2) Remain with the patient during coughing episodes; encourage sips of water.
(3) Explain all procedures to the patient before attempting to initiate them.
(4) Orient the patient to the hospital environment, equipment, and routine.
(5) Encourage verbalization of fear and anxiety.
(6) Reinforce the physician's explanations, and clarify misconceptions about the disease, treatment plan, and prognosis.
b. Ineffective airway clearance related to excessive mucous production and broncho-spasm
Goal: Patient will maintain a patent airway.
Interventions:
(1) Take the patient's temperature every 4 hours or as ordered.
(2) Take the patient's blood pressure, respiration, and pulse as ordered.
(3) Assess the level of consciousness, and report any decrease in level to the physician.
(4) Elevate the head of bed to semi-Fowler's position.
(5) Place side rails up for safety and support.
(6) Administer humidified oxygen by the method and at the rate ordered.
(7) Order IPPB from Respiratory Therapy.
(8) Administer medication as ordered (bronchodilators, expec-

torant, steroid, antibiotics, Ispurel nebulization).

   (9) Encourage fluids. (Instruct the patient to *avoid cold fluids*.)

  (10) Assess sputum for color, tenacity, and amount.

  (11) Collect sputum for culture and sensitivity.

  (12) Suction PRN.

c. Ineffective breathing pattern related to decreased lung expansion during acute attack

  Goal: Patient will resume an effective breathing pattern.

  Interventions:

   (1) Monitor arterial blood gases.

   (2) Monitor for signs and symptoms of ineffective breathing (shallow respiration, diaphoresis, dyspnea, use of accessory muscle).

   (3) Place the patient in high Fowler's position.

   (4) Administer humidified oxygen as ordered.

   (5) Maintain a patent airway.

   (6) Administer medications as ordered.

   (7) Remain with the patient during an acute attack.

   (8) Instruct in, and assist with, diaphragmatic and pursed-lip breathing.

   (9) Increase activity as tolerated.

  (10) Assess the patient after bronchodilator treatment.

d. Fluid volume deficit related to increased respiratory distress and diaphoresis

  Goal: Patient will maintain adequate hydration status.

  Interventions:

   (1) Encourage fluid intake to at least 2500 cc per day unless contraindicated.

   (2) Provide liquid-to-soft diet.

   (3) Encourage the patient to eat the prescribed diet.

   (4) Administer parenteral fluids as ordered.

   (5) Record intake and output.

   (6) Weigh the patient daily or as ordered.

e. Knowledge deficit regarding self-care management

  Goal: Patient, family, and significant other will demonstrate and verbalize understanding of home-care and follow-up instructions.

  Interventions:

   (1) Explain the importance of preventing future attacks.

    (a) Avoid known irritants.

    (b) Avoid stressful situations.

    (c) Express anxieties and fears.

    (d) Encourage communication with significant other and/or family.

   (2) Provide adequate humidity.

    (a) Use humidifier (provide information on humidifiers and the need to clean them).

    (b) Inform the patient that nonflowering plants can increase humidity by 5% to 10%.

   (3) Instruct the patient to avoid persons with infections, especially upper respiratory infections.

   (4) Instruct the patient not to smoke, and to avoid persons who smoke.

   (5) Explain the importance of breathing exercises.

   (6) Explain the importance of diet and fluids.

    (a) Force 2000 to 3000 ml of fluid daily unless contraindicated.

    (b) Avoid weight gain.

    (c) Eat balanced, nutritious meals.

   (7) Reinforce the importance of keeping outpatient appointments.

   (8) Discuss symptoms to report to the physician: upper respiratory infection, flu, elevated temperature.

   (9) Discuss medications: names, dosages, times of administration, purposes, and side effects.

  (10) Demonstrate proper use of inhalers and maintenance of the container.

  (11) Explain the importance of taking medications as ordered.

6. Evaluation

  a. Patient is free from anxiety and/or fear.

  b. Patient's airway is patent.

  c. Patient breathes normally.

  d. Patient's hydration status is adequate.

  e. Patient and family demonstrate an

understanding of home-care and follow-up instructions.

E. **Pulmonary Emphysema** Destruction of lung tissue with permanent overinflation of the alveoli.
1. Causes
   a. Exact cause unknown.
   b. Familial predisposition.
   c. Environmental pollution (smoking, air pollution, allergens, infectious agents).
2. Assessment
   a. Observe general appearance for thinness, face color (face may be pale or ruddy to ruddy-cyanotic, caused by hypoxia and hypercapnia); exertional dyspnea (present earlier in the disease but eventually occurring at rest); and prolonged expiration phase of respiration.
   b. Inspect chest for barrel shape, a reduction in the normal use and rise and fall of the chest during ventilation, or reduction in diaphragmatic movement, and use of accessory muscles for breathing.
   c. Observe cough and sputum (morning cough that produces thick, viscous sputum; cough is spasmodic and is initiated by minimal exertion, such as talking).
   d. Auscultate lungs for wheezing, rales, and faint breath sounds.
   e. Measure temperature and vital signs; respirations tend to be shallow and rapid.
   f. Percuss lungs for hyperresonance.
3. Patient care management. *See* Unit Eight, Alterations in Respiration and Carbon Dioxide Exchange, Section B: Patient Care Management, page 292.
4. Nursing diagnoses/goals/interventions. *See* Chronic Obstructive Pulmonary Disease, page 378.

F. **Pulmonary Heart Disease (cor pulmonale)** A condition in which the right ventricle enlarges (with or without failure) as a result of diseases that affect the structure or function of the lung.
1. Causes: chronic obstructive pulmonary disease, deformities of the thoracic cage, pulmonary embolus.
2. Assessment
   a. Inspect feet and legs for edema, and neck veins for engorgement.
   b. Palpate abdomen for liver enlargement and ascites.
   c. Auscultate heart for a loud pulmonic second sound and heart murmur.
   d. Observe the patient for confusion and drowsiness.
3. Patient care management: oxygen therapy, digitalization, sodium restriction, diuretic therapy, rest.
4. Nursing diagnoses/goals/interventions. *See* Chronic Obstructive Pulmonary Disease, page 378.

Alterations in Behavior

A. Dementia
   Dementia A permanent, progressive deterioration of mental function characterized by confusion, impaired judgment, forgetfulness, and personality changes. Five percent of 65 and older suffer cognitive impairment; 15% experience mild to moderate impairment; 66% of nursing home residents have significant impairment. Psychiatric disabilities in dementia are depression, agitation, wandering, combativeness, anxiety, hallucinations, delusional ideation.
   The two most common types of *dementia* are multi-infarct dementia and Alzheimer's disease.
   1. Multi-infarct dementia
      This condition results from repeated strokes that cause complete deterioration of cerebral tissue within a circumscribed area. Onset is gradual or sudden, and the course is marked by a cyclical worsening and lessening of signs and symptoms.
      The early phase of multi-infarct dementia shows a gradual progression of impaired intellectual functioning and partial memory lapses; symptoms include dizziness, headache, decreased physical and mental vigor, and vague physical complaints. Delirium may result from insufficient cerebral circulation.
   2. Alzheimer's disease
      The disease is characterized by brain atrophy and the presence of neurofibrillary tangles, granulovascular changes, neuritic (senile) plaques, and reduced cholinergic enervation. Symptoms appear gradually, beginning with impaired memory and progressing to language and motor difficulties. The cause is unknown.
      The first stage lasts from 2 to 4 years and is marked by spatial and time disorientation, inappropriate affect, decreased concentration, transient paranoia, careless dressing

or grooming, impaired judgment, forgetfulness, perceptual disturbances, and memory loss.

The second stage, lasting up to 7 years, is marked by more profound changes and loss of independence; symptoms include inability to recognize familiar persons or to interpret the environment, poor comprehension, nocturnal restlessness, apraxia, ravenous appetite without weight gain, complete disorientation, wandering, hoarding, inability to read or write, communication difficulties, hypertonia, and both short- and long-term memory loss.

The last stage occurs during the final year and is marked by a blank facial expression, paraphasia, irritability, hyperorality, seizures, inability to recognize family members, loss of appetite, emaciation, and total dependence.

Duration of the illness varies from 5 to 14 years before death occurs. Factors that contribute to death include pneumonia or other infections, malnutrition, and dehydration.

3. Assessment for dementia
   a. Assess personality changes in the patient.
   b. Assess the patient's orientation to time, place, and person.
   c. Assess the patient for memory gaps.
   d. Assess the patient's physical status.
   e. Assess the patient's coping patterns of behavior in dealing with the neurological deficit.
   f. Assess the patient's communication pattern.
   g. Assess the attitude of the family and significant others toward the patient's condition.
   h. Assess the patient's decision-making ability.
   i. Assess interpersonal dynamics between the patient, his/her family, and significant others.
   j. Assess the patient's environmental support system and its potential for assisting the patient to deal with his/her condition.

4. Patient Care Management for dementia
   a. Medical management of the specific cause.
   b. Rehabilitation and retraining programs.
   c. Family counseling.

d. Crisis intervention.
e. Supportive psychotherapy.
f. Psychotropic drugs, antidepressants. (Observe caution in the use of drugs with anticholinergic properties.)

5. Nursing diagnoses/goals/interventions for Alzheimer's disease
   a. Self-care deficit: hygiene, nutrition, and toileting related to forgetfulness, confusion, regressed behaviors
      Goal: The patient will receive help to maintain hygiene status, drink a minimum of 1500 cc daily, maintain mobility as much as possible, and take prescribed medications.
      Interventions:
      (1) Assess the patient's ability to care for self; provide assistance as required.
      (2) Keep self-care and personal items within reach.
      (3) Provide adequate food and fluid intake.
      (4) If the patient is bedridden, have him/her perform range-of-motion exercises.
      (5) Assess medication ordered for drugs known to lower serum folate levels (e.g., barbiturates, Dilantin, primidone, nitrofurantion, some analgesics, and possible phenothiazines—Mellaril, Thorazine, Compazine, Phenegran), also alcohol.
      (6) Assist the family in setting realistic goals for the patient at home.
   b. Altered thought process related to forgetfulness, confusion, and inability to perceive realistically or interact appropriately with others
      (1) Reorient the patient to surroundings, routines, and so on.
      (2) Provide safety (windows safe and secure, side rails up, call bell within patient's reach, night light near bed).
      (3) Keep surroundings as quiet as possible.
      (4) Provide active listening.
      (5) Do not confront the patient about confabulation of facts. (This serves the purpose of maintaining ego integrity.)
      (6) Do not confront the patient about inappropriate behavior.

(7) Avoid unnecessary use of restraints.

(8) Assist the patient in maintaining communication with his/her family and/or significant others.

(9) Give simple, clear, short explanations of procedures and routines.

(10) Document changes in the patient's responses.

(11) Teach the family to assess the patient's response to therapy.

(12) If possible, assign the same nurses for each shift.

(13) Introduce yourself before taking care of the patient.

c. Grieving related to loss of functioning and role

d. Knowledge deficit regarding prognosis, grief and mourning process, treatment, medications, and community resources
Goal: Family will receive emotional support and information about disease process and prognosis.
Interventions:

(1) Assess the family members' stage of loss; offer to spend time with them for the purpose of ventilation of feelings and concerns.

(2) Accept the family members' feelings in the time of actual loss, when the patient is diagnosed, when plans are being made for long-term care, and as they anticipate the gradual deterioration in intellectual functioning and finally death.

(3) Assess the family members' knowledge of the disease process and prognosis; clarify information and teach as needed; help them understand, accept, and cope with the patient's behavior.

6. Evaluation for Alzheimer's disease

a. The patient maintains hygiene with assistance.

b. The patient ingests an adequate number of calories to maintain weight.

c. The patient takes medication daily as ordered.

d. The patient is oriented to time, place, and person.

e. The patient interacts with others in socially appropriate ways.

f. The family understands the disease proc-

ess, the prognosis, and the prescribed medical regimen.

g. The family has the names of available community resource groups, a social worker, and a mental health counselor for crises and for coping with chronic illness.

7. Nursing diagnoses/goals/interventions for Multi-infarct dementia

a. Self-care deficit: total, related to confusion, forgetfulness, and regressed behaviors
Goal: Patient will perform some activities of daily living with minimal necessary assistance, drink a minimum of 1500 cc daily, maintain or attain the desired weight, participate in exercise and rest periods daily, and ambulate with assistance.
Interventions:

(1) Assist with self-care; allow the patient to do as much as possible.

(2) Keep expectations realistic.

(3) Record vital signs and intake and output at least once daily, and weight, twice a week.

(4) Offer frequent feedings of high-calorie, low-volume protein between meals; assist with meals.

(5) Assist with choice of clean apparel appropriate to the climate.

(6) Supervise medication consumption; observe for side effects.

b. Altered thought processes (disorientation, forgetfulness, confusion) related to cerebral pathology
Goal: Patient will be oriented to time, place, and person; interact voluntarily with others, make some decisions and choices related to care and activities, and reminisce to integrate life experiences.
Interventions:

(1) Get the patient's attention before speaking; say his/her name; wait for eye contact; speak slowly, distinctly, and loud enough to be heard; turn off radio and television; and shut out other distractions.

(2) Give the patient choices when possible, but avoid meaningless, unnecessary changes (e.g., in room decor, roommate, routines).

(3) Answer questions repeatedly as

necessary; use short, simple sentences; reinforce verbal communication with gestures; build on sensible statements of the patient to strengthen reality-based conversation.

(4) Provide orientation to time, place, and person every hour; use clock, calendars, signs, pictures, and written reminders; put patient's picture and name (in big letters) on the door to the room and on the bed.

(5) Use concrete symbols (photographs, tangible creations, and products) of the patient's past.

(6) Encourage the patient to review the past in order to remember and savor happy events, friendships, trips, achievements.

(7) Celebrate special events in the patient's life (e.g., birthdays, anniversaries, religious days); observe customary national holidays with parties, special refreshments, and entertainment.

(8) Utilize volunteers to visit or write letters for the patient.

(9) Arrange for meaningful occupational therapy.

c. Ineffective individual coping related to confused state and uncontrolled, intense feelings (e.g., fear, anxiety, anger, sadness, depression)

Goal: Patient will communicate feelings and concerns and will utilize previous and new coping methods and measures.

Interventions:

(1) Observe, describe, and record the patient's common behavior patterns; identify cues that trigger adverse reactions and plan to avoid or control these; note whether the patient is agitated by certain topics of conversation or situations.

(2) Recognize that episodes of paranoia, aggression, temper tantrums, delusion, anxiety, despondency, rigid orderliness, fear, fantasy, apathy, and/or stubbornness may occur from time to time.

(3) Administer medication as ordered to control antisocial behavior.

(4) Ask family and friends to identify successful coping mechanisms used by the patient.

(5) Use therapeutic touch to show concern; also give small gifts.

(6) Respect the patient's need for privacy (space, time, possessions).

d. Knowledge deficit regarding prognosis, treatment, medications, community resources

Goal: Patient and family will discuss the treatment plan and follow-up care, including the medication schedule and side effects to watch for, and will use appropriate community resources.

Interventions:

(1) Assist the family to understand the disease process, to accept the patient's behavior, and to work through their feelings of guilt, helplessness, depression, and love.

(2) Explain the medication schedule, possible side effects, and treatment plan.

(3) Consult with the occupational therapist.

(4) Discuss the community resources (day-care or respite facility, residential facility, support groups).

(5) Discuss the follow-up care and the symptoms to report to the physician.

(6) Instruct the family in techniques to reorient the patient to time, place, and persons.

8. Evaluation for Multi-infarct dementia

a. Patient performs the activities of daily living with assistance.

b. Patient maintains desired weight and ingests sufficient fluids and electrolytes.

c. Patient exhibits normal bowel elimination.

d. Patient is oriented to time, place, and person.

e. Patient reminisces about life experiences.

f. Patient interacts appropriately with others.

g. Patient participates in some decisions about the activities of daily living.

h. Patient has fewer episodes of uncontrolled mood swings.

i. Patient demonstrates increased ability to communicate feelings.

j. Patient and family understand the chronic disability and the prescribed medical regimen; family indicates willingness to keep the patient oriented to reality and interacting with others.

   k. Patient and family understand the need for continuing medical and nursing supervision and for consultation.

   l. Family has information about community resource groups.

B. Delirium

Delirium   DSM IV defined as an organic brain syndrome that has as an essential feature a clouded state of consciousness manifested by:

1. Decreased ability to maintain attention to external stimuli.
2. Decreased ability to shift attention to new stimuli.
3. Presence of rambling, irrelevant, or incoherent speech.

At least two of the following are present:

1. Reduced consciousness.
2. Hallucinations, illusions, misinterpretations.
3. Disturbances of sleep/wake cycle.
4. Increased or decreased psychomotor activity, memory impairment.

There is an acute onset consisting of hours or a few days.

1. Characteristics of delirium in persons 65 and over
   a. Stress of physical illness, environmental change, and trauma frequently give rise to delirium.
   b. It occurs in 10% of psychiatric admissions.
   c. It occurs in 15–40% of medical/surgical hospital admissions.
   d. There is a higher prevalence in hip fracture and open heart surgery.
   e. It is generally reversible.
   f. It often goes unrecognized.
   g. There are high morbidity and mortality rates.

2. Causes of delirium

   Delirium is to the elderly what fever is to the young. The majority of individuals presenting with delirium suffer from specific physical illness.
   a. Medication and/or alcohol intoxication.
   b. Medication withdrawal—sedatives, hypnotics.
   c. Metabolic imbalances—vitamin deficiencies, organ failure.
   d. Environmental change, severe psychological stress.
   e. Endocrine disorders.

   f. Cardiovascular disorders.
   g. Neurological disorders and trauma.
   h. Blood dyscrasias.

3. Patient care management
   a. Determining and treating underlying cause(s).
   b. Maintaining physiologic balance with hydration, nutrition, oxygen supply, and electrolyte balance.
   c. Haloperidol 0.5–2.0 mg b.i.d. for agitation.

DELIRIUM VS. DEMENTIA

	Delirium	Dementia
Onset	acute	usually insidious, chronic, unless reversible
Consciousness	brief	static
Orientation	abnormal	some defects
Memory	recent defective	recent and later remote defective
Attention	always impaired	may be intact
Perception	frequently disturbed; contents vivid	misperceptions may be absent
Thinking	disorganized; contents rich	impaired; contents empty, stereotyped
Judgment	poor	poor
insight	may be present in lucid intervals	may be absent, variable

4. Nursing diagnoses/goals/interventions
   a. Altered thought processes related to physiological or psychological stressors; sensory-perceptual limitations
   Goals
   (1) The patient will experience appropriate and adequate sensory and motor stimuli.
   (2) The patient will differentiate reality from nonreality.
   (3) The patient will maintain usual level of orientation.
   (4) The patient will experience optimal contact with reality relative to condition.
   (5) The patient will not experience injuries.
   (6) The patient will demonstrate ability to perform activities of daily living, with assistance, if necessary.
   (7) The patient and/or significant other will participate in treatment/discharge plan.
   (8) The patient and/or significant other

will demonstrate appropriate coping strategies.

Interventions

(a) Provide patient with consistent, nurturing caregivers and a consistent routine.

(b) Maintain a respectful attitude and discuss appropriate subjects with the patient.

(c) Explain all procedures in a simple manner and introduce unfamiliar persons who interact with the patient.

(d) Provide opportunities for the patient to interact with others, as appropriate.

(e) Discuss current and past events with the patient.

(f) Use the patient's name when speaking to him/her.

(g) Maintain good room lighting (i.e., curtains open to denote day or night; prevention of shadows).

(h) Place familiar objects and personal possessions in the patient's room.

(i) Monitor sleep/wake patterns (see also care plan for sleep pattern disturbance).

(j) Monitor noise and activity levels in the patient's environment.

(k) Assist or encourage the patient to move about in bed at least every 2 hours and/or to be up in a chair or ambulate twice a day, as appropriate.

(l) Ensure that hearing aids, glasses, prosthetic devices are worn.

(m) Utilize meaningful touch while providing nursing care, and evaluate response to touch.

(n) Observe for distorted interpretations of internal or external stimuli.

(o) Assist with problem solving and differentiation between internal and external stimuli.

(p) Evaluate verbal and nonverbal behavior in response to internal or external stimuli.

(q) Avoid belittling the patient when he/she misinterprets stimuli.

(r) Validate interpretation of internal or external stimuli.

(s) Use a calm, slow approach during interacting.

(t) Establish communication patterns that neither support nor challenge non-reality based thinking and that divert non-reality-based thinking into reality.

(u) Reorient the patient to reality concisely and simply; when the patient has poor short-term memory, focus on feelings, not facts.

(v) Set limits on inappropriate behavior.

(w) Implement measures to divert the patient from inappropriate behaviors, such as distraction or removing the patient from the situation.

(x) Positively reinforce reality-based thinking and behaviors.

(y) Observe for indications of hallucinations, suicidal behavior, and/or delusions.

(z) Review medication history for potential drug-drug or drug-food interactions, side effects, underdosage or overdosage, and toxicity, and consult with physician and/or pharmacist, as appropriate.

(aa) Place clock and calendar within line of vision, and call attention to these items often.

(bb) Assess neurological/mental status on admission and on an ongoing basis; report changes immediately.

(cc) Encourage the patient to validate his/her thoughts and decisions.

(dd) Institute safety measures, such as bed in low position, side rails up, no smoking while alone, call light within reach.

(ee) Judiciously evaluate the use of arm, leg, hand, and/or chest restraints.

(ff) Structure the environment to remove potential hazards and to demarcate areas in which the patient may move around.

(gg) Stay with the patient when he/she is frightened, anxious, agitated, restless, etc.

(hh) Perform ongoing assessments according to appropriate assessment criteria, and intervene promptly when indicated.

(ii) Identify events that increase the patient's anxiety, fear, confusion, and altered thought processes.

(jj) Monitor laboratory work with diagnostic studies to detect abnormalities.

(kk) Document therapeutic interventions and the patient's response.

(ll) Help the patient to identify self-care deficits.

(mm) Assist the patient in ADL routine to maximize functioning.

(nn) Encourage/monitor the patient's daily nutrition and fluid intake.

(oo) Break activities into small, clear, simple, one-command steps, and allow the patient adequate time to complete activity.

(pp) Do not force the patient's participation in care.

(qq) Involve significant others in the treatment/discharge plan, particularly if the patient's thought processes remain altered.

(rr) Help patient/significant other to identify community support programs, such as support groups, home health agencies, church-based programs.

(ss) Provide educational opportunities for the patients/significant others to learn to deal effectively with altered thought processes and/or disease processes.

(tt) Encourage patient and/or significant other to express feelings.

5. Evaluation

a. The patient demonstrates optimal contact with reality, relative to his/her condition, as evidenced by appropriate verbal and nonverbal behaviors.

b. The patient experiences no sensory overload or deprivation, as evidenced by verbal and nonverbal indicators.

c. The patient verbalizes accurate interpretation of internal and external stimuli.

d. The patient demonstrates an absence of or a decrease in non-reality-based thinking, relative to his/her condition.

e. The patient remains oriented to time, place, person, and self, relative to his/her condition.

f. The patient utilizes visual and verbal clues to maintain orientation.

g. The patient validates thoughts and decisions with the nurse and/or significant other.

h. The patient experiences no injury to self or others as a result of altered thought processes.

i. The patient assists with activities of daily living, as far as he/she is able.

j. The patient or significant other actively participates in the treatment/discharge planning.

k. The patient or significant other verbally identifies the community support systems available.

C. Depression in the elderly (*see* Unit Eight)

1. Risk factors for the 65 and over

a. Changes in physical function

(1) Functional limitations in strength/ambulation.

(2) Sensory losses.

(3) Medically imposed limitations.

b. Changes in support network

(1) Geographic dislocation.

(2) Loss of caregivers due to death/illness.

(3) Unplanned retirement.

(4) Lack of confiding relationships.

2. Somatic disorders associated with depression

a. Neurological disorders

(1) Parkinson's disease.

(2) Dementing illness.

(3) Cerebrovascular disease.

(4) Myasthenia.

(5) CNS neoplasms.

(6) Multiple Sclerosis.

b. Endocrine disorders

(1) Hypothyroidism.

(2) Apathetic hypothroidism.

(3) Cushing's disease/syndrome.

(4) Addison's disease.

(5) Panhypopituitarism.

(6) Parathyroid disease.

c. Systemic disorders

(1) Occult malignancy.

(2) Infectious processes.

(3) Congestive heart failure.

(4) Renal failure/dehydration.

(5) Obstructive pulmonary disease.

(6) Anemia.

DEMENTIA OF DEPRESSION AND ORGANIC DEMENTIA

Similarities:

- Lack of self care
- Restlessness
- Irritability
- Loss of creativity
- Somatic complaints
- Disorientation
- Memory and concentration problems

Differences:

	Organic Dementia	Dementia of Depression
• Onset	Slow, insidious onset	Rapid onset
• Course	Progressive, cumulative	Rapid, uneven
• Diurinal	Symptoms worse at night	Little variation throughout the day
• Insight	Often unaware of cognitive deficit, usually denies problem	Complains of memory loss, emphasizes problem
• Response	Approximate	Apathetic—"I don't know"
• Self-Worth	Emphasizes trivial accomplishments	Emphasizes failures
• Impairment	Greater impairment of recent memory and orientation	Greater impairment of attention and concentration
• Affect	Inappropriate, shallow, or labile	Constricted
• Physical	No neurovegetive signs	Possible dysfunctions in sleep, appetite, bowel, sexual habits

---

D. **Suicide** A harmful act directed toward oneself and aimed at terminating a life situation perceived as intolerable.

1. Dynamics/characteristics
   a. Incidence
      (1) Three times as many men as women commit suicide.
      (2) The rate is high for black youths, alcoholics, and American Indians.
      (3) Among professionals, physicians, police officers, and dentists are at a higher risk.
   b. The rates for adolescents and people over 50 years of age have been increasing.
   c. Precipitating factors: Recent withdrawal from alcohol or substance abuse; recent changes in behavior or activities of daily living (e.g., retirement); loss of job, home or capabilities; changes in location or environment; changes in financial situation; cultural isolation.
   d. Methods used: The most widely used modes to actualize the suicidal act are drugs, including alcohol, and narcotics. Jumping or hanging are the most frequently used method in hospitals. Suicides occur at hospitals at a much greater rate than elsewhere. It is most often the medical and surgical patients who attempt suicide, more so than the neuro-psychiatric patients. Suicide attempts occur most often in hospital settings during a change of shift, at mealtime, or on weekends.
   e. Related emotions: hostility, aggression, guilt, ambivalence, hopelessness, helplessness, despair.
   f. Important assumptions about suicide.
      (1) A suicidal person gives many direct and indirect clues about his/her self-destructive intentions.
      (2) An attempt to commit suicide is often considered to be a desperate cry for help from a person in a state of intolerable stress.
      (3) Most suicides occur 3 months after the beginning of improvement in the patient's condition, when his/her drive and energy levels have increased sufficiently for the person to act on his/her feelings and thoughts.

2. Assessment
   a. Assess prodromal clues to suicide: verbal clues, behavioral clues (direct or indirect), presence of a complex life situation.
   b. Assess the patient's ability to communicate his/her feelings to others.
   c. Assess the lethality of the object/substance/act used in the suicide attempt.

d. Assess the patient's mood. Depressed? Angry? Hostile?

e. Assess the patient for possible drug or alcohol use as a means of coping.

f. Evaluate the patient's environmental support system and its potential in helping him/her to cope with the situation.

g. Assess the events or circumstances that may have precipitated the suicide attempt.

h. Assess the patient's perception of his/her situation (feeling of hopelessness).

i. Assess the patient's coping patterns of behavior in the face of stress. Is the patient impulsive?

j. Assess the risk factors (poverty, family history of suicide, acute or chronic physical or mental illness, loss of loved one(s), social isolation, loneliness, retirement).

3. Patient care management

a. Treatment: immediate hospitalization and continuous surveillance, supportive counseling for patient and family, psychotherapy.

b. Health promotion
   (1) Crisis intervention.
   (2) Anticipatory guidance and counseling.
   (3) Identification of risk factors related to health and adjustment problems.
   (4) Health education—use of community resources (where to obtain help).
   (5) Working with survivors of suicide attempts because they are considered at risk.

4. Nursing diagnoses/goals/interventions

a. Risk for violence: self-directed, related to suicide ideation
   Goal: Patient will not harm self.
   Intervention:
   (1) Provide a safe environment. Take away sharp objects (scissors, nail files, razor blades), toxic substances, straps, and other potentially dangerous objects (e.g., medications).
   (2) Follow hospital procedure for suicide prevention.
   (3) Tell patient, talking on a one-to-one basis, what you are doing; observe sleeping and eating habits; observe attitude; accompany at all times, even to bathroom; allow only permissible family and friends to be in attendance.
   (4) Be alert for both verbal and nonverbal cues ("good-bye," giving away prized possessions).
   (5) Convey genuine interest in the patient's welfare by making it known to him/her that you will do everything possible to prevent the person from taking any self-destructive actions.
   (6) Take all suicide threats seriously. Note that plans are more lethal when they are specific.
   (7) Monitor changes in affect. Calmness or cheerfulness that is new to patient's affect may signal that the patient's mind is made up to attempt to commit suicide, and that the patient has formulated an effective plan to do so.
   (8) Let the patient know that you understand something of what he/she is experiencing.
   (9) Evaluate behavior before discontinuing suicide prevention and before discharge.

b. Ineffective individual coping related to feeling of hopelessness, powerlessness
   Goal: Patient will identify causes of feelings.
   Interventions:
   (1) Encourage patient to discuss the painful feelings that preceded suicidal thoughts.
   (2) Urge regular attendance of group therapy.
   (3) Correct distorted perceptions.
   (4) Teach art of requesting and accepting assistance when it is needed.

c. Self-esteem disturbance related to maturational or physiological factors
   Goal: Patient will develop a feeling of increased self-worth and an ability to initiate and maintain social relationships.
   Interventions:
   (1) Encourage the patient to do as much self-care as possible.
   (2) Help the patient to express his/her feelings.
   (3) Reassure the patient, but do not give false reassurances and promises.

(4) Structure time so the patient is kept distracted and busy. Encourage peer group activities.

(5) Do not allow the patient to reinforce negative ideas about himself/herself. Respond to self-deprecatory remarks in a positive way.

d. Knowledge deficit regarding support services and constructive methods of life management
Goal: Patient will recognize and utilize individual or community assistance as needed. Family will recognize signs of impending suicide attempts and will identify resources available.
Interventions:

(1) Discuss discharge plan and evaluate patient's acceptance of the need for mental health counseling.

(2) Determine what resources are most compatible and appropriate for patient follow-up.

(3) Teach family and peers the warning signs of suicide.

(4) Involve family as much as possible.

(5) Provide information regarding available community support groups, hotlines, suicide prevention and crisis intervention centers, and local mental health facilities.

(6) Initiate appropriate referrals after consultation with physicians/family/friends. Arrange first contact prior to discharge from hospital.

5. Evaluation
Patient:
a. Does not attempt suicide.
b. States fewer occurrences of suicidal ideation.
c. Participates in planning for care.
d. Expresses hopeful feelings in at least one area.
e. Expresses positive feeling about himself/herself.
f. Attends group therapy regularly and participates occasionally.
g. States no presence of suicide ideation.
h. Identifies and has telephone numbers of private and community support groups and health centers providing assistance for suicidal individuals.
i. Agrees to call a designated person before attempting suicide.

Alterations That Interfere with the Meeting of Sexual Needs

A. Urinary Incontinence
1. Definition—an involuntary loss of urine.
2. Causes
a. Urinary tract infection.
b. Vaginal infection or irritation.
c. Constipation.
d. Effects of medicine.
e. Weakness of muscles that hold the bladder in place.
f. Weakness of the bladder itself.
g. Weakness of the urethral sphincter muscles.
h. Overactive bladder muscles.
i. Blocked urethra (possibly from prostate enlargement).
j. Hormone imbalance in women.
k. Neurologic disorders.
l. Immobility (not being able to move around).
3. Types
a. **Urge incontinence** Involuntary loss of urine associated with an abrupt and strong urge to void.
b. **Stress incontinence** The involuntary loss of urine during coughing, sneezing, laughing, or other physical activities that increase abdominal pressure.
c. **Overflow incontinence** Involuntary loss of urine associated with over-distension of the bladder. This type of incontinence may have a variety of presentations, including frequent or constant drinking, or there may be urge or stress incontinence symptoms.
Urinary incontinence is a symptom and not a condition in itself.
4. DIAGNOSTIC MEASURES: (*See* chart on page 394)
a. History.
b. Physical examination with additional tests.
c. Urinalysis.

5. Pharmacologic treatment
a. Drugs for incontinence due to detrusor overactivity:
(1) Anticholinergic/antispasmodic agents. The purpose of these drugs is to relax the bladder and increase bladder capacity.
(Note: All anticholinergic drugs are contraindicated in patients with narrow-angle but not wide-angle glaucoma.)

(2) Propantheline. Recommended at 7.5–30 mg in the fasting state, t.i.d.–q.i.d. (higher dossages may be needed).

(3) Oxybutynin.* Recommended at 2.5–5 mg, p.o., t.i.d.

(4) Tricyclic agents. Imipramine** and doxepin may be beneficial at 10–100 mg, p.o./d, initially in divided doses.

(5) Dicyclomine hydrochloride. Clinical experience suggests that this drug is as effective as other anticholinergic agents in controlling detrusor over-activity. Dose is 10–20 mg, t.i.d., p.o.

b. Drugs for incontinence due to urethral sphincter insufficiency.

(1) Alpha-adrenergic agonist agents. These drugs increase urethral resistance by stimulation of urethral smooth muscle acting on alpha-adrenergic receptors in the urethra.

(2) Phenylpropanolamine (PPA). The recommended dose is 25–75 mg, p.o., q. 12h.
(Note: These drugs should be used with caution in patients with hypertension, hyperthyroidism, cardiac arrhythmias, and angina.)

c. Estrogen supplementation therapy. Estrogen replacement in post-menopausal women may restore urethral mucosal coaptation. Estrogen replacement should be given with a progestin when endometrial tissue is present. (Atrophic vaginitis should be treated cyclically with conjugated estrogen, 0.3–1.25 mg/d, p.o., or vaginally, 2 g or fraction/d). Progestin 2.5–10 mg/d continuous or intermittent.

d. Combined alpha-adrenergic agonist and estrogen supplementation therapy. Combination therapy may be considered when an initial single drug therapy fails.

6. Surgery
Surgery is sometimes needed to help treat the cause of incontinence. Surgery can be used to:

a. Return the bladder neck to its proper position in women with stress incontinence.

b. Remove tissue that is causing a blockage.

c. Replace or support severely weakened pelvic muscles.

d. Enlarge a small bladder to hold more urine.

SURGICAL MANAGEMENT OF UI*

UI type	Cause	Treatment
Stress	Hypermobility	Retropubic suspension Needle endoscopic suspension
Stress	Intrinsic sphincter deficiency	Sling (mostly female) Artificial sphincter Urethral bulking
Urge	Refractory detrusor instability	Augmentation cystoplasty
Overflow	Obstruction	Relieve obstruction
	Nonobstructive	Intermittent catheterization Other

*Source: "Urinary Incontinence in Adults—Quick Reference Guide for Clinicians," U.S. Department of Health and Human Services, Public Health Services AHCPR, 1992, p. 7.

---

7. Patient care management

a. Behavioral techniques
Behavioral techniques teach the patient ways to control his/her own bladder and sphincter muscles. They work well for certain types of urinary incontinence. Two types of behavioral techniques are commonly used: bladder training and pelvic muscle exercises. The patient may also be asked to change the amount of liquid that he/she drinks and to drink more or less water depending on the bladder problem.

(1) **Bladder training** Used for urge incontinence, and may also be used for stress incontinence. Both men and women can benefit from bladder training. People learn different ways to control the urge to urinate. Distraction (thinking about other

---

*Drugs marked with a single asterisk have been officially approved by the FDA for the indicated use. The remainder are not approved but are commonly used.

**Imipramine is officially approved by the FDA for enuresis in children but not for adults.

things) is just one example. A technique called prompted voiding—urinating on a schedule—is also used. This technique has been quite successful in controlling incontinence in nursing home patients.

(2) **Pelvic muscle exercises** Called Kegel exercises; used for stress incontinence. The Kegel exercises help to strengthen weak muscles around the bladder.

COMMON TESTS USED TO DIAGNOSE URINARY INCONTINENCE

Name of test	Purpose
Blood tests	Examines blood for levels of various chemicals.
Cystoscopy	Looks for abnormalities in bladder and lower urinary tract. It works by inserting a small tube into the bladder that has a telescope for the doctor to look through.
Post-void residual (PVR) measurement	Measures how much urine is left in the bladder after urinating by placing a small soft tube into the bladder or by using ultrasound (sound waves).
Stress test	Looks for urine loss when stress is put on bladder muscles usually by coughing, lifting, or exercise.
Urinalysis	Examines urine for signs of infection, blood, or other abnormality.
Urodynamic testing	Examines bladder and urethral sphincter function (may involve inserting a small tube into the bladder; x-rays also can be used to see the bladder).

From: "Urinary Incontinence in Adults: A Patient's Guide," U.S. Department of Health and Human Services, Public Health Service, AHCPR, 1993.

---

b. Other measures and supportive devices
(1) Intermittent self-catheterization.
(2) Indwelling catheters.
(3) Suprapubic catheters.
(4) External collection of catheters.
(5) Penile clamps.
(6) Pessaries.
(7) Absorbent pads or garments.

INTERNAL CATHETERS

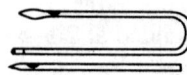

Intermittent (two lengths shown)

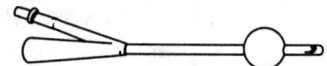

Indwelling

EXTERNAL CATHETERS

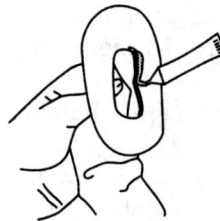

Hollister Female Urinary Pouch

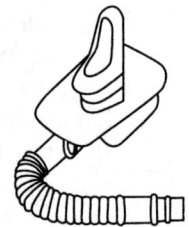

Hollister Female Urinary Incontinence System

ADULT DIAPERS

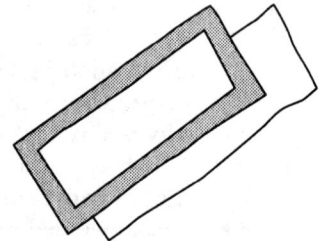

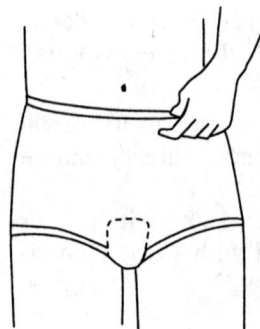

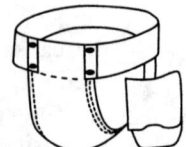

Source: *Bladder Control for Women and Bladder Control for Men,* Patient Education Press: Plainfield, New Jersey, 1989, pp. 29–30.

8. Nursing diagnoses/goals/interventions
   a. Fluid volume deficit related to inadequate fluid intake.
      Goal: The patient will drink 2000 mL of appropriate fluid in each 24-hour period.
      Intervention
      (1) Assess the patient's preference in liquids and provide those liquids.
      (2) Explain the reason to drink an adequate amount of fluid.
      (3) Increase hydration level by:
         (a) Encouraging fluid intake of 1200 mL 7:00 A.M. to 3:00 P.M., 600 mL 3:00 P.M. to 7:00 P.M., 200 mL 7:00 P.M. to 7:00 A.M., and limiting fluids after 7:00 P.M. to avoid urgency at night or enuresis.
         (b) Keeping accurate intake and output records, noting volume of each voiding and incontinence pattern.
         (c) Discouraging the use of caffeinated beverages and artificial sweeteners.
      (4) Involve the patient in planning for fluid intake.
   b. Stress incontinence related to:
      (1) High intra-abdominal pressure.
      (2) Sphincter weakness.
      (3) Overdistension of bladder.
      Goals
      (1) The patient will demonstrate an absence of, or decreased episodes of, incontinence.
      (2) The patient will state techniques that increase bladder control.
      (3) The patient will state how he/she can alter some factors contributing to incontinence.
      Interventions
      (1) Assess the incontinence patterns.
      (2) Increase bladder capacity as follows:
         (a) Determine the time lapsed between the urge to void and actual voiding; respond promptly to a request for assistance in toileting.
         (b) After the patient is placed on the toilet, encourage the patient to "hold off" urinating as long as possible.
         (c) Give positive reinforcement for efforts.

      (d) Discourage frequent voiding as a result of habit or anxiety and not need.
      (3) Instruct the patient in techniques that strengthen the sphincter and muscle control relating to urination by:
         (a) Teaching Kegel exercises.
         (b) Starting and stopping stream while voiding.
         (c) Instructing the patient to schedule voiding or setting a voiding schedule that involves drinking a measured amount of fluid and voiding at specific times. (This requires a commitment of both staff and patient for consistency.)
      (4) Teach healthy nutritional habits by:
         (a) Encouraging daily intake of fiber, fresh fruits and vegetables, and fluids to ensure regular bowel elimination and avoid abdominal pressure on bladder.
         (b) Avoiding use of laxatives and enemas that develop dependency.
         (c) Advising that caffeinated beverages and grapefruit juice act as diuretics as well as bladder irritants.
         (d) Encouraging the patient to respond promptly to urge to defecate.
   c. Functional incontinence related to:
      (1) Decreased dexterity of upper extremities.
      (2) Cognitive, perceptual, or psychosocial deficits interacting with environment.
      Goals:
      (1) The patient will demonstrate exercises that improve mobility, dexterity, and urine-controlling muscle.
      (2) The patient will state factors contributing to functional incontinence.
      Interventions:
      (1) Discuss with the patient the incontinent episodes, reenact with him/her exactly what occurs, and discuss possible solutions:
         "What goes through your mind when you first realize you have to urinate?"
         "How easy is it to remove clothing in order to urinate?"

(2) Encourage the patient to schedule toileting upon arising in morning; after meals, before bedtime, before becoming involved in a lengthy activity, and before and after exercise.

(3) Resolve environmental barriers by:
  (a) Providing call light.
  (b) Having bedpan or commode within reach at night.
  (c) Installing grab bars around toilet.
  (d) Using raised toilet seat.
  (e) Leaving bathroom door ajar if it is difficult to turn knob.
  (f) Using night light in bedroom and bathroom.

(4) Discuss appropriate clothing, use of Velcro instead of zippers and buttons, loops at waist of underpants to hook fingers through and remove paints easily and quickly.

(5) Discuss with the patient types of activities preferred—walking, dancing, swimming, aerobics, knitting, sewing, painting—and arrange a routine that will maintain walking muscle strength, and hand and finger dexterity:
  (a) Kegel exercises for pelvic floor muscles 3 times a day for 10 minutes each time; should see improvement within 2 weeks if done consistently.
  (b) Water exercise classes or measuring out a mile walk within nursing home halls. (A chalkboard or bulletin board at the end of the mile to mark of achievement is positive reinforcement.)
  (c) Regularly scheduled group exercise classes.
  (d) Manual-dexterity activities (sewing, knitting, etc.).
  (e) Positive reinforcement for exercising.

(6) Avoid encouragement of incontinence or negative reinforcement by routine use of pads, diapers, or other depersonalizing procedures, since they trap urine and enhance bacterial growth.

(7) Avoid placing patient on toilet following incontinence episode, unless overflow incontinence has been identified; if incontinence occurs, assist with clean-up as quickly as possible and with minimal conversation; this should not be a socializing event.

d. Self-esteem disturbance related to urinary incontinence after recent hospitalization
Goals:
(1) The patient will attain continence by following nursing care plan and mutually determined goals.
(2) The patient will identify personal strengths.
Interventions:
(1) Assess cognition, motivation to be continent, and willingness to participate in the care plan through communication and mental status testing.
(2) Encourage verbalization of anger, frustration, helplessness; explore previously used coping techniques when problems arise; convey to the patient that incontinence can be controlled, and discuss mutual goals to give a sense of control; explore and stress positive personality characteristics
(3) Encourage the patient to discuss recent hospitalization and to air feelings about the use of indwelling catheter.
(4) Encourage the use of clothes that are easily and quickly removed.
(5) Anticipate continence and demonstrate a positive attitude.
(6) Encourage the return of social activities.
(7) Assist with grooming.
(8) Suggest limited use of incontinent pads and garment for social outings.

e. Risk for urinary infection related to altered immune response (age-related) and recent catheter insertion
Goals:
(1) The patient will experience prompt detection of urinary tract infection.
(2) The patient will demonstrate habits that decrease the potential for urinary tract infection.
Interventions:
(1) Instruct the patient to report any "feverish" feelings, chills, lower abdominal discomfort, urgency in voiding, dysuria, lower back or flank pain, changes in color, odor or amount of urine, return or increase of incontinence.

(2) Instruct the patient to report any symptoms of infection, the most common in the elderly being "not feeling well," loss of appetite, odorous urine, lack of clear urine, and increased disorientation.

(3) Request an order for urinalysis.

(4) Note white blood cell count and bacterial level.

(5) Stress the importance of maintaining optimal fluid intake to prevent urinary tract infections, urinary stasis, dehydration, and concentrated urine.

(6) Teach the patient the importance of changing clothes and cleansing perineum promptly if incontinent.

(7) Review the use of cranberry juice to maintain acidity of the urine and prevent infection; avoid caffeinated beverages and artificial sweeteners.

(8) Reinforce hygiene measures such as:

    (a) Washing hands after each toileting.

    (b) Cleansing perineal area from front to back when bathing or after toileting.

    (c) Showering instead of bathing, to prevent bacteria from entering urethra.

    (d) Completely emptying the bladder, which is achieved most effectively by upright or forward-bent position during voiding.

f. Other nursing diagnoses

(1) Overflow incontinence related to:

    (a) Obstruction/stricture.

    (b) Absent or impaired motor/sensory impulses or weak musculature.

(2) Total continuous incontinence related to:

    (a) Anatomical fistula.

    (b) Spinal cord lesion at or below reflex arc.

(3) Reflex incontinence related to:

    (a) Spinal cord lesion above conus medullaris.

(4) Urge incontinence related to:

    (a) Bladder irritability.

    (b) Small bladder capacity.

    (c) Overdistension of bladder.

9. Evaluation

  a. The patient is hydrated.

  b. The patient has bladder control.

  c. The patient is free from bladder infection.

B. Management of the Patient Undergoing Prostatectomy

1. Causes: prostatic hyperplasia, malignancy of the prostate.

2. Types

  a. **Suprapubic prostatectomy** Removal of the gland through an incision in the bladder. The incidence of incontinence is low.

  b. **Perineal prostatectomy** Removal of the gland through an incision in the perineum.

  c. **Transurethral resection** Removal of the gland with an endoscopic instrument. Impotence is low, but incontinence occurs frequently.

  d. **Retropubic prostatectomy** Removal of the gland through a low abdominal incision. Incontinence and impotence occur infrequently.

  e. **Total prostatectomy** Removal of the gland and seminal vesicles. There is a high incidence of impotence, incontinence, and rectal injury.

C. Nursing diagnoses/goals/interventions

1. Pain related to surgical intervention, bladder spasm, and urinary retention

Goal: Patient will verbalize a decrease in pain.

Interventions:

  a. Administer antispasmodic and anticholinergics as ordered.

  b. Intermittently irrigate urethral and suprapubic catheters as ordered; use sterile normal saline and sterile syringe; instill solution gently—never force; continue to irrigate until solution is clear.

2. Hematuria, acute urinary retention, urinary diversion related to surgery

Goal: Patient will show no signs or symptoms of urinary retention, or of obstruction to the flow of urine; intake and output will be balanced; patient will void normally after removal of catheter.

  a. Monitor continuous bladder irrigation to cleanse the bladder and prevent clot formation.

  b. Observe straight drainage.

  c. Tape drainage tube to inner aspect of thigh for external bladder traction.

  d. Maintain intake and output, including the amount of fluid used for irrigation.

  e. Instruct the patient to avoid sitting for prolonged periods.

  f. Encourage adequate amounts of fluids.

g. Observe drainage bag, dressing, and incision site for excessive bleeding.

h. Monitor vital signs.

i. Maintain continuous bladder irrigation (CBI); use sterile saline as ordered for irrigation; maintain sterility of irrigating equipment.

j. Maintain patency of urethral and suprapubic catheters.

k. Observe for signs and symptoms of urinary retention.

l. After catheter removal, measure urine output after each voiding, catheterize to check for residual urine as ordered, and report if greater than 500 mL.

3. Risk for infection related to presence of cathethers in bladder and presence of wound
Goal: Patient will show no signs of urinary tract infection.
Interventions:

a. Take the patient's temperature every 4 hours; report elevation above 101°F.

b. Note character of urine; report if cloudy.

c. Maintain closed drainage system.

d. Observe for signs and symptoms of urinary tract infection.

e. Encourage coughing and deep breathing.

f. Monitor suprapubic catheter for drainage around site and for redness, swelling, and pain around site.

4. Body image disturbance in self-concept related to fear of impotence, loss of male identity, and urinary incontinence
Goal: Patient will verbalize feelings related to change in body image to care giver or significant other and will resume activities of daily living.
Interventions:

a. Encourage the patient to express his feelings.

b. Actively listen to what the patient says.

c. Answer questions honestly.

d. Encourage adaptive coping behavior.

e. Explain that some urinary incontinence is normal at first.

f. Assure the patient that the surgical site will heal and good urinary control with return.

g. Teach and encourage the patient to practice perineal exercises; include significant other in teaching.

h. Explain that a dry ejaculation will occur for the first few months; reassure that normal ejaculation will return (patients with perineal surgery will not be able to maintain an erection).

i. Explain that the ability to impregnate is gone (except with simple TURP, transurethral resection prostatectomy).

j. Encourage communication with the significant other.

5. Knowledge deficit regarding postoperative routine, symptoms to report to physician, and home-care and follow-up instructions
Goal: Patient and/or significant other will verbalize understanding of postoperative routine, symptoms to report to physician, and home-care and follow-up instructions.
Interventions:

a. Teach the patient signs and symptoms to report immediately: heavy bleeding, difficulty in voiding, incisional redness, elevated temperature, and pain on walking.

b. Teach the patient the names of medications, the administration schedule, dosages, purposes, and side effects.

c. Provide other patient education.

  (1) Drink ample amounts of fluids to avoid dehydration.

  (2) Avoid coffee, tea, and cola drinks, and alcohol for 1 month after surgery.

  (3) Shower daily.

  (4) Do not engage in sexual activity for 1 month or as instructed by physician.

  (5) Avoid over-the-counter medications unless approved by the physician.

  (6) Keep appointments with the clinic or physician.

  (7) Do perineal exercise to regain urinary control (tense the muscles by pressing the buttocks together).

  (8) Avoid straining at stool and heavy lifting.

  (9) Avoid long automobile rides and strenuous exercise.

D. Evaluation

1. Patient verbalizes a decrease in pain.

2. Patient shows no signs of urinary retention.

3. Patient's urine flows freely through the catheter.

4. Patient's intake and output are balanced.

5. Patient voids after catheter is removed.

6. Patient shows no signs of infection.

7. Patient and/or significant other can verbalize the postoperative routine, symptoms to report to the physician, and home-care management and follow-up.

Other Alterations of Health

A. Pressure Ulcers
1. Definition—Localized area of tissue necrosis that develops when soft tissue is compressed between a bony prominence and an external surface for a prolonged period of time.
2. Staging[1]
   a. Stage 1 (1)—Non-blanchable erythema of intact skin; the heralding lesion of skin ulceration. Discoloration of skin, warmth, or hardness also may be indicators.

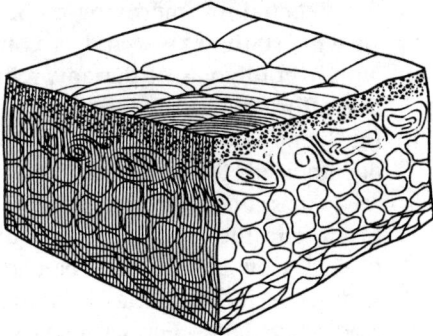

Staging definitions recognize these assessment limitations:
   (1) Identification of Stage 1 pressure ulcers may be difficult in patients with darkly pigmented skin.
   (2) When eschar is present, accurate staging of the pressure ulcer is not possible until the eschar has sloughed or the wound has been debrided.
   b. Stage II (2)—Partial thickness skin loss involving epidermis and/or dermis. The ulcer is superficial and presents clinically as an abrasion, blister, or shallow crater.

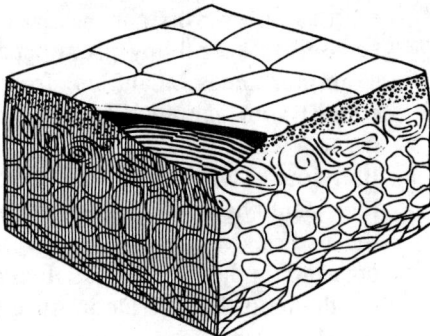

   c. Stage III (3)—Full thickness skin loss involving damage or necrosis of subcutaneous tissue that may extend down to, but not through, underlying fascia. The ulcer presents clinically as a deep crater with or without undermining of adjacent tissue.

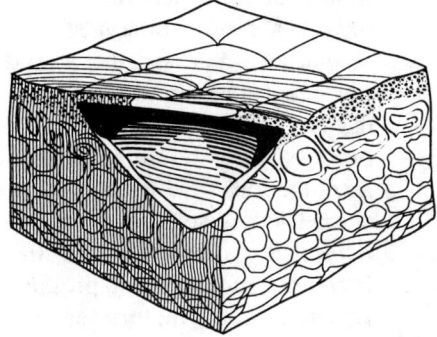

   d. Stage IV (4)—Full thickness skin loss with extensive destruction, tissue necrosis, or damage to muscle, bone, or supporting structures (e.g., tendon, joint capsule).

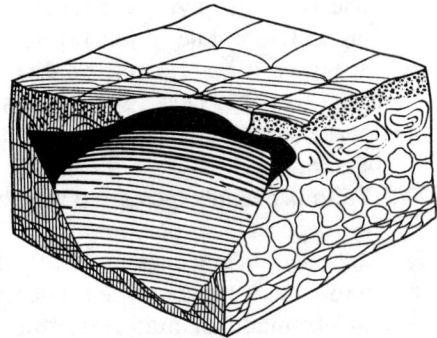

3. Risk assessment tools and risk factors[2]
   Bed- and chair-bound individuals or those with impaired ability to reposition should be assessed for additional factors that increase the risk of developing pressure ulcers. These factors include immobility, incontinence, nutritional factors such as inadequate dietary intake and impaired nutritional status, and altered level of consciousness. Individuals should be assessed on admission to acute care and rehabilitation hospitals, nursing homes, home care programs, and other health care facilities. A systematic risk assessment can be accomplished by using a validated risk assessment tool such as the Braden Scale or the Norton Scale. Pressure ulcer risk

[1]*Pressure Ulcers in Adults: Prediction and Prevention, Clinical Practice Guideline, Number 3;* Rockville, MD: Agency for Health Care Policy and Research, 1992, p. 8.
[2]*Pressure Ulcers in Adults: Prediction and Prevention, Clinical Practice Guideline, Number 3*, Rockville, MD; Agency for Health Care Policy and Research, 1992, pp. 13–14.

should be reassessed at periodic intervals.

4. Skin care and early treatment[3]
   a. All individuals at risk should have a systematic skin inspection at least once a day, with particular attention to the bony prominences; results are documented.
   b. Skin should be cleansed at time of soiling and at routine intervals.
   c. Avoid hot water, and use a mild cleansing agent that minimizes irritation and dryness of the skin. During the cleansing process, care should be taken to minimize the force and friction applied to the skin. There is some association between dry, flaky, or scaling skin and an increased incidence of pressure ulcers. Environmental factors leading to skin drying, such as low humidity (less than 40%) and exposure to cold, should be minimized. Dry skin should be treated with moisturizers.
   d. Avoid massage over bony prominences. The scientific evidence for using massage to stimulate blood flow and avert pressure ulcer formation is not well established. There is preliminary evidence suggesting it may lead to deep tissue trauma.
   e. Minimize skin exposure to moisture due to incontinence, perspiration, or wound drainage. When these sources of moisture cannot be controlled, underpads or briefs made of materials that absorb moisture and present a quick-drying surface to the skin should be used. Topical agents that act as barriers to moisture should be used.
   f. Skin injury due to friction and shear forces should be minimized through proper positioning, transferring, and turning techniques. In addition, friction injuries may be reduced by the use of lubricants.
   g. Adequate dietary intake of protein and calories should be maintained. When apparently well-nourished individuals develop an inadequate dietary intake of protein or calories, caregivers should first attempt to discover and correct the factors compromising intake and offer support with eating. Other nutritional supplements

or support may be needed. If dietary intake remains inadequate and if consistent with overall goals of therapy, more aggressive nutritional intervention such as enteral or parenteral feedings should be considered. For nutritionally compromised persons, a plan of nutritional support and/or supplementation should be implemented to meet individual needs and the overall goals of therapy.
   h. Maintain current activity level, mobility, and range of motion if appropriate. If the potential for improving mobility and activity status exists and is consistent with overall goals of therapy, rehabilitation efforts should be instituted.
   i. Interventions should be monitored and documented. Specific details are needed on who should provide the care, how often, and the supplies and equipment needed. How the care is to be undertaken should be individualized, written, and readily available. Furthermore, results of the interventions and the care being rendered, and adjustment in the interventions, as indicated by the outcomes should be documented. To ensure continuity, documentation of the plan of care must be clear, concise, and accessible to every caregiver.

5. Mechanical forces and support surfaces[4]
   a. Individuals in bed assessed to be at risk for developing pressure ulcers should be repositioned at least every 2 hours if consistent with overall patient goals. A written schedule for systematically turning and repositioning the individual should be used. Positioning devices such as pillows or foam wedges should be used to keep bony prominences (for example, knees or ankles) from direct contact with one another, again according to a written plan.
   b. Individuals who are completely immobile should have a care plan that includes the use of devices that totally relieve pressure on the heels, most often by raising them off the bed. Donut-type devices should not be used. Ring cushions are known to cause venous congestion and edema. Although few studies have docu-

[3]Ibid., pp. 15–22.
[4]Ibid., pp. 22–26.

mented their deleterious effects, one study of at-risk patients found that ring cushions (donuts) are more likely to cause than to prevent pressure ulcers.

c. Other recommendations include not positioning the individual directly on the trochanter when the side-lying position is used and maintaining the head of the bed at the lowest degree of elevation consistent with medical conditions and other restrictions. The amount of time the head of the bed is elevated should be limited. Anyone assessed to be at risk for developing pressure ulcers should be placed on a pressure-reducing device when lying in bed—such as foam, static air, alternating air, or gel mattresses. Lifting devices such as a trapeze or bed linen should be used to move, rather than drag, individuals who cannot assist during transfers and position changes.

d. Uninterrupted sitting by at-risk individuals in chairs or wheelchairs should be avoided. If consistent with overall patient management goals, the individual should be repositioned, shifting the points under pressure, at least every hour or be put back to bed. Individuals who are able to move should be taught to shift weight every 15 minutes. For individuals who sit in wheelchairs or on other sitting surfaces, the use of a pressure-reducing device such as those made of foam, gel, air, or a combination is indicated—but not donut-type devices. Positioning in the chair should include consideration of postural alignment, distribution of weight, balance and stability, and pressure relief. A written plan for the use of positioning devices and schedules may be helpful for chair-bound individuals.

6. Wound types
   a. Red wound (granulating)
      (1) Dressing
          (a) Gauze dressing moistened with saline.
          (b) Hydrocolloids.
          (c) Hydrogels.
          (d) Transparent films.
      (2) Therapies
          (a) Nutritional support.
          (b) Support surfaces.

   b. Yellow wound (slough necrosis)
      (1) Dressing
          (a) Exudate absorbers.
          (b) Hydrocolloids, hydrogels, transparent films for autolysis.
          (c) Moist gauze dressings.
      (2) Therapies
          (a) High pressure irrigation.
          (b) Surgical debridement.
          (c) Nutrition support.
          (d) Hydrotherapy with whirlpool.
          (e) Electric stimulation.

   c. Black wound
      (1) Dressing
          (a) Debriding agents—Elase, Collagenase, Travase.
          (b) Hydrocolloids, hydrogels, transparent films for autolysis.
      (2) Therapies
          (a) High-pressure irrigation.
          (b) Hydrotherapy.
          (c) Laser or surgical debridement.
          (d) Nutritional support.
          (e) Oxygen.
          (f) Support surface.

7. Nursing diagnoses/goals/interventions
   a. Risk for impaired skin integrity related to poor nutrition, immobility, incontinence, sensory deficits.
      Goal: The patient's skin will remain intact with absence of redness or mottling.
      Interventions:
      (1) Assess for areas of redness over bony prominences and pressure points.
      (2) Ambulate as ordered. Limit chair sitting to 1 hour. Foam cushion in chair. Shift position every 15 minutes while in chair.
      (3) Change position at least every 2 hours.
      (4) Apply external catheter (male) or pouches (female) to maintain dryness. Apply ABD pad to rectal area for fecal incontinence.
      (5) Keep linen smooth. Use cloth underpad next to buttocks. (Avoid Chux or plastic-lined pad.)
      (6) Apply alternating air mattress overlay.
      (7) Apply Duoderm Extra Thin to both hips and heels and sacrum.

Apply transparent film to other areas prone to breakdown.
(8) Apply heel protectors.
(9) Apply elbow protectors.
(10) Use a "lift sheet" when positioning patient.
(11) Encourage patient to use overhead trapeze, if indicated.
(12) Assess nutritional status.
  (a) Weigh weekly and record.
  (b) Observe dietary intake.
  (c) Monitor lab values (hemoglobin, hematocrit, and albumin).
  (d) Observe for edema of lower extremity, sacral areas, and pulmonary.
  (e) Observe for poor skin turgor, dry tongue, and dry mucous membrane.
  (f) Fluid intake of 2000–3000 cc in 24 hours, unless contraindicated.
  (g) Nutrition consultation for albumin 3.0 mgn and below.
(13) Bathe with mild soap, partial bath every other day to prevent dryness of skin.
(14) Moisturize skin daily and prn.
(15) Apply skin barrier cream to perineum after cleaning when patient is soiled.

Nursing diagnosis:
(1) Impaired skin integrity related to poor nutrition, immobility, incontinence, sensory deficit.
  (a) Stage I pressure ulcer.
    Goal: The patient's skin will be intact and without redness or mottling.

Interventions:
(1) Apply Hydrocolloid Extra-thin to both hips and heels and sacrum.
(2) Assess and record wound characteristics weekly.
(3) Keep area clean and dry.
(4) Place on support surface for pressure reduction.
  (a) Stage II pressure ulcer
    Goal: The patient will demonstrate progressive healing by increasing the amounts of epithelium.

Interventions:
(1) Assess and document size of ulcer base weekly (length, width, depth).
(2) Describe status of ulcer weekly in nurses' notes.
(3) Cleanse with sterile normal saline.
(4) Cover pressure ulcer with dressing that maintains a moist environment (wet dressing, transparent dressing, Hydrocolloid).
(5) Place on alternating air mattress overlay for pressure relief.
  (a) Stage III or IV pressure ulcer
    Goal: The patient will demonstrate progressive healing as evidenced by decreasing dimensions of ulcer base and the presence of granulation tissue.

Interventions:
(1) Assess and document size of ulcer base weekly (length, width, depth).
(2) Describe ulcer characteristics in nurses' notes (granulation, epithelialization, necrotic tissue) weekly.
(3) Observe for infection (redness, induration, fever, edema at site, and purulent drainage).
  (a) For a clean, noninfected, nondraining ulcer, cleanse with normal saline. Apply moist normal saline dressing every 8 hours or use Hydrogel, cover with gauze, hydrocolloid, or transparent dressing (hydrocolloid contraindicated for diabetes). Change every other day or 3 times a week.
  (b) For a non-granulating draining ulcer, cleanse with a mixture of half normal saline and half hydrogen peroxide. Rinse with normal saline. Apply exudate absorber or cover with foam dressing or ABD pad. Secure with transparent dressing or nonallergenic tape. Change every other day.

(c) If there is slough necrosis or eschar in the wound, cleanse with a mixture of half normal saline and half hydrogen peroxide. Rinse with normal saline and apply hydrogel. Cover with foam dressing or ABD pad. Change daily.

OR

Use an enzymatic debrider (Elase or Collagenase). Apply and cover with 4 × 4 gauze dressing, tape window frame style. Apply polysporin powder first, if foul odor is present. When applying Elase, cover with non-adhering petrolatum dressing before applying gauze dressing.

(d) After eschar and/or necrosis have been removed and the wound is clean, apply hydrogel if crater is present. Change every 3 days.

(4) Infection. After debridement, use Elase or Collagenase (hydrogel for crater). Culture the wound and treat as per policy, and/or physician's orders.

(a) Administer parenteral antibiotics as ordered.

(b) Cleanse with a mixture of half hydrogen peroxide and half normal saline followed by normal saline rinse.

(c) Use enzymatic debrider or hydrogel if necrosis is present.

(d) Dress with gauze dressing; hydrocolloid is contraindicated for infection and patients with diabetes mellitus.

(e) Change dressing daily.

(5) Therapeutic support surfaces

(a) For more than 2 intact turning surfaces, use an alternating air mattress overlay.

(b) For 2 or less turning surfaces, use a kinetic therapy bed.

8. Evaluation

a. The patient's skin will remain intact.

b. The patient's pressure ulcer will demonstrate progressive healing.

c. The patient will become afebrile.

Meeting the Needs of the Terminally Ill Patient

DYNAMICS/CHARACTERISTICS OF DEATH AND DYING

1. Dying is a time of many changes—physical, mental, emotional.
2. Responses to death and dying are determined by our social and cultural orientations. Advances in medicine and technology are aimed at eradication of illness, elimination of pain, and prolongation of life—all of which negate the reality of death and dying.

3. The health-care givers' awareness of their feelings toward their own mortality is important if they are to assist their patients and their families to cope with death and dying.
4. When patients do not improve and face imminent death, health-care givers tend to feel a sense of helplessness and hopelessness and perhaps even of failure. It is imperative, therefore, that all health-care givers deal with their own attitudes, feelings, and orientations about death before they address a dying patient's needs.

5. Each individual responds to his/her own terminal illness uniquely (reactions to helplessness, pain, disability, imminent separation from loved ones, etc.).
6. Elizabeth Kubler-Ross, in *On Death and Dying* (New York: Macmillan, 1969) has identified patterns of reactions to the dying process as follows:
   a. Denial—"No, not me." Avoidance or refusal to acknowledge the diagnosis; allows the person to mobilize inner coping resources.
   b. Anger—"Why me?" Difficult stage; characterized by anger, envy, resentment, feeling of being abandoned; people around the patient are often targets of his/her anger; understanding is very important.
   c. Bargaining—"Yes, me, but..." An attempt to postpone death by offering behavior change (may be associated with guilt feelings); completing unfinished tasks before death; bargains usually made with God.
   d. Depression—"What's the use?" Feeling of great loss; person begins to mourn for loss of health, income, job, and independence, and in anticipation of impending losses (family, friends, the future); patient may feel shame and guilt for causing sorrow to loved ones and being a "burden" to them; patient becomes less verbal, and family, friends, and staff find this difficult.
   e. Acceptance—"Yes, me. I am ready." Time for peace; person comes to terms with reality; person wants to be left alone at this time; person's communication becomes more nonverbal.

ASSESSMENT

1. Be familiar with the physical signs of impending death.
2. Assess your own perceptions and feelings about death and dying.
3. Assess your own thoughts and feelings about the patient.
4. Assess the patient's patterns of behavior—how he/she is coping with pain, his/her own feelings, and the impending separations; his/her fears, expectations, and resources; and his/her role in the family.
5. Assess the patient's family—the members' perception of the patient's illness and diagnosis; their feelings about the patient and the manner in which they manage these feelings; their pattern of communication with the patient and within the family; the way they are coping; their support system and resources.
6. Assess the environment—is the patient's environment conducive to expression of feelings; does the environment promote patient participation in his/her own care?
7. Assess the patient's condition (if the condition permits) and the family's understanding of issues related to Do Not Resuscitate (DNR) choices. (Adhere to all applicable state regulations and appropriate policies and procedures of the health care institution.) Review with the patient and/or family Advanced Directives. Assist in clarification of information.

PATIENT CARE MANAGEMENT

1. Symptomatic care according to the patient's disease condition.
2. Pain relief.
3. Comfort measures.
4. Respect for patient's rights.

NURSING DIAGNOSES/GOALS/ INTERVENTIONS

1. Alteration in body image related to the debilitating changes imposed by the disease process
   Goals:
   a. Patient will be able to express feelings about the effects of the debilitating changes in his/her body.
   b. Patient will be able to accept the debilitating changes imposed by his/her illness.
   c. Patient will be able to assist in his/her own care.
   Interventions:
   a. Realize that physical care and emotional care go hand in hand.
   b. Consider the patient's physical deterioration and loss of physical strength during his/her participation in self-care. Do not rush the patient through any procedure. Provide periods of rest between nursing procedures.
   c. Anticipate pain. Provide comfort measures and administer pain relief before the patient becomes aware of the pain.
   d. Promote open communication. Allow the patient to express all his/her feelings and emotions without judgment.
   e. Institute comfort measures.
   f. Assist the patient in validating his/her perception of reality.
2. Alteration in comfort: pain related to the disease process

Goals:
 a. Patient will verbalize relief from pain.
 b. Patient will verbalize some degree of comfort.
 c. Patient will verbalize feeling of being in control of his/her life (not dependent on the care givers in all aspects of his/her care).
Interventions:
 a. Assess the patient's need for pain relief.
 b. Anticipate the patient's pain, and provide comfort measures and pain relief before the patient becomes aware of the pain.
 c. Allow the patient to participate in his/her own care.

3. Risk for social isolation related to the patient's decreased verbal communication and withdrawal
Goals:
 a. Patient will acknowledge the presence and care of those around him/her by interacting and verbalizing his/her feelings, especially fears related to dying.
 b. Family members and health-care givers will continue to communicate with the patient.
 c. Patient will be open to express his/her feelings.
Interventions:
 a. Accept the patient's needs for privacy.
 b. Do not withdraw from the patient (mutual withdrawal).
 c. Communicate with the patient by means of words, touch, and presence.
 d. Observe the patient's patterns of coping.
 e. Involve the family in the care of the patient.
 f. Avoid probing into the patient's feelings.
 g. Provide for physical comfort measures.
 h. Make frequent visits.
 i. Provide information to the patient as needed.

4. Anticipatory grieving related to impending losses (life, family, friends, the entire world) as a result of the disease process
Goals:
 a. Patient will be able to express his/her feelings about dying.
 b. Patient and his/her family will be able to share their feelings about their impending losses.
 c. Patient and his/her family will be able to maintain open communication and physical closeness throughout the dying process.

Interventions:
 a. Respect the patient. Accept the patient's denial and anger; encourage him/her to express feelings of rage, resentment, and depression. This expression helps the patient to relieve guilt feelings and be less fearful.
 b. Be honest in responding to the patient's questions.
 c. Support the patient and his/her family in dealing with their emotions.
 d. Maintain verbal communication with the patient even when he/she becomes reluctant to communicate verbally.
 e. Provide an environment where the patient may be able to reminisce and recount events in his/her life.
 f. Be nonjudgmental.
 g. If the patient's condition permits, allow him/her to participate in self-care to decrease feelings of helplessness, dependence, and loss of control.
 h. Provide health promotion measures.
  (1) Assist the patient and his/her family to cope with impending death.
  (2) Allow the family members to assist in the care of the patient as much as possible. This helps them to deal with their feelings effectively.
  (3) Encourage the family to express their feelings of grief and concern toward the dying person.
  (4) Prepare children for the reality of death when the subject arises naturally (e.g., when a pet dies). In the case of death in the family, be honest in answering questions. Assist children to express their feelings; allow them to attend the services with the family if desired.

EVALUATION

1. Patient achieves and maintains the highest possible quality of life during the dying process.
2. Patient is able to express and validate his/her own feelings about own death and dying.
3. Patient and family are able to cope effectively with the permanent separation that they face.
4. Patient is able to make realistic decisions about his/her life situation.
5. Patient is pain free during the dying process.

Appendix I

AHA's Patient's Bill of Rights*

1. The patient has the right to considerate and respectful care.

2. The patient has the right to obtain from his physician complete current information concerning his diagnosis, treatment, and prognosis in terms the patient can be reasonably expected to understand. When it is not medically advisable to give such information to the patient, the information should be made available to an appropriate person in his behalf. He has the right to know, by name, the physician responsible for coordinating his care.

3. The patient has the right to receive from his physician information necessary to give informed consent prior to the start of any procedure and/or treatment. Except in emergencies, such information for informed consent should include but not necessarily be limited to the specific procedure and/or treatment, the medically significant risks involved, and the probable duration of incapacitation. Where medically significant alternatives for care or treatment exist, or when the patient requests information concerning medical alternatives, the patient has the right to such information. The patient also has the right to know the name of the person responsible for the procedures and/or treatment.

4. The patient has the right to refuse treatment to the extent permitted by law and to be informed of the medical consequences of his action.

5. The patient has the right to every consideration of his privacy concerning his own medical care program. Case discussion, consultation, examination, and treatment are confidential and should be conducted discreetly. Those not directly involved in his care must have the permission of the patient to be present.

6. The patient has the right to expect that all communications and records pertaining to his care should be treated as confidential.

7. The patient has the right to expect that within its capacity a hospital must make reasonable response to the request of a patient for services. The hospital must provide evaluation, service, and/or referral as indicated by the urgency of the case. When medically permissible, a patient may be transferred to another facility only after he has received complete information and explanation concerning the needs for and alternatives to such a transfer. The institution to which the patient is to be transferred must first have accepted the patient for transfer.

8. The patient has the right to obtain information as to any relationship of his hospital to other health care and educational institutions insofar as his care is concerned. The patient has the right to obtain information as to the existence of any professional relationships among individuals, by name, who are treating him.

9. The patient has the right to be advised if the hospital proposes to engage in or perform human experimentation affecting his care or treatment. The patient has the right to refuse to participate in such research projects.

10. The patient has the right to expect reasonable continuity of care. He has the right to know in advance what appointment times and physicians are available and where. The patient has the right to expect that the hospital will provide a mechanism whereby he is informed by his physician or a delegate of the physician of the patient's continuing health care requirements following discharge.

11. The patient has the right to examine and receive an explanation of his bill regardless of source of payment.

12. The patient has the right to know what hospital rules and regulations apply to his conduct as a patient.

*Reprinted with the permission of the American Hospital Association.

PART III

Model Examinations

Model NCLEX-RN Examination I

To stimulate the actual test conditions, use the computer program packaged with this book. If you do not have access to a computer, use Model Examinations I and II to practice answering the types of questions you will encounter on the actual NCLEX using CAT. Allow a maximum of five hours for each Model Examination.

Directions:

1. Read each question carefully before looking at the answer choices.
2. When you are sure that you understand the question, select the choice that provides the correct answer.
3. In marking the answer sheet, use a pencil and blacken the circle that corresponds to your answer.

①　②　●　④

If it becomes necessary to change an answer, erase the original one completely.

4. Don't spend too much time on a question to which you don't know the answer. If you can eliminate one or more choices as clearly incorrect, select the best answer from the remaining ones.
5. Since there is no penalty for guessing, answer every question.

ANSWER SHEET FOR MODEL EXAMINATION I

1. ① ② ③ ④	51. ① ② ③ ④	101. ① ② ③ ④	151. ① ② ③ ④
2. ① ② ③ ④	52. ① ② ③ ④	102. ① ② ③ ④	152. ① ② ③ ④
3. ① ② ③ ④	53. ① ② ③ ④	103. ① ② ③ ④	153. ① ② ③ ④
4. ① ② ③ ④	54. ① ② ③ ④	104. ① ② ③ ④	154. ① ② ③ ④
5. ① ② ③ ④	55. ① ② ③ ④	105. ① ② ③ ④	155. ① ② ③ ④
6. ① ② ③ ④	56. ① ② ③ ④	106. ① ② ③ ④	156. ① ② ③ ④
7. ① ② ③ ④	57. ① ② ③ ④	107. ① ② ③ ④	157. ① ② ③ ④
8. ① ② ③ ④	58. ① ② ③ ④	108. ① ② ③ ④	158. ① ② ③ ④
9. ① ② ③ ④	59. ① ② ③ ④	109. ① ② ③ ④	159. ① ② ③ ④
10. ① ② ③ ④	60. ① ② ③ ④	110. ① ② ③ ④	160. ① ② ③ ④
11. ① ② ③ ④	61. ① ② ③ ④	111. ① ② ③ ④	161. ① ② ③ ④
12. ① ② ③ ④	62. ① ② ③ ④	112. ① ② ③ ④	162. ① ② ③ ④
13. ① ② ③ ④	63. ① ② ③ ④	113. ① ② ③ ④	163. ① ② ③ ④
14. ① ② ③ ④	64. ① ② ③ ④	114. ① ② ③ ④	164. ① ② ③ ④
15. ① ② ③ ④	65. ① ② ③ ④	115. ① ② ③ ④	165. ① ② ③ ④
16. ① ② ③ ④	66. ① ② ③ ④	116. ① ② ③ ④	166. ① ② ③ ④
17. ① ② ③ ④	67. ① ② ③ ④	117. ① ② ③ ④	167. ① ② ③ ④
18. ① ② ③ ④	68. ① ② ③ ④	118. ① ② ③ ④	168. ① ② ③ ④
19. ① ② ③ ④	69. ① ② ③ ④	119. ① ② ③ ④	169. ① ② ③ ④
20. ① ② ③ ④	70. ① ② ③ ④	120. ① ② ③ ④	170. ① ② ③ ④
21. ① ② ③ ④	71. ① ② ③ ④	121. ① ② ③ ④	171. ① ② ③ ④
22. ① ② ③ ④	72. ① ② ③ ④	122. ① ② ③ ④	172. ① ② ③ ④
23. ① ② ③ ④	73. ① ② ③ ④	123. ① ② ③ ④	173. ① ② ③ ④
24. ① ② ③ ④	74. ① ② ③ ④	124. ① ② ③ ④	174. ① ② ③ ④
25. ① ② ③ ④	75. ① ② ③ ④	125. ① ② ③ ④	175. ① ② ③ ④
26. ① ② ③ ④	76. ① ② ③ ④	126. ① ② ③ ④	176. ① ② ③ ④
27. ① ② ③ ④	77. ① ② ③ ④	127. ① ② ③ ④	177. ① ② ③ ④
28. ① ② ③ ④	78. ① ② ③ ④	128. ① ② ③ ④	178. ① ② ③ ④
29. ① ② ③ ④	79. ① ② ③ ④	129. ① ② ③ ④	179. ① ② ③ ④
30. ① ② ③ ④	80. ① ② ③ ④	130. ① ② ③ ④	180. ① ② ③ ④
31. ① ② ③ ④	81. ① ② ③ ④	131. ① ② ③ ④	181. ① ② ③ ④
32. ① ② ③ ④	82. ① ② ③ ④	132. ① ② ③ ④	182. ① ② ③ ④
33. ① ② ③ ④	83. ① ② ③ ④	133. ① ② ③ ④	183. ① ② ③ ④
34. ① ② ③ ④	84. ① ② ③ ④	134. ① ② ③ ④	184. ① ② ③ ④
35. ① ② ③ ④	85. ① ② ③ ④	135. ① ② ③ ④	185. ① ② ③ ④
36. ① ② ③ ④	86. ① ② ③ ④	136. ① ② ③ ④	186. ① ② ③ ④
37. ① ② ③ ④	87. ① ② ③ ④	137. ① ② ③ ④	187. ① ② ③ ④
38. ① ② ③ ④	88. ① ② ③ ④	138. ① ② ③ ④	188. ① ② ③ ④
39. ① ② ③ ④	89. ① ② ③ ④	139. ① ② ③ ④	189. ① ② ③ ④
40. ① ② ③ ④	90. ① ② ③ ④	140. ① ② ③ ④	190. ① ② ③ ④
41. ① ② ③ ④	91. ① ② ③ ④	141. ① ② ③ ④	191. ① ② ③ ④
42. ① ② ③ ④	92. ① ② ③ ④	142. ① ② ③ ④	192. ① ② ③ ④
43. ① ② ③ ④	93. ① ② ③ ④	143. ① ② ③ ④	193. ① ② ③ ④
44. ① ② ③ ④	94. ① ② ③ ④	144. ① ② ③ ④	194. ① ② ③ ④
45. ① ② ③ ④	95. ① ② ③ ④	145. ① ② ③ ④	195. ① ② ③ ④
46. ① ② ③ ④	96. ① ② ③ ④	146. ① ② ③ ④	196. ① ② ③ ④
47. ① ② ③ ④	97. ① ② ③ ④	147. ① ② ③ ④	197. ① ② ③ ④
48. ① ② ③ ④	98. ① ② ③ ④	148. ① ② ③ ④	198. ① ② ③ ④
49. ① ② ③ ④	99. ① ② ③ ④	149. ① ② ③ ④	199. ① ② ③ ④
50. ① ② ③ ④	100. ① ② ③ ④	150. ① ② ③ ④	200. ① ② ③ ④

MODEL NCLEX-RN EXAMINATION I

This examination covers the full spectrum of the NCLEX Examination Blueprint.

1. A primipara who is 37 weeks pregnant comes to the prenatal clinic for a weekly checkup. It is noted during the examination that lightening has occurred. Which of the following should the nurse tell this patient?

   (1) She should go into labor within the next 4 weeks.
   (2) She should limit her activities.
   (3) She should expect her membranes to rupture shortly.
   (4) She should feel less pressure on the lower extremities.

2. During the first prenatal visit, the nurse meets with the couple to discuss the pregnancy. While taking the family history, the nurse learns that this young couple moved to the city 3 months ago from a small town a thousand miles away. Based on this information which of the following areas is MOST important to assess?

   (1) Health history.
   (2) Socioeconomic history.
   (3) Support systems.
   (4) Educational background.

3. A 25-year-old primipara has been pre-eclamptic. Which of the following criteria would indicate successful management of her condition during active labor?

   (1) Decreased contractions.
   (2) Respiratory rate < 16.
   (3) Absence of seizures.
   (4) Absent reflexes.

4. A patient is to undergo outpatient intracapsular extraction of the cataract of the right eye. Which of the following situations could be cause for cancellation of the surgery upon arrival at the facility?

   (1) Patient complains of dryness of mouth.
   (2) Patient complains of arthritic pain of both hands.
   (3) Patient arrives without an escort.
   (4) Patient's significant other does not support decision to have surgery.

5. The nurse is completing a history and assessment of a 70-year-old diabetic patient being admitted into a geriatric unit. Which question would be MOST helpful in eliciting information for an admission assessment?

   (1) Who told you that dates could be included in your diet?
   (2) Do you take daily laxative?
   (3) What do you do when you become shaky?
   (4) You are not having problems with giving yourself insulin, are you?

6. A college student has had a right nephrectomy after an automobile accident. His post-surgery intravenous order reads: (1) 1000 ml. of dextrose in 0.45% saline, (2) 1000 ml. of Ringer's lactate, (3) 1000 ml. of dextrose in 0.45% saline. To ensure that the above IV fluids run for 24 hours, the nurse should set the infusion pump at which rate? (The infusion set delivers 10 drops/ml).

   (1) 35 drops per minute.
   (2) 26 drops per minute.
   (3) 40 drops per minute.
   (4) 21 drops per minute.

7. A 50-year-old woman is receiving warfarin (Coumadin) after replacement of a heart valve. Which of the following statements would indicate that she needs more health teaching regarding the medication?

   (1) "My legs feel heavy."
   (2) "I always take aspirin for headaches."
   (3) "I think I am getting the flu."
   (4) "I ate a chocolate bar the day before yesterday."

8. A physician has prescribed a scopolamine transdermal patch to prevent motion sickness. The nurse should instruct the patient to

   (1) continue to wear while showering.
   (2) apply patch to any hairy surface.
   (3) wear gloves when applying the patch.
   (4) rub the patch for five minutes after application.

9. A 54-year-old woman with 3 married children is admitted to a psychiatric unit because of severe depression. She has lost 20 pounds over a period of 3 weeks. She keeps repeating that she is "better off dead" and that she is "a nobody." Which of the following nursing interventions would provide the patient the GREATEST therapeutic support?

   (1) Convince the patient that her family loves and needs her.
   (2) Help the patient focus attention on how much she has to live for.
   (3) Help the patient recognize the need to express her feelings.
   (4) Advise her to look at the bright side of life.

10. The nurse is reviewing medication administration with the mother of a 2-year-old asthmatic who is recovering from pneumonia. Which of the responses by the mother indicates an understanding of the importance of medication compliance?

    (1) "I can give my child her medicines before breakfast and at bedtime. That way I will not forget."
    (2) "As long as my child feels good, I don't worry about missing a pill or two."
    (3) "These pills are very expensive, so I space them further apart."
    (4) "My child stays with me during the weekdays, so I make sure she gets the medicine then."

11. Which of the following nursing strategies would help a patient deal with feelings of dejection and hopelessness?

    (1) Explain to the patient the dynamics of depression using simple terminologies.
    (2) Invite the patient to recreational therapy to keep her mind off her problems.
    (3) Sit next to the patient for a while but remain silent until the patient initiates the conversation.
    (4) Tell the patient that everyone becomes depressed at some point in their lives.

12. The nurse approaches a 6 year old to administer her preoperative injection. The child asks, "Is this going to hurt?" Which of the following replies indicates the MOST effective nursing intervention?

    (1) "If you lie very still, it won't hurt."
    (2) "Injections don't hurt brave boys and girls."
    (3) "Yes, it will hurt, but I'll stay with you until it stops."
    (4) "Yes, but it will only hurt for a little while."

13. In order to alleviate gastric discomfort after medication administration, the nurse should instruct the patient to take medication

    (1) with breakfast.
    (2) in divided doses.
    (3) with an antiemetic.
    (4) in the evening.

14. Which of the following clinical manifestations is indicative of hemorrhage following a tonsillectomy?

    (1) Dark brown blood emesis.
    (2) Shallow respiration.
    (3) Flushed face.
    (4) Frequent swallowing.

15. To avoid the most common medication error, the nurse should

    (1) question the use of multiple tablets to provide a single dose.
    (2) refuse to interpret illegible handwriting.
    (3) investigate an atypical drug name.
    (4) check medications in question with another nurse.

16. During crutch walking using the 3-point gait, the patient's weight is borne on:

    (1) both crutches.
    (2) both wrists and palms.
    (3) both axilla and chest wall.
    (4) the non-affected limb.

17. Penicillin 250 mg. PO every 6 hours has been ordered. When the nurse enters the room to administer the first dose, the patient states he was on penicillin two years ago and developed hives. Based on this information the nurse should

    (1) administer the drug as ordered and observe for a reaction.
    (2) administer the drug with Benadryl to decrease the chance of reaction.
    (3) withhold the drug and inform the physician of the patient's allergy.
    (4) administer the drug intravenously to bypass gastric absorption.

18. A 55-year-old male bank manager came to the emergency room with a complaint of chest pain. While a complete diagnostic workup is being done, which of the following nursing interventions may be initiated to ease his chest pain?

    (1) Connect patient to cardiac monitor.
    (2) Elevate the head of his stretcher.
    (3) Administer nitroglycerin tablet.
    (4) Administer nasal oxygen 2-4 ml.

19. The nurse reviewing the physician's orders for a head injury patient should question the use of which of these drugs?

    (1) Decadron.
    (2) Phenobarbital.
    (3) Morphine.
    (4) Maalox.

20. Which of the following actions will be MOST effective in helping a patient who is apprehensive and crying to cope with her labor?

    (1) Promote relaxation through reassurance and comfort measures.
    (2) Explain the physiological mechanisms of labor so the patient understands what is happening.
    (3) Distract the patient with other activities.
    (4) Allow the patient to remain agitated if that is her method of coping.

21. A woman in labor should be encouraged to void frequently so that

    (1) the descent of the presenting part is not hindered.
    (2) catheterization is not necessary.
    (3) urine specimens are available to monitor labor.
    (4) rupture of the bladder does not occur.

22. Initial assessment of abdominal distension due to flatulence is BEST done by

    (1) auscultating the abdomen for bowel sounds.
    (2) palpating the abdomen for movement of gas.
    (3) inspecting the abdomen for movement of flatus.
    (4) observing the patient for the passage of gas.

23. A 25-year-old male is having peritoneal dialysis. Which of these interventions by the nurse would be appropriate to minimize his confusion?

    (1) Administering a tranquilizer.
    (2) Providing reality orientation.
    (3) Applying wrist and ankle restraints.
    (4) Providing radio or taped music.

24. A cardiac patient complains of headache shortly after he started using nitroglycerin ointment. The headache is an example of which of the drug's side effects?

    (1) First-pass.
    (2) Local.
    (3) Systemic.
    (4) Anesthetic.

25. A patient who has been diagnosed with chronic myelogenic leukemia is being treated with mithramycin. The nurse selects the nursing diagnosis "risk for injury." This diagnosis is related to

    (1) seizures.
    (2) bleeding tendencies.
    (3) ataxia.
    (4) psychotic reactions.

26. Which of these conditions that accompanies leukemia necessitates that the nurse apply pressure to an injection site longer than usual?

    (1) Leukopenia.
    (2) Thrombocytopenia.
    (3) Leukocytosis.
    (4) Hemophilia.

27. A patient has a Hickman-Broviac catheter. The nurse should follow which of these procedures during the change of dressing?

(1) Place the patient flat, remove the old dressing, and cover with a gauze dressing.
(2) Place the patient in a supine position, remove old dressing, don sterile gloves, cleanse the area first with alcohol then with povidone, cover with transparent dressing.
(3) Place the patient in semi-Fowler's position, cleanse the area with sterile saline solution, and apply povidone before covering with a gauze dressing.
(4) Place the patient flat in bed, don sterile gloves, cleanse the area with saline solution, and cover with a gauze dressing.

28. The physician ordered 2 units of packed cells to be infused. After checking the blood unit with another nurse, the nurse will

(1) monitor the flow rate at 100 drops per minute.
(2) infuse the cells with 5% dextrose.
(3) start the infusion at 20 drops per minute.
(4) observe the patient after infusion for signs of reaction.

29. A nurse interviews a newly admitted patient in a psychiatric unit. Which of the following statements by the nurse is likely to elicit valuable information about the patient's perception of his condition?

(1) "Please tell me why you decided to come to the hospital for treatment."
(2) "Please describe what you are feeling right now."
(3) "Why do you think you are sick?"
(4) "I am here to help you solve your problems. Please feel free to share them with me."

30. A family discovered that their 75-year-old mother, who is hospitalized for treatment of chronic myelogenic leukemia, is receiving a blood transfusion. They questioned the nurse as to the reason. The nurse's BEST response should be

(1) "Your mother is very ill right now and needs the blood transfusion."
(2) "I will have the doctor talk to you."
(3) "Your mother's red blood cells are low because of chemotherapy. This will make her feel better."
(4) "Because of the chemotherapy, your mother is unable to make new red cells; we hope this works."

31. During a nurse-patient interaction, the nurse must utilize various techniques to keep the flow of ideas, thoughts, and feelings moving. Which of the following techniques would achieve this objective?

(1) Keep the patient talking.
(2) Use silence to allow patient to ventilate.
(3) Use words that are likely to encourage the patient to communicate with the nurse.
(4) Use only direct words to keep the conversation focused.

32. Which of the following toys is MOST appropriate for a 3 year old in a mist tent?

(1) Raggedy Ann doll.
(2) Crayons and coloring book.
(3) Bean bag.
(4) Plastic nesting blocks.

33. A culture and sensitivity of the cerebrospinal fluid confirm that a child has meningococcal meningitis. To prevent the spread of infection the nursing staff instructs all people who come in contact with the patient to

(1) wash their hands frequently.
(2) wear a mask.
(3) wear gowns and gloves.
(4) wear mask, gowns, and gloves.

34. A 9-year-old boy has juvenile rheumatoid arthritis. He is to be discharged from the hospital. He was very active in sports before his hospitalization. Which of the following sports could he now participate in?

(1) Baseball.
(2) Skiing.
(3) Swimming.
(4) Hockey.

35. During the administration of packed red cells, the patient complains of shaking and chills. The patient has a fever of 101.6°F. The BEST action by the nurse should be

(1) stop the infusion of red blood cells and infuse 0.9% sodium chloride.
(2) slow the drip rate to 20 drops per minute until symptoms subside.
(3) continue the infusion and administer acetaminophen and antihistamines.
(4) continue the infusion, but observe and record vital signs every 15 minutes.

36. A labor patient's amniotic fluid is greenish in color. In a vertex presentation, the nurse's assessment of this sign would be
    (1) polyhydramnios.
    (2) intrauterine infection.
    (3) staining from Betadine used for examination.
    (4) fetal distress.

37. A nursing diagnosis appropriate for a patient with peptic ulcer and receiving a regimen of antacids and propantheline (Probanthine) would be
    (1) diarrhea related to Probanthine.
    (2) sexual dysfunction related to side effects of antacids.
    (3) altered oral mucosa membrane related to side effects of Probanthine.
    (4) hyperthermia related to the stress of peptic ulcer disease.

38. A post-hysterectomy patient refuses to ambulate because she is experiencing considerable pain. She fears that it would intensify upon ambulation. The appropriate nursing intervention is to
    (1) allow her to remain in bed.
    (2) administer an analgesic.
    (3) notify the physician.
    (4) assist her with ambulation.

39. Ten units of platelets are to be infused. The platelets should be administered
    (1) within 10 minutes.
    (2) over an hour.
    (3) within 2 hours.
    (4) over 30 minutes.

40. The BEST method to evaluate the effectiveness of a patient's coughing and deep breathing exercises is to
    (1) measure his temperature.
    (2) percuss the lung field.
    (3) measure the amount of sputum expectorated.
    (4) auscultate the lung.

41. While straightening the patient's bed, the nurse finds a radium needle among the linen. The appropriate action for the nurse is to
    (1) remove the radium needle with rubber-gloved hands.
    (2) place the radium implant in an emesis basin.
    (3) notify the nuclear medicine department.
    (4) advise the patient to replace the radium implant.

42. Adjustment to cataract glasses will be enhanced if the patient is instructed by the nurse to
    (1) wear glasses only when reading.
    (2) practice looking through the center of the glasses.
    (3) wear glasses when leaving familiar surroundings.
    (4) practice improving his peripheral vision.

43. A patient is experiencing a considerable amount of chest pain upon coughing. Which of the following actions would NOT be helpful in promoting an effective coughing mechanism?
    (1) Assisting the patient to ambulate.
    (2) Splinting the wound site anteriorly and posteriorly while the patient coughs.
    (3) Administering frequent small doses of narcotics to relieve pain.
    (4) Teaching the patient to assume an erect, upright position when coughing.

44. A patient has returned to the ambulatory department medical clinic to have his tine test read. The area injected with purified protein derivative (PPD) has a blisterlike elevation containing fluid. The BEST information to give the patient is
    (1) "You have a negative reaction to the PPD."
    (2) "You have tuberculosis."
    (3) "You will need a chest X-ray and sputum testing."
    (4) "You have a positive reaction to the PPD."

45. The physical therapist reports that a patient refuses to do her exercises because she is experiencing too much pain. Which of the following actions would be MOST effective in getting the patient to comply with her therapy?

(1) Explain to the patient the importance of cooperating in her exercise program.
(2) Suggest to the physician that the exercise program be canceled.
(3) Administer pain medication a half hour before exercises.
(4) Advise the therapist to continue to encourage the patient to exercise.

46. A 42-year-old stock broker, who is a cocaine addict, was admitted by his wife into a drug rehabilitation center. Which of the following responses by his wife indicate an understanding of the BEST approach to take with her husband?

(1) "He really does not have a bad problem, only his work is stressful."
(2) "I tell him all the time that taking drugs and drinking will ruin his life."
(3) "I will no longer make excuses for him; we need to face the problem together."
(4) "He gets mad when I talk about the problem, so it's best to let him quit on his own."

47. An 82-year-old widow is admitted to a hospital because of alternating periods of confusion and lucidity. She is extremely agitated and disoriented. As the nurse approaches, she screams, "Go away! What are you doing in my house?" Which of the following nursing approaches would be MOST likely to provide support for the patient during her confused state?

(1) Place her in a room close to the nurses' station.
(2) Discourage family members from bringing familiar things from home so that she may get used to hospital objects.
(3) See to it that her room is well lighted at night.
(4) Allow her family to stay with her in the evening until bedtime.

48. An 86-year-old woman is hospitalized. She becomes extremely frightened and confused. She states, "I want to get out of this jail!" Which of the following nursing approaches would MOST likely prevent recurrence of confusion?

(1) Establishing a routine for the patient.
(2) Letting her develop her own day-to-day routine.
(3) Letting her help the nurse develop her day-to-day activities.
(4) Asking her to memorize her daily routine activities.

49. A 70-year-old male was admitted to the coronary care unit with a diagnosis of unstable angina. He is placed on telemetry and is to begin isosorbide dinitrate (Isordid tembids) sustained-release 40 mg. tablets. In addition to the nitrate therapy, nifedipine (Procardia) 10 mg. P.O. every 6 hours will be given. The nurse should observe the patient for

(1) hypotension.
(2) tremors.
(3) hyperkalemia.
(4) tetany.

50. A patient is admitted to the labor room at 40 weeks gestation. The nurse collects the following data: contractions are every 3 minutes lasting 45 seconds; membranes are intact; bloody show is present. Which of the following information should be added to the admission history?

(1) The patient's reaction to pain.
(2) The time and description of last food intake.
(3) The date of last prenatal visit.
(4) Health histories of other children.

51. Which of the following statements by a patient with angina pectoris indicates adequate understanding concerning administration of coronary vasodilators?

(1) "I will only have to take pills for a few weeks."
(2) "I can take the long-acting pill anytime during the day."
(3) "If I get a headache, I should stop taking the pills."
(4) "The nitroglycerin is not habit-forming, so I can take as needed."

52. A patient is being treated conservatively for glaucoma. The aim of glaucoma management is to
    (1) inhibit the production of aqueous fluid.
    (2) dilate the pupil to allow for an increase in aqueous fluid drainage.
    (3) prevent the production of aqueous fluid.
    (4) increase visual acuity and production of aqueous fluid.

53. During discharge planning, a mother asks what she should do if her 3 year old develops symptoms of croup at home. The MOST appropriate response by the nurse would be
    (1) "Call your local emergency squad immediately."
    (2) "Further attacks can be prevented by teaching the child appropriate breathing exercises."
    (3) "Take the child into the bathroom, close the door, and turn on a hot shower."
    (4) "Give the child fluids in order to liquefy her secretions."

54. Which of these places should a patient with a pacemaker be advised to avoid?
    (1) Hotels and motels.
    (2) Churches and community centers.
    (3) Theaters and cinema houses.
    (4) Fast-food restaurants.

55. A patient is ready to leave the rehabilitation center, post-cerebrovascular accident. The nurse should advise the wife prior to discharge to
    (1) assist her husband with communication by completing sentences for him.
    (2) encourage her husband to carry out self-care activities.
    (3) feed and bathe her husband and assist with dressing.
    (4) restrict visitors during the evening and holidays.

56. Which of the following variations from the normal routine labor and delivery should a nurse expect for a cardiac patient?
    (1) Not being placed on a fetal monitor.
    (2) Being allowed to only lie on back.
    (3) Vital signs measured every 2 hours.
    (4) Membranes will be ruptured earlier than usual.

57. A patient with acute cholecystitis is being prepared for a cholecystectomy. Which of these drugs, if ordered for pain relief, may cause adverse effects in this patient?
    (1) Nubain.
    (2) Codeine.
    (3) Percodan.
    (4) Demerol.

58. A patient from the nursing home was admitted to a medical unit with a diagnosis of urinary tract infection. Gentamicin via intravenous piggyback is ordered. It will be important for the nurse to monitor which of the following in relation to gentamicin administration?
    (1) Calcium level.
    (2) Creatinine level.
    (3) Sodium level.
    (4) Magnesium level.

59. A child with croup has an increased respiratory rate. Of the following assessment findings, which one should the nurse report immediately?
    (1) Flaring nostrils with each inspiration.
    (2) Restlessness followed by extreme fatigue.
    (3) Substernal retractions.
    (4) Emesis of undigested food.

60. An 84 year old complains of inability to sleep at night while being hospitalized. She was given Nembutal at 10 P.M. The next day she was drowsy and wanted to sleep instead of eating her breakfast. The nurse is aware that this effect is MOST probably due to
    (1) reduced hepatic function.
    (2) reduced cardiac function.
    (3) gentamicin interaction.
    (4) delayed toxic effect.

61. Which of the following must the nurse consider crucial when handling a situation involving a patient's angry verbal abuse directed toward her/him?
    (1) The nurse's awareness of her/his own patterns of response to anger-provoking situations.
    (2) The nurse's ability to recognize anger in the patient.
    (3) The nurse's ability to redirect the patient's anger to more constructive outlets.
    (4) The nurse's ability to assist the patient in accepting the feeling of anger.

62. A schizophrenic patient demonstrates a steady improvement in relating with other patients and staff members on the unit. Which of the following activities is MOST appropriate at this time?

(1) Introducing the patient into a group therapy session.
(2) Having the patient sit and interact with a friendly patient.
(3) Selecting two nonthreatening, nonverbal patients and getting them involved in a card game with the patient.
(4) Sitting and talking with the patient in the company of a friendly patient.

63. After the registered nurse had made the patient assignments for the day, a licensed practical nurse complained, "I have had the same assignment for three weeks, and I am tired of it." The registered nurse should

(1) confirm with her that her complaint is legitimate and change her assignment.
(2) confirm with her that the complaint is legitimate but state that her assignment would be changed the following day.
(3) discuss her complaint with the supervisor at the end of the day.
(4) request to speak with her and the collective bargaining representative at the end of the day.

64. A patient is admitted to the medical intensive care unit in acute respiratory distress related to status asthmaticus. The nursing history reveals that he has NIDDM (non-insulin dependent diabetes mellitus) which is controlled by oral medication. Because he is receiving Solu-Medrol glucocorticoids, the nurse is aware of the risk for

(1) reduced blood glucose levels.
(2) increased effect of hypoglycemic agents.
(3) reduced effectiveness of Solu-Medrol.
(4) increased blood glucose levels.

65. A mother brings her baby to the well baby clinic for immunization. Which of the following findings would contraindicate immunization at this time?

(1) Anemia.
(2) Malnutrition.
(3) Active infection.
(4) Slowed development.

66. Which of these methods should be used to monitor the chest dressing after a mastectomy?

(1) Inspecting the anterior aspect of the dressing.
(2) Lifting the lower edge of the anterior dressing.
(3) Removing the dressing over the axilla.
(4) Inspecting the posterior dressing and the area under the patient.

67. A 32-year-old woman is admitted to a psychiatric unit for evaluation after terrorizing her co-workers with a knife. She is verbally abusive. One afternoon, she starts hitting another female patient without any apparent provocation. The other patient is removed from her presence. Which of the following statements by the nurse would be appropriate handling of the patient's behavior?

(1) "Why did you hit that patient?"
(2) "You will have to stay in the seclusion room to keep you away from other patients."
(3) "Hitting others is dangerous. I am not going to allow you to repeat this behavior."
(4) "I am going to discuss your behavior with other patients at the next ward meeting."

68. A 6 month old is admitted to the pediatric unit with a diagnosis of gastroenteritis. His mother states that he has had 5 to 6 watery, green stools every day for the last 3 days. To which of the following rooms should this baby be assigned?

(1) A private room, with a sink, located across from the nurses' station.
(2) A 2-bedded room, now occupied by a 6-month-old infant with bronchitis.
(3) A private room, located next to the dirty utility room.
(4) A 2-bedded room, now occupied by a 1-month-old infant with pyloric stenosis.

69. A patient is to start the weaning process from a tracheotomy. The nurse should proceed in which of the following ways?

(1) Insert the plug in the outer cannula, and instruct the patient to call if she experiences respiratory distress.

(2) Deflate the cuff, insert the plug, and remove the plug after 5 minutes, observing the patient during this period for respiratory distress.

(3) Suction the patient's tracheotomy thoroughly, and instruct the family to stay at the bedside while the plug is in the inner cannula.

(4) Suction the patient, remove and soak the inner cannula in hydrogen peroxide for five minutes, rinse in saline.

70. Neomycin and lactulose will increase the mental functioning of a patient with hepatic coma by

(1) increasing serum potassium level.

(2) increasing serum sodium level.

(3) reducing bacterial production of ammonia in the intestines.

(4) preventing intestinal infection.

71. Which of the following activities is MOST appropriate for a hospitalized 5 year old who is allowed to go to the playroom?

(1) Joining a group of boys and girls who are playing house.

(2) Looking at a stamp collection that belongs to an 8-year-old boy.

(3) Playing by himself with a racing car.

(4) Building a block tower next to another child who is also playing with blocks.

72. After a baby receives the diphtheria and tetanus toxoid and pertussis (DPT) vaccine, the nurse should teach the mother about potential side effects, which include

(1) mild arthralgia and lymphadenitis.

(2) abdominal pain and tremor.

(3) anorexia and fretfulness.

(4) paralysis and hypertension.

73. A patient is given belcomethasone (Vanceril) inhaler prn for asthma attacks. Which statement indicates adequate understanding of its use?

(1) "Since it is habit forming, I should not use it every day."

(2) "If I have to use the drug more that prescribed, I will call the doctor."

(3) "Nausea and vomiting are side effects to be expected with this drug."

(4) "I should keep the inhaler in a dry, warm place when it is not in use."

74. A 46-year-old woman came to the health clinic with symptoms of postmenopause syndrome. The nurse takes a diet history and will encourage a high dietary intake of

(1) potassium.

(2) sodium.

(3) calcium.

(4) vitamin C.

75. The nurse is preparing to suction a patient with a tracheotomy. Before inserting the catheter, the nurse should

(1) insert hydrogen peroxide into the tracheotomy.

(2) remove the inner cannula.

(3) administer 100% oxygen via ambu bag.

(4) ask the patient to cough.

76. Which of the following would be an appropriate intervention for a patient who is being admitted for threatened abortion?

(1) Reassure her that everything will be fine.

(2) Allow her to verbalize her feelings about this threat to her pregnancy.

(3) Explain to her that spontaneous abortion is nature's way of expelling defective embryos.

(4) Reassure her that, if she does abort, she will still be able to have other children.

77. The nurse is taking the health history of a college student who is suspected to have infectious hepatitis (hepatitis A). Which of the following statements would be important in establishing the diagnosis?

(1) "I gave blood 3 weeks ago."

(2) "I had clams for lunch last summer."

(3) "My roommate had the same symptoms 1 month ago."

(4) "During my surgery 3 months ago, I received a pint of blood."

78. A patient with left-sided hemiplegia, homonymous hemianopsia, and some aphasia regains consciousness. The nurse, who is present when the patient awakens, notices his confusion. The appropriate action at this time is to

(1) walk over to his right side and inform him that he has had a "stroke."
(2) notify the physician.
(3) allow the patient to recover from his confusion.
(4) walk over to the patient's left side and reassure him.

79. An ambulatory 80-year-old female nursing home resident is admitted to the hospital for treatment of urinary tract infection (UTI). The patient has reported to the nursing staff, within an hour of consuming a meal, that she had not been fed. The nurse would describe this behavior in her nurse's notes as

(1) long-term memory intact.
(2) registration/retention unimpaired.
(3) orient to time, place, and person.
(4) short-term memory impaired.

80. A measure to cope with urinary incontinence in a male patient is to

(1) restrict fluids.
(2) insert an indwelling catheter.
(3) apply an external catheter.
(4) apply a diaper.

81. A 63-year-old male with a possible cerebrovascular accident of the left cerebral hemisphere is brought into the emergency room. In which of these body and head positions should the nurse place the patient?

(1) On back, head turned to right side.
(2) Body turned to right side, head positioned to left side.
(3) Body and head positioned to left side.
(4) Body positioned on right side and head turned to the left side.

82. Discharge teaching for patients after surgery for a detached retina should include advising the patient which of the following activities can be performed at home?

(1) Reading a book.
(2) Watching television.
(3) Playing tennis.
(4) Swimming.

83. Two days after having a colostomy, a patient refuses to look at her stoma during the dressing change. The appropriate action by the nurse is to

(1) encourage her to look at the stoma.
(2) notify the doctor.
(3) continue to change the dressing.
(4) teach a family member to change the dressing.

84. A patient who is an admitted cocaine addict also admits to drinking a "glass or two" of vodka along with cocaine daily. The nurse is aware that the combination of alcohol and cocaine use represents

(1) dual addiction.
(2) cross tolerance.
(3) mixed addiction.
(4) dual tolerance.

85. A patient appears withdrawn after a mastectomy although her recovery is uneventful. The nurse can be helpful during this period by

(1) allowing the patient time alone so that she can reflect on her surgery.
(2) encouraging the patient to talk to her family.
(3) offering the patient the name of a support group.
(4) encouraging the patient to become involved in her exercises.

86. Which of the following factors in a mother's history would put a newborn at risk for infection?

(1) Rupture of membranes more than 24 hours before delivery.
(2) Bleeding episodes during the second trimester.
(3) Urinary tract infection during her third trimester.
(4) Use of Pitocin during labor.

87. A patient is placed on Coumadin 10 mg. daily. The nurse will check which of the following laboratory data daily?

(1) Prothrombin time (PT).
(2) Partial thromboplastin time (PTT).
(3) Lee-White clotting time (LWCT).
(4) Activated clotting time (ACT).

88. Which of these items should both a patient with a pacemaker and a diabetic carry on their person?

(1) Identification card or bracelet.
(2) Eye drops and nitroglycerin tablets.
(3) Glucose tablets and candy.
(4) Batteries and eyeglasses.

89. A patient is admitted to a mental hospital. The patient has a history of attempted suicide by drug overdose. The nurse should implement which of the following interventions FIRST?

(1) Obtain blood sample for drug toxicity screen.
(2) Assess neurological function.
(3) Measure vital signs.
(4) Elevate the legs to increase circulation.

90. A patient arrives in the emergency room in acute respiratory distress. He also has an extensive rash and heart palpitations. A nursing assessment reveals that he recently began taking penicillin for bronchitis. Which of the following drugs, if ordered, would the nurse question?

(1) Vasopressors.
(2) Antihistamines.
(3) Bronchodilators.
(4) Antibiotics.

91. The nurse is developing a nursing care plan for a patient after eye surgery. A nursing diagnosis that should be included in the nursing care plan is

(1) pain related to pressure.
(2) risk for pressure ulcer.
(3) risk for injury related to postoperative alteration in visual acuity.
(4) disturbed self-concept related to chronic disease.

92. A patient has been taking an antihistamine for symptoms associated with sinusitis. To minimize the side effect of sedation, the nurse should teach the patient before discharge to

(1) take the antihistamine at bedtime.
(2) ingest extra coffee during the day.
(3) combine the antihistamine with a central nervous system stimulant.
(4) continue to perform usual activities despite drowsiness.

93. A nursing home resident has been admitted to a geriatric floor. The patient wanders around the floor during waking hours. A nursing intervention to prevent fatigue and injury is to

(1) restrain the patient with leather cuffs in bed.
(2) maintain bedrest with side-rails up.
(3) place the patient in a Geri-chair with lap table, and assist with ambulation every 2 hours.
(4) apply a body restraint and place the patient in a Geri-chair at the nurse's station.

94. A patient having a bone marrow transplant is placed on which of the following isolations after the conditioning phase?

(1) Strict isolation.
(2) Respiratory isolation.
(3) Isolation precaution.
(4) Protective isolation.

95. Which of the following would NOT affect the severity of withdrawal symptoms in the drug-addicted newborn?

(1) The withdrawal symptoms exhibited by the mother.
(2) The length of addiction of the mother.
(3) The amount of drug-dosage the mother has ingested.
(4) The time between the mother's last dose and delivery.

96. Aluminum hydroxide is an antacid administered to patients with chronic renal failure because it

(1) reduces the potential for constipation.
(2) prevents absorption of phosphate from the gastrointestinal tract.
(3) blocks absorption of calcium from the gastrointestinal tract.
(4) interferes with nitrogen and protein assimilation.

97. The physician treating a 46-year-old woman, newly diagnosed as diabetic, prescribed that she be taught insulin administration. This patient's ability to effectively internalize the procedure for self-administration of insulin may be MOST affected by

(1) type of syringe.
(2) previous health care experience.
(3) cultural background.
(4) recent diabetic diagnosis.

98. An 18 month old is brought to the emergency room with second and third degree burns on both her hands. The nurse in the emergency room does an initial assessment of the child. Which of the following findings should be communicated immediately to the physician?

(1) Pallor, a temperature of 101°F, and a blood pressure of 90/60.

(2) Flushed face, a pulse rate of 100, and a respiratory rate of 26.

(3) Poor skin turgor, a blood pressure of 100/68, and a pulse rate of 90.

(4) Cold, clammy skin, a pulse rate of 140, and a respiratory rate of 36.

99. The purpose of administering heparin before starting hemodialysis is to

(1) dissolve blood cells.

(2) reduce inflammation.

(3) prevent clotting of the blood.

(4) reduce bleeding.

100. A patient is to have a saphenous vein coronary artery bypass graft procedure (CABG). He and his wife are anxious about his surgery. Which of these nursing interventions would do the MOST to reduce their anxiety?

(1) Providing information about the upcoming surgery.

(2) Introducing them to someone who has undergone this surgery.

(3) Directing them to refer all questions to the surgeon.

(4) Allowing them to ventilate their feelings about the impending surgery.

101. A nurse comes to talk to a patient. The patient says, "Go away, I don't want to talk today." Which of the following responses by the nurse would be MOST appropriate?

(1) "If you don't want to talk now, I'll leave. Call me whenever you're ready. I will be in the day room."

(2) "I'll sit here with you for a while."

(3) "Why don't you want to talk today?"

(4) "Have I done something today that you don't like?"

102. Which of the following statements indicates successful patient teaching concerning digoxin use?

(1) "I will only have to take this drug for a month or two, until my heart heals."

(2) "If I miss a dose, I should eliminate it and not take two in one day."

(3) "If I have any nausea or vomiting I should stop taking the medicine."

(4) "A little swelling in my feet or ankles is not uncommon with this medicine."

103. A 4 month old is brought to a sickle-cell screening clinic. The Sickledex test performed on the baby is positive. The nurse should tell the mother

(1) "Your baby has sickle-cell anemia."

(2) "Your baby does not have sickle-cell anemia or sickle-cell trait."

(3) "We do not know if your baby has sickle-cell trait or sickle-cell anemia."

(4) "We need to do a sickle-cell prep."

104. Which of the following statements indicates an understanding of the hypertensive treatment regime?

(1) "If I miss a dose, I should take 2 at the next dosage time."

(2) "I should take pills when I feel like my blood pressure is high."

(3) "For relaxation, I plan to soak in our hot tub everyday."

(4) "I am not supposed to stop taking the drug if I feel dizzy."

105. Which of the following nursing diagnoses can be used for patients with bulimia and anorexia nervosa?

(1) Altered nutrition: less than body requirement related to self-starvation.

(2) Body image disturbance related to overestimation of size of body.

(3) Ineffective individual coping related to inability to control eating habit.

(4) Knowledge deficit regarding coping with nutrition.

106. Which of the following behaviors by a 58-year-old cardiac patient indicates successful patient teaching?

    (1) Neglecting to report symptoms such as nausea.

    (2) Reporting a weight gain of over two pounds per week.

    (3) Taking the pulse rate once a week.

    (4) Maintaining yearly blood pressure check-ups.

107. A patient has joint rigidity secondary to Parkinson's disease. Which of the following interventions will prevent joint deformity?

    (1) Application of hot packs, twice daily.

    (2) Participation in a daily progressive exercise program.

    (3) Maintaining bedrest during periods of stiffness.

    (4) Passive range-of-motion exercises, 3 times a week.

108. When assessing a patient with chronic bronchitis for evidence of bronchial obstruction, the nurse should observe the patient for

    (1) bronchial breath sounds.

    (2) use of accessory muscles.

    (3) slowed pulse.

    (4) prolonged inspiration.

109. The nurse assesses that a patient is positively motivated to learn about his cardiac medication because he

    (1) states that he will take his medication as ordered.

    (2) avoids having his wife attend the teaching session.

    (3) misses 50% of the questions on the medication pretest.

    (4) asks many questions about his health and medication.

110. In order to promote desired learning outcomes, the nurse would use which of the following as a positive reinforcer?

    (1) Separation.

    (2) Money.

    (3) Smiling.

    (4) Punishment.

111. A 68-year-old male was diagnosed as having Parkinson's disease and was placed on L-Dopa, 250 mg., PO 3 times a day for 3 weeks. He is returning to the clinic for evaluation of his treatment. Which of the following would indicate that the patient is compliant with medication administration?

    (1) Weight gain of 2 lbs.

    (2) Patient holds thermometer in mouth.

    (3) Masklike facial expression.

    (4) Complaint of rigidity of shoulders and neck.

112. A patient's blood pressure is to be measured to assess the occurrence of postural hypotension. The nurse should measure the patient's blood pressure in

    (1) both arms, sitting and standing.

    (2) left arm, sitting.

    (3) left arm, sitting and standing.

    (4) both arms, sitting.

113. Which of the following statements indicates the need for further teaching concerning the use of beclomethasone (Varicin) via metered-dose inhaler?

    (1) "I should fully inhale before depressing the cartridge."

    (2) "I should wait 1 to 2 minutes before taking a second inhalation."

    (3) "It is best to use only 1 to 2 puffs at a dosage schedule."

    (4) "The nebulizer cartridge should be shaken well before using."

114. A patient with chronic obstructive pulmonary disease (COPD) is admitted to the emergency room. Which of the following oxygen concentrations would be MOST appropriate?

    (1) 100% per non-rebreather mask.

    (2) 28% per Venturi mask.

    (3) 60% per aerosol mask.

    (4) 80% per reservoir mask.

115. Depression is considered to be a precursor of suicide. Which of the following nursing actions could prevent future suicide attempts?

    (1) Letting the patient know that the health care team will not allow her to do anything that is potentially self-destructive.
    (2) Keeping the patient in a seclusion room at all times.
    (3) Diverting the patient's attention away from suicide by focusing all conversations on the patient's hobbies and interests.
    (4) Describing behavior on the patient's progress record.

116. A psychotic patient becomes extremely agitated and highly delusional. He paces up and down the halls all day and all night. He has not slept for several nights. Which of the following nursing diagnoses should the nurse add to her nursing care plan?

    (1) Sleep pattern disturbance related to physiological disturbance caused by anxiety.
    (2) Knowledge deficit regarding recognition and effective management of anxiety.
    (3) Ineffective individual coping related to perception of situation.
    (4) Disturbances in self-concept related to instability of interpersonal relationship.

117. A 65-year-old widow is admitted to a psychiatric unit. She states that her life is not worth living anymore because she is "useless and no good to anybody." Her 3 children are all married with families. She has numerous physical complaints. She is unable to concentrate and has a poor memory. She is preoccupied with thoughts of death. Which of the following nursing diagnoses should the nurse add to the patient's care plan?

    (1) Knowledge deficit related to loss.
    (2) Ineffective individual coping related to irrational avoidance of situations.
    (3) Anxiety related to irrational thoughts or guilt.
    (4) Sleep pattern disturbance related to recurrent nightmares.

118. A 67-year-old female is hospitalized for a diagnostic workup for abdominal pain. Prior to barium studies, the patient complained of increasing abdominal pain with rigidity or vomiting. The nurse's BEST response would be to

    (1) administer analgesics and narcotics by intramuscular injection.
    (2) inform the physician and prepare to cancel barium studies.
    (3) prepare to give barium via intravenous route and keep NPO.
    (4) prepare to give barium sulfate via a nasogastric tube.

119. A new mother is concerned that her baby might catch "germs" from her while breast-feeding. The MOST important measure she should be taught to prevent bacterial contamination of the baby is

    (1) wearing sterile pads inside her bra.
    (2) not allowing anyone in the room while she breast-feeds.
    (3) washing her hands before each feeding.
    (4) cleansing her nipples daily with an antiseptic solution.

120. During her second trimester, a pregnant woman tells the nurse she is experiencing constipation. Which of the following would be the MOST appropriate intervention for this problem?

    (1) Milk of magnesia every night at bedtime.
    (2) Increased fat and protein in the diet.
    (3) Increased cellulose and fluid in the diet.
    (4) Dulcolax suppository every morning.

121. A 20-year-old primipara in her second trimester of pregnancy is being screened in the antipartal clinic for gestational diabetes. Her fasting blood glucose level is 160 mg/dl. She asked her nurse if she had diabetes. The nurse should reply

    (1) "We will need a second fasting blood glucose tomorrow."
    (2) "Yes, you have diabetes mellitus."
    (3) "No, your blood glucose level is within normal range."
    (4) "No, you have an elevated blood glucose because you are pregnant."

122. The first muscle of choice for an intramuscular injection for a 3 month old is the

(1) vastus lateralis.
(2) dorsogluteal.
(3) ventrogluteal.
(4) deltoid.

123. A woman delivers her first child who has a meningomyelocele. The woman tells the nurse she knows this happened because she smoked and was not careful about her diet during her pregnancy. The nurse should reply

(1) "Yes, smoking can cause a variety of defects in the unborn child."
(2) "We don't know the cause of defects such as your baby's."
(3) "I'm sure that smoking and a poor diet did not cause the defect."
(4) "It's true that you gained a lot of weight during your pregnancy."

124. A patient was given naloxone (Narcan) 0.1 mg. IV in order to reverse the effects of narcotics administered during surgery. The nurse should assess the patient after Narcan administration for

(1) respiratory difficulty.
(2) dry mouth.
(3) intense pain.
(4) urine output.

125. A patient has been admitted in a chemical dependency unit with intoxication of an unknown substance. He demonstrates severe anxiety and panic. Which of the following nursing actions should the nurse initiate immediately?

(1) Restrain to prevent injury to self.
(2) Administer antipsychotic medication.
(3) Implement seizure precaution.
(4) Provide a quiet environment.

126. A 63-year-old male with a history of uncontrolled hypertension is brought unconscious to the emergency room. Which of the following statements by the wife should be included on the assessment form?

(1) "My husband has had several attacks of weakness of the arms and legs during the last 3 weeks."
(2) "My husband's father died from cancer of the prostate."
(3) "High blood pressure runs in my family."
(4) "My husband has a high pressure job."

127. A postoperative nursing diagnosis that should be included in a nursing care plan of a patient after a colostomy is

(1) anxiety related to loss of bowel control.
(2) potential impairment of skin integrity related to bedrest.
(3) body image disturbance related to change or loss of body function.
(4) sexual dysfunction related to altered body image.

128. A 45-year-old patient with a history of alcohol abuse is hospitalized with swelling of the legs and abdomen. In the past two weeks he has vomited moderate amounts of blood and is presently disoriented. In view of the patient's admitting health history and symptoms, his initial assessment should include

(1) observing the arms and hands for flapping tremors.
(2) auscultating the chest for congestion.
(3) inspecting the skin for dryness.
(4) percussing the chest for rales.

129. A patient on heparin therapy complains of headache and requests medication. Which of the following NSAIDS (non-steroidal anti inflammatory drugs), if ordered, would be used?

(1) Aspirin.
(2) Acetaminophen.
(3) Ibuprofen.
(4) Idomethacin.

130. During suctioning the nurse should remember to

(1) lubricate the catheter with tap water before insertion.
(2) apply suction during the insertion of the catheter.
(3) apply suction for 10 seconds.
(4) maintain the patient's head in a neutral position.

131. A patient with exophthalmic goiter has had a subtotal thyroidectomy. Which of the following symptoms, should they occur, be reported immediately to the physician?

(1) Decreased blood pressure.
(2) Dyspnea.
(3) Drop in pulse rate.
(4) Headache.

132. A patient has had an elevated temperature for 3 days. Both her skin and her sclera are jaundiced and her urine is dark in color. In view of the patient's symptoms, which of the following assessment techniques should be part of the physical assessment?

    (1) Observe the mental state.
    (2) Palpate the abdomen.
    (3) Percuss the abdomen.
    (4) Auscultate the abdomen.

133. A nurse aide has been complaining about her assignment to the patients and her peers. She also complained about time for breaks, poor organization, and the charge nurse's personality. As the charge nurse on the floor you should

    (1) ignore the problem; it will eventually solve itself.
    (2) report the incident to the supervisor.
    (3) confront the nurse aide at the nurse's station and inquire why she is dissatisfied with her assignment.
    (4) arrange for a meeting with the nurse aide in the conference room to discuss her complaints.

134. Discharge teaching for a patient receiving Coumadin therapy would include

    (1) take 2 pills in 1 day if a daily dose is missed.
    (2) avoid drinking liquor, beer, or wine.
    (3) eat a diet high in leafy green vegetables.
    (4) take over-the-counter medicine as needed.

135. The primary purpose of using combination chemotherapy in the treatment of Hodgkin's disease is to

    (1) prevent resistance of the tumor to one drug.
    (2) prevent recurrence of the disease.
    (3) reduce pain and complication.
    (4) reduce the tumor mass with minimal toxic effect.

136. An asthmatic is receiving oral theophylline. The nurse should observe the patient for which of the following side effects?

    (1) Difficulty voiding.
    (2) Drowsiness.
    (3) Palpitations.
    (4) Confusion.

137. A patient is recovering from a craniotomy. He is receiving mannitol. Which of the following outcomes BEST represents therapeutic effects of mannitol therapy?

    (1) Improved neurological status.
    (2) Improved intercranial pressure.
    (3) Decreased peripheral edema.
    (4) Enhanced creatinine clearance.

138. A school nurse conducting a health screening clinic of adolescents should refer which of these adolescents for further diagnostic follow-up?

    (1) An adolescent with a convex curve in the upper back and a concave curve in the lower back when bent forward at the waist.
    (2) An adolescent with eruption of wisdom teeth upon oral examination.
    (3) An adolescent with proliferation of pubic and axillary hair, and swelling of breasts upon physical examination.
    (4) An adolescent with patches/areas of papules on the face, neck, shoulder, and upper chest.

139. A patient is admitted to a psychiatric unit because of severe withdrawal and regressive behavior. The patient is unable to attend to his personal hygiene and his personal appearance begins to deteriorate. The nurse would add which of the following nursing diagnoses to the patient's nursing care plan?

    (1) A symbolic effort to eradicate a painful life experience.
    (2) A symbolic retreat to an earlier level of adjustment that proved successful.
    (3) Banishment of unacceptable wishes from the patient's consciousness.
    (4) The turning of interest inward to a total self-preoccupation.

140. A patient tells the nurse that she feels like she is trapped in a cave. "Oh, why am I saying this to you? You don't know what it's like to be trapped like this." What should the nurse's response be?

    (1) "I guess I don't."
    (2) "Trapped? What do you mean by being trapped in a cave?"
    (3) "Why do you feel trapped?"
    (4) "Being trapped anywhere must be an uncomfortable feeling."

141. An adolescent patient is admitted to a psychiatric unit with a diagnosis of borderline personality disorder. Which of the following nursing diagnoses should be included in his nursing care plan?

(1) Risk for violence: self-directed or directed at others related to inability to control anger.

(2) Ineffective individual coping related to anxiety.

(3) Altered thought process related to misinterpretation of reality.

(4) Knowledge deficit regarding available community resources.

142. A patient is placed on Premarin to ease the symptoms of postmenopausal syndrome. Patient teaching included restricted sodium intake and regular weight checks. Additional teaching should include

(1) reducing intake of vitamin C.

(2) avoiding large meals.

(3) taking medication after meals.

(4) preventing excessive sun exposure.

143. A patient receives NPH Humulin insulin at 7:30 A.M. At what time of the day would the nurse be alert to the potential for a hypoglycemic reaction?

(1) After breakfast.

(2) At midnight.

(3) Before bedtime.

(4) Before supper.

144. The wife of a patient who has had a cerebrovascular accident wished to know whether her husband will be permanently paralyzed. The nurse's explanation should be

(1) "He should regain some function; much of his paralysis is due to edema of the brain tissue."

(2) "No, his present symptoms are part of a hysterical reaction."

(3) "New neurons will not regenerate to replace the damaged cells; therefore the symptoms will not subside."

(4) "He will regain all of his original muscle strength."

145. Which of the following would be MOST likely to precipitate acidosis in a pregnant diabetic?

(1) Decrease in salt intake.

(2) Decreased activity.

(3) Nausea and vomiting.

(4) Hypertension.

146. A patient recently diagnosed with AIDS is being treated at a clinic specializing in health care for AIDS patients. While providing care for the patient after 6 months of Zidovudine (AZT) therapy, the nurse will be mindful of which of the following?

(1) Respiratory isolation.

(2) AIDS transmission precautions.

(3) Isolation precaution.

(4) No precaution necessary.

147. A patient is to have a left pneumonectomy. Which of these measures, if taught preoperatively, will be of benefit to the patient after surgery?

(1) Turning and positioning.

(2) Coughing and deep breathing techniques.

(3) Use of the incentive spirometer.

(4) Suctioning and deep breathing techniques.

148. A 78-year-old patient has been admitted to the geriatric unit. A week later according to the nurse's notes, the patient has not passed stool in 4 days. Prior to giving her a laxative, the nurse will check for evidence of

(1) confusion.

(2) fecal impaction.

(3) anxiety.

(4) urinary incontinence.

149. A 20-year-old male was involved in a motorcycle accident. At the scene of the accident, he complained of inability to move his extremities. X-rays taken in the emergency room show vertebral damage at C_4. Which of these findings exhibited by the patient on admission will necessitate immediate intervention?

(1) Irregular breathing pattern.

(2) Temperature of 100°F.

(3) Headache.

(4) Sluggish bowel sounds.

150. A patient with cirrhosis due to alcoholism is admitted to the intensive care unit (ICU). His abdomen is distended and firm and he has pitting edema of the lower extremities. He is to receive lactulose (Cephulac) every 4 hours. The nurse will anticipate which of the following effects of the drug?

    (1) Nausea and vomiting.
    (2) Frequent stools.
    (3) Tremors and muscle spams.
    (4) Skin rash.

151. A 45-year-old woman is admitted to a psychiatric unit after a suicide attempt. She is described by her husband as "an outgoing, highly ambitious, sensitive person who gets along with nearly everyone." She has no previous suicide attempts. Her 18-year-old daughter was diagnosed with acute leukemia a month ago. The woman has lost 15 pounds over the last 3 weeks. She has lost her appetite. She refuses to eat and drink. She sits on her bed, staring at the floor. Which of the following nursing interventions is a priority in caring for this patient?

    (1) Physical needs.
    (2) Safety needs.
    (3) Activity needs.
    (4) Self-care needs.

152. A patient is bleeding profusely from an above-the-knee stump. The appropriate nursing intervention is to

    (1) reinforce the dressing.
    (2) apply a tourniquet above the stump.
    (3) notify the physician.
    (4) elevate the stump.

153. A patient has a prolonged labor due to uterine dysfunction. In the first 12 hours postpartum, the nurse will assess frequently for signs of

    (1) toxemia.
    (2) uterine atony.
    (3) abdominal distention.
    (4) urinary tract infection.

154. Which of the following combinations of maternal and fetal blood have the potential for incompatibility?

    (1) Rh-positive mother with Rh-positive baby.
    (2) Rh-positive mother with Rh-negative baby.
    (3) Rh-negative mother with Rh-negative baby.
    (4) Rh-negative mother with Rh-positive baby.

155. Milk of magnesia is ordered prn every evening for a patient. The nurse should assess for evidence of renal disease because this drug contains a large concentration of

    (1) purine.
    (2) iron.
    (3) potassium.
    (4) sodium.

156. An 18 month old has burns and multiple bruises over the body. Child abuse is suspected. The nurse interviews the child's parents to obtain a health history. Which of the following information would the nurse include in her notes?

    (1) The toddler had all of the immunizations that are appropriate for this age.
    (2) The mother and father give different versions of how the toddler received the burns and bruises.
    (3) Both parents were extremely upset over the toddler's injuries.
    (4) The mother asked to stay with the child in the emergency room.

157. Which of the following actions by a patient with tuberculosis demonstrates that he does NOT fully understand his drug therapy?

    (1) He takes pyridoxine along with other drugs.
    (2) He takes his daily tuberculin medication in divided doses.
    (3) He reports side effects to his physician.
    (4) He asks the pharmacist for the drugs by name.

158. Post-prostatectomy, a patient is having continuous bladder irrigation. The patient is experiencing bladder spasm. A nursing intervention that can relieve the spasm is

    (1) administering an analgesic.
    (2) clearing the drainage apparatus of obstruction.
    (3) increasing the flow of solution through the bladder drainage.
    (4) applying warm compresses to the lower abdomen.

159. Neomycin is administered to a patient with acute cirrhosis. While on neomycin therapy, the nurse will check the daily lab work for elevation of

    (1) white blood cells.
    (2) amylase.
    (3) creatinine.
    (4) $T_3 T_4$.

160. Which of these nursing diagnoses should the nurse include in a nursing care plan of a patient who has attempted suicide?

   (1) Knowledge deficit regarding constructive methods of life management.
   (2) Self-care deficit related to confusion and forgetfulness.
   (3) Altered thought processes related to cerebral pathology.
   (4) Ineffective coping related to anxiety.

161. When teaching a patient about signs and symptoms of hypoglycemia, the nurse should include which of the following signs?

   (1) Sweating.
   (2) Increased urination.
   (3) Intense thirst.
   (4) Weight loss.

162. The nurse is developing a nursing care plan for a patient with congestive heart failure with pulmonary edema. A nursing diagnosis that should be included in the plan of care is

   (1) risk for fluid volume excess related to right-sided heart failure.
   (2) ineffective individual coping related to external stressors.
   (3) altered comfort related to inflammation and infection.
   (4) risk for caregiver role strain related to long-term care.

163. A patient with rheumatoid arthritis is being placed on drug therapy with ibuprofen (Motrin) 200 mg. three times a day. The nurse at the clinic should provide him with which of the following information about this drug?

   (1) Wear a hat outdoors to prevent sun exposure.
   (2) Expect water retention and weight gain.
   (3) Use in conjunction with aspirin for relief of pain.
   (4) Take with food to reduce gastric irritation.

164. After successful treatment of thyroid crisis, a patient is being discharged with Propyltheouraid (PTU) 30 mg. and Lugol's solution 0.3 ml. 3 times a day as ordered. Which of the following foods should be eliminated from his diet?

   (1) Seafood.
   (2) Alcohol.
   (3) Green vegetables.
   (4) Citrus fruits.

155. While assisting a patient to breast-feed her infant, the nurse tells her to place the brown pigmented area around the nipple well into the baby's mouth. This position of the nipple would

   (1) promote erection of the nipple.
   (2) minimize breast engorgement.
   (3) make the infant feel more secure.
   (4) improve the efficiency of the baby's sucking.

166. The nurse can prevent infection of the sac of an infant with meningomyelocele by

   (1) handling the infant carefully.
   (2) changing diapers often.
   (3) covering the sac with a sterile moist dressing.
   (4) positioning the infant in a prone or side-lying position.

167. An alcoholic patient whose condition is improving tells the nurse that he does not think he will be able to stop drinking alcohol. The BEST response by the nurse is

   (1) "Why do you think you will never be able to stop drinking?"
   (2) "I'm sure that if you try you'll be able to stop drinking."
   (3) "You think that you'll never be able to stop drinking?"
   (4) "It's worth trying."

168. A terminally ill patient becomes very quiet and verbally uncommunicative. Friends and relatives who visit the patient try to cheer him up. This pattern of behavior on the part of his visitors reflects

   (1) a very strong supportive attitude.
   (2) a lack of open acknowledgment of the dying patient's situation.
   (3) a healthy response to the dying process.
   (4) hopefulness.

169. Which of the following interventions will facilitate maintenance of adequate nutrition in an infant with hydrocephalus?

   (1) Offering her thickened feedings.
   (2) Supporting her head during feeding.
   (3) Handling her minimally after feeding.
   (4) Positioning her on her left side after feeding.

170. A 6 year old has been diagnosed with Type I diabetes, insulin dependent diabetes mellitus. The potential nursing diagnosis category that BEST fits the clinical situation is

(1) altered growth and development.
(2) self-care deficit.
(3) anxiety.
(4) sleep pattern disturbance.

171. A nurse is assigned to administer an enema to a child with Hirschsprung's disease. Which of the following solutions should be utilized?

(1) Tap water.
(2) Soap suds.
(3) Sodium phosphate.
(4) Normal saline.

172. Which of these statements by a mother of a diabetic child indicates a need for further education?

(1) "It is important to accurately prepare the dosages of insulin."
(2) "The insulin should be injected at a 90 degree level."
(3) "Some kind of sugar should always be available in case of reaction."
(4) "Periods of increased exercise will mean my child will need more insulin."

173. A new mother in the postpartum unit states that she had no opportunity to use the ointment she received at the clinic for pruritus and a thick, curdlike vaginal discharge before she was admitted in labor. This information should alert the nursery staff to

(1) place her baby in newborn isolation.
(2) observe her baby for ophthalmia neonatorum.
(3) inspect umbilical cord.
(4) assess eyes for thrush.

174. Which of the following individuals taking care of an elderly patient is most at risk for caregiver role strain?

(1) A 45-year-old female who employs 2 12-hour companions for her elderly parent.
(2) A 63-year-old retired teacher caring for her mother.
(3) A 50-year-old widower who has recently moved back home to take care of his elderly father.
(4) An unemployed 30-year-old male bus driver living with his mother who has recently been diagnosed with Alzheimer's.

175. A 60-year-old male leukemia patient is receiving an allogenic bone marrow transplant. During the conditioning stage, he is receiving total body irradiation. A nursing diagnosis that should be added to the patient nursing care plan is

(1) altered nutrition less than body requirement related to persistent nausea and vomiting.
(2) pain related to impaired circulation for ambulation.
(3) risk for self-concept disturbance related to appearance changes.
(4) risk for injury related to decreased tactile sensation.

176. A patient strikes the nurse and later apologizes, saying, "I am sorry. I really didn't mean it. I don't know why I did it." What would be the nurse's MOST appropriate response?

(1) "Don't worry about it, I know you didn't mean to hurt me."
(2) "As long as you realize that what you did was wrong, I forgive you."
(3) "I was really surprised. Why did you do it?"
(4) "You must have had a very strong feeling about something that made you angry."

177. A patient with a history of schizophrenia has been readmitted to the psychiatric unit. He is placed on thiothixene (Navane). After 2 weeks of therapy the patient complains of difficulty in swallowing and chewing. The nurse also notices that the patient is experiencing muscle spasms of face, neck, legs, and arms. The nurse informs the physician and is aware that these symptoms relate to

(1) excessive anticholinergic effects of the medication.
(2) psychotic effect of schizophrenia.
(3) extrapyramdial reaction to the medication.
(4) manifestation of situational crisis of hospitalization.

178. A 45-year-old diabetic is placed on an oral hypoglycemic agent, chloropropamide (Diabanese). If he takes Diabanese at 8 A.M., he should expect the drug's peak activity to be at

(1) 12:00 midnight.
(2) 8:00 P.M.
(3) 4:00 P.M.
(4) 10:00 P.M.

179. A patient is being seen in the clinic because of difficulty in sleeping. In addition she complains of feeling "panicked" when in crowded situations. She is to begin treatment with Xanax 0.5 mg. PO 3 times a day. The clinic nurse should focus on which of the following during the assessment stage?

(1) Response to phobic situations.
(2) Physiological symptoms only.
(3) Response to counseling.
(4) Psychological symptoms only.

180. During assessment, a patient who sustained back injuries in an accident 5 years ago described the pain as nagging and burning. It was also stated "the pain is the focus of my life." These symptoms are the characteristic of which type of pain?

(1) Chronic.
(2) Psychologic.
(3) Phantom.
(4) Acute.

181. The BEST method to check a dressing for bleeding after a thyroidectomy is to

(1) loosen the edge of the dressing and lift it to permit direct observation of the wound.
(2) press the skin surrounding the incision.
(3) turn the patient's head to the side to permit full visualization of the dressing.
(4) slip a hand under the patient's neck and shoulders to feel for dampness of the dressing or bed linen.

182. A patient during and after a bone marrow transplant must *avoid* which of the following until white blood cells return to normal?

(1) Cooked fruits and vegetables.
(2) Flowers and plants in the bedroom.
(3) Shellfish and aged cheese.
(4) Household pets.

183. The nurse notes tiny, pearly white spots on the nose and forehead of a newborn she is admitting to the nursery. The nurse should

(1) place the newborn in the isolation nursery.
(2) notify the physician immediately.
(3) do nothing beyond recording presence in nurse's note.
(4) cleanse areas with a betadine solution twice a day.

184. A patient with open-angle glaucoma is to begin treatment with pilocarpine .25% 2 ghs. every 6 hours. The nurse should include in her teaching that

(1) eyelids should be covered with a warm compress after administration of eyedrops.
(2) dryness of the mouth and throat may occur.
(3) visual acuity will be reduced in dim light.
(4) a burning sensation indicates that the drug dose should be increased.

185. The nurse is taking the health history of a 5 year old who is suspected to have acute glomerulonephritis. Which of the following statements by the mother would be important in establishing the diagnosis?

(1) "The family attended a family reunion a week ago."
(2) "My husband had a bladder infection a week ago."
(3) "My child had a sore throat about 10 days ago."
(4) "My father died of kidney cancer 10 years ago."

186. The nursing care plan for a juvenile diabetic will include the nursing diagnosis of altered nutrition: less than body requirements related to

(1) decreased glucagon secretion.
(2) impaired utilization of insulin.
(3) impaired glucose transport.
(4) excessive energy expenditure.

187. A patient came to the emergency room complaining of feeling "anxious" and stated that she had tingling in feet and hands. An arterial blood gas reveals respiratory alkalosis. The nurse should prepare to treat her with

(1) sodium bicarbonate.
(2) mechanical ventilation.
(3) oxygen therapy.
(4) rebreather bag.

188. Which of the following reactions to a painful procedure would be expected from a child suspected to be abused?

(1) Crying throughout the procedure.
(2) Accepting pain without protest.
(3) Assisting the nurse during the procedure.
(4) Striking out at the nurse.

189. An 85 year old is transferred from a nursing home to the geriatric unit of an acute care facility. The admitting diagnosis is dehydration. During the admission process, the nurse will be aware of which of the following clinical signs of dehydration?

    (1) Poor skin turgor.
    (2) Moist, clammy skin.
    (3) Abdominal cramps.
    (4) Pink, frothy sputum.

190. A 27-year-old mother of a newborn baby boy is admitted to a psychiatric unit because of recurring thoughts of suffocating her baby. She admits that these thoughts are senseless because she loves her baby. She states that these thoughts are terrifying and she is compelled to wash her hands repeatedly whenever these thoughts "occupy" her mind. She states that she is unable to control it. The appropriate nursing diagnosis for the patient's behavior is

    (1) anxiety related to irrational thoughts of guilt.
    (2) impaired social interaction related to overt hostility.
    (3) activity intolerance related to fatigue.
    (4) altered family process related to adjustment requirement.

191. A 60-year-old bone marrow transplant patient is being conditioned with total body irradiation (TBI) and cyclophosphamide. The nurse should inform the patient and family beforehand that

    (1) no visitors are allowed during the phase of the treatment.
    (2) the patient must wear a mask after completion of treatment whenever leaving the room.
    (3) visitors need not take any special precaution during this phase of treatment.
    (4) the patient would be placed in a 2-bedded room in the general population of the floor.

192. The nurse schedules a conference with the parents of a newly diagnosed juvenile diabetic. Which of the following interventions would the nurse implement FIRST?

    (1) Discuss the genetic aspect of insulin dependent diabetic mellitus.
    (2) Teach the family blood glucose testing and the administration of insulin.
    (3) Allow the parents to verbalize their feelings about the child's illness.
    (4) Discuss the way insulin acts in the body and its relationship to blood sugar levels.

193. The nurse, during the transitional assessment of an infant following delivery, should report which of the following findings to the physician?

    (1) Flexion posture maintained, arms flexed at the elbow and rested on the chest, legs flexed at the knees and thighs rested on abdomen.
    (2) Eyes tightly closed, lids edematous, and sclera white and clean.
    (3) Asymmetry of right gluteal and thigh fold and limited abduction of the right leg.
    (4) Flexion of hands and soles of the feet when they are touched near the base of the digits.

194. Which of the following instructions given by the nurse would a mother in labor be able to respond to after an epidural block?

    (1) "Pant whenever you feel a contraction."
    (2) "One more push with the next contraction."
    (3) "Turn on your side if you feel more confortable."
    (4) "Call me if you feel faint."

195. When assessing a woman who is 6 hours postpartum, the nurse finds the fundus 3 finger breadths above the umbilicus and displaced to the left of the midline. The nurse should

    (1) administer a prn dose of oxytocin.
    (2) gently massage the fundus until it becomes firm.
    (3) notify the team leader.
    (4) ask the patient to void.

196. A 65 year old is brought to the emergency room in hyperglycemic hyperosmolar non-ketatic (HHNK) syndrome. The nurse is aware that intravenous therapy is ordered to

    (1) provide potassium and necessary electrolytes.
    (2) administer calcium chloride to prevent tetanus.
    (3) restore adequate vascular volume.
    (4) administer hyperosmotic intravenous fluid.

197. A 67-year-old patient is experiencing pain after a tooth extraction. The nurse administers aspirin and codeine together for pain relief. This is an example of which type of effect?

    (1) Synergistic.
    (2) Antagonistic.
    (3) Potentiated.
    (4) Additive.

198. After surgery, which of the following nursing interventions will reduce swelling of the stump of a below-the-knee amputation?

    (1) Elevating the stump on pillows.
    (2) Wrapping the stump with an Ace bandage.
    (3) Applying a pressure dressing to the stump.
    (4) Elevating the foot of the bed.

199. The physician has ordered a nutrition solution to run for 24 hours. The nurse realizes that it will not finish within this time period. The nurse should

    (1) increase the flow rate.
    (2) decrease the flow rate.
    (3) recalculate the finishing time.
    (4) notify the physician.

200. An adolescent is brought to the emergency room in diabetic ketoacidosis (DKA). An arterial blood gas reveals metabolic acidosis. The nurse is aware that intravenous therapy is ordered to

    (1) provide potassium and necessary electrolytes.
    (2) administer calcium chloride to prevent tetanus.
    (3) restore adequate vascular volume.
    (4) administer hyperosmotic intravenous fluid.

ANSWER KEY

1.	1	41.	3	81.	3	121.	1	161.	1
2.	3	42.	2	82.	2	122.	1	162.	1
3,	3	43.	1	83.	3	123.	2	163.	4
4.	3	44.	3	84.	3	124.	3	164.	1
5.	3	45.	3	85.	3	125.	1	165.	4
6.	4	46.	3	86.	1	126.	1	166.	3
7.	2	47.	4	87.	1	127.	3	167.	3
8.	1	48.	1	88.	1	128.	1	168.	2
9.	3	49.	1	89.	3	129.	2	169.	3
10.	1	50.	2	90.	4	130.	3	170.	1
11.	3	51.	4	91.	3	131.	2	171.	4
12.	3	52.	1	92.	1	132.	2	172.	4
13.	1	53.	3	93.	3	133.	4	173.	4
14.	4	54.	4	94.	4	134.	2	174.	4
15.	1	55.	2	95.	1	135.	4	175.	1
16.	2	56.	3	96.	2	136.	3	176.	2
17.	3	57.	4	97.	4	137.	1	177.	3
18.	4	58.	2	98.	4	138.	1	178.	2
19.	3	59.	2	99.	3	139.	2	179.	1
20.	4	60.	1	100.	2	140.	2	180.	1
21.	1	61.	1	101.	2	141.	1	181.	4
22.	1	62.	4	102.	2	142.	3	182.	1
23.	2	63.	2	103.	3	143.	4	183.	3
24.	3	64.	4	104.	4	144.	1	184.	3
25.	2	65.	3	105.	2	145.	3	185.	3
26.	2	66.	4	106.	2	146.	2	186.	3
27.	2	67.	3	107.	2	147.	3	187.	4
28.	3	68.	1	108.	2	148.	2	188.	2
29.	2	69.	2	109.	4	149.	1	189.	1
30.	3	70.	3	110.	3	150.	3	190.	1
31.	3	71.	1	111.	2	151.	1	191.	2
32.	4	72.	3	112.	1	152.	2	192.	3
33.	4	73.	2	113.	1	153.	2	193.	3
34.	3	74.	3	114.	2	154.	4	194.	4
35.	1	75.	3	115.	4	155.	4	195.	4
36.	4	76.	2	116.	1	156.	2	196.	3
37.	3	77.	3	117.	3	157.	2	197.	4
38.	2	78.	1	118.	2	158.	2	198.	4
39.	1	79.	4	119.	3	159.	3	199.	3
40.	4	80.	3	120.	3	160.	1	200.	2

RATIONALES

1. **1** Lightening is the settling of the uterus back into the pelvis. This occurs up to 4 weeks before delivery in primiparas. At this time pressure on the lower extremities increases, sometimes causing leg cramps. Frequency of urination also recurs at this time. **Nursing process:** Planning. **Client need:** Health promotion/maintenance. **Cognitive level:** 3.

2. **3** The recent move to the city provides the potential for this couple to be without any significant others to turn to if they need assistance with the pregnancy. The nurse should find out whether they have any family members in the vicinity. She should also ask about close friends and affiliations with churches and other organizations to which they may belong. **Nursing process:** Assessment. **Client need:** Health promotion/maintenance. **Cognitive level:** 3.

3. **3** If the patient's condition had progressed to eclampsia, the patient would have had seizures. Therefore the absence of seizures demonstrates successful control. **Nursing process:** Evaluation. **Client need:** Health promotion/maintenance. **Cognitive level:** 4

4. **3** Ambulatory surgery patients must have an escort after surgery. Someone must stay with the patient until the first postoperative visit the day following cataract surgery. **Nursing process:** Assessment. **Client need:** Safe, effective care environment. **Cognitive level:** 3.

5. **3** Hypothetical questions are useful in determining patient comprehension of previously learned material. Choice 4 places the patient on the defensive and prevents the patient from offering information. **Nursing process:** Evaluation. **Client need:** Health promotion/maintenance. **Cognitive level:** 4.

6. **4** The following formula is used:

$$\frac{\text{Total volume infused} \times \text{Drops/ml}}{\text{Total time of infusion (min.)}}$$

$$= \text{Drops per minute}$$

$$\frac{3000 \times 10}{1440 \text{ min.}} = \frac{30,000}{1440}$$

$$= 20.80, \text{ or } 21 \text{ drops per minute}$$

Nursing process: Analysis. **Client need:** Physiological integrity. **Cognitive level:** 4.

7. **2** Both warfarin and aspirin can alter blood's ability to coagulate by decreasing blood clotting factor VII. A drug interaction between the two may result in bleeding. **Nursing process:** Evaluation. **Client need:** Physiological integrity. **Cognitive level:** 4.

8. **1** Transdermal scopolamine patches are applied behind the ear and are not affected by water. **Nursing process:** Implementation. **Client need:** Health promotion/maintenence. **Cognitive level:** 3.

9. **3** A depressed patient is usually unable to verbalize feelings toward the appropriate object. These feelings, specifically anger, are sometimes directed inward causing overwhelming subjective distress. The patient may be able to deal with these feelings once they are identified. **Nursing process:** Planning. **Client need:** Psychosocial integrity. **Cognitive level:** 3.

10. **1** This response indicates a desire to fit the medication schedule into the family's routine, thereby increasing compliance. **Nursing process:** Evaluation. **Client need:** Health promotion/maintenance. **Cognitive level:** 4.

11. **3** Remaining with the patient conveys acceptance of her feelings and the nurse's interest in the patient. **Nursing process:** Planning. **Client need:** Psychosocial integrity. **Cognitive level:** 3.

12. **3** Simple, truthful explanations of procedures provide a basis for establishing trust with the school-age child. The nurse should remain with the child after the procedure in order to encourage her to verbalize her feelings. **Nursing process:** Implementation. **Client need:** Psychosocial integrity. **Cognitive level:** 3.

13. **1** Administering a medication with meals may decrease a drug's gastrointestinal side effect. **Nursing process:** Planning. **Client need:** Health promotion/maintenance. **Cognitive level:** 3.

14. **4** When a child is hemorrhaging after a tonsillectomy, he or she will swallow the excess blood. **Nursing process:** Assessment. **Client need:** Physiological integrity. **Cognitive level:** 3.

15. **1** The most common medication error is administration of the wrong dose. This activity could easily lead to administration of an over or under dose of a drug. **Nursing process:** Assessment. **Client need:** Health promotion/maintenance. **Cognitive level:** 3.

16. **2**   The three-point gait allows for partial weight bearing or no weight bearing. The crutches and the involved leg are moved forward together, with the weight taken on the wrists and the palms. **Nursing process:** Assessment. **Client need:** Physiological integrity. **Cognitive level:** 3.

17. **3**   The ocurrence of hives following penicillin administration indicates that the patient has developed an allergy to the drug and should not receive penicillin or related preparations again. **Nursing process:** Implementation. **Client need:** Health promotion/maintenance. **Cognitive level:** 4.

18. **4**   Only this option would both ease the chest pain and could be initiated without a physician's order. The chest pain is due to poor circulation of blood carrying oxygen to the myocardium. Administering 100% oxygen saturates the blood cells, therefore increasing the amount of oxygen going to the damaged myocardium. **Nursing process:** Implementation. **Client need:** Physiological integrity. **Cognitive level:** 3.

19. **3**   Morphine should not be administered to a patient with a head injury because it depresses respiration. Increased intracranial pressure also causes decreased respiration; therefore, this drug would mask the symptom. **Nursing process:** Assessment. **Client need:** Safe, effective care environment. **Cognitive level:** 3.

20. **1**   The most important principle of nursing care during the active phase of labor is comfort. The patient should be kept dry and cool. She needs constant reassurance and should not be left alone. Relaxation and rest should be encouraged, with frequent back rubs and mouth care, between contractions. The patient should be positioned in whatever way she is most comfortable. **Nursing process:** Planning. **Client need:** Health promotion/maintenance. **Cognitive level:** 3.

21. **1**   A full bladder will impede the descent of the presenting part because it fills the space through which the fetus needs to pass. It also significantly increases the amount of discomfort during contractions because the presenting part causes pressure on the distended bladder. **Nursing process:** Analysis. **Client need:** Health promotion/maintenance. **Cognitive level:** 3.

22. **1**   The presence of bowel sounds is a more definitive measure of the intestines' mobility that leads to the decreasing of abdominal distension. **Nursing process:** Assessment. **Client need:** Physiological integrity. **Cognitive level:** 4.

23. **2**   Providing reality orientation lessens mental confusion. The other actions would increase the patient's confusion. **Nursing process:** Planning. **Client need:** Psychosocial integrity. **Cognitive level:** 3.

24. **3**   A systemic effect such a headache resulting from vasodilation of cerebral vessels occurs due to absorption of the drug through the skin. **Nursing process:** Analysis. **Client need:** Physiological integrity. **Cognitive level:** 3.

25. **2**   Mithromycin causes bone marrow depression. The thrombocytopenia is cause for the bleeding that occurs when this drug is administered. **Nursing process:** Analysis. **Client need:** Physiological integrity. **Cognitive level:** 4.

26. **2**   Thrombocytopenia (decreased platelets) occurs because the rapid proliferation of leukocytes prevents the bone marrow from developing platelets. This condition coexists with the patient's disease process. **Nursing process:** Implementation. **Client need:** Physiological integrity. **Cognitive level:** 3.

27. **2**   Sterile gloves are used when changing the Hickman dressing. The site is cleansed, using a circular motion, with alcohol; then povidone is applied and the site is covered with a transparent, waterproof dressing. **Nursing process:** Implementation. **Client need:** Physiological integrity. **Cognitive level:** 4.

28. **3**   Blood is started at 20 drops per minute for the first 10 minutes. If no reaction is noted, the rate may be increased to 50 to 70 drops per minute. **Nursing process:** Implementation. **Client need:** Physiological integrity. **Cognitive level:** 3.

29. **2**   Encouraging the patient to describe rather than to explain what he is feeling is less threatening to the patient who may not have any insight into what is happening to him at that time. **Nursing process:** Assessment. **Client need:** Physiological integrity. **Cognitive level:** 3.

30. **3**   The nurse should inform the family of the reason for the transfusion and allay their

fears. **Nursing process:** Implementation. **Client need:** Physiological integrity. **Cognitive level:** 4.

31. **3**   The nurse should encourage the patient to verbalize his thoughts, feelings, and ideas by using therapeutic interviewing techniques such as reflecting, use of open-ended questions, and broad openings. **Nursing process:** Planning. **Client need:** Psychosocial integrity. **Cognitive level:** 3.

32. **4**   A Raggedy Ann doll or a beanbag would be inappropriate as they would become moist because of the increased humidity in the mist tent. Crayons are inappropriate as the toddler could insert one into the tracheostomy opening. Plastic nesting blocks are the safe choice. **Nursing process:** Implementation. **Client need:** Safe, effective care environment. **Cognitive level:** 3.

33. **4**   Meningococcal meningitis is readily transmitted to others by droplet infection from nasopharyngeal secretions. Protection from droplets includes the use of mask, gown, and gloves. **Nursing process:** Planning. **Client need:** Safe, effective care environment. **Cognitive level:** 3.

34. **3**   Management of juvenile rheumatoid arthritis includes physical therapy of the involved joints. Exercise in a swimming pool allows freedom of movement with support and minimal gravitational pull. **Nursing process:** Planning. **Client need:** Health promotion/maintenance. **Cognitive level:** 3.

35. **1**   If problems develop, the infusion can be stopped and the normal saline solution turned on. **Nursing process:** Implementation. **Client need:** Physiological integrity. **Cognitive level:** 3.

36. **4**   Greenish staining indicates the passage of meconium. In a vertex presentation, meconium is indicative of fetal distress. It would not be significant in a breech presentation. **Nursing process:** Assessment. **Client need:** Physiological integrity. **Cognitive level:** 3.

37. **3**   A very common side effect of Probenthine is dryness of the mouth; therefore this nursing diagnosis is appropriate. **Nursing process:** Analysis. **Client need:** Physiological integrity. **Cognitive level:** 3.

38. **2**   A patient who is experiencing pain often finds it difficult to follow through with prescribed activities because the pain becomes the center of attention. After the pain is relieved, the patient is able to cooperate. **Nursing process:** Implementation. **Client need:** Physiological integrity. **Cognitive level:** 4.

39. **1**   Platelets are administered quickly within 10 minutes. **Nursing process:** Implementation. **Client need:** Physiological integrity. **Cognitive level:** 3.

40. **4**   Auscultation of the lung allows the nurse to obtain information about the functioning of the respiratory system and about the presence of any obstruction in the passages. **Nursing process:** Implementation. **Client need:** Physiological integrity. **Cognitive level:** 3.

41. **3**   If long-handled tongs and a lead container are not available, the nurse should notify the nuclear medicine department so that it can remove the radium. **Nursing process:** Implementation. **Client need:** Safe, effective care environment. **Cognitive level:** 4.

42. **2**   Since there is loss of peripheral vision with the removal of the lens, clear vision is possible only through the center of the glasses. Peripheral vision is poor with cataract glasses because of the optical distortion created by the strong lenses. **Nursing process:** Implementation. **Client need:** Health promotion/maintenance. **Cognitive level:** 3.

43. **1**   Although ambulation *may* encourage the patient to deep breathe, the other measures will definitely be helpful to promote and/or support effective coughing. **Nursing process:** Implementation. **Client need:** Physiological integrity. **Cognitive level:** 4.

44. **3**   The presence of an area of vesiculation (a blisterlike area with fluid) is indicative of a positive reaction. A definitive diagnosis is made after the tubercle bacillus is found in the sputum. A chest X ray is also needed to establish the presence or absence of calcification or cavities in the lung. **Nursing process:** Analysis. **Client need:** Health promotion/maintenance. **Cognitive level:** 4.

45. **3**   A patient's refusal to cooperate with the therapist is probably due more to the pain that occurs with exercise than to a lack of motivation; therefore, the most beneficial action would be to administer pain medication beforehand so that the patient can perform his or her exercises. **Nursing process:** Planning. **Client need:** Physiological integrity. **Cognitive level:** 4.

46. **3**   This response reflects an understanding of the need to confront the problem rather than deny it. **Nursing process:** Evaluation. **Client need:** Health promotion/maintenance. **Cognitive level:** 4.

47. **4**   Allowing the patient's family to stay with her until bedtime would likely help her maintain a grasp of reality. **Nursing process:** Planning. **Client need:** Psychosocial integrity. **Cognitive level:** 3.

48. **1**   Establishing a routine for the patient promotes a feeling of security because of the sameness of activities. A routine also reduces the patient's need for decision making at the time of confusion. **Nursing process:** Planning. **Client need:** Psychosocial integrity. **Cognitive level:** 4.

49. **1**   Nifedipine (Procardia) reduces peripheral resistance, and along with concurrent use of nitrates, can cause hypotension with initial administration. **Nursing process:** Implementation. **Client need:** Physiological integrity. **Cognitive level:** 3.

50. **2**   There is always the possibility that general anesthesia will be used during delivery, so the time and the type of the last meal are vital information. The patient's reaction to pain is an important assessment to make, but it is not part of the history. **Nursing process:** Assessment. **Client need:** Health promotion/maintenance. **Cognitive level:** 4.

51. **4**   Nitroglycerin tablets are not habit-forming and can be taken as needed. It should be stressed, however, that if chest pain becomes severe and is not relieved with nitroglycerin, the physician should be notified. **Nursing process:** Evaluation. **Client need:** Health promotion/maintenance. **Cognitive level:** 3.

52. **1**   The objective of the management of glaucoma is to decrease the intraocular pressure to a level at which progression of the disease is halted. Inhibiting the production of aqueous fluid and facilitating its drainage will decrease the intraocular pressure. **Nursing process:** Assessment. **Client need:** Physiological integrity. **Cognitive level:** 3.

53. **3**   The warm, moist air provided by running hot water in the shower will help to decrease the laryngeal obstruction due to edema and spasms. **Nursing process:** Planning. **Client need:** Health promotion/maintenance. **Cognitive level:** 3.

54. **4**   Many fast-food restaurants use microwave ovens, which interfere with the electrical impulse of the pacemaker. Weapon detectors at airports will detect the presence of a pacemaker but will not interfere with its electrical impulse. **Nursing process:** Assessment. **Client need:** Health promotion/maintenance. **Cognitive level:** 4.

55. **2**   The patient should be encouraged to carry out all self-care activities on the unaffected side, such as eating, combing hair, brushing teeth, bathing, and shaving with an electric shaver. If the patient is given enough time, he will be able to complete questions on his own. **Nursing process:** Planning. **Client need:** Health promotion/maintenance. **Cognitive level:** 3.

56. **3**   Changes in vital signs provide an early indication of any change in cardiac status. **Nursing process:** Assessment. **Client need:** Health promotion/maintenance. **Cognitive level:** 4.

57. **4**   Meperidine (Demerol) may cause biliary tract spasm. **Nursing process:** Planning. **Client need:** Safe, effective care environment. **Cognitive level:** 3.

58. **2**   Gentamicin is a nephrotoxic agent; therefore, creatinine levels should be checked as a reflection of renal function. **Nursing process:** Implementation. **Client need:** Safe, effective care environment. **Cognitive level:** 3.

59. **2**   The degree of prostration is an important guideline in determining the extent of respiratory embarrassment. If the child's energy is depleted, she will be unable to sustain the effort needed for respiration. **Nursing process:** Assessment. **Client need:** Physiological integrity. **Cognitive level:** 3.

60. **1**   The reduced metabolism of barbiturates by the liver is partly responsible for the "hangover" effect seen in the elderly. **Nursing process:** Assessment. **Client need:** Safe, effective care environment. **Cognitive level:** 3.

61. **1**   Because verbally aggressive patients usually evoke anger in the health care giver, the nurse must be aware of her or his own patterns of response. This awareness will help the nurse in dealing with the patient and her or his own anger therapeutically. **Nursing process:** Analysis. **Client need:** Psychosocial integrity. **Cognitive level:** 3.

62. **4**   Reintroducing the patient gradually to the realities of social interaction is important. This gives the patient an opportunity to test

out newly learned interaction skills without the threats of rejection. **Nursing process:** Planning. **Client need:** Psychosocial integrity. **Cognitive level:** 4.

63. **2**   The nurse should not change the assignment made for the day, since this would disrupt the working of the whole staff. The staff should be told that if a particular assignment is desired, the head nurse should be notified the day before so that it may be considered. **Nursing process:** Analysis. **Client need:** Safe, effective care environment. **Cognitive level:** 4.

64. **4**   Glucocorticoids increase blood sugar levels, particularly in those patients with diabetes mellitus who are taking hypoglycemia agents. **Nursing process:** Analysis. **Client need:** Safe, effective care environment. **Cognitive level:** 3.

65. **3**   Evidence of an active infection, such as high fever, is a contraindication to immunization. **Nursing process:** Assessment. **Client care:** Health promotion/maintenance. **Cognitive level:** 3.

66. **4**   Because of gravity and the patient's position during the first 8 to 12 hours after surgery, the anterior dressing is usually dry. Therefore, the posterior site should be inspected for bleeding. **Nursing process:** Planning. **Client need:** Physiological integrity. **Cognitive level:** 3.

67. **3**   The approach makes the patient aware of her behavior and its consequences. This awareness will help the patient understand the appropriate limits set on her behavior. The statement focuses on the patient's behavior, not on her as a total person. **Nursing process:** Implementation. **Client need:** Psychosocial integrity. **Cognitive level:** 4.

68. **1**   Infants admitted to the pediatric unit with diarrhea are isolated until the results of a stool culture are known. Gastroenteritis may be caused by an organism that is communicable by fecal contamination. A location near the nurses' station facilitates close observation of the infant. A sink is essential for proper handwashing. **Nursing process:** Planning. **Client need:** Safe, effective care environment. **Cognitive level:** 4.

69. **2**   During the weaning process, the nurse stays with the patient, to assess for respiratory distress and to intervene whenever necessary. The proper order of procedure is given in choice 2. **Nursing process:** Implementation. **Client need:** Physiological integrity. **Cognitive level:** 4.

70. **3**   Ammonia-forming bacteria are found in the colon. Neomycin reduces intestinal bacteria, and lactulose prevents the formation of ammonia. **Nursing process:** Assessment. **Client need:** Physiological integrity. **Cognitive level:** 3.

71. **1**   Children in the preschool years engage most often in dramatic play. They enjoy imitating the adults in their environment. **Nursing process:** Planning. **Client need:** Safe, effective care environment. **Cognitive level:** 3.

72. **3**   Common adverse effects related to DPT vaccine include anorexia and fretfulness, in addition to redness and pain at the site of injection. **Nursing process:** Implementation. **Client need:** Health promotion/maintenance. **Cognitive level:** 3.

73. **2**   Although there are fewer side effects with a steroidal inhaler (local application) than with the systemic route, overuse and abuse can lead to hypothalamic-pituitary-adrenal (HPA) suppression. **Nursing process:** Evaluation. **Client need:** Health promotion/maintenance. **Cognitive level:** 3.

74. **3**   Postmenopausal women should increase their dietary intake of calcium in order to prevent osteoporosis. **Nursing process:** Implementation. **Client need:** Health promotion/maintenance. **Cognitive level:** 3.

75. **3**   Preoxygenation with 100% oxygen for one to two minutes supplies oxygen at the time when the patient's oxygen need is compromised. Also, suctioning removes oxygen along with mucus. **Nursing process:** Implementation. **Client need:** Physiological integrity. **Cognitive level:** 3.

76. **2**   The first thing the nurse should do is ascertain how the patient is perceiving what is happening. Once she finds out what the patient's fears are, she can deal with them. She should never assume that the patient is feeling something, as in choice 4, as she may introduce a fear that the patient is not experiencing. The nurse should also never reassure a patient that everything will be fine when there is no way of telling what the outcome of a particular situation will be. **Nursing process:** Implementation. **Client need:** Health promotion/maintenance. **Cognitive level:** 3.

77. **3**   The incubation period for infectious hepatitis is usually 30 days. Viral infection is rarely transmitted by blood transfusion. Fecal-oral contact is the usual route of transmission, which would occur in this situation of close proximity. **Nursing process:** Assessment. **Client need:** Physiological integrity. **Cognitive level:** 4.

78. **1**   The patient should be approached via the unaffected visual field. Some confusion is expected from cerebral edema still present after the cerebrovascular accident. It is appropriate to alleviate whatever anxiety the patient experiences by giving correct information. **Nursing process:** Implementation. **Client need:** Physiological integrity. **Cognitive level:** 4.

79. **4**   Long-term memory usually remains during normal aging. Short-term memory, involved in acquisition, retention, and retrieval of information, is impeded later in life. Major illness, UTI, and anxiety due to a new environment lead to forgetfulness. **Nursing process:** Assessment. **Client need:** Psychosocial integrity. **Cognitive level:** 4.

80. **3**   Choices 2 and 4 would predispose a patient to infection of the bladder and the skin, respectively. Choice 1 would cause dehydration and eventually lead to urinary infection. **Nursing process:** Planning. **Client need:** Physiological integrity. **Cognitive level:** 3.

81. **3**   Asymmetry of the face is a sign of paralysis. The side of the body that is governed by the side of the brain affected by the thrombosis of hemorrhage becomes paralyzed. This patient has right sided weakness and left facial weakness. This position allows drainage of secretions and prevents aspiration; also the patient should not lie on the paralyzed side. **Nursing process:** Implementation. **Client need:** Physiological integrity. **Cognitive level:** 4.

82. **2**   The other recreational activities listed place too much strain on the retina. Reading requires rapid eye movement, which is contraindicated for a patient who has had a detached retina. Reading may not be allowed for two to three weeks. **Nursing process:** Implementation. **Client need:** Health promotion/maintenance. **Cognitive level:** 3.

83. **3**   The patient should gradually be included in the process of changing the colostomy when she demonstrates that she is ready for this step. Involvement in the dressing process may encourage her to look at the stoma. **Nursing process:** Implementation. **Client need:** Health promotion/maintenance. **Cognitive level:** 3.

84. **3**   Mixed addiction is a condition in which the person is dependent in more than one substance, such as cocaine and alcohol. **Nursing process:** Analysis. **Client need:** Psychosocial integrity. **Cognitive level:** 3.

85. **3**   Mastectomy support groups provide an opportunity for the patient to talk with other women who have had similar surgery. Such groups also provide information and assistance. **Nursing process:** Assessment. **Client need:** Psychosocial integrity. **Cognitive level:** 3.

86. **1**   Once the membranes are ruptured, the infant's protection from external organisms is compromised. When membranes have been ruptured more than 24 hours, the chance of infection is greatly increased. **Nursing process:** Assessment. **Client need:** Safe, effective care environment. **Cognitive level:** 4.

87. **1**   Initial Coumadin therapy is based on daily prothrombin time. **Nursing process:** Evaluation. **Client need:** Safe, effective care environment. **Cognitive level:** 3.

88. **1**   If a patient has an accident or experiences battery malfunction, the identification card or bracelet will contain the information needed to render safe health care, such as the doctor's name; type, model, rate, and manufacturer of pacemaker; and hospital where it was inserted. **Nursing process:** Planning. **Client need:** Health promotion/maintenance. **Cognitive level:** 3.

89. **3**   The first action should be to take a set of vital signs as a baseline assessment. **Nursing process:** Assessment. **Client need:** Psychosocial integrity. **Cognitive level:** 3.

90. **4**   This patient presents signs and symptoms related to an anaphylactic reaction to penicillin. Emergency treatment includes epinephrine, antihistamines, bronchodilators, and vasopressors. **Nursing process:** Planning. **Client need:** Safe, effective care environment. **Cognitive level:** 4.

91. **3**   High risk for injury is related to postoperative alteration in visual acuity. These patients would be wearing an eye shield or patch on the operated eye, thereby compromising the field of vision. **Nursing process:**

Analysis. **Client need:** Physiological integrity. **Cognitive level:** 4.

92. **1**   Taking antihistamines at bedtime will reduce the effect of sedation. **Nursing process:** Implementation. **Client need:** Health promotion/maintenance. **Cognitive level:** 3.

93. **3**   These patients have a lot of energy. They also need sensory stimulation. Walking provides for both. **Nursing process:** Implementation. **Client need:** Safe, effective care environment. **Cognitive level:** 4.

94. **4**   Protective isolation prevents the patient from bacteria, viruses, and fungi in the normal environment. After the chemotherapy treatment, the white blood cells are reduced; therefore, infections are a risk. The hospital room will be private and virtually germfree. **Nursing process:** Implementation. **Client need:** Safe, effective care environment. **Cognitive level:** 3.

95. **1**   Length of addiction, dose of drugs, and time between last dose and delivery all affect the amount of drugs the infant has been exposed to and the blood level of the drugs at birth. **Nursing process:** Evaluation. **Client need:** Physiological integrity. **Cognitive level:** 4.

96. **2**   Aluminum hydroxide is used to treat hyperphosphatemia, common in renal failure patients, because it prevents absorption of phosphate from the G.I. tract. **Nursing process:** Planning. **Client need:** Physiological integrity. **Cognitive level:** 3.

97. **4**   A recent diagnosis may increase the patient's stress and anxiety level, thus interfering with effective learning. **Nursing process:** Assessment. **Client need:** Health promotion/maintenance. **Cognitive level:** 4.

98. **4**   The vital signs in choice 4 are indicative of burn shock. This condition is life threatening and must be treated immediately by the physician. **Nursing process:** Analysis. **Client need:** Physiological integrity. **Cognitive level:** 4.

99. **3**   Heparin is administered to prevent clotting of the blood as it circulates through the machine. **Nursing process:** Planning. **Client need:** Physiological integrity. **Cognitive level:** 3.

100. **2**   This option would do the most to reduce the patient's anxiety because it would allow them to ask questions and share concerns with someone who has had this surgery. **Nursing process:** Implementation. **Client need:** Psychosocial integrity. **Cognitive level:** 4.

101. **2**   This response conveys the nurse's acceptance of the patient's feelings. **Nursing process:** Implementation. **Client need:** Psychosocial integrity. **Cognitive level:** 3.

102. **2**   Patients should be taught not to try to "catch up" on missed dosages by taking two pills in one day. **Nursing process:** Evaluation. **Client need:** Physiological integrity. **Cognitive level:** 4.

103. **3**   A Sickledex screening test does not adequately distinguish between sickle-cell trait and sickle-cell anemia. This distinction is made by a hemoglobin electrophoresis, which separates the various types of hemoglobin, making it possible to identify the type and amount of hemoglobin present. **Nursing process:** Analysis. **Client need:** Physiological integrity. **Cognitive level:** 4.

104. **4**   Patients should be taught not to discontinue medication. If the patient has adverse side effects, then she should contact the nurse or physician. **Nursing process:** Evaluation. **Client need:** Health promotion/maintenance. **Cognitive level:** 4.

105. **2**   Only this nursing diagnosis can be made for both conditions. Choices 1 and 4 relate only to anorexia nervosa and choice 3 relates only to bulimia. **Nursing process:** Analysis. **Client need:** Psychosocial integrity. **Cognitive level:** 4.

106. **2**   Evidence of increasing weight may indicate congestive heart failure and should be reported to the physician or nurse. **Nursing process:** Evaluation. **Client need:** Health promotion/maintenance. **Cognitive level:** 4.

107. **2**   A progressive exercise program will keep the joints flexible and prevent joint deformity. **Nursing process:** Planning. **Client need:** Physiological integrity. **Cognitive level:** 3.

108. **2**   Signs of bronchial obstruction include the use of accessory muscles, wheezing on ascultation, increased heart rate, and/or mental status changes. **Nursing process:** Assessment. **Client need:** Physiological integrity. **Cognitive level:** 3.

109. **4**   By posing questions, an individual displays motivation by desiring greater knowledge about practical health care. **Nursing process:** Assessment. **Client need:** Health promotion/maintenance. **Cognitive level:** 4.

110. **3** Smiling is an example of a universal nonverbal positive reinforcer. **Nursing process:** Implementation. **Client need:** Health promotion/maintenance. **Cognitive level:** 3.

111. **2** Levodopa does not stop the progression of the pathology associated with Parkinsonism, but it improves symptoms and prolongs life. The major symptomatic relief is associated with rigidity and tremors. **Nursing process:** Assessment. **Client need:** Health promotion/maintenance. **Cognitive level:** 4.

112. **1** Assessment for the presence of postural hypotension consists of measuring the blood pressure while standing and sitting. Any change in position would elicit an episode of hypotension. **Nursing process:** Implementation. **Client need:** Health promotion/maintanence. **Cognitive level:** 3.

113. **1** The puff of medication must be delivered at the beginning of inhalation to ensure that the distal airway receives the dosage. **Nursing process:** Evalution. **Client need:** Physiological integrity. **Cognitive level:** 4.

114. **2** Patients with chronic obstructive pulmonary disease are at risk for oxygen-induced hypoventilation. Oxygen should be delivered at the lowest rate possible, while at the same time reducing the threat of hypoxemia. **Nursing process:** Evaluation. **Client need:** Physiological integrity. **Cognitive level:** 4.

115. **4** Communication among members of the staff is critical in preventing suicide. Observations of the patient's behavior must be documented in the patient's progress record. This information is valuable in evaluating the patient's progress and in developing the patient's nursing care plan. **Nursing process:** Implementation. **Client need:** Psychosocial integrity. **Cognitive level:** 3.

116. **1** The physiological disturbance caused by anxiety is reflected in a disturbance in sleep pattern. **Nursing process:** Assessment. **Client need:** Psychosocial integrity. **Cognitive level:** 4.

117. **3** Anxiety experienced by the patient is without identifiable cause. The anxiety can be vague or intense. It occurs as a reaction to some unconscious threat to biological integrity. **Nursing process:** Analysis. **Client need:** Psychosocial integrity. **Cognitive level:** 4.

118. **2** Barium administration is contraindicated in patients with perforation of the gastrointestinal tract or intestinal obstruction. If signs of perforation or obstruction are observed, such as increased abdominal pain, rigidity, or nausea, the physician should be informed. **Nursing process:** Implementation. **Client need:** Physiological integrity. **Cognitive level:** 4.

119. **3** Organisms are easily transported on the skin to form areas of contamination that have been touched. The hands are a common source of bacteria. The breasts need only normal cleansing to prevent any transport of organisms. Sterile technique is not necessary. **Nursing process:** Planning. **Client need:** Health promotion/maintenance. **Cognitive level:** 3.

120. **3** The best treatment for constipation is prevention. Cellulose creates bulk in the bowel and thus increases peristalsis. Fluids soften the stool. Laxatives and suppositories should be avoided if at all possible. **Nursing process:** Planning. **Client need:** Health promotion/maintenance. **Cognitive level:** 3.

121. **1** A second fasting blood-glucose is needed before a definite diagnosis of gestational diabetes mellitus is made. This type of diabetes exists only during pregnancy. The symptoms disappear after childbirth. It is not to be confused with latent diabetes, which is precipitated by pregnancy. **Nursing process:** Analysis. **Client need:** Health promotion/maintenance. **Cognitive level:** 4.

122. **1** The choice for intramuscular injection is the vastus lateralis. This muscle is selected because the others are too small. **Nursing process:** Assessment. **Client need:** Health promotion/maintenance. **Cognitive level:** 3.

123. **2** The mother of a child with a congenital defect often feels that she is to blame for the child's abnormality. At present, the cause of meningomyelocele is unknown. **Nursing process:** Implementation. **Client need:** Health promotion/maintenance. **Cognitive level:** 3.

124. **3** Narcan is a narcotic antagonist; when administered, the patient will experience intense pain. **Nursing process:** Implementation. **Client need:** Physiological integrity. **Cognitive level:** 3.

125. **1** This action should be initiated first. Once the patient is calm, he may be placed in a quiet, uncrowded environment with little or no visual or interpersonal stimuli, windows, or furniture. **Nursing process:** Planning. **Client need:** Psychosocial integrity. **Cognitive level:** 4.

126. **1** Transient ischemic attacks (TIA) are caused by cerebral thrombosis (disturbance of the carotid or middle cerebral artery). Usually prodromal signs precede the severe attack. These attacks are reversible and may last from 10 to 30 minutes. The residual deficit does not last more than 24 hours. TIA's may serve as a warning of impending stroke, which has its greatest incidence in the first month after the first attack. **Nursing process:** Assessment. **Client need:** Physiological integrity. **Cognitive level:** 4.

127. **3** It is expected that some disturbance in body image will occur. Sexual dysfunction, on the other hand, is not expected to occur, although altered sexuality patterns related to change or loss of body part may be expected. **Nursing process:** Analysis. **Client need:** Health promotion/maintenance. **Cognitive level:** 3.

128. **1** Ammonia accumulates in the blood when the liver is unable to metabolize toxins such as those produced from the breakdown of blood in the intestinal tract following gastrointestinal bleeding. This interferes with the function of the central nervous system, causing symptoms such as flapping tremors of the arms and hands. **Nursing process:** Analysis. **Client need:** Physiological integrity. **Cognitive level:** 4.

129. **2** All of these NSAID's except acetaminophen affect platelet function. The interaction between heparin and the other medications would increase the potential for bleeding. **Nursing process:** Analysis. **Client need:** Safe, effective care environment. **Cognitive level:** 3.

130. **3** Suctioning removes oxygen as well as mucus; therefore, suctioning should not last for more than 10 seconds. **Nursing process:** Implementation. **Client need:** Physiological integrity. **Cognitive level:** 3.

131. **2** Dyspnea, noisy breathing, voice changes, and stridor are signs of recurrent laryngeal nerve damage. **Nursing process:** Assessment. **Client need:** Physiological integrity. **Cognitive level:** 3.

132. **2** Palpate the abdomen (upper right quadrant) for tenderness and hepatomegaly. **Nursing process:** Assessment. **Client need:** Physiological integrity. **Cognitive level:** 3.

133. **4** A confrontation should not take place in front of the staff because it disrupts the professional and working environment. The problem is not likely to solve itself, and the charge nurse has a responsibility to tackle it. **Nursing process:** Assessment. **Client need:** Safe, effective care environment. **Cognitive level:** 3.

134. **2** Drinking alcoholic beverages may increase the potential for bleeding by affecting hepatic metabolism. **Nursing process:** Implementation. **Client need:** Health promotion/maintenance. **Cognitive level:** 3.

135. **4** The combination of drugs increases the magnitude of tumor kill. Different toxicities permit the use of four drugs at full clinical dose without cumulative toxicity. **Nursing process:** Evaluation. **Client need:** Physiological integrity. **Cognitive level:** 4.

136. **3** Side effects of theophylline frequently include palpitations, nervousness, insomnia, and frequent urination. **Nursing process:** Implementation. **Client need:** Safe, effective care environment. **Cognitive level:** 3.

137. **1** A therapeutic outcome of mannitol therapy for a patient with increased intracranial pressure would be best demonstrated by improved neurological status. **Nursing process:** Evaluation. **Client need:** Physiological integrity. **Cognitive level:** 4.

138. **1** The adolescent has scoliosis and needs to be referred to an orthopedic clinic. The nurse will observe a convex curve in the upper back and a compensating concave curve in the lower back when the child bends forward at the waist. All of the other physical findings are normal for adolescents. **Nursing process:** Assessment. **Client need:** Health promotion/maintenance. **Cognitive level:** 3.

139. **2** According to psychoanalytic views, regressive behavior is a symbolic retreat to a more primitive level of adjustment used successfully by the patient during early years. Although regression provides a temporary feeling of security, it usually does not enhance the patient's coping abilities. **Nursing process:** Analysis. **Client need:** Psychosocial integrity. **Cognitive level:** 4.

140. **2** This response is most likely to elicit more information from the patient. It also gives the patient an opportunity to recognize and describe her own feelings. **Nursing process:** Implementation. **Client need:** Psychosocial integrity. **Cognitive level:** 3.

141. **1** The anger felt by the borderline personality is a result of inability to develop and achieve autonomy. Frustration with the

problems of adolescence results in the projection of violence onto the present situation or inward to the self. **Nursing process:** Analysis. **Client need:** Psychosocial integrity. **Cognitive level:** 4.

142. **3**   Nausea and vomiting are common side effects of estrogen therapy and can be reduced if estrogen is taken on a full stomach. **Nursing process:** Implementation. **Client need:** Health promotion/maintenance. **Cognitive level:** 3.

143. **4**   The most likely time for insulin reaction to occur in a patient who is taking an intermediate acting insulin in the morning is prior to supper. NPH Humulin's onset is 2–4 hours and it peaks between 4–12 hours. **Nursing process:** Analysis. **Client need:** Physiological integrity. **Cognitive level:** 3.

144. **1**   Choice 1 is the best answer because it conveys correct information. **Nursing process:** Implementation. **Client need:** Physiological integrity. **Cognitive level:** 3.

145. **3**   Nausea and vomiting make it impossible to regulate dietary intake. These conditions render insulin computation very difficult and disturb the equilibrium of insulin maintenance. **Nursing process:** Assessment. **Client need:** Phsysiological integrity. **Cognitive level:** 4.

146. **2**   AIDS patients receiving AZT are still able to transmit the virus to others, therefore appropriate precaution needs to be observed. **Nursing process:** Planning. **Client need:** Safe, effective care environment. **Cognitive level:** 3.

147. **3**   For best results the use of the incentive spirometer should be taught preoperatively. **Nursing process:** Planning. **Client need:** Physiological integrity. **Cognitive level:** 4.

148. **2**   Laxatives are contraindicated if there is evidence of abdominal obstruction or if the patient has a fecal impaction. **Nursing process:** Assessment. **Client need:** Physiological integrity. **Cognitive level:** 3.

149. **1**   The physical findings after injury to the spinal cord are dependent on the level of damage. Damage to the cervical spine at this level produces abnormal breathing. Although the other findings are important and the patient may exhibit all of them, only choice 1 necessitates immediate intervention. **Nursing process:** Assessment. **Client need:** Physiological integrity. **Cognitive level:** 3.

150. **3**   The action of Lactulose in the bowel is the conversion of ammonia to ammonium for evacuation in the stool. This reduction in the ammonia level alleviates some of the symptoms associated with hepatic failure. **Nursing process:** Evaluation. **Client need:** Physiological integrity. **Cognitive level:** 3.

151. **1**   In severe depression, the patient's physiological status becomes compromised. The physical needs, such as nutrition, sleep/rest, elimination, medications, and fluid and electrolyte balance are priority. **Nursing process:** Planning. **Client need:** Psychosocial integrity. **Cognitive level:** 4.

152. **2**   A tourniquet should be kept at the bedside. The bleeding is probably caused by slipping of a ligature. The appropriate action is to control the bleeding with a tourniquet until the bleeder can be ligated. **Nursing process:** Implementation. **Client need:** Physiological integrity. **Cognitive level:** 3.

153. **2**   Prolonged labor tires the uterine muscles, and this can cause lack of tone and relaxation. The fact that there was uterine dysfunction in the patient's labor makes it more likely that the uterus will relax in the initial postpartum period. **Nursing process:** Assessment. **Client need:** Health promotion/maintenance. **Cognitive level:** 4.

154. **4**   Rh incompatibility is an antigen-antibody reaction. The problem occurs when an antigen (the Rh factor) in the baby's blood causes an antibody reaction in the mother's blood. **Nursing process:** Evaluation. **Client need:** Safe, effective care environment. **Cognitive level:** 3.

155. **4**   Because of high concentration of sodium, magnesium hydroxide should be given cautiously to patients with renal disease. **Nursing process:** Assessment. **Client need:** Physiological integrity. **Cognitive level:** 3.

156. **2**   Parents who abuse their children display predictable patterns of behavior. They offer contradictory stories concerning the origin of the child's injuries. **Nursing process:** Assessment. **Client need:** Health promotion/maintenance. **Cognitive level:** 4.

157. **2**   Antituberculosis drugs are most effective when administered in a single dose on an empty stomach upon arising. **Nursing process:** Evaluation. **Client need:** Health promotion/maintenance. **Cognitive level:** 3.

158. **2**   Blocked catheters can lead to bladder spasm. Relief of obstruction often alleviates

pain without the need for analgesia. **Nursing process:** Implementation. **Client need:** Physiological integrity. **Cognitive level:** 3.

159. **3** Patients with normal renal function excrete the small amount of neomycin which is absorbed systemically. If renal impairment is present, the drug may accumulate and cause further renal damage. **Nursing process:** Assessment. **Client need:** Physiological integrity. **Cognitive level:** 3.

160. **1** The patient can become a constructive member of society rather than elect to be self destructive when provided with the opportunity to gain knowledge regarding effective ways to handle problems. **Nursing process:** Analysis. **Client need:** Psychosocial integrity. **Cognitive level:** 4.

161. **1** Sweating is an early sign of hypoglycemia and is related to the release of epinephrine as a compensatory response. **Nursing process:** Implementation. **Client need:** Health promotion/maintenance. **Cognitive level:** 3.

162. **1** The etiological factor that completes the nursing diagnosis is inefficient pumping of the heart. **Nursing process:** Analysis. **Client need:** Physiological integrity. **Cognitive level:** 3.

163. **4** A common effect of ibuprofen use is gastric irritation. If this should occur, the drug should be taken with food, milk, or an antacid. **Nursing process:** Implementation. **Client need:** Health promotion/maintenance. **Cognitive level:** 3.

164. **1** Patients on antithyroid medications should be taught to eliminate iodine rich foods such as seafood. **Nursing process:** Implementation. **Client need:** Physiological integrity. **Cognitive level:** 3.

165. **4** This action compresses the lactiferous sinuses behind the areola and draws milk into the baby's mouth when he sucks. **Nursing process:** Implementation. **Client need:** Health promotion/maintenance. **Cognitive level:** 3.

166. **3** The primary goal of the nurse is to guard against interruption of the integrity of the sac in order to prevent infection leading to meningitis. Covering the sac helps maintain its integrity. **Nursing process:** Implementation. **Client need:** Health promotion/maintenance. **Cognitive level:** 3.

167. **3** The use of reflective questions can elicit more information about the patient's thoughts, feelings, and experiences. **Nursing process:** Assessment. **Client need:** Psychosocial integrity. **Cognitive level:** 3.

168. **2** Most dying persons know the reality of their conditions. Open acknowledgment of their feelings with family members, friends, and caregivers will facilitate their coming to terms with these feelings and the validation of their perception of the reality of feelings. Open communication provides support during this difficult period for everyone involved. **Nursing process:** Assessment. **Client need:** Psychosocial integrity. **Cognitive level:** 3.

169. **3** Infants with hydrocephalus are prone to malnutrition because of inadequate food intake and frequent vomiting. Handling the infant after feeding can precipitate an episode of vomiting. **Nursing process:** Implementation. **Client need:** Health promotion/maintenance. **Cognitive level:** 4.

170. **1** Children with diabetes mellitus are at risk for altered growth and development related to the effects of impaired glucose regulation. **Nursing process:** Analysis. **Client need:** Physiological integrity. **Cognitive level:** 4.

171. **4** Only isotonic enemas are utilized because repeated use of tap water may cause water intoxication and phosphate enemas may cause hypertonic dehydration and shock. **Nursing process:** Implementation. **Client need:** Physiological integrity. **Cognitive level:** 4.

172. **4** Periods of increased exercise may require a reduced insulin dosage because exercise increases glucose utilization. **Nursing process:** Evaluation. **Client need:** Health promotion/maintenance. **Cognitive level:** 4.

173. **4** A thick, curdlike vaginal discharge is characteristic of monilial vaginitis, caused by *Candida albicans,* a fungus. If the neonate is exposed to this fungus during delivery, it can develop thrush, which is a monilial infection of the mouth. **Nursing process:** Analysis. **Client need:** Health promotion/maintenance. **Cognitive level:** 4.

174. **4** This caregiver is inexperienced. This young person may have difficulty with role reversal. Social isolation may occur because of new caregiver's role. Also there is a possibility of a lack of support system. **Nursing process:** Assessment. **Client need:** Health promotion/maintenance. **Cognitive level:** 4.

175. **1**   Side effects during conditioning procedures are nausea and vomiting, mucositis, fluid and electrolyte imbalance, and dermatological reactions. **Nursing process:** Analysis. **Client need:** Physiological integrity. **Cognitive level:** 4.

176. **4**   This response focuses on acknowledging the patient's feelings about her environment that may have triggered the patient's behavior and that the violent act was an unintentional reflex action. This is also an opportunity for the nurse to assist the patient in recognizing that her behavior was unacceptable. **Nursing process:** Evaluation. **Client need:** Psychosocial integrity. **Cognitive level:** 3.

177. **3**   All of the symptoms indicate extrapyramidal side effects. They generally occur within the first 2 days or weeks of treatment. The symptoms subside within 6 months after the drug is discontinued. **Nursing process:** Evaluation. **Client need:** Psychosocial integrity. **Cognitive level:** 3.

178. **2**   Diabinese is a long acting first generation sulfonylurea. It onsets in 1 hour and peaks 12 hours later. **Nursing process:** Planning. **Client need:** Physiological integrity. **Cognitive level:** 3.

179. **1**   During assessment, it is important for the nurse to determine the physical as well as psychological symptoms that the patient is experiencing. The nurse should focus on the response to the anxiety as the cause of the illness. **Nursing process:** Assessment. **Client need:** Psychosocial integrity. **Cognitive level:** 3.

180. **1**   Chronic pain is usually burning or nagging and may become the pathology altering the patient's lifestyle. **Nursing process:** Planning. **Client need:** Psychosocial integrity. **Cognitive level:** 3.

181. **4**   This method should be used periodically to check for bleeding. Because of the position of the patient's head, the nurse should also check the neck dressing and the pillow for blood. **Nursing process:** Implementation. **Client need:** Physiological integrity. **Cognitive level:** 3.

182. **1**   The patient must avoid all of the choices except cooked fruits and vegetables. Flowers and plants have fungi and bacteria. Shellfish and aged cheese contain bacteria. Household pets carry bacteria/dandruff and viruses in their hair. **Nursing process:** Evaluation. **Client need:** Safe, effective care environment. **Cognitive level:** 4.

183. **3**   Milia are tiny white papules appearing on the face of the neonate as a result of unopened sebaceous glands. They disappear spontaneously within a few weeks. **Nursing process:** Implementation. **Client need:** Safe, effective care environment. **Cognitive level:** 4.

184. **3**   Pilocarpine produces miosis and contraction of the ciliary muscles. Patients using pilocarpine will experience reduced visual acuity in dim light as a result of miotic action on pupils and ciliary muscles. **Nursing process:** Implementation. **Client need:** Safe, effective care environment. **Cognitive level:** 3.

185. **3**   Glomerulonephritis occurs 10–14 days after an infection with the Beta hemalytic streptococcus. The disease typically occurs secondary to streptococcal pharyngitis. **Nursing process:** Analysis. **Client need:** Physiological integrity. **Cognitive level:** 4.

186. **3**   Children with insulin-dependent diabetes mellitus experience impaired glucose transport secondary to an insufficient production of insulin. **Nursing process:** Analysis. **Client need:** Physiological integrity. **Cognitive level:** 3.

187. **4**   Respiratory alkalosis is caused by excessive loss of carbon dioxide. It is treated by eliminating the cause and helping the patient breathe more deeply and slowly. A rebreather bag helps to retain carbon dioxide. **Nursing process:** Implementation. **Client need:** Psychosocial integrity. **Cognitive level:** 3.

188. **2**   Abused children accept pain without protest. They have learned that crying often precipitates abusive behavior. They generally mistrust all adults and don't expect adults to provide comfort. **Nursing process:** Assessment. **Client need:** Psychosocial integrity. **Cognitive level:** 3.

189. **1**   A clinical sign of dehydration is poor skin turgor with dry tongue and mouth. **Nursing process:** Assessment. **Client need:** Physiological integrity. **Cognitive level:** 3.

190. **1**   Obsessive compulsive behavior, such as frequent handwashing, is a manifestation of anxiety. **Nursing process:** Analysis. **Client need:** Psychosocial integrity. **Cognitive level:** 4.

191. **2**   After treatment with cyclophosphamide and total body radiation, the patient's immune system is suppressed/reduced because of destruction of white blood cells. Infection is a very serious risk for patients receiving chemotherapy. **Nursing process:** Implementation. **Client need:** Physiological integrity. **Cognitive level:** 4.

192. **3**   Before beginning to teach, the nurse should encourage the family members to verbalize their feelings. Insulin-dependent diabetes mellitus is a life-long disorder requiring meticulous attention to daily care. The family must first learn to accept this situation. **Nursing process:** Implementation. **Client need:** Health promotion/maintenance. **Cognitive level:** 3.

193. **3**   The head of the femur does not lie entirely within the acetabulum in infants with congenital dislocated hips. Thus there is limited abduction of the leg on the affected side. All of the other findings are normal. **Nursing process:** Assessment. **Client need:** Physiological integrity. **Cognitive level:** 4.

194. **4**   An epidural is usually administered in the latter part of the first stage of labor to block sensation of contractions. The patient in labor is unable to follow instruction in options 1–3. After a nerve block, the mother is positioned on her back with head slightly elevated. **Nursing process:** Evaluation. **Client need:** Physio-logical integrity. **Cognitive level:** 4.

195. **4**   Displacement of the fundus to either side of the midline usually indicates a full bladder. The first action to be taken would be to have the patient void. If a full bladder was the problem, the fundus will return to its normal location and become firm. **Nursing process:** Evaluation. **Client need:** Health promotion/maintenance. **Cognitive level:** 3.

196. **3**   Patients with HHNK are often severely dehydrated and need to have adequate volume restored. **Nursing process:** Planning. **Client need:** Physiological integrity. **Cognitive level:** 3.

197. **4**   An additive effect occurs when two drugs with the same effect, such as aspirin and codeine, are combined. The result is an enhanced effect. **Nursing process:** Implementation. **Client need:** Physiological integrity. **Cognitive level:** 3.

198. **4**   Elevation of the foot of the bed lessens edema of the stump and hastens venous return. Elevation of the stump on pillows should be avoided. **Nursing process:** Implementation. **Client need:** Physiological integrity. **Cognitive level:** 3.

199. **3**   An increase in infusion flow rate will increase the blood and urine glucose level. The goal of TPN is also to have the parenteral nutrition solution run continuously at a constant rate. **Nursing process:** Implementation. **Client need:** Physiological integrity. **Cognitive level:** 4.

200. **2**   Patients with metabolic acidosis are severely dehydrated and need adequate volume restored. **Nursing process:** Planning. **Client need:** Physiological integrity. **Cognitive level:** 3.

Self-Analysis Chart

After you have completed the model NCLEX exam I and checked your answers, fill in the chart below. In the columns under "Reason for Error" list the number of each kind of error you made for each phase of the nursing process. The results will indicate the kinds of errors you made most frequently, so that you can take steps to minimize them. For example, if you have many errors under "Misread Problem," you need to slow down and read the questions more carefully. Note such specific details as the age of the patient, the symptoms described, the tests and/or procedures performed, and the drug(s) prescribed.

NURSING PROCESS	NUMBER OF QUESTIONS	NUMBER CORRECT	NUMBER INCORRECT	REASON FOR ERROR			
				FAULTY JUDGMENT	LACK OF KNOWLEDGE	MISREAD PROBLEM	WRONG GUESS
Assessment	47						
Analysis	30						
Planning	35						
Implementation	64						
Evaluation	24						
Total	200	—	—	—	—	—	—

Model NCLEX-RN Examination II

To stimulate the actual test conditions, use the computer program packaged with this book. If you do not have access to a computer, use Model Examinations I and II to practice answering the types of questions you will encounter on the actual NCLEX using CAT. Allow a maximum of five hours for each Model Examination.

Directions:

1. Read each question carefully before looking at the answer choices.
2. When you are sure that you understand the question, select the choice that provides the correct answer.
3. In marking the answer sheet, use a pencil and blacken the circle that corresponds to your answer.

① ② ● ④

If it becomes necessary to change an answer, erase the original one completely.

4. Don't spend too much time on a question to which you don't know the answer. If you can eliminate one or more choices as clearly incorrect, select the best answer from the remaining ones.
5. Since there is no penalty for guessing, answer every question.

ANSWER SHEET FOR MODEL EXAMINATION II

1. ① ② ③ ④	51. ① ② ③ ④	101. ① ② ③ ④	151. ① ② ③ ④
2. ① ② ③ ④	52. ① ② ③ ④	102. ① ② ③ ④	152. ① ② ③ ④
3. ① ② ③ ④	53. ① ② ③ ④	103. ① ② ③ ④	153. ① ② ③ ④
4. ① ② ③ ④	54. ① ② ③ ④	104. ① ② ③ ④	154. ① ② ③ ④
5. ① ② ③ ④	55. ① ② ③ ④	105. ① ② ③ ④	155. ① ② ③ ④
6. ① ② ③ ④	56. ① ② ③ ④	106. ① ② ③ ④	156. ① ② ③ ④
7. ① ② ③ ④	57. ① ② ③ ④	107. ① ② ③ ④	157. ① ② ③ ④
8. ① ② ③ ④	58. ① ② ③ ④	108. ① ② ③ ④	158. ① ② ③ ④
9. ① ② ③ ④	59. ① ② ③ ④	109. ① ② ③ ④	159. ① ② ③ ④
10. ① ② ③ ④	60. ① ② ③ ④	110. ① ② ③ ④	160. ① ② ③ ④
11. ① ② ③ ④	61. ① ② ③ ④	111. ① ② ③ ④	161. ① ② ③ ④
12. ① ② ③ ④	62. ① ② ③ ④	112. ① ② ③ ④	162. ① ② ③ ④
13. ① ② ③ ④	63. ① ② ③ ④	113. ① ② ③ ④	163. ① ② ③ ④
14. ① ② ③ ④	64. ① ② ③ ④	114. ① ② ③ ④	164. ① ② ③ ④
15. ① ② ③ ④	65. ① ② ③ ④	115. ① ② ③ ④	165. ① ② ③ ④
16. ① ② ③ ④	66. ① ② ③ ④	116. ① ② ③ ④	166. ① ② ③ ④
17. ① ② ③ ④	67. ① ② ③ ④	117. ① ② ③ ④	167. ① ② ③ ④
18. ① ② ③ ④	68. ① ② ③ ④	118. ① ② ③ ④	168. ① ② ③ ④
19. ① ② ③ ④	69. ① ② ③ ④	119. ① ② ③ ④	169. ① ② ③ ④
20. ① ② ③ ④	70. ① ② ③ ④	120. ① ② ③ ④	170. ① ② ③ ④
21. ① ② ③ ④	71. ① ② ③ ④	121. ① ② ③ ④	171. ① ② ③ ④
22. ① ② ③ ④	72. ① ② ③ ④	122. ① ② ③ ④	172. ① ② ③ ④
23. ① ② ③ ④	73. ① ② ③ ④	123. ① ② ③ ④	173. ① ② ③ ④
24. ① ② ③ ④	74. ① ② ③ ④	124. ① ② ③ ④	174. ① ② ③ ④
25. ① ② ③ ④	75. ① ② ③ ④	125. ① ② ③ ④	175. ① ② ③ ④
26. ① ② ③ ④	76. ① ② ③ ④	126. ① ② ③ ④	176. ① ② ③ ④
27. ① ② ③ ④	77. ① ② ③ ④	127. ① ② ③ ④	177. ① ② ③ ④
28. ① ② ③ ④	78. ① ② ③ ④	128. ① ② ③ ④	178. ① ② ③ ④
29. ① ② ③ ④	79. ① ② ③ ④	129. ① ② ③ ④	179. ① ② ③ ④
30. ① ② ③ ④	80. ① ② ③ ④	130. ① ② ③ ④	180. ① ② ③ ④
31. ① ② ③ ④	81. ① ② ③ ④	131. ① ② ③ ④	181. ① ② ③ ④
32. ① ② ③ ④	82. ① ② ③ ④	132. ① ② ③ ④	182. ① ② ③ ④
33. ① ② ③ ④	83. ① ② ③ ④	133. ① ② ③ ④	183. ① ② ③ ④
34. ① ② ③ ④	84. ① ② ③ ④	134. ① ② ③ ④	184. ① ② ③ ④
35. ① ② ③ ④	85. ① ② ③ ④	135. ① ② ③ ④	185. ① ② ③ ④
36. ① ② ③ ④	86. ① ② ③ ④	136. ① ② ③ ④	186. ① ② ③ ④
37. ① ② ③ ④	87. ① ② ③ ④	137. ① ② ③ ④	187. ① ② ③ ④
38. ① ② ③ ④	88. ① ② ③ ④	138. ① ② ③ ④	188. ① ② ③ ④
39. ① ② ③ ④	89. ① ② ③ ④	139. ① ② ③ ④	189. ① ② ③ ④
40. ① ② ③ ④	90. ① ② ③ ④	140. ① ② ③ ④	190. ① ② ③ ④
41. ① ② ③ ④	91. ① ② ③ ④	141. ① ② ③ ④	191. ① ② ③ ④
42. ① ② ③ ④	92. ① ② ③ ④	142. ① ② ③ ④	192. ① ② ③ ④
43. ① ② ③ ④	93. ① ② ③ ④	143. ① ② ③ ④	193. ① ② ③ ④
44. ① ② ③ ④	94. ① ② ③ ④	144. ① ② ③ ④	194. ① ② ③ ④
45. ① ② ③ ④	95. ① ② ③ ④	145. ① ② ③ ④	195. ① ② ③ ④
46. ① ② ③ ④	96. ① ② ③ ④	146. ① ② ③ ④	196. ① ② ③ ④
47. ① ② ③ ④	97. ① ② ③ ④	147. ① ② ③ ④	197. ① ② ③ ④
48. ① ② ③ ④	98. ① ② ③ ④	148. ① ② ③ ④	198. ① ② ③ ④
49. ① ② ③ ④	99. ① ② ③ ④	149. ① ② ③ ④	199. ① ② ③ ④
50. ① ② ③ ④	100. ① ② ③ ④	150. ① ② ③ ④	200. ① ② ③ ④

MODEL NCLEX-RN EXAMINATION II

This examination covers the full spectrum of the NCLEX Examination Blueprint.

1. A nurse was approached by a 45-year-old neighbor because her 80-year-old mother, who had been very active all of life, had started becoming confused in the evening. The mother lives alone in another part of town and lately the mother's neighbors had reported to the daughter that she would wander about the apartment halls at night. She would also become agitated when questioned as to where she was going or if she needed assistance. The daughter asked the nurse, "What should I do?" Which of the following advice would be helpful?

    (1) "Make arrangements immediately to have your mother placed in a nursing home."
    (2) "Have your mother move in with you so you can observe her behavior."
    (3) "Talk to Social Service, so that a home health aide may be hired for your mother."
    (4) "Visit your mother in the evening to observe her behavior. Then if necessary, have her medically evaluated."

2. A 30-year-old female has experienced a loss of appetite and has lost 10 pounds in the last month. Her temperature has been elevated to 99–100°F for the last 2 weeks. She has a familial history of systemic lupus erythematosis (SLE). She has been admitted to the hospital for a work-up/diagnosis. Which of the following symptoms related to lupus should the nurse bring to the physician's attention?

    (1) Pre-menstrual constipation relieved by a mild laxative.
    (2) Rash over the cheeks and the bridge of the nose after sunbathing.
    (3) Episodes of sinus headaches during the spring and fall.
    (4) Periods of muscular ache after a game of tennis.

3. The nurse is preparing the medication for a patient with a gastrointestinal tube (GTT). One of the medications is a sustained-release tablet and the others are liquids. Before administering the medications, the nurse should

    (1) crush the tablet.
    (2) mix the drug with an antacid.
    (3) obtain the liquid form of the medication.
    (4) mix tablet with liquid medication.

4. An indwelling catheter is removed after a prostatectomy and the patient is experiencing urinary frequency and dribbling. Which of these statements would alleviate the patient's anxiety concerning this situation?

    (1) "Complete urinary control may never return."
    (2) "Dribbling will always be a problem."
    (3) "Urinary control will return slowly."
    (4) "A urinary bag may give you more security."

5. A 55-year-old female has a left upper quadrantectomy of the left breast. She is then taken to the recovery room. Her left arm and hand should be placed in which of these positions?

    (1) Elbow at the level of the heart, and hand above the elbow.
    (2) Arm and hand at the same level.
    (3) Elbow at the level of the heart, and hand below the heart.
    (4) Arm above the level of the shoulder.

6. Which of the following nursing interventions will do the MOST to help a prospective father accept his new role during pregnancy?

    (1) Explain the physiological and psychological changes he can expect in the mother.
    (2) Tell him you will give the mother emotional support so he won't have to worry about her.
    (3) Let him verbalize his feelings about the pregnancy and fatherhood.
    (4) Encourage him to think about his role in the pregnancy.

7. A 4 year old is brought to the pediatric emergency room with partial thickness burns of head, neck, and right shoulder. Which of these statements by the parent would prompt the nurse to immediately inform the physician?

   (1) "We have two sets of twins at home and they never got burned."
   (2) "I have been so busy that the baby did not receive all the shots."
   (3) "The baby started walking at 12 months old."
   (4) "I feel so bad about this child getting this terrible burn."

8. A 45-year-old male was admitted to a psychiatric unit because of acute delirium tremens. He has been a heavy drinker for the past 10 years. He becomes very restless and tells the nurse, "Those men are trying to shoot me. Let me out of here before they kill me." Which of the following nursing interventions would be MOST helpful?

   (1) Tell the patient, "Lie down and go to sleep."
   (2) Tell the patient, "Rest or I will tie you in bed."
   (3) Reassure the patient, "No one is trying to shoot you."
   (4) Tell the patient, "You must really be very frightened about something. I will stay with you for a while."

9. The nurse ran into a patient's room after hearing a loud scream. Upon entering the room, she sees the patient in bed, having a grand mal seizure. The nurse should immediately

   (1) place the side rails in the upright position.
   (2) place a tongue blade between his teeth.
   (3) restrain the patient's movement.
   (4) turn the patient's head to the side.

10. A male infant with an elevated indirect bilirubin of 13 mg is placed under a Bililite. Which of the following actions by a graduate nurse indicates that she does not fully understand the standard of care for this infant?

    (1) Changes the infant's position every 2 hours while receiving the treatment.
    (2) Covers the infant's scrotal area during treatment.
    (3) Administers feeding and water to the infant while under the light.
    (4) Leaves the infant unclothed during treatment.

11. Which of the following is MOST likely to cause lead poisoning in a toddler?

    (1) Eating vegetables sprayed with insecticide.
    (2) Playing with toys decorated with paint.
    (3) Ingesting paint and/or plaster chips.
    (4) Inhaling fumes from a local chemical factory.

12. A 75-year-old male had surgery for a noncancerous obstruction of the colon. After placing the patient in the surgical intensive care unit (SICU) for close observation of chronic obstructive respiratory disease, the operating surgeon went out of town for the weekend. On Friday evening after surgery, the patient was alert, stable, and responsive to verbal commands until shortly after midnight when he began to hallucinate. The staff nurse made a diagnosis of delirium tremens. The patient was treated with diazepam (Valium) stat. The patient's only relative, a sister who he was not close to, but was listed as next of kin by patient on admission, was called because his blood pressure had increased and his blood gases were deteriorating. The patient had signed himself into the hospital and signed his own operating consent. The patient had not executed a health care power of attorney to give decision-making rights to his sister. Further the patient had no advance directive (living will, durable power of attorney for health care or health care proxy). The resident suggested to the sister that a DNR (do not resuscitate) order was needed because the patient was at risk for myocardial infarction or cerebral vascular accident. The resident wrote the order and the staff nurse filled out the paper form and the sister signed it. The patient survived the weekend and was generally alert and oriented by Sunday morning. Was the DNR order appropriate and on whose behalf was the nurse acting?

    (1) The DNR order was appropriate and the nurse was acting in the physician's and hospital's behalf.
    (2) The DNR order was inappropriate and the nurse was acting on the behalf of the physician and hospital.
    (3) The DNR order was inappropriate and the nurse was not working on behalf of the patient.
    (4) The DNR order was appropriate and the nurse was acting on the behalf of the patient.

13. A 22-year-old woman is admitted to a psychiatric unit after experiencing panic while driving to work. She states that while driving on the highway she felt her heart pounding, her head spinning, and her hands trembling. She decided to return home. Once inside the house, she felt relieved. Consequently, she started avoiding outdoor activities. She dreaded the thought of being outside. She has been absent from work frequently. In planning the patient's care, the nurse should

(1) recognize that the patient's condition is not incapacitating.
(2) explain to the patient that her fears are irrational.
(3) realize that the patient recognizes that her fears are unreasonable but is unable to control them.
(4) encourage the patient to confront what it is she is afraid of until she overcomes her fear.

14. A 75-year-old female, a resident of a nursing home, was admitted into the hospital with a right hip fracture. She wears glasses but the nursing home did not send them to her. Although the patient was experiencing some pain, she was oriented to time, place, and person. Beginning surgery on the hip was done the next day. Twenty four hours after surgery, during the late afternoon and early evening hours, she became disoriented and agitated and began screaming. This behavior continued throughout the night, only to disappear around daybreak. Which of the following diagnoses relating specifically to this behavior should the nurse include in the patient's nursing care plan?

(1) Risk for self-directed violence related to disease process.
(2) Acute confusion related to poor vision.
(3) Fear related to the unknown.
(4) Ineffective individual coping related to anxiety.

15. The BEST approach to evaluating the effectiveness of nutrition therapy for a person with diabetes is

(1) maintaining blood glucose, weight, lipids, blood pressure, and renal status.
(2) adherence to establishes dietary plan as shown in detailed food diary.
(3) ability to control complications such as hypoglycemia, hypertension, and heart disease.
(4) adherence to established insulin, exercise, and dietary regimen.

16. A 50-year-old patient who has had diabetes for 3 years told the nurse in the diabetic clinic that she would like to achieve good glycemic control. She does self monitoring of blood glucose twice daily. The nurse should advise her to

(1) avoid any change in her food intake and activity pattern.
(2) take extra insulin when she is experiencing additional stress.
(3) test her blood glucose level seven times per day to determine the effects of food intake and activity patterns.
(4) test blood glucose before taking insulin or oral hypoglycemic agents and base dose on current readings.

17. A 4-year-old child receives a transfusion of packed cells. He complains of a sharp pain in his back and chills. The nurse takes his vital signs and finds that the child's pulse and respirations are above normal limits and that he has an elevated temperature. The MOST appropriate intervention by the nurse at this time is to

(1) slow down the transfusion and assess the child's vital signs every 15 minutes.
(2) stop the transfusion, place the child in a semi-Fowler's position, and notify the head nurse.
(3) slow down the transfusion and administer an antihistamine as ordered by the physician.
(4) stop the transfusion, send a sample of urine to the laboratory, and notify the physician.

18. A 2-year-old child with acquired immunodeficiency syndrome has been hospitalized. The pediatric nursing staff should be mindful that the risk of infection transmission and exposure to disease may more than likely occur during which of the following nursing procedures?

(1) Bathing.
(2) Diaper change.
(3) Feeding.
(4) Physical assessment.

19. Which of the following medications are generally prescribed for a child with cystic fibrosis?

(1) Electrolyte replenishers and antidiarrheal agents.
(2) Pancreatic enzymes and water-miscible vitamins.
(3) Expectorants and vitamin C.
(4) Antibiotics and antihistamines.

20. An infant with meningomyelocele should be placed in which of the following positions during the preoperative period?

   (1) Supine position with the head slightly elevated.
   (2) Side-lying position with the head lower than the feet.
   (3) Semi-Fowler's position with legs maintained in abduction.
   (4) Prone position with hips slightly flexed.

21. Children with sickle-cell crisis often have joint pain. Which of the following nursing interventions is appropriate to decrease joint pain?

   (1) Immobilize the joint and apply ice packs.
   (2) Administer aspirin and apply cool compresses.
   (3) Perform passive range of motion exercises and apply warm compresses.
   (4) Elevate the extremity and avoid movement of the joint.

22. An 80-year-old patient has a nasogastric tube in place. Intermittent feeding of Jevity 250 ml every 4 hours has been ordered. The nurse aspirated the gastric content with a syringe before starting the feeding. The returned gastric content was 50 ml and greenish color. The nurse should

   (1) return the gastric content to the stomach, then administer feeding as ordered.
   (2) dispose of gastric content, notify the physician.
   (3) return the gastric content to the stomach, then send patient down for gastrointestinal X rays.
   (4) Dispose of gastric content, proceed to administer water instead of ordered feeding.

23. On the fourth day postpartum, a breast-feeding mother's breasts are hard and tender and her temperature is 100.4°F. The nurse should suspect

   (1) a breast abscess.
   (2) mastitis.
   (3) breast engorgement.
   (4) cystic breasts.

24. A 60-year-old female is admitted to the hospital with a rectal temperature of 104°F. Her respirations are rapid and shallow aggravated by coughing. The physician's admission orders include bedrest, sputum for culture and sensitivity, and ampicillin, 1 gm every 6 hours. Before initiating her antibiotic therapy, the nurse should

   (1) place a NO SMOKING sign on her door.
   (2) measure her temperature.
   (3) have her inhale humidified air.
   (4) collect sputum for culture and sensitivity.

25. Which of the following discharge instructions should the nurse give to a patient with emphysema?

   (1) Restrict daily fluid intake to 4 glasses a day.
   (2) Administer oxygen at no more than 1 to 2 liters per minute.
   (3) Restrict diet to 1000 calories per day.
   (4) Inhale bronchodilator 2–3 puffs from nebulizer when needed.

26. A primipara with preexisting diabetes mellitus should be taught which of the following?

   (1) Carbohydrates should be cut by 20% and protein increased.
   (2) Limit carbohydrate intake at breakfast.
   (3) Increase carbohydrates to reduce urinary ketones.
   (4) Restrict calories to control weight gain during second and third trimesters.

27. In dealing with a patient who is manipulative, which of the following strategies should be used?

   (1) Constantly remind the patient what behavior is acceptable and what is not.
   (2) Limit only those behaviors that are clearly destructive to the patient and others.
   (3) Discuss the patient's unacceptable behavior during ward meetings to give the patient an opportunity to justify it.
   (4) Remind the patient of the nurse's authority and accountability for patient care.

28. When teaching nutrition to a child who has diabetes, it is BEST to
    (1) begin with a more precise meal plan and then teach flexibility.
    (2) give general guidelines and let the child prepare own meals.
    (3) give parents a list of "good" and "bad" foods to build menus for the whole family.
    (4) use the exchange system to promote a balanced and structured diet.

29. Prior to administering Fluorouracil (5FU) the nurse should check which of the following laboratory data?
    (1) Sodium and potassium.
    (2) Sedimentation rate and sodium.
    (3) White blood cell count and platelets.
    (4) Liver enzymes and amylase.

30. An 80-year-old patient had a gastrostomy tube placed 2 days ago. She is now receiving an ordered enteral feeding, osmolite-HN, full strength at a rate of 150 ml/hour. Three hours after the first feeding, the patient started having diarrhea. The nurse, being mindful of the complications of enteral feeding should FIRST
    (1) discontinue the enteral feeding.
    (2) decrease the feeding rate.
    (3) request a change in enteral formula.
    (4) request a nutritional consult.

31. A suicidal patient is placed on suicide precautions. Which of the following should the nurse tell the patient?
    (1) "These precautionary measures are designed for your own good."
    (2) "You will be physically restrained if you become overtly self-destructive."
    (3) "The staff will be watching you constantly to protect you from hurting yourself."
    (4) "Suicide precautions means isolating you in a locked, quiet room."

32. A patient refuses to sit in a chair offered by the nurse during a ward meeting. The patient claims that, "They are trying to destroy me. They have planted a bomb under this chair." He accuses the nurse as "one of them." Which of the following strategies would be MOST helpful in dealing with the patient's delusional system?
    (1) Sit in the chair to prove that the chair is safe.
    (2) Tell the patient, "No one is trying to destroy you and I am certainly not one of those who you think want to kill you."
    (3) Allow the patient to select his own chair.
    (4) Ask the patient, "Why do you think anyone would plot to destroy you?"

33. Which of the following information would the nurse give a pregnant cardiac regarding her second stage of labor?
    (1) She will not be brought to the delivery room.
    (2) She will not be allowed to push.
    (3) She will not be able to receive any pain medication.
    (4) She will not be able to receive any anesthesia.

34. Which one of the following is the BEST indication of an elderly patient's risk for falls?
    (1) Periods of confusion.
    (2) Prior history of falls.
    (3) Poor vision and hearing.
    (4) Taking more than 3 medications daily.

35. An 18-year-old patient was admitted to the intensive care unit with tonic/clonic seizure. He sustained a head injury 2 years ago from a motorcycle accident. He stopped taking his diphenylhydantoin (Dilantin) over a year ago because he had not had a seizure in a year. The physician ordered a loading dose of diphenylhydantoin (Dilantin) intravenously, and blood to be drawn for a peak and trough serum level. Which of the following actions by the nurse indicates she understands the physician's orders?

(1) Obtain serum specimens for trough level; administer Dilantin, then obtain serum specimen for peak level.

(2) Administer Dilantin IV, obtain peak serum level specimen 1/2 hour later, and a trough serum level 1/2 hour before next dose.

(3) Administer Dilantin, obtain peak serum level specimen 1/2 hour later, and trough serum level 1 hour after Dilantin administration.

(4) Obtain specimen for peak serum level followed by a trough serum level; based on levels, administer Dilantin IV.

36. A patient is placed on a monoamine (MAO) inhibitor for severe depression. The nurse should teach him to avoid which of the following foods?

(1) Fish.
(2) Eggs.
(3) Chicken.
(4) Red wine.

37. A patient approaches the nurse demanding a pass to leave the ward immediately. The nurse should handle the patient's demands by saying:

(1) "I have to let your doctor know about your request."

(2) "Don't you know the rules about passes on this unit?"

(3) "Your request is unreasonable."

(4) "Something must have happened that made you want to leave at once today. You may wish to talk about it."

38. A 13-year-old girl who has been prescribed a Milwaukee brace tells the nurse, "I'm not going to wear the brace to school. I'm only going to wear it at home." The nurse should interpret this statement as

(1) rebellion against adult authority.
(2) concern about her body image.
(3) anger at having scoliosis.
(4) fear of bodily harm.

39. A 6 year old is admitted to the pediatric unit with a diagnosis of acute glomerulonephritis. Which of the following data from the child's health history is a direct correlation to this diagnosis?

(1) He has a history of otitis media.
(2) He had impetigo 10 days ago.
(3) He has frequent urinary tract infections.
(4) He had pharyngitis 2 weeks ago.

40. Which of these statements by a patient recently placed on a monoamine (MAO) inhibitor indicates the need for further patient teaching?

(1) "I usually take my medication at bedtime."

(2) "I do not drink alcohol beverages while I am on the medication."

(3) "I only eat cottage and cream cheese."

(4) "I had my brother driving me around to complete my errands."

41. A patient with tuberculosis voices concerns about taking "so many pills." The BEST explanation the nurse can give the patient for receiving more than one medication is based on which of the following?

(1) Administration of 2 or more drugs minimizes the danger that a drug-resistant organism will emerge.

(2) Because of the extreme virulence of your disease, many drugs have to be administered to bring it under control.

(3) The current antituberculosis drugs are ineffective alone; therefore, they must be given in combination.

(4) Using a combination of drugs will bring the disease under control.

42. Which type of delivery should the nurse anticipate for a pregnant cardiac?

(1) Spontaneous vaginal delivery.
(2) Cesarean section.
(3) Low forceps delivery.
(4) Vacuum extraction.

43. A primipara has been diagnosed as having gestational diabetes mellitus. The dietary treatment for her would require

(1) cutting carbohydrates by 20% and increasing protein.
(2) limiting carbohydrate intake at breakfast.
(3) increasing carbohydrates to reduce urinary ketones.
(4) restricting calories to control weight gain during second and third trimesters.

44. A patient is to be discharged on cyclophosphamide (Cytoxan) orally. Discharge teaching will include

(1) taking Cytoxan with meals.
(2) doubling doses if one is missed.
(3) taking Cytoxan at bedtime.
(4) drinking plenty of fluids.

45. The physician writes an order for an IV bolus of a bronchodilator for an asthmatic patient. The nurse should know

(1) to prepare a piggyback infusion in 0.9% normal saline to run for 20–30 minutes.
(2) to dilute medication in a 1000 ml bag of dextrose and water, to run for 24 hours.
(3) to administer medication, full strength, intravenously over 1 hour.
(4) that the medication would be administered in full concentration, intravenously over 1–2 minutes.

46. A patient is ordered an aspirin rectal suppository as needed for fever. The nurse is aware that the medication is

(1) administered with its covering intact.
(2) stored in the refrigerator.
(3) mixed with a gel before insertion.
(4) expelled within 2 minutes after insertion.

47. When a pediatric nurse tries to take an admission history on a 3 year old, the child's mother bursts into tears and cannot answer any questions. Which of the following actions should the nurse take?

(1) Continue to take the history.
(2) Encourage the mother to verbalize her fears concerning her child's illness.
(3) Ask the mother to assist in the admission physical assessment.
(4) Ask the mother to join her husband in the waiting room.

48. A 19-year-old male is admitted to a psychiatric hospital for evaluation after vandalizing several school buildings in his neighborhood and threatening to kill his teachers. One afternoon, he comes running out of his room screaming, shouting obscenities, and striking at anything in sight. Which of the following actions is required when dealing with the patient's behavior at this time?

(1) Allow him to continue his expression of anger.
(2) Let him know that you understand his feelings.
(3) Tell him that his behavior is totally irrational and that you will not allow it to continue.
(4) Call for help in order to control him until he calms down.

49. A 25-year-old female is admitted to a psychiatric unit because she accuses her co-worker of plotting against her. She refuses food because "it is poisoned." Which of the following responses by the nurse would be appropriate?

(1) "No one is trying to poison you."
(2) "Who do you think is trying to harm you?"
(3) "If you continue to refuse food, we may have to force feed you."
(4) "I do not believe the food is poisoned. If you wish, you may select the food you like from the tray."

50. A diabetic patient was advised by her doctor to switch from animal intermediate insulin to human insulin. The nurse should tell the patient which of the following?

(1) "You will require a late night snack."
(2) "You will need to increase your calorie intake during the day."
(3) "You will require an afternoon snack."
(4) "You will require a higher dose of regular insulin."

51. Which of the following is the rationale for placing an infant with meningomyelocele on intake and output?

(1) These infants often have congenital malformations of the kidneys.
(2) These infants have impaired bowel and bladder functioning.
(3) These infants are susceptible to rapid changes in fluid balance.
(4) These infants have difficulty ingesting fluids because of a poor sucking reflex.

52. A 34-year-old male has acute thrombophlebitis of the right leg. He is on complete bedrest and receiving heparin therapy. The nurse observed the patient twisting a towel tightly around his right thigh. When asked why, the patient stated, "it eases the pain." After assessing the patient and administering pain medication, the nurse should

   (1) inform the patient to request pain medication whenever needed in the future.
   (2) inform the patient that tying a towel around his thigh would cut off blood circulation to his foot.
   (3) assist the patient in identifying methods of reducing pain without jeopardizing his health.
   (4) ask the physician to either order a stronger dose of the drug he is currently receiving or switch to another drug.

53. A patient who has been diagnosed as having an eating disorder describes herself as "a very fat person." Which of the following responses by the nurse would be MOST appropriate?

   (1) "You don't look fat at all."
   (2) "Why do you say you're fat?"
   (3) "I don't understand why you think you're fat."
   (4) "You seem to think you are fat but I see you as very thin."

54. A combination of antineoplastic drugs is administered in cancer therapy because

   (1) toxic effects will not develop.
   (2) each of the drugs will destroy different types of cancer cells.
   (3) drug resistance will develop more slowly.
   (4) smaller dosages may be given.

55. Which of these lunches is allowed on a renal diet?

   (1) Bacon, lettuce, and tomato sandwich on white bread and diet soda.
   (2) Frankfurter and sauerkraut on a roll and a bottle of beer.
   (3) Turkey sandwich on whole wheat bread, lettuce and tomato salad, and tea.
   (4) Orange and grapefruit salad with cottage cheese and cracker and black coffee.

56. Which of these actions should be performed before a peritoneal catheter is inserted?

   (1) Weighing the patient.
   (2) Measuring temperature.
   (3) Measuring blood pressure.
   (4) Emptying the bladder.

57. A post-hysterectomy patient has a Foley catheter to straight drainage. The nurse notices the absence of urine flowing through the drainage tube and the fact that the amount of urine in the bag has not increased in the last hour. The nurse should

   (1) call the physician.
   (2) palpate the bladder to determine if it is distended.
   (3) notify the head nurse that the patient is not producing urine.
   (4) check the Foley and drainage tube for blockage.

58. Which of the following interventions is appropriate to use with a pregnant woman who is narcissistic?

   (1) Tell her she is acting silly.
   (2) Agree that she should be very concerned about herself.
   (3) Divert her attention by focusing your health teaching on the baby.
   (4) Focus your health teachings on her comfort.

59. A patient is admitted to a hospital for the third time because of a metastatic lung cancer. The patient knows that his illness is terminal. One day he says to the nurse, "I want to live a little longer to see all my children finish college." In light of this statement, which of the following nursing diagnoses should be added to this patient's nursing care plan?

   (1) Knowledge deficit related to the process of loss resolution.
   (2) Powerlessness related to inevitable death.
   (3) Grieving related to loss.
   (4) Ineffective individual coping related to fearful response.

60. A new graduate nurse was asked to witness a consent for surgery by the chief resident. She joined the resident and the patient discussing the surgery. The resident stopped the conversation so that the nurse could sign the consent. She signed the consent after witnessing the patient signature. The action by the nurse is

   (1) illegal.
   (2) legal.
   (3) unethical.
   (4) immoral.

61. A new graduate nurse is administering medication through a feeding tube. Which of these actions indicates that she needs more training on the procedure for administering medication through a feeding tube?

   (1) Tablets are crushed to a fine powder, then mixed with formula in container for administration.
   (2) Tablets are crushed to a fine powder and mixed with water, then administered separately.
   (3) Flush the tube with 50 mL of water prior to giving and after medication and before reinstituting tube feeding.
   (4) Administer liquid form of the ordered medication through the feeding tube.

62. The audibility of fetal heart tones is NOT affected by which one of the following?

   (1) The position of the fetus.
   (2) The amount of amniotic fluid.
   (3) The thickness of the abdominal wall.
   (4) The thickness of the placenta.

63. Which of the following actions by a patient would do the MOST to prevent the spread of tuberculosis during hospitalization?

   (1) Covering the mouth and nose with a tissue when coughing or sneezing.
   (2) Wearing a mask.
   (3) Avoiding face-to-face contact with others.
   (4) Taking antituberculosis drugs as prescribed.

64. To ensure glycemic control, type II diabetes requires calorie restriction and

   (1) elimination of alcohol and simple sugar.
   (2) weekly contracts with the dietitian to promote adherence.
   (3) increased oral hypoglycemic agents (OHAs) to enhance fat metabolism.
   (4) smaller meals and snacks spaced throughout the day.

65. The nurse administering the chelating agents BAL and calcium disodium edetate (EDTA) to a toddler should

   (1) plan a rotation schedule of injection.
   (2) administer injections in the deltoid.
   (3) monitor blood work for vitamins and minerals level.
   (4) restrict fluid intake.

66. The major goal in nutrition care of an adolescent diabetic is maintenance of normal weight gain and growth. A common deterrent to achieving this goal is

   (1) overactive counterregulatory hormones.
   (2) adolescent food aversions and food jags.
   (3) erratic eating and insulin schedules.
   (4) overrestriction of calories.

67. A patient is admitted to a psychiatric unit because of chronic alcoholism. He is to undergo detoxification. Detoxification can be BEST explained to the patient as

   (1) a cure for alcoholism.
   (2) the first step in a treatment process for the patient with a problem with alcohol.
   (3) a treatment best handled in a stimulating and challenging environment.
   (4) a form of aversion therapy.

68. A patient is to have a below-the-knee amputation. He appears to have many questions concerning his upcoming surgery. Which of the following interventions would reduce the anxiety surrounding the amputation?

   (1) Teach him crutch walking.
   (2) Instruct him in arm exercises.
   (3) Arrange for a visit from a rehabilitated amputee.
   (4) Inform the patient about phantom pain.

69. A 38-year-old mother of 2 children is admitted to a hospital because of severe epigastric pains and vomiting. She felt dizzy and fainted. Her friend who brought her to the hospital describes her as a noncomplainer who keeps everything to herself. She is a single parent and supports her elderly parents who live with her and her children. She works as a manager in a local department store. Which of the following factors must be considered by the nurse when assessing the patient's immediate needs?

   (1) Her home environment and support system.
   (2) The extent of her physical illness.
   (3) Her ability to express her feelings and emotions.
   (4) Her patterns of handling stressful situations.

70. A child in a mist tent starts crying and pulling on the canopy in an effort to get out of the tent. The nurse should

(1) explain the purpose of the mist tent and remain with the child until the crying stops.
(2) apply clove hitch restraints.
(3) give a bottle of clear fluids to calm the child.
(4) call the pediatrician and request medication for sedation.

71. A male quadraplegic was hospitalized for a respiratory infection. During the evening he began to experience headache and an anxious feeling. He complained to the nurse. The nurse should immediately

(1) assess the bladder for fullness.
(2) administer urecholine stat.
(3) massage the lower abdomen.
(4) auscultate both lungs.

72. A senior citizens' group requested information on cataracts. When talking to the group, the MOST important point that the nurse should make is

(1) cataract is a rare condition and is a symptom of a medical condition.
(2) cataract is a normal part of aging; most people have cataract in both eyes.
(3) cataracts block some of the light to the eye but would not cause blindness.
(4) cataracts occur in both eyes and deteriorate at the same time.

73. A mother of 2 young children is admitted to a psychiatric hospital because of recurring thoughts of harming her children. The patient scrubs and washes her hands so frequently that her skin is bleeding. Her diagnosis is obsessive-compulsive disorder. Her actions thus serve which of the following purposes?

(1) To reduce anxiety.
(2) Self-punishment.
(3) To get attention.
(4) To maintain personal hygiene.

74. The supervisor asked a registered nurse on a medical surgical unit to work overtime on the coronary unit where she was assigned to complete care for 2 patients. One of the patients had a "cardiac arrest." He was resuscitated but is brain dead. When asked why she did not notify anyone concerning changes on the monitor, the nurse stated, "This was my first time in the coronary care unit and I cannot read a monitor." Who is liable?

(1) Only the nurse, because she did not recognize her own limitations.
(2) Only the supervisor, because she should have known that the nurse was not coronary care unit experienced.
(3) Both the nurse and the supervisor.
(4) The health care facility.

75. A 35-year-old female has been experiencing periods of gastric pain for 6 months. She is admitted to the hospital for complete diagnostic evaluation. She is to have a gastrointestinal series. The patient asks the nurse whether she will experience pain during the gastrointestinal series. Which of these statements by the nurse would be an accurate and appropriate answer to the patient's question?

(1) "There will be no pain."
(2) "Don't worry about the sensation you will have."
(3) "You may be uncomfortable during the procedure, but you should not experience pain."
(4) "Most patients state that they do not have pain."

76. Which of these is an acceptable alternative to physical restraints for a patient with sundown syndrome?

(1) Side rails in up position.
(2) Wheelchair with self releasing belts.
(3) Dimming the room light.
(4) Geri-chair with fixed lap board/tray.

77. A 75-year-old nursing home resident has been transferred to the hospital for treatment of pneumonia. The patient cries, yells continuously, and tries to pull off the oxygen mask. The physician has ordered all of the following. Which should the nurse consider FIRST to deal with the patient's behavior?

(1) Mitten or wrist restraint.
(2) Haldol .25 mgm prn.
(3) Move to private room when available.
(4) 12 hour companions.

78. In counseling a victim of sexual assault, which of the following approaches would assist the person in coping with the crisis?

    (1) Acknowledging the victim's painful experience and preparing the victim for possible delayed psychological reactions.
    (2) Developing an action plan for the patient whose decision-making ability may have been compromised by the experience.
    (3) Reassuring the victim that the painful memories of the assault will eventually dissipate in time.
    (4) Referring the victim to a psychiatrist for psychotherapy.

79. A child who has been treated for lead poisoning has normal blood levels and is ready to be discharged. Which of the following should be included in the discharge teaching to her mother?

    (1) The importance of having the blood lead level checked every 2 months.
    (2) Strategies to prevent the child from putting nonedible objects into her mouth.
    (3) Signs and symptoms of developmental delays.
    (4) Move from her present apartment as soon as possible.

80. A type A positive infant of an RH negative mother is having an exchange transfusion for hemolytic disease. Which type blood would be used?

    (1) A positive.
    (2) A negative.
    (3) O positive.
    (4) O negative.

81. A child is receiving vincristine for acute lymphoblastic leukemia. Which of these symptoms should be immediately reported to the physician?

    (1) Diarrhea.
    (2) Anorexia.
    (3) Skin rash.
    (4) Constipation.

82. A 65-year-old diabetic patient has been admitted to the intensive care unit with hyperglycemic hyperosmolar nonketotic (HHNK) syndrome. Monitoring the laboratory data, the nurse would expect

    (1) serum glucose level of 1000mg/dl.
    (2) serum potassium of 4.5 mEq/L.
    (3) serum pH level of <7.38.
    (4) elevated serum ketones.

83. Which of the following plays a major role in the prevention of diabetic ketoacidosis (DKA)?

    (1) Self monitoring of blood glucose.
    (2) Urine testing for glucose.
    (3) Avoiding changes in food intake.
    (4) Increasing oral hypoglycemic agents.

84. During the first trimester of pregnancy hypoglycemia is often a problem for women with preexisting diabetes because

    (1) "morning sickness" leads to dehydration and decreased need for insulin.
    (2) The hormones of pregnancy intensify the action of oral hypoglycemic agents.
    (3) There is increased sensitivity to insulin.
    (4) Oral hypoglycemic agents cross the placenta diverting them from circulating blood.

85. A patient is to have 3-bottle water seal chest drainage. The nurse should be mindful that

    (1) bottle #3 controls the amount of suction applied.
    (2) bottle #1 acts as a seal to keep air from being drawn into pleural cavity.
    (3) bottle #2 controls suction and provides water seal.
    (4) bottle #3 acts as water seal and collection of drainage.

86. A patient is to have his chest tube removed. The nurse should instruct the patient to

    (1) take a deep breath and hold it until the physician removes the tube.
    (2) cough while the physician removes the tube.
    (3) lay on affected side while the tube is removed.
    (4) alternate between coughing and deep breathing while the nurse removes the tube.

87. Which of these safety measures should be performed every 8 hours without fail when caring for a patient on continuous mechanical ventilation?

    (1) Provide humidified air.
    (2) Suction endotracheal tube.
    (3) Check ventilatory alarms.
    (4) Monitor response to ventilation.

88. An 18-month-old child fractured his femur when he fell out of his crib. He is admitted to the pediatric unit and placed in Bryant's traction. A nursing diagnosis that should be added to the child's nursing care plan is

    (1) risk for impaired skin integrity related to friction/shearing of leg bandage.
    (2) altered nutrition less than body requirement related to immobility.
    (3) impaired swallowing related to position while in traction.
    (4) risk for infection related to trauma.

89. Hip flexion deformity could be prevented in a patient with paresis or paralysis by

    (1) keeping the bed in a semi-Fowler's position.
    (2) alternating the position of the bed during the day.
    (3) placing a trochanter roll along the external aspect of the hip.
    (4) keeping both feet in contact with the footboard.

90. Which of the following nursing diagnoses should be included in a nursing care plan of a patient with a cerebrovascular accident?

    (1) Unilateral neglect related to disturbed perceptual ability.
    (2) Anxiety related to prescribed therapy.
    (3) Pain related to disease condition.
    (4) Risk for infection related to disease process.

91. A patient is to be discharged after a left mastectomy. The MOST important thing that the nurse can teach her is how to

    (1) schedule shopping, housework, or gardening.
    (2) contact a visiting nurse.
    (3) perform self-examination of the right breast.
    (4) limit her social activities.

92. The mother of a 3 year old asked the nurse when she should give her child a tepid sponge bath for an elevated temperature. The nurse responded,

    (1) "After an antibiotic is given."
    (2) "Thirty minutes after the administration of an antipyretic."
    (3) "When the child's temperature is below 104°F (40°C)."
    (4) "When irritability and crying are present."

93. The nurse should monitor which of the following lab values on a routine basis while a patient is on Cytoxan?

    (1) Liver enzymes.
    (2) Uric acid levels.
    (3) Calcium.
    (4) Potassium.

94. A 69-year-old patient is given Dulcolax to relieve constipation. After bowel evacuation the patient is placed on Metamucil daily. The nurse should include which of the following interventions in her plan of care?

    (1) Administer at least 8 oz. of fluid with medication.
    (2) Mix medication with evening meal.
    (3) Add patient's medication to the Metamucil.
    (4) Discontinue Metamucil if no bowel movement is noted in 4 hours.

95. If the firstborn of an Rh-negative woman who has never before been pregnant develops pathological jaundice, it usually indicates that the mother could have been previously sensitized by a

    (1) blood transfusion.
    (2) hydatidiform mole.
    (3) venereal disease.
    (4) vaccination.

96. When a newborn's fontanelles are inspected, which of the following observations would suggest an abnormality?

    (1) The posterior fontanelle is smaller than the anterior.
    (2) The anterior fontanelle is diamond shaped.
    (3) The anterior fontanelle bulges.
    (4) The posterior fontanelle is difficult to palpate.

97. Which of the following statements by a patient receiving Cytoxan indicates the need for further patient teaching?

    (1) "I may lose my hair due to this chemotherapy."
    (2) "Soft toothbrushes will reduce bleeding of the gums."
    (3) "Red urine means that I am getting rid of the medication."
    (4) "I should weigh myself and report unexpected weight gain."

98. A patient who has undergone axillary node dissection for the treatment of breast cancer should be instructed by the nurse to

(1) reduce dietary carbohydrates for two weeks.
(2) limit arm movement on the affected side for one month.
(3) eliminate citrus juices from the diet for three weeks.
(4) avoid shaving the affected underarm for two weeks.

99. While preparing a medication, the nurse notes that the physician has doubled the usual dosage of the drug. She should

(1) administer the drug according to the new order.
(2) check the orders with several other staff nurses before administering the drug.
(3) record that an overdosage was ordered.
(4) check with the doctor concerning the dosage ordered.

100. Which of the following safety interventions for falls is controversial?

(1) Use of Geri-chair.
(2) Non-skid footwear.
(3) Use of side rails.
(4) Use of nightlight.

101. The nurse is taking an 80-year-old patient's history with the assistance of the patient's care giver. Which of these incidents would signal that the patient may be abused?

(1) The care giver has little knowledge of the elder's medical conditions.
(2) The patient is disoriented.
(3) The care giver handles the elder's finances.
(4) The care giver is involved in many community activities.

102. A 3-year-old child has nephrotic syndrome. She has proteinuria and generalized edema. Which of the following nursing interventions should receive the HIGHEST priority?

(1) Recording intake and output.
(2) Monitoring blood pressure.
(3) Daily weighing.
(4) Frequent skin massage.

103. A 7-year-old child has classic hemophilia. He has fallen in the school playground and injured his knee. When the child arrives at the emergency room, the nurse should immediately

(1) assess mobility by performing passive range of motion to the child's knee.
(2) elevate the child's leg and apply warm compresses to the injured area.
(3) administer an analgesic and wait until it is effective before implementing further nursing care.
(4) immobilize the child's leg and apply an ice pack locally.

104. During an acute psychotic episode, patients can become frightened of their own bizarre sensory experiences. They also fear losing control over their own impulses. Which of the following nursing interventions would help the patient to feel less frightened?

(1) Assure the patient that his sensory experiences will disappear in no time.
(2) Let the patient know that the staff will assist him in maintaining control.
(3) Keep the patient in a well-lighted, stimulating environment at all times.
(4) Keep potentially harmful objects out of the patient's reach.

105. Which of the following laboratory values found in a patient suspected of having disseminated intravascular coagulation should be brought to the attention of the physician immediately?

(1) An elevated hemoglobin level.
(2) A shortened prothrombin time.
(3) A drop in hematocrit.
(4) A prolonged partial thromboplastin time (PTT).

106. A registered nurse is observing a new graduate suctioning a patient. Which of the following actions by the graduate nurse would indicate to the registered nurse that the graduate nurse needs more instruction in suctioning technique?

(1) Installing normal saline into airway, then applying suction while inserting the catheter.
(2) Administering oxygen via manual resuscitation bag then inserting the catheter gently.
(3) Suctioning for 10–15 seconds, applying suction while withdrawing the catheter.
(4) Selecting a #16 French catheter for a #8 airway, don sterile glove, then proceed to suction patient.

107. A patient on a mechanical ventilator requires suctioning. The nurse should perform which of the following actions to ensure the patient does not experience hypoxemia?

(1) Hyperoxygenation using a resuscitation bag.
(2) Hyperinflation by pressing the sigh button on the ventilator.
(3) Hyperoxygenation by deflating the cuff on the tracheotomy tube.
(4) Hyperinflation by using intermittent positive pressure breathing.

108. A mother asked the nurse on the pediatric unit to "look in" on her daughter. The child is breathing with the use of accessory muscles in the chest, ribs, and neck and also displaying nasal flaring. The nurse should FIRST

(1) notify the pediatrician.
(2) start administering cardiopulmonary resuscitation.
(3) administer nasal oxygen.
(4) apply a pulse oximeter.

109. A registered nurse notes that a physician had ordered digoxin in a larger dose than the usual therapeutic one. When she called the supervisor and explained the situation, the supervisor told her to give the medication as ordered. She gave the drug, and the patient suffered a toxic reaction. Is the nurse liable even though she was following the physician's order?

(1) Yes. After speaking to the supervisor, she should have checked with the physician.
(2) Yes. On her own, she should have reduced the dose to the usual amount.
(3) No. The supervisor's order absolved the nurse.
(4) No. A nurse has no responsibility to question a physician's order.

110. Which of the following interventions would be appropriate for an elderly, hospitalized patient who becomes confused in the evening?

(1) Relocate the patient in a 2-bedded room from the window bed to the bed by the door.
(2) Arrange for a volunteer or family to visit in late afternoon and early evening.
(3) Restrict fluids in the evening to control incontinence.
(4) Apply physical restraints to prevent the patient from harming him- or herself.

111. A patient comes to the outpatient psychiatric center for electroconvulsive therapy. Which of the following situations will necessitate canceling and/or rescheduling the treatment for another day?

(1) Patient had not eaten for 12 hours.
(2) Patient comes for treatment unaccompanied.
(3) Patient feels confused and depressed.
(4) Patient is unemployed.

112. A measure that will prevent a complication of a radium implant in the cervix is

(1) insertion of a nasogastric tube.
(2) withholding food and fluids for 24 hours.
(3) administration of a saline douche.
(4) insertion of an indwelling catheter.

113. Which of the following procedures during the admission routine will be MOST threatening to a 4 year old?

(1) Assessing his pulse and respirations.
(2) Obtaining his height and weight.
(3) Collecting a urine specimen.
(4) Taking his rectal temperature.

114. Which of the following measures will prevent complications that commonly occur after gallbladder surgery?

(1) Maintenance of bedrest.
(2) Assisting the patient with ambulation at least twice a day.
(3) Preoperative teaching of leg exercises.
(4) Assisting and encouraging coughing and deep breathing.

115. A newborn has been diagnosed as having a tracheoesophageal fistula. The primary objective of the nursing care is to

(1) maintain fluid and electrolyte balance.
(2) prevent upper respiratory infections.
(3) maintain a patent airway.
(4) prevent atelectasis and pneumothorax.

116. During recovery immediately after electroconvulsive therapy, the nursing priority is

(1) reorienting the patient upon awakening.
(2) administering oxygen to prevent hypoxia upon awakening.
(3) applying restraints to prevent harm to self or others upon awakening.
(4) administering acetaminophen for headache upon awakening.

117. A 15-year-old male has an ostomy. His mother would like to know what sports he could safely participate in. The nurse should recommend which of the following?

    (1) Football.
    (2) Hockey.
    (3) Tennis.
    (4) Soccer.

118. A 20-year-old patient with Crohn's disease has just had an ileostomy. Which of the following statements indicates that he needs further patient teaching?

    (1) "I am to avoid gas forming foods such as cabbage and onions."
    (2) "I can either take or place a deodorizing pill in the pouch to control odor."
    (3) "I should shower with my appliance in place."
    (4) "I will irrigate my ileostomy daily."

119. Which of the following actions by the nurse demonstrates that she needs further training in caring for the patient with an ostomy?

    (1) She empties the content of the pouch into the toilet.
    (2) She tapes the pouch in place when it leaks.
    (3) She changes the pouch when it is leaking.
    (4) She cleanses the skin around the stoma with warm tap water.

120. A child with meningitis has assumed the opisthotonus posture. Which of the following is the optimal position for him?

    (1) Side-lying position.
    (2) Prone position.
    (3) Supine position.
    (4) Semi-Fowler's position.

121. A 25-year-old man is admitted to a psychiatric unit after accusing his neighbors of stealing his money and threatening their lives. He was found running naked in the street. He states that he hears voices telling him to destroy "anything that moves." His speech is tangential and thoughts are disorganized. Which of the following approaches should be taken when talking to this patient?

    (1) Speak to the patient in abstract terms.
    (2) Give elaborate explanations.
    (3) Speak in short, simple sentences.
    (4) Interrupt the patient whenever his thoughts don't make sense.

122. A preterm infant is more likely to develop anemia than a full term infant because he has

    (1) impaired ability to manufacture immune globulins.
    (2) immature white blood cells.
    (3) decreased liver glycogen stores.
    (4) deficient liver stores of iron.

123. A nurse is assigned to observe the mother-child interaction with a family that is suspected of child abuse. The BEST approach to establish rapport with the mother would be to

    (1) provide suggestions for discipline.
    (2) explain the child's progress in the hospital.
    (3) acknowledge parental strengths.
    (4) explain the child's developmental needs.

124. A female patient with cancer of the right breast with bone metastasis is complaining that the pain medication is not relieving her pain. The patient is receiving meperdine (Demerol) 100 mgm IM every 3 hours prn for pain. The nurse should notify the physician and recommend changing to another opioid analgesic and

    (1) giving the analgesic around the clock.
    (2) continuing to give on a prn basis.
    (3) Giving a bolus dose, then following a prn schedule.
    (4) Alternating with a nonsteroidal anti-inflammatory drug (NSAID).

125. Which of these items can a visitor NOT bring to a bone marrow transplant patient during the period of engraftment?

    (1) Canned soda.
    (2) A new magazine or book.
    (3) Posters or photographs.
    (4) Candy or junk food.

126. A patient who is suffering an acute myocardial infarction is being seen in the emergency department. The patient is to receive thrombolytic therapy. The nurse should be aware that

    (1) an informed consent is needed.
    (2) medication should be administered within 2 hours.
    (3) A 12 lead electrocardiogram is not needed before therapy.
    (4) Isoenzymes should be done only after therapy.

127. A 13 year old receives NPH insulin every morning at 7:30 A.M. At what time would it be appropriate for the nurse to provide the child with a snack?

(1) 11:00 in the morning.
(2) 3:30 in the afternoon.
(3) 9:30 in the evening.
(4) 11:00 in the evening.

128. A 65-year-old housewife is diagnosed as having increased ocular pressure during her yearly eye examination. She asks the nurse, "Why didn't I exhibit symptoms of increased eye pressure?" The MOST appropriate and accurate explanation is:

(1) "The impairment of peripheral vision occurs gradually."
(2) "The condition was diagnosed in its early stage."
(3) "Impairment of vision does not occur in this condition."
(4) "No symptoms occur in this condition."

129. A mother called the nurse at the pediatric well baby clinic because her 8 month old had been exposed to rubella and had not been vaccinated. The nurse should instruct the mother to

(1) not worry because the baby has natural immunity at this age.
(2) immediately bring baby in for an MMR (mumps, measles, rubella) vaccination.
(3) immediately bring the baby in for serum immunoglobin.
(4) observe the baby for 72 hours for a temperature over 101°F.

130. In planning strategies for dealing with a verbally abusive and openly aggressive patient, the nurse must understand that

(1) the patient's behavior is consciously motivated.
(2) the patient perceives the nurse as a disciplinarian.
(3) the patient's behavior most probably represents the only way of coping known to the patient.
(4) the patient will probably abandon unacceptable behaviors if positive reinforcements are provided at all times for her other behaviors.

131. A patient expresses to the nurse her fears that she will experience severe pain after surgery. The appropriate nursing intervention is to

(1) refocus her attention from the idea of pain.
(2) explain that medication for pain will be available.
(3) reassure her that the pain will disappear soon.
(4) reassure her that little pain is associated with this surgery.

132. An unvaccinated 4-year-old child has been exposed to *Haemophilus influenza* type B (Hib). The mother should be instructed to

(1) bring the child to the well baby clinic for antibiotic treatment.
(2) quarantine the child for 15–20 days.
(3) bring the child for 3 doses of Hib vaccine given at 3-month intervals.
(4) bring the child for one dose of Hib vaccine.

133. The physician ordered cimetadine (Tagamet) and antacids for a patient with a gastric ulcer. The nurse should instruct the patient to

(1) take both medications before meals.
(2) take the antacids before each meal and Tagamet in morning and evening.
(3) take the antacids before meals and Tagamet after meals.
(4) take the antacids 1 hour before or after Tagamet.

134. A patient was given a drug intramuscularly. The patient immediately developed difficulty in breathing; the skin became pale, cool, and clammy. The patient's blood pressure fell from 130/90 to 90/60. The nurse should immediately

(1) prepare epinephrine for IV administration.
(2) prepare narcon for administration.
(3) increase the IV infusion rate.
(4) administer amoxicillin intravenously.

135. A 50-year-old female postmastectomy patient is to have a bone marrow transplant (BMT). Which of the following statements made by her demonstrates she does NOT understand this treatment?

(1) "A bone marrow transplant will replenish my bone marrow reserves."
(2) "Where am I going to get bone marrow? I have no relative and I cannot use mine."
(3) "My bone marrow will be harvested when I am in remission."
(4) "I will be hospitalized for about 10 days post-transplant."

136. Which of the following activities is MOST appropriate for a 6-year-old boy who is on bedrest for acute glomerulonephritis?

(1) Playing Chinese checkers with the nurse.

(2) Swapping baseball cards with an 8-year-old boy who has had an appendectomy.

(3) Reading comic books and watching television.

(4) Playing cards with a 5 year old who has pneumonia.

137. An HIV-positive patient was tested for tuberculosis and the test was negative. The nurse should be mindful that

(1) a negative reading for immunosuppressed patients suggests that the patient had been in contact with mycobacterium tuberculosis.

(2) false positive occurs often among immuno-suppressed patients.

(3) the patient probably does not have tuberculosis.

(4) false negative occurs among immuno-suppressed patients.

138. A preeclamptic woman was given large doses of magnesium sulfate just before delivery. The nurses in the nursery should be instructed to observe the newborn during the first 48 hours for

(1) increased reflexes.

(2) convulsions.

(3) increased urine output.

(4) depressed reflexes.

139. A 65-year-old widower with a history of congestive heart failure is dyspneic with cyanosis of the nailbeds and lips, is anxious, and has pitting edema of the feet and ankles. His dyspnea is due primarily to

(1) accumulation of serous fluid in alveolar spaces.

(2) obstruction of bronchi by mucoid secretions.

(3) compression of lung tissue by a dilated heart.

(4) restriction of respiratory movement by ascites.

140. A patient with esophageal varcies has a Sengstaken-Blakemore tube in place. The nurse, being mindful of possible complications, would keep which of the following at the bedside?

(1) A hemostat.

(2) A pair of scissors.

(3) A Venturi mask.

(4) A tracheostomy set.

141. Which of the following statements by a diabetic patient taking Glucotrol indicates that there is a need for further patient teaching?

(1) "If my glucose level continues to rise, I will call my doctor."

(2) "I take my pills 30 minutes before breakfast."

(3) "I do not skip meals."

(4) "The pills are the same as insulin."

142. A patient receiving insulin for diabetes mellitus is receiving a form of therapy that can be compared to which of the following?

(1) Thyroid for cretinism.

(2) Streptomycin for tuberculosis.

(3) Cortisone for rheumatoid arthritis.

(4) Morphine for severe pain.

143. A patient is to receive a short course of radiation after mastectomy. The benefit of this treatment is

(1) stimulation of the body's defense mechanism.

(2) destruction of malignant cells not removed by surgery.

(3) facilitation of scar healing.

(4) halting of keloid formation.

144. An intravenous drug abuser who is HIV (human immunodeficiency virus) positive is being discharged from the hospital. Which of the following instructions should the nurse include in discharge teaching?

(1) Disposal of soiled tissues and garbage.

(2) Restriction of visitors who are ill or otherwise infected.

(3) Weighing the patient every other week.

(4) Restriction of fluid intake.

145. Which of these methods would be MOST effective in determining whether a nasogastric tube is still in the abdomen?

    (1) Inserting a small amount of air quickly and listening with a stethoscope.
    (2) Checking to see whether the tape anchoring the tube is undisturbed.
    (3) Placing the end of the tube in a glass of water and observing it for bubbles.
    (4) Aspirating the nasogastric tube for stomach content.

146. A male patient is being admitted into the hospital for a bone marrow transplant. Which of the following items should he NOT bring with him?

    (1) Two pairs of glasses.
    (2) Single edged razor.
    (3) Three or four new magazines or books.
    (4) Stereo/cassette radio with cassettes.

147. The goal of nurses on a medical surgical unit is to prevent and decrease the number of falls on their unit. The nurses should be mindful that patients need to manifest which of the following characteristics to be placed on "fall precaution"?

    (1) Emotional problems.
    (2) Mental status change.
    (3) Communication deficit.
    (4) Advanced age.

148. The nurse plans to explain preoperative procedures, the operating room, the recovery room, and postoperative procedures to a child. Which of the following interventions should be implemented FIRST?

    (1) Explain to her the need for preoperative medications.
    (2) Tell her that her parents will be waiting in her room for her.
    (3) Describe the appearance of the recovery room and the operating room.
    (4) Ask her to tell what she knows about the operation.

149. A patient diagnosed with angina pectoris has been placed on nitrate therapy. During the first 24 hours the nurse should monitor the patient for headaches and

    (1) increased blood pressure.
    (2) orthostatic hypotension.
    (3) anorexia.
    (4) increased heart rate.

150. Which of the following recreational activities would be MOST appropriate for a suspicious patient?

    (1) Card game of solitaire.
    (2) Playing chess with the nurse.
    (3) Making ceramic pots.
    (4) Playing basketball with other patients.

151. A patient on digitalis preparation returns to the outpatient clinic with a complaint of anorexia, nausea and vomiting, and visual disturbance. The nurse should

    (1) instruct the patient to decrease dose.
    (2) have blood drawn for digitalis level.
    (3) instruct patient to discontinue medication.
    (4) prepare the patient immediately for an intravenous dose of digitalis.

152. A patient with a recent bout of depression is receiving imipramine (Tofranil). The patient returned to the outpatient psychiatric center. The patient complained that the medication makes him very drowsy and interferes with his performance at work. The nurse should instruct the patient to

    (1) take the drug at night.
    (2) discontinue the medication.
    (3) avoid drinking large amounts of fluids.
    (4) take the drug with food or milk.

153. The area around an infusion site is cold to the touch and swollen. The action the nurse should take in this situation is to

    (1) reset the drip rate.
    (2) remove the IV.
    (3) apply warm compresses.
    (4) notify the physician.

154. A 6 month old is diagnosed with isotonic dehydration. Which of the following is the best way to assess the baby's level of dehydration each shift?

    (1) Measure weight.
    (2) Measure intake and output.
    (3) Assess skin turgor.
    (4) Palpate his anterior fontanel.

155. A mother is concerned about food allergies. She asked the nurse how to introduce new foods to her infant. The nurse should instruct her to

(1) "Avoid foods that you and your husband are allergic to until the infant is 2 years old."
(2) "Avoid all hypoallergenic foods until age 5, then introduce new foods."
(3) "Offer new foods one at the time, well cooked and in small quantities."
(4) "Offer new foods in combination, if allergies do not occur within 4 hours, integrate into diet."

156. A patient is complaining of epigastric fullness, abdominal distention, profuse sweating, and palpitations after eating. The patient is 2 weeks postgastrectomy. The nurse should instruct the patient to

(1) drink liquids with meal.
(2) eat several small meals a day.
(3) take an antacid before meal.
(4) eat a high carbohydrate diet.

157. A female nursing home resident was admitted to the geriatric unit with a diagnosis of pneumonia. The patient is demonstrating the following behavior: sleeps during the day and is awake during the night; disoriented as to time, place, and person, and is becoming agitated. Considering that all of these are ordered or would be ordered if requested by the nurse, she should FIRST

(1) administer ordered Haldol.
(2) apply restraints.
(3) administer Ativan.
(4) relocate to a private room.

158. A 2-year-old child has celiac disease. The nurse is counseling his parents about the child's diet. Which of these statements by the parents indicates they do not understand the dietary regimen?

(1) "We bake our own whole wheat bread so that our child will be able to eat sandwiches."
(2) "We do not give our child raw fruits and vegetables."
(3) "We make sure our child takes his vitamins and minerals as prescribed."
(4) "Our child has snacks between his meals."

159. A multipara age 60 years old is experiencing stress incontinence. During her yearly gynecology exam at the women's health clinic she asked her nurse what non-surgical measure can be used to control this problem. The nurse should instruct the patient to

(1) buy incontinence pads.
(2) decrease fluid intake.
(3) perform Kegel exercises.
(4) perform abdominal twist exercises.

160. The method to determine whether a patient is eliminating retained fluid is through monitoring of the patient's

(1) weight.
(2) vital signs.
(3) intake and output.
(4) skin turgor.

161. A patient states that he is allergic to a medication the doctor prescribed. The appropriate action for the nurse in this situation is to

(1) withhold the medication and notify the doctor.
(2) give the medication and then, if the patient has a reaction, notify the doctor.
(3) record the information on the chart after administering the dose.
(4) administer the medication via a different route.

162. Previously unconscious, a patient in the intensive care unit (ICU) is thrashing about wildly in bed. Presuming that all of the following measures are ordered, which one should the nurse initiate FIRST?

(1) Apply restraints.
(2) Administer phenobarbital.
(3) Decrease sensory stimuli.
(4) Insert a padded tongue blade.

163. A patient has had a modified mastectomy and is to be discharged from the hospital in 48 hours. She asked the nurse what activity she would be allowed to engage in at home. The nurse should discourage her from

(1) vacuuming or mopping.
(2) using the telephone.
(3) playing cards.
(4) combing her hair.

164. A 22-year-old gymnast sustained a head injury during practice. She lost consciousness immediately after her injury. She is brought to the emergency room. Her blood pressure was 100/80, pulse 80, respiration 20. Which of the following groups of symptoms would be indicative of increasing intracranial pressure?

(1) Blood pressure 90/70, pulse 110, respiration 44.
(2) Blood pressure 180/80, pulse 66, respiration 14.
(3) Blood pressure 110/68, pulse 40, respiration 22.
(4) Blood pressure 120/90, pulse 94, respiration 18.

165. A patient has recently had a baby. She tells the nurse at the well baby clinic that her 3-year-old son is very jealous of her new sister. Which of the following interventions should the nurse recommend to the patient?

(1) Allow the toddler to feed the new baby.
(2) Buy a pet for the toddler.
(3) Plan a special time each day to spend with the toddler.
(4) Discuss the toddler's feelings with him.

166. In planning the care of a psychotic patient who is experiencing hallucinations, which of the following interventions is considered critical?

(1) Setting fewer limits in order to allow for more expression of feelings.
(2) Maintaining constant observation.
(3) Providing more opportunities for interaction with others.
(4) Constantly negating the patient's hallucinatory ideations.

167. A newborn's first stool passed was thick, blackish green, and sticky. The nurse should

(1) record the passage and description of stool in nurse's notes.
(2) notify the physician immediately.
(3) send stool specimen to lab for culture and sensitivity.
(4) observe the newborn for jaundice and further passage of black stools.

168. A 36-year-old housewife and mother of 3 children ages 14, 12, and 10, is brought to the emergency room by a friend who found her extremely confused, disoriented, and hallucinatory. Her diagnosis is delirium tremens. Which of the following nursing interventions would be therapeutic for this patient?

(1) Physical restraint, companion, and seizure precaution.
(2) Seizure precaution, well-lighted room, and sedatives.
(3) Sedatives, side rails up, and physical restraint.
(4) Non-stimulating environment, side rails up, and avoidance of caffeine.

169. A 4 year old is admitted to the pediatric unit for repair of an inguinal hernia. Which of the following toys should the nurse provide for the child in order to help him cope with the hospital experience?

(1) Pounding board.
(2) Doctor and nurse puppets.
(3) Coloring book and crayons.
(4) Big Bird and Ernie dolls.

170. Which of the following methods would be LEAST helpful in identifying the early signs of dehydration in an adult?

(1) Measuring the blood pressure.
(2) Measuring the central venous pressure.
(3) Inspecting the peripheral veins for filling.
(4) Monitoring the urine output.

171. An infant is to have a lumbar puncture. The nurse should place and maintain the child in which of the following positions during the procedure?

(1) Sitting position, buttocks placed in middle of bed and/or examining table.
(2) Side lying, nurse's hands holding the neck and the thigh in flexed position.
(3) Mummy restraint holding the child in prone position.
(4) Side lying position, nurse holding child's hands and feet to prevent movement.

172. A 25-year-old vegetarian in her first trimester is concerned about her diet while pregnant. The nurse should advise her to

(1) drink 3 glasses of whole milk daily, take multivitamins daily, eat green leafy vegetables and fruits, and drink decaffeinated or herbal tea.

(2) eat no more than 3 eggs weekly, take multivitamins daily, eat green leafy vegetables and fruits, and drink decaffeinated or herbal tea.

(3) drink soy milk, take daily supplements of multivitamins, B_{12}, calcium, vitamin D, iron and zinc, and eat a combination of legumes and whole-grain cereals or nuts and whole-grain cereals.

(4) eat meat high in protein and iron such as liver and beef, drink 3 glasses of milk daily and take multivitamins with minerals daily.

173. Which of the following actions must be avoided by the nurse in dealing with a patient with antisocial personality?

(1) Discussing the patient's attitude and behavior.

(2) Limiting what the patient can and cannot do.

(3) Assisting the patient in recognizing limitations.

(4) Making false promises.

174. A pregnant 15 year old in her first trimester has lactose intolerance and refuses to drink milk. The nurse should instruct her to try

(1) eating low-fat dairy products.

(2) eating custards, aged cheese, and yogurt.

(3) drinking milk only in the morning and at bedtime.

(4) eating ice cream instead of drinking milk.

175. Which of the following nursing interventions are appropriate for a patient with a third-degree laceration after delivery?

(1) Complete bedrest.

(2) High-roughage diet.

(3) Increased fluids.

(4) Abdominal exercises.

176. A young couple in a new community is expecting their first child and would like to take a childbirth preparation class. Which of the following should be recommended to them?

(1) One-to-one childbirth classes.

(2) Group classes.

(3) Parenting classes.

(4) Hypnosis classes.

177. A cardiac woman in her eighth month of pregnancy called the nurse in the antepartal clinic because over the last 5 days she has developed a wet cough with dyspnea, her face and extremities are edematous, and she complains of "palpitation." The nurse should advise her to

(1) ignore the symptoms, they are normal for the latter part of the pregnancy.

(2) make an appointment to see the physician as soon as possible.

(3) immediately come to the antepartal clinic.

(4) ask her mother to stay with her until she delivers.

178. A patient with a diagnosis of gestational diabetes mellitus has missed several appointments. When asked the reason for the missed appointments, she stated: "I did not feel good." The BEST reply by the nurse should be

(1) "That is not a good reason for not seeing the physician."

(2) "Instead of canceling, call and let us know how you feel."

(3) "Come anyway, we will fix you up."

(4) "Whenever you feel sick, do not hesitate to call the office."

179. A patient who is a heavy smoker has had several bouts of respiratory infection in the past year. The reason is

(1) lack of specific immunity to the virus.

(2) presence of fewer phagocytes.

(3) retention of a large amount of tracheobronchial secretions.

(4) reduction in number of T-cells.

180. A 45-year-old mother of 5 noticed a lump in her breast while showering. She consults her family physician, and upon examination he palpates a 2-cm enlargement in the upper outer quadrant of the left breast. The axillary nodes are also enlarged. The presence of enlarged lymph nodes in the patient's axilla may be interpreted as

(1) indication that the tumor cells have not spread beyond this point.

(2) indication that inflammation has occurred.

(3) indication that cells have metastasized from the primary site.

(4) the beginning of a breast abscess.

181. A patient has had a pacemaker for 2 years. The pacemaker is fixed at 72 beats/minute. He calls the medical cardiac outpatient department because he has been experiencing dizziness, hiccups, and palpitations. His pulse rate is 80. The nurse should instruct him to

(1) ignore the symptoms, they are normal for patients with pacemakers.

(2) make an appointment to see the physician as soon as possible.

(3) immediately come to the medical cardiac clinic.

(4) ask his wife to stay with him when the symptoms occur.

182. A prenatal patient who is at term has the following obstetrical history:

1989 — spontaneous abortion — 12 weeks.
1990 — NSVD — living female — 39 weeks.
1991 — NSVD — living male — 32 weeks.
1992 — NSVD — living male — 40 weeks.
1993 — NSVD — stillborn — 38 weeks.

The proper way to record this patient's parity is

(1) gravida 3 para 3.

(2) gravida 4 para 6.

(3) gravida 6 para 4.

(4) gravida 5 para 3.

183. A 50-year-old woman is being treated for thrombophlebitis. Suddenly, she experiences a sharp, stabbing chest pain and dyspnea. Until the physician arrives, the nurse should

(1) encourage patient to cough and deep breath.

(2) perform postural drainage.

(3) place patient in a sitting upright position.

(4) administer a stat dose of Coumadin.

184. A Jackson-Pratt drain was inserted after a radical modified mastectomy. During the first 8 hours, 25 ml was removed from the drain. The nurse should

(1) notify the physician.

(2) do nothing; this amount of drainage is acceptable.

(3) examine the drain and tube for collapse.

(4) assess the wound for redness.

185. A patient tells the nurse, "I called my employers and informed them that I am dying. I know I'm dying very soon." Which of the following responses by the nurse would be MOST appropriate?

(1) "Don't talk like that. Your condition is improving."

(2) "We are all going to die. No one knows when. When your time is up, then that's the time to go."

(3) "What makes you think you are dying soon? Let's talk about it."

(4) "Let's not talk about dying. Let's talk about living. Your children are so precious. Are they coming today to visit?"

186. A patient diagnosed as having angina pectoris is returning to the cardiac outpatient clinic. The patient is on aspirin 325 gm daily, nitroglycerin, and Lopressor. Which of the following statements by the patient indicates he needs further patient teaching?

(1) "I ran out of aspirin so I took Tylenol."

(2) "I take my nitroglycerin before I climb several flights of stairs."

(3) "I quit smoking."

(4) "Plain aspirin upsets my stomach so I take Ecotrin."

187. An 80-year-old nursing home resident has been admitted to the hospital with an infected pressure ulcer of the sacrum, stage IV. The ulcer base is covered with yellow slough necrosis and the patient's serum albumin is 2.4 gm/dl. A referral should be made to

(1) nutritional services.

(2) physiotherapy.

(3) plastic surgery.

(4) podiatry.

188. A diabetic patient with a serum cholesterol of 290 mg/dl. is being treated with Mevacor, a cholesterol lowering drug. Which of the following statements would indicate the need for further patient education?

    (1) "I try to eat wholesome; I drink three glasses of whole milk daily and eat little or no beef."

    (2) "I have changed my eating habits and now eat turkey, fish, and chicken instead of beef."

    (3) "I make my chili con carne with ground turkey and kidney beans."

    (4) "I cannot eat cheeseburgers until my serum cholesterol is lowered."

189. A 65-year-old diabetic patient with peripheral vascular disease is hospitalized for a fractured hip. The nurse would like to prevent skin breakdown. The patient should be placed on

    (1) an eggcrate mattress overlay.

    (2) an alternating air mattress overlay.

    (3) an air fluidized therapy.

    (4) a water bed overlay.

190. If one of the bottles in the water-seal chest drainage system breaks, the nurse should immediately

    (1) reconnect the remaining tubes to one of the bottles.

    (2) obtain a new water-seal system.

    (3) clamp the tube as close to the chest as possible.

    (4) remove the chest tube.

191. A manipulative patient is evoking angry feelings in the nurse. The initial action by the nurse to handle her own feelings is to

    (1) analyze the meaning of the patient's behavior.

    (2) ask the patient, "Is it your intention to make me angry?"

    (3) ask herself what is causing her to feel angry.

    (4) confront the patient about his unacceptable behavior.

192. An 85-year-old patient is on enteral feedings. Which of the following physician's orders for enteral feeding would you question?

    (1) Tube feeding 300 mL bolus every four hours.

    (2) Administer 100–150 mL of water via enteral tube every 6 hours.

    (3) Progressive feeding: 1/2, 3/4 and full strength over 3 days.

    (4) Continuous feeding at 50 mL/hr via feeding pump.

193. A 50-year-old elementary school teacher diagnosed with hypertension has not been taking her Lasix as prescribed, once daily. Her reason for noncompliance is "When I take the pill with breakfast, I have to urinate by 9 A.M. and I am not allowed to leave my class alone." The nurse should instruct her to

    (1) ask the physician for a note allowing bathroom privilege as needed.

    (2) ask the principal for coverage in the morning.

    (3) take the pill after school hours.

    (4) take the pill on the weekend so she can use the toilet as needed.

194. A patient is being taught to take his radial pulse. When he returns the demonstration, which of these actions would indicate that he does NOT fully understand the procedure?

    (1) He takes his pulse for 30 seconds, then doubles the result to obtain the pulse rate.

    (2) He uses the first 3 fingers to palpate the pulse.

    (3) He positions the hand that is being measured palm up.

    (4) He records the rate and rhythms of the pulsations.

195. A patient is being taught pursed-lip breathing exercises. Which of the following benefits should a patient derive from breathing exercises?

    (1) Maintenance of negative intrathoracic pressure.

    (2) Facilitation of inhalation.

    (3) Improvement of oxygen transportation.

    (4) Promotion of effective coughing.

196. When the nurse sees a prenatal patient for the first time, the patient complains of being "so sick to my stomach." Which of the following responses should the nurse use to reassure the patient and assess her complaint of nausea?

    (1) "This is a common occurrence during the early part of pregnancy, and you need not worry."
    (2) "This is a common occurrence due to all the changes going on in your body."
    (3) "This is a common occurrence because of bodily changes during pregnancy. Can you tell me when you feel sick to your stomach?"
    (4) "You should discuss this with the doctor when she/he examines you."

197. A patient receiving enteral feeding has developed diarrhea. The nurse should

    (1) slow the feeding rate.
    (2) request an order for antidiarrheal.
    (3) increase the amount of water administered between feedings.
    (4) collect a stool specimen.

198. A 34-year-old mother of a 1-month-old baby girl is admitted to a hospital because she is not able to move her right arm. She tells the nurse that it happened suddenly. A thorough neurological examination and diagnostic work-up revealed no organic basis for her symptom. Which of the following nursing approaches would be MOST appropriate?

    (1) Sympathize with the patient's suffering.
    (2) Confront the patient with the unreality of her symptoms by saying to the patient, "It's all in your mind."
    (3) Divert her attention away from her symptom.
    (4) Prove to the patient that she is not as sick as she thinks she is.

199. During the daily patient re-assessment, the nurse observed that an 80 year old on enteral feeding had a decreased urine output, the urine was dark, and the mucous membrane of the mouth was dry. The nurse should

    (1) notify the physician immediately.
    (2) increase or ensure the patient receives adequate amounts of "free water."
    (3) request a nutritional consult.
    (4) start an intravenous of Ringer's lactate.

200. A patient's enteral feeding tube is clogged. The best method to handle this situation is to

    (1) irrigate the feeding tube with cranberry juice or a carbonated beverage.
    (2) connect the feeding tube to intermittent suction.
    (3) irrigate with gentle pressure using water and a 50 ml piston syringe.
    (4) Call the physician to change the tube.

ANSWER KEY

1.	4	41.	1	81.	4	121.	3	161.	1
2.	2	42.	3	82.	1	122.	4	162.	2
3.	3	43.	2	83.	1	123.	3	163.	1
4.	3	44.	4	84.	3	124.	1	164.	2
5.	1	45.	4	85.	3	125.	4	165.	3
6.	3	46.	2	86.	1	126.	1	166.	2
7.	2	47.	2	87.	3	127.	2	167.	1
8.	4	48.	4	88.	1	128.	1	168.	4
9.	1	49.	4	89.	2	129.	3	169.	2
10.	3	50.	3	90.	1	130.	3	170.	1
11.	3	51.	2	91.	3	131.	2	171.	2
12.	3	52.	3	92.	2	132.	4	172.	3
13.	3	53.	4	93.	1	133.	4	173.	1
14.	2	54.	3	94.	1	134.	1	174.	2
15.	1	55.	3	95.	1	135.	2	175.	3
16.	4	56.	4	96.	3	136.	2	176.	2
17.	4	57.	4	97.	3	137.	4	177.	3
18.	2	58.	4	98.	4	138.	4	178.	4
19.	2	59.	2	99.	4	139.	1	179.	3
20.	4	60.	2	100.	3	140.	2	180.	3
21.	3	61.	1	101.	1	141.	4	181.	3
22.	1	62.	4	102.	3	142.	1	182.	3
23.	3	63.	1	103.	4	143.	2	183.	3
24.	4	64.	4	104.	2	144.	2	184.	3
25.	2	65.	1	105.	4	145.	4	185.	3
26.	3	66.	4	106.	1	146.	2	186.	1
27.	2	67.	2	107.	2	147.	2	187.	1
28.	1	68.	3	108.	3	148.	4	188.	1
29.	3	69.	2	109.	1	149.	2	189.	2
30.	2	70.	1	110.	2	150.	1	190.	3
31.	3	71.	1	111.	2	151.	2	191.	3
32.	3	72.	2	112.	4	152.	1	192.	1
33.	2	73.	1	113.	4	153.	2	193.	3
34.	2	74.	3	114.	4	154.	1	194.	1
35.	2	75.	3	115.	3	155.	3	195.	3
36.	4	76.	2	116.	1	156.	2	196.	3
37.	4	77.	2	117.	3	157.	1	197.	1
38.	2	78.	1	118.	4	158.	1	198.	3
39.	4	79.	2	119.	2	159.	3	199.	2
40.	1	80.	2	120.	1	160.	1	200.	3

RATIONALES

1. **4**   The daughter needs to see the behavior that the neighbors reported. If they are right, the patient would need a full evaluation by her physician before any intervention, social or medical, is implemented. **Nursing process:** Assessment. **Client need:** Psychosocial integrity. **Cognitive level:** 4.

2. **2**   Sunlight causes rashes to occur when a patient has systemic lupus erythematosis. They are precipitated or worsened by exposure to ultraviolet rays and most often appear as a "butterfly" rash over the nose and cheeks. **Nursing process:** Evaluation. **Client need:** Physiological integrity. **Cognitive level:** 4.

3. **3**   The pharmacy should be contacted to obtain a liquid form or regular tablet of the medication. Sustained-release products should never be crushed, because this will destroy the sustained release property. The patient will receive an increased number of daily doses of the non-sustained release tablet. **Nursing process:** Implementation. **Client need:** Physiological integrity. **Cognitive level:** 3.

4. **3**   Urinary frequency and incontinence may occur after a transurethral resection. The patient should be assured that the return to urinary control is slow but will occur. **Nursing process:** Implementation. **Client need:** Safe, effective care environment. **Cognitive level:** 3.

5. **1**   This position minimizes the development of edema because it allows drainage of the hand and arm, since the lymph nodes have been removed. Acute edema of the arm and hand is also associated with trauma to the axillary vessel during surgery. **Nursing process:** Implementation. **Client need:** Physiological integrity. **Cognitive level:** 3.

6. **3**   The father needs to know what to expect from the pregnancy. He also needs to explore his feelings about the pregnancy and fatherhood and to verbalize them. The nurse will give the mother emotional support, but she should not negate the father's role in also providing such support. **Nursing process:** Implementation. **Client need:** Health promotion/maintenenace. **Cognitive level:** 3.

7. **2**   A tetanus history is obtained on admission and tetanus toxoid administered if appropriate. When there is no history of immunization, human antitoxin should be administered. The nurse should ascertain what immunization was not received. Recommended schedule is as follows: Diphteria-pertussis-tetanus (DPT) immunizations are administered at bimonthly intervals beginning at age 2 months for 3 doses; oral trivalent polio vaccine is administered at 2 months and at 4 months of age; measles, mumps, and rubella (MMR) immunizations are administered at 15 months: Diphteria-pertussis-tetanus and oral trivalent polio boosters are given at 18 months. Haemophilus influenza type b (Hib) polysaccharide vaccine is given at 24 months. **Nursing process:** Analysis. **Client need:** Health promotion/maintenance. **Cognitive level:** 3.

8. **4**   This statement conveys an acknowledgment of what the patient is experiencing and also reassures him that he will be safe. **Nursing process:** Implementation. **Client need:** Psychosocial integrity. **Cognitive level:** 3.

9. **1**   Once a seizure has begun the nurse's responsibility is to safeguard the patient from injury. The patient should not be touched, held down, or turned during the tonic and clonic stage of the seizure. **Nursing process:** Implementation. **Client need:** Physiological intgegrity. **Cognitive level:** 3.

10. **3**   All the options are right except choice 3. The infant should be removed from the Bililite, fed, then returned to the Bililite. The unclothed infant is exposed to fluorescent lights, which change the indirect bilirubin into a water-soluble form that is excreted in the bile and urine. The infant should only be removed from the light for feeding. **Nursing process:** Evalution. **Client need:** Health promotion/maintenance. **Cognitive level:** 3.

11. **3**   Developmentally, both infants and toddlers place many nonfood substances into their mouths. The majority of cases of lead poisoning are caused by repeated ingestion of chips of interior or exterior lead-base paint. Older housing in disrepair is a major contributing factor to lead poisoning in young children. **Nursing process:** Analysis. **Client need:** Health promotion/maintenance. **Cognitive level:** 3.

12. **3**   The patient had exhibited decision-making capacity prior to the onset of delirium tremens. No advance directive, either written or verbal, was present. The facts as

presented did not illustrate any awareness by the sister of her brother's prior wishes. In his present condition, the patient had rights. He had the right to be treated as a person in the strictest sense, to have wishes followed if they were known, and to assume that his medical condition would be managed aggressively in the absence of any statement to the contrary by him. Further, until the professional staff knew the patient's wishes with respect to resuscitation and life-sustaining measures, all interventions were appropriate. The staff nurse did not seem to understand that the DNR order ethically could be completed only by the patient as an autonomous individual, by the patient's surrogate when the patient is permanently incompetent or by a designated power of attorney. The nurse was not acting as the patient's advocate, but as an advocate for the physician and institution (see the American Nurses Association "Code for Nurses with Interpretive Statement," Planks 1, 2, and 3). **Nursing process:** Evaluation. **Client need:** Health promotion/maintenance. **Cognitive level:** 4.

13. **3** The phobic person recognizes that the fear associated with an object, activity, or situation is irrational, but is unable to control phobic responses. **Nursing process:** Planning. **Client need:** Psychosocial integrity. **Cognitive level:** 4.

14. **2** These are classic symptoms of sundown syndrome. Because of dwindling environmental light as evening approaches, lack of orienting cues, poor vision, and admission into a strange environment, the patient becomes disoriented. Another nursing diagnostic category this may be is "altered thought processes." **Nursing process:** Analysis. **Client need:** Psychosocial integrity. **Cognitive level:** 4.

15. **1** Medical nutrition therapy is critical for achieving and maintaining optimal glycemic control. Monitoring of all of these is the tool for evaluating the effectiveness of the MNT. **Nursing process:** Evaluation. **Client need:** Health promotion/maintenance. **Cognitive level:** 3.

16. **4** Blood glucose monitoring provides feedback to help with insulin and/or carbohydrate adjustment. Whether to decrease medication or increase the carbohydrate intake is an individualized decision based on the person's diabetes management goals.

Nursing process: Implementation. **Client need:** Health promotion/maintenance. **Cognitive level:** 4.

17. **4** When a child receiving a blood transfusion experiences a hemolytic reaction, the transfusion must be discontinued immediately to prevent renal failure and death. The physician must be notified and urine specimens sent to the laboratory to assess for the presence of hemoglobin, which is indicative of intravascular hemolysis. **Nursing process:** Implementation. **Client need:** Physiological integrity. **Cognitive level:** 3.

18. **2** Handwashing and use of universal precautions (gloves) is of extreme importance especially during diaper change. The diaper must be disposed of immediately and properly. **Nursing process:** Implementation. **Client need:** Health promotion/maintenance. **Cognitive level:** 3.

19. **2** Pancreatic enzymes are administered before each meal to replace those that are unavailable for digestion because of obstruction of the pancreatic ducts. The child with cystic fibrosis is unable to absorb fat; thus vitamins that are naturally fat soluble must be replaced by synthetic water-miscible vitamins. These include vitamins A, D, E, and K. **Nursing process:** Evaluation. **Client need:** Physiological integrity. **Cognitive level:** 3.

20. **4** During the preoperative period the infant is placed in a prone position to minimize tension to the sac and decrease the possibility of rupture. **Nursing process:** Implementation. **Client need:** Physiological integrity. **Cognitive level:** 3.

21. **3** Passive exercises to the involved extremity promote circulation. Heat promotes vasodilation, which will help to decrease the sickling phenomenon. **Nursing process:** Implementation. **Client need:** Physiological integrity. **Cognitive level:** 3.

22. **1** The greenish or bile color gastric content indicates that the nasogastric tube is correctly placed; therefore, the feeding may be given. If over 100 ml of feeding was aspirated, the nurse would have returned the gastric content and either slowed down the rate or turned off the feed, then returned in 1–2 hours to re-assess the residual gastric content. **Nursing process:** Implementation. **Client need:** Physiological integrity. **Cognitive level:** 4.

23. **3**   Breast milk "comes in" on the third or fourth day postpartum. Engorgement usually occurs until the woman's body adjusts to the baby's demand for milk. The breasts will be hard and tender, and it is usual to run a low-grade fever. This is an inflammatory process, not an infection. **Nursing process:** Analysis. **Client need:** Health promotion/maintenance. **Cognitive level:** 3.

24. **4**   Sputum should be collected for bacteriological studies before initiating antibiotic therapy. **Nursing process:** Implementation. **Client need:** Physiological integrity. **Cognitive level:** 4.

25. **2**   Because the patient has chronic CO_2 retention, hypoxia is the stimulus to breathe. Too much oxygen suppresses the hypoxic drive and death may occur. The oxygen flow rate should be low—only 1–2 liters per minute. **Nursing process:** Implementation. **Client need:** Physiological integrity. **Cognitive level:** 4.

26. **3**   Ketonuria in pregnancy is a signal that starvation, ketosis, is occurring. In the second and third trimester the diet should be increased 100–300 Kcal/day over prepregnancy needs. Food and blood glucose monitoring records are used to meet glycemia control goals and prevent or correct ketosis. **Nursing process:** Implementation. **Client need:** Physiological integrity. **Cognitive level:** 3.

27. **2**   This approach is aimed at assisting the patient to identify those behaviors that are unacceptable and those feelings associated with them so that he may be able to explore socially acceptable means of coping. **Nursing process:** Implementation. **Client need:** Psychosocial integrity. **Cognitive level:** 3.

28. **1**   Four categories of approaches are: give general guidelines; prepare menu planning systems; teach a simplified carbohydrate-counting approach; and teach the exchange list. **Nursing process:** Implementation. **Client need:** Health promotion/maintenance. **Cognitive level:** 4.

29. **3**   Because Fluorouracil's side effect is bone marrow depression, patients receiving this drug should be assessed for a WBC of more than 3,500 mm or platelet below 100,000/mm. **Nursing process:** Assessment. **Client need:** Physiological integrity. **Cognitive level:** 3

30. **2**   The infusion rate should be slowed to 80–100 ml/hr. The diarrhea is probably due to fast infusion. Osmolite Hn is isotonic and lactose free, therefore the diarrhea could not be attributed to the formula. The feeding should not be discontinued, although the other options should be considered. A nutritional consult should be requested and done before the formula is changed. **Nursing process:** Implementation. **Client need:** Physiological integrity. **Cognitive level:** 4.

31. **3**   It is important for the patient to know that people are interested in his welfare and safety. Suicidal persons are usually afraid of the consequences of their own impulses. Knowing that the staff will be at hand to prevent self-destructive behavior promotes feeling of security and importance needed by the person who has felt hopeless, useless, and not needed. **Nursing process:** Implementation. **Client need:** Psychosocial integrity. **Cognitive level:** 3.

32. **3**   Allowing the patient to select his own chair gives him the opportunity to safely examine reality. **Nursing process:** Implementation. **Client need:** Psychosocial integrity. **Cognitive level:** 3.

33. **2**   The mechanism involved in pushing would place too great a strain on her cardiovascular system at this stage. **Nursing process:** Implementation. **Client need:** Health promotion/maintenance. **Cognitive level:** 3.

34. **2**   Most elderly patients who fall in the hospital have a history of multiple falls in the community. **Nursing process:** Assessment. **Client need:** Physiological integrity. **Cognitive level:** 3.

35. **2**   In order to ensure that a therapeutic drug level is maintained, serum monitoring of drug level may be performed. Serum drug concentrations are a guide to therapy. In monitoring serum levels, two blood levels are usually obtained: the peak level, drawn $1/2$ hour after the medication is totally administered, and the trough level, drawn $1/2$ hour before the next dose. Peak levels monitor possible toxic levels, whereas trough levels monitor whether or not the level remains within the therapeutic range. These blood levels are then used to determine the next dose of the medication. **Nursing process:** Analysis. **Client need:** Physiological integrity. **Cognitive level:** 4.

36. **4**   Patients receiving MAO inhibitors are placed on a low-tyramine diet. The diet helps

to prevent adverse reaction such as palpitation, severe headache, and hypertension. The diet excludes aged cheese, fermented sausages, broad beans and pods, fruits such as bananas, avocadoes, canned figs and raisins, cultured dairy products, chocolate and products made with chocolate, caffeine, beer and ale, wines, yeast extract, licorice, soy sauce, and food products made with soy. **Nursing process:** Implementation. **Client need:** Psychosocial integrity. **Cognitive level:** 4.

37. **4** This statement acknowledges the patient's feelings and conveys the nurse's willingness to explore with the patient what she is experiencing at that time. **Nursing process:** Implementation. **Client need:** Psychosocial integrity. **Cognitive level:** 3.

38. **2** Adolescents are undergoing many normal bodily changes. Illness increases their concern about their body image. Nursing process: **Nursing process:** Analysis. **Client need:** Psychosocial integrity. **Cognitive level:** 3.

39. **4** Acute glomerulonephritis is related to a previous infection with group A Beta hemolytic streptococci. Following an initial streptococcal infection, there is generally a latent period of 7 to 14 days before the onset of glomerulonephritis. **Nursing process:** Analysis. **Client need:** Physiological integrity. **Cognitive level:** 4.

40. **1** An adverse effect of monoamine inhibitors is insomnia; therefore the medication should be given in the A.M. Other adverse effects are hyperreflexia, confusion, tremors, mania, fatigue, and memory impairment. The patient should be instructed not to drive a car, operate machinery, or engage in other activities requiring alertness until aware of drug effects. **Nursing process:** Evaluation. **Client need:** Safe, effective care environment. **Cognitive level:** 4.

41. **1** Simultaneous administration of several drugs is the current trend to reduce the chance of the emergence of resistance and to increase tuberculostatic effects. This answer does not overwhelm the patient and gives him accurate information. **Nursing process:** Implementation. **Client need:** Physiological integrity. **Cognitive level:** 4.

42. **3** A low forceps delivery eliminates the need for her to push during her second stage of labor. She would probably be given epidural anesthesia for the second stage, so that she is not stressed by the discomfort from the extremely intense contractions of this stage. **Nursing process:** Planning. **Client need:** Health promotion/maintenance. **Cognitive level:** 3.

43. **2** The specific components of an ideal diet to promote an optimal outcome for gestational diabetes mellitus have not yet been determined. One goal that appears to be consistent is the attention given to limiting carbohydrate intake at breakfast. Hyperglycemia may occur after breakfast in diet-controlled gestational diabetes mellitus unless carbohydrates are restricted. Some women can tolerate only 30 g. or less carbohydrates at breakfast; larger amounts are tolerated later in the day. In addition to limited carbohydrate at breakfast, frequent small feedings throughout the day may facilitate blood glucose control without the need for insulin. Only human insulin should be used, to reduce the likelihood of insulin-antibody formation in both mother and fetus. **Nursing process:** Implementation. **Client need:** Physiological integrity. **Cognitive level:** 3.

44. **4** Bladder toxicity is related to Cytoxan therapy especially on long term oral use. Drinking plenty of fluids reduces the risk of developing complications. **Nursing process:** Implementation. **Client need:** Physiological integrity. **Cognitive level:** 3.

45. **4** A bolus is a concentrated dose of medication given over a short period of time. Most bolus IV medications are given over 1–2 minutes. **Nursing process:** Implementation. **Client need:** Physiological integrity. **Cognitive level:** 3.

46. **2** Suppositories are designed to melt at body temperature, so they are stored in the refrigerator or in a cool place. Most rectal suppositories are packed in foil wrappers. **Nursing process:** Analysis. **Client need:** Physiological integrity. **Cognitive level:** 3.

47. **2** When a nurse assesses anxiety in the parent of a hospitalized child, the first priority is to determine the reason for the anxiety. **Nursing process:** Implementation. **Client need:** Psychosocial integrity. **Cognitive level:** 3.

48. **4** Calling for help is a practical and safe action to protect the patient and others during this emotional outburst. **Nursing process:** Implementation. **Client need:** Psychosocial integrity. **Cognitive level:** 4.

49. **4**   This response provides an opportunity for the patient to safely examine reality. The nurse acknowledges the patient's experience without making a judgement as she shares her own perception of reality. **Nursing process:** Implementation. **Client need:** Psychosocial integrity. **Cognitive level:** 3.

50. **3**   Both human regular and intermediate-acting insulins generally peak earlier than animal insulins. Patients switching from an animal intermediate insulin to a human may find that the earlier peak necessitates a midafternoon snack or other adjustment in management. **Nursing process:** Implementation. **Client need:** Physiological integrity. **Cognitive level:** 3.

51. **2**   An infant with a meningomyelocele often has a neurogenic bladder because of defective nerve supply to the bladder, which affects both sphincter and detrusor tone to produce overflow incontinence with constant dribbling of urine. Poor anal sphincter tone leads to lack of bowel control. **Nursing process:** Evaluation. **Client need:** Physiological integrity. **Cognitive level:** 3.

52. **3**   Before the patient can be taught healthful ways to alleviate the pain of thrombophlebitis, assess the patient's prior experiences with pain and what has helped in the past. Teach pain reduction techniques, such as elevation of the part, resting the part whenever needed, application of warm, moist compresses, and wearing support or antiembolis stockings. The pain is peripheral and related to the inflammatory process. **Nursing process:** Planning. **Client need:** Physiological integrity. **Cognitive level:** 3.

53. **4**   Patients with eating disorders such as anorexia nervosa perceive themselves as overweight even if they are actually grossly underweight for their height and age. It is important to present the fact about the patient's weight as the nurse sees it in an objective and non-judgmental manner. **Nursing process:** Implementation. **Client need:** Psychosocial integrity. **Cognitive level:** 3.

54. **3**   With the administration of a combination of drugs, resistance to specific drugs develops more slowly. **Nursing process:** Evaluation. **Client need:** Physiological integrity. **Cognitive level:** 3.

55. **3**   Fruits and fruit juices are not allowed on this diet. **Nursing process:** Evaluation. **Client need:** Physiological integrity. **Cognitive level:** 3.

56. **4**   The bladder may be perforated if it is inflated while the catheter is being inserted. **Nursing process:** Implementation. **Client need:** Physiological integrity. **Cognitive level:** 3.

57. **4**   The nurse should first check to see whether the Foley is blocked, the drainage tube is kinked, or the patient is lying on the tube. **Nursing process:** Implementation. **Client need:** Physiological integrity. **Cognitive level:** 3.

58. **4**   Narcissism is common early in pregnancy. The woman is very concerned with her own well-being. The baby does not seem real to her yet, so health teaching concentrated on the baby is not significant to her. Since she feels it is her life that is being disrupted, she will be most responsive to health teaching focused on her. It would be untherapeutic to tell her she is silly, and encouraging her in her excessive concern will only increase it. **Nursing process:** Implementation. **Client need:** Psychosocial integrity. **Cognitive level:** 3.

59. **2**   The patient has entered the second stage of grieving. It is an attempt at postponing death until a certain task is completed. These requests are usually made to God and provide a way for the patient to deal with the situation in small increments. **Nursing process:** Analysis. **Client need:** Psychosocial integrity. **Cognitive level:** 4.

60. **2**   A nurse witnessing a consent form merely certifies the identity of the person who signs it. The major responsibility for obtaining informed consent resides with the physician or his surrogates. A proper consent has two major components: an oral explanation and a written consent form. If either the explanation or the consent form is flawed, the consent process is open to question. **Nursing process:** Evaluation. **Client need:** Safe, effective care environment. **Cognitive level:** 3.

61. **1**   Medications are to be administered separately. Do not mix all the medication for 1 dosing time in 1 container. Flush with at least 5 ml of water between medications. **Nursing process:** Implementation. **Client need:** Physiological integrity. **Cognitive level:** 3.

62. **4**   The fetal heart is not auscultated in the vicinity of the placenta. Since the fetus is

free floating in the amniotic fluid in utero, the fetal heart is usually audible in an area of the uterus other than where the placenta is attached. **Nursing process:** Evaluation. **Client need:** Health promotion/maintenance. **Cognitive level:** 3.

63. **1**   A face mask need be worn only when a patient leaves his room to go to another area of the hospital. The other methods are more effective at preventing the spread of tuberculosis. **Nursing process:** Implementation. **Client need:** Physiological integrity. **Cognitive level:** 4.

64. **4**   Because of the impaired insulin secretions in these persons, smaller meals and snacks, spaced more frequently throughout the day may prevent exaggerated postmeal hyperglycemia. **Nursing process:** Implementation. **Client need:** Physiological integrity. **Cognitive level:** 3.

65. **1**   Both EDTA and BAL are viscous solutions and are administered deep intramuscularly. They are administered every 4 hours for 5 days. A rotation schedule for each series of injections is essential to prevent tissue damage and to ensure maximun tissue absorption. For toddlers, only the vastus lateralis, ventrogluteal, and gluteal sites are used. **Nursing process:** Implementation. **Client need:** Physiological integrity. **Cognitive level:** 3.

66. **4**   Overrestriction of calories may be a consequence of the common, erroneous belief that restricting food, rather than adjusting insulin, is the way to control blood glucose. **Nursing process:** Evaluation. **Client need:** Physiological integrity. **Cognitive level:** 3.

67. **2**   Detoxification is the first step in a treatment process for alcoholism that involves withdrawing the person from alcohol in a supervised environment. **Nursing process:** Implementation. **Client need:** Physiological integrity. **Cognitive level:** 3.

68. **3**   All of these interventions should be done in the preoperative period, but only choice 3 will effectively relieve the anxiety that the patient is experiencing. **Nursing process:** Planning. **Client need:** Physiological integrity. **Cognitive level:** 3.

69. **2**   While all the other choices are important, the extent of the patient's physical illness must be promptly assessed because her condition can be life-threatening if not corrected at once. **Nursing process:** Assessment. **Client need:** Psychosocial integrity. **Cognitive level:** 3.

70. **1**   An increase in energy expenditure on the child's part will result in increased respiratory distress. The nurse should explain the procedure to her in terms that she will understand in order to decrease the child's anxiety. **Nursing process:** Implementation. **Client need:** Safe, effective care environment. **Cognitive level:** 3.

71. **1**   The symptoms that the patient is experiencing is autonomic dysreflexia, also called hyperreflexia. It is an exaggerated autonomic nervous system response to a noxious stimulus, most often a distended bladder. **Nursing process:** Evaluation. **Client need:** Physiological integrity. **Cognitive level:** 4.

72. **2**   Cataract is a normal part of aging. About half of Americans aged 65 to 74 have cataracts. About 70% of those over the age of 75 have this condition. One eye may be worse than the other because cataracts develop at a different rate. **Nursing process:** Implementation. **Client need:** Physiological integrity. **Cognitive level:** 3.

73. **1**   The ritualistic behavior demonstrated by the patient is an attempt to handle anxiety-provoking situations. The anxiety is associated with persistent undesirable and uncontrollable thoughts and repetitive, irresistible, and stereotyped acts. **Nursing process:** Evaluation. **Client need:** Psychosocial integrity. **Cognitive level:** 3.

74. **3**   Both are liable: the supervisor for placing a nurse without coronary care experience in that unit, and the nurse for not recognizing her own limitations. **Nursing process:** Evaluation. **Client need:** Safe, effective care environment. **Cognitive level:** 4.

75. **3**   It is essential that the sensation to be experienced be described as accurately as possible. Choice 3 does this best. **Nursing process:** Evaluation. **Client need:** Psychosocial integrity. **Cognitive level:** 3.

76. **2**   A Geri-chair with a fixed lap board or tray does not allow the patient any freedom; therefore, it is a restraint. Self-releasing belts or self-releasing torso supports offer assistance to prevent sliding in a wheelchair and can be released and/or removed by the patient. **Nursing process:** Planning. **Client need:** Safe, effective care environment. **Cognitive level:** 3.

77. **2**   Age is a predisposing factor to delirium. The use of a low-dose neuroleptic such as Haldol should be initiated first. Once the pneumonia has been resolved the patient should return to the pre-illness state. **Nursing process:** Implementation. **Client need:** Psychosocial integrity. **Cognitive level:** 4.

78. **1**   Acknowledging the victim's painful experience promotes a feeling of security. Preparing the victim for possible delayed psychological reactions enables the victim to develop a realistic plan of action to prevent potentially dangerous residual responses. **Nursing process:** Planning. **Client need:** Psychosocial integrity. **Cognitive level:** 3.

79. **2**   Lead poisoning can easily recur if the child again ingests lead paint chips. The child must be supervised and guided toward activities other than pica. **Nursing process:** Implementation. **Client need:** Health promotion/maintenance. **Cognitive level:** 3.

80. **2**   The transfusion is always given with the baby's own type blood if possible. However, Rh-negative blood would be given so that the fresh blood supply would not be destroyed by the maternal antibodies. Once there no longer are any Rh-positive cells to destroy, the antibodies will be absorbed. **Nursing process:** Analysis. **Client need:** Health promotion/maintenance. **Cognitive level:** 3.

81. **4**   Vincristine is a plant alkaloid that may cause alopecia and neurotoxicity, including numbness, ataxia, weakness, and foot drop. Constipation may occur because of adynamic ileus. **Nursing process:** Assessment. **Client need:** Physiological integrity. **Cognitive level:** 3.

82. **1**   In HHNK syndrome there is very high blood glucose, without ketones. Glucose levels range from 400 to 2800 mg/dl with an average of just over 1,000 mg/dl. This condition is seen in type II diabetics. **Nursing process:** Evaluation. **Client need:** Physiological integrity. **Cognitive level:** 4.

83. **1**   Diabetic ketoacidosis can be prevented if diabetics performed self-monitoring of blood glucose (SMBG). Insulin dosage is calculated based on the blood glucose level. SMBG also evaluates the effectiveness of the meal plan and enhances flexibility of food choices. SMBG coordinates the diabetes management plan. **Nursing process:** Evaluation. **Client need:** Physiological integrity. **Cognitive level:** 3.

84. **3**   The two major reasons why hypoglycemia is more likely at this time are: 1) an overall lowering of basal blood glucose of 9 to 14 mg/dl and 2) an increased sensitivity to insulin. The importance of between-meal snacks should be stressed. **Nursing process:** Analysis. **Client need:** Physiological integrity. **Cognitive level:** 3.

85. **3**   The 3-bottle system provides a third bottle to control the amount of suction applied. This bottle contains 3 tubes. The short tubing extends from water seal to suction bottle, a long glass tube extends below the water level (20 cm) and is open to the atmosphere. The amount of suction is determined by the depth to which the tube is submerged; a short piece of tubing leads to the suction source of the control bottle. **Nursing process:** Evaluation. **Client need:** Physiological integrity. **Cognitive level:** 3.

86. **1**   The patient is instructed to perform the valsalva maneuver which aids in the removal of the chest tube and allows full expansion of the lung. **Nursing process:** Implementation. **Client need:** Physiological integrity. **Cognitive level:** 3.

87. **3**   The other measures should be performed at more frequent intervals. **Nursing process:** Implementation. **Client need:** Physiological integrity. **Cognitive level:** 3.

88. **1**   In Bryant's traction the hips are flexed at a 90° angle and both legs are suspended by pulleys and weights. The weights are attached to the legs by bandages. The skin under the bandage should be observed for sloughing on both legs. **Nursing process:** Evaluation. **Client need:** Physiological integrity. **Cognitive level:** 4.

89. **2**   Hip flexion deformity is most often caused by maintaining the hip in a flexion position for an extended period of time (sitting in a semi-Fowler's position in bed). Patients are advised to alternate the position of the bed several times a day. **Nursing process:** Implementation. **Client need:** Physiological integrity. **Cognitive level:** 3.

90. **1**   Unilateral neglect is a state in which an individual is unable to attend to or "ignores" the hemiplegic side of the body and/or objects, persons, or sounds on the affected side of the individual's environment. The nursing diagnosis is specific for patients with cerebrovascular accident, cerebral tumor,

brain injury/trauma and/or cerebral aneurysms. **Nursing process:** Evaluation. **Client need:** Physiological integrity. **Cognitive level:** 3.

91. **3** Patient education in regard to breast self-examination is important because 50% of patients experience tumor recurrence in the remaining breast. **Nursing process:** Implementation. **Client need:** Health promotion/maintenance. **Cognitive level:** 4.

92. **2** If sponging is done before the administration of antipyretic, the hypothalamus will try to offset the lowered body temperature and the child will shiver. Shivering causes the temperature to rise even more as the body tries to conserve heat. The child should be covered with a light blanket. **Nursing process:** Implementation. **Client need:** Health promotion/maintenance. **Cognitive level:** 3.

93. **1** Liver dysfunction may be noted in patients taking Cytoxan, liver enzymes such as SGOT, SGPT LDH. These studies are based on release of enzymes from damaged liver cells. These enzymes are elevated in liver cell damage. **Nursing process:** Evaluation. **Client need:** Physiological integrity. **Cognitive level:** 3.

94. **1** Metamucil should be administered in juice or fluid followed by at least 8 ounces of fluid to prevent intestinal impaction or obstruction. **Nursing process:** Implementation. **Client need:** Physiological integrity. **Cognitive level:** 3.

95. **1** If an Rh-negative woman receives Rh-positive blood, she will form anti-Rh-positive antibodies. These antibodies will destroy the baby's red blood cells both in utero and immediately after delivery. **Nursing process:** Evaluation. **Client need:** Health promotion/maintenance. **Cognitive level:** 3.

96. **3** A bulging anterior fontanelle would indicate increased intercranial pressure. **Nursing process:** Assessment. **Client need:** Health promotion/maintenance. **Cognitive level:** 3.

97. **3** Red urine or hematuria should be reported immediately. This is due to hemorrhagic cystitis and is related to Cytoxan therapy. Sudden weight gain may indicate retention of water resulting from syndrome of inapropriate antidiuretic hormone (SIADH), also related to Cytoxan therapy. **Nursing process:** Evaluation. **Client need:** Physiological integrity. **Cognitive level:** 4.

98. **4** A patient who has undergone axillary node dissection should not shave the affected underarm or apply depilatory cream or strong deodorant to it for at least two weeks. **Nursing process:** Implementation. **Client need:** Physiological integrity. **Cognitive level:** 4.

99. **4** Whenever there is a problem with a doctor's order, the nurse should verify the order with the original source—the doctor. **Nursing process:** Evaluation. **Client need:** Safe, effective care environment. **Cognitive level:** 3.

100. **3** Side rails in the up position may be used to assist the elderly in moving or turning in bed. If they are used as a deterrent to falls, they may be the cause of injury as the patient tries to get out of bed to use the bathroom by climbing over or around the siderails. **Nursing process:** Evaluation. **Client need:** Safe, effective care environment. **Cognitive level:** 4.

101. **1** Lack of interest in condition or needs of an elder demonstrates a low level of commitment to meeting the individual's need. The spiritual values held by the family enable them to transcend the problem of agony and the stress on the caregiver. **Nursing process:** Assessment. **Client need:** Safe, effective care environment. **Cognitive level:** 3.

102. **3** When edema is present, the child must be weighed daily. Maintenance of constant weight is the best index of overall fluid balance. **Nursing process:** Planning. **Client need:** Physiological integrity. **Cognitive level:** 4.

103. **4** Hemorrhage into the joints is a frequent occurrence with children having hemophilia. It is treated by immobilization of the joint and application of cold to promote vasoconstriction. **Nursing process:** Assessment. **Client need:** Physiological integrity. **Cognitive level:** 4.

104. **2** The knowledge that the staff will not allow the patient to lose control over his own impulses promotes a sense of security in the immediate environment. **Nursing process:** Implementation. **Client need:** Psychosocial integrity. **Cognitive level:** 3.

105. **4** The full picture of the mechanism involved in DIC consists of decreased circulating platelets, prolonged thrombin time, prothrombin time, and partial thromboplastin time. The last three prolonged values mean

the enzymes that are the most instrumental in connecting fibrinogen into fibrin are in short supply. **Nursing process:** Evaluation. **Client need:** Physiological integrity. **Cognitive level:** 4.

106. **1**   Normal saline is no longer recommended for normal pulmonary hygiene because it can contribute to decrease in oxygenation by introducing liquid into the lungs. Suction is never applied while inserting the catheter because doing so removes air from the patient's airway, contributes to hypoxemia and damages the mucosa. Suctioning should only be applied for 10 to 15 seconds. The catheter should be inserted smoothly, rather than jabbing up and down. **Nursing process:** Implementation. **Client need:** Physiological integrity. **Cognitive level:** 4.

107. **2**   Hyperoxygenation is not enough; the patient must simultaneously receive hyperinflation, which involves raising the tidal volume. Hyperinflation helps prevent hypoxemia because it increases functional residual capacity—the amount of air in the lung after exhalation. The best method is to use the ventilator sigh control so that hyperinflation can be provided by simply pressing the sigh button. **Nursing process:** Implementation. **Client need:** Physiological integrity. **Cognitive level:** 3.

108. **3**   Children have a fast metabolism rate, so they have a great oxygen requirement. When a child's oxygen needs are not satisfied, they breathe faster—which is an early sign of respiratory deterioration. Because they are susceptible to hypoxia, oxygen should be administered immediately. Pulse oximeters are to be used for monitoring oxygen saturation, not to indicate the need for oxygen. **Nursing process:** Implementation. **Client need:** Physiological integrity. **Cognitive level:** 4.

109. **1**   The nurse is licensed and is responsible for her actions. She had the knowledge to recognize the dosage as not therapeutic and should have had the judgment to check the physician. A statement by the supervisor does not remove the nurse's personal responsibility for her own actions. The supervisor and the physician may also be liable. **Nursing process:** Evaluation. **Client need:** Safe, effective care environment. **Cognitive level:** 4.

110. **2**   The volunteer and family will provide social and sensory stimulation, which will enable the patient to experience optimal

contact with reality. Dehydration (electrolyte imbalance) is one of the conditions that may cause confusion, so fluids should not be restricted. **Nursing process:** Implementation. **Client need:** Safe, effective care environment. **Cognitive level:** 4

111. **2**   Patients must be accompanied by a responsible adult to and from the outpatient treatment. If a patient comes alone, the doctor will cancel the treatment. Patients are confused after treatment and may not remember coming to or leaving the hospital. It may take 6 months for memory to return to normal. The companion should remain with the patient for 8 hours after treatment. **Nursing process:** Evaluation. **Client need:** Physiological integrity. **Cognitive level:** 4.

112. **4**   A Foley catheter is inserted to keep the bladder deflated, thereby decreasing the risk of the bladder's being burned by the radium implant. **Nursing process:** Planning. **Client need:** Physiological integrity. **Cognitive level:** 3.

113. **4**   The preschooler's concept of body integrity is poorly developed. These children fear that intrusive procedures, such as taking a rectal temperature, will cause bodily mutilation. These fears are related to their psychosexual level of development. **Nursing process:** Evaluation. **Client need:** Health promotion/maintenance. **Cognitive level:** 4.

114. **4**   The incidence of pneumonia is high in patients with gallbladder surgery because the incision is high in the abdominal wall and the postoperative discomfort experienced causes the patients to inhibit ventilating movements. The nurse, by splinting the wound and/or teaching the patient to do the same, can encourage coughing and deep breathing with a relative minimum of pain. Coughing allows the patient to expectorate mucus and deep breathing allows him/her to inflate the lungs, encouraging proper ventilation. **Nursing process:** Analysis. **Client need:** Physiological integrity. **Cognitive level:** 3.

115. **3**   In tracheoesophageal fistula, one portion of the esophagus consists of a blind pouch and the other portion is connected to the trachea by way of the fistula. The infant is in danger of aspirating secretions and must be suctioned continuously to maintain a patent airway. **Nursing process:** Evaluation. **Client need:** Physiological integrity. **Cognitive level:** 3.

116. **1** The patient is confused and agitated upon awakening since there is no memory of what has happen or of where he/she is. If agitation persists, pulse oximeter readings can determine if it is due to hypoxia. If the patient is hypoxic, oxygen is administered. **Nursing process:** Evaluation. **Client need:** Safe, effective care environment. **Cognitive level:** 4.

117. **3** The patient must avoid contact sports. During contact sports injury may occur in the abdominal area. **Nursing process:** Implementation. **Client need:** Health promotion/maintenance. **Cognitive level:** 4.

118. **4** An ileostomy should never be irrigated because it cannot be regulated and irrigant may cause intense abdominal cramping, distention, and perforation. **Nursing process:** Evaluation. **Client need:** Health promotion/maintenance. **Cognitive level:** 4.

119. **2** A leaking pouch should never be taped. Taping traps any drainage between the skin and pouch and causes irritation. **Nursing process:** Evaluation. **Client need:** Health promotion/maintenance. **Cognitive level:** 4.

120. **1** When the child with meningitis assumes an opisthotonus posture, he flexes his head and legs backward; thus a prone or supine position would be inappropriate. A semisitting position will cause increased head pain. **Nursing process:** Implementation. **Client need:** Physiological integrity. **Cognitive level:** 3.

121. **3** Because of the patient's disordered thoughts and perceptions, short, simple sentences should be used when talking to him. Schizophrenic patients are not able to deal with abstractions. It is believed that ability to filter or synthesize incoming stimuli from the environment is impaired. As a result, the patient responds indiscriminately to all stimuli, causing thought disorganization. **Nursing process:** Implementation. **Client need:** Psychosocial integrity. **Cognitive level:** 3.

122. **4** Iron stores are built up during the last month of gestation, when growth has been completed. The preterm infant does not have the last month of gestation. **Nursing process:** Evaluation. **Client need:** Health promotion/maintenance. **Cognitive level:** 3.

123. **3** The nurse interacting with the parents must be noncritical. Parental strengths are acknowledged in order to increase self-esteem. This helps to establish rapport. After rapport has been established, the nurse may then proceed to teach the parents about discipline and other aspects of child growth and development. **Nursing process:** Implementation. **Client need:** Psychosocial integrity. **Cognitive level:** 3.

124. **1** This schedule would prevent pain from building up and becoming severe. Demerol is short-acting and not recommended for cancer pain management. Morphine is potent and lasts up to 4 hours and is a better choice for this patient. **Nursing process:** Evaluation. **Client need:** Safe, effective care environment. **Cognitive level:** 4.

125. **4** No food items should be brought into the hospital other than canned soda. The other items are allowed. The magazines and books must be new. **Nursing process:** Implementation. **Client need:** Safe, effective care environment. **Cognitive level:** 3.

126. **1** Although thrombolytic drugs are beneficial and sometimes life-saving, they are potentially dangerous agents, associated with definite risk of hemorrhage, which is often difficult to manage; therefore the patient must be informed of this risk before starting therapy. **Nursing process:** Implementation. **Client need:** Physiological integrity. **Cognitive level:** 4.

127. **2** A snack is provided at the peak of insulin action. NPH insulin is an intermediate-acting insulin with a peak action of 6 to 8 hours; thus a snack must be provided at midafternoon. **Nursing process:** Evaluation. **Client need:** Physiological integrity. **Cognitive level:** 3.

128. **1** The symptoms occur gradually, often going unnoticed. Over a period of time, however, elevated intraocular pressure causes visual impairment. If uncorrected, blindness may result. **Nursing process:** Implementation. **Client need:** Physiological integrity. **Cognitive level:** 3.

129. **3** Measles immunoglobulin is an alternative for a child too young to receive the measles vaccine. All susceptible persons who have been exposed to measles should be vaccinated within 72 hours. The measles vaccination schedule begins at 15 months of age. **Nursing process:** Implementation. **Client need:** Health promotion/maintenance. **Cognitive level:** 4.

130. **3** Aggression occurs as a defense response to anxiety and loss of self-esteem. This state-

ment reflects the nurse's understanding of the dynamics of the patient's behavior. This understanding will help the nurse to develop a care plan based on the patient's needs. **Nursing process:** Analysis. **Client need:** Psychosocial integrity. **Cognitive level:** 3.

131. **2**   Anxiety can best be alleviated by information and clarification. In this case, the patient needs to know that pain medication will be available when needed. **Nursing process:** Implementation. **Client need:** Physiological integrity. **Cognitive level:** 3.

132. **4**   Unimmunized children who are 15 months to 5 years of age should be given a single dose of one of the Hib vaccines then immunized with one of three vaccines, given at one month intervals. **Nursing process:** Implementation. **Client need:** Health promotion/maintenance. **Cognitive level:** 3.

133. **4**   The purpose of administering the H_2 antagonist (Tagamet) and an antacid is to assure adequate pain relief; therefore the antacid should be taken one hour before or after the Tagamet. **Nursing process:** Implementation. **Client need:** Physiological integrity. **Cognitive level:** 4.

134. **1**   The patient is having an anaphylactic reaction; epinephrine is used for anaphylaxsis. Rapid intravenous injection usually causes a prompt elevation of blood pressure. Pulse pressure may increase significantly. It also relaxes the bronchiolar smooth muscles. **Nursing process:** Implementation. **Client need:** Physiological integrity. **Cognitive level:** 4.

135. **2**   Donor services for bone marrow may be allogenic (unrelated person or a sibling) or autologous, the patient's own bone marrow harvested (gathered) when the malignancy is in remission. **Nursing process:** Evaluation. **Client need:** Physiological integrity. **Cognitive level:** 3.

136. **2**   School-age children prefer activities with peers of the same sex. Choice 4 is incorrect because children with acute glomerulonephritis are susceptible to respiratory infections. **Nursing process:** Implementation. **Client need:** Health promotion/maintenance. **Cognitive level:** 3.

137. **4**   False negatives are common among patients whose immune systems are so severely impaired that they are unable to mount a response to the small amount of purified protein derivatives injected under the skin surface, even though they are infected. These patients are anergic. **Nursing process:** Evaluation. **Client need:** Physiological integrity. **Cognitive level:** 4.

138. **4**   The patient should be observed for depressed reflexes, depressed respiration, and tetany. The antidote to magnesium sulfate depression or respiratory depression, hypotonia, and tetany is calcium. **Nursing process:** Assessment. **Client need:** Health promotion/maintenance. **Cognitive level:** 4.

139. **1**   Increased pulmonary venous pressure leads to transudation of fluid from the pulmonary capillaries, causing dyspnea. **Nursing process:** Evaluation. **Client need:** Physiological integrity. **Cognitive level:** 4.

140. **2**   A pair of scissors should be kept at the bedside in case the gastric ballon breaks causing the esophageal ballon to move up and occlude the patient's airway. The scissors are used to cut the tube at the esophageal inflation port and remove it. **Nursing process:** Evaluation. **Client need:** Physiological integrity. **Cognitive level:** 4.

141. **4**   Oral hypoglycemic agents lower blood glucose by stimulating the pancreas to release more insulin and decreasing the liver production of glucose. These drugs cannot be used to treat patients with type I diabetes since they are unable to produce any insulin. **Nursing process:** Evaluation. **Client need:** Physiological integrity. **Cognitive level:** 4.

142. **1**   Thyroid is replacement therapy, similar to insulin for diabetes mellitus. **Nursing process:** Evaluation. **Client need:** Physiological integrity. **Cognitive level:** 4.

143. **2**   Radiation is commonly administered to destroy malignant cells not removed by surgery when the axillary nodes have been found to contain tumor cells. **Nursing process:** Evaluation. **Client need:** Physiological integrity. **Cognitive level:** 3.

144. **2**   Since the patient is immunosuppressed, exposure to ill or infected individuals should be avoided. **Nursing process:** Implementation. **Client need:** Health promotion/maintenance. **Cognitive level:** 3.

145. **4**   Choice 2 may be used with option 4. **Nursing process:** Implementation. **Client need:** Physiological integrity. **Cognitive level:** 3.

146. **2**   Only an electric razor is allowed during the conditioning period. The patient's platelets supply will be diminished; there-

after, bleeding is a complication. **Nursing process:** Evaluation. **Client need:** Physiological integrity. **Cognitive level:** 4.

147. **2**   Mental status changes such as disorientation, confusion, and inability to make purposeful decisions are behaviors that result in falls. These patients need mental status assessment and appropriate management based on assessment results. **Nursing process:** Evaluation. **Client need:** Safe, effective care environment. **Cognitive level:** 4.

148. **4**   The first step in the teaching-learning process is to determine the child's present knowledge. Further explanations are then planned. **Nursing process:** Implementation. **Client need:** Physiological integrity. **Cognitive level:** 3.

149. **2**   The generalized vasodilatation effect of the drug causes headaches because of effect on the cerebral blood vessels and causes orthostatic hypotension due to vasodilation of the peripheral vascular system. **Nursing process:** Implementation. **Client need:** Physiological integrity. **Cognitive level:** 3.

150. **1**   A game of solitaire does not involve open competition with others, which can be threatening to the patient. This game allows the patient to compete with himself without the potential threat of losing to someone else which would call for defense of the self. **Nursing process:** Planning. **Client need:** Psychosocial integrity. **Cognitive level:** 3.

151. **2**   These are symptoms of digitalis toxicity. A serum digitalis level must be drawn for a definitive diagnosis so that the appropriate management could be initiated that day before another dose is taken. **Nursing process:** Implementation. **Client need:** Physiological integrity. **Cognitive level:** 4.

152. **1**   Peak plasma concentration of Tofranil is attained within 2 to 4 hours. Therefore if taken at night, daytime sedation would be less of a problem along with other side effects of dry mouth and blurred vision. **Nursing process:** Implementation. **Client need:** Physiological integrity. **Cognitive level:** 4.

153. **2**   The IV has infiltrated (is no longer in the vein). It must be removed and restarted in a different site. The fluid in the tissue will absorb without long-term effect. **Nursing process:** Implementation. **Client need:** Physiological integrity. **Cognitive level:** 3.

154. **1**   An infant's weight provides important data about the state of hydration. Changes in weight reflect the severity of dehydration as well as the degree of recovery. **Nursing process:** Assessment. **Client need:** Physiological integrity. **Cognitive level:** 3.

155. **3**   A careful schedule for introducing new foods can quickly identify the offending agent. If local inflammation occurs, such as swelling of the lip or urticaria around mouth, the food must by avoided and not reintroduced for 6 months. **Nursing process:** Implementation. **Client need:** Health promotion/maintenance. **Cognitive level:** 4.

156. **2**   The patient is experiencing dumping syndrome. Food and fluid are moved quickly into the small intestines, the hypertonic content draws fluid (extracellularly) from the plasma, thereby decreasing the circulating blood volume. If the patient avoids fluids with meals and eats several small meals, the food will move slowly into the jejunum, thus preventing the reported symptoms. **Nursing process:** Implementation. **Client need:** Physiological integrity. **Cognitive level:** 3.

157. **1**   Haldol should be administered. The patient is experiencing delirium, possibly due to a septic condition secondary to pneumonia. The signs and symptoms exhibited are classic signs as described in the DMS IV manual for delirium related to general condition. Haldol is an antipsychotic drug, therefore it should be used for the psychotic behavior exhibited. Ativan is an antianxiety medication, therefore inappropriate. The behavior of these patients worsens if isolated, therefore option 4 is inappropriate. **Nursing process:** Implementation. **Client need:** Physiological integrity. **Cognitive level:** 4.

158. **1**   Celiac disease is an inborn error of metabolism that triggers a toxic reaction to gluten, a protein contained in wheat and rye flours. Thus, foods containing these flours must be omitted from the child's diet. **Nursing process:** Evaluation. **Client need:** Health promotion/maintenance. **Cognitive level:** 4.

159. **3**   Kegel exercises are a technique that strengthens the sphincter and muscle control relating to urination. The exercise consists of starting and stopping the urine stream while voiding until the muscle is isolated, then the patient performs exercises to pre-

vent involuntary urination. **Nursing process:** Implementation. **Client need:** Physiological integrity. **Cognitive level:** 3.

160. **1**   The pattern of daily weights provides an accurate account of fluid loss or retention by the body. **Nursing process:** Assessment. **Client need:** Physiological integrity. **Cognitive level:** 3.

161. **1**   Until the patient's assertions have been checked out with his doctor, the medication should not be administered. Many patients are knowledgeable about medications; therefore it is best to treat such a statement as the truth. **Nursing process:** Implementation. **Client need:** Safe, effective care environment. **Cognitive level:** 3.

162. **2**   Administration of phenobarbital will sedate the patient and thereby prevent him from harming himself. Restraints may increase restlessness. The patient should be restrained only when all other measures fail. Reduction of sensory stimuli while caring for a restless patient may prevent increasing confusion and hyperactivity. **Nursing process:** Planning. **Client need:** Physiological integrity. **Cognitive level:** 4.

163. **1**   Household chores that require a lot of arm movement should be avoided. The patient should not lift, push, or carry heavy objects for 6 to 8 weeks. **Nursing process:** Implementation. **Client need:** Physiological integrity. **Cognitive level:** 4.

164. **2**   Cerebral edema following head trauma increases the bulk of brain tissue, thereby placing pressure on the structure that controls vital signs. Slowing of the pulse, change in respiration rate, and widening pulse pressure or increased systolic pressure are symptoms of increasing intracranial pressure. **Nursing process:** Assessment. **Client need:** Physiological integrity. **Cognitive level:** 4.

165. **3**   The toddler resents the arrival of a new sibling because now mother and father are sharing their love and attention with someone else. The child requires attention also, and parents should set aside a time each day to spend exclusively with the other child. **Nursing process:** Implementation. **Client need:** Health promotion/maintenance. **Cognitive level:** 3.

166. **2**   Constant observation is most critical because command hallucinations are considered to be the most dangerous sensory disturbance experienced by psychotic patients.

Nursing process: Planning. **Client need:** Psychosocial integrity. **Cognitive level:** 3.

167. **1**   Meconium, a thick, blackish green, sticky stool, is the first stool passed by the newborn. It is the result of digested amniotic fluid that the newborn swallowed in utero. **Nursing process:** Implementation. **Client need:** Health promotion/maintenance. **Cognitive level:** 4.

168. **4**   Care of the patient with delirium tremens should include general safety, a nonstimulating environment, and measures to correct physiological imbalances caused by alcohol. **Nursing process:** Implementation. **Client need:** Physiological integrity. **Cognitive level:** 4.

169. **2**   Play with doctor and nurse puppets allows the child to imitate the activities he/she sees in the hospital. Play is one of the child's most effective ways of dealing with the stress of hospitalization. **Nursing process:** Implementation. **Client need:** Psychosocial integrity. **Cognitive level:** 3.

170. **1**   Choices 2, 3, and 4 identify dehydration more efficiently and quickly than measuring the blood pressure. Eventually, in dehydration, the blood pressure drops, but by that time the patient may be irreversibly affected. **Nursing process:** Assessment. **Client need:** Physiological integrity. **Cognitive level:** 3.

171. **2**   Children are best controlled on the side lying position with the head flexed and knees drawn toward the chest. **Nursing process:** Implementation. **Client need:** Physiological integrity. **Cognitive level:** 3.

172. **3**   Vegetarians must receive adequate protein from unrefined grains such as brown rice and whole wheat, legumes such as beans, split peas, lentils, nuts in large quantities, and a variety of cooked and fresh vegetables and fruits. A combination of these foods will provide adequate protein. **Nursing process:** Evaluation. **Client need:** Physiological integrity. **Cognitive level:** 3.

173. **1**   Lengthy discussions with a patient with antisocial personality about his attitudes and behavior is likely to create the impression that unacceptable behavior is open to discussion and hence, may be sanctioned. The discussion may lead into a "power struggle" between the patient and the nurse. **Nursing process:** Planning. **Client need:** Psychosocial integrity. **Cognitive level:** 3.

174. **2**   Milk is sometimes tolerated in cooked form such as custards. Fermented dairy products such as cheese and yogurt are sometimes tolerated. Lactose enzymes maybe used to alleviate the problem. They may be purchased in tablets or liquids. Lactose-treated milk is available commercially in some grocery stores. **Nursing process:** Implementation. **Client need:** Health promotion/maintenance. **Cognitive level:** 3.

175. **3**   Increased fluid is a natural stool softener. One of the goals of intervention in a third-degree laceration is to make the stool as soft as possible, so that there is no strain on the anal sutures during bowel movements. Also, the softer the stool, the less pain the patient will experience. **Nursing process:** Implementation. **Client need:** Physiological integrity. **Cognitive level:** 3.

176. **2**   Group classes will prevent the couple from being isolated. Childbirth preparation classes usually cover preparation for labor and delivery. Members are encouraged to increase the group's cohesiveness. **Nursing process:** Evaluation. **Client need:** Health promotion/maintenance. **Cognitive level:** 4.

177. **3**   This patient's progressive symptoms are typical of congestive heart failure, the heart's signal of decreased ability to meet the demands of pregnancy. **Nursing process:** Evaluation. **Client need:** Health promotion/maintenance. **Cognitive level:** 4.

178. **4**   Gestational diabetes management requires frequent physician visits and monitoring of blood glucose levels. These patients should call their physician whenever they feel ill or "out of sorts." Many times the problem may be solved over the telephone. **Nursing process:** Implementation. **Client need:** Health promotion/maintenance. **Cognitive level:** 4.

179. **3**   Even though patients have chronic productive coughs, they are not able to expectorate all of the tracheobronchial secretions. These secretions are an excellent medium for bacterial growth. **Nursing process:** Evaluation. **Client need:** Physiological integrity. **Cognitive level:** 4.

180. **3**   The usual pattern of metastatic spread is the extension from the breast to the axillary nodes, the internal mammary nodes, and the supra-clavicular nodes. Fifty percent of women with lumps for 1 month have involvement of the lymph nodes; at 6 months, 68% have positive axillary nodes. **Nursing process:** Analysis. **Client need:** Physiological integrity. **Cognitive level:** 3.

181. **3**   The patient is experiencing pacemaker failure. The signs are pulse above 60 beats/minutes or about 5 beats minus below set rate, dizziness, faintness, palpitations and hiccups. At the medical clinic he will be seen, have an EKG, and be admitted to the coronary care unit or intensive care unit from the clinic. **Nursing process:** Implementation. **Client need:** Physiological integrity. **Cognitive level:** 4.

182. **3**   Gravida refers to the number of times a woman has been pregnant, including the present pregnancy. Para refers to the number of pregnancies delivered at viable term. The patient's spontaneous abortion at 12 weeks would not count as a para. **Nursing process:** Implementation. **Client need:** Health promotion/maintenance. **Cognitive level:** 4.

183. **3**   This patient's chest pain is probably due to a pulmonary embolus. The onset of pain is sudden and may be constant or intermittent. Coughing, swallowing, and deep breathing can aggravate the pain. After placing patient in upright position, oxygen may be administered. **Nursing process:** Implementation. **Client need:** Physiological integrity. **Cognitive level:** 4.

184. **3**   Eight hours after a radical modified mastectomy, the drainage should be more than 25 ml but should not exceed 200 ml in 8 hours. The drainage tube should be checked for blockage. **Nursing process:** Implementation. **Client need:** Physiological integrity. **Cognitive level:** 4.

185. **3**   Providing an atmosphere where the patient is able to freely verbalize feelings about death will help the patient deal with the dying process. All other responses convey discomfort and avoidance to confront issues related to dying. **Nursing process:** Implementation. **Client need:** Psychosocial integrity. **Cognitive level:** 3.

186. **1**   Aspirin prevents blood clot formation that can block the coronary arteries and cause a myocardial infarction, whereas Tylenol does not. **Nursing process:** Evaluation. **Client need:** Physiological integrity. **Cognitive level:** 4.

187. **1**   A nutritional consult is needed to calculate the daily calories needed to bring serum albumin to 3.5 gm/dl. Healing will not

occur because the patient is malnourished. **Nursing process:** Evaluation. **Client need:** Physiological integrity. **Cognitive level:** 4.

188. **1**   Whole milk contains 5.0 gm of saturated fat per cup. Turkey and chicken without the skin contains 1 gm (for 2 medium size pieces). Cheddar cheese (6.0 gm per 1 oz.) and other aged cheeses are high in saturated fat. Beans contain 0.3 gm per cup. **Nursing process:** Evaluation. **Client need:** Physiological integrity. **Cognitive level:** 4.

189. **2**   Alternating air mattress is the support surface of choice. The air cells inflate enough to support the patient yet deflate enough to allow the skin to relax so that blood can return. If blood does not return, tissues will begin to die. **Nursing process:** Implementation. **Client need:** Physiological integrity. **Cognitive level:** 3.

190. **3**   Clamping the chest tube prevents atmospheric pressure from entering the pleural space and causing collapse of the lung. **Nursing process:** Implementation. **Client need:** Physiological integrity. **Cognitive level:** 3.

191. **3**   Analysis of one's own feelings should precede all other actions. Once the nurse has identified the cause of these feelings, she will be better equipped to handle the situation. **Nursing process:** Analysis. **Client need:** Phychosocial integrity. **Cognitive level:** 3.

192. **1**   Bolus enteral feedings are the major cause of diarrhea. If the feeding is to be given intermittently, it would have to be administered at a rate of 5–10 ml/min., therefore only 100 ml would be delivered in 2 hours. **Nursing process:** Evaluation. **Client need:** Physiological integrity. **Cognitive level:** 3.

193. **3**   Lasix duration for action by oral administration is 4 to 6 hours. If the diuretic is taken at 3 or 4 P.M. she should not be awaken during the night. **Nursing process:** Evaluation. **Client need:** Physiological integrity. **Cognitive level:** 4.

194. **1**   The pulse should be taken for 1 full minute so that irregularities in rate and rhythm may be noted. **Nursing process:** Evaluation. **Client need:** Physiological integrity. **Cognitive level:** 3.

195. **3**   The goal of breathing exercises is to allow complete exhalation and emptying of the lungs. Pursed-lip breathing, or positive pressure breathing, provides for the maintenance of positive pressure in the lung, thereby preventing alveolar collapse and improving transportation through the alveoli. **Nursing process:** Analysis. **Client need:** Physiological integrity. **Cognitive level:** 3.

196. **3**   This answer reassures the patient that what is happening to her is normal, but does not negate her feelings of discomfort. By seeking information about the symptom, the nurse can plan appropriate intervention to alleviate the discomfort. **Nursing process:** Implementation. **Client need:** Health promotion/maintenance. **Cognitive level:** 3.

197. **1**   Diarrhea is often caused by too fast a feeding rate. Slowing the rate may help especially if the feeding is hypertonic. The feeding may also be diluted. A stool specimen is needed when diarrhea is antibiotic induced and caused by *Clostridum difficile*. **Nursing process:** Implementation. **Client need:** Physiological integrity. **Cognitive level:** 3.

198. **3**   Sympathizing with the patient will reinforce her use of the physical symptoms in dealing with her emotional conflicts. Confronting her with the unreality of her physical problem will make her cling more to the symptoms to justify their existence. The nurse must divert the patient's attention away from her physical symptoms toward activities in which she may be able to experience success and feel good about herself. **Nursing process:** Evaluation. **Client need:** Psychosocial integrity. **Cognitive level:** 4.

199. **2**   These are signs of dehydration. The patient should receive 1 ml of water per kilocalorie consumed or 30 ml of water per kilogram of body weight per day. The patient feeding usually contains some water, usually between 300–500 ml. Therefore add free water to make up the difference. **Nursing process:** Evaluation. **Client need:** Physiological integrity. **Cognitive level:** 4.

200. **3**   Cranberry and carbonated beverages are questionable as to their ability to clear clogs. Thirty ml to 50 ml of water in a 50 ml piston syringe, applying gentle pressure alternating with suction is the recommended method. **Nursing process:** Implementation. **Client need:** Physiological integrity. **Cognitive level:** 3.

Self-Analysis Chart

After you have completed the model NCLEX exam II and checked your answers, fill in the chart below. In the columns under "Reason for Error" list the number of each kind of error you made for each phase of the nursing process. The results will indicate the kinds of errors you made most frequently, so that you can take steps to minimize them. For example, if you have many errors under "Misread Problem," you need to slow down and read the questions more carefully. Note such specific details as the age of the patient, the symptoms described, the tests and/or procedures performed, and the drug(s) prescribed.

NURSING PROCESS	NUMBER OF QUESTIONS	NUMBER CORRECT	NUMBER INCORRECT	REASON FOR ERROR			
				FAULTY JUDGMENT	LACK OF KNOWLEDGE	MISREAD PROBLEM	WRONG GUESS
Assessment	14						
Analysis	17						
Planning	13						
Implementation	53						
Evaluation	103						
Total	200	___	___	___	___	___	___

INDEX

Documentation for Barron's NCLEX/CAT-RN Simulation Disk

This documentation applies to either the Windows or the Macintosh disk that is packaged with this book.

The disk must be installed on the hard drive of your computer before you can run it.

The Macintosh disk needs a computer with a
- minimum of 4 megabytes of RAM
- 68030 processor or better
- System 7 or better
- hard disk with 2.5 MB

The Windows disk needs a computer with a
- minimum of 4 megabytes of RAM
- Windows 3.1
- hard disk with 2.5 MB
- VGA monitor

Installation

To install the disk on your hard drive, first boot the machine in the normal way.

Macintosh

1. Put the Barron's disk into the disk drive. Double-click on the disk icon to open it.
2. Locate the NCLEX-RN Installer icon and double-click on it.
3. When a Barron's NCLEX-RN dialogue box appears, click on the Continue button.
4. Click on Install to accept the Barron's NCLEX-RN folder or use the install dialogue to navigate to your preferred destination disk/folder.
5. When a dialogue box appears, informing you that installation was successful, choose Quit. Eject the disk from your disk drive and store it in a safe place.
6. To open Barron's NCLEX/CAT-RN Simulation, double-click on the NCLEX-RN icon in the NCLEX-RN folder (or in the folder you created).

Windows

1. Put the Barron's NCLEX/CAT-RN disk into the floppy disk drive.
2. Under the File menu in the Program Manager, select Run.
3. Type A:setup (Substitute the correct drive letter of your disk drive).
4. Follow the instructions that appear on the screen.
5. When installation is finished, remove the disk from the drive and store in a safe place.
6. To open Barron's NCLEX/CAT-RN Simulation, double-click on the NCLEX-RN icon in the NCLEX-RN group.

About Barron's NCLEX/CAT-RN Simulation

The disk packaged with this book includes multiple-choice questions that cover the full spectrum of the NCLEX Examination Blueprint. You can use the questions in three ways: in Testing Mode, Learning Mode, or Review Mode.

The examinations in the Testing Mode have been designed to closely simulate the testing conditions of the actual NCLEX/CAT-RN, the licensure examination that is administered using Computerized Adaptive Testing under the auspices of the National Council of State Boards of Nursing. Passing or failing the Barron's NCLEX/CAT-RN Simulation should not be taken as a predictor of whether you will pass or fail the actual NCLEX/CAT-RN. However, after you complete a test, the program will display the results and allow you to analyze your strengths and weaknesses. This information can be used to determine the areas in which you need further study.

Testing Mode

As with the actual NCLEX/CAT-RN, you will have a maximum of five hours to complete the test. The pass/fail formula of the Testing Mode is based on a point system designed to simulate as closely as possible the actual passing standard set by the National Council. After a minimum number of questions (75) have been answered, testing will stop as soon as your performance is calculated to be above the simulated passing standard. The test will also stop when the maximum number of questions (265) have been answered or when the five hour limit is reached.

You may take a test in the Testing Mode as often as you wish. Each question will be selected by the program based upon how you answered the previous question. The total number of questions administered before the test is concluded will depend upon your pattern of correct and incorrect responses. Therefore, each time you enter the Testing Mode you will receive a different exam.

Learning Mode

The Learning Mode will allow you to receive feedback for every answer choice. By selecting Solution Preferences, you will be able to decide when you prefer the computer to display the solution (after every answer or only after the correct answer is given). There are four practice sets in the Learning Mode. Each set contains 100 questions.

Review Mode

The Review Mode allows you to review the previous exam taken in the Testing Mode. Each answer choice chosen is displayed. The correct answer is also displayed in cases where you chose an incorrect response. An explanation of the correct answer can be viewed by clicking on the Solution button.

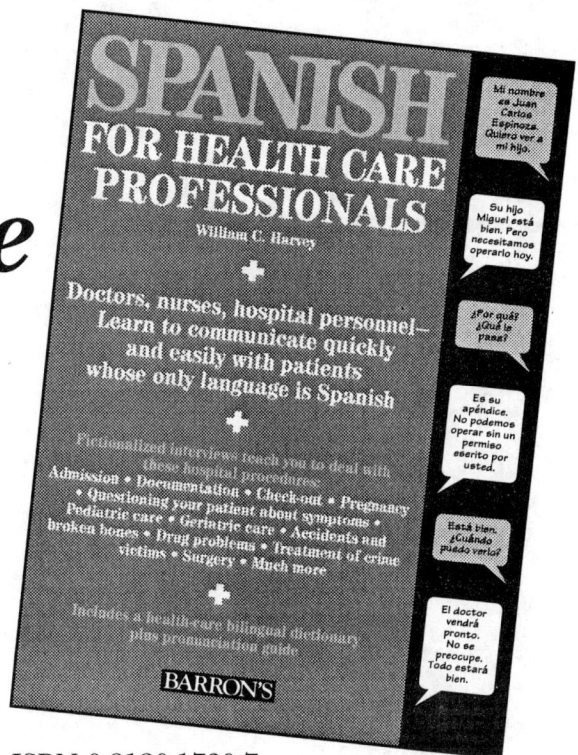